NETWORK MANAGEMENT
CONCEPTS AND PRACTICE
A HANDS-ON APPROACH

J. Richard Burke

An Alan R. Apt Book

PEARSON
Prentice
Hall

Pearson Education, Inc.
Upper Saddle River, New Jersey 07458

Library of Congress Cataloging-in-Publication Data

Burke, Richard (James Richard)
   Network management : concepts and practice, a hands on approch / J.
Richard Burke.
      p.   cm.
   ISBN 0-13-032950-9
   1.   Computer networks—Management.   I. Title.
   TK5105.5 .B866 2004
   004.6′068—dc21

                                                            2003003918

Vice President and Editorial Director, ECS: *Marcia J. Horton*
Publisher: *Alan Apt*
Associate Editor: *Toni D. Holm*
Editorial Assistant: *Patrick Lindner*
Vice President and Director of Production and Manufacturing, ESM: *David W. Riccardi*
Executive Managing Editor: *Vince O'Brien*
Managing Editor: *Camille Trentacoste*
Production Editor: *Patty Donovan*
Director of Creative Services: *Paul Belfanti*
Creative Director: *Carole Anson*
Art Director: *Jayne Conte*
Cover Designer: *Bruce Kenselaar*
Cover Photo Image: *George E. Tice*
Art Editor: *Greg Dulles*
Manufacturing Manager: *Trudy Pisciotti*
Manufacturing Buyer: *Lynda Castillo*
Marketing Manager: *Pamela Schaffer*

 © 2004 by Pearson Education, Inc.
Pearson Education, Inc.
Upper Saddle River, New Jersey 07458

Printed in the United States of America

10 9 8 7 6 5 4 3 2 1

ISBN 0-13-032950-9

Pearson Education Ltd., *London*
Pearson Education Australia Pty. Ltd., *Sydney*
Pearson Education Singapore, Pte. Ltd.
Pearson Education North Asia Ltd., *Hong Kong*
Pearson Education Canada, Inc., *Toronto*
Pearson Educación de Mexico, S.A. de C.V.
Pearson Education—Japan, *Tokyo*
Pearson Education Malaysia, Pte. Ltd.
Pearson Education, *Upper Saddle River, New Jersey*

*This book is dedicated to three special people
who have always been there for me:
my mother, Evelyn; my aunt Theresa; and my mentor,
Rev. D. Bradley Murray, S.J.*

PREFACE

The title of this book is *Network Management: Concepts and Practice. A Hands-on Approach.*

A NEW APPROACH

Network Management: Concepts and Practice. A Hands-on Approach uses Network Management System (NMS) software to demonstrate each network management concept described. Thus, it shows the student how to practice network management. In addition to the demonstrations illustrated in the book, we arranged to include the NMS used for the demonstrations with the book. Therefore, students will be able to practice network management techniques at any time.

NETWORK MANAGEMENT PROTOCOLS IMPLEMENTED

This book concentrates on the implementation of the Simple Network Management Protocol (SNMP) because of its pervasive use in the enterprise. Most of this use is provided by SNMPv1. In addition, we give a complete description of SNMPv3 and demonstrate its use. SNMPv3 is now an Internet Standard that provides "industrial strength" authentication and encryption. The student is also introduced to the use of the Desktop Management protocol and Web-based Management.

SUMMARY OF FEATURES

- Uses an NMS that focuses on the fundamentals of network management
- Describes the responsibilities of a network manager
- Provides step-by-step configuration of desktop and network devices
- Provides comprehensive descriptions of RMON1 and RMON2 MIBs and uses them to display and analyze network traffic
- Provides tables which organize the details of network implementation and management strategies

- Provides tables that divide the broad range of network management concepts into manageable descriptions
- Demonstrates how to access, compile and use device-specific enterprise MIBs
- Provides a summary of commercial NMSs categorized by capability and cost
- Includes over 300 figures that demonstrate network management details.
- Includes Review Questions and Exercises at the end of each chapter

CONTENT OVERVIEW

Readers of this book should have had a course in networking fundamentals or experience in that area. However, for those needing some review, we have included Chapter 1 that provides an overview of networking components. In addition, Chapters 2 and 3 introduce the reader to network management vocabulary and the basic principles of network management.

Chapter 1 provides an overview of networking concepts, shows photographs of the devices that will be used on the demonstration network, and explains the functions of the devices.

Chapters 2 and 3 describe what network management is all about. Chapter 2 discusses the responsibilities of a network manager, defines network management vocabulary, provides an example of how remote network management is done and documents the history of network management development. Chapter 3 discusses network implementation and network management strategies and gives tables of issues that should be considered for each. Also described are the ISO Network Management Categories and examples of each are given. In addition, the chapter summarizes the capabilities and costs of current network management systems (NMS). Finally, different network management strategies are examined and one selected for this book.

Chapters 4 and 5 provide step-by-step configuration of demonstration network components. Chapter 4 configures desktop components and Chapter 5 configures network components such as hubs, switches, routers, and probes.

Chapter 6 examines details of the SNMPv1 protocol, the structure of the MIB tree, explains SNMPv1 commands and arguments, uses a command line utility to execute SNMPv1 commands, introduces the Meterware/Analyzer NMS, and captures and analyzes SNMPv1 frames.

Chapter 7 explains the Structure of Management Information (SMIv1), the ASN.1 definitions of MIB objects and how to create them, and implements enterprise objects.

Chapters 8 and 9 examine RMON1 and RMON2 MIB objects and how to use an NMS and a probe to capture and analyze objects that measure network traffic statistics. RMON2 objects provide traffic statistics for protocols up to the Application Layer.

Chapters 10 and 11 describe other important network management protocols. Chapter 10 discusses the Desktop Management Interface (DMI) standard, demonstrates how it is used to access desktop attributes, and how the desktop attribute

format can be mapped to the MIB format for remote access by an NMS that uses
SNMPv1. Chapter 11 discusses Web-based management and demonstrates the use
of a web browser to access object values from an embedded SNMPv1 web server
on a Cisco switch.

Chapter 12 demonstrates configuration and use of SNMPv3, the new IETF
Standard for authentication and encryption of SNMP messages. David Spakes of
SNMP Research International co-authors this chapter. The history of the transition
from SNMPv1 to SNMPv2 to SNMPv3 is reviewed, operational enhancements in
SNMPv2 are explained and authentication of users and encryption of messages for
a SNMPv3 agent are demonstrated using a SNMPv3 command line interface. In addition, the chapter uses a GUI Wizard, in development at SNMP Research, to configure authentication for a SNMPv3 agent, demonstrates the SNMPv3 Enterpol
NMS in development at SNMP Research and shows how to use the Enterpol application, Simple Policy Pro, to distribute configurations throughout the enterprise.

Six Appendices are included that support chapter material, provide advanced
material, and provide an essential reference for the student. Appendix A reviews IP
addressing and subnetting. Appendix B supports Chapter 7 by providing additional
material on Abstract Syntax Notation 1 (ASN.1). Appendix C is rfc 1213 which is a
description of each of the objects in MIB-II. Appendix D explains the Basic Encoding Rules used to create packets sent over the "wire." Appendix E describes other
approaches to information management that are in use today and Appendix F
demonstrates other useful tools on the CD-ROM

INSTRUCTOR INFORMATION

Network management is complicated by the large number of objects, their associated, often long, names and the use of lower and upper case in precise ways to represent these names. This situation can certainly be a barrier to learning the subject.
To be certain that the student knows that what is typed represents an object name,
object names are typed exactly as they appear in the standards. Because of this
some sentences start with lowercase letters. For further clarity, we have tried to use
bolding of text to call attention to words that introduce new concepts or words on
which we wish to focus the reader's attention.

An "Instructor CD-ROM" has been created that includes answers to chapter
Review Questions and solutions to chapter Exercises. In addition, it includes all the
figures in the book. These can be used directly to create PowerPoint classroom
presentations. We have also included all the tables because they provide a framework for class discussions and a focus for chapter material.

CONTACT US

Your comments and suggestions are welcome. They can be sent via email to
jamesrichardburke@att.net

ACKNOWLEDGMENTS

I wish to thank the following reviewers for making the suggestions that allowed the organization and content of the book to be improved greatly; Ron Fulle/ Rochester Institute of Technology; Phillip Rawles/Purdue University; David Hayes/San Jose State University; Ashok Goel/Michigan Tech; Mansoor Alam/ University of Toledo; Christos Douligeris/UC San Diego and University of Piraeus (Greece); Mani Subramania/Georgia Tech.; George Polyzos/UC San Diego; and Andy Bierman/Cisco Systems, Inc., IOS Technologies Division, San Jose.

In addition, I would like to thank all the people at Prentice Hall who contributed to the development and production of a work like this. With their care for detail, the product is of much greater value to the reader. I especially thank my publisher, Alan Apt, who recognized the need for the book and was patient with the author through some trying times. Associate Editor, Toni Dianne Holm was responsible for guiding the development of the front cover and back cover of the book as well as the format and content of the preface. Jake Warde did his usual quality job of coordinating the reviews and the production of the Instructor CD-ROM. The authors managed to generate some difficult editing problems during the production phase of this book. Thanks to the positive attitude and expertise of Patty Donovan of Pine Tree Composition, Inc., they were resolved.

The author came to depend on many people who provided support of one kind or another just out of interest in the topic of this book. It is a pleasure to thank them for making this all come together. From the beginning, Fred Mendez of Apptitude, the principal tester of the Analyzer NMS, provided expert guidance that enabled the full capability of Analyzer to be applied to the capture and analysis of RMON objects. He also provided hardware support of the probes. Fredrik Noon of HiFn, an original developer of Analyzer, edited the software to make it available as a student CD-ROM. Management at HiFn, previously at Technically Elite and then Apptitude where first Meterware and then Analyzer were developed, made significant contributions to this book. They donated the Analyzer NMS software and two state-of-the-art probes for the demonstration network. Special thanks are due to Chris Kember, John Metzger and John Feldmeir for this.

Luis Hernandez of IBM in Research Triangle Park arranged for the loan of an IBM IntelliStation ZPRO workstation and the technical services of Michael Redd to support it. In addition, Donald Plotnick of IBM Tivoli Systems provided guidance on the use of their DMI browser and agent.

Special thanks are due to Mohammad Fatmi, who was manager of the North Carolina State University (NCSU) campus network facilities at the time this book was started. He helped to design and setup the demonstration network, loaned the CISCO switches and router that was used, and provided much helpful documentation.

Howard Holgate of the Cisco Internet Telephony Services loaned a Cisco router with an installed IOS supporting SNMPv3. Further assistance in this regard was provided by Jeff Case of SNMP Research. Jeff made available their Enterpol SNMPv3 NMS, Simple Policy Pro software, several command line utilities, and the support of Faith McCullough and Sandra McLeod. The author would also like to thank John Sancho, CEO of Castle Rock Computing, for the offer to use their SNMPc5 NMS that is compatible with all current versions of SNMP and for providing an evaluation disk of that product.

Professor Mladen Vouk of the NCSU Computer Science Department loaned a workstation and other peripheral devices.

The Micromuse London office donated its Netcool/OMINIbus "Real Time Fault Management for Service Providers and Enterprises" product for evaluation. It is discussed in Appendix E. Technical assistance was provided by Dennis Stavroyiannopoulos and administrative assistance by Jane Scotland, Nicole Fortenberry and Sonia Ramanah.

J. RICHARD BURKE

BRIEF TABLE OF CONTENTS

CONTENTS

TABLE OF FIGURES

CHAPTER 1

NETWORKING COMPONENTS

This chapter will:

- Review communication architecture concepts
- Describe the functions of the OSI Reference Model layers
- Compare the OSI Reference Model and the TCP/IP communication architectures
- Explain the structure of frames used on an Ethernet LAN
- Describe the functions performed by network devices
- Show the physical connectivity of the demonstration network devices

It is expected that readers of a book on network management will be familiar with network technology. If that is not the case for some users of this book, Chapter 1 reviews the functions performed by network devices and the communication architecture that are required for network devices to communicate and thus network management to take place. In addition, Chapters 4 and 5 are devoted to configuration management of devices on the demonstration network.

Understanding network technology is important for network design as well as for effective network management implementation. Network management requires communication between devices on the network. The software components that implement this communication are combined to form what is called communication architecture. Each device on a network needs to implement some or all of this architecture in order to communicate with other devices. The communication architecture is the "fuel" that powers the network and enables network management. Thus we begin this chapter with a discussion of communication architectures.

1.1 COMMUNICATION ARCHITECTURES

A communication architecture integrates many protocols and the software that implements them. These parts can be developed independently of one another as long as the developers adhere to the standards that specify the interface between them, i.e., how the parts will communicate with one another. A communication architecture is often referred to as a protocol stack for reasons to be seen below.

An example of communication architecture is the OSI Reference Model that was introduced in International Standard ISO/IEC 7498-1, "Open System Interconnection-Basic Reference Model" **[Ref 1]. [Refs 2-3]** are books that discuss this architecture in detail. The ISO/IEC standard came about because it was recognized that a standardized environment for the development of network communication software was needed. It was envisioned that such a standardized environment would provide a way of thinking about these software components and how they should work together. The OSI Reference Model is shown in **Figure 1.1**.

This is a high-level model that simply says there are seven categories of functions that need to be performed in order to achieve communication between net-

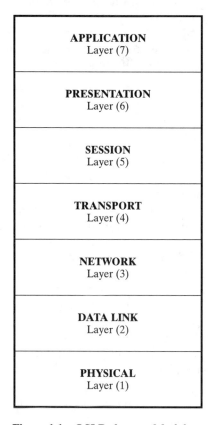

APPLICATION
Layer (7)

PRESENTATION
Layer (6)

SESSION
Layer (5)

TRANSPORT
Layer (4)

NETWORK
Layer (3)

DATA LINK
Layer (2)

PHYSICAL
Layer (1)

Figure 1.1 OSI Reference Model

worked devices. However, the model appropriately does not specify how to implement the functions. The functions in each layer are defined by protocols, which are implemented in software. The software must be installed on each device on the network for communication to take place.

The software in each layer provides services to the layer above it. Thus, depending on the requirements of the communication and the devices that are communicating, software in all layers of this model may have to provide services. For example, if an application on one computer wanted information stored on another computer, it would need to communicate with a database management system on the other computer. In this case, all layers of the stack in each computer would provide services. Another example of such communication is what this book is all about; namely a management application on a Management Station requesting information from the agent process on a Management Agent. We discuss the nature of this communication in Chapter 2.

In addition to specifying the categories of functions that need to be performed to achieve communication, the OSI Reference Model implies that there is a need to divide the communication architecture implementation into seven distinct functional layers that can be developed independently of each other. This approach greatly simplifies the development process and allows improvements of software in one layer to be made without affecting the software developed for other layers. This layered approach may clarify why the architecture is called a protocol "stack." Let's describe the functions these layers perform and how they are implemented in practice. To get a picture of the functions provided by these layers as they are discussed, the hypothetical network shown in **Figure 1.2** is provided.

LAN 1 contains two segments connected by a bridge. Segment 1 has two devices connected to the segment by a hub. Segment 2 contains two devices networked by perhaps a 10BASE2 "thin" coax. LAN 2 is networked to LAN 1 by a satellite wide area network (WAN) that connects two routers. LAN 2 has one segment.

1.1.1 Physical Layer

This layer defines the electrical, mechanical, functional and procedural specifications for the hardware that connects a device to the network. For example, a standard that is developed for the Physical layer would specify a connector's size and shape, the exact number of pins it should have, the signals that can be used on the circuits attached to those pins and the functions performed by each circuit. This is the layer where bits are transformed into voltages. The Electronic Industries Association/Telecommunications Industries Association (EIA/TIA) standard 232-E is a good example of a Physical layer specification **[Ref 4]**. Repeaters and hubs make use of the Physical layer only. **Figure 1.2** shows a LAN segment that includes a 3COM LinkBuilder FMS II hub.

1.1.2 Data Link Layer

This layer specifies the procedures that are followed in order to achieve reliable point-to-point transfer of information between two devices. The ISO/IEC 8802-3 standard **[Ref 5]** specifies an implementation of the OSI Data Link layer protocols

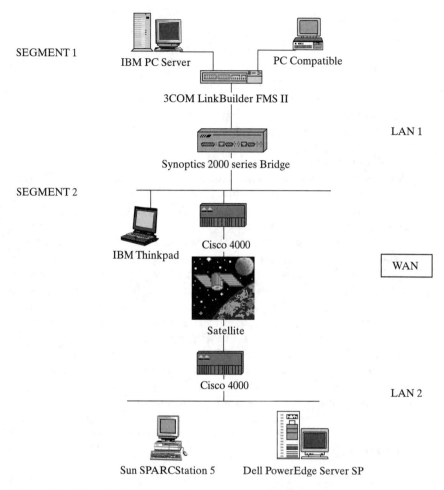

Figure 1.2 Hypothetical Network Consisting of Two LANs Linked by a Satellite WAN

for Ethernet multi-access media. In this implementation, the OSI Data Link layer is divided into two sublayers: the Logical Link Control **(LLC)** sublayer and the Medium Access Control **(MAC)** sublayer. This division provides a convenient distribution of labor into functions that ensure reliable transmission using acknowledgments between stations (LLC sublayer) and functions that ensure orderly access to a particular network medium (MAC sublayer).

For devices attached to an Ethernet LAN, as shown in the figure, the MAC sublayer implements the Carrier Sense Multiple Access with Collision Detection **(CSMA/CD)** access method. CSMA means that a computer waits until there is no signal from any other computer on the LAN before transmitting a message. CD means that this approach does not always work, collisions of signals do occur and two or more computers wanting to send messages wait different amounts of time before trying to send their messages again. This approach reduces the probability that a collision will occur the next time. The MAC sublayer constructs a **frame,** the basic unit of information transfer from one device to another on the network. (Frames are discussed later in this chapter.) Devices communicating with other devices on the same network are only interested in the hardware addresses of those devices. The hardware source and destination addresses are added to the frame by the MAC sublayer. A different MAC specification would be used by the routers to send frames to the WAN implemented in the figure by a satellite network.

A good example of a device that uses only the Physical and Data Link layer protocols, is the **bridge.** A Synoptics bridge is shown in **Figure 1.2** connecting two Ethernet LAN segments. Its job is to look at the MAC destination field of the frame received at its input port and decide if the frame should be forwarded to the segment on its output port. If the destination of a frame is a device on the input segment of the bridge there is no point in forwarding the frame to the output segment. This procedure reduces unnecessary segment traffic. In order to perform its function, the bridge has to know the hardware addresses on each segment. As soon as a bridge is powered up, it learns these addresses from the frames it receives and stores them in the bridge table. Bridges can be configured to transmit a frame if the destination address is not in the bridge table.

1.1.3 Network Layer

In contrast to the point-to-point information transfer function of the Data Link layer, the Network layer provides the mechanisms for transporting a packet from the source network to the destination network. **[Ref 6-7] Packets** are messages constructed by the network layer and higher layers of the protocol stack. The packet of one layer is encapsulated in the packet of the next lower layer and all become part of the frame. (We will discuss packets later in this chapter.) The packets are encapsulated in a **header** and **trailer** by the MAC sublayer to form a complete frame that is ready for transmission. In a multinetwork system, such as the Internet, **routers** connect networks There are two Cisco routers in **Figure 1.2.** Each connects a LAN to a WAN satellite network that allows the LANs to communicate. It is the router's job to pass the packet to the network that will move it closer to its destination. This requires that the router be provided with the network addresses of the source and destination devices. A function of the Network layer is to provide these addresses. A router is called a network layer device because it is controlled by protocols up to and including the network layer.

1.1.4 Transport Layer

We must use more specific terminology when describing the Transport layer. We use the TCP/IP **[Ref 6-7]** terminology because the TCP/IP communication architecture is what is implemented in this book. (See **Figure 1.4** for a comparison of the TCP/IP communication architecture to the OSI Reference Model.) The TCP/IP Transport layer provides "reliable" and "unreliable" transport protocols. The reliable protocol, which is called the Transport Control Protocol (TCP), provides the mechanisms that enable "end-to-end" reliability. For example, it will ensure that data sent from the Dell server on LAN 2 is the data received by the PC Compatible on Segment 1 of LAN 1. It accomplishes this by the use of automated acknowledgment frames and automated retransmissions if necessary. TCP provides end-to-end error detection and recovery. TCP is also responsible for requesting a specific type of service for the packet. For example, the requested service could be: 1) use the fastest networks or 2) use the least expensive networks.

The "unreliable" transport protocol, which is called the User Datagram Protocol (UDP), places no constraints on the network. Best-effort delivery from the source device to the destination device is all that is required. UDP is used when speed is of the essence and the effort spent on ensuring reliability using TCP is not cost-effective. The Simple Network Management Protocol **(SNMP),** employed in this book, uses the UDP Transport layer protocol. Whether it is TCP or UDP that is used, process-to-process communication is requested by specifying the source and destination ports of the communicating processes. A port is a number that serves as an ID for a process that is either sending or receiving a packet. A port ID is mapped to an address in memory by the operating system.

1.1.5 Session Layer

The TCP/IP protocol stack does not specify Session or Presentation layers. This is an example of the flexibility of the OSI architecture concept, which does not dictate how the required functionality will be implemented. The functions of Session and Presentation layers are included in the TCP/IP Application layer. It is therefore useful to have some appreciation of the OSI Session and Presentation layers.

The Session layer is a software-implemented switching system. **[Ref 7-8]** The Session layer provides the mechanisms necessary to "open" and "close" multiple logical connections between processes on different PCs. These logical connections are called sessions. A logical connection exists when two processes in different computers are able to send packets to one another. Many logical connections can use the same physical connection and the same Presentation layer connection. The Presentation layer connections map to the Application layer processes that are linked by the session.

1.1.6 Presentation Layer

The Presentation layer **[Ref 8]** provides a common representation of data transferred between peer application layer entities on different stations. (See description of the Application layer that follows.) Application layer entities describe information in a generic, computer-language-independent format. This format is useful for the management of information. The format used is called abstract syntax notation.one **(ASN.1). (See Ref 9** and **Appendix B).** ASN.1 represents information in a hierarchical structure. However, the layers below the Presentation layer use information in a format that is practical for transmission across the network. This format is called **transfer syntax.** It is a byte stream formatted according to Basic Encoding Rules **(BER). (**See **Appendix D).** The Presentation layer translates between ASN.1

syntax and transfer syntax in a way that is acceptable to the communicating stations. The Presentation layer also translates transfer syntax into machine language used by the computer that hosts it. The Presentation layer is responsible for compression and encryption of information and the reverse processes. The ASN.1 format is also used to describe the structure of management information **(SMI)** for the MIB objects you will see in Chapter 7.

1.1.7 Application Layer

The Application layer eliminates the need for each application program to include code for every service. This is analogous to the advantage that an Application Program Interface **(API)** provides for application program access to the local operating system. The Application layer has no OSI Reference Model layer above it. Thus, formerly, it provides no services to a higher layer. However, the Application layer exists to provide services needed by application programs. In the language of the OSI Reference Model **[Ref 2]**, the Application layer contains **application entities** that provide various services to applications. Application entities are broken down into **application-service elements** which provide different functions needed. The **System Management Application Entity (SMAE)**, for example, is the entity that provides the primary support to network management applications. SMAE contains the **Remote Operations Service Element (ROSE)**, which is used to implement communication for all applications. The Common Management Information Protocol **(CMIP)** makes use of ROSE to send and receive protocol data units (PDUs). CMIP is the OSI analogy to SNMP.

There are two types of application service elements: Common Application Service Elements and Specific Application Service Elements. As the names imply, Common Application Service Elements provide service generally useful to a variety of application programs provided by vendors, while Specific Application Service Elements service the additional needs of particular application programs. An example of a Specific Application Service Element is the File Transfer Access Management Protocol **(FTAM).** Probably more familiar is the analogous TCP/IP **File Transfer Protocol (FTP).**

As we can see from this brief discussion of the OSI Application layer, this layer provides the OSI Reference Model with many of its extensive and valued capabilities. In contrast to the TCP/IP architecture, for example, the presence of distinct Presentation and Session layers provides added flexibility. Taken together, these capabilities make the OSI Reference Model the architecture of choice. It was designed to be so because all needed aspects were built-in from the beginning of its development. Because of the concomitant complexity, however, widespread implementation of the pure OSI Reference Model has been slow.

Now that we have described each layer in the OSI Reference Model protocol stack, it is probably clearer to the reader why a communication architecture is developed in pieces. Each piece alone is a big design and implementation job. Please consult the references at the end of the chapter to learn more details than could be presented here.

1.2 FRAMES

In order to send information over the network to another device, the sending device uses its communication architecture to create a frame and the receiving device uses its communication architecture to process the frame. The frame contains all the information necessary for it to reach the other device whether it resides on the same LAN or on any LAN in the world.

The frame is constructed in the following manner for the OSI Reference Model:

1. The application program makes a request for data that reside on another device.
2. The request is passed to the appropriate application-layer-entity in the Application layer that provides its part of the service requested by the application program.
3. The application-layer-entity constructs an Application layer protocol data unit **(PDU).** A PDU consists of the **data** passed by the application program and a **header**, which contains information that will be used by the application-layer-entity in the receiving device to process the PDU.
4. The Application layer PDU is then passed to the appropriate presentation-layer-entity. This entity constructs a Presentation layer protocol data unit (PDU) that consists of a Presentation layer header added to the Application Layer PDU. The Presentation layer header contains information that will enable the presentation-layer-entity in the receiving device to process the Presentation Layer PDU and enable the device to display the data appropriately, for example. As was discussed above, Presentation layer entities provide a very important additional function. They negotiate a transfer syntax for the communication with the destination device. When a transfer syntax is acceptable to both parties, the PDU provided by the application-layer-entity in ASN.1, is translated into transfer syntax and passed to the appropriate Session Layer entity.
5. PDUs continue to be constructed and passed to the layers below. This process of passing PDUs from one layer to another, with each layer adding its header, continues until the Network layer PDU is received by the Data Link layer.
6. The frame is constructed in the Data Link layer. The Network Layer PDU is encapsulated in a Data Link layer header and a Data Link layer trailer. The Medium Access Control (MAC) sub-layer of the Data Link layer does this encapsulation. Thus, the headers and trailers are usually called MAC headers and trailers.

Figure 1.3 shows what the frame looks like in the case of the ISO\IEC Standard MAC frame.

The descriptions of the fields in the MAC header and trailer are as follows:

Preamble—allows the circuitry in the receiving network interface card (NIC) to reach steady state synchronization with the received frame timing.

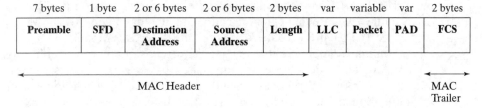

7 bytes	1 byte	2 or 6 bytes	2 or 6 bytes	2 bytes	var	variable	var	2 bytes
Preamble	**SFD**	**Destination Address**	**Source Address**	**Length**	**LLC**	**Packet**	**PAD**	**FCS**

MAC Header   MAC Trailer

Figure 1.3   ISO/IEC Standard 8802-3 (ANSI/IEEE Standard 802.3) MAC Frame Format

Start Frame Delimiter (SFD)—a sequence of bits that tells the receiver that a frame is being received.

Destination Address—the hardware address of the destination device. The typical Ethernet hardware address is 6 bytes.

Source Address—the hardware address of the source device. It is also typically 6 bytes. This address is stored in Read Only Memory (ROM) on the network interface card (NIC).

Length—the number of bytes in the packet.

LLC—logical link control. Provides reliable communication between devices on the same LAN.

Packet—the data supplied by the application program and all of the headers added by the Application layer through the Network layer.

PAD—bytes added if the total length of the frame is less than required by the CSMA/CD protocol (64 bytes).

FCS—Frame Check Sequence. The source applies an algorithm to the bytes in the destination address, source address, length, LLC, packet and PAD fields to produce a value for the FCS. The receiver applies the same algorithm to the same fields in the received frame. If the result is the original FCS, the frame is assumed to have been received without transmission error.

The minimum frame size in a 10Mb/s implementation of a CSMA/CD procedure is 64 bytes. The maximum frame size is 1518 bytes.

There is also a frame structure called the Ethernet II frame which was the first frame format to be used on Ethernet networks. The distinction between them is that the Ethernet II frame uses a Type field instead of a Length field and no LLC field. The Type field identifies the protocol used in the next layer, the network layer.

1.3 TCP/IP PROTOCOL STACK

Although this is a chapter on network devices, you have seen from what has been discussed so far that network devices are helpless without a communication architecture. Thus, when we discuss devices we are assuming that the communication architecture is an integral part of the device.

The TCP/IP protocol stack is installed on the devices on our demonstration LAN and we will use that communication architecture. **Figure 1.4** shows a comparison of the TCP/IP protocol stack and the OSI Reference Model.

You immediately see that the TCP/IP stack is not an exact replication of the OSI Reference Model. It does the job however because the necessary OSI Session and Presentation functions are included in the TCP/IP Application layer as has been mentioned. The Application layer contains many application support protocols. **SNMP,** and **HTTP** used by the Web Browsers, are included among them. Both will be used in this book for network management. Another distinction you will notice is that the "Data Link" layer is implemented differently. The Network Interface Layer does what its name implies: it provides a connection from the higher level protocols to media access implementations. It does not provide the reliable point to point functionality of the OSI Data Link LLC sublayer. But this was not a role intended for TCP/IP. As mentioned above, the additional Presentation and Session layers of the OSI Reference Model provide more functional flexibility and they can be enhanced without disturbing the Application layer software. Therefore, it might be fair to say that the OSI Reference Model "had it all" from its inception, but it is possible to produce sufficient capability with the TCP/IP architecture with less complexity.

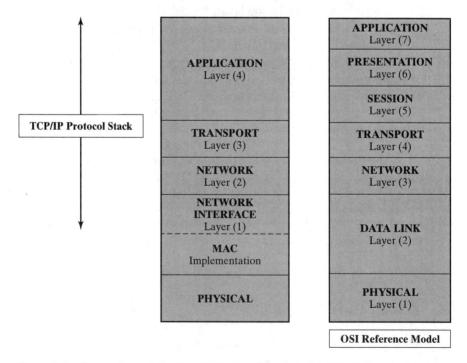

Figure 1.4   Comparison of the TCP/IP Protocol Stack to the OSI Reference Model

Figure 1.5 shows the functionality of the TCP/IP Network Interface Layer. For the TCP/IP environment, the Network Interface Layer will include software that implements the Network Device Interface Specification **(NDIS).** This software provides an interface to the higher levels of the TCP/IP protocol stack as well as an interface to drivers for various media access specifications. One such specification that we are using for our Ethernet is ISO/IEC Standard 8802-3 (ANSI/IEEE Standard 802.3). Interfaces to drivers for other media access specifications, such as Fiber Distributed Data Interface (FDDI) can be included. Drivers are written for the NICs that they control. Having NDIS allows the higher layers of the protocol stack to be independent of the media access implementation that is used as long as the stack complies with NDIS.

So as not to leave the reader with only an overview of networking concepts, in what follows we introduce you to the demonstration network used in this book and describe its components. Pictures of the components have been included so that the reader will see what they look like and how connections to them are actually made. We think that having this physical view will help the reader visualize how networking and network management are implemented as we work through later chapters.

1.4 THE DEMONSTRATION NETWORK

The demonstration network is a LAN. LANs typically host workstations, servers, hubs, switches, repeaters, bridges, routers and probes. Our demonstration network is shown in **Figure 1.6**.

It is a small network but it includes most of the devices that are used on a LAN. There are two types of communication media being used. Subnet 1 uses only

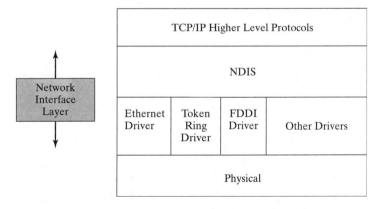

Figure 1.5   The Functions of the TCP/IP Network Interface Layer

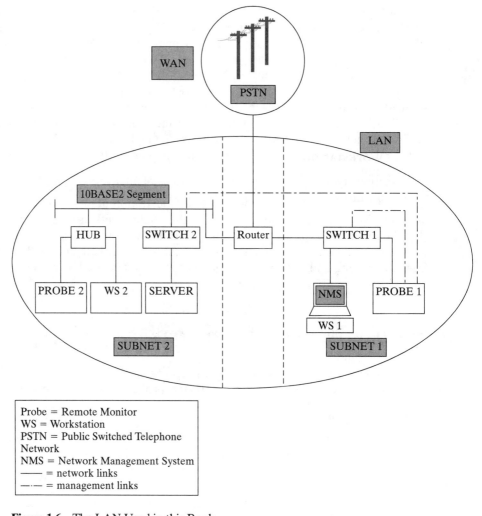

Figure 1.6 The LAN Used in this Book

10BASET media. Subnet 2 uses10BASET and 10BASE2 media.(See the discussion under Repeaters, that follows, for the definition of these communication media terms.) We will see in later photos in this chapter that:

- The switches have RJ-45, AUI and serial connectors.
- The hub has coaxial BNC, AUI and serial connectors.
- The router has AUI Ethernet and serial connectors.
- The Ethermeter probe has BNC and serial connectors.
- The Fastmeter probe has RJ-45 and serial connectors.
- PCs have either BNC or RJ-45 connectors.

When necessary, an AUI transceiver/adapter is used to adapt from AUI connectors to RJ-45 or BNC connectors. **Figure 1.7** shows these adapters as well as an NT4.0/95 modem with RJ-11 connectors for the wall line and telephone connections.

AUI connectors were designed for connection to a cable that runs from a computer to the Medium Attachment Unit (MAU) on a 10BASE5 cable. BNC connectors are used to connect 10BASE2 cable to the adapter in the computer. RJ-45 connectors are eight pin connectors for 10BASET cables that connect the computer adapter to a hub. Now let's examine the typical computers on a network.

1.4.1 Workstations

Workstations typically make use of the services of all layers of a protocol stack because they process the requests of application programs for information on servers. There are two workstations on the network. They are labeled WS1 and WS2. WS1 is a IBM PS/2 Multimedia Unit. It hosts the Windows NT 4.0 Workstation operating system. It also hosts a copy of the Meterware NMS application programs that will be used to access network management information from network devices and remote monitors. WS2 hosts the Windows 95 operating system and another copy of the Meterware NMS. It will also be used to demonstrate the acquisition of management information. WS1 is attached to subnet 1 by its RJ-45 connection to Switch 1. WS2 attaches to subnet 2 by its BNC connection to the hub.

1.4.2 Servers

Servers also make use of all layers of the protocol stack because they respond to requests from application programs on other computers. The server on this network, labeled Server, hosts the Windows NT 4.0 Server operating system. WS1, WS2 and

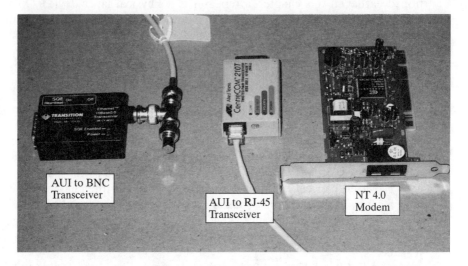

Figure 1.7 AUI, BNC and RJ-45 type connectors used for network physical connectivity. Also shown is a modem for the Windows NT4.0 operating system that uses the standard RJ-11 telephone jack connectors.

Server implement the client/server architecture. WS1, WS2 and Server also form a Windows NT 4.0 Domain. The domain concept will be discussed in Chapter 4. Server will be used in the demonstration of acquisition of management information. Server is attached to subnet 1 by its RJ-45 connection to Switch 2.

1.4.3 Repeaters

The length of a LAN is limited by the CSMA/CD specification. A signal from a station that is sending must propagate to the farthermost station that may be waiting to send a message before the listening time of that station ends. The number of stations on a LAN segment is limited because each station taps off some of the energy in the signal. Incorporating **repeaters,** which amplify the signal between segments, can extend the length of a LAN beyond its single segment minimum. Such repeaters are used on 10BASE2 and 10BASE5 LANs.

The CSMA/CD specification allows the 10BASE2 LAN to have three coaxial segments containing up to 30 devices each. The length of each segment is limited to 185 meters. Such a LAN can therefore have 90 attached devices when repeaters are used between segments. The terminology 10BASE2 means 10Mb/s transmission rate, BASE stands for baseband, which means the full bandwidth is available for the transmission and 2 stands for 185 meters rounded off.

The terminology 10BASE5 means the segments with devices attached can be 500 meters in length and up to 100 devices can be attached to each. **[Ref 10-11]** Thus if repeaters are used, a 10BASE5 LAN can have 300 devices attached. However, being about 0.5in in diameter, the 10BASE5 cable is much less flexible than 10BASE2 cable which is less than 0.25in in diameter Thus 10BASE5 installations are only practical in permanent installations. More often than not these days, hubs rather than 10BASE2 or 10BASE5 media are used to construct LANs. As mentioned earlier in this chapter, a repeater is a Physical layer device. Only Physical layer protocols apply to it. The repeater does not examine information in a frame but simply amplifies and re-transmits it. We have not included a repeater in the demonstration network.

1.4.4 Hubs

A **hub** is a repeater with many input and output ports. Like a simple repeater, it is considered a Physical layer device. Every transmission received by the hub on one port is amplified and re-transmitted out of all other ports. Like the simple repeater, the hub does not examine information in any field of the frame. Hubs are used mostly today to construct LANs. This choice was enabled by the availability of category 5 twisted pair cable and more recent upgrades to the characteristics of category 5 cable. In the past, only coaxial cable could be used for 10Mb/s transmission rates over any practical distance. Now category 5 twisted pair cable can be used for transmission rates up to 100Mb/s over100 meter distances and gigabit rates are feasible.

Figure 1.8 and **Figure 1.9** show the front and back of the 3COM hub. This hub connects Probe 2 and WS2 to 10BASE2 coaxial cable using BNC connectors. Hubs can be constructed using coaxial cable BNC connectors, twisted pair connectors or

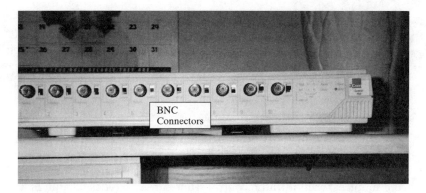

Figure 1.8 Front of 3COM Hub

a combination of both. The hub used here has BNC connectors on the front and one Attachment Unit Interface (AUI) connector on the back. Each 10BASE2 cable is attached using a BNC "T" connector with one end of the "T" terminated by a 50 ohm resistor, the characteristic impedance of the cable, to eliminate reflections of the signal. (See the AUI to BNC Transceiver in Figure 1.7 for an example of how a "tee" connection with terminator looks.) As **Figure 1.6** suggests, there are three cables connected to the hub, two on the front and one on the back.

An external AUI-to-BNC transceiver is attached to the AUI connector on the left of **Figure 1.9**. We are using this transceiver to make a connection to the BNC connector on the back of Switch 2. Also, shown in the middle of **Figure 1.9** is the management unit that has been added so that we can manage the hub using Meterware/Analyzer. Near the center of that unit is a 25 pin serial connector that will be used to configure the hub in Chapter 5. This connector can also be hooked up, via an RS-232 cable, to a modem for remote configuration.

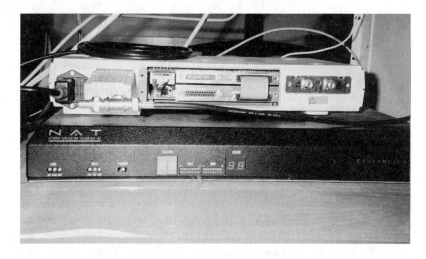

Figure 1.9 Back of 3COM Hub

Twisted pair hubs use RJ-45 connectors. The cables also use RJ-45 connectors and contain two twisted pairs. One twisted pair transmits information from an attached device to the hub and the other twisted pair is used to transmit information from the hub to the attached device. The maximum length of a segment between a hub and a device is 100 meters.

1.4.5 Bridges

In the devices previously described, the protocol stack was not used to read the information in the frames received and thus there was no control of traffic flow to or from other devices. As you might expect, this is often undesirable. **Bridges** provide the simplest form of traffic control. There are two types of bridges: transparent and translating.

The **transparent bridge** divides a LAN into segments that use the same media access control specification and it controls what traffic is passed between the segments. When the bridge receives a frame from one segment, it stores the source address in a database called a **bridge table**. By learning the source addresses, the bridge learns which devices are on which segments. Later, when a bridge receives a frame, if the destination address is that of a device with a source address on the segment from which the frame was received, the bridge discards the frame. If the bridge has not learned where a destination address is, it can be configured so that the frame will be forwarded. A bridge is called a MAC device because it uses information in the MAC header, i.e., the hardware address, to make decisions. The bridge reads no other information in the frame and when the frame is forwarded, it is unmodified. Thus a bridge protocol stack will only use Physical and Data Link layer protocols. **Translating bridges** connect networks using different MAC layer specifications, for example Ethernet and Token Ring. In this case, the bridge translates the MAC header of one into the MAC header of the other.

Bridges perform another important function: errors and collisions that take place on one segment are not propagated to devices on the other segment. Bridges can be used to construct complex networks depending on how they are configured. A **switch** is a multiport bridge. The router on our network can be configured to operate as a bridge. Rather than using bridges on our network, we are using switches because they provide more functionality. This use of switches rather than bridges is commonplace today.

1.4.6 Switches

As just mentioned, a switch is a multiport bridge. Thus the switch has more forwarding options. The switch stores a source hardware address and the port through which it was received in the **switch table**. If a switch receives a frame containing a destination hardware address that is not in its switch table, the switch can be configured to forward the frame out of all ports that have connected links. So for example, suppose Switch 1 in **Figure 1.6** has just been turned on and receives a frame containing the WS1 destination hardware address and the Probe 1 source address. But the WS1 destination hardware address is not in its switch table so the frame will be forwarded to both WS1 and the Router. Now the switch knows the port to which Probe 1 is attached. Thus if a frame containing the destination address of Probe 1 is received the frame will be forwarded only to Probe 1.

Switches are typically configured to forward incoming frames to outgoing ports based on destination MAC addresses associated with those ports in the switch table. However, switches can be configured to drop frames based on MAC destination addresses or to redirect frames to other MAC addresses. Some ports can also be configured as secure ports which means only frames from a specified set of other ports will be forwarded to them.

Today, switches are often used to construct Ethernet LANs. This is called **Switched Ethernet.** Unlike LANs based on hubs or cable, switched Ethernet enables simultaneous communication between multiple ports without collision. Switches can also be used to construct virtual LANs **(VLANs).** A VLAN is a LAN created by isolating a set of ports and the attached devices from the rest of the ports on the switch. Other ports do not see collisions on the VLAN. A switch can support multiple VLANs.

Higher layers of the protocol stack are now being implemented in switches. You will often hear the terms layer 3 switching and layer 4 switching, meaning that entities in the Network and Transport layers, respectively are being employed to decide how the frame should be handled. Use of layer 4 entities would, for example, enable the switch to give re-transmission priority to frames requiring a higher quality of service **(QoS).** As the capability of switches increases, it is becoming more difficult to differentiate them from routers. **Figure 1.10** shows the fronts of Switch 1 and Switch 2 sitting on the Fastmeter probe which is discussed below.

Switch 2 is almost identical to Switch 1 except that Switch 1 has an optical fiber 100 Mb/s Ethernet port. We will talk about these switches in great detail in Chapter 5 when we configure them and all devices on the network. For now, lets point out a few features. The fronts of the switches contain 24 10 Mbps RJ-45 connectors numbered left to right from 1 to 24. The two connectors on the far right are numbered 26

Cisco
Switches

Fastmeter
Probe (front)

Figure 1.10   Fronts of Cisco Catalyst 1900 Switches and Fastmeter

and 27. These are RJ-45 100Mbps connectors. They would typically be connected to other switches to create a backbone. The backs of the switches have AUI connectors. These connectors are numbered 25. On Switch 2, we use this AUI connector and a transceiver to connect the switch to the 10BASE2 cable as mentioned above. The back of the switches also contains RJ-45 connectors which can be used to configure the switch by connecting it to a PC, the network or, using a modem and the PSTN.

1.4.7 Routers

Like bridges and switches, **routers** isolate network segments into collision domains. Each domain is unaware of collisions in other domains. In addition, routers further isolate subnets and networks by using the Network layer in the protocol stack. An entity in the Network layer reads the Network layer header in the packet to find the destination network address. It then looks up the address in the routing table. The **routing table** is a list of mappings of network addresses to ports (IP Interface Addresses) that will get the packet to the destination network by the best means. The best means could be the shortest distance, the minimum time, the maximum throughput, etc. The routing table for a small network can be constructed manually (statically). For large networks, it is necessary to have it done automatically (dynamically) using routing protocols that learn routes from other network routers. A router is primarily distinguished from bridges and switches by the fact that routers connect networks and use network addresses to do so. Thus the router is only interested in network addresses and in getting packets from one network to another.

    Table 1.1 shows a hypothetical routing table. Since this routing table is that of a very small network, it could be created and maintained manually (statically).

    Implementations of routing protocols cause packets to be sent to routers on other networks to which the sending router is directly connected. These packets both send and request information. The Routing Information Protocol **(RIP)** sends a message every 30 seconds that includes all the information in the routing table of the sending router. The Open Shortest Path First **(OSPF)** protocol uses a more efficient paradigm. In the case of OSPF, only updates to the routing table are typically sent. Thus, in a short time, every router on the network will have the type of information shown in **Table 1.1**. Of course, on a typical network, there will be many

Table 1.1 Hypothetical Routing Table

Destination (IP Network Address)	Mask for	Distance (hops)[a]	Route (IP Interface Address)
Network 1	Network 1	0	A
Network 2	Network 2	0	B
Network 3	Network 3	1	C
Network 4	Network 4	1	D
Network 5	Network 5	2	E
Network 6	Network 6	3	F
Network 4	Network 4	2	G

[a]A hop is a traversal of one router.

more entries than shown in this table **[Ref 12].** Other routing protocols will be discussed and configured in Chapter 5.

The destination column in **Table 1.1** lists the IP addresses of networks that this router has learned. The second column contains the **masks** for those networks. When the router receives a packet, it performs the logical AND operation on the received IP address and all masks until it finds an IP network address in the first column. (See **Appendix A** for a detailed discussion of IP addressing, subnet masks and the logical AND process.) From the data in the third column, labeled "distance," the router knows the number of hops from itself to the other networks for each of its network interfaces. The number of hops is the number of routers the packet must traverse to reach the destination network. If the RIP is being used, the router sends the packet out of the interface that will produce the least number of hops. Notice that there are two routes available from this router to Network 4. The router will choose Route D because it has the least number of hops.

Figure 1.6 shows that our router connects two subnets. **Figure 1.11** shows the back of the actual router.

On the left is the AUI-to-BNC transceiver that connects the router to the AUI-to-BNC transceiver on the back of Switch 2 on subnet 2. On the right is the AUI-to-RJ-45 transceiver that connects the router to a RJ-45 port on Switch 1 which is on Subnet 1. When a router connects subnets, what happens when the router receives a frame? Let's say the frame comes from another LAN though the PSTN serial connector which is the connector on the far left. The router applies a **subnet mask** to the address in the destination field of the Network Layer header. As described for the network masks in **Table 1.1**, the application of the logical AND will extract the address of the subnet to which the packet should be routed. The connector on the far right is a 25-pin serial connector that can be used to configure the router with an attached PC. We will have much more to say about this when we configure the router in Chapter 5 using this configuration method.

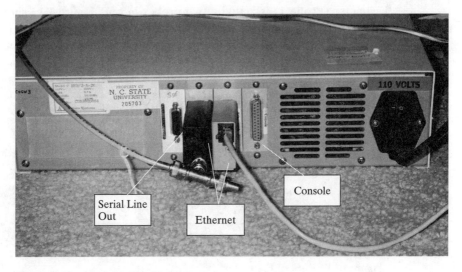

Figure 1.11   Back of Cisco AGS Router

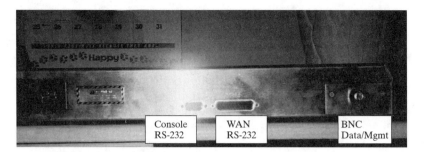

Figure 1.12   Back of Ethermeter

1.5.8 Probes

Figure 1.12 and Figure 1.13 show the backs of the two probes that will be used to capture network traffic.

Probes are invaluable tools for learning about the details of the communication between devices. Probes can be placed on any segment of a global network and the information they gather transferred to the Management Station for analysis of the traffic on that segment. Thus probes are also called remote monitors.

Our two probes have different network physical attachments and capabilities. The Ethermeter, (Probe 2), is attached to the hub on Subnet 2 using a BNC connector. Traffic capture and probe management are done using the same port. Ethermeter will detect and capture any traffic that reaches the Subnet 2 side of the router. Ethermeter has two other ports. The one on the far left is a serial DB-9 RS-232 port and the other is a serial DB-25 RS-232 port. Both can be used to configure Ethermeter with a PC and a crossover cable. A crossover cable, often called a null-modem cable, is often needed to connect the transmit pins of each device to the receive pins of the other. The WAN RS-232 connector can be used to attach a modem for remote configuration.

Fastmeter (Probe 1) is actually two probes in one. **Figure 1.13** shows that it has four ports. The **Management Port** is attached to Switch 1. This port is used by an NMS such as Meterware/Analyzer to request and receive SNMP management traf-

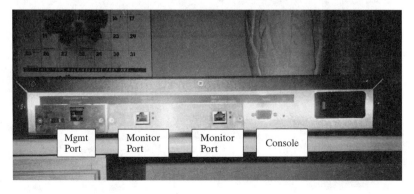

Figure 1.13   Back of Fastmeter

fic. Fastmeter has two other ports called **monitor ports**. Thus Fastmeter can monitor two network segments simultaneously. We have attached one monitor port to Switch 2 on Subnet 2 and one monitor port to Switch 1 on Subnet 1 to capture traffic on each of those switches simultaneously. The attachment to Switch 2 allows Fastmeter to capture the same traffic as Ethermeter.

In **Figure 1.6**, the dashed lines from Fastmeter to the switches indicate the monitoring functions of Fastmeter. Fastmeter also has a serial DB-9 RS-232 port on the far right that is used to configure it directly using a crossover cable and a PC or remotely using a modem and an RS-232 cable. This port can also can be used for out of band management by connecting it to a management station.

The Management Agent on Fastmeter is enhanced over that on Ethermeter. Fastmeter's management agent captures both RMON1 and RMON2 MIB variables. The RMON1 MIBs are examined in Chapter 8. Also, Fastmeter captures protocol traffic in all layers of the OSI Reference Model. Thus, for example, Fastmeter captures SNMP, FTP and Web application layer traffic for analysis by Meterware/Analyzer.

Now that we have reviewed networking components and how they may be configured to implement a working network, in Chapter 2 we discuss the principles of network management, how they are implemented using the network itself, as well as the history of network management development.

CHAPTER SUMMARY

This chapter provided an overview of networking components and communication architectures. These topics will be visited again in detail when we demonstrate some aspects of ISO Configuration Management in Chapters 4 and 5. The functions of the layers in the OSI Reference Model were described. The OSI Reference Model was compared to the TCP/IP protocol stack that we are using on our network devices and the differences explained. It was shown how frames are constructed by the protocol layers. An explanation was given of the functions of networking devices and the layers of the TCP/IP stack they implement. The physical connectivity of the devices on the network was shown via photos and explained.

REVIEW QUESTIONS

1. What was the purpose of creating the OSI Reference Model?
2. The OSI Reference Model has seven layers performing seven categories of functions necessary for computer communication. The TCP/IP protocol stack has only four layers. What functionality, if any, is missing in the TCP/IP protocol stack?
3. SNMP is part of which layer in the TCP/IP protocol stack?
4. A Network Management System (NMS) is part of which layer if any in a protocol stack?
5. What two elements does a PDU contain?
6. What headers would an SNMP packet contain?

7. What protocol does a web browser use?

8. Why might you want to configure a switch to drop frames intended for a particular device?

9. What is the advantage of a switched LAN over a 10BASE2 LAN?

10. Are switches always layer-2 devices?

11. What is the advantage of networking using hubs versus using coaxial cable?

12. Why do you think 10BASET segments connecting devices to hubs are limited to 100 meters in length?

13. What is the purpose of a bridge table?

14. What mappings do switch tables contain?

15. What mappings do routing tables contain?

16. How does the Ethernet II frame differ from the ISO/IEC 802.3 frame?

17. What is the purpose of the Network Device Interface Specification (NDIS)?

EXERCISE

1. Too often in a computer lab, a computer classroom or an organization, the user of a computer network is not exposed to how the network is connected and it is often difficult to get someone to describe the connectivity or to find a network diagram, if it exists. Find out from your instructor or your network administrator, how your network is connected and draw a diagram of it. Include the access to other campus networks and the Internet.

REFERENCES

1. ISO Standard 7498-1 "Open System Interconnection-Basic Reference Model" For access to this and other standards that will be listed in chapter references, see http://www.ansi.org/.

2. "SNMP, SNMPv2 and CMIP: The Practical Guide to Network Management," William Stallings, Addison Wesley, 1993, p. 541.

3. "Open Networking with OSI." Adrian Tang and Sophia Scoggins, Prentice Hall, 1992.

4. TIA/EIA Standard 232-E, "Interface Between Data Terminal Equipment and Data Circuit Terminating Equipment Employing Serial Binary Data Interchange."

5. ISO/IEC 8802-3 "Carrier sense multiple access with collision detection (CSMA/CD) access method and physical layer specifications."

6. "Internetworking with TCP/IP, Volume I, Principles. Protocols and Architecture," Second Edition, Douglas E. Comer, Prentice Hall, 1991.

7. "A Guide to TCP/IP on Microsoft Windows NT 4.0," Richard Burke and Mohammad Fatmi, Course Technology (International Thomson Publishing,) 1998, p. 10.

8. "Open Networking with OSI,: op. cit., p. 200.

9. "SNMP, SNMPv2 and CMIP": op. cit., p. 568

10. "ISO/IEC 8802-3," op. cit., p. 133

11. " A Guide to TCP/IP on Microsoft Windows NT 4.0" opcit., p. 16.

12. Ibid., pp. 156–172.

CHAPTER 2

OVERVIEW OF NETWORK MANAGEMENT

This chapter will:

- Describe responsibilities of a network manager
- Define network management vocabulary
- Discuss network management principles
- Provide an example of network management implementation
- Identify new network management approaches
- Document the evolution of network management

As the title of the chapter suggests, we intend to give the reader an initial perspective on network management, why the need for network management has increased and how the concepts and implementations evolved. The reader is introduced to the general network management recipe with a step-by-step example. The example provides a framework that is filled in by the details given in later chapters.

2.1 WHAT IS NETWORK MANAGEMENT?

2.1.1 The Early Days

The job of the network manager in the early days of network management was mostly a local one. This was possible because connectivity of interest was mostly local, networks were not large and there were not that many networks. The network manager was primarily concerned with attaching PCs, workstations and a server to a LAN using Network Interface Cards (NICs), installing and configuring operating systems on PCs, workstations and servers, installing protocol stacks, configuring NIC I/O addresses, Direct Memory Access (DMA) addresses and Interrupts so as not to conflict with other NIC selections and configuring protocol stacks. The Ping application was usually employed to ensure that all devices on the network could communicate with one another. Ping sends a message to a device identified by its IP address and waits for a reply from that device.

To control access to information on a network server, the manager might write a script for the server that would be executed when the user at the PC or workstation logged on. The script would provide a uniform view to all users and only provide access to drives, folders or files that the user or group of users needed. The manager would perform coordination activities for the PCs and workstations. He or she would also install a print server application on the server or a stand-alone print server PC to manage the print jobs from each of the PCs and workstations. After all, sharing a printer was one of the main purposes of networks in the first place.

If the network were to be divided into segments or subnets, say one for each department in the organization, a bridge or router, respectively, would be used to connect them. If a subnet, the manager would configure a router table to enable connectivity according to network address, subnet address and subnet mask. Connectivity to remote networks required more router configuration and installation and maintenance of *Wide Area Network* (WAN) interfaces but this was not often required.

Next, it was necessary to install user applications on PCs and workstations and to ensure that they were interfacing correctly with the operating system. Then, application support programs (APIs) appeared on the scene to support easy access to the protocol stack and thereby the server. Sometimes such support programs were an integral part of the protocol stack and sometimes not. Given all of these duties, it was still possible for the network manager to accomplish them in a timely manner because the number of devices to be managed was small by today's standards.

2.1.2 Maintenance

All of the duties mentioned above configure the initial state of the network only. Network **performance** is not optimized, there will be software and hardware **failures** and network resources will change. Thus, maintaining the network will demand much of the manager's time. In addition, the manager is usually required to make estimates of the network **capacity** that will be necessary to meet the growing demands of the organization and to find ways of providing that capacity within budget. One can add to this list of duties the need to **account** for usage of the network so that charges can be assessed and applied to cost centers. Then there was need for some minimal **security**. Configuration of user IDs, passwords and file rights or permissions, at a minimum, was needed to control access to private and perhaps sensitive information. Given all of these responsibilities, it was just possible for the network manager to keep up with his duties on a small LAN, if he or she worked extra hours.

Note

The words in bold in the paragraph above are also the formal names of the management categories that were defined by the International Organization for Standards **[Ref 1]**.

The above paragraphs imply that the network manager does everything. Given the size of today's enterprise networks, even with the software tools available, network "management" has divided into specialties. For example, one specialty includes administrative functions, such as backing up servers, adding and deleting users, installing operating systems and applications and maintaining security. These tasks are typically done by people who, for example, have Novell's Certified NetWare Administrator (CNA) training or perhaps Microsoft's Certified Professional (MCP) training.

Then there are the network engineers who may have received Novell's Certified NetWare Engineer (CNE) or the Microsoft Certified System Engineer (MCSE) certificates that provide training in network technologies, network support, network service and network management. These people are responsible for the health of the network and its availability to the user. When we use the term network manager, we are thinking of those in the latter group who use the tools of network management to monitor and control the network resources. It should be noted that there is no clear line of distinction between the roles of network professionals and that it is not necessary to have a certificate to perform the necessary functions.

2.1.3 Information Explosion

As the information age came upon us and the number of Internet users grew exponentially, the number of users on organizational networks (Intranets) also grew along with the number of such networks. In addition, as knowledge became an essential ingredient for a company's success, the demand for networks to provide intra-organizational connectivity as well as global access using the Internet, grew dramatically. With such growth came the demand for applications that would enable all this information to be used effectively.

Software that enabled applications to communicate with applications on other machines was now more in demand. (Enter client/server systems) **[Ref 2].**

Such software provided interfaces to protocol stacks and the network. These interfaces are analogous to the Application Program Interfaces (APIs) on the local computer that simplify access to the operating system and other local programs. You will often hear the term **middleware** used for programs that provide these interfaces.

2.1.4 Network–Based Management

The reader can easily see that the workload for the network manager had gotten so great that all of it could not be handled locally or be effective and timely. Also, as networks have grown larger and more complicated, many other demands on the network manager have arisen. The network manager needed to find more efficient ways to determine and control the state of network. The Simple Network Management Protocol (SNMP) **[Ref 3-8],** the Management Information Base (MIBs) **[Ref 9-11]** and network management systems (NMS) were developed that could be used by the network manager to remotely control values of device parameters. For remote network traffic monitoring, the Remote Monitor (RMON1) standard **[Ref 12-14]** was later added. This standard allowed the manager to access the agent on a "probe" that captured traffic on the segment to which it was attached and analyze the statistics of that traffic. The long-term goal of network management is automatic detection of potential network problems and correction of these problems before they become network failure points. A modern example of this approach is discussed in Appendix E.

Some of the references listed above are called Requests for Comments (RFCs). If the reader is not familiar with RFCs, it is important to know that these are the "Proposed Standards" for the Internet community in the United States. All RFCs are available on the Internet. Yahoo provides a number of ways to access them. Our preference from Yahoo is **[Ref 15]**. **[Ref 16]** is equivalent and provides other information about the Internet Engineering Task Force (IETF) that oversees Internet standards development. In both of these references, the RFCs are hyperlinked for rapid access. The primary body of non-proprietary networking knowledge consists of the IETF RFCs and the IEEE and ISO standards.

2.2 SOME NETWORK MANAGEMENT VOCABULARY

Network management today is mostly a combination of local and remote configuration and management with software. Remote network management is accomplished when one computer is used to monitor, access and control the configuration of other devices on the network. **Figure 2.1** shows a simple network management environment.

The managing device is called a **Management Station** and the managed device is called a **Management Agent.** In this example, the station and agent are using the Public Switched Telephone Network (PSTN) to communicate. A management agent hosts software that provides access to information about the device that is hosting it. A management station hosts management software called the Network

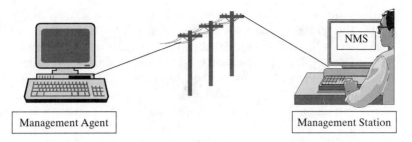

Figure 2.1 Simple Network Management Environment

Management System (NMS). The NMS consists of applications that enable the station to access, display and analyze the information provided by the agent. The management agent can be a computer, as shown in **Figure 2.1**, or another device, such as a hub, router or switch.

Figure 2.2 depicts management terminology and functionality in more detail.

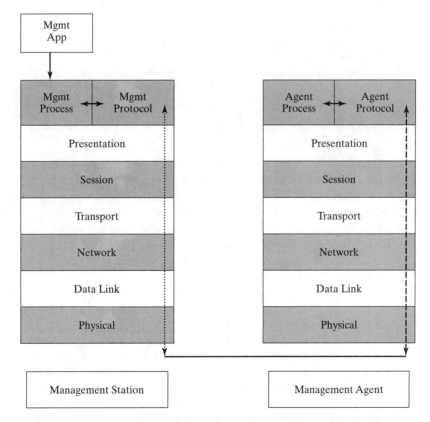

Figure 2.2 Protocol Stacks on the Management Station and the Management Agent

If the terminology is not clear at this time, don't worry, we will come back to it often. The terminology we use is that defined in the Open Systems Interconnection (OSI) Reference Model specified by the International Organization for Standards (ISO) **[Ref 1]**. ISO Standards can be obtained from the WebSite of the American National Standards Institute (ANSI) given in **[Ref 17]** by clicking on the "Standards Information" button. Also, there are many standards that are published by the International Telecommunications Union (ITU) that are relevant. For example, the standard that we refer to as **[Ref 1]** was originally an ITU standard with the title X.200. It was initiated by the ITU-T technical committee that was originally the International Consultative Committee for Telegraphy and Telephony (CCITT), a French standards organization. To access the ITU-T Standards (called Recommendations) go to **[Ref 18]**

Figure 2.2 shows flow of network management information between a Management Station and a Management Agent. To make this happen, two or more software modules are added to both the Management Station and the Management Agent. One of these is the program that enables transport of management information between two devices. This program implements the network management protocol. SNMP is an example of a network management protocol.

> **Note**
>
> There are distinctions between modules, programs and processes that are not important to us in the context of this book. A program is executable code. A process is a program that is active. A module is code that may not be executable by itself.

Another program added is called a **management process** on the Management Station and an **agent process** on the Management Agent. The management process services management application programs and provides an interface to the network management protocol, e.g., SNMP. The agent process is an integrator of processes (called subagents) that access information requested by a network management application and also serves as an interface to the network management protocol. An overview of what agent code embodies and its role as integrator can be found in **[Ref 9]**.

A management application is a readily available application that you buy from a vendor. A collection of management applications is typically called a Network Management System (NMS). The agent process can run on any device such as a PC, workstation, server, router, hub, and switch. The agent process collects the values of a specified set of variables when a request is made by the Management Station. The virtual store of such values is called the Management Information Base (MIB). The MIB is called a virtual store because the values are actually maintained by the managed sub-systems of the device **[Ref 9]**. The management application program queries the agent's MIB, obtains the results and displays them in readable form on the management station.

2.3   A NETWORK MANAGEMENT EXAMPLE

The following are the basic steps that take place when a management application wishes to obtain the value of a MIB variable on a Management Agent. **Figure 2.2** is the software architecture that implements these steps.

1. A management application belonging to the NMS calls for the service of the management process.
2. The management process calls the program that implements the **network management protocol,** e.g., SNMP.
3. The network management protocol implementation constructs a request packet. This packet is embedded in a frame constructed using the protocol stack. The frame is sent to the program on the Management Agent that implements the network management protocol, e.g. SNMP. In SNMP, a typical request packet is called a Get-Request packet.
4. The implementation of the network management protocol on the Management Agent causes the request packet to be passed to the agent process.
5. The agent process accesses the value of the requested variable (perhaps with the help of a subagent) and passes it to the program that implements the network management protocol.
6. The network management protocol constructs the response packet that is embedded in the frame constructed by the protocol stack and the frame is sent to the Management Station. In SNMP, the response packet is called a Get-Response packet.
7. At the management station, the program that implements the network management protocol receives the response packet. Implementation of this protocol causes the response packet to be passed to the management process.
8. The management process either passes the requested value to the application program that displays it, perhaps using a Graphical User Interface (GUI), or stores it in memory for later retrieval.

Implementation of these steps constitutes the overhead that is incurred when network management over a network is implemented. This overhead includes, for example, the number of CPU cycles used by the management application program and the network management protocol in constructing a request packet and the number of control bytes supplied by the protocol stack layers that are necessary to ensure that the packet gets to the port of the processing module. In addition, storage used on management stations and management agents may be significant for large networks. It is convenient to have a dedicated Management Station on the network so that management processing does not interfere with other processing. Beyond these overhead considerations, the network manager has to be concerned about the amount of traffic being generated by network management packets. Too much network management traffic creates a new problem. There is always a trade-off to be defined.

The diagram in **Figure 2.2** shows OSI Reference Model protocol stacks on the Management Station and the Management Agent. As we discussed in Chapter 1, there are seven layers in the OSI Reference Model protocol stack. The top layer is the Application layer. It contains the network management protocol, e.g., SNMP, and the agent or management processes. The Application layer will also contain other protocols and service processes, e.g., FTP, HTTP, SMTP. They are not relevant for this discussion and thus have not been shown for clarity. We are also not concerned at this time with the necessary functions that are performed by lower layers of the protocol stack that were discussed in Chapter 1.

2.4 ADDITIONAL NETWORK MANAGEMENT PROTOCOL CAPABILITIES

Network management protocols can construct requests for multiple values in a single message. The agent process retrieves each value and puts them in the Get-Response packet in the order in which they were requested. Accessing multiple values in one Get-Request packet speeds up the access process. In addition, there are commands that make it possible to traverse the management information data structure (MIB) on the Management Agent in logical order. For SNMP, this is accomplished with the Get-Next-Request command These commands and their implementation will be examined in detail in Chapter 6: SNMP.

Network management protocols also enable the Management Agent to send unsolicited messages to the Management Station. These messages, called **traps,** are sent, for example, if a device goes from the powered-up to the powered-down state and when there is a Get-Request that does not contain the correct community name, the SNMP password. There are many other trap messages that are used, as we will see.

In addition to accessing information from standard network devices such as computers, routers and switches, information can also be accessed from other network devices called probes or remote monitors **(RMON).** The use of the words remote monitor may seem redundant since most network monitoring is of a remote device. However, remote monitoring and the RMON standard refer to monitoring activity (traffic) on a network segment, not a particular device. Thus, the Management Agent is remote from (not a part of) the devices it is monitoring. A remote monitor can be configured to capture and store all or selected groups of frames that it receives on the network segment to which it is attached. Thus, remote monitors provide information about traffic between devices on a network segment. Such information includes, among other things, hardware and network addresses of source and destination devices, the protocols that are being used and statistics about usage of the segment by specific devices.

The Management Station accesses information captured by the remote monitor using the procedures described above in steps 1–8. It also may, automatically poll the monitors on a regular basis for updates of information.

2.5   NETWORK MANAGEMENT ENHANCEMENTS

The capabilities of network management applications continue to expand as the need arises and technology advances. Included in these expansions are fault, capacity, resource and trending management. New categories of management such as Service Level Agreements (SLA) **[Ref 19-20]** and Management by Policy **[Ref 21]** and their metrics have become important. In addition, the number of network management approaches has increased. Included in these new approaches are Web-based Management **[Ref 22]** and Desktop Management **[Ref 23]**. We talk about these approaches in Chapters 10 and 11.

There are also more management application programs available They provide a wide range of data analysis and decision-making capabilities. However, it is important to emphasize at this point that all management application programs depend on the protocols and databases that are the focus of this book. Furthermore, no matter how comprehensive the management application, what is important is that the application provide information important to the network manager and display it in a manner that is easy to comprehend.

As promised, let's now look at the evolution of network management. It is useful to do so because the resulting perspective will provide the reader with an appreciation of how we got to where we are and the rationale for today's and future approaches to network management. This understanding will also enable the reader to evaluate evolving approaches to network management. As you will see, a lot happened in the short time period between when network management was first thought to be necessary and today.

2.6   EVOLUTION OF NETWORK MANAGEMENT

2.6.1   OSI Reference Model

About 10 years before people working in the field of data networks began to see a need for remote and/or automated network management, those associated with data networks and the International Organization for Standards (ISO) recognized that growth in the use of communication over distributed networks required a formal protocol architecture specification that would promote uniformity in standards development. In 1977, the ISO established a subcommittee to develop such an architecture. The result was the Open Systems Interconnection **(OSI)** Reference Model, ISO Standard 7498-1 **[Ref 1]**, which was published in 1984. The stated purpose of this Reference Model was to "provide a common basis for the coordination of standards developments for the purpose of system interconnection, while allowing existing standards to be placed in perspective within the overall Reference Model." This Reference Model is usually used to explain the functionality of protocol stacks as was done in Chapter 1.

2.6.2 SGMP

In March of 1987, a few network engineers in the United States began an effort to develop a network management protocol for gateways **[Ref 8].** (This reference provides an interesting look at the controversy surrounding network management developments at the time.) By November of 1987, this effort led to RFC 1028, the Simple Gateway Monitoring Protocol **(SGMP) [Ref 24].** The goal of the SGMP developers was to minimize the complexity of software needed for gateway management and the number of commands to which gateway agents would have to respond. Thus only two types of commands were viewed essential: "get" the value of a variable and "set" (change) the value of a variable.

During the time frame in which SGMP was developed, those continuing to enhance the Open Systems Interconnection (OSI) Reference Model began to develop a network management protocol to add to the OSI suite of protocols. A group in the United States therefore thought that the long-term solution would be to add the OSI network management protocol to the existing Internet TCP/IP architecture rather than pursue SGMP. This approach was called **CMOT** (CMIP over TCP) where **CMIP** is Common Management Information Protocol. CMIP is contained in the Application layer of the OSI protocol stack. CMIP is defined in ISO standard 7498-4 **[Ref 25].** See **[Ref 5]** for a good description of it.

2.6.3 CMIP

As was mentioned in Chapter 1, in the OSI Reference Model protocol stack, CMIP plays a role similar to that of SNMP in the TCP/IP protocol stack. Upon request from the management application, CMIP creates the protocol data unit and maps it to a Remote Operations Service Element (ROSE) protocol that supports communications between all distributed applications in the OSI environment. Referring back to **Figure 2.2**, in the OSI environment, CMIP and ROSE are part of a Management Process that is very comprehensive. For all applications, including management, the OSI application layer provides more application services than does the TCP/IP application layer.

Included among the additional capabilities of the CMIP are eleven management operations (commands) rather than the five supported by SNMP and the ability to operate over a variety of protocol stacks including TCP/IP. By making extensive use of object-oriented modeling concepts, CMIP provides more detailed representation of MIB objects, the ability to create objects, and objects that inherit the properties of other objects. In addition, the ability to define the scope of object filtering according to attributes leads to much greater control of its Get operation. These capabilities also lead naturally to a larger MIB with objects that have many attributes not present in MIB definitions used by SNMP.

There has been a price to pay for these capabilities at the Application and other layers of the OSI Reference Model. Long development times and complexity have kept the industry from adopting it pervasively. In short, the difference between CMIP and SNMP can be best stated by the SNMP motto: "Keep it Simple." A thorough discussion of OSI System Management Concepts, including CMIP, is given in **[Ref 5].**

2.6.4 SNMP

As a result of controversy over the SGMP and CMOT approaches, the Internet Activities Board (IAB), the body that was responsible for all Internet research and development in the United States at the time, convened a subcommittee in February 1988 to identify the best approach to follow. The decision was that both approaches would be pursued. Eventually the CMOT approach was found too difficult to implement and was abandoned. However, an enhanced version of SGMP, called the Simple Network Management Protocol **(SNMP)** was developed **[Ref 3].** Several groups worked on this management system definition. Work on the Internet-standard Network Management Framework was also initiated (see below). This framework encompasses SNMP. By 1989, SNMP had become the defacto operational standard for network management of TCP/IP-based networks.

2.6.5 More History

A little more history is appropriate at this point. At about the same time that development of the OSI Reference Model protocol architecture was initiated, universities in the United States were developing protocols that would enable communication between a small number of their computers for collaborative research. This effort was supported by the DOD Advanced Research Projects Agency **(ARPA)** and led to the non-proprietary set of protocols known as TCP/IP. **[Ref 26]** The TCP/IP protocols were an intrinsic part of the Unix operating system developed at UC Berkeley. Eventually corporations took notice of the TCP/IP protocols and use began to grow. However, as mentioned, it was expected that the TCP/IP protocols, and thus SNMP, would be a temporary measure until completion of the OSI protocols.

This was not to be the case. SNMP became so widespread and the OSI protocols were so slow in developing that SNMP became the dominant network management protocol. Even so, a study of the details of the OSI Reference Model Standard 7498-1 and its protocols is very worthwhile. The standard describes the protocols and their interactions in great detail. Such detail is difficult to find elsewhere. Although TCP/IP and SNMP are today the dominant protocol stack and network management protocol, respectively, the OSI Reference Model and CMIP are in use.

2.6.6 Network Management Framework

In August 1988, the Internet Activities Board (IAB) assigned a working group the task of creating an Internet Standard Network Management Framework to define the components required for network management of TCP/IP networks. This resulted in three RFCs. RFC 1155 **[Ref 27]** defined the Structure of Management Information **(SMI)**. SMI makes use of Abstract Syntax Notation One **(ASN.1)**. ASN.1 was developed to enable specification of the OSI Reference Model and is the language used to define SMI managed objects. For discussion of ASN.1, see **[Ref 9, 28, 29]** and **Appendix B** of this book. As explained above, the agent process accesses the value of an object requested in an SNMP Get-Request packet. Object values are stored in a data structure on the Management Agent. RFC 1156 defines this data structure and calls it the Management Information Base **(MIB)[Ref 9-11]**. The requested object is referenced using the language of SMI (a subset of ASN.1). Finally, RFC 1157 defines the Simple Network Management Protocol, SNMP **[Ref 3]**.

2.6.7 History Table

Table 2.1 provides a summary of the evolution of the computerized network management developments described above and lists other relevant events. We have not discussed all of these developments in this chapter but they will be addressed in other parts of this book. As you can see, 1988 and 2002 were busy years for network management development. There are many informative articles available in *Network World, Data Communications,* and *Network Computing* magazines about network management and related topics during this time. In addition, the magazines refer to vendor products that are improving the state-of-the art in network management applications. We refer to these in the appropriate chapters.

2.7 HISTORY GRAPH

Figure 2.3 is a graph of the data in the **Table 2.1**. While being less accurate than the History Table, the graph gives us a birds-eye-view of the technology and protocols that have made possible or impacted the development of network management. What is not included in the table or shown on the graph are the tools being developed that, using the current protocols, are providing added value that make network management more powerful for the enterprise. We discuss such tools in Appendix E.

The only axis on the graph that has meaning is the ordinate where years are shown. However, we have attempted to show the dependence of one development on others by placing it directly over ones on which it depended. For example, RMONI depended on RMONII. The height of the boxes is intended to give an indication of the time frame over which major development indicated in the box took place. The width of the box has no meaning and is chosen only to accommodate the included text.

Table 2.1 Evolution of Network Management (References are those at end of chapter)

Date	Event	Reference
1968	ARPA funds development of packet switching networks	• RFC 1120 Internet Activities Board. V. Cerf. Sep-01-1989. (Obsoleted by RFC1160) • RFC 1160 Internet Activities Board. V. Cerf. May-01-1990. (Obsoletes RFC1120)
1974	TCP/IP concept proposed	Cerf V., and R. Kahn, "A Protocol for Packet Network Interconnection," IEEE Trans. on Communications, Vol. COM-22, No. 5, pp. 637–648, May 1974. [Ref 26]
1976	Ethernet developed	Metcalfe, R., and D. Boggs, "Ethernet: Distributed Packet for Local Computer Networks," Communications of the ACM, Vol. 19, No. 7, pp. 395–404, July 1976.
1978	OSI Reference Model development initiated	
1983	OSI Reference Model becomes international standard	ISO/IEC 7498 (CCITT X.200) [Ref 1]
1987	SGMP development started ASN.1 developed	[Ref 24] ISO 8824, Parts 1–4
1988	IAB initiates study of SGMP and CMIP SNMPv1 becomes Interim Draft Standard SNMPv1 becomes Draft Standard IAB initiates development of Internet Standard Network Management Framework (SMI) Draft Standard MIB I developed	 Interim RFC 1028 (SNMPv1) Draft RFC 1098 (SNMPv1) Draft RFC 1065 (SMI) Draft RFC 1066 (MIB I) [Ref 10]
1989	CMOT approach abandoned SNMP becomes the defacto standard for TCP/IP management	
1990	SMI becomes Recommended Standard SNMPv1 becomes Recommended Standard MIB I becomes Recommended Standard	RFC 1165 (SMI) RFC 1157 (SNMP) [Ref 3] RFC 1156 (MIB I) [Ref 11]
1991	MIB II RMONI	RFC 1213 (MIB II) RFC1271 (RMONI) [Ref 12]
1993	SNMPv2 Proposed SNMPv2 Security SNMPv2 MIB SNMPv2 SMI	RFC 1441 (SNMPv2 Management Framework) RFC 1446 (SNMPv2 Security Protocols) RFC 1450 (SNMPv2 MIB) RFC 1442 (SNMPv2 Structure of Management Information)
1995	RMONI	RFC1757 [Ref 13]
1997	RMONII	RFC2021
1998	Desktop Management Interface (DMI) Specification v2.0s Web-based Management Initiative	• http://www.dmtf.org/sped/dmis • Network Computing, Feb 2001, p. 57 • http://www.dmtf.org/standards/standard-wbem.php
1999	SNMPv2 Management Frameworks SNMPv3 Security	RFC 2571 RFC 2574 (User-based Security Model)
2002	SNMP Management Frameworks SNMPv3 Security SNMP VACM SNMP MIB	RFC 3411 std 62 RFC 3414 (User-based Security Model), std 62 RFC 3415 (View-based Access Control Model), std 62 RFC 3418, std 62

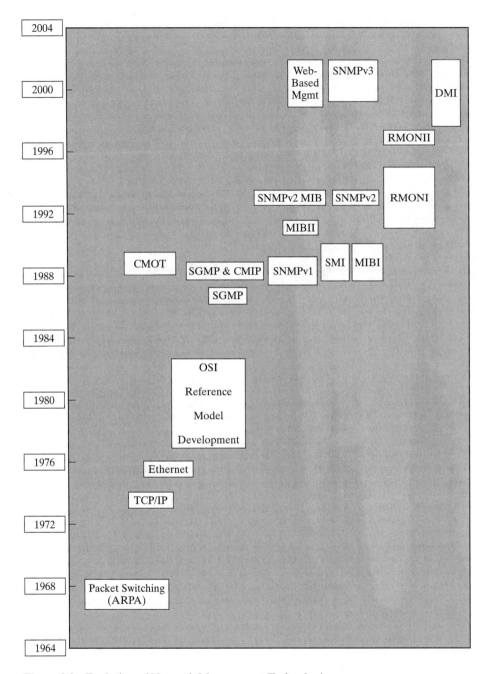

Figure 2.3 Evolution of Network Management Technologies

CHAPTER SUMMARY

This chapter provided a perspective on network management. It described the responsibilities of a network manager. It showed that these responsibilities became too many to be handled locally when the onset of the information age greatly increased the number and size of networks to be managed. This situation led to the development of a remote approach to network management. The chapter included a discussion of the terminology and fundamental principles of network management and an example of remote network management was given. The history of the development of network management was described and referenced. The reader was introduced to the importance of RFCs and the material in the chapter gives reference to many RFCs.

REVIEW QUESTIONS

1. What is the principle difference between the SGMP and the SNMP?
2. What is a MIB?
3. What principle feature did the RMON1 standard add to the MIB-2 standard?
4. What is the function of an agent process on a Management Agent?
5. Should we always strive for more network management?
6. What network management protocol does the OSI protocol stack use?
7. What function does CMIP play in the OSI Reference Model?
8. Why are some vendors hesitant to incorporate an SNMP agent on their devices?
9. Did SNMP become a de facto or de jure Internet standard?

EXERCISES

1. Make a list of network management functions that are done manually and locally today.
2. Make a list of network management functions that are done locally using software today.
3. Make a list of network management functions that are done locally and automated.
4. Make a list of network management functions that can be done remotely.
5. Make a list of network management functions that are automated and done remotely.

You may not be able to contribute to all of these lists at this point but add to them from what you learn in later chapters. For example, see the tables in Chapter 3. You will find these lists enlightening and perhaps surprising, as did the author.

REFERENCES

1. ISO Standard 7498-1, "Open System Interconnection-Basic Reference Model."
2. "A Guide to TCP/IP on Microsoft Windows NT 4.0," Richard Burke and Mohammad Fatmi, Course Technology, 1998.
3. RFC 1157, "A Simple Network Management Protocol." J.D. Case, M. Fedor, M.L. Schoffstall, C. Davin, May 1, 1990.
4. "The Simple Book, An Introduction to Management of TCP/IP-based Internets," Marshall T. Rose, Prentice Hall Series in Innovative Technology, 1991, p. xxi.
5. "SNMP, SNMPv2 and CMIP: The Practical Guide to Network Management Standards," William Stallings, Addison Wesley, 1993.
6. "The Simple Book, An Introduction to Internet Management," Second Edition, Marshall T. Rose, Prentice Hall Series in Innovative Technology, 1994.
7. "Total SNMP: Exploring the Simple Network Management Protocol," Sean Harnedy, CBM books, 1994.
8. "How to Manage Your Internet using SNMP," Marshall T. Rose and Keith McCloghrie, PTR Prentice Hall, 1995.
9. "Understanding SNMP MIBs," David Perkins and Evan McGinnis, Prentice Hall PTR, 1997, Chapter 5.
10. RFC 1066, "Management Information Base for Network Management of TCP/IP-Based Internets," K. McCloghrie, M.T. Rose. Aug-01-1988. (Obsoleted by RFC1156.)
11. RFC 1156, "Management Information Base for Network Management of TCP/IP-Based Internets," K. McCloghrie, M.T. Rose. May-01-1990. (Obsoletes RFC1066.)
12. RFC1271, "Remote Network Monitoring Management Information Base," S. Waldbusser. Nov-01-1991. (Obsoleted by RFC1757.)
13. RFC 1757, "Remote Network Monitoring Management Information Base," S. Waldbusser. February 1995. (Format: TXT=208117 bytes) (Obsoletes RFC1271) (Obsoleted by RFC2819) (Status: DRAFT STANDARD.)
14. RFC 2819, "Remote Network Monitoring Management Information Base," S. Waldbusser. May 2000. (Format: TXT=198676 bytes) (Obsoletes RFC1757) (Also STD0059) (Status: STANDARD.)
15. "RFC Index," http://www.csl.sony.co.jp/cgi-bin/hyperrfc?rfc-index.txt.
16. "The Internet Engineering Task Force (IETF)," http://www.ietf.org/.
17. "American National Standards Institute (ANSI)," http://www.ansi.org/.
18. "International Telecommunications Union (ITU)," http://www.itu.int/publications/itut/itutrec.htm.
19. "Sinking in the Service Management Sea, Bruce Boardman, Network Computing, November 1, 1998, p. 130.
20. "SLA Monitoring Tools," Data Communications, February 1999.
21. "Policy Based Network Management," Joel Conover, Network Computing, November 29, 1999, p. 44.
22. "Web Management," http://joe.lindsay.net/webbased.html#wbem.
23. "Desktop Management," http://www.dmtf.org/spec/dmis.html.
24. RFC 1028, "Simple Gateway Monitoring Protocol," J. Davin, J.D. Case, M. Fedor, M.L. Schoffstall. Nov-01-1987. (Status: HISTORIC.)

25. ISO Standard 7498-4 "Open Systems Interconnection-Basic Reference Model, Management Framework."

26. "A Protocol for Packet Network Interconnection," Cerf V, and R. Kahn, IEEE Transactions on Communications, Vol. COM-22, No 5, pp. 637–648, May 1974.

27. RFC 1155, "Structure and Identification of Management Information for TCP/IP-based Internets."

29. ISO Standard 8824, Parts 1-4, "Abstract Syntax Notation One."

29. "SNMP, SNMPv2 and CMIP: The Practical Guide to Network Management Standards," William Stallings, Addison Wesley, 1993, p. 541

CHAPTER 3

NETWORK IMPLEMENTATION AND MANAGEMENT STRATEGIES

This chapter will:

- Explain why a network implementation strategy is needed
- Examine the principles of network design
- Explain why a network management strategy is needed
- Describe network management categories and related activities
- Classify current network management tools according to functionality
- Examine different network management strategies
- Select a management strategy for this book

The computer network is the central nervous system of most organizations today. This is because information, and the rate at which it can be obtained and distributed, is key to the economic success of companies in the information age. Thus organizations must have a network that is available and reliable. Since networks consist of a complicated set of hardware and software components, reliability comes at the cost of redundancy, diligence, manpower and management. Chapter 2 provided a brief introduction to current network management implementation concepts and to why it was necessary to implement these concepts as networks grew in number and size. Because an organization's network is so critical to its functionality, before implementing anything, it is important to design a network implementation and management strategie that fit the corporation's needs. In this chapter, we examine how to think about such designs.

3.1 WHY A NETWORK IMPLEMENTATION STRATEGY SHOULD BE DESIGNED

We said in the previous paragraph that an implementation strategy is needed because the network is now essential to the organization. Because of the distributed, rather than centralized, nature of networks, and the large size of current networks, the implementation choices are many and often costly. The optimal implementation will depend on the business model of the organization, its size, the geographical distribution of the organization's components, the size of the network to be managed, the network technologies available and the homogeneity of the network hardware and software components. In addition, it is no longer acceptable just to design and implement a network that optimally services the needs of the organization today. One must anticipate future requirements and take into account scalability of design and technology choices. A strategy is needed so that all of these issues will be considered when deciding on the implementation choice. Obviously the design of such a strategy is a major responsibility and implementation design can be considered an important part of network management.

3.2 WHY A NETWORK MANAGEMENT STRATEGY SHOULD BE DESIGNED

In the previous chapter, we talked about the many functions of network managers and administrators. Because of these many functions, on a university campus, for example, some network management, network administration and system administration is often delegated from the campus level to the department to which a network or subnet has been assigned. This management approach is beneficial just as it is beneficial to distribute Internet domain management.

However, there is often limited current awareness at the campus level of resource inventory and resource configuration changes at the department level. Yet, campus network management is responsible for the overall health of the campus network. Unilateral changes in resource inventory, resource configurations and numbers of hosted applications at the department level can place unexpected loads on the campus system which reduce performance and availability, cause packets to be dropped and make fault detection and correction more difficult.

We know from experience that department level network managers will be required or want to meet with campus level network managers on a regular basis to coordinate activities and needs. However, we also know from experience that such meetings will not always take place and that department level network managers want the flexibility to support the department needs as they see fit in a timely manner. We are using the university campus as an example here, but these issues arise in any organization. Thus, we are led to believe that there is a need for a process by which the campus level can monitor and coordinate all network management activities of all departments. The design of this process is the design of a network management strategy.

3.3 NETWORK IMPLEMENTATION STRATEGY DESIGN

You will see later in this chapter that the International Organization for Standards (ISO) has defined five network management categories. One of the reviewers of this book said that he/she likes to think of network implementation design as a sixth category. We agree with that because the optimum implementation design will clarify the design of management strategy. Let's consider some of the choices involved in an implementation design.

Networks come small, medium and large. A small network is typified by a LAN that connects computers in a university laboratory or in one department of a company. A LAN that connects several departments in a university or company typifies a medium size network. A large network is typically one that connects geographically distributed units of an organization using WAN components. Such a network will consist of LANs connected by WANs. A large network could be global, i.e., connecting different divisions of a company in different countries. The Internet and the Public Switched Telephone Network are examples of WANs. The hardware and software used to implement LANs is usually under the control of the company's chief information officer. On the other hand, the WAN may make use of networks that are leased by the company and over which the company has no control. Nevertheless, it is essential that the WAN provide available and reliable links between all units of the company. The network implementation and management design challenges are obviously greater in this environment. **Figure 3.1** illustrates

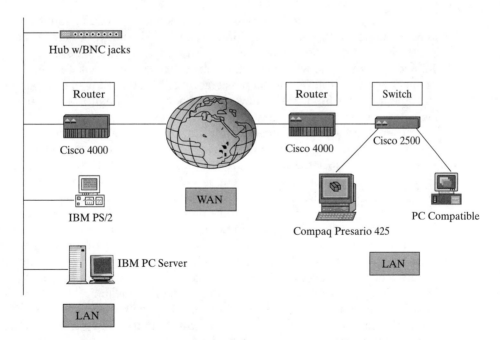

Figure 3.1 Typical Network Connectivity and Components

typical connectivity and components included in any implementation and for which a management strategy needs to be developed.

Let's make a table of issues the designer of a network implementation might need to address. These issues, by category, are listed in Table 3.1. Because of the extent of such a design process, we are only able to indicate some of the many considerations. However, this may be sufficient to give one a feel for how to begin in a real situation.

Each of these categories requires extensive planning. Each must then be integrated into a coherent enterprise network design. Finally, the design must be modified to meet budget availability and to be consistent with the business model of the organization. For a more comprehensive analysis, that includes discussion of the relationship between the business and technical aspects of the process, see **[Ref 1].** Once you have thought through some of the issues listed in the above table, you may be ready to make use of one of the advanced network design tools available. For a review of all the wonderful things these can do for you, see **[Ref 2].**

3.4 NETWORK MANAGEMENT CATEGORIES

The fundamental premise of good network management is maintaining availability of resources to the user. Tools to support the network manager in this endeavor are many and their number continuously increases. It is up to the network manager to find the tools that will be most helpful. We list some of these tools and give references to them later in the chapter.

Before searching for such tools, it is first necessary to think about what needs to be managed. To this end, it is helpful to consider the network management categories defined by the ISO, read the standard in **[Ref 3]** where these categories are defined and then read what the authors referenced in this book define to be management activities relevant to these categories. The network manager can then extract the activities he or she believes are important to monitor and manage from the point of view of the organization.

There is no universal categorization, however, and any categorization of activities is a useful starting point for developing a management strategy. One such categorization and associated metrics are shown in **Table 3.2**. The metrics define the meaning of the category and give examples of what needs to be considered and/or measured. For example, Windows NT 4.0 Server has a User Manager tool that includes a **Policy** Menu. One of the items on this menu is **User Rights**. It gives the network administrator the ability to define the last metric under Policies in **Table 3.2** for a variety of user rights. Another example is the tool OMNIbus by Micromuse Inc. that addresses the Category **Faults** and metric **Proactive Prevention.** Appendix E describes this tool, which prioritizes SNMP alarms so potential faults that have the greatest probability of affecting network availability will be addressed first. The choice of these priorities is influenced by the business model of the organization. Windows NT 4.0 Server also has a tool that includes a large number of server **Performance** metrics such as total processor use, interrupts/sec, queue length and bytes/sec received.

Table 3.1 Network Implementation Design Analysis

Category	Issues

Geographical Distribution	1. Office
	  • Subnets
	  • LAN
	2. Department (many offices)
	  • Subnets
	  • LAN
	3. Division (many departments)
	  • LAN
	  • WAN
	4. Organization (many divisions)
	  • Local
	    ❑ LAN
	    ❑ MAN
	    ❑ WAN
	  • National
	    ❑ WAN
	  • Global
	    ❑ WAN

Subnets	1. How many
	  • Connectivity
	    ❑ Bridges
	    ❑ Switches
	    ❑ Routers
	2. Ethernet
	  • Wireless
	    ❑ Number of receivers
	  • 10BASET
	    ❑ Location of hub(s)
	  • 10BASE2
	  • 10BASE5
	  • How many IP addresses
	    ❑ Static addresses
	    ❑ Addresses supplied by DHCP

LAN	1. How many
	2. Domain names
	3. DNS (Domain Name Service) configuration
	4. Network address
	5. Subnets
	  • How many
	5. Connectivity
	  • Switched Ethernet
	  • Router
	6. Ethernet
	7. Token Ring
	8. FDDI (Fiber Distributed Data Network)

(continued)

Table 3.1 *Continued*

Category	Issues
MAN (Metropolitan Area Network)	1. Connectivity between LANs ❑ FDDI ❑ SONET(Synchronous Optical Network) ❑ LAN ❑ ATM ❑ SMDS (Switched Multi-megabit Data Service) ❑ DQDB (Dual Queue Dual Bus) ❑ Ethernet
WAN	1. Connectivity between LANs or MANs ❑ PSTN ❑ X.25 ❑ TI-T3 ❑ SONET ❑ Frame Relay ❑ SMDS ❑ ATM ❑ Distribution of services
Bandwidth Requirements	1. Video Bandwidth • Constant • Time Dependent • Bandwidth on Demand 2. Audio Bandwidth • Constant • Time Dependent • Bandwidth on Demand 3. Teleconferencing Bandwidth
Media Requirements	1. Cable 2. Wireless 3. Microwave 4. Satellite 5. Optical Fiber
Technology	1. What is available now 2. Minimum required for the job 3. Technology improvements during next 5 years 4. Required to support expected growth
Service Level Agreements (SLA)	1. Specified bandwidth available at any time 2. Specified bandwidth available during specified time periods 3. Bandwidth on demand
Security Requirements	1. Location of firewalls 2. Firewall capabilities 3. Location of proxy servers 4. Encryption and authentication needs 5. Network Intrusion Detectors (NID)
Budget	1. To support resources of optimum network 2. To support resources of minimum network

Table 3.2   A Network Management Categorization and Associated Metrics

Category	Metrics
Reliability	• Transmission error rates • Dropped packets • Link failures
Faults	• Proactive prevention • Detection • Location • Correction time
Availability	• Mean time between failures (MTBF) of network

Performance	• Time to provide a response to the user
	  ❑ Processor total use
	  ❑ Processor interrupts/sec
	  ❑ Processor queue length
	  ❑ Transmit packet lengths

Throughput	• Bytes per second that a user can expect to transmit reliably • Guaranteed throughput based on Service Level Agreement (SLA)
Data	• Packet throughput
Voice	• Ordered packet throughput
Video	• Link bandwidth • Bandwidth on demand
Use	• Packets/sec • Transactions/sec
Resource Use	• Application software • Network devices • Services • Permanent storage • CPU
Policies	• Traffic • What's critical • How many network control packets • Which threshold alarms • Alerts on what events • What's non-critical • Backup—what and how often • Application testing • Software upgrades—how often • Administration • Type of service availability required • Security level required • Firewall protection requirements • Network intrusion detection needs • Number of software license requirements • User rights requirements and how distributed among which users
Redundancy	• Number of redundant systems required • Critical alternate paths
User Support	• Automatic responses to user questions about procedures • Automatic responses to user questions about network problems • Automatic reporting of problems and solutions to users and to a database

Table 3.3   ISO Network Management Categories

Performance Management

Fault Management

Configuration Management

Security Management

Accounting Management

Whatever the network management strategy employed, it will include elements from the categories listed in Table 3.2. Which categories are considered important will depend on the nature of the business that uses the network, the size of the network, the primary purpose of the network, the types of hardware and software that are to be managed, the philosophy of the network manager, the availability of management tools from vendors, and cost trade-offs.

A formal network management categorization has been defined by the International Organization for Standards (ISO)**[Ref 3].** This categorization is shown in **Table 3.3**. In the sections that follow **Table 3.3**, we use other tables to divide each category into sub-categories and give examples of associated network management activities. These sub-categories should not be considered unique or exhaustive. We will see demonstrations of many of them in Chapters 8, 9, and 12.

3.4.1 Performance Management

As indicated in **Table 3.2**, the performance of a network is determined by the network's ability to satisfy the needs of multiple users. Thus, network performance management is concerned with throughput, percentage utilization, error rates and response times. Performance management involves the activities shown in **Table 3.4**. As shown there, **"Collecting Baseline Utilization Data"** is a performance management category. It is a specific example of the more general category **"Collecting a History of Utilization Data."** An activity in this category is sampling counts of the number of IP packets that are received by a device during the sampling intervals at different times of day and on different days. This number can be used to determine if the number of received packets is increasing over time signaling a pending capacity problem for the device. The management software included with this book is used to do such sampling in Chapters 8 and 9. In these same chapters, you will see examples of setting **Notification Thresholds** and how the device uses SNMP packets to make the network manager aware when such thresholds are exceeded.

In the design of a network, its expected performance can be anticipated by creating **simulations** of network performance using different device and network parameters. This approach is the holy grail of network design. Depending on the tool used, it can be a profitable exercise and certainly is necessary for some networks. Some good examples of such tools for network design are given in **[Refs 2,4,5]. [Ref 6]** describes simulations of SNMP device agents and lists the vendors that make them. One can then create a virtual network of different agents against

Table 3.4 Performance Management Sub-Categories and Related Activities

Collecting Baseline Utilization Data	• Measuring link utilization using a probe • Counting packets received/transmitted by a specific device • Measuring device processor usage • Monitoring device queue lengths • Monitoring device memory utilization • Measuring total response times
Collecting a History of Utilization Data	• Measuring utilization and response times at different times of the day • Measuring utilization and response times on different days over an extended period
Capacity Planning	• Manually graphing or using a network management tool to graph utilization as a function of time to detect trends • Preparing trend reports to document projected need for and the cost of network expansion
Setting Notification Thresholds	• Having a network management tool poll devices for values of critical parameters and graphing these values as a function of time • Setting polling intervals • Setting alarms/alerts on those parameters when the threshold is reached or a percentage of it is reached • Initiating an action when the threshold is reached such as sending a message to the network manager
Building Databases	• Having the network management tool create a database of records containing device name, parameter, threshold and time for off-line analysis • Using the database to extract time dependence of utilization • Using the time dependence of parameters to decide when network upgrades will be necessary to maintain performance
Running Network Simulations	• Using a simulation tool to develop a model of the network • Using the model's parameters and utilization data to optimize network performance
Latency	• Query/Response time interval

which an NMS can be tested. In principle, one can then practice SNMP management without a network. This approach is not a panacea as the author points out, but it may be a useful starting point if equipment is not available.

3.4.2 Fault Management

Fault Management is the process of proactive prevention or the detection, isolation and correction of abnormal behavior on the network. It can simply mean monitoring for breaks in cables, printer jams or workstations that are down; i.e., things that result in slow network response. For LANs, it can mean monitoring traffic in search of excessive packet collisions or retransmissions. It includes configuration of alarms that will automatically let the manager know when critical thresholds are exceeded. A goal of fault management is to use trend analyses to predict faults and change network conditions so that the network is always available to the user.

Table 3.5 lists some Fault Management sub-categories and related activities. Connectivity Testing is an example. **Physical connectivity** can be tested using a cable tester designed for the purpose and obtained from Black Box or other network hardware vendors. **Software connectivity** between two devices can be tested

Table 3.5 Fault Management Sub-Categories and Related Activities

Prioritization	• Prioritize faults in the order in which they should be addressed • Use in-band management packets to learn about important faults • Identify which fault events should cause messages to be sent to the manager • Identify which devices should be polled and at what intervals • Identify which device parameter values should be collected and how often • Prioritize which messages should be stored in the manager's database
Timeliness Required	• Management Station is passive and only receives event notifications • Management Station is active and polls for device variable values at required intervals • Application periodically requests a service from a service provider
Physical Connectivity Testing	• Using a cable tester to check that links are not broken

Software Connectivity Testing	• Using an application that makes a request of another device that requires a re sponse.
	  ❏ The most often used application for this is Ping.Exe. It calls the Internet Control Message Protocol (ICMP) which sends periodic Echo Request messages to a selected device on a TCP/IP network
	  ❏ Application on one device makes a request of an application on another device

Device Configuration	• Devices are configured conservatively to minimize chances of dropped packets
SNMP Polls	• Devices are periodically polled to collect network statistics
Fault Reports Generated	• Thresholds configured and alarms generated • Text media used for report • Audio media used for report • A color graphical display used to show down devices • Human manager is notified by pager
Traffic Monitored	• Remote monitors used • Protocol analyzers used • Traps sent to Network Management Station • Device statistics monitored
Trends	• Graphical trends generated to identify potential faults

by sending a text message from one device to another using the ping.exe application and the Internet Control Message Protocol (ICMP) described in **[Ref 7].** If the physical link and the software required for communication are working correctly, the device that receives the message will return the same message to the sender. **SNMP polls** are another way that connectivity between a management station and an agent station can be tested. The management station reports that a device has not responded to a poll. Since SNMP polls are often used periodically anyway to collect statistics from devices, connectivity testing comes free. **Alarms** are fundamental to automated fault prevention. We will see how alarms are configured in Chapter 8 and demonstrate their use. Monitoring of **Device Statistics** relative to device specifications is another good fault prevention tool. If for example, a router has a specified packet throughput limit and the average packet rate is 80% of that limit, it is time to upgrade the router or reroute some of the traffic. Appendix E describes an application that periodically sends requests for service to service provider devices to check on their availability as part of a larger fault prevention effort. This is an example of active management in which **timeliness** of information is key.

3.4.3 Configuration Management

For a network, configuration management includes network configuration and device configuration. Network configuration is often called capacity management because the main concern is topology redesign and adding or redistributing resources to provide the capacity necessary to handle the traffic. Our configuration focus in this book is device configuration as shown in Table 3.6. Device configuration, whether done **locally** or **remotely**, is important enough that Chapters 4 and 5 are devoted to it. **Automated configuration** is becoming a more important part of network management as the sizes of networks grow. The use of the Dynamic Host Configuration Protocol (**DHCP**) and Domain Name Services (**DNS**) addresses provided by Internet Service Providers (ISPs) are examples. NMSs also help in this area with **auto-discovery** of network devices and duplicate IP addresses. NMSs also use **SNMP** messages to determine and store device configurations.

The Desktop Management Interface (DMI) standard discussed and demonstrated in Chapter 10 was developed to enable more desktop configuration capability. SNMP can then be used to access such details remotely. Thus using SNMP, DMI and a DBMS (e.g., Access) cooperatively, presents us with the opportunity to remotely build a global device configuration database. This is really what is needed for network management at the organizational level.

Another configuration feature is software that provides **extensions** to SNMP MIB 2 for more detailed management. An example is the Windows NT 4.0 Server Resource Kit that provides an extension to the NT 4.0 Server SNMP service. This extension may now be included in the SNMP service of the latest service packs. We will see in Chapter 10 that this extension allows us to use the NMS included with this book to manage DHCP, FTP and WWW services.

3.4.4 Security Management

Security Management has become an important component of network management as financial transactions and e-business have become pervasive in Internet traffic. In addition, a more recent concern is terrorism. Security Management is the process of controlling access to network resources with authentication, encryption, authorization policies, firewalls and network intrusion detectors. These mechanisms limit access to hosts, network devices, files and applications to a degree that depends on the user and the user's access method (e.g., local or remote access) and provide notification of attempted or actual breaches of security. Authenticating messages sent between devices so that the receiver knows the transmitter is an example of a security technique. We will see an elementary example of this technique used by SNMPv1. SNMPv3 was developed to enable secure exchanges of SNMP messages. SNMPv3 will be discussed and demonstrated in Chapter 12. **Table 3.7** lists some sub-categories of Security Management and related activities.

Table 3.6 Configuration Management Sub-Categories and Related Activities

Configuration (Local)	• Choice of medium access protocol
	• Choice of correct cabling and connectors
	• Choice of cabling layout
	• Determining the number of physical interfaces on devices
	• Setting device interface parameter values
	  ❑ Interrupts
	  ❑ I/O addresses
	  ❑ DMA numbers
	  ❑ Network layer addresses (e.g., IP, NetWare, etc)
	• Configuration of multiport devices (e.g., hubs, switches and routers)
	• Use of the Windows Registry
	• Comparing current versus stored configurations
	• Checking software environments of devices
	• SNMP service

Configuration (Remote)	• From the network management station
	  ❑ Disabling device ports
	  ❑ Redirecting port forwarding
	  ❑ Disabling devices
	  ❑ Comparing current versus stored configurations
	  ❑ Configuring routing tables
	  ❑ Configuring security parameters such as community strings and user names
	  ❑ Configuring addresses of management stations to which traps should be sent
	• Verifying integrity of changes

Configuration (Automated)	• Using the Dynamic Host Configuration Protocol (DHCP) to configure IP addresses • Using Plug and Play enabled NICs for automatic selection of interrupts and I/O addresses • Domain Name Services (DNS) addresses provided • Trap messages from agents

Inventory (Manual)	• Maintaining records of cable runs and the types of cables used
	• Maintaining device configuration records
	• Creating network database containing for each device:
	  ❑ Device types
	  ❑ Software environment for each device
	  ❑ Operating systems
	  ❑ Utilities
	  ❑ Drivers
	  ❑ Applications
	  ❑ Versions
	  ❑ Configuration files (.ncf, .ini, .sys)
	  ❑ Vendor contact information
	  ❑ IP address
	  ❑ Subnet address

Inventory (Automated)	• Auto-discovery of devices on the network using an NMS • Auto-determination of device configurations using an NMS • Creation of a network database • Auto-mapping of current devices to produce a network topological map • Accessing device statistics using an NMS and the Desktop Management Protocol

Table 3.7   Security Management Sub-Categories and Related Activities

Applying Basic Techniques	• Identifying hosts that store sensitive information • Management of passwords • Assigning user rights and permissions • Recording failed logins • Setting remote access barrier codes • Employing virus scanning • Limiting views of the Enterprise network • Tracking time and origin of remote accesses to servers
Identifying Access Methods Used	• Electronic mail • File transfer • Web browsing • Directory service • Remote login • Remote procedure call • Remote execution • Network monitors • Network management system
Using Access Control Methods	• Encryption • Packet filtering at routers • Packet filtering at firewalls • Source host authentication • Source user authentication
Maintenance	• Audits of the activity at secure access points • Executing security attack programs (Network Intrusion Detection) • Detecting and documenting breaches
Accessing Public Data Networks	• No restrictions—hosts are responsible for securing all access points • Limited access—only some hosts can interface with the Public Data Network using a proxy server
Using an Automated Security Manager	• Queries the configuration database to identify all access points for each device • Reads event logs and notes security-related events • Security Manager shows a security event on the network map • Reports of invalid access point attempts are generated daily for analysis

3.4.5 Accounting Management

Accounting Management is the process of measuring the usage of network resources in order to distribute costs and resources. An example of Accounting Management is monitoring the use of a server by users in a specific department and charging the department accordingly. Accounting Management sub-categories and related activities are listed in **Table 3.8**. Accounting management principles are not addressed in this book.

Table 3.8 Accounting Management Sub-Categories and Related Activities

Gather Network Device Utilization Data	• Measure usage of resources by cost center • Set quotas to enable fair use of resources • Site metering to track adherence to software licensing

Bill Users of Network Resources	• Set charges based on usage.
	• Measure one of the following
	  ❑ Number of transactions
	  ❑ Number of packets
	  ❑ Number of bytes
	• Set charges on direction of information flow

Use and Accounting Management Tools	• Query usage database to measure statistics versus quotas • Define network billing domains • Implement automatic billing based on usage by users in the domain • Enable billing predictions • Enable user selection of billing domains on the network map
Reporting	• Create historical billings trends • Automatic distribution of billing to cost centers • Project future billings by cost center

Of the ISO Management Categories, this book will discuss and demonstrate concepts that address all but Accounting Management. Although Accounting Management will not be treated, it should be noted that Accounting Management components of a Network Management System (NMS) provide essential support on enterprise networks.

3.5 MANAGEMENT TOOLS

Now that options for network management priorities have been examined and perhaps prioritized, the network manager must select which of the available management tools best meet his or her needs. Vendors have addressed network management requirements in many ways. Some provide only management products required by large networks while others provide management products that are more cost effective for small or medium size networks. Products that are designed to manage enterprise networks address all of the ISO categories listed in **Table 3.3**. Products that address smaller networks typically focus on queries that determine the state of specific device parameters. Thus, network management tools are available for a wide range of network types. A particular product may address only some of the ISO management categories. Within those categories, varying degrees of capability are provided.

Table 3.9 has been constructed to provide the reader with a listing of some of the NMS tools that we think are of interest because of their relevance to the content of this book and/or because of general interest in the capabilities provided. The material for this table was generated first by examining **[Refs 8-13]**. Because of the dates of these references, those that looked most relevant were used to access the

Table 3.9   Current Network Management Tools

Company	Product	URL	Comments
Apptitude (HiFn)	Meterware/ Analyzer	http://www. hifn.com	NMS used in this book. Is a complete SNMPv1 tool. It is only available with the book. Apptitude was a leader in SNMP management software and hardware for many years. HiFn develops integrated circuits for encryption.
SNMP Research International	• EnterPol • CIAgent • SNMPv3 Wizard	http://www.snmp.com/index.html	EnterPol is a SNMPv3 NMS. CIAgent is an agent. CIAgent is a free download. SNMPv3 Wizard is an agent configuration tool. The company has many other products. The company has been a leader in the SNMP field.
Castlerock	SnmpC	http://www.castlerock.com/	The Work Group Edition 5.1 is appropriate for small networks. It supports SNMPv3, as does the Enterprise edition that provides other capabilities. Cost of the Work Group Edition is $995.00 The company has been a leader in the SNMP field.
Solar Winds	Engineers Edition	http://solarwinds.net/	Provides a number of management tools ranging in price from $145 to $1995. The $1995.00 package is Web-enabled. The Engineers Edition at $995.00 looks like the most attractive for users of this book in that it contains most of the featuresof the HiFn Analyzer.
MG-SOFT	Net Inspector Lite	http://www.mg-soft.si/	Net Inspector Lite is $495.00. It looks like a good choice for readers of this book. MG-SOFT provides many other more comprehensive products and products can be enhanced by proxy front-end modules. There are also products that support SNMPv3.
Triticom	LANdecoder SNMP Manager	http://www.triticom.com/	LANdecoder SNMP Manager is a simple, easy to use SNMP Manager for Microsoft Windows environment. With it, you can query and control any SNMP-capable device on your network. It can operate standalone or be integrated with Triticom's LANdecoder 32 V 3.2., a network analyzer. The price of LANdecoder SNMP manager is $995.00.
Finisar	Shomiti Surveyor	http://www.finisar-systems.com/	Shomiti Systems is now part of Finisar. The Surveyor product is a comprehensive network hardware manager. A free download is available.

(*continued*)

Table 3.9 *Continued*

Company	Product	URL	Comments
Acterna	Link View Classic 7.2	http://www.acterna.com/	A software based network analyzer at a price of $995.00. Includes a traffic generator. Excellent graphics Also available is Advanced Ethernet Adapter which provides promiscuous capture of packets. Price is then $2700.00.
Network Instruments	Observer 8	http://www.netinst.com/html/observer.html	Supports Ethernet, Token Ring, FDDI, GigaBit and Windows 98/ME and NT/2000/XP. Includes capture for protocol analysis. Price is $995.00.
Precision Guesswork	LANwatch32 v6.0	http://www.guesswork.com/snmptool.html	Described to be an easy-to-use command-line application that allows you to GET a variable, SET a variable, get the NEXT variable, or even get all the variables. Provides programs for receiving ALERTS, as well as a simple monitoring program that allows you to tell if your hosts are SNMP reachable, IP reachable, or not reachable. Allows you to remotely monitor, gather and change networking information from hosts on your network, enabling you to diagnose existing problems on the network, predict where problems are likely to occur, pinpoint faulty routers and interfaces, and, in general, exert control over your network.
Cisco	Small Network Management	http://www.cisco.com/warp/public/cc/pd/wr2k/wrsnms/	Cisco produces many network management products. These products seem most appropriate for audience of this book.
	LAN Management	http://www.cisco.com/warp/public/cc/pd/wr2k/lnmn/	
3COM	Network Supervisor 3.5	http://www.3com.com/products/en_US/detail.jsp?tab=features&pathtype=purchase&sku=3C15100C	This free package can be downloaded from this site. Other packages are available from this site also.
Computer Associates	Unicenter Network and Systems Manager 3.0	http://www3.ca.com/Solutions/SubSolution.asp?ID=2846	This is the basic network infrastructure management package. There are add-on applications available such as a performance application.
Enterasys	NetSight Element Mgr.	http://www.enterasys.com/products/items/NS-EM/	Element Manager is the basic network management package. Policy Manager incorporates the business model into the management process.
	NetSight Policy Mgr.	http://www.enterasys.com/products/items/NETSIGHT-PM/	

Company	Product	URL	Comments
Sunrise Telecom	LAN Explorer	http://www.sunrisetelecom.com/lansoftware/lanexplorer.shtml	A comprehensive NMS, comparable to Analyzer but also containing packet capture and analysis capabilities. $799.00 per license.
HP	Toptools	http://www.hp.com/toptools/prodinfo/overview.intro.html	Toptools is a comprehensive hardware management product. It has many plug-ins for specific hardware. All its features can be integrated into your enterprise management platforms such as hp Open-View Network Node Manager, Microsoft SMS, CA Unicenter TNG, IBM Tivoli Enterprise Management and Tivoli NetView.
IBM	Tivoli Netview 7.1	http://www.tivoli.com/products/index/netview/	This comprehensive management product also correlates and manages events for systematic management of faults.
Groupe Bull S. A. EVIOIAN (A Bull Company)	Openmaster SLM	http://www.bull.com/	Monitoring and control functions encompass systems management, network management, and application management, and it can manage software configurations, hardware assets and batch production. It also works at a higher level, addressing the underlying business needs in a business-oriented way, to provide measurable business value.
Compuware	Network Vantage	http://www.compuware.com/products/vantage/networkvantage/	Formerly called Ecoscope, monitors network performance by monitoring protocol and application traffic. Part of a suite called Vantage.
NetScout	nGenius Real Time Monitor	http://www.netscout.com/products/rtm.htm	Real time voice, video and data traffic. Part of the nGenius Suite.
Nortel	Optivity 6.0 Network Management System	http://www.nortelnetworks.com/products/01/optivity/net_mgmt/index.html	Optivity Network Management System is a comprehensive network management solution. Its key features include fault management, performance analysis, reporting, and access level security.
BGS	Patrol Connect SNMP	http://www.bgs.com/products/proddocview.cfm?id=7263	There are many Patrol products by BGS. Connect SNMP seems the most appropriate for this book. BGS products cover all aspects of network management.
Network Associates Sniffer Technologies	Sniffer Basic	http://www.sniffer.com/products/sniffer-basic/default.asp?A=2	Sniffer Technologies is one of three product lines of Network Associates. Sniffer Basic is one of a suite of Sniffer Technologies products. Its current price is $2163.00.

(continued)

Table 3.9 *Continued*

Company	Product	URL	Comments
Solcom	VirtualEyz	http://www.solcom.com/home. asp?menu=homepage&hdr=shim	Is intended for the Windows NT Platform. Is managed by an ISP and maintained by Solcom.
Heroix	Robomon for Windows	http://www.heroix.com/Downloads/ pdf/Broch_RMNT.pdf	Part of a suite of management products for both Windows and Unix.
NetIQ	End2End Performance Monitor	http://www.netiq.com/products/ e2e/default.asp	End2End Performance Monitor Suite monitors the performance of networked applications from the end-user's point of view to pinpoint whether a problem is with the client, network or server. It includes optional modules for more detailed analysis of these problems.
Ace°Com	Enterprise Tele-management	http://www.acecomm.com/ solutions/en/en.htm	A comprehensive solution including all ISO network management categories.

latest data for **Table 3.9** from Internet web pages. In addition, there is a major database of network management products maintained by SNMP Research International **[Ref 14]**. We have included many listings from that database in the table here.

There is significance to the order in which the products are listed. Those nearest the top of the table are considered to provide many of the capabilities of the Meterware/Analyzer tool used in the book. In addition, we felt that that these provided the required amount of capability while being attractively priced for the likely audience of this book. Products nearer the bottom of the list provide more capability and are oriented toward enterprise management needs such as service level and policy management, storage of network collected information for correlation analyses and being able to monitor objects for many network media. It can be expected that these will demand a higher price. The prices shown in **Table 3.9** are those we were able to obtain reliably from the company on the Internet. Most of the products that we would expect to demand a higher price did not provide the price information. **[Ref 15]** is a recent comparison of "low-cost" products. All but one are included in Table 3.9. For future network management options, we recommend that the reader consult *Network World* and *Network Computer* trade journals. *Data Communications* is no longer published.

It is not necessarily the best strategy to buy the network management tool that is the most expensive. Such a tool may be overkill for accessing the management information you want and may require more expertise to use it effectively than you want to develop. Also, since different vendor's products provide different management capabilities, two tools that cost the same may be appropriate for your network size but emphasize different services. Therefore, it is important that a management strategy for your network be carefully devised before selecting a management tool. The following example network management configurations attempt to clarify these points.

3.6 NETWORK MANAGEMENT CONFIGURATIONS

There are two network management configurations: Centralized and Distributed. Let's look at the centralized case first. In both cases the client/server model of network communication is implemented. **[Refs 16-17]**

3.6.1 Centralized Configuration

The network in **Figure 3.2** consists of three nodes that are LANs and a backbone node to which the LAN nodes are connected. The number of devices on these LANs is meant to represent a LAN of many such devices. In this configuration, management is centralized to the Network Management Station on the backbone network. The Management Station could also have been part of one of the LANs. The Management Station hosts the NMS and a Management Information Base (MIB). The network manager gathers information about activities on the LANs by using the NMS and SNMP packets to query the agents on the LAN devices. The word probe is another name for a remote monitor as discussed in Chapter 1. The device agents copy and store information from transmitted and received packets.

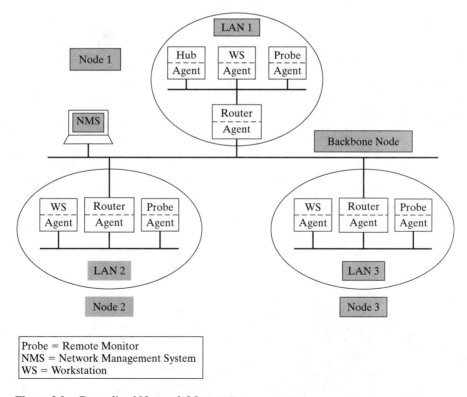

Figure 3.2   Centralized Network Management

The agents on the probes copy and store packets on the network segment to which they are attached when requested to do so by the NMS. One disadvantage to the centralized NMS configuration shown is that failure of a router shuts down all management of the LAN to which it is connected.

3.6.2 Distributed Configuration

The network shown in **Figure 3.3**, uses distributed network management and would be a good choice for an Enterprise network in which there are more backbone devices and more LAN devices. It is a more robust system. The LANs are managed by a Local Administrator using the local NMS while a Central Administrator manages backbone devices using an NMS host attached to the backbone network.

A LAN NMS could be one that has only the capability necessary to provide the type of management required by that network while the NMS on the backbone might need to be more comprehensive for its functions. For example, from **Table 3.9**, one might select an NMS near the top of the table for the LANs and one near the bottom of the table for the backbone NMS. Each node's NMS maintains a MIB for that node only. This reduces storage requirements for each Management System

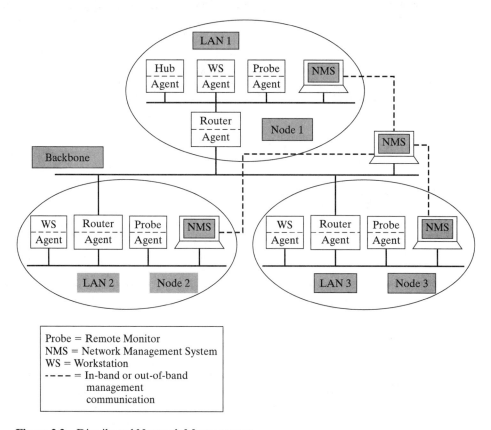

Figure 3.3 Distributed Network Management

that can become quite large because many tables of many objects have to be stored. The backbone NMS could maintain a MIB for each LAN and each LAN could keep its MIB updated. Thus, the backbone NMS would have a complete Enterprise view. The backbone NMS can also query a LAN NMS to obtain management information about devices on that LAN. In this case, the LAN NMS is an agent for the backbone NMS. A LAN NMS could also query the backbone NMS for information about the status of devices on other LANs. In this case, the backbone NMS becomes an agent for the LAN NMS. This arrangement provides a hierarchy of Management Station and Management Agent communication using either in-band management over the network or out-of-band management over a dedicated management network. This communication is indicated by the dashed lines in **Figure 3.3**. An important advantage of this hierarchy is that in case of a network fault, some level of network management will probably be available.

These decentralized features of distributed management serve another important function these days. Because the business of an organization now relies on its network, it has become important to correlate distributed events so that better management decisions can be made. These decisions involve the relationship of the business model of the organization and the health of the network. There is now software that makes such a correlation possible and we will see examples of it in Appendix E. Some of the tools listed in **Table 3.9** include this capability. An automated distributed hierarchy also makes possible effective distribution of the management load. In the example of **Figure 3.3**, if the backbone NMS (the manager of managers) is automatically provided with the management status of each LAN by messages from those LANs, then a coordinated management discipline across the entire network will be in effect. This approach is similar to that of domain management on the Internet that works so well.

3.7 SELECTED MANAGEMENT STRATEGY

As can be seen from the discussion thus far, many network implementations, management policies and strategies as well as configurations to implement those policies and strategies are possible. There are also a variety of NMS tools available to implement network management. There may or may not exist a management tool that implements all of the functions required by a management policy and strategy. Some compromise will be necessary unless a new network management tool is written. The compromise must be made based on what is best for the organization and not just on the tools or technology that are available.

The network we use to demonstrate management concepts implements a centralized strategy. Only one LAN with two subnets is managed. The reason for this choice is that we wish to demonstrate management fundamentals with the simplest network that will allow us to include the principal devices used on networks today. Distributed management introduces other concepts that are not germane to the purpose of this book. The TCP/IP protocol stack **[Refs 16-17]** and the Simple Network Management Protocol (SNMP) **[Ref 18-22]** are used to query the SNMP agents on each device. SNMPv1 is chosen for demonstration in all but Chapter 12 because it is the dominant network management protocol used in today's network environments and is the simplest to implement. SNMPv1 clearly elucidates the essential principles of network management that the student should learn. There are three versions of SNMP: SNMPv1, SNMPv2 and SNMPv3 **[Ref 21].** Among the improvements of version 2 over version 1 are expanded data types, improved efficiency in retrieving information and richer error handling. SNMPv3 is SNMPv2 plus commercial grade security and administration features. SNMPv2 and SNMPv3 are discussed, configured and implemented in Chapter 12.

An NMS needs access to the MIB on the devices it manages. The MIB is a virtual database that is managed by the device's agent. **Instances** of device objects are stored in the MIB data structure and retrieved by the agent from this data structure when a query is received from the NMS. As will be seen in detail later, an instance is the word used to represent an object's value. There are four types of MIBs. MIB I, MIB II, which is an extension of MIB I that has more objects, proprietary MIBs and RMON MIBs. MIB I and MIB II are standard MIBs whose properties are defined by Internet Request for Comments (RFCs). MIB II is a superset of MIB I and is the

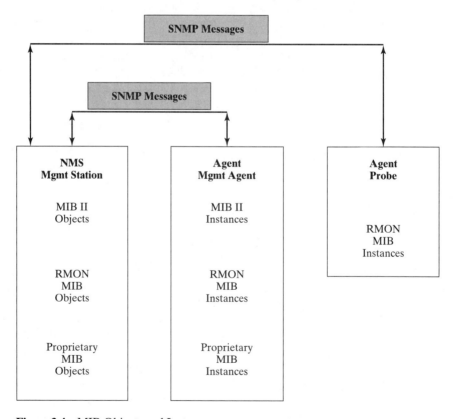

Figure 3.4 MIB Objects and Instances

only one we will refer to from this point on. Proprietary MIBs have additional objects that are specific to a particular device. RMON MIBs contain objects relevant to segment traffic captured by probes. (RMON MIBs are considered part of MIB II.) RMON objects are supported by probes and some multiport devices such as the switches we use on our network. In order for an NMS to access instances of objects stored in MIB data structures, the NMS must have compiled lists of these objects installed on the computer that hosts the NMS. Proprietary MIBs can usually be obtained from the vendor in text form and then compiled by your NMS.

Figure 3.4 summarizes the relationships between the NMS, MIB objects, device agents, RMON agents and their instances. The arrows indicate the flow of SNMP messages.

We have chosen the NMS Meterware/Analyzer from **Table 3.9** because we found it attractive for the concepts we wanted to demonstrate in this book. Other NMSs from the top of the table could have been chosen. Thus, we believe that it is possible to use one of those NMSs when following the exercises in the book because we have chosen to demonstrate fundamental concepts that are not dependent on Meterware/Analyzer. The other side of the coin is that we believe Meterware/Analyzer provides at least as much capability as other NMSs appropriate for this book and the transition would not be difficult.

CHAPTER SUMMARY

The concepts of network implementation and management strategies were discussed. The importance of selecting a network management strategy that will satisfy the current and projected long-term needs of the organization was explained. We examined the ISO Network Management Categories by dividing them into tables of sub-categories that defined metrics for each. The general network management environment and the centralized and distributed network management configurations available to implement that environment were described. A table of current NMS tools was constructed. This table contains features of the tools and vendor URLs. A management configuration was selected for this book.

REVIEW QUESTIONS

1. Why is a network important to organizations today?
2. Write down three reasons why a network implementation strategy is important.
3. What do you think is the most costly aspect of implementing a network for an organization?
4. Do you think remote network management is worth the bandwidth required?
5. Assuming you think remote network management is important, write down three reasons that a network management strategy is needed.

6. The ISO has defined five categories of network management. Can you pick one that is the most important? If not why?
7. What do you think is the most important criteria to apply when choosing a network management system?
8. Write down one practical example of an activity for each of the five types of ISO Management Categories that comes to mind from your experience.
9. There are now three versions of SNMP. Why have we chosen to emphasize version 1 in this book?
10. What is the distinction between variables in MIB II and those in Proprietary MIBs?
11. If you had your choice, for a large network would you implement a centralized or distributed network management strategy and why?

EXERCISES

1. Using your good and bad experiences, design an optimum network for a college classroom.
   - Show the connectivity of all devices
   - Label all devices
   - Describe the media used
   - Describe the need for the devices you have chosen
   - Explain how you would physically connect the devices in the most convenient way in the classroom
   - Assume you must have connectivity to other classrooms
   - Assume you must have connectivity to the Internet
   - Assume there is connectivity to a campus management facility
2. If you were going to use a NMS to manage the devices in the hypothetical network you designed in Exercise 1, what are examples of the most important information you would like to have available?

REFERENCES

1. Network Computing, October 1, 2001, "Can You Build It?" p. 53.
2. Network World, "Designing Networks: Tools of the Trade," December 3, 2001, pp. 42–46.
3. International Standard ISO/IEC 7498-4, "Information Processing Systems—Open Systems Interconnection—Basic Reference Model—Part 4: Management Framework.
4. Network Computing, "Making Sense of Network Chaos," April 17, 2000, pp. 69–84.
5. Network Computing, "NetRule 4.0," June 11, 2001, pp. 40–42.
6. Network Computing, "SNMP SIM SUITES," December 10, 2001, pp. 86–89.
7. Internet Control Message Protocol (ICMP), Request for Comments RFC 0792.
8. Data Communications, "Distributed Net Management: In Search of Solutions," McGraw-Hill; Feb. 1996, pp. 101–112.
9. Data Communications, "Network and Systems Management Listing," McGraw-Hill, August 21, 1996, pp. 195–208.
10. Data Communications, "Guaranteed Service?" McGraw-Hill, June 1997, pp. 84–94.

11. Data Communications, "RMON 2: A Window on the Enterprise," McGraw-Hill, September 1997, pp. 87–93.

12. Data Communications, "A Reasoned Approach to Network Management," McGraw-Hill, March 1998, pp. 30–32.

13. Data Communications, 1998 Global Networking Directory, "Network and Systems Management," Supplement to Data Communications, pp. 159–173.

14. "Network Monitoring Software," http://netman.cit.buffalo.edu/nm-bin/showprods.cgi?db=MONITORING

15. Network Computing, "Network Management on $1.19 A Day," February, 2003, pp. 32–46.

16. "Internetworking with TCP/IP, Volume I, Principles. Protocols and Architecture," Second Edition, Douglas E. Comer, Prentice Hall, 1991.

17. "A Guide to TCP/IP on Microsoft Windows NT 4.0," Richard Burke and Mohammad Fatmi, ITP Course Technology, 1998, p. 10.

18. "The Simple Book: An Introduction to Management of TCP/IP-based Networks," Marshall T. Rose, Prentice Hall, 1991.

19. "How to Manage Your Network Using SNMP," Marshall T. Rose and Keith McCloghrie, PTR Prentice Hall, 1995.

20. "SNMP, SNMPv2 and CMIP," William Stallings, Addison Wesley, 1993.

21. "SNMP, SNMPv2, SNMPv3 and RMON 1 and 2, Reading, Mass., Addison Wesley, 1998.

22. "Total SNMP," Sean Harnedy, CBM Books, 1994.

CHAPTER 4

CONFIGURATION: CLIENT/SERVER COMPONENTS

This chapter includes configuration of:

- Network Interface Cards
- Windows 95
- Windows NT 4.0 SERVER
- Windows NT 4.0 Workstation
- The TCP/IP Protocol Suite
- SNMP Management Agents
- Microsoft Networks
- Discussions of:
  - NetBIOS over TCP/IP
  - Domain Name Service (DNS)
  - Windows Internet Name Service (WINS)
  - Windows NT 4.0 Domains

This chapter and the one that follows provide examples of the local configuration category in **Table 3.6 of Chapter 3**. Such configuration is not only a typical component of network management, but also provides the baseline for effective SNMP management over the network. It is the purpose of this chapter and the next to provide that baseline.

You will see also that successful device configuration requires the careful application of a methodology and documentation of that methodology.

This is true even if there are only a few devices on the network. The time it takes to troubleshoot a network is usually inversely proportional to the care taken in documenting device configuration. What one often thinks is that the configurations will be remembered. This is almost never the case. Thus the configuration practices described in this chapter and Chapter 5 will simplify network management if followed and documented.

In Chapter 1: Networking Components, all of the hardware and software necessary for the operation of a LAN were discussed. If this discussion were sufficient, we would now be able to power-up the LAN devices, load the networking software and begin communication between devices. What is missing is the configuration of the software that will make each device and application recognizable to every other device and application. It is a bit like getting the people on each end of the telephone line to speak the same language.

One reason network configuration is not easy is that most networks are heterogeneous, consisting of computers with different operating systems, utility software and applications. It is typical to have computers running DOS, Macintosh, Windows 95/98, Unix, Linux, Windows NT 4.0/2000 Workstation and SERVER and Novell's NetWare operating systems. The latest addition is Windows XP. These operating systems create and store files in different formats and may use different protocol stacks with different network addressing schemes.

We saw in Chapter 1 that NDIS specifications were written so that different protocol stacks could link to different network adapter cards (NICs) using different Data Link protocol layer implementations. NICs connect the motherboard to the network media. Software is needed to control the output of NICs. Such software is typically called a NIC driver. In order for the driver to be able to communicate over different LAN media, it also must be written to the NDIS specification, or in the case of NetWare, to the Open DataLink Interface (ODI) specification. Legacy adapter cards often require manual setting of the Interrupt Request (IRQ) number, the input/output (I/O) address and the Direct Memory Access (DMA) address. Each of these must be specified so as not to be the same as those chosen for other legacy adapter cards on the LAN. Fortunately, "Plug-N-Play" adapter cards are now common. The system BIOS works with these cards to automatically configure their parameters at startup so as not to have values that conflict with one another or with legacy adapter cards.

In addition to enabling the protocol stack to link to the network media, the protocol stack itself on each PC must be configured. (We will on occasion use the terms PC and Workstation to refer to computers on a LAN that host programs.) This configuration includes a wide range of choices that will be discussed.

The configuration of PCs is usually done when the operating system is being installed because the installation file asks you to supply configuration information. Even if you do so, it is likely that you will want to change it at some later time. Much of the configuration information requested is similar for most operating systems. There are three PCs on the network used for this book. That network is shown again in **Figure 4.1**. We will begin our configurations by discussing Asynchronous Communications, a topic relevant to all PCs.

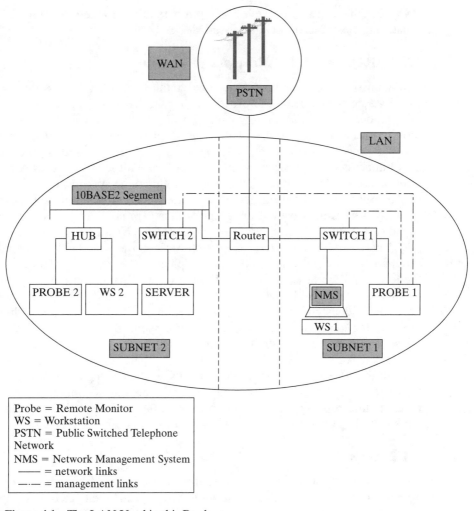

Figure 4.1   The LAN Used in this Book

4.1 ASYNCHRONOUS COMMUNICATIONS

Whether the device is external to the system box (e.g., a printer) or internal to the system box (e.g., the system clock), there has to be an organized process whereby devices communicate with the processor. This organization is provided by assigning a different combination of Interrupt Request (IRQ) number and Input/Output (I/O) addresses with each device. Sometimes a Direct Memory Access (DMA) number is needed. The available number of IRQs is limited so there is "competition" for them among devices. The assignment of these parameters is an important concern of the network administrator. On a typical Industry Standard Architecture

(**ISA**) bus there are 16 possible IRQ numbers in the range from 0 to 15. There is usually no constraint on I/O addresses.

4.1.1 IRQs and I/O Addresses

The 16 possible IRQ numbers correspond to the 16 lines on the ISA bus that can be used by a device to signal the processor that service is needed. The processor uses this number, or, more accurately a number derived from it called a "vector," to determine the memory address of the "**interrupt handler**" program that should be called to process the interrupt. Sixteen sounds like plenty of interrupt request numbers, but actually a significant number of them are automatically confiscated by devices on the system board such as the system timer, the system clock, the keyboard, the interrupt controller itself, and others. After this, there are nine left. Let's include a floppy drive and two hard drives. Now there are six lines left for use by, say, a sound card, a printer, a network card and a modem. Now there are two lines left.

These two lines would be assigned to serial ports. An IBMPC can control four serial ports, but usually not that many are physically available. In IBMPC parlance, the four ports are labeled COM 1 through COM 4. When only two IRQ lines are available, COM 1 and COM 3 share IRQ4 and COM 2 and COM 4 share IRQ3, but not simultaneously. The COM labels are synonyms for the base I/O addresses that are used for communication between the ports and the CPU. These I/O addresses are set by the System BIOS at startup. COM 1 is assigned 3F8H and COM 2 is assigned 2F8. An I/O program is called whenever there is data received or data to be transmitted. These programs contain the bus address of the device that receives or transmits data through the port. However, before any communication can take place, an interrupt request from the port must be handled. We see next how this is done with the Universal Asynchronous Receiver/Transmitter (**UART**).

4.1.2 UARTs

All device interrupts are processed by the UART. **Figure 4.2**, from the book, "Programmers Guide to Serial Communications," by Joe Campbell, **[Ref 1],** is helpful here.

The figure illustrates the interrupt structure of the IBM PC that is provided by the National Semiconductor 8259 UART chip. The latest of these chips has the number 16550. It is backward compatible with the 8259. The 16550 is used in most computers these days.

In **Figure 4.2**, we see some examples of devices connected to the Peripheral Interrupt Controller (PIC) of the UART. The UART controls all connections between devices and the processor. The UART performs many functions and contains several registers, two of which, of course, are the registers that contain data received and data waiting for transmission. The Interrupt Mask Register can be used to block an interrupt from being passed to the processor. For reasons that don't need to be discussed here, the IRQ number is added to the number in the Offset register and the result is used by the CPU as an index to the vector table. The index provides the processor with the memory address of the interrupt handler corresponding to the particular device that sent the interrupt. On the right of **Figure 4.2**, you can see the memory addresses associated with the COM 1 and COM 2 interrupts.

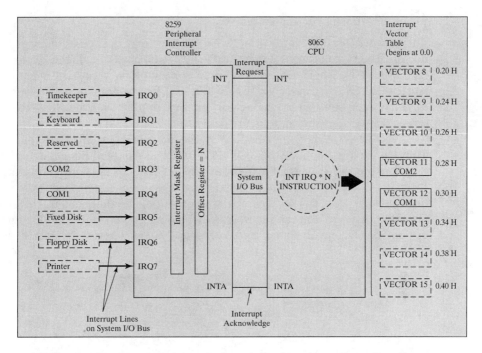

Figure 4.2   National Semiconductor 8259 Peripheral Interrupt Controller. (*Source:* Campbell, *C Programmer Guide to Serial Communication,* © 1994, p. 602. Reprinted by permission of Pearson Education, Inc., Upper Saddle River, NJ.)

The bottom line is that 16 bus lines have been quickly used up and there may be other devices you want to add, such as a scanner. This situation can easily lead to IRQ and I/O conflicts unless the network administrator is careful in the assignment. As mentioned above, there is some relief these days for avoiding conflicts because of the availability of "Plug-N-Play" adapters which provide a range of IRQ and I/O combinations from which the BIOS selects at power-up. Nevertheless, the number of IRQs is still limited. If a computer has devices that are supported by both legacy (configured by setting switches or by software) and Plug-N-Play adapters, it is best to configure the legacy adapters first and then let the Plug-N-Play adapters chose from what is left.

> **Note**
>
> One can disable a device in the System/Device Manager page of Control Panel of Windows 95 to get access to its IRQ and I/O address. However, it is likely that you will also need to physically detach the device from the system bus so that the I/O address will be freed up if it is a COM port.

We will use communication between asynchronous serial COM ports on our PCs and asynchronous serial ports, called Consoles, on the devices to be configured. Now let's configure a serial device, the network interface card.

4.1.3 Network Interface Card (NIC)

The network interface card (or network adapter) may contain as many as four connectors. The types are twisted pair, 10BASE2 (thin coax), AUI (thick coax) and optical fiber. Also, there may be only one connector on a card. Our network uses twisted pair (RJ-45), thin coax (BNC) and AUI Connectors. To see how the card on WS2 has been configured, in Control Panel we double click the Network icon. The screen displayed is shown in **Figure 4.3**.

It shows "the network components that have been installed" on the computer. The NIC on this computer, SN-3200 PCI Ethernet Adapter, is highlighted. SN-3000 PCI Ethernet Adapter is a Plug-N-Play NIC. PCI stands for Peripheral Component Interface. The **PCI** bus is a high-speed bus that is designed to speed up communication between processor and memory and other devices that need it. This NIC is attached to that bus. You can see what settings were chosen by the BIOS at power-up by opening Control Panel and clicking System, Device Manager, Network

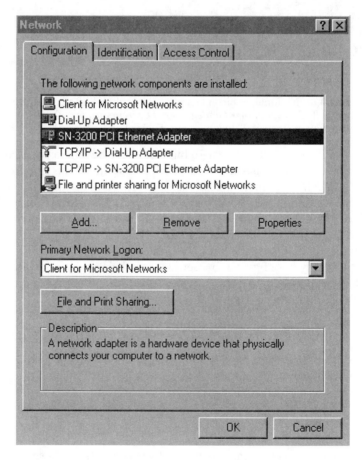

Figure 4.3 Network components configured on WS2

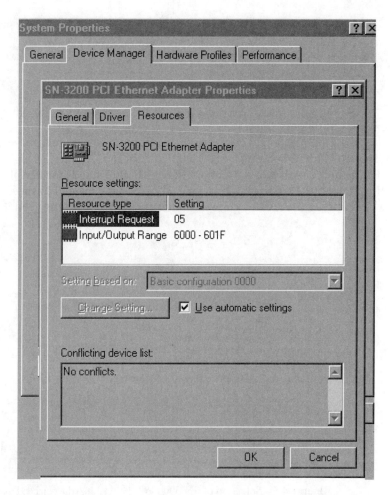

Figure 4.4   Resources chosen by System BIOS for the SN-3000 PCI
Ethernet Adapter

Adapters, SN3200 PCI Ethernet Adapter, Properties, and Resources. **Figure 4.4**
shows the resources chosen.

When Windows 95 was installed on WS2 it provided a "Universal Driver" that
could support this NIC. Highlighting SN-3200 PCI Ethernet Adapter and clicking
Properties in Figure 4.3 generates **Figure 4.5**, which shows that the NIC supports
drivers that are written to either the NDIS or ODI interface.

The driver that supports either 32 bit or 16 bit application NDIS is selected
because the TCP/IP protocol stack has been written to the NDIS specification and
it is desirable to support both 32 and 16 bit applications (e.g., DOS applications).
Clicking bindings shows, in **Figure 4.6**, that the NIC is bound to the TCP/IP protocol stack. This was the only stack loaded so there was no choice to be made.

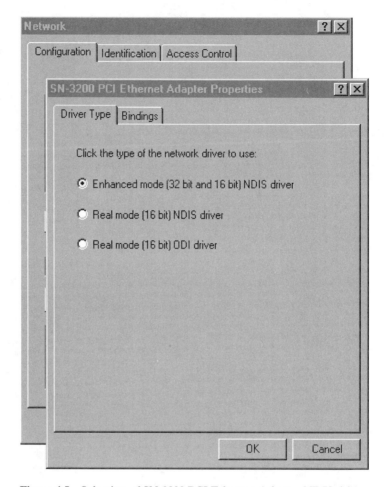

Figure 4.5   Selection of SN-3000 PCI Ethernet Adapter NDIS driver

4.2   WINDOWS 95

Although having been displaced by later Windows products, Windows 95 is still a typical and useful network client. Configuring it is very similar to configuring Windows 98, Windows NT4.0 Workstation, Windows 2000 or Windows XP.

4.2.1 TCP/IP Protocol Stack

Highlighting "TCP/IP → SN3200 Ethernet Adapter," on the Network page, and clicking Properties generates **Figure 4.7**. This is the dialog box where all of the TCP/IP parameters are set for use by the Internet (IP) layer of the stack. The "IP Address" tab allows the computer to have either an IP address specified or obtained automatically from the Dynamic Host Configuration Protocol **(DHCP).** If you want to use DHCP, it is checked here and configured on the computer that

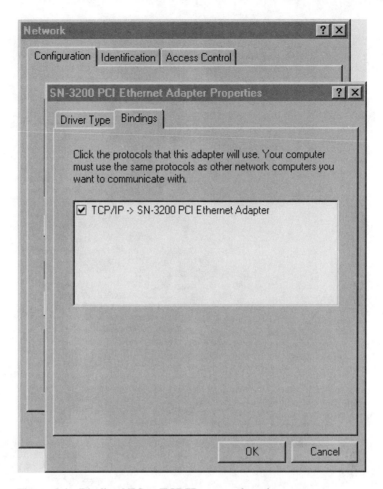

Figure 4.6 Binding NIC to TCP/IP protocol stack

hosts the Windows NT 4.0 SERVER. (See **[Refs 2 and 5]** for a description of DHCP configuration). We have selected "Specify an IP address": 192.192.192.241. The subnet mask is set to 255.255.255.248. **Table 4.1** shows the Ethernet and IP addresses of all devices on the LAN.

From the IP Address and the subnet mask, the Internet Protocol (IP) can determine that this computer is on a subnet, that the subnet address is 192.192.192.240 and that there can be up to six devices on the subnet. IP therefore knows that if it wants to send a packet to an address that is not in the range 192.192.192.241 to 192.192.192.246 it must send the packet to a router on the network. (See **Appendix A** for a discussion of IP addresses, subnet masks and subnet addresses.)

Gateway

Clicking the "Gateway" tab provides the dialog box shown in **Figure 4.8**. Use the "Add" button to add gateway addresses to the "Installed gateways" box. The first gateway address listed is used as the default gateway. If this computer wants to

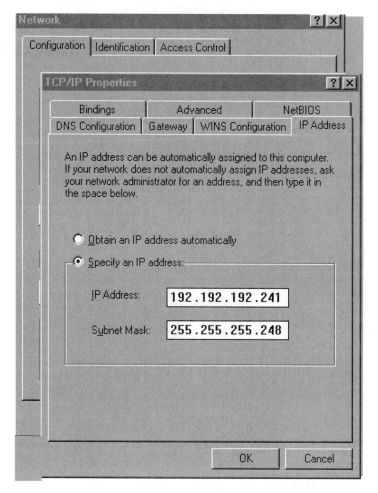

Figure 4.7 Configuration of TCP/IP properties for WS2

send a packet to a device with an address not in the range 192.192.192.241 to 192.192.192.246, it will send the packet to the default router 192.192.192.243. Gateway is another term used for a router. However, the term "gateway" is more precisely intended to apply to a device that can translate the contents of a frame from the format created by one communication architecture to that of the communication architecture used by the network to which the frame is being routed.

Domain Name Service

Click the **DNS** Configuration tab to get the dialog boxes shown in **Figure 4.9**. DNS is the service that is used on the Internet to resolve (translate) domain names to IP addresses. We want to enable DNS so that domain names can be converted automatically to IP addressees on our domain. Raleigh has been arbitrarily selected

Table 4.1   LAN IP, ETHERNET and SUBNET ADDRESSES (Subnet Mask = 255.255.255.248)

DEVICE	IP ADDRESS	ETHERNET ADDRESS	SUBNET ADDRESS
SUBNET 1			192.192.192.232
Probe 1	192.192.192.235	00-80-52-E0-18-3C	
Switch 1	192.192.192.236	00-E0-1E-74-5B-40	
WS 1	192.192.192.233	10-00-5A-D4-5C-E9	
Router	192.192.192.234	00-00-0C-06-16-95	
SUBNET 2			192.192.192.240
Router	192.192.192.243	00-00-0C-06-16-96	
WS 2	192.192.192.241	00-40-05-44-A7-DC	
SERVER	192.192.192.242	00-20-35-E4-1D-2B	
Switch 2	192.192.192.244	00-50-50-E0-F5-40	
Hub	192.192.192.245	08-00-4E-07-B7-E6	
Probe 2	192.192.192.246	00-00-A3-E0-18-82	

as the domain name. (This network resides in Raleigh, N.C. We will talk more about domain names and the rules that apply later in this chapter.) The DNS host is assigned the name SERVER. We click the Add button to provide the IP address of the DNS server, which is 192.192.192.242. There are no other DNS servers on the network. The last dialog box is the "Domain Suffix Search Order." This mouthful means "include everything that is in a fully qualified domain name except the computer name." Since our network is not attached to the Internet, what we provide here is the name Raleigh. Thus the DNS domain name of server is server.raleigh. If our network were attached to the Internet, we would need to have a name of the form server.Raleigh.com or server.Raleigh.net, for example. These names would then be considered **fully qualified domain names**.

Windows Internet Name Service

The resolution of NetBIOS names to IP addresses is provided for members of Windows NT 4.0 domains by the Windows Internet Name Service **(WINS).** WINS is configured on the Windows NT 4.0 SERVER and on the WINS client. Let's say the WINS client is the computer running Windows 95. Clicking the WINS tab shown in **Figure 4.7** produces the screen shown in **Figure 4.10**.

On this tab, you enable WINS Resolution and type in the IP addresses of the primary and secondary WINS servers. As this screen shows, we have only a Primary WINS SERVER on our network. Its address is 192.192.192.242, the same address as the domain server, SERVER. When we examine the configuration of the Windows NT 4.0 SERVER later, you will see that NetBIOS name resolution can be established by defining the resolution in a static database or by letting the WINS server learn the resolution from network traffic.

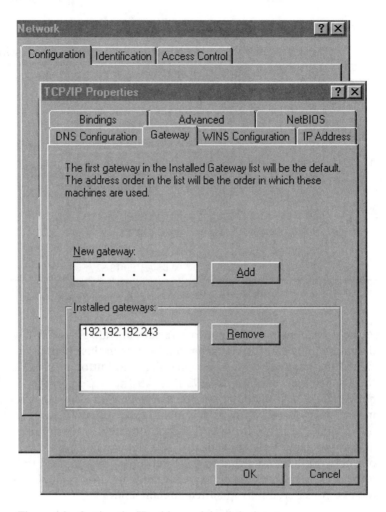

Figure 4.8   Setting the IP address of the default gateway

4.2.2 Client for Microsoft Networks

Figure 4.11 shows **Figure 4.4** again, this time with the "Client for Microsoft Networks" component highlighted. The Description box says that this component enables this computer to connect to other Microsoft Windows computers and share their files and printers. This is sufficient if you are sharing files and printers among Windows 95 computers. If you want to share your Windows 95 files with Windows NT servers and workstations and with computers running Windows for Workgroups, you must also add the "File and Print Sharing" component to this computer.

You click the "Files and Print Sharing" button and fill in the check box for sharing files and the check box for sharing printers that appears there. If you don't do these things, your computer will be removed from **Network Neighborhood**.

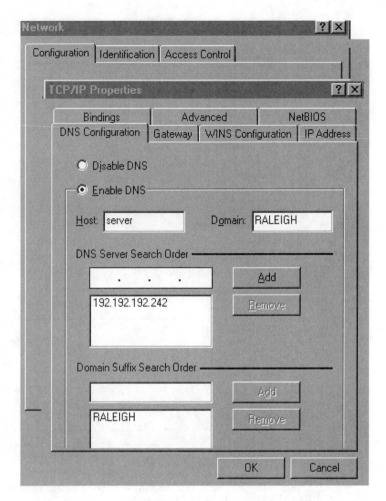

Figure 4.9   Configuring the Domain Name Service (DNS)
parameters for WS 2

Even though it may show up on the Network Neighborhood screen, its files and
printers will not be accessible. If you try to access this computer from an NT computer on the network, for example, you will get a message that the network path to
this computer cannot be found. This happens because the NT computer gets no
reply from this computer when the Network Neighborhood program runs and tries
to establish a communication link.

Referring again to **Figure 4.11**, "Client for Microsoft Networks" is selected in
the box "Primary Network Logon." The other choice is "Windows Logon" which
logs the user onto WS2 only. With the choice of "Client for Microsoft Networks,"
the computer can either log on to a Windows NT Domain or on to a workgroup in
which computers are running Windows for Workgroups. WS2 is part of a domain

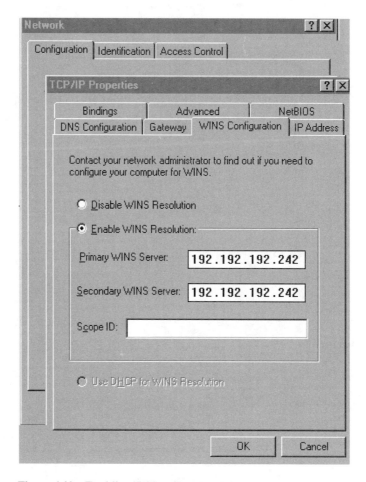

Figure 4.10 Enabling WS2 to have NetBIOS names resolved to IP addresses by the WINS server

that is configured on the Windows NT 4.0 SERVER. The name of the computer that is running Windows NT 4.0 SERVER is SERVER. The other domain member is the computer running Windows NT 4.0 Workstation. It has the name WS1. We will examine the configuration of SERVER later in this chapter.

Note

Don't confuse Windows NT domains with the Domain Name Service (DNS) domains used on the Internet. They are compatible and work together, but the primary purpose of Windows NT domains is to provide a logical network for authenticating computers, users and the rights of users on the domain. A domain is not a specific physical network.

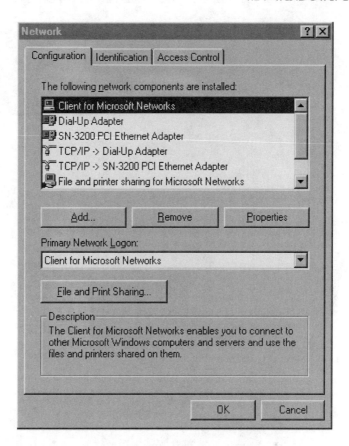

Figure 4.11   Configuring Client for Microsoft Networks

In order for WS2 to log on to the domain, one more configuration step is needed. In **Figure 4.11**, click the Identification tab to get **Figure 4.12**. There you see that the domain configured on SERVER has the name Raleigh. Click the checkbox "Log on to Windows NT computers." Then SERVER will be able to authenticate the logon of WS2 to the Raleigh domain. If we would then click Network Neighborhood, we would see the name WS 2 in the list along with any other members of the domain Raleigh that are logged on.

"Client for Microsoft Networks" can get access to another computer on the same subnet by knowing only the Network Basic Input Output System Protocol (NetBIOS) name of the destination computer, for example, SERVER. The NetBIOS interface to the application will access the NetBIOS Extended User Interface (NetBEUI) protocol stack to do this. However, NetBEUI does not include a Network layer and cannot route packets. If the destination computer is on the other side of a router, e.g., WS 1, the TCP/IP protocol stack and an IP address are necessary. If these are available, the NetBIOS interface will redirect the packets to the TCP/IP stack instead of to the NetBEUI stack. This is referred to as **NBT** or "NetBIOS over TCP/IP."

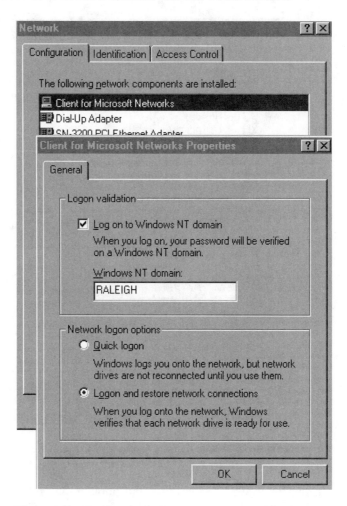

Figure 4.12 Configuring WS2 for logon and authentication by domain SERVER

4.2.3 SNMP

To manage WS2, we need to configure its SNMP agent. To access the necessary screens, open Control Panel and double-click the Network icon to get the screen shown on the left of **Figure 4.13**.

In the textbox, you see in "The following network components are installed" dialog box that the Microsoft SNMP Agent is listed and thus installed. If it is not listed, click the Add button to get a screen where you highlight Services and then click Add. You are provided with the screen on the right of **Figure 4.13** where you select the Manufacturer of the program (Microsoft in this case) and then highlight SNMP Service. Click Add to install the SNMP service. No configuration of the

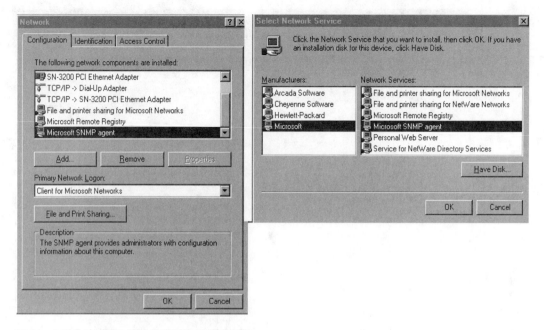

Figure 4.13   Configuring the WS2 SNMP Agent

SNMP Management Agent for Windows 95/98 is possible. We will see that our Windows NT 4.0 SERVER gives us more SNMP configuration flexibility.

The Microsoft SNMP Agent for Windows 95 provides MIB-2 variables. It also provides two values for the Community String that must be used by Management Stations that wish to access MIB-2 variables. The Community String required to read a MIB-2 value is "public." The Community String required to set a MIB-2 value is "private." Now that the Management Agent is installed on WS2, we will be able to access the MIB-2 values it collects when we use the Management Station application in later chapters.

4.3   WINDOWS NT 4.0 SERVER

We are aware of two excellent references that describe all aspects of Windows NT SERVER 4.0. They are described in **[Ref 3-4].** Ref 4 is more advanced. It provides in-depth configuration information making extensive use of the Registry.

4.3.1   SERVER Manager

SERVER Manager is one of the primary tools used to configure the use of the server. The SERVER Manager tool in Windows NT 4.0 SERVER is in the Administrative Tools Group on the Start menu. To open it, Click Start, Programs, Administrative Tools and SERVER Manager. The SERVER Manager screen is shown in **Figure 4.14**.

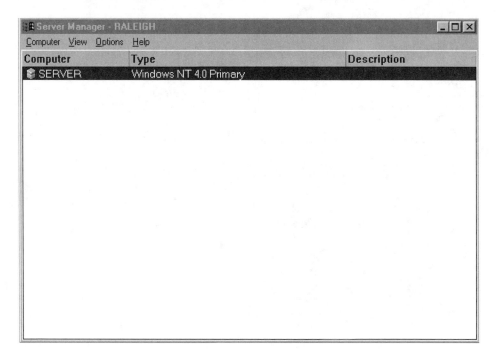

Figure 4.14   SERVER Manager showing the Primary Domain Controller, SERVER

Windows NT domains provide a logon service that makes it possible for the user to do a logon once and gain access to all computers on any domain in which the user and the user's computer are registered. Access to files on these computers is well controlled by **sharing** server directories and setting **permissions** as to what can be done with files in those directories either by domain users or groups of domain users. There are **trust relationships** between domains that can be configured to make multidomain access secure. The subject of multiple NT domains is quite comprehensive and beyond the scope of this chapter. See **[Ref 3-5]** for more information. We will focus on the configuration of one domain.

Computers must be added to the domain to become members. Only a person with Administrator-level rights, such as Administrator, can do this. Our server, SERVER, is a Primary Domain Controller (PDC). This selection can only be made when Windows NT 4.0 SERVER is being installed. When there is also a Backup Domain Controller (BDC) or more than one domain, the PDCs synchronize with the BDC and with other PDCs so that all data on all domains is current and consistent.

There are two steps required to add a domain member:

1. Click "Add to Domain" on the server Computer pull-down menu and enter the computer name in the dialog box.
2. On the computer being added, enter its name and the domain name on the "Identification" tab of the Network page. When the added computer is

restarted, it sends out Discovery frames that contain its NetBIOS name. When the server replies, it includes in the reply frame an ID that is used by the added computer to identify itself to the server from that point on.

Note

The following was necessary in Windows NT 4.0 Service Pack (SP) 3. It is possible that the problem was fixed in later SPs. In SP3, if you delete a member computer name from SERVER Manager and then want to add it again, you need to do the following: 1) on the computer whose name was deleted, change from Domain to Workgroup and then add any name such as XYZ; 2) restart the computer; 3) change from Workgroup XYZ to the previous domain name; 4) add the computer name in SERVER Manager; 5) restart the computer whose membership you are reestablishing.

4.3.2 User Manager for Domains

User Manager for Domains is the other primary tool for configuring the server. The Administrator (we will use Administrator to represent any user who has Administrator-level privileges) has to decide who is allowed to logon to domain computers and what rights they will have for controlling the network. The Administrator does this by using the "User Manager for Domains" utility that is in the Administrative Tools Group. **Figure 4.15** shows the User Manager for Domains screen.

By default three users are listed: Administrator, Guest and IUSER_ SERVER. The last is the account for an Anonymous User of the Microsoft Internet Information SERVER (**IIS**). The panel at the bottom shows the various groups to which users and rights can be assigned. Other users can be added to the domain on this screen and their rights on the domain defined.

Double clicking Guest, for example, brings up the screen shown in **Figure 4.16** called "User Properties." Here the Administrator controls the password for the Account and its restrictions. The restrictions are accessed from Account on the Policies menu. Also on the Policies menu is the User Rights item. From there, user rights to control domain resources are set.

A **token,** containing all of the user parameters set in SERVER Manager and User Manager is created. When a user logs on to a domain, the user's "token" is passed to any resource that the user tries to access. All parameters in the token have to match those defined for the resource in order for it to be accessed.

4.3.3 TCP/IP Protocol Stack

On the Network page of SERVER, click the Protocols tab, highlight TCP/IP Protocol and click Properties. This brings up the Microsoft TCP/IP Properties page shown on the bottom screen of **Figure 4.17** where IP addresses are configured.

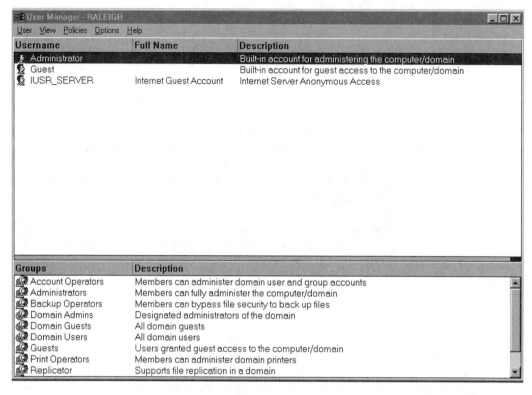

Figure 4.15 User Manager for Domains Configuration

IP addresses are currently specified so the Dynamic Host Configuration Protocol (DHCP) server is not being used. If the DHCP server were configured on SERVER, we could create a range of IP addresses from which the DHCP server would assign an address to SERVER and to a client that logged on. **[Ref 5]** discusses how to configure DHCP in detail.

The IP address of SERVER, the Primary Domain Controller (PDC), is 192.192.192.242, the subnet mask, a constant of the LAN, is 255.255.255.248, and the Default Gateway address is 192.192.192.243 for the subnet on which the PDC resides and the Adapter is IBM Etherjet ISA Adapter.

Clicking the "WINS Address" tab, we see in Figure 4.20 that the "Primary WINS SERVER" has the IP address 192.192.192.242 and there is no "Secondary WINS SERVER." "Enable DNS Windows Resolution" is checked so that DNS and WINS can collaborate on NetBIOS and DNS domain name resolution. Neither LMHOSTS nor Scope ID will be used.

Windows Internet Name Service (WINS)

Having specified the IP Address of the WINS server, we now access the WINS Manager to examine the tools that enable the configuration of name resolu-

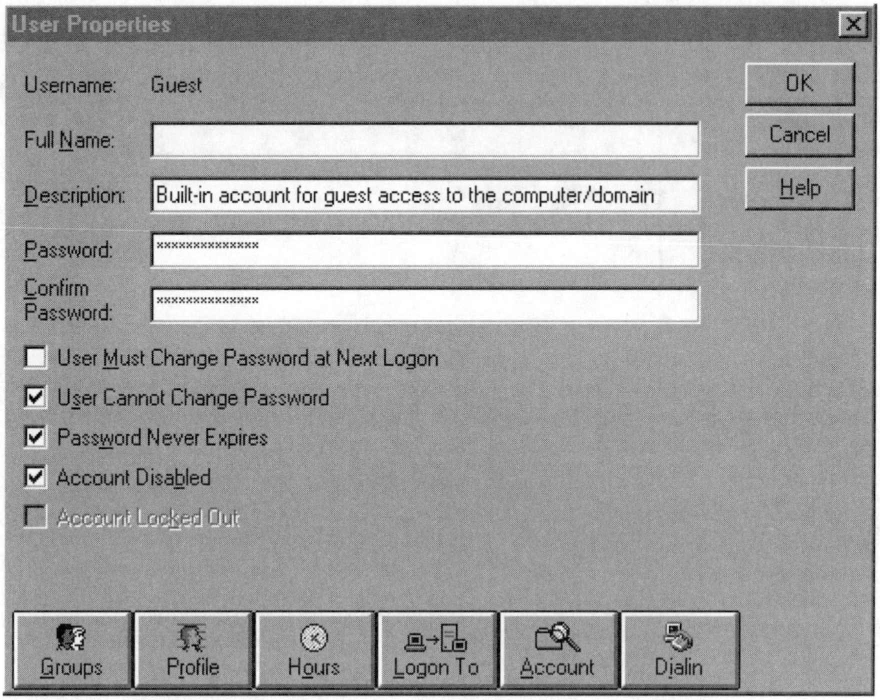

Figure 4.16 Configuring Domain User Logon

tion and its other aspects. Configuration of these tools requires more discussion than we can give here but you can find that discussion in the associated Help menus or in **[Ref 3,5]**.

Figure 4.18 shows the initial WINS Manager Screen. This screen is accessed by selecting Programs from the Start menu, then selecting Administrative Tools and from there, WINS Manager.

In the left panel, we see the IP address, 192.192.192.242, that was assigned to the WINS server in **Figure 4.17**. In the right panel, some statistics on IP address queries received and releases of NetBIOS names have been collected. On the Mappings pull-down menu, clicking Static Mappings produces the screen shown in the foreground of **Figure 4.19**. These are just examples and not the NetBIOS names that we are using our LAN.

This screen shows resolutions of NetBIOS names to IP addresses that is fixed. In addition you see other names associated with these computers. These names are the services provided by these computers that are automatically registered with the WINS SERVER program when the computers log onto the domain.

It is not necessary to statically map NetBIOS names to IP addresses as done here. This will be done dynamically by the WINS server utility when a domain computer logs on. The computer automatically sends its NetBIOS name and IP address

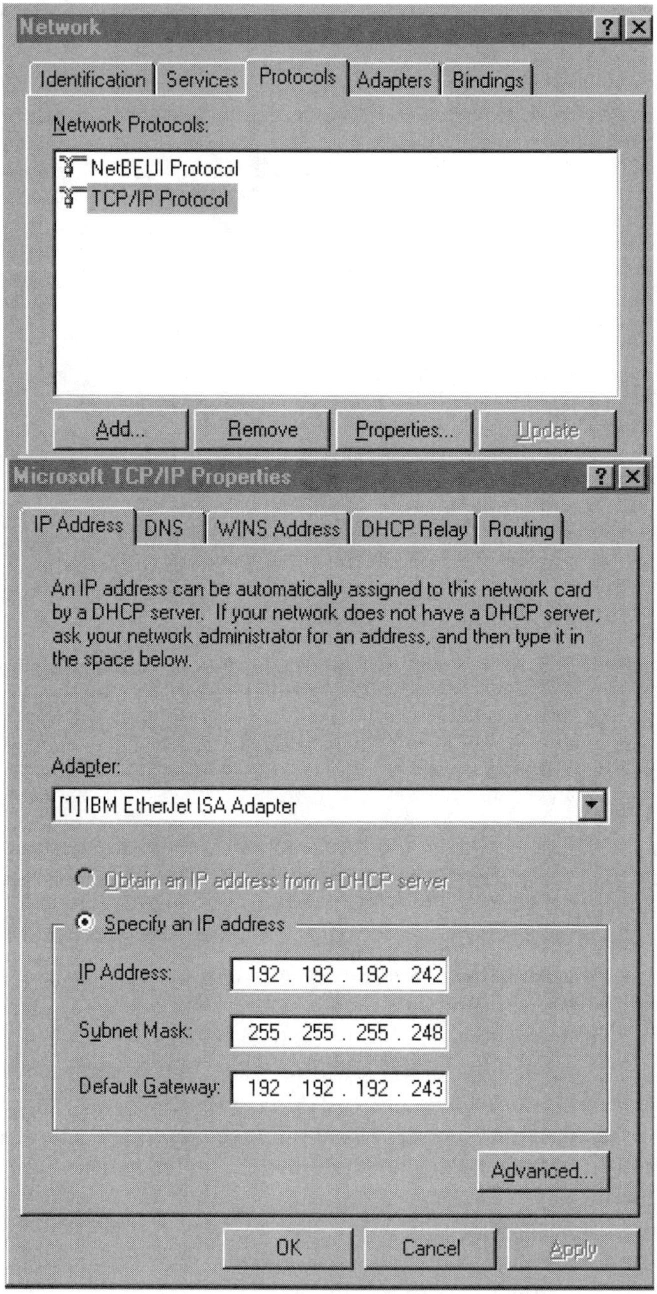

Figure 4.17 Configuring SERVER TCP/IP Properties

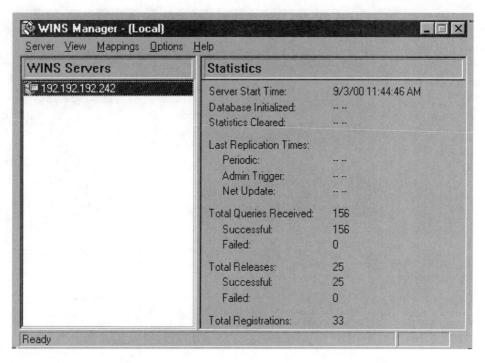

Figure 4.18 WINS Manager screen

to the WINS server utility and it is added to the WINS database. To see the current database, click "Show Database" on the "Mappings" menu.

You can configure the WINS utility to remove database entries at times you set by using "Configuration" in the "SERVER" pull down menu. When there are other WINS servers on the domain or in other domains, these servers synchronize among themselves so that each has a current copy of each other's database. This collaboration significantly increases the likelihood than an IP address will be found when a computer wanting to send a packet makes a query. Thus removing a WINS database entry must be time controlled and that is done automatically after the user removes the entry.

Another advantage to having the WINS service is that it can provide the latest NetBIOS names to the static Domain Name Service (DNS). DNS uses these names and the DNS domain name to form a Fully Qualified Domain Name. This collaboration is established on the domain server as shown on the screen in **Figure 4.20** by checking "Enable DNS for Windows Resolution."

There are other topics that need to be addressed for a complete configuration of the WINS Name Service that will not be needed for this book. For more information about this and other items mentioned below, see the associated Help menu or **[Ref 3–5].**

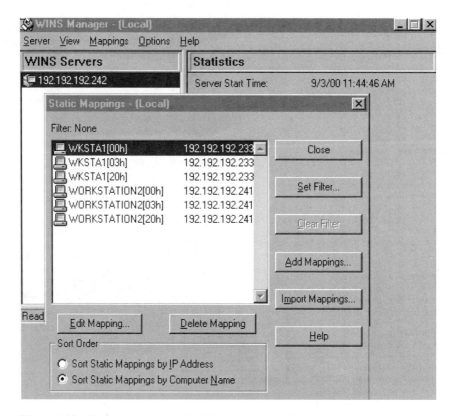

Figure 4.19   Static Mappings of NetBIOS Names to IP Addresses

Domain Name Service

Figure 4.21 shows the dialog boxes on the DNS tab of the TCP/IP Protocol Properties page (Microsoft TCP/IP Properties).

The Primary Domain Controller is the host of the DNS server. DNS is managed by the DNS Manager utility that is in the Administrative Tools group. Clicking DNS Manager brings up the screen shown in **Figure 4.22**.

In the left panel, you see listed the IP address of the computer that is hosting the DNS server. Clicking the IP address shows SERVER Statistics in the right panel. The right panel contains a list of queries to the DNS database for IP addresses corresponding to DNS domain names, as well as certain responses to queries. Double clicking the IP address of our DNS server host provides a list of DNS databases that can be managed. **Cache** contains the domain names and IP addresses of the Internet root servers such as .com, .net, .org etc. The next three databases, arpa, net, and raleigh contain reverse-look-up records that have been created. A **reverse-look-up record** is one that provides the NetBIOS name given the IP address. We will not discuss reverse-look-up records further because they are outside the scope of this book. For more detailed information, see the associated Help

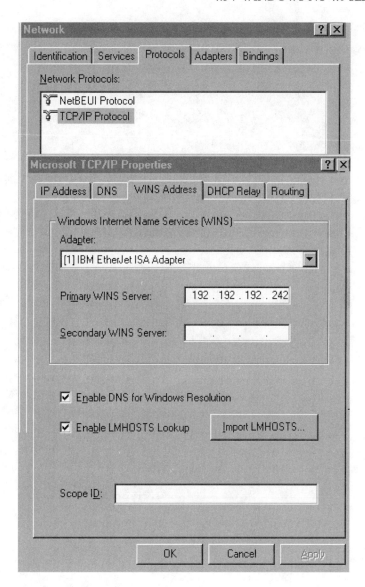

Figure 4.20 Establishing collaboration between WINS and DNS name services

menu or **[Ref 5]**. The last database, raleigh, contains a listing of NetBIOS names to IP addresses for the Raleigh DNS domain.

4.3.4 Network Interface Card

Figure 4.23 shows the Network dialog box of Windows NT 4.0 SERVER that is accessed, as usual, from Control Panel. This is where the NetBIOS name of the server and the domain it controls is established.

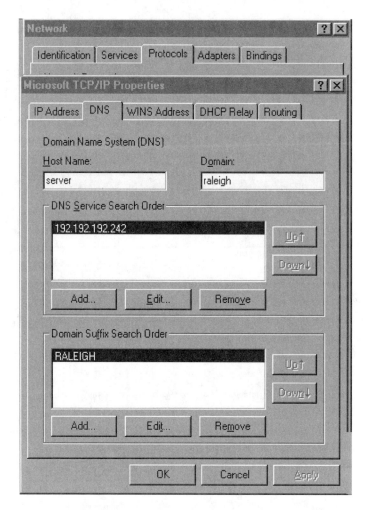

Figure 4.21 Configuring DNS for SERVER

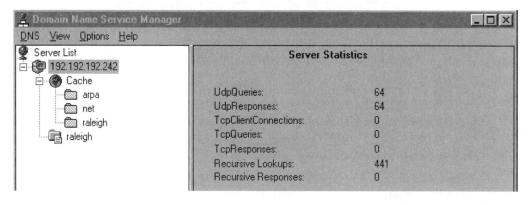

Figure 4.22 DNS Manager

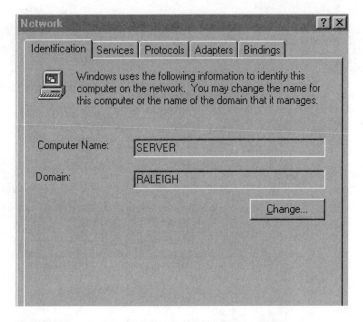

Figure 4.23   Configuration of SERVER Network Interface

Clicking Adapters, we see in **Figure 4.24** that an IBM Etherjet ISA adapter is being used. Windows NT 4.0 did not provide a driver for this adapter. Thus, when the operating system was loaded and the driver was requested, "Have Disk" was selected so that the driver could be installed from diskette. The IBM Etherjet ISA adapter is also a Plug-N-Play adapter like the SN3200 installed on WS2. In addition, it is user configurable. Using software provided, you can let the BIOS select any values of IRQ, I/O address or DMA number from ranges of values or configure the values manually.

To see what values were selected for this adapter, let's use the **Windows NT 4.0 Diagnostics Tool.** This tool is a help to the network manager in many situations. Windows NT 4.0 Diagnostics is in the Administrator Tools group. Click Resources, Devices, highlight IBMEIMP and then click Properties. **Figure 4.25** shows the settings that were chosen by the system BIOS.

The driver that was installed for this Etherjet adapter was written to the NDIS standard.

4.3.5 SNMP

To manage SERVER we need to configure SNMP as we did for WS2 earlier in this chapter. Here you will see distinctions between capability provided by the Windows 95 Microsoft SNMP Agent and that of the Windows NT 4.0 SP4 SNMP Agent.

On Control Panel, double-click the Network icon. In the Network dialog box, select the Services tab and then select the SNMP Service if it is listed. If it is not,

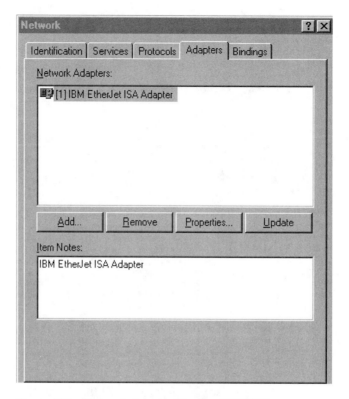

Figure 4.24 Network Adapter Used by SERVER

click the Add button to get the Select Network Service screen where you can select SNMP service and then install it by clicking OK.

Figure 4.26 shows the Services tab of the Network dialog box on the left when the SNMP service has been installed. Highlight SNMP Service and click the Properties button to get the screen shown on the right where the Agent tab is selected.

Management Agent

In the Contact text block, type in the name of the person who is responsible for maintaining the server configuration. Then type in the location of the server. As the text at the top of the Agent tab indicates, this information will provide values for the sysContact and sysLocation MIB variables in the System Group of MIB-2 We will use MIB variables like these to capture and analyze SNMP packets in Chapter 6: SNMP.

"Services" (not shown) are listed in the bottom panel. When checked (✓), they provide information that can be stored in MIB-2 variables to be accessed by a Management Station. For example, End-to-End refers to TCP MIB variables, Internet refers to the IP MIB and Datalink refers to Ethernet hardware address variables. Since all of this data (services) may be stored by Windows NT 4.0 SNMP Management Agent, all boxes are checked.

Next click the Security Tab to obtain the screen shown in **Figure 4.27**.

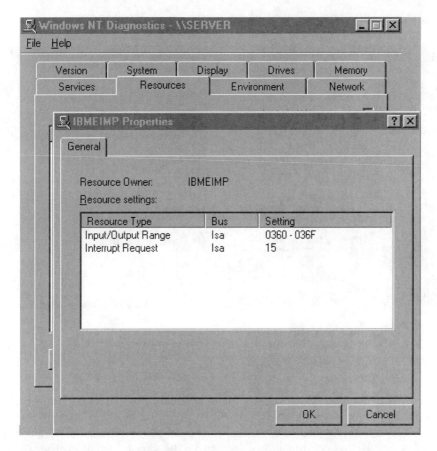

Figure 4.25 Using NT Diagnostics to determine I/Os and IRQ for SERVER

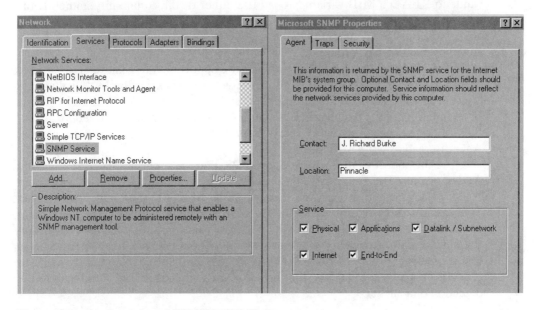

Figure 4.26 Configuration of SERVER SNMP Agent

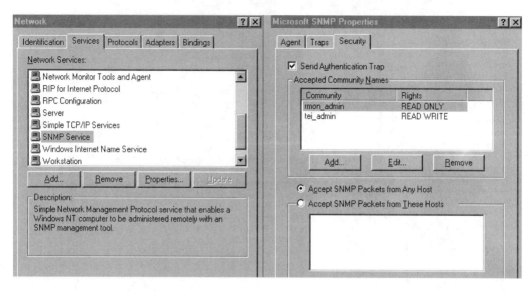

Figure 4.27   Configuring SNMP Agent Security

Security

The "Accepted Community Names" dialog box has two columns. The Community column shows names that will be accepted by the Management Agent on the server. These names must be included in SNMP packets from Management Stations. The Rights column shows access to MIB variables that each of the community names provides. If the management application on a Management Station only wants to READ a MIB variable, it can use either of the community names. If the management application wants to be able to either set (WRITE) or READ a variable, it must use the community name tei_admin. Other choices of Rights can be selected by clicking the Add button.

The bottom, right dialog box provides the opportunity to achieve another level of security beyond community name. Here you can click on the button that says "Accept SNMP Packets from These Hosts" and then click the Add button to type-in IP or Internet Packet Exchange (IPX) names or addresses as shown in **Figure 4.28**.

Now packets from only "safe" hosts will be allowed by the Management Agent to read or write MIB variables

At the top of the screen in **Figure 4.28**, there is a check box next to "Send Authentication Trap." A **trap** is an unsolicited message sent from a Management Agent to a Management Station. Traps are used to inform a Management Station of events that may require action by the Station or the responsible network manager. If the box is checked, a trap will be sent to a specified (on the Traps tab) Management Station. An example of such a trap message is: a Management Station sends a message to the Management Agent with an incorrect community name or requests an action for which it does not have a Right. Such a trap could lead to the detection of a hacker.

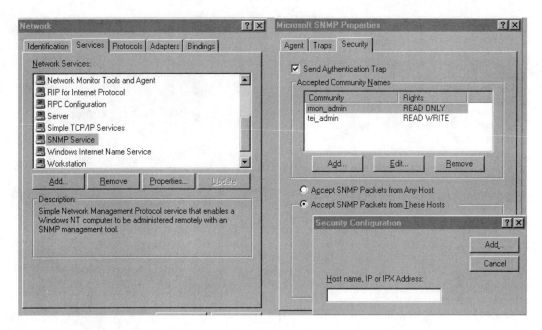

Figure 4.28 Configuring IP Addresses for Computers that can access SERVER SNMP Agent

Traps

Next click the Traps tab to get the screen in **Figure 4.29**. The Community Name text block is where you enter the name that will be used by the SERVER in trap messages. This name must be the same as that configured by the receiving Management Station for receiving trap messages.

The text box labeled "Trap Destinations," shows which Management Stations should receive trap messages. There is only one shown, the IP address of WS1, which hosts Meterware. Sometimes there is more than one Management Station that is legally configured to access a Management Agent. In that case, you may want more than one or all Management Stations to get the trap messages. In some network devices, you can configure traps to be sent when a value exceeds some threshold. Under such circumstances, in a distributed management system of the type discussed in **Chapter 3**, you may want a trap sent to the local management station and to a higher-level management station. To add a Management Station to the list, click the Add button and type in the IP address in the text box that appears.

4.4 WINDOWS NT 4.0 WORKSTATION

The Windows NT 4.0 SERVER operating system is designed to handle multiple requests for its services simultaneously. It is the manager of a Windows NT domain. Thus it has the capability to create and authenticate a domain of computers and

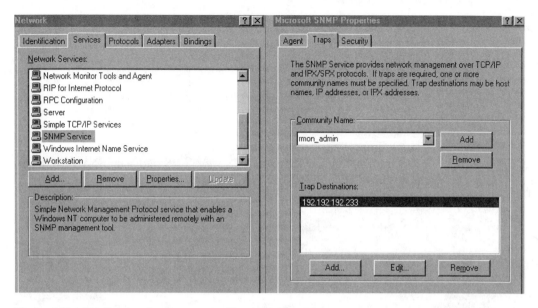

Figure 4.29   Configuring the Community Name for Trap Messages

users. In contrast, the focus of the Windows NT 4.0 Workstation operating system is the use of one machine by one user at a time.

Not surprisingly, Windows NT 4.0 SERVER package includes more service programs. These include DHCP, DNS, WINS, Remote Access Service (RAS), and the Internet Information SERVER (IIS) which is an FTP, Gopher and WWW server.

We are using the Windows NT 4.0 workstation on our network primarily as the host of the SNMP manager, Meterware and as a member of a Windows NT 4.0 domain.

In the next chapter, we configure the devices that provide the network infrastructure that enables communication for the clients and servers discussed in this chapter. These devices include a hub, two switches, a router and two probes which support SNMP management activities.

CHAPTER SUMMARY

This chapter stepped through the configurations of the Client/SERVER devices used on our LAN. These configurations include computers hosting the Windows 95, Windows NT 4.0 Workstation and the Windows NT 4.0 SERVER operating systems. The characteristics of asynchronous communications between peripheral devices and client and server computers were discussed. This discussion focused on IRQ numbers, I/O addresses, DMA numbers because their selection is key to the correct use of computers on networks. The TCP/IP suite was configured for two clients and a server. A Windows NT 4.0 domain was configured for these clients and the server. Microsoft Networking was configured to enable communication on the domain. It was shown that using NetBIOS over TCP/IP enables Microsoft Networks for a routing environment The distinction between the Windows NT 4.0 Workstation and the Windows NT 4.0 SERVER operating systems was discussed. Some services included with Windows NT 4.0 SERVER but not with Windows NT 4.0 Workstation were examined. These are DHCP, WINS and DNS. The additional services provided by the server package, RAS and IIS, were not discussed because, although important, they are not relevant to the scope of this book. References to information on RAS and IIS were provided. The SNMP Management Agent was installed on WS2 and SERVER and configured.

REVIEW QUESTIONS

1. What is the purpose of having IRQs?
2. What happens when an interrupt occurs?
3. If there are both legacy and Plug-N-Play NICs on your computer, why is it best to configure the legacy NICs first?
4. What role does the system BIOS have regarding the operation of Plug-N-Play NICs?
5. Why are the NDIS and ODI specifications so important to network communications?
6. What does it mean to bind a protocol stack to a NIC?
7. The IP addresses of the devices on our network all begin with the three fields 192.192.192. To what class do such network addresses belong?
8. What is the purpose of having a default gateway?
9. What capability does NBT provide?
10. What is the value of creating a Windows NT domain?
11. What advantage is provided by having WINS and DNS server processes collaborate?
12. What is the purpose of configuring a Community Name for the SNMP agent?
13. What is the purpose of an SNMP trap?
14. What is the primary difference between Windows NT 4.0 SERVER and Workstation operating systems?

EXERCISES

1. From the MSDOS command line or from Run on the Start menu, type either **winipcfg** on a Windows 95 platform or **ipconfig** on a Windows NT 4.0 platform to show how your computer is configured. Be sure to click the "More Information" button to get all the configuration information. Print out the screen and use it for a reference that relates your computer configuration to the configuration done in this book.
2. Access the SNMP service on a machine available to you to see if SNMP is configured. If it is, write down the value of each variable. If is not, write down what variables can be configured.

3. If you have a Windows NT 4.0, Windows 2000 or Windows XP SERVER on your network, use it to access the WINS Service and examine the WINS database. List the WINS NetBIOS names and IP addresses you see there.

REFERENCES

1. "Programmers Guide to Serial Communications," Joe Campbell, SAMS Publishing, a Division of Prentice Hall, Inc., 1994.
2. "Windows 95 Unleashed," Ed Tiley et al., SAMS Publishing, 1995.
3. "Inside Windows NT SERVER 4," Drew Heywood et al., New Riders, 1997.
4. "Windows NT SERVER 4, " Karanjit S. Siyan et al., New Riders, 1997.
5. "A Guide to TCP/IP on Microsoft Windows NT 4.0," Richard Burke and Mohammad Fatmi, International Thomson, Course Technology, 1998.

CHAPTER 5

CONFIGURATION: INFRASTRUCTURE COMPONENTS

This chapter describes configuration of:

- Hubs
- Switches
- Routers
- Routing Information Protocol (RIP)
- Open Shortest Path First Routing Protocol (OSPF)
- Border Gateway Routing Protocol (BGP)
- Probes
- SNMP Management Agents for all devices

This chapter provides demonstrations of a major part of network management, that of configuration management of the devices that make up the network infrastructure. Hubs, switches and routers make up the bulk of this infrastructure, which makes it possible for PCs to communicate over LANs, WANs, the Internet, Intranets and Extranets. To summarize from Chapter 1:

- A hub is a multiport repeater. When a hub receives a frame it amplifies the signal and distributes it to all other ports on the hub.
- A switch is a multiport bridge. When a switch receives a frame, it amplifies the signal, looks at the MAC address to determine which port should retransmit the frame to get it to the intended network device

and sends it to that port. The switch can be configured to disconnect any attached device, to discard frames intended for an attached device, to send frames with a specific hardware address to another hardware address instead and to copy a frame to a mirror port which can send it to an attached traffic monitor.

- The function of routers is to get the packet to a destination network. The router reads the header created by the Network layer of the protocol stack on the source computer. The router can be configured to filter by protocol, source network address or destination network address. The router uses its routing table to determine which of its ports will provide the "shortest" path to the destination network and sends the packet out of that port. Routers implement routing protocols to inform other routers of information they have in their routing tables.

In order to make our discussions of the configuration of these infrastructure components concrete, they must be referenced to real devices. This means that the configuration steps described will of course not be identical to those appropriate to devices on your network. However, it is expected that your configuration steps will be similar and that having done it for the devices on the demonstration network will make it much easier to do on your own network.

5.1 HUBS

The hub on our network is a 3COM Link builder FMS Coaxial Hub Model 3C16250. In order for this hub, and others that could be stacked with it, to be managed, an FMS Management Module, Model 3C16030, has been installed. **Figures 5.1 and 5.2** show the front and back of the 3COM hub that we saw in Chapter 1.

Two of the BNC connectors in **Figure 5.1** connect the hub to WS 2 and Probe 2 as shown in **Figure 5.3**, the demonstration network for the book.

In **Figure 5.2**, the Management Module is the lower of the two modules shown in the center. The connector on the left, next to the power plug, is an AUI connector. In the case of our network, this connector is attached to an external transceiver that allows the hub to be connected to the 10BASE2 cable that goes to Switch 2. There are three ways to manage/configure this hub and the switches and routers.

Figure 5.1 Front of 3COM Hub

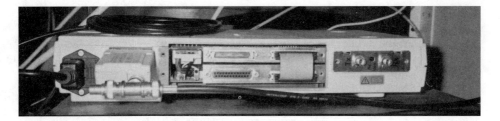

Figure 5.2   Back of 3COM Hub

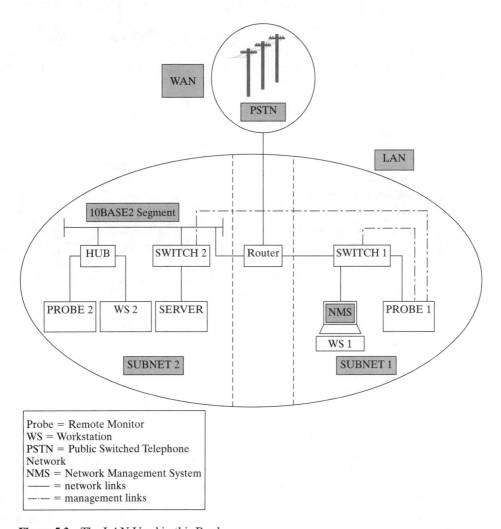

Figure 5.3   The LAN Used in this Book

1. Connect to the Management Module DB-25 RS-232 serial connector in the center of that module. This is referred to as "out-of–band management" because the network is not being used. The procedure is as follows:
   - Connect the serial connector of a computer to the module serial connector using a crossover cable
   - Use a VT100 Terminal Emulator program such as Windows HyperTerminal to access the menus of the management program on the hub
   - For remote management of the hub, use an RS-232 cable to connect a modem to the serial connector on the Management Module and connect the modem to the RJ-11 telephone jack in the wall. Then use a VT100 Terminal Emulator program to access the hub management menus.

2. Connect to the Management Module over the network using Telnet. This is an example of "in-band management" because the network is used. The procedure is as follows:
   - Connect the computer's serial connector to the Management Module serial connector using a crossover cable
   - Use a VT 100 emulator (e.g., HyperTerminal) to access the menus of the management program
   - Display the Setup screen
   - Use the VT 100 terminal emulator to enter the IP address, subnet mask and default router for the hub
   - Logoff from the VT100 interface
   - Open the Telnet application (provided with all Windows Operating Systems)
   - Highlight the IP address of the hub
   - Click "Connect."

3. Connect to the Management Module over the network using the Simple Network Management Protocol (SNMP) (in-band management). The procedure is as follows:
   - Connect the computer's serial connector to the Management Module serial connector using a crossover cable
   - Use a VT 100 emulator (e.g., HyperTerminal) to access the menus of the management program
   - Display the Setup screen
   - Use the VT 100 emulator to enter the IP address, subnet mask and default router of the hub
   - Logoff from the VT 100 interface
   - Reset the management module from the reset button on the back of the hub
   - Open the NMS on the management station
   - Select the hub from the network display
   - Apply the management tools to the hub.

An advantage of out-of-band management is that it works if the network is down. Since out-of-band management will be used on other devices that will be

Table 5.1 Network Device Configurations (Subnet Mask = 255.255.255.248)

Device	IP Address	Ethernet Address	Subnet Address
SUBNET 1			192.192.192.232
Probe 1	192.192.192.235	00-80-52-E0-18-3C	
Switch 1	192.192.192.236	00-E0-1E-74-5B-40	
WS 1	192.192.192.233	10-00-5A-D4-5C-E9	
Router	192.192.192.234	00-00-0C-06-16-95	
SUBNET 2			192.192.192.240
Router	192.192.192.243	00-00-0C-06-16-96	
WS 2	192.192.192.241	00-40-05-44-A7-DC	
Server	192.192.192.242	00-20-35-E4-1D-2B	
Switch 2	192.192.192.244	00-50-50-E0-F5-40	
Hub	192.192.192.245	08-00-4E-07-B7-E6	
Probe 2	192.192.192.246	00-00-A3-E0-18-82	

configured, we will demonstrate management of the Hub with in-band management using Telnet. Let's assume that out-of–band management through the Management Module serial connector was used to configure the hub's IP address and subnet mask which are 192.192.192.245, 255.255.255.248, respectively as you see in **Table 5.1**.

A Windows 95 or similar computer has a Telnet VT100 emulator shortcut installed in the Programs group in the Start menu. This shortcut is shown in **Figure 5.4**. Clicking Telnet brings up the screen shown in **Figure 5.5**. If you click "Connect," the submenu provides two opportunities: "click the IP address of the hub 192.192.192.245" to access it using the network or "click Remote System" to get access to a remote device using a modem.

We connect to the hub by clicking its IP address. This accesses the hub introductory management screen shown in **Figure 5.6** with OK highlighted. Pressing the Enter key generates the screen shown in **Figure 5.7** where User Name and Password must be entered. For our discussion, we assume that the administrator is creating a user, so he or she enters the User Name and Password. For this 3COM hub, the Enter key is used to move between fields. After entering the appropriate text, the Enter key is used to move to OK, where it is used again to get to the Main Menu screen shown in **Figure 5.8**. Here different management submenus may be selected.

Table 5.2 summarizes the capabilities that the submenus provide. Only some of these hub management features will be discussed at this point.

Before a user can manage the hub, an administrator has to create a security level for the user. So lets look first at the second item in **Table 5.2**, User Access Levels.

5.1.1 User Access Levels

The tab key is used to move the highlight to "User Access Levels" on the screen shown in **Figure 5.8** and the Enter key gets us to the screen shown in **Figure 5.9**.

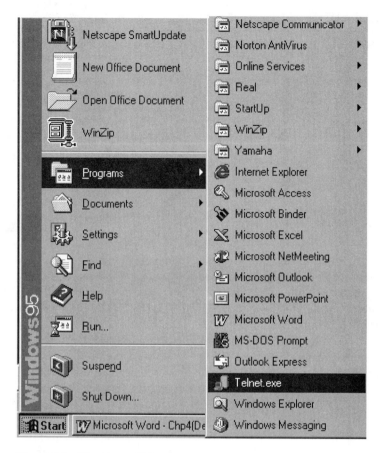

Figure 5.4 Shortcut to Telnet.exe

Local Security

Selecting "Local Security" and pressing the Enter key gets us the screen in **Figure 5.10** where you set the access level you want the user to have. The labels on the left indicate the three ways the hub can be managed. For example, we are now using Telnet. The labels at the top of the table are the choices for access level with the highest access level being "security." Any combination of management/access level can be disabled. We will leave all combinations enabled. However, it may be desirable in some circumstances to disable all remote management possibilities so that the management can only be done locally.

Create User

Having selected the access element of the matrix, with OK highlighted, Enter is pressed to return to the previous menu. Here we select "Create User" and press Enter to get the screen shown in **Figure 5.11**.

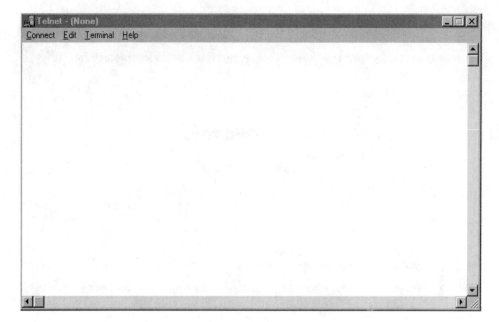

Figure 5.5 Telnet Connection Screen

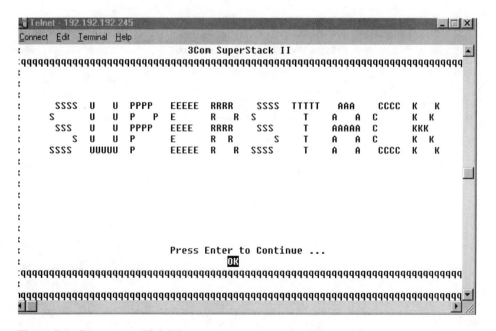

Figure 5.6 Doorway to Hub Management

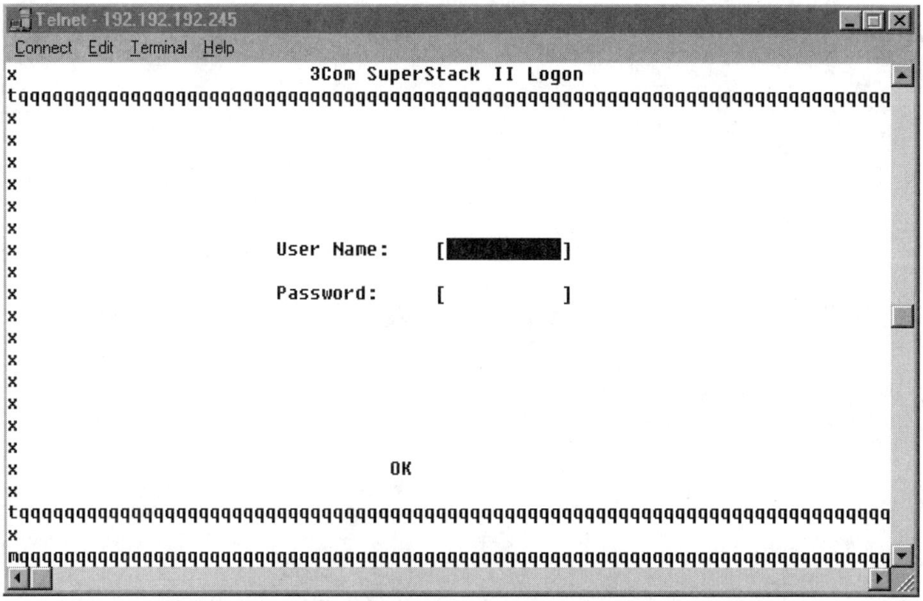

```
┌─────────────────────────────────────────────────────────────────────────┐
│ ▓ Telnet - 192.192.192.245                                      _ □ ×     │
├───────────────────────────────────────────────────────────────────────────┤
│ Connect  Edit  Terminal  Help                                             │
├───────────────────────────────────────────────────────────────────────────┤
│x                      3Com SuperStack II Logon                          ▲ │
│tqqqqqqqqqqqqqqqqqqqqqqqqqqqqqqqqqqqqqqqqqqqqqqqqqqqqqqqqqqqqqqqqqqqqqqqqq  │
│x                                                                          │
│x                                                                          │
│x                                                                          │
│x                                                                          │
│x                                                                          │
│x                           User Name:   [▓▓▓▓▓▓▓▓]                        │
│x                                                                          │
│x                           Password:    [        ]                       │
│x                                                                        ░ │
│x                                                                          │
│x                                                                          │
│x                                                                          │
│x                                                                          │
│x                                                                          │
│x                                  OK                                      │
│x                                                                          │
│tqqqqqqqqqqqqqqqqqqqqqqqqqqqqqqqqqqqqqqqqqqqqqqqqqqqqqqqqqqqqqqqqqqqqqqqqq  │
│x                                                                          │
│mqqqqqqqqqqqqqqqqqqqqqqqqqqqqqqqqqqqqqqqqqqqqqqqqqqqqqqqqqqqqqqqqqqqqqqqqq ▼│
│ ◄                                                                       ► │
└───────────────────────────────────────────────────────────────────────────┘
```

Figure 5.7   3COM Hub User and Password Security Configuration

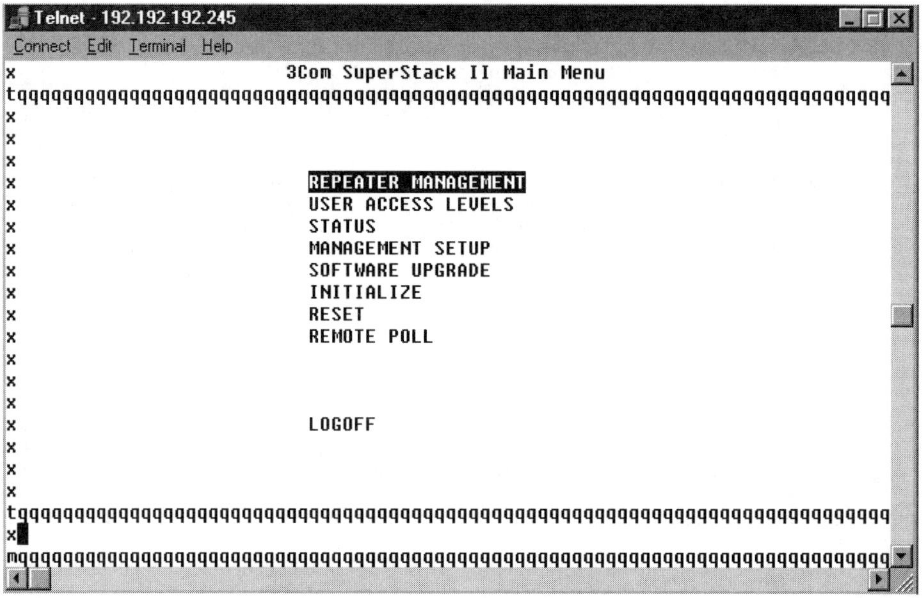

```
┌─────────────────────────────────────────────────────────────────────────┐
│ ▓ Telnet - 192.192.192.245                                      _ □ ×     │
├───────────────────────────────────────────────────────────────────────────┤
│ Connect  Edit  Terminal  Help                                             │
├───────────────────────────────────────────────────────────────────────────┤
│x                     3Com SuperStack II Main Menu                       ▲ │
│tqqqqqqqqqqqqqqqqqqqqqqqqqqqqqqqqqqqqqqqqqqqqqqqqqqqqqqqqqqqqqqqqqqqqqqqqq  │
│x                                                                          │
│x                                                                          │
│x                                                                          │
│x                        REPEATER MANAGEMENT                               │
│x                        USER ACCESS LEVELS                                │
│x                        STATUS                                            │
│x                        MANAGEMENT SETUP                                  │
│x                        SOFTWARE UPGRADE                                  │
│x                        INITIALIZE                                        │
│x                        RESET                                           ░ │
│x                        REMOTE POLL                                       │
│x                                                                          │
│x                                                                          │
│x                        LOGOFF                                           │
│x                                                                          │
│x                                                                          │
│x                                                                          │
│tqqqqqqqqqqqqqqqqqqqqqqqqqqqqqqqqqqqqqqqqqqqqqqqqqqqqqqqqqqqqqqqqqqqqqqqqq  │
│x▓                                                                         │
│mqqqqqqqqqqqqqqqqqqqqqqqqqqqqqqqqqqqqqqqqqqqqqqqqqqqqqqqqqqqqqqqqqqqqqqqqq ▼│
│ ◄                                                                       ► │
└───────────────────────────────────────────────────────────────────────────┘
```

Figure 5.8   Main Hub Management Screen

Table 5.2 Submenus of the 3COM Hub Management Module

Submenu	Functions
Repeater Management	• Management of a stack of hubs consisting of 1 to 8 units (hubs) connected together. Three management activities, Statistics, Setup and Resilience, are available for all security access levels • Management of one unit in the stack • Management of one port of a unit
User Access Levels	• Local security: configure what rights the user has for each type of access level assigned • Create User • Delete Users • Edit User
Status	Management module information such as hardware and software versions and the fault log
Management Setup	IP addresses, subnet masks and default routers for TCP/IP and SPX/IPX can be configured here
Software Upgrade	This screen can be used to download newer versions of the Management Module software
Initialize	Can be used to return the non-volatile RAM to its initial values. Should be used as a troubleshooting tool with great care because the system will be changed considerably from its current state
Reset	Resets the entire stack of units. Removes configuration data but not management setup data. Equivalent to depressing the reset button on the back of the unit
Remote Poll	If there is a management module on a remote device, poll the remote device to see if it is connected

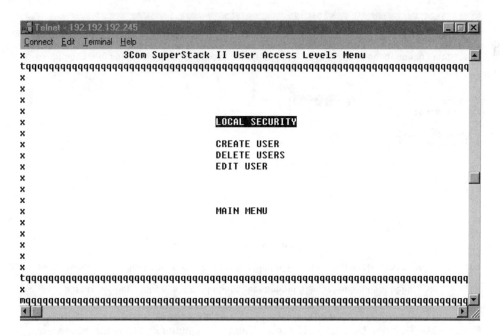

Figure 5.9 Configuring User Access Levels

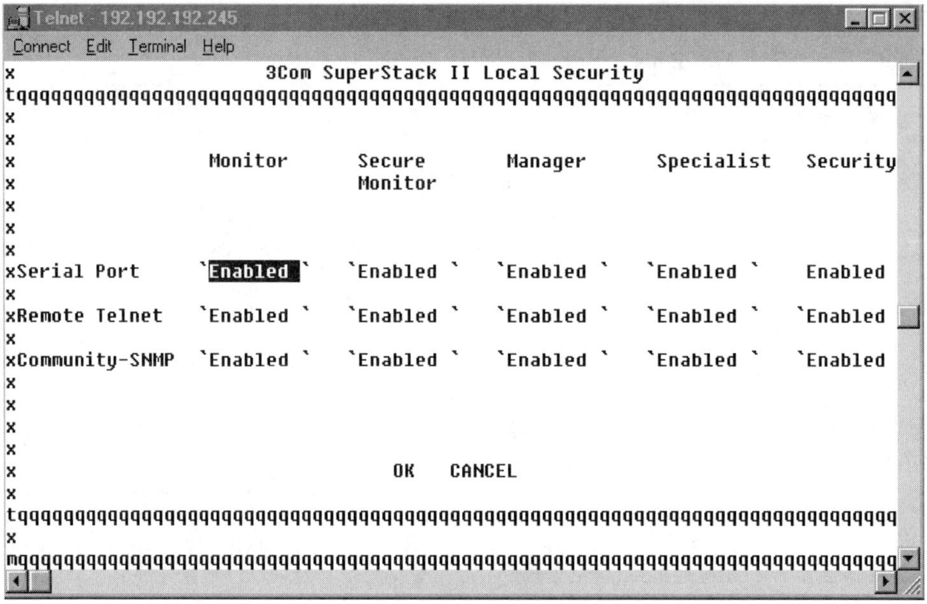

```
Telnet - 192.192.192.245                                        _ □ ×
Connect  Edit  Terminal  Help
x                    3Com SuperStack II Local Security           ▲
tqqqqqqqqqqqqqqqqqqqqqqqqqqqqqqqqqqqqqqqqqqqqqqqqqqqqqqqqqqqqqqqqqqqqqqqqq
x
x
x               Monitor       Secure        Manager      Specialist   Security
x                             Monitor
x
x
xSerial Port   `Enabled `     `Enabled `    `Enabled `   `Enabled `   Enabled
x
xRemote Telnet `Enabled `     `Enabled `    `Enabled `   `Enabled `   `Enabled  ▯
x
xCommunity-SNMP `Enabled `    `Enabled `    `Enabled `   `Enabled `   `Enabled
x
x
x
x
x                        OK    CANCEL
x
tqqqqqqqqqqqqqqqqqqqqqqqqqqqqqqqqqqqqqqqqqqqqqqqqqqqqqqqqqqqqqqqqqqqqqqqqq
x
mqqqqqqqqqqqqqqqqqqqqqqqqqqqqqqqqqqqqqqqqqqqqqqqqqqqqqqqqqqqqqqqqqqqqqqqqq ▼
◄▐ ▐                                                              ▶
```

Figure 5.10   Access Level Matrix

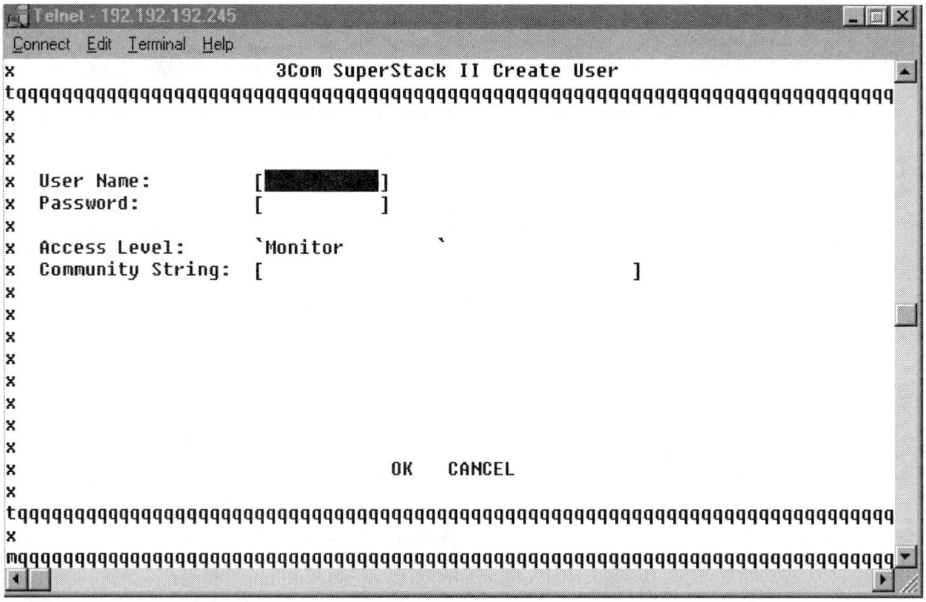

```
Telnet - 192.192.192.245                                        _ □ ×
Connect  Edit  Terminal  Help
x                    3Com SuperStack II Create User              ▲
tqqqqqqqqqqqqqqqqqqqqqqqqqqqqqqqqqqqqqqqqqqqqqqqqqqqqqqqqqqqqqqqqqqqqqqqqqqq
x
x
x
x   User Name:          [▮▮▮▮▮▮▮▮]
x   Password:           [        ]
x
x   Access Level:       `Monitor            `
x   Community String:   [                              ]
x
x
x
x
x
x
x
x
x                        OK    CANCEL
x
tqqqqqqqqqqqqqqqqqqqqqqqqqqqqqqqqqqqqqqqqqqqqqqqqqqqqqqqqqqqqqqqqqqqqqqqqqqq
x
mqqqqqqqqqqqqqqqqqqqqqqqqqqqqqqqqqqqqqqqqqqqqqqqqqqqqqqqqqqqqqqqqqqqqqqqqqqq ▼
◄▐ ▐                                                              ▶
```

Figure 5.11   Defining User ID and Password, and the Community String for the Access Level selected in Figure 5.10

SNMP

This 3COM hub Management Module provides a SNMPv1 Management Agent. To access it from a Management Station, the Community String needs to be configured. The assignment of community string names was discussed in **Chapter 4**. Any name can be chosen as long as it is identical to what will be configured on the Management Station. The community string is a field in SNMP packets that is used as a password for communication between Management Stations and Management Agents. After assigning the Community Name, the hub can be managed. We will discuss SNMP and its use in detail in the next chapter.

Now that the user has been assigned an ID, a Password and a Security Level, we can examine the capabilities provided by the Repeater Management submenu shown in **Table 5.2**. The tab key is used to highlight Repeater Management on the Main Menu in **Figure 5.8** and Enter is pressed to get the screen shown in **Figure 5.12**.

5.1.2 Repeater-level Management Options

Statistics—In **Figure 5.13**, we see statistics for all ports on the 3COM hub. If we had a stack of hubs, we would be seeing cumulative statistics for all ports on all hubs. As you can see, management at the Repeater Management level provides limited information and is read-only regardless of access level.

Setup—**Figure 5.14** shows that our stack of hubs only contains one unit. Unit Capacity says that the stack can support eight units. The hub is shown operational.

Resilience—The screen shown in **Figure 5.15** indicates what resilience means. A port can be configured to have a backup port. If the connection on the

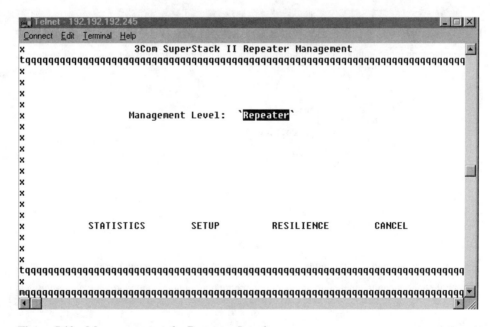

Figure 5.12 Management at the Repeater Level

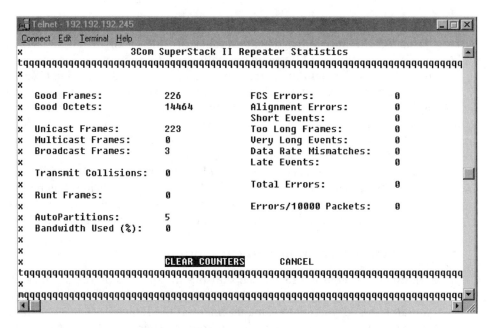

Figure 5.13 Snapshot of Hub Port Statistics

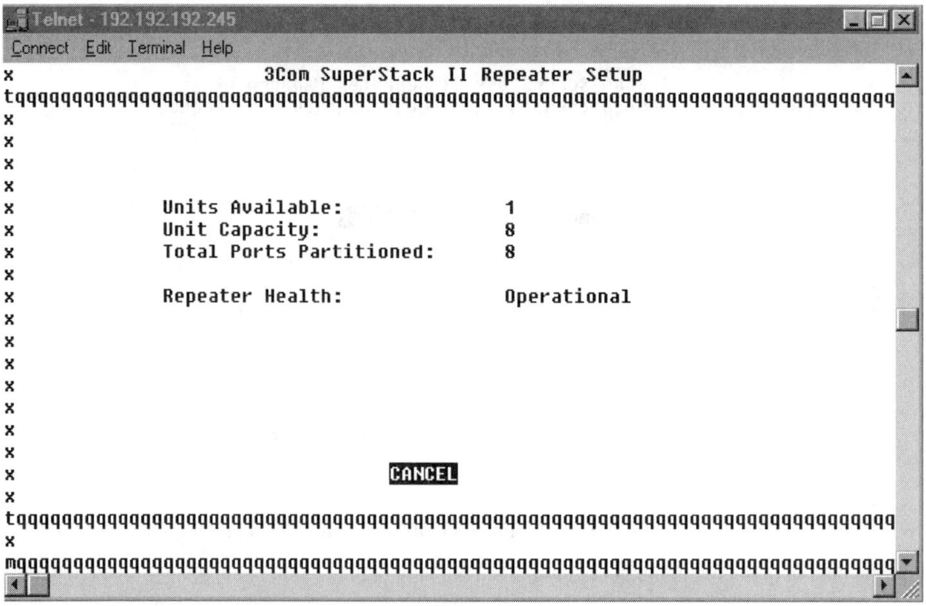

Figure 5.14 Hub Status

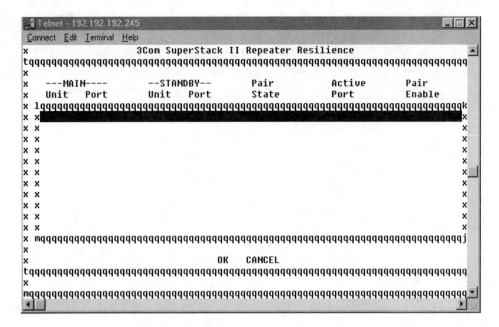

Figure 5.15   Port Resilience Configuration

main port fails, the backup port takes over. The FMS Management Module that is installed in our hub does not have this capability. It is available in the FMS II Management module.

Under Repeater Management there are two other management options, Unit Management and Port Management.

5.1.3 Unit Management and Port Management Options

For the management module on this hub, to get to Unit and Port management we first have to highlight Repeater Management in **Figure 5.8** and then press Enter to get **Figure 5.12**. Here the space bar is used to toggle from Repeater to Unit. Then, pressing Enter, we get **Figure 5.16**.

The values in this figure describe Unit 1, the hub we are configuring. As you can see from **Figures 5.1** and **5.2**, the Port Capacity is 12 because there are 10 BNC ports on the front of the hub and two ports on the back. One of those on the back is the AUI port on the far left and the other is the pair of 10BASEFL optical fiber ports on the far right used for connecting the hub stack.

To get to a port on Unit 1, we return to **Figure 5.12**, toggle to Port using the space bar and press Enter to get port information. Port 5 is the port to which WS 2 is attached and is the only port active on Unit 1 at this time. The result is shown in **Figure 5.17**.

Port 5 is selected and thus the menu items shown can be applied to it by selecting them. We select Setup to get the screen shown in **Figure 5.18**.

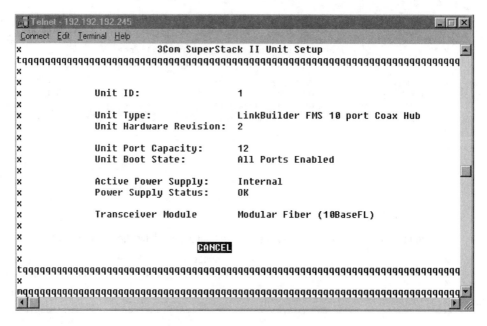

Figure 5.16   Unit Hardware Characteristics

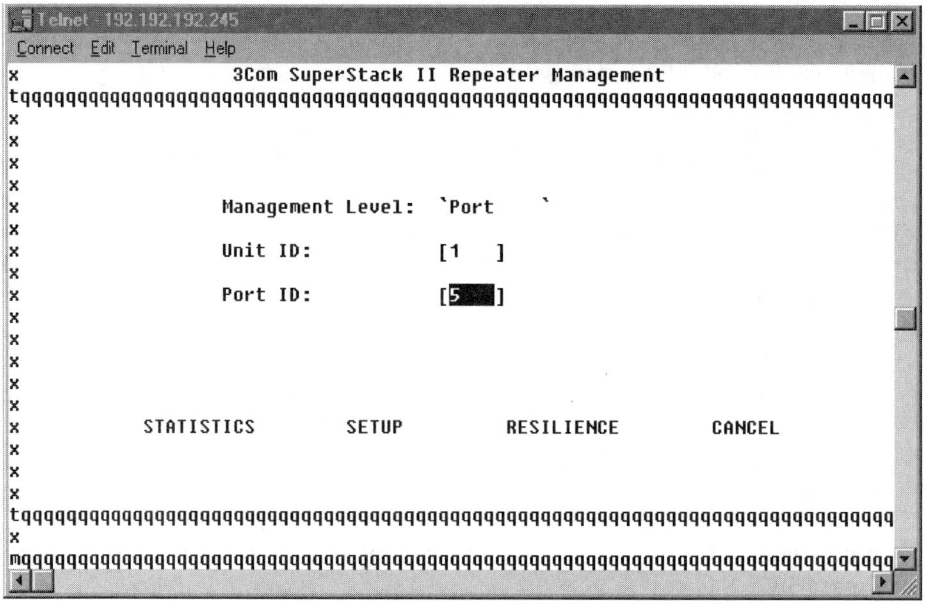

Figure 5.17   Port Management Level for Unit 1

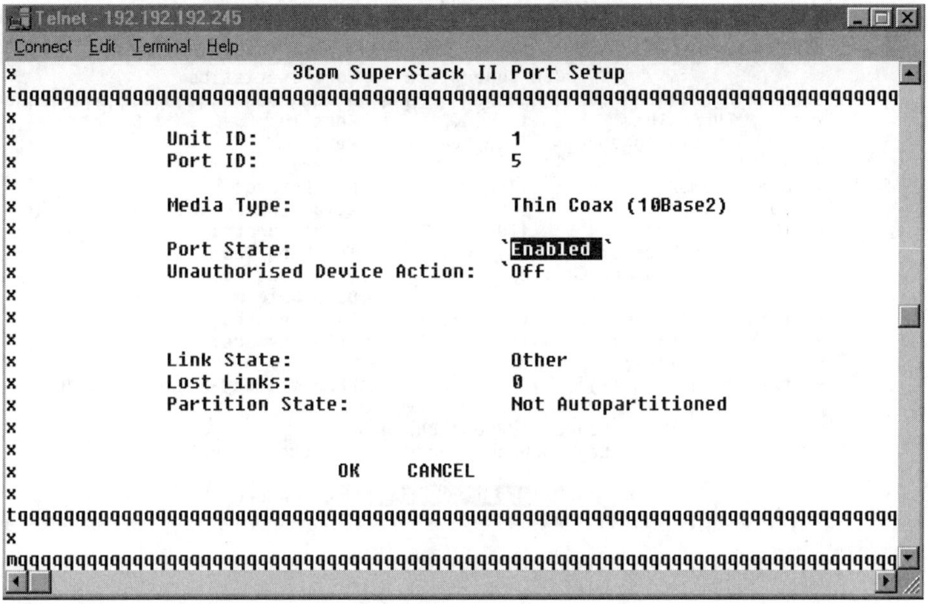

Figure 5.18   Port Setup

Using Port State, you can enable or disable a port. In addition, the Management Module reads the hardware and network address in the first packet received by the port. If either changes, a Trap is sent to the Management Station and/or the port is shut down automatically. If the Partitioned State shows Autopartitioned, the port has been shut down this way (i.e., partitioned off) because it is not operating properly.

Next select Port Statistics in Figure 5.17 to get the statistics shown in **Figure 5.19**.

Here we see a snapshot of all frames into and out of Port 5. More interesting are the two lines at the bottom of the screen. Relevant to the discussion of **Figure 5.18**, the first says that there have been no "source address changes" and that the last hardware source address received was 00400544A7DC, the NIC on WS 2.

We do not need to address the other items on the Main Menu at this time, so this concludes the discussion of hub management using Telnet. We will return to SNMP management of the hub in a later chapter. Now let's look at switch configuration, a more extensive subject.

5.2 SWITCHES

5.2.1 Hardware Configuration

There are two switches on the network, which have been labeled Switch 1 and Switch 2 as shown in **Figure 5.3**. Both are Cisco Catalyst 1900 Series switches. We will configure only Switch 2 because the process is identical for Switch 1. Switch 2 can also be configured using the Web. We will discuss that approach in Chapter 11.

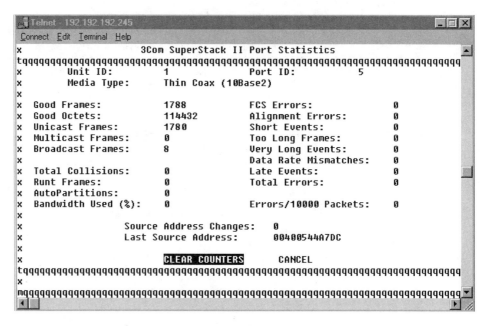

Figure 5.19   Unit 1, Port 5 Statistics

If you have a switch from another supplier, the approach to configuration used here will be similar.

The characteristics of the ports on the front and back of the switches are described in **Table 5.3**. One 10Mbps RJ-45 port is connected to SERVER. The AUI port on the back uses a 10Mbps transceiver with a coaxial cable connector to connect that port to the 10Base2 coaxial cable.

Before we configure the switch's management module, we will examine the important manual configuration capabilities provided by the controls on the front of the switch. The LEDs on the left side provide a number of functions. There are five types: System, RPS, STAT, UTL and FDUP The System LEDs are described in **Table 5.4.**

Table 5.5 describes the information provided by the port LEDs. The port LEDs operate in different modes that are selected by the Mode button. In **STAT** mode, the LEDs indicate the status of the port and its link. In bandwidth utilization (**UTL**) mode, only combinations of green LEDs are meaningful and only meaningful for the switch as a whole. Different combinations reflect different switch present and peak bandwidth utilization. In Full Duplex (**FDUP**) mode, ports with lit LEDs are operating in 20Mbps mode.

Probably the most common use of the port LEDs is in Stat mode when one can just look at the lights to see which links are operational (solid green) and which are operational and active (blinking green).

The default port operational mode is half-duplex and 10Mbps. 10BaseT ports operate only in half-duplex mode. If a port on a switch can operate in Full Duplex mode, the device on the other end of the link must be able to operate in this mode

Table 5.3 Ports on Cisco Catalyst 1900 Switch 2

Type	Number of Ports	Description

10BASET	24 ports (on front)	• 10Mbps bandwidth in half duplex mode
		• Connect to workstations, servers, hubs and routers
		• Rule of thumb.
		    • Use a straight-through cable if only one device being connected is marked with an X. (In the device marked with an X, crossover takes place in the device)
		    • Use a crossover cable if both devices are marked with Xs
		• Maximum of 100 meters between switch and attached device

AUI	1 port (on back)	• 10Mbps bandwidth in half-duplex mode • Connect to Ethernet transceiver that connects to thick or thin coaxial cable, fiber optic cable or UTP cable • Use crossover cable if the transceiver is used to convert to a 10BaseT RJ-45 connection • Maximum of 100 meters between switch and attached device
100BaseT	1port (on front)	• 100Mbps bandwidth in half-duplex mode • Connect to workstations, servers, hubs and routers with compatible band-width and to other switches to form a backbone • Rule of thumb is same as for 10BaseT type
100BaseFX	1 port (on front)	• 100Mbps bandwidth • Uses multimode optical fiber cable to connect devices • Maximum of 2 kilometers between switch and attached device
Console	1 port (on back)	• Serial port used for device configuration • Can be connected to a modem for remote configuration • Requires a crossover cable between the console connector and the serial connector on a PC serial port
RPS	1 (on back)	• Connector for Redundant Power Supply

Table 5.4 System LEDs on Switch 2

Type	Color (Status)	Function
System	Off	System not powered up
	Green	Normal operation
	Amber	Some Power on Self Test(s) (POST) failed
RPS	Off	Redundant Power Supply (RPS) is not being used. Standard (Internal) Power Supply is being used. The RPS is not supplied with the switch. It is an option
	Green	RPS is being used
	Amber	RPS is not operational or not being used correctly
	Flashing Amber	Both RPS and the Standard power supply are powered up and power is being supplied by the standard supply

Table 5.5 Port LEDs on Switch 2

Mode	Port LED Color	Status
STAT		When selected (lighted) by pressing the Mode button, the colors of the port LEDs indicate the status of the port
	None	The port is not connected to a device or the device and/or port are not working
	Green	Link is operational but there is no activity
	Flashing Green	Activity on the link
	Alternating Green and Amber	Error frames are being detected on the link • CRC errors • Collisions • Alignment
	Amber	Port is not forwarding frames • Disabled by management • Suspended by Spanning Tree Protocol because of network loops • Suspended because of address violation
UTL	Green	• Ports 1 → 8 means current bandwidth is less than 6Mbps • Ports 9 → 16 means current bandwidth is between 6 and 120 Mbps • Ports 17 → 24 means current bandwidth is between 120 and 280 Mbps • The LED of the highest port in a group will be blinking • The peak bandwidth is indicated by the highest solid green LED in the group
FDUP	Green	• Port is operating in Full Duplex Mode (20Mbps)

also. Operating 10Mbps ports in Full Duplex mode provides a link bandwidth of 20Mbps. 100Mbps 100BaseT ports can operate in Full-Duplex mode.

5.2.2 Management Module Configuration

We will use out-of-band management for configuration of the management module. When we discuss Web-based management in Chapter 11, we will also show how this switch can be managed using web-based management with a graphical user interface (GUI). For this switch, a crossover cable is needed between the console port on the back of Switch 2 and the serial port on the computer used in Virtual Terminal Emulation (VTE) mode. Server will be used in VTE mode for this configuration.

Console Port

First, we configure the serial communication link between Switch 2 and Server. To do this in Windows NT 4.0 SERVER, select Start, Programs, Accessories Hyperterminal, and then Hyperterminal again. This brings up the New Connection screen and a dialog box, shown in **Figure 5.20**, in which you must type a name for the connection and select an icon for it.

"Your connection" has been entered as an example and the first telephone icon has been selected. Serial Port B on the Server is configured as COM2 and it is connected to the console port on Switch 2. If we now go to Control Panel and click Ports, we can get a complete description of COM2, which is shown on the three screens on the left of **Figure 5.21**.

By clicking Settings on the top screen, the middle screen appears showing the required communicating settings. Clicking Advanced in the middle screen, the bot-

Figure 5.20 Naming the Hyperterminal Connection

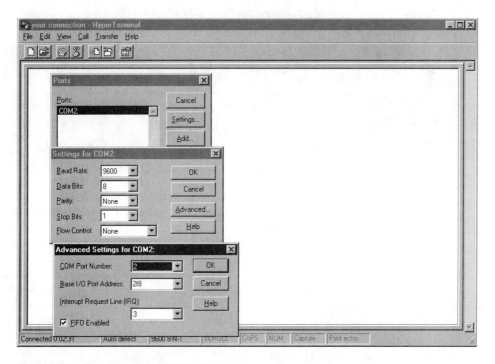

Figure 5.21 Configuration of COM 2

Figure 5.22 Catalyst 1900 Management Console Introduction Screen

tom screen appears showing that COM2 has an I/O address of 2f8 and an IRQ of 3 as expected from what has been said about this subject in Chapter 4.

You will immediately be able to tell if your configuration is right by pressing Enter once. If all is well, Switch 2 will send the message you see in **Figure 5.22**.

> **Note**
>
> As for the hub, the procedures used below to configure the Cisco Catalyst 1900 switch may be different in detail from what is necessary for your hardware.

If you don't get this message it is because you did not use a crossover cable or your communications settings, such as baud rate or Flow Control, are incorrect. You can check that you are really looking at Switch 2 by the Ethernet Address. Type in the password, if one has been configured, and then press Enter for the Main Menu as shown in **Figure 5.23**.

You can modify the Password on the Main Menu screen if you type "C" to get Console Settings.

Network Management

The first submenu to examine in **Figure 5.23** is Network Management. Type "N" to get the Network Management screen shown in **Figure 5.24**.

We are interested in the IP Configuration and SNMP Management items.

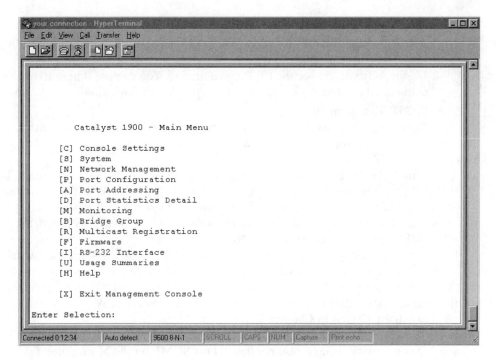

Figure 5.23   Main Menu of Catalyst 1900 Management Console

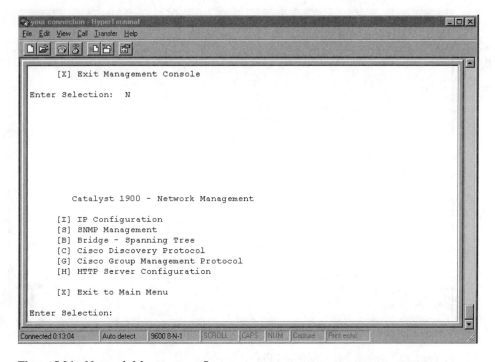

Figure 5.24   Network Management Screen

a. **IP Configuration**

Type "I" to get **Figure 5.25**, which shows the current IP Configuration settings for Switch 2.

Under Actions, you see the [P] **Ping** command. You can use it here to test the connectivity of the links attached to any port on the switch.

b. **SNMP Management**

Returning to **Figure 5.24**, type "S" to get the SNMP Management Configuration screen shown in **Figure 5.26.**

This screen provides a good summary of SNMP configuration options. The first two lines provide the screens for setting the READ and WRITE Community Strings. Typing "R" brings up the screen shown in **Figure 5.27** that says, under Actions, "this command configures the community string the switch will recognize on all SNMP read (Get) requests." Get Requests are the SNMP commands used by the Management Station to get values of the MIB variables from the Switch 2 agent. In the case of this switch, these are values of the standard MIB-2 variables. Additional Enterprise MIB values, specific to this Cisco switch, can be accessed if the Management Station has those MIB variables installed. We will install them when we discuss MIBs in **Chapter 7**.

The Current setting of the **READ** Community String is rmon_admin. This READ community string is also configured for SNMP on the Management station.

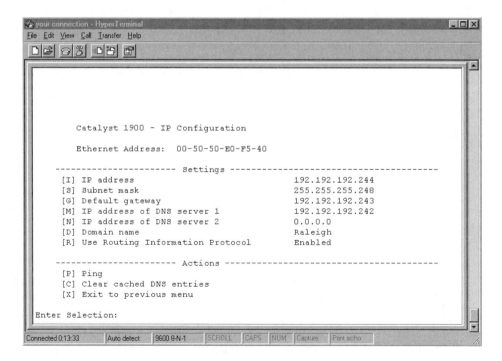

Figure 5.25 Switch 2 IP Configuration

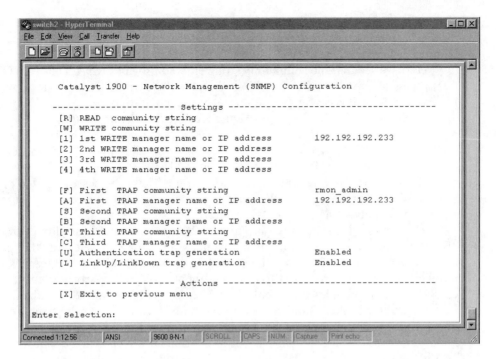

Figure 5.26   SNMP Agent Configuration

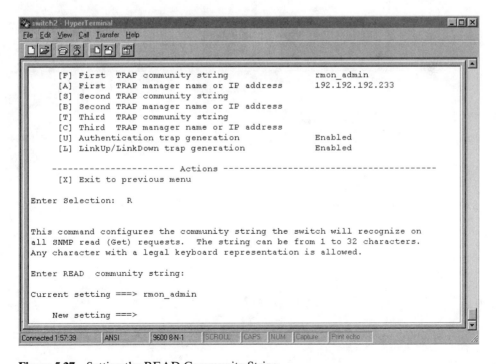

Figure 5.27   Setting the READ Community String

This is what we want so we do not change it. Any Management Station that uses the Switch 2 community string can read its MIB values. Pressing Enter takes us back to **Figure 5.26** where we type "W" to get the screen shown in **Figure 5.28**.

Here we see that the community string entered provides READ and **WRITE** (set) access to Switch 2 MIB variables. We leave the current setting of tei_admin because this is what is configured on the Management Station.

The numbers [1] through [4] in **Figure 5.26** provide the opportunity to select a number of WRITE managers. Write Managers are those given the privilege to set MIB values on the switch. Selection requires providing the IP address of the Write Manager Station. The current selection is 192.192.192.233, the IP address of WS1, the Management Station that hosts Meterware. These choices are used to protect the WRITE privilege. If no Write managers are identified, any manager knowing the community string can set MIB values.

The Letters [F] through [C] in **Figure 5.26** enable the configuration of three TRAP Community String/Trap manager pairs. One pair is selected, the pair rmon_admin/192.192.192.233. As mentioned in the case of the hub, a TRAP is an unsolicited message that is sent to a management station if a particular event occurs. This switch provides two events for which traps will be sent: the Authentication trap and the LinkUp/LinkDown trap. An Authentication trap will be sent if the management agent on the switch receives a Get or Set Request containing a community string that is not recognized. A LinkUp/LinkDown trap will be sent when a port is transitioned from a disabled/suspended status to an enabled status or from enabled to disabled/suspended status.

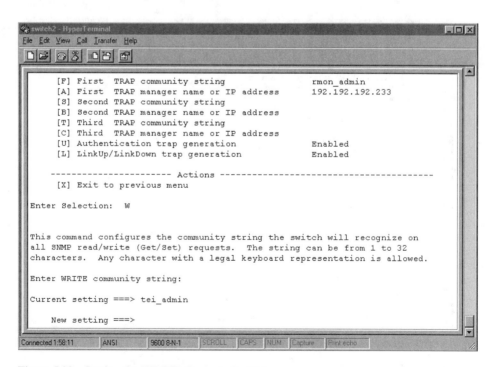

Figure 5.28   Setting the WRITE Community String

The configuration of the management agent on Switch 2 is now complete and the MIB values can be accessed from the Management Station.

Port Configuration

The next item on the Main Menu in **Figure 5.23** we need to visit is [P] Port Configuration. Typing "P" brings up the screen in **Figure 5.29**.

The ports you want to configure are "identified" here. There are two Switch 2 ports in use: Server, the IBM IntelliStation ZPRO, is connected to Port 3 and the AUI port on the back of the switch is connected to the 10Base2 cable. Type "3" and press Enter to get **Figure 5.30**.

At this time the important things to notice are "Description/name of port" which is ZPRO, "Status of Port" is Enabled and "Full Duplex" mode is disabled. These are the correct port configuration values. Each item on this menu can be used to change these values and other values that we do not need to discuss here.

Port Addressing

The next configuration step is Port Addressing. On the screen in **Figure 5.30**, under Related Menus, "A" is typed to go to the Port Addressing screen, **Figure 5.31**. At the top of that screen, on the second line, you see:

Address: Static 00-20-35-E4-1D-2B

Figure 5.29 Selecting a Port to Configure

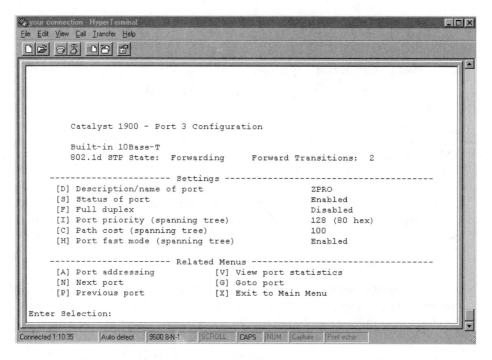

Figure 5.30 Port 3 Configuration

Figure 5.31 Port 3 Addressing

Table 5.6 Static Address Settings

Menu Item	Description
Address Table Size	• The upper limit of the number of addresses that a secured port can have. There is no limit on unsecured ports
Addressing Security	• Reduces usage of a port to a specified list of static addresses. • Violations may cause port disablement.
Flood Unknown Unicasts	• A Unicast is a frame destined for one device • If enabled, any frame that has an Ethernet destination that is not in the address table will be transmitted out of all ports.
Flood Unregistered Multicasts	• A Multicast is a frame that is destined for a set of devices • If enabled, a frame received for a multicast address that has not been registered with the switch, will be transmitted out of all ports • This menu item can be used to control which ports will allow this.

This statement says that this Ethernet address has been statically mapped to Port 3 in the switch's Ethernet address table. It means that any frame that has this Ethernet destination address will be transmitted out of Port 3 to SERVER. Port 3 could have a hub attached to it and accordingly there could be a number of Ethernet destination addresses that could be statically mapped to Port 3. Table 5.6 describes static mapping settings. Static mapping is not a practical approach to constructing a switch address table, however. It is usually best to let the switch learn Port-to-Ethernet Address mappings from the source addresses in the frames it receives through the port.

The items listed under "Actions" in **Figure 5.31** are those which a Network Manager will often implement. Lets look at the screen generated when "L," under "Actions," is typed. This screen is shown in **Figure 5.32**. At the bottom of the figure, we see a list of addresses, according to Type, Address and Accepted Source Ports. Currently there is only the static address for the IBM ZPRO Server. Accepted Source Ports are Unrestricted. This means that the switch will forward any frame that includes the IBM ZPRO destination address to that computer. Since this is not always desirable, typing "D" in **Figure 5.31** allows the network manager to "Define restricted static address." Then only frames that have these restricted Ethernet Source Addresses will be forwarded to Static Address: 00-20-35-E4-1D-2B.

Now let's look at the Port Addressing menu for the other active port on Switch 2, the AUI port. Returning to the Main Menu (**Figure 5.23**), "A" is typed to get the screen where the AUI port can be identified. Then AUI is typed and Enter is pressed for the screen shown in **Figure 5.33**.

On the second line of **Figure 5.33** you see:

Address : Dynamic 00-40-05-44-A7-DC

Here the word "Dynamic" appears. This dynamic address is the Ethernet address of WS 2. This means that Switch 2 has learned that any frame that has this Ethernet destination address should be transmitted out of its AUI port. The switch learned

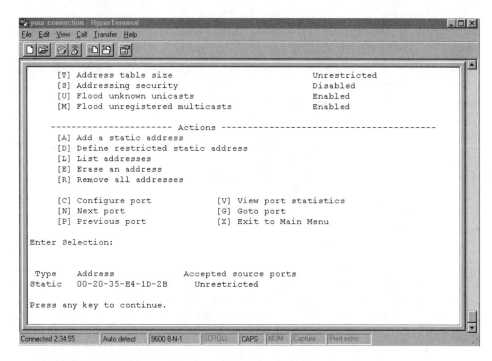

Figure 5.32   List of Accepted Source Ports for Destination Port 3

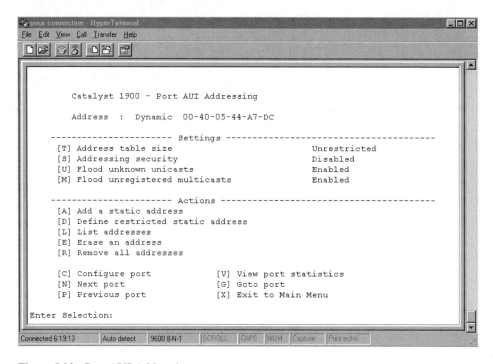

Figure 5.33   Port AUI Addressing

this mapping from reading a frame containing WS2's Ethernet source address received at the AUI port. If you refer to the demonstration network in **Figure 5.3**, you will see that this interpretation is correct.

The other thing to note about dynamic addresses is that they are stored in the switch address table for a limited time. The switch assumes that if it has not seen the address in that time limit, the source is inactive or turned off and there is no sense wasting good memory space on it. You can set this timeout on the System submenu on the Main Menu. It is called **Address Aging Time** there.

Monitoring

We go to the switch Main Menu again (Type "X") and then type "M" to look at the Monitoring configuration screen shown in **Figure 5.34**. This screen provides an essential tool for the network manager. It makes it possible to have a copy of frame activity on any or all ports sent to a Monitor port on the switch. This monitor port can be connected to a probe that will store these frames for analysis by a protocol analyzer. The Apptitude Fastmeter on our network has two Mirror ports which are attached to the Monitor ports on Switch 2 and Switch 1. Thus all frames entering or leaving any or all ports on these switches can be captured simultaneously. We rely on this capability often in Chapters 8 and 9.

Typing "C" in **Figure 5.34** provides a screen on which capturing can be enabled or disabled. It is Enabled here. Typing "M" in **Figure 5.34** provides a screen where the Monitoring port is selected. See **Figure 5.35**.

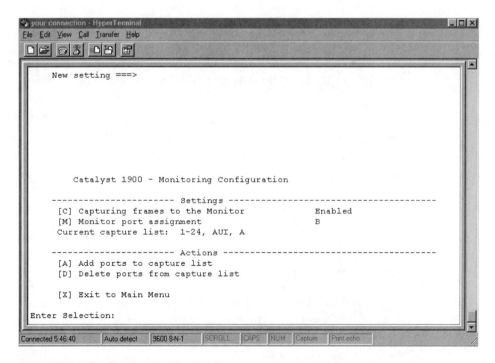

Figure 5.34 Configuring the Monitor Port

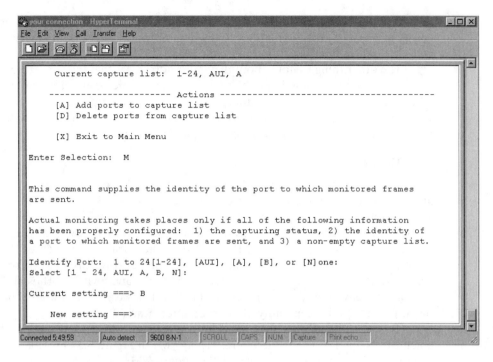

```
Current capture list:  1-24, AUI, A

---------------------- Actions ----------------------------------------
[A] Add ports to capture list
[D] Delete ports from capture list

[X] Exit to Main Menu

Enter Selection:  M


This command supplies the identity of the port to which monitored frames
are sent.

Actual monitoring takes places only if all of the following information
has been properly configured:  1) the capturing status, 2) the identity of
a port to which monitored frames are sent, and 3) a non-empty capture list.

Identify Port:  1 to 24[1-24], [AUI], [A], [B], or [N]one:
Select [1 - 24, AUI, A, B, N]:

Current setting ===> B

   New setting ===>
```

Figure 5.35 Monitor Port Selection

Any port can be selected to be the monitor port. In this case, the 100BaseT Port B is selected. The current ports that will be captured are ports 3 and AUI. These are the only active ports on Switch 2. However, ports to be captured can be added or deleted by using the [A] and [D] items listed under "Actions" in **Figure 5.35**.

Port Statistics Detail

The last screen we will examine for Switch 2 is a screen that is also valuable to the network manager for troubleshooting, as you will see by example below. On the Main Menu (**Figure 5.23**), we access Port Statistics Detail by typing "D." This provides the opportunity to select a port to view. Typing "3" we get the screen shown in **Figure 5.36**. Here we can see if the number of frames being received and transmitted by a port appear reasonable and if any errors are being reported. If the Receive Statistics errors are large in any category, then the manager will want to find out which devices are sending frames to the port and, if access is possible, check the statistics of those devices. If the Transmit Statistics errors are large, then the switch port may be at fault. Using the other switch management tools we have already discussed, the switch port can be disabled or the frames received from a particular device will not be forwarded, for example. At this time, everything for port 3 looks normal.

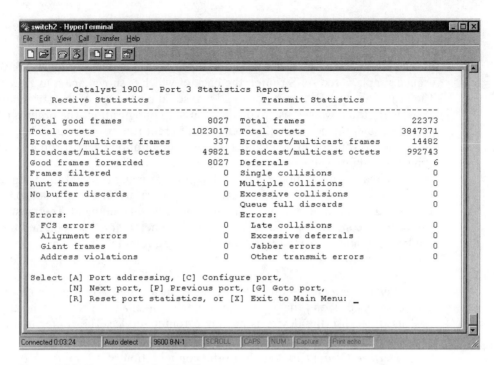

Figure 5.36 Port 3 Statistics Detail

Just before this section was written however, the screen in **Figure 5.36** showed that Receive Statistics for Port 3 were zero but Transmit Statistics were normal. This meant that IBM ZPRO was not sending frames to Port 3. We could see from the LED on the front of the switch that the link to the IBM ZPRO was active so it was not a hardware problem. We also found by using the Ping command on the switch that the peer network layers on the switch and the IBM ZPRO were communicating. (Remember, the Ping command is an application that causes a series of identical messages to be sent from the Internet Control Message Protocol (ICMP) in the Network layer on the switch to the ICMP in the Network layer on the IBM ZPRO. This results in identical messages being sent back if there is a software link between those layers.) Thus it seemed like the disconnect was in a higher layer of the protocol stack Rebooting the IBM ZPRO restored the connection as Receiver Statistics began to be collected. A possible explanation is that some software in a layer above the Network layer did not load the first time the IBM ZPRO was powered up.

This completes the configuration of Switch 2 using its Console Port. We could have configured the switch over the network using Telnet or using Web Management. Web Management, as mentioned above, is possible for this switch because it contains a web server in its firmware. All configuration methods provide the same capability. We now examine how to configure a router.

5.3 ROUTERS

In this section, we discuss configuration of the router shown in **Figure 5.3**. We are using a simple Cisco AGS router, the back of which is shown again in **Figure 5.37**. The router has two Ethernet ports and two serial ports. One of the serial ports is a Console port that we will use to demonstrate its configuration. The other is a WAN port. Although the configuration steps for different routers will vary, what we configure on this router will be included in the configuration of most routers. Routers of more capability will have more configuration possibilities.

The management modules of routers provide many configuration commands. Thus they are usually sorted into categories. There are also many subcommands and associated parameters for each command and subcommand. The most important of these commands, subcommands and parameters for this book and their use will be listed and explained in a table. All can be found in the manuals that come with the router.

Global Commands—apply to the router as a whole. An example of a Global Command is one that gives the router its hostname. The word hostname is used because the device is hosting a router service. The router is therefore often referred to as a server.

Interface Commands—apply to the configuration of an interface such as an Ethernet interface.

Line Commands—apply to serial ports.

Router Commands—configure routing protocols such as the Routing Information Protocol (**RIP**) and the Open Shortest Path First protocol (**OSPF**).

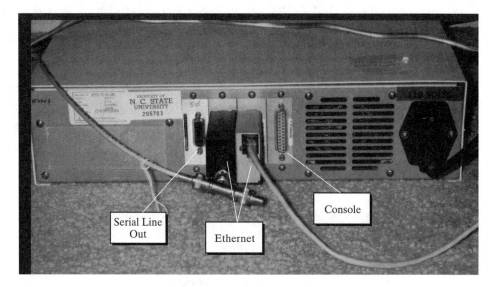

Figure 5.37   Back of Cisco AGS Router

5.3.1 Setup

All commands are typed at a Command prompt. The Command prompts on the Cisco router used here have two levels of user access. They are **"Hostname >"** and **"Hostname #"**. The difference is that the Hostname # prompt provides access to all router configuration commands and requires a password.

There is a Setup program that will run automatically if configuration of the router is being done the first time. Setup will walk you through the process of configuring your router. You can also access Setup at a later time by typing Setup at the "Hostname #" prompt.

Figures 5.38 and **5.39** show the Setup dialog that ran when Setup was typed at the Hostname # prompt. These screens show the current choices for configuration values of this router.

Global Commands

The screen in **Figure 5.38** shows some of the global commands that can be configured.

In the first line under "Configuring global parameters," we are changing the hostname from **Router 234/243** to **Router 1**. In the next line, the password to use with the hostname# prompt is "burke." In later lines, notice some of the many protocols that can be configured and interpreted by this router. At this point, we have

Figure 5.38 Router Global Commands

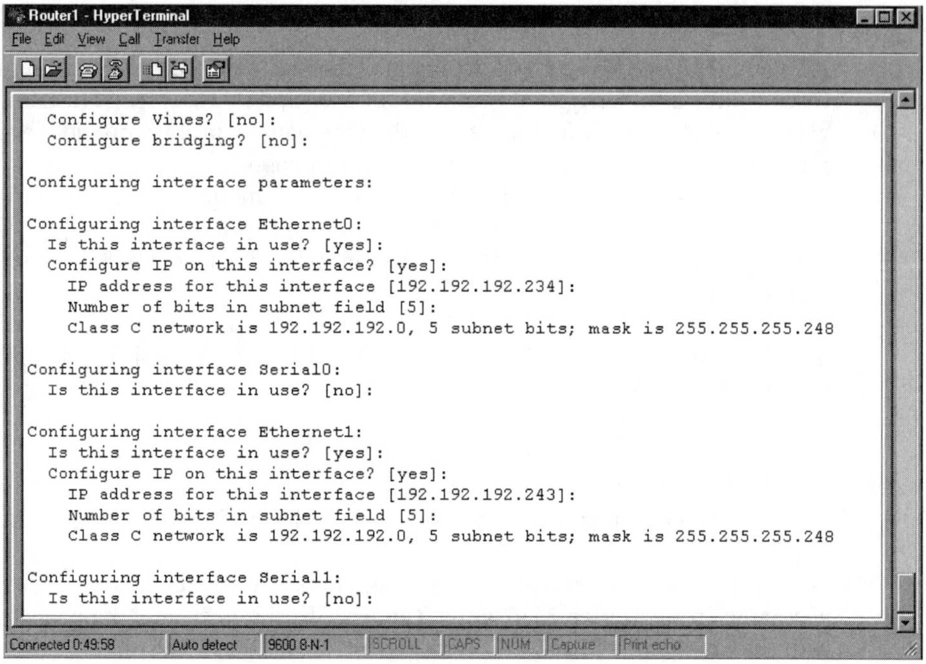

```
╔═ Router1 - HyperTerminal ════════════════════════════ _□×╗
║ File  Edit  View  Call  Transfer  Help                   ║
║  ┌──┬──┐ ┌──┬──┐ ┌──┬──┐ ┌──┐                            ║
║  │  │  │ │  │  │ │  │  │ │  │                            ║
║  └──┴──┘ └──┴──┘ └──┴──┘ └──┘                            ║
║ ┌──────────────────────────────────────────────────┐ ▲ ║
║ │   Configure Vines? [no]:                          │   ║
║ │   Configure bridging? [no]:                       │   ║
║ │                                                   │   ║
║ │ Configuring interface parameters:                 │   ║
║ │                                                   │   ║
║ │ Configuring interface Ethernet0:                  │   ║
║ │   Is this interface in use? [yes]:                │   ║
║ │   Configure IP on this interface? [yes]:          │   ║
║ │     IP address for this interface [192.192.192.234]: │   ║
║ │     Number of bits in subnet field [5]:           │   ║
║ │     Class C network is 192.192.192.0, 5 subnet bits; mask is 255.255.255.248 │   ║
║ │                                                   │   ║
║ │ Configuring interface Serial0:                    │   ║
║ │   Is this interface in use? [no]:                 │   ║
║ │                                                   │   ║
║ │ Configuring interface Ethernet1:                  │   ║
║ │   Is this interface in use? [yes]:                │   ║
║ │   Configure IP on this interface? [yes]:          │   ║
║ │     IP address for this interface [192.192.192.243]: │   ║
║ │     Number of bits in subnet field [5]:           │   ║
║ │     Class C network is 192.192.192.0, 5 subnet bits; mask is 255.255.255.248 │   ║
║ │                                                   │   ║
║ │ Configuring interface Serial1:                    │   ║
║ │   Is this interface in use? [no]:                 │ ▼ ║
║ └──────────────────────────────────────────────────┘   ║
║ Connected 0:49:58 │ Auto detect │ 9600 8-N-1 │ SCROLL │ CAPS │ NUM │ Capture │ Print echo ║
╚══════════════════════════════════════════════════════════╝
```

Figure 5.39 Global and Interface Commands

only chosen to configure two protocols: IP and RIP. We will configure IP and RIP, as well as OSPF and BGP routing protocols, later in this chapter. **BGP** is the Border Gateway Protocol. Continuing to answer the questions by pressing the Enter key, in **Figure 5.39** we are given the opportunity to choose configuration of the (Banyon) Vines protocol and bridging. (Remember that this router can also be used as a bridge.)

Interface Commands

Now we come to "Configuring interface parameters."

1. **Interface Ethernet0**

   With the next line, we begin the configuration of Ethernet0. For our network, Ethernet0 is the router interface on Subnet 1. IP is to be configured on this interface and the interface IP address has been given the value 192.192.192.234. Values for the other parameters, "Number of bits in the subnet field," the address of the Class C network, and the Subnet Mask have been determined by the router from information already provided. See **Appendix A** for a discussion of how this is done.

2. **Interface Serial0**

   Moving on to further questions on this screen, we are presented with the opportunity to configure interface Serial0. This is the WAN interface. We are not using it at this time so we will not configure it.

3. **Interface Ethernet1**

   The Interface Ethernet1 configuration process is the same as that for Interface Ethernet0 except the IP address is 192.192.192.243. This router interface is on Subnet 2.

4. **Interface Serial1**

   This is the Console interface that can be configured from the Main Router Menu.

At this point, based on the global parameters we selected to configure, the configuration is complete for this router. If we were to press the Enter key again, the router would show the configuration we had created and we would be given the opportunity to save it in the router's non-volatile RAM. On this router that is simply done by typing **"write memory"** at the "hostname#" prompt. To see what was saved at any later time, type **show configuration** at this prompt. When the router is started again at a later date it will use the stored configuration. You can erase non-volatile memory by typing the command **write erase** at the "hostname#" prompt.

5.3.2 Command-line Configuration of Commands and Subcommands

The Setup program has enabled us to do a lot of the router configuration quite easily. To specify more configuration details or to add router capabilities that were not configured in Setup, it is necessary to use command-line configuration commands and subcommands. There are many commands and subcommands so they are not something that you remember the first time you use a router. In the beginning, you have to look them up in the manuals that come with the router. Eventually, you will remember those you use most often.

Let's take a look at some commands and subcommands that are very useful and learn how they are used. We will configure our router with a command line utility from scratch as if we had not used Setup. A command line-based configuration utility is not as user friendly as a Web-based server but may be more instructive the first time through. This router is too old to have a Web server installed.

Starting from scratch then, we open the Hyperterminal connection to the Console port on the router. Press the Enter key once to get the prompt router1>. Then we type enable and Enter to get the password prompt. We then press Enter and type the password to get the prompt **router 1#** in **Figure 5.40**

Write erase is typed at the prompt "router1#" to erase non-volatile RAM so that we can start configuration with a clean slate. [OK] on the next line indicates that non-volatile memory has been erased. We start configuration on the third line.

Typing the command **"configure"** at the prompt provides access to the configuration subcommands. You are asked if you are "Configuring from terminal, memory or network." Terminal, enclosed in square brackets [], is the default. We are configuring from terminal. The next two lines are instructions provided by the router.

The screen after the router instructions is blank until we add what you see in **Figure 5.40**. So what configuration commands and subcommands do we use from

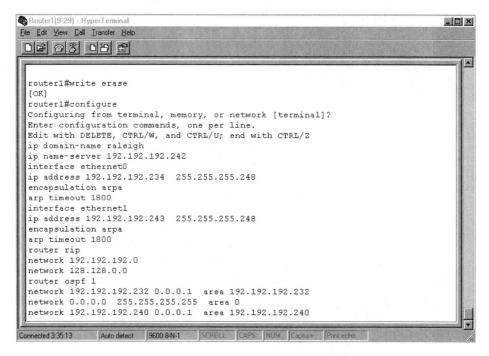

```
router1#write erase
[OK]
router1#configure
Configuring from terminal, memory, or network [terminal]?
Enter configuration commands, one per line.
Edit with DELETE, CTRL/W, and CTRL/U; end with CTRL/Z
ip domain-name raleigh
ip name-server 192.192.192.242
interface ethernet0
ip address 192.192.192.234  255.255.255.248
encapsulation arpa
arp timeout 1800
interface ethernet1
ip address 192.192.192.243  255.255.255.248
encapsulation arpa
arp timeout 1800
router rip
network 192.192.192.0
network 128.128.0.0
router ospf 1
network 192.192.192.232 0.0.0.1  area 192.192.192.232
network 0.0.0.0  255.255.255.255  area 0
network 192.192.192.240 0.0.0.1  area 192.192.192.240
```

Figure 5.40   Command-Line Configuration of the Router

this point on? The router configuration program does not tell us. However, there is a command called **show?** that gives a list of commands and subcommands. You can also get them from the manuals. You then type them in line by line. If you make a syntax mistake the router will tell you. The next two lines in **Figure 5.40** are Global Configuration Commands. They inform the router that it is in domain "raleigh" and that the IP address of the computer hosting the Domain Name Service (DNS) in domain raleigh is 192.192.192.242 (SERVER). It is useful to have a table of some typical commands and subcommands for quick reference. These are listed in **Table 5.7**.

Interface Ethernet0

On the next line, the configuration command "interface ethernet0," specifies that the lines you type (until you type another configuration command) are sub-commands that configure interface ethernet0. Encapsulation "**arpa**" configures the router to use the Ethernet II frame. The Ethernet II frame includes a Type field immediately after the Source Address field. This Type field contains the ID of the Network layer protocol that starts in the following field. If Encapsulation "**iso 1**" were chosen, the router would construct frames using the IEEE 802.3 frame which is shown in **Figure 1.3** of **Chapter 1**.

Arp timeout "1800," specifies that the Address Resolution Protocol (**ARP**) table will retain Ethernet-IP Address mappings for 1800 seconds (30 minutes). (See

Table 5.7   Router Configuration Commands, Subcommands, Parameters and Functions

Commands	Subcommands	Parameters	Functions
enable			Generates the # prompt at which all subcommands can be executed
password		xxxxxxxxx	If set, is required to use the configure command
configure			Command that starts the configuration program
ip domain-name		name	"name" specifies the name of the Internet domain to which the router belongs
ip name-server		ip address	"ip address" sets the IP address of the computer that is hosting the DNS for the network
interface		ethernet no. serial no.	"ethernet no." specifies the Ethernet to be configured "serial no." specifies the serial line to be configured
	ip address	address subnet mask	"address" sets the IP address for the router interface "subnet mask" sets the subnet mask for the router
	encapsulation	arpa iso	"arpa" configures the router to us the Ethernet II frame "iso1" configures the router to use the IEEE 802.3 frame
	arp timeout	seconds	"seconds" specifies the time that the router will keep an IP Ethernet address mapping in the ARP cache. The default is 240 seconds
access-list		list	"list" specifies which IP addresses will be accepted/ rejected at this router interface
		permit	Used before "list" to "permit" only those IP addresses specified in "list"
		deny	Used before "list" to "deny" the IP addresses specified in "list"
		source	Specific IP source address permitted or denied by "permit" or "deny," respectively
		source mask	Range of IP source addresses that can be permitted or denied with "permit" or "deny"
no access-list			Deletes the entire list specified in "list"
router	rip		Specifies the RIP routing protocol will be configured on the router
	network		Specifies the directly connected networks that will receive RIP routing protocols from "router"
router	ospf	#	Specifies the OSPF routing protocol will be configured on "router"
	network		Specifies a range of addresses that OSPF will advertise to neighboring routers reachable from "router"
router	bgp		Specifies the BGP routing protocol will be configured on "router"
	network		Specifies the IP addresses on a network that the BGP will advertise to routers outside the autonomous system it borders
	neighbor		Specifies the IP address and the Autonomous System number of a router to which BGP will advertise the network it borders

the discussion of ARP in **Appendix A)**. The default for this subcommand is four minutes. When you are setting up or testing a network, it is often helpful to have the ARP table retained for longer than four minutes.

Interface Ethernet1

The next line is the command interface ethernet1. The three subcommands that follow configure this interface as was done for ethernet0.

5.3.3 Routing Protocols

router "rip" is the command/subcommand combination that enables RIP configuration. **[Ref 1]** The subcommand **"network"** specifies the attached networks to which RIP will send the routing table of router. Network 192.192.192.0 is our Class C network. There is no other router on our network to receive the routing table. Network 128.128.0.0 is a hypothetical Class B network that makes a Point-to-Point Protocol **(PPP) [Ref 5-7]** connection, using a modem, to the PSTN. A characteristic of RIP is that it sends its entire routing table every 30 seconds to the networks specified in its network subcommands. Our router would receive routing table messages from other routers if there were any. If our router did not receive a RIP message from another router in 240 seconds, it would delete the routes provided by that router as being unreliable.

router ospf 1 is the command/subcommand/parameter combination that enables OSPF configuration. We will briefly describe how OSPF is configured below and we will configure it on the router. However, OSPF is a comprehensive and complex protocol. Thus to use it effectively, it is necessary to refer to the OSPF standard **[Ref 2]**. Also, see **[Ref 7-8]**.

Like RIP, OSPF is an Interior Routing Protocol **(IRP)** for an Autonomous System **(AS)**. IRP is the label given to a routing protocol that is used in an AS. OSPF is a more efficient routing protocol than RIP. For example, whereas a RIP router sends its routing table to all directly attached routers every 30 seconds, an OSPF router only sends routing table changes when they occur. An Autonomous System is a system under one Administration. It contains a set of one or more networks using the same routing protocol that is independent of routing protocols used in other Autonomous Systems on the network. **Figure 5.41** is a modification of **Figure 5.3**, providing a visual description of our AS.

Autonomous Systems are connected by **AS Boundary Routers** which may, for example, use the Border Gateway Protocol **(BGP) [Ref 3,4]** to communicate with one another. Each Autonomous System consists of one or more **Areas** which are connected by **Area Border Routers**. Our router is a border router. It would also be a Boundary Router if it were connected to a router in another AS. One purpose of Autonomous Systems and Areas is to reduce routing protocol traffic. Be aware that the terminology just used can be confusing but is correct.

The command **router ospf 1** enables configuration of the OSPF routing process that has the ospf-process id of 1 as a parameter. A particular OSPF

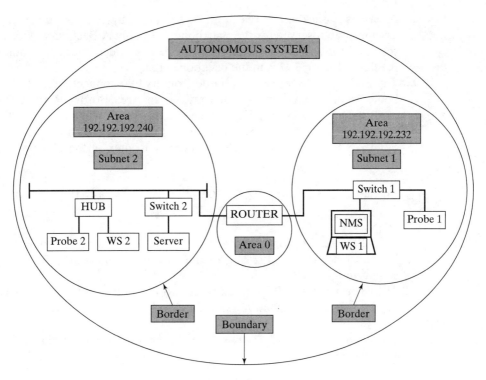

Figure 5.41 Autonomous System with Three Areas

process controls the routing in an AS. The id = 1 is the identifier of the process and the AS.

The subcommand **Network** 192.192.192.232 0.0.0.1 area 192.192.192.232 determines the following, assuming that our LAN is an AS.

a. **Area 192.192.192.232** is an area of an Autonomous System. We have chosen the area label 192.192.192.232 because we are making Subnet 1 this Area. You can give an Area any unique number label .

b. The **parameters** 192.192.192.232 and 0.0.0.1 immediately following the subcommand "Network" determines the router will advertise to other routers that it has access to addresses in the range 192.192.192.233 to 192.192.192.239.

This **range** of addresses is determined by the parameter 0.0.0.1, which is called a **wildcard mask**. It is used much like an IP mask. In this example, 0.0.0.1 specifies that the last digit in the last field of the IP address can be anything in the allowed device addresses but that all other decimal digits in the address are as specified.

The subcommand **Network** 0 255.255.255.255 area 0 specifies that:

   a. Area 0 is a **Backbone Area** of an Autonomous System. The label "0" is pre-assigned and reserved for the Backbone Area only. A Backbone Area must be specified for any AS. It is the network that provides inter-area connectivity. Router in **Figure 5.41** is in the backbone area.

   b. The Backbone Area contains border routers that connect Areas to the backbone. As mentioned above, our router is an Area Border Router. The wildcard parameter 255.255.255.255 means that Router will advertise all devices in the Backbone Area to areas to which it is connected. Of course in the case our LAN there is only one device, namely Router, in the backbone area so there is nothing to advertise.

The subcommand **Network** 192.192.192.240 0.0.0.1 area 192.192.192.240 specifies that:

   a. Area 192.192.192.240 is an area of our Autonomous System and that this area has the label 192.192.192.240. In the case of our network, this area corresponds to Subnet 2

   b. The wildcard mask 0.0.0.1 specifies that Router will advertise that it has access to addresses in the range 192.192.192.241 to 192.192.192.249 to all other routers.

The first six lines in **Figure 5.42** are repeats of the last six lines in **Figure 5.40**. Thus we continue the discussion with the seventh line.

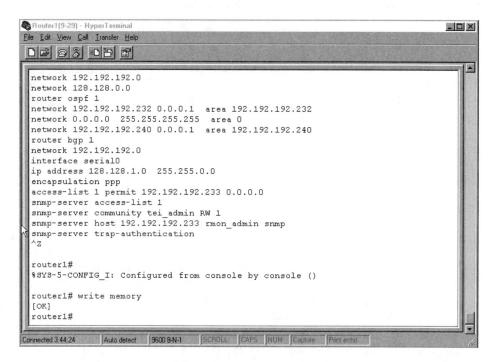

Figure 5.42   BGP, Serial and SNMP Configuration of Router

router bgp 1 on the seventh line is the command that starts the BGP routing process. See **[Ref 3,4]** for a complete description of BGP. The number 1 is the ID used to identify the router to BGP routers on other Autonomous Systems and to tag the information that is passed to other BGP routers.

The subcommand **Network** 192.192.192.0 advertises that network 192.192.192.0 is in Autonomous System 1. In the case of our network, this is the only network within AS 1. As mentioned above, Router is the Autonomous System Boundary Router.

Serial Interface

Interface serial0 is the command/subcommand combination that initializes the configuration of the router serial interface with the ID=0. We will assume that this interface will connect to a modem. Thus its subcommands specify that:

a. The IP address and network mask assigned to this interface are 128.128.1.0 and 255.255.0.0, respectively.
b. The Point to Point Protocol (**PPP**) **[Refs 5-7]** encapsulation will be used to send IP packets over the Public Switched Telephone Network (PSTN) to a router on another Autonomous System over the network 128.128.0.0.

Now let's examine the SNMP configuration of the router.

5.3.4 SNMP

Access-list in Figure 5.42 is a Global Configuration Command that allows one to create a list of devices that are permitted or denied access to another device. We have created the access-list with the following parameters:

a. Has the identifier 1
b. **Permits** management access by a device if
  1. The device IP address is 192.192.192.233 (WS1 on our network) or
  2. The device has an IP address that satisfies the criteria specified by the wildcard mask 0.0.0.0 As implemented by OSPF, the use of 1's in the mask permits access to devices with a range of IP addresses. The use of all zeros here means that only a device with the specified address, 192.192.192.233, has access.

The SNMP configuration begins with the next line **snmp-server access-list 1**, which specifies that the server will use the list, list 1, specified above.

Snmp-server community tei_admin RW 1 specifies that its community name is tei_admin, that it provides Read/Write (RW) access and that the access-list is 1.

Snmp-server host 192.192.192.233 rmon_admin snmp configures **trap** messages as follows:

• 192.192.192.233 means that the host for trap messages is the Management Station with the IP address 192.192.192.233,

- rmon_admin means that the trap community name is rmon_admin
- snmp means that all SNMP traps will be sent

Snmp-server trap-authentication specifies that a Trap message will be sent to the Management Station in the event a message requesting access to a MIB variable has an incorrect community string.

We have now configured the router variables that will enable it to satisfy the operational needs of our network and that of this book. Many other options could be configured to optimize router operation for a specific network. We have configured the management agent on the router to enable the Management Station to access the values of its MIB-2 variables.

As you can see from the description of the configuration of the router on the demonstration network, it is a detailed task and one that is critical to the operation of the network.

We will now examine the Fastmeter probe and what is necessary to configure it for our network. We also have an Ethermeter probe on the network. Its configuration will not be discussed because its capability is included in that of Fastmeter, which is an enhanced Ethermeter.

5.4 PROBES

Ethermeter (Probe 2) and Fastmeter (Probe 1) are the two probes on our network. Both can capture frames that appear on the network segment to which they are attached. Ethermeter supports RMON variables. These variables, which are an extension to MIB-2, contain values relevant to network traffic. Fastmeter supports RMON and RMON 2 variables. RMON 2 is an extension of RMON. All frames captured by these probes can be transferred to Meterware/Analyzer for protocol analysis. Meterware/Analyzer is capable of analyzing protocols implemented in the seven layers of the OSI Reference Model. You will see the power of such analysis as we begin to use Meterware/Analyzer to examine SNMP packets in the next chapter.

Configuration of Fastmeter must be done out-of-band from the console using Hyperterminal as we have done for other device configurations. Its configuration is similar in many ways to what has been done on the switches and the router. **Figure 5.43** shows the Fastmeter main menu. We need only explore the first menu item, so "1" is chosen to get **Figure 5.44**.

There are three items on this menu that are of primary interest to us now: Interface, Security and Trap configurations. **Figure 5.45** shows Interfaces Configuration.

The Fastmeter manual uses the MIB terminology **ifIndex,** as we will see in Chapter 7: to identify its three interfaces to the network. **ifIndex** is an object in the MIB-2 **ifTable. ifIndex.1** identifies the probe management interface which is connected to the network by a 10Mbps port on Switch 1. The management interface is the interface that is queried by an NMS and transmits captured data to Meterware/Analyzer. **ifIndex.2** is connected to a 100Mbps port on Switch 1. This is the interface of Fastmeter, which captures all traffic from the Switch 1 mirror port. **ifIndex.3** is connected to a 100Mbps port on Switch 2. This is the interface of Fast-

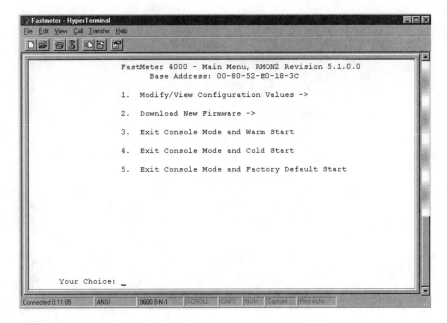

Figure 5.43   Fastmeter Main Menu

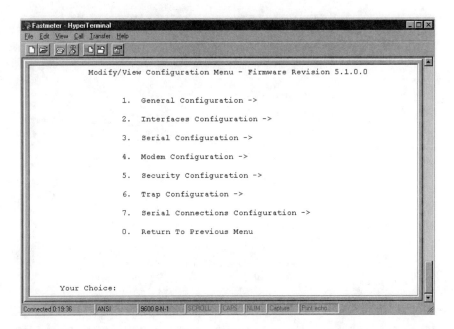

Figure 5.44   Fastmeter Configuration Menu

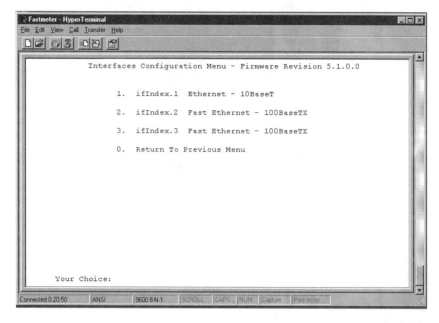

Figure 5.45 Fastmeter Interfaces. (See Figure 1-13 for a physical picture of these interfaces.)

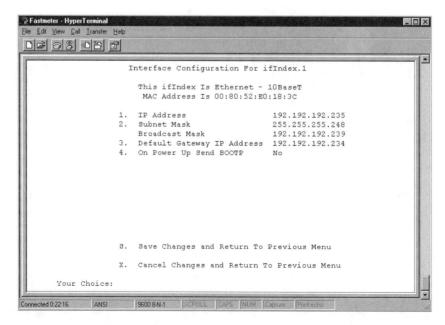

Figure 5.46 IP Configuration of Fastmeter ifIndex.1, the Management Port

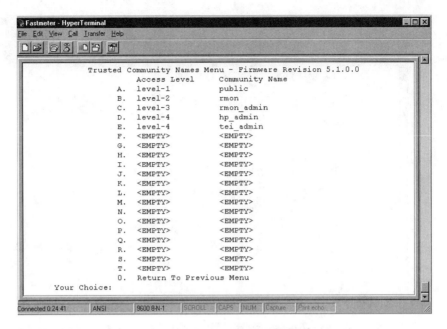

Figure 5.47 Fastmeter Access Levels and Associated Community Names

meter, which captures all traffic from the Switch 2 mirror port. These mirror ports are discussed in the Switch section of this chapter.

Figure 5.46 shows the IP configuration of Fastmeter if Index.1. This screen is used to change these configurations if desired.

The Fastmeter Security Configuration menu item in **Figure 5.44** enables the configuration of Trusted Community Names and Trusted Client IP Hosts. We saw this two-level security when we configured SERVER. **Figure 5.47** shows the Trusted Community Names list for Fastmeter. Fastmeter uses four levels of Trusted Community Names that are defined in **Table 5.8.**

The associated Community Names can be changed in **Figure 5.47**. Other Community Names for these access levels can be added. Hp_admin refers to printer management. This table provides an example of the MIB view concept that we discuss in Chapter 7. The SNMP Community Name in **Table 5.8** determines which MIB objects will be accessible to the management station. For example, the

Table 5.8 Fastmeter Levels of Trusted Community Names

Level	Community Name	Rights
1	public	Read-only access, no rmon access
2	rmon	Read-only access including rmon, no capture buffer access
3	rmon_admin	Read-only access, read-write access to rmon
4	hp_admin	Read-write access to all MIBs
4	tei_admin	Read-write access to all MIBs

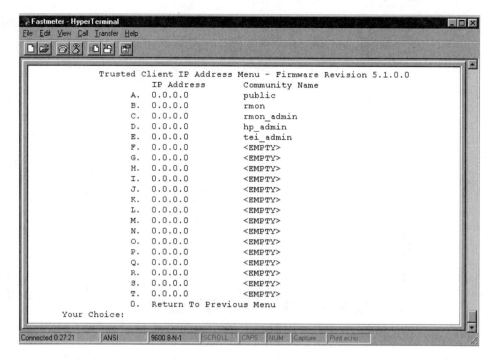

Figure 5.48   Trusted Client IP Addresses

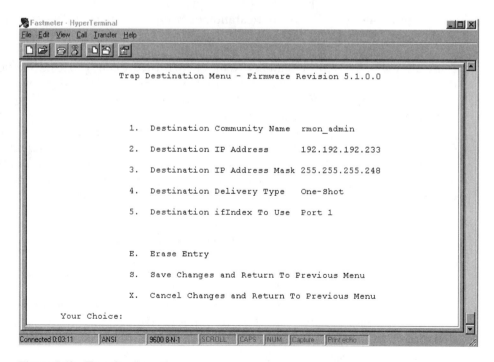

Figure 5.49   Trap Configuration

password "rmon" is not sufficient for a management station to access packets captured by the probe for analysis.

The Trusted Client IP hosts list is shown in **Figure 5.48**. In line E, for example, we could insert the IP address, 192.192.192.233 of WS1 to enable Meterware/Analyzer to have the highest level of access to Fastmeter.

Figure 5.49 provides the last of the SNMP configuration menus. It shows that the IP address 192.192.192.233 (WS1) is to receive Trap messages from Fastmeter and that only one message (one-shot) will be sent. These parameters can be changed on this screen.

Fastmeter is now configured to have its management agent process requests for MIB 2, and RMON 2 values from the Meterware/Analyzer application on Management Station WS1 and to capture packets from all ports on Switch 1 and Switch 2. In the next chapter, you will see how Meterware/Analyzer and Fastmeter are used together to capture and analyze SNMP packets.

Now that we have reviewed networking concepts, the principles of network management and configured all the devices on the demonstration network, in the following chapters of the book, we will focus on the practice of network management using SNMP and the Network Management System (NMS) Meterware/Analyzer.

CHAPTER SUMMARY

The steps to set up both in-band and out-of-band configuration of hubs, switches and routers were explained. In this chapter, in-band configuration (Telnet) was used to configure the hub while out-of-band configuration was used to configure the switches, the probes and the router. A table showing the configuration of all devices on the network was provided. Significant attention was paid to the use of LEDs on the switches for monitoring and configuration. The configuration requirements of each device were outlined and a configuration for each was demonstrated. The SNMP agent on each device was configured so that MIB values could be accessed. Particular attention was paid to the many forwarding options that can be configured for the switches and to the mirror ports that can be configured to capture frames from any or all ports for analysis. The CISCO router command structure was presented. A set of commands from this structure appropriate for our needs was documented in a table, explained and used to configure the router. The step-by-step configuration of the router is shown in screen captures as it is being done. Routing protocols RIP, OSPF and BGP were described and configured on the router. The configuration of the probe Fastmeter was presented.

REVIEW QUESTIONS

1. How would you know if a cable is a crossover cable?
2. What is a DTE and what is a DCE?
3. When is a crossover cable necessary when configuring a device?
4. What is the advantage of being able to do out-of-band management of a device?

5. What is the principle way that hubs are distinguished from switches?
6. Community Names must be recognized by the device SNMP agent and known by the Management Station. How do you think this cooperation arranged?
7. Why is it important to identify WRITE managers on CISCO switches?
8. When an Ethernet address is associated with a switch port, to what device does that address refer?
9. What is the difference between a static address and a dynamic address?
10. How is a dynamic address obtained by a device?
11. What is a Restricted Static Address?
12. What is meant by Address Aging Time?
13. What capability is provided by a switch Monitor Port?
14. What is a principal difference in the way RIP routers and OSPF routers communicate with neighbor routers?
15. What is the advantage of creating an SNMP Access List on a router?
16. What is the difference between MIB-2 and RMON MIB variables?

EXERCISES

1. Find out the IP address of a hub, switch or router on your network and use Telnet to get the introductory Management screen.
2. Make a list of the operating characteristics of the switch discussed in this chapter that can be configured.
3. If your network is not too large, see if you can get the information necessary to make a table for your network like that shown in Table 5.1, Network Device Configurations.
4. Use out-of-band management or Telnet to examine the SNMP configuration of a router on your network. Document the configuration in a table. Make three columns: one that describes the configuration; one that specifies "Adequate" or "Inadequate"; and one that specifies how to correct an "Inadequate" configuration.
5. If you have a Cisco switch or a switch from another vendor on your network with similar LED modes, document the status of STAT, UTL and FDUP modes for the switch and what each status means.
6. Find out if the switch has a mirror port configured and which ports are being mirrored.

REFERENCES

1. RFC 1058, "The Routing Information Protocol."
2. RFC 2328, "OSPF version 2."
3. RFC 1771, "A Border Gateway Protocol 4 (BGP-4)."
4. RFC 1772 "Application of the Border Gateway Protocol in the Internet."
5. RFC 1661, "The Point-to-Point Protocol."
6. RFC1662, "PPP in HDLC-like Framing."
7. "A Guide to TCP/IP on Microsoft Windows NT 4.0," Richard Burke and Mohammad Fatmi, International Thomson, Course Technology, 1998.
8. OSPF: Anatomy of an Internet Routing Protocol," John T. Moy, Addison Wesley, 1998.

CHAPTER 6

SNMP

This chapter:

- Reviews the components of a network management system
- Examines the fields of the SNMP packet
- Describes the SNMP Protocol Data Unit
- Explains the structure of the MIB tree
- Introduces MIB-2 objects and object identifiers
- Explains SNMP commands and arguments
- Demonstrates the results of SNMP commands
- Discusses the components and use of SNMP security
- Introduces NMS MIB Browsers
- Demonstrates the capture and analysis of SNMP frames using an NMS

In the section "Evolution of Computerized Network Management" of Chapter 2, you were introduced to the rationale for the development of the Simple Network Management Protocol (SNMP) and you learned how SNMP was brought into existence. In this chapter, we will discuss SNMP in detail so that it will be clear how this protocol enables the transfer of information between a Management Agent and a Management Station. The fundamentals of information transfer are formally provided by ISO/IEC 7498-1 "Open Systems Interconnection-Basic Reference Model." **[Ref 1].** The formalism for application of the Basic Reference Model to management information transfer is provided by ISO/IEC 7498-4 "Management Framework." **[Ref 2]. [Ref 3]** provides an exposition of these formalities that is more readable.

The next chapter, "Management Information Base (MIB)," will explain the formal definition of management information, called objects, in detail. However, in order to discuss SNMP, we need to introduce the concepts of objects, Object Identifiers and the Structure of Management Information (SMI) in this chapter.

6.1 REVIEW OF MANAGEMENT STATION/MANAGEMENT AGENT COMMUNICATION

Figure 6.1 portrays the network management client/server model for the specific case of the TCP/IP protocol stack, the SNMP management protocol and the Ethernet medium access control (MAC) specification that we are using on our network.

Figure 6.1 is a diagram of the basic components of a network management environment. These components consist of:

1. A Management Application hosted by the Management Station
2. Management processes
3. SNMP
4. Management MIB
5. A communication architecture
6. Agent processes
7. Agent MIB

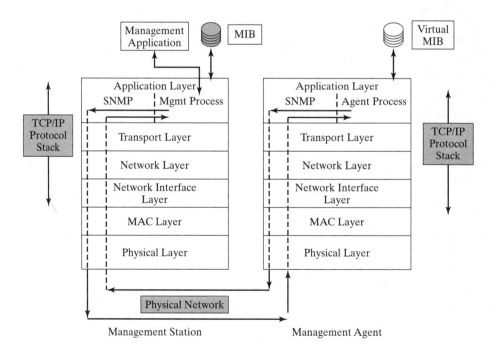

Figure 6.1 Components of a TCP/IP-based Network Management Environment

The use of these components for communication between a Management Station and a Management Agent is as follows:

6.1.1 Management Application

A management application consists of a program that requests access to information stored on a Management Agent. The information is displayed to the user at the Management Station using other programs. These displays typically map to some or all of the ISO Network Management Categories, defined in Chapter 2, namely: Fault Management, Configuration Management, Performance Management, Security Management and Accounting Management. Graphical displays of the analyses relevant to these categories are provided by some NMS suites of applications. The NMS we are using and included with this book is Meterware/Analyzer originally developed by Apptitude, Inc.

6.1.2 Management Process

The management application is supported by one or more management processes, which are Application-level programs. For example, one of these processes will provide a function that accesses the MIB variable requested by a management application from the MIB data structure and then passes it to the SNMP module. In **Figure 6.1**, the icon for the MIB data structure is a hard drive.

6.1.3 Management Station SNMP

An SNMP packet containing a version number, a community string, an SNMP command and a list of variables is passed to the Transport layer in the TCP/IP protocol stack. This layer and lower layers create other headers that enable the formation of a frame that is sent over the network to the Management Agent.

6.1.4 Management Agent SNMP

The MAC layer on the Management Agent receives the frame constructed on the Management Station, passes the enclosed packet to the TCP/IP protocol stack for processing and finally the SNMP component of the packet is passed to the SNMP module in the Application layer. An SNMP process extracts the MIB variable and passes it to the appropriate Agent Process.

6.1.5 Agent Process

An Agent process performs the functions necessary to map the variable to the subsystem that has stored the value and returns the value to SNMP. SNMP creates the SNMP header and sends the header, the variable and the variable's current value to the TCP/IP Transport layer. A frame is created by the MAC layer and transmitted to the Management Station where it is processed and the variable's value returned to the Management application.

From what we've discussed you can see that the essential components of network management implementation are

1. The MIB on the Management Station, which stores MIB variables
2. The management application software that requests, displays and analyzes MIB values
3. SNMP that constructs request and reply messages and
4. The agent process on the Management Agent that maps the variable requested to the subsystem where the value is stored and returns the value to the SNMP module.

In this chapter, we will examine the SNMP version 1 packet and the encoding of SNMP messages for transmission over the network. There are now three versions of SNMP. SNMPv1 is the version that is pervasive in networks today. In the next chapter, we examine how the MIB objects that are used by SNMP are described and formatted using the language ASN.1.

6.2 THE SNMP PACKET

To examine how SNMP does its job, we first discuss the packet structure. The format for coding the fields in the packet is explained in **Appendix D**. The use of this format, the Basic Encoding Rules **(BER),** is demonstrated in this chapter **[Ref 4-5]**. The SNMPv1 packet is shown in **Figure 6.2**.

- **Version** is the version of SNMP that is being used by the Management Station and Management Agent on this network. From this point on, we will refer to SNMPv1 as SNMP. SNMP actually encodes version 1 with a "0" in the Version field.
- **Community Name** is an SNMP "password." Management Stations and Management Agents must use community names that match or frames will be discarded. This gives the Management Agent control over which Management Station can access which MIB variable value, if any. In addition, both the Management Station and the Management Agent must use the same version of SNMP or frames will be discarded. The SNMP Community Name is not encrypted and thus provides no security against network intrusion. Since this issue has become of greater importance in recent years, more attention is being paid to implementation of SNMPv3.
- The **Protocol Data Units (PDUs)** for the SNMP Get-Request, Get-Next-Request and Set-Request contain the fields shown in **Figure 6.3**.
  - ❑ **Request ID** field is an integer that numbers the request sent from the Management Station to the Management Agent. This field is also used in

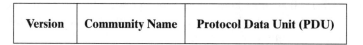

Version	Community Name	Protocol Data Unit (PDU)

Figure 6.2 The SNMPv1 Packet

Request ID	Error Status	Error Index	VarBindList

Figure 6.3 Fields of SNMP GetRequest, GetNextRequest, and SetRequest Protocol Data Units (PDUs)

the response from the Management Agent so that SNMP on the Management Station can correlate requests and responses.

❑ **Error Status** field has the value "0" in all Get-Request messages. In Get-Response messages, it is used by the Management Agent to inform the Management Station that the PDU was either received correctly or that an exception occurred. If the latter, a non-zero value is returned. There are six possible non-zero object values:

⇒ **noError** = 0,

⇒ **tooBig** = 1 = "PDU has too many bytes",

⇒ **noSuchName** = 2 = "there is no object with this name"

⇒ **badValue** = 3 = "integer identifying the PDU type is bad"

⇒ **readOnly** = 4 = "incorrect implementation of SNMP"

⇒ **genErr** = 5 = "unspecified errors of other types."

❑ **Error Index** is an integer, starting with one, in the Get-Response message, which identifies the first variable in the VarBindList that caused an error code to appear in the Error Status field. When the PDU is a request from the Management Station, the Error Status and Error Index fields have the value zero.

❑ **VarBindList** is a list of Variable ID and Variable Value pairs as shown in **Figure 6.4**

⇒ **Variable ID** contains the Object Identifier of the variable defined in the Structure of Management Information (SMI) specification. The Object Identifier defines the path to the object in the MIB tree.

⇒ **Variable Value** contains the value of the variable which could be, for example, an integer, an octet string, or an IP address.

Since a Management Station may request the values of a number of variables in a single request packet, the VarBindList may contain several pairs of the fields shown in **Figure 6.4**, there being one pair for each value requested.

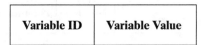

Variable ID	Variable Value

Figure 6.4 VarBindList Pairs

6.3 SNMP COMMANDS

SNMP specifies 5 commands **[Ref 6-7]**. The numbers in parentheses are the codes for the associated PDUs

- **Get-Request** (0) requests a value or set of values from a Management Agent MIB.
- **Get-Next-Request** (1) requests the value of the next lexicographically larger Object Identifier in a MIB tree given the present Object Identifier. (The precise meaning of this statement requires an examination of the Structure of Management Information that will be discussed below and in the next chapter.) If used repeatedly, the Get-Next-Request command allows the Management Station to "walk" the entire MIB tree to get the values of all variables without specifying the identifiers of any variables.
- **Get-Response** (2) is a response from the Management Agent to the Management Station supplying the requested value(s).
- **Set-Request** (3) sets (changes) a value in the Management Agent MIB. A change could, for example, cause an action such as shutting down the device.
- **Trap** (4) is an unsolicited message from a Management Agent to a Management Station that is initiated by an alarm/event pair on the Management Agent. The purpose of Traps is to inform the Management Station of events that may require action by a network manager. **[Ref 8]**

The Trap command uses the PDU shown in **Figure 6.5**.

- **Enterprise** contains an Object Identifier, defined by an authorized vendor, for the device subsystem that created the trap message.
- **Agent Address** is the IP address of the network device.
- **Generic Trap Number** contains an integer representing one of seven traps defined in SNMP RFC 1157 **[Ref 6]**. An example is the integer "2" that indicates a link on the device is down.
- **Specific Trap Number** contains a code. The Management Station might then require a proprietary MIB for that device in order to interpret the number.
- **Time Stamp** contains the time in 1/100ths of a second since the agent on the device was initialized.

Enterprise	Agent Address	Generic Trap Number	Specific Trap Number	Time Stamp	VarBindList

Figure 6.5   SNMP Trap Protocol Data Unit (PDU)

- **VarBindList** may contain some or all of the information shown in **Figure 6.4** as well as other troubleshooting information. For example, an Object Identifier and an associated value that identifies a specific failure may be provided.

6.4   STRUCTURE OF MANAGEMENT INFORMATION (SMI)

In the previous section, we examined the fields in messages exchanged between Management Station and Management Agent. These messages cause values in the Management Agent MIB to be read or set. The Variable ID field in **Figure 6.4** contains the Object Identifier of the object to be read in the case of a Get-Request PDU or Get-Next-Request PDU and the Variable Value field contains "0." In the case of the Set-Request PDU and the Get-Response PDU, the Variable Value field fields contains the value of the object being set or returned, respectively.

In order for the Management Agent to find a requested value, there must be a data structure that the Agent process can use. Using this data structure, the Agent process maps Object Identifiers to values stored by device subsystems. A subsystem could be the NIC and the value could be its hardware address. The MIB has a hierarchical tree structure. Each object in the MIB has an Object Identifier (the Variable ID in **Figure 6.4**) that defines its location in the tree. Each object has a name. Groups of objects that are related are also defined. Each object has a type such as "integer." Types can be **simple** or **constructed**. An object that is of type simple has only one value, whereas an object that is of type constructed contains other objects that are of simple type, but which may not be the same simple type.

ASN.1 specifies the types of objects that may be defined and the format for defining them. This format will contain, for example, the name of the object, its type, whether it is accessible by a Management Station, and if so, whether it is read-only, read-write or not accessible, and a brief text description of the object. The language used to define MIBs is described in **RFC 1155**, The Structure of Management Information (SMI)**[Ref 9].** The SMI is a specification of how information is to be managed on TCP/IP networks. The SMI makes use of parts of Abstract Syntax Notation One **(ASN.1),** defined in **[Ref 10]** to formally define a MIB object. Also see **Appendix B** for a discussion of ASN.1. terminology.

Some of the objects in the SMI object tree, starting from the tree root, are shown in **Figure 6.6**. Those that are highlighted, including **mgmt (2)** and some under it, and some under **private** are of interest to us in this book. Each node in the tree has a name and an Object Identifier. This identifier is constructed by the set of numbers, separated by a dot (.) that defines the path to the object from the tree root. The number "0," representing the root node is not used. For example, the identifier for the object with the name **sysDescr(1)** is constructed by following the path indicated by the shaded boxes in **Figure 6.6**. Thus the Object Identifier for sysDescr (1) is:

1.3.6.1.2.1.1.1

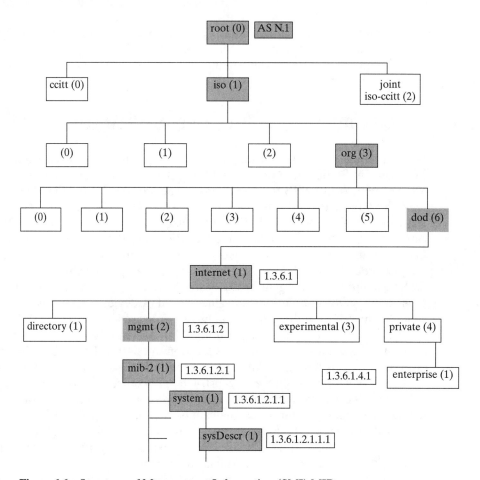

Figure 6.6 Structure of Management Information (SMI) MIB

There are many objects in a MIB and they are all identified according to this scheme. Thus, the tree can be indefinitely deep. As mentioned above, MIB objects that are related, for example, objects that contain information about the interfaces of a network device, would be in one group. The current MIB standard is MIB-2. It originally contained 10 groups with the names: system, interfaces, address translation (at), internet protocol (ip), internet control management protocol (icmp), transmission control protocol (tcp), unreliable datagram protocol (udp), exterior gateway protocol (egp), transmission, and simple network management protocol (snmp). Thirteen more groups, called extensions have been added. We will see some of these later. Some of the groups contain many objects and some of these objects are tables of other objects. **[Ref 11]**

There are still not enough objects in MIB-2 to satisfy the needs of all users and vendors. Thus most vendors have created proprietary MIBs for their devices. Those MIBs are listed under the **enterprise** node which is a sub-node of **private (4)** in **Figure 6.6**. Vendors usually make those MIBs available so that they can be compiled and loaded onto the Management Station to enable access to the additional objects on their devices. An important extension to MIB-2 was provided by the Remote Monitoring Standard, RMON. Chapter 8 is devoted to the RMON Specification. The RMON objects contain information about traffic on network segments.

We will see later that Meterware/Analyzer and other network management systems (NMSs) provide a graphical interface that makes it easy to retrieve MIB values from a Management Agent. However, we will examine the underlying details and "do it the hard way" first.

To appreciate how MIB values are identified and retrieved and to get a complete picture of the retrieval process, it is best to begin by examining the more general case of the retrieval of an object's value from a table. To make this interesting and practical, we will use the IP Routing Table, shown in **Table 6.1**, as an example. First, let's expand the view of the mib-2 (1) object shown in **Figure 6.6** to expose the **ipRouteTable** object. The result is shown in **Figure 6.7**.

6.5   SNMP COMMANDS AND ARGUMENTS

ip is one of 10 objects contained in the original mib-2. Notice that Group (9) is missing. It is reserved for OSI MIB objects. The ip object in turn contains 23 objects and the **ipRouteTable (21)** is one of those. The ipRouteTable contains the **ipRouteEntry(1)** object that contains 13 **column objects**. An instance of the ipRouteTable object is all the values in the table. An instance of a column object is one of the values in the column.

6.5.5 GetRequest Command

Suppose the Management Station wants to access an instance of the column object **ipRouteNextHop**, what Object Identifier would need to be provided to SNMP?

The object **ipRouteTable** has the identifier	**1.3.6.1.2.1.4.21**
The object **ipRouteEntry** has the identifier	**1.3.6.1.2.1.4.21.1**
The object **ipRouteNextHop** has the identifier	**1.3.6.1.2.1.4.21.1.7**

ipRouteNextHop is the Object Identifier for the column but how do we access an **instance** of ipRouteNextHop? In other words, what row should be selected? SNMP makes use of Index objects to select the row. One or more column objects can be Index objects. More than one Index object is sometimes necessary to unambiguously identify the row. The ipRouteTable uses one index object, the ipRouteDestination object. Thus, for example, if the ipRoute NextHop instance in the third row of **Table 6.1** is desired, and the ipRouteDestination index object for that row has the value 10.3.4.5, the Management Station would supply the following instance identifier to SNMP:

1.3.6.1.2.4.21.1.7.10.3.4.5.

Table 6.1 ipRouteTable = 1.3.6.1.2.1.4.21

ipRoute Dest (1)	ipRoute ifIndex (2)	ipRoute Metric 1 (3)	ipRoute Metric 2 (4)	ipRoute Metric 3 (5)	ipRoute Metric 4 (6)
10.3.4.3	1				
10.3.4.4	2				
10.3.4.5	3				

The instance identifier is constructed by appending the Index instance(s) for the desired row, 10.3.4.5 in this case, to the column Object Identifier, 1.3.6.1.2.4.21.7.

If we were using a command line interface to the SNMP application, the following command would be typed at the prompt:

GetRequest (1.3.6.1.2.4.21.1.7.10.3.4.5) or,

GetRequest (ipRouteNextHop.10.3.4.5).

This command would result in 1.3.6.1.2.4.21.1.7.10.3.4.5 being put in the Variable ID field in **Figure 6.4**.

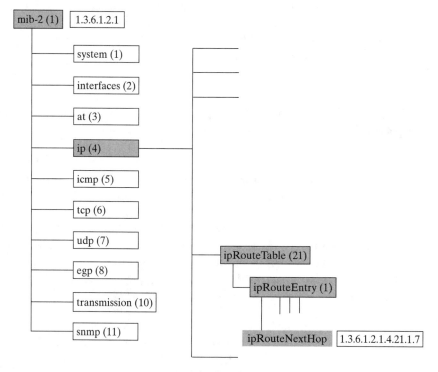

Figure 6.7 mib-2 objects (left) and ip (4) objects (right)

ipRoute NextHop (7)	ipRoute Type (8)	ipRoute Protocol (9)	ipRoute Age (10)	ipRoute Mask (11)	ipRoute Metric 5 (12)	ipRoute Info (13)

If more than one instance in the row were desired, say ipRouteifindex and ipRouteNextHop, the command would be:

GetRequest (1.3.6.1.2.1.4.21.1.2.10.3.4.5 , 1.3.6.1.2.1.4.21.1.7.10.3.4.5) or,

GetRequest (ipRouteifIndex.10.3.4.5 , ipRouteNextHop.10.3.4.5).

Let's use a SNMP command-line program[1] to try out some SNMP commands. We will use the mib-2 System group as a test so as not to introduce the details required by an ipRouteTable. For the Command Prompt windows that follow, refer to the diagrams in **Figures 6.6 and 6.10** for the lexicographical ordering and Object Identifiers of the objects we discuss.

> **Note**
>
> Lexicographical order is dictionary order. The Object Identifiers in **Figure 6.6** enforce lexicographical order. If a number in Object Identifier1, beginning on the left, is less than the corresponding number in Object Identifier2, Object Identifier1 precedes Object Identifier2 in lexicographical order.

In **Figure 6.8**, we attempt to access the object sysDescr of Server. The first command line is wsnmp −h server get sysDescr. **wsnmp** is the SNMP application on Server, **−h server** indicates that the Agent to be accessed is on Server, **get** is the GetRequest command and **sysDescr** is the name of the scalar object whose value is being requested. As discussed earlier, the response "error-status = 2 <noSuchName>" indicates that the Agent does not recognize the entity sysDescr and "error-index = 1" means that the first object in the GetRequest command is in error. In this example, there is only one object value being requested. The Object ID returned, 1.3.6.1.2.1.1.1, is the Object ID of sysDescr.

So what went wrong? The problem is that according to SNMP rules, the GetRequest command must request an instance of an object and sysDescr is not an instance. You see in the following command line, when sysDescr.0 is requested, the

---

[1]The wsnmp utility was made available by Donald Plotnick of IBM Tivoli Systems.

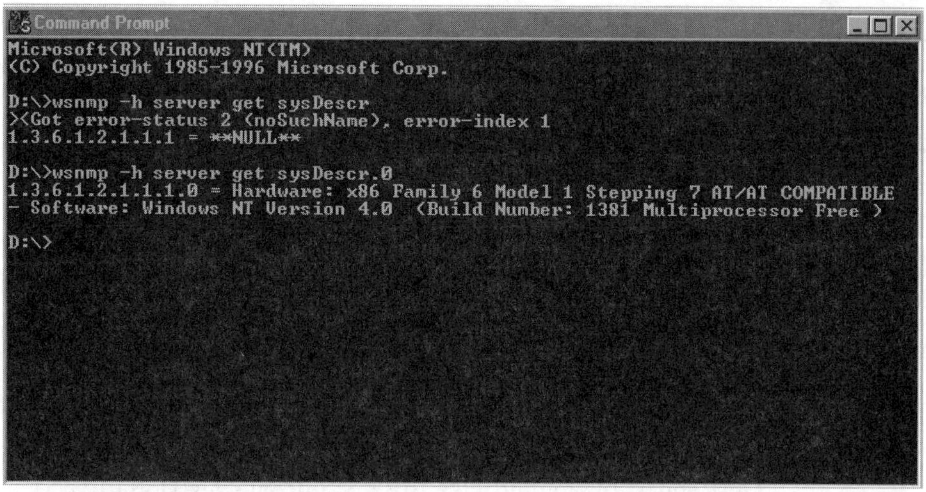

Figure 6.8 Using GetRequest to Access Server Object sysDescr

correct response for Server is received. As we discussed for the ipRouteTable, instances of objects there had identifiers that appended values of Index objects. Therefore, for consistency, SNMP requires this for simple objects also. The instance of a simple object is indicated by appending "**. 0** " to the Object Identifier as in sysDescr.0. This indicates it is a scalar object having only one value.

GetNextRequest Command

Let's see what happens if we use the GetNextRequest command in **Figure 6.9** instead of the GetRequest command. The **getnext** command in the first command line produces the desired result. This is because the getnext command retrieves the next object in lexicographical order, that is sysDescr.0.

The following "getnext sysDescr.0" command returns 1.3.6.1.2.1.1.2.0, the Object Identifier of sysObjectID.0, because sysObjectID.0 is the next object in lexicographical order that has a value. The value is 1.3.6.1.4.1.311.1.1.3.1.3. As **Figure 6.6** indicates, this is the value of a node in the enterprises branch (1.3.6.1.4.1) of the SMI tree. The number representing the enterprise is 311, which is IBM. Thus, the

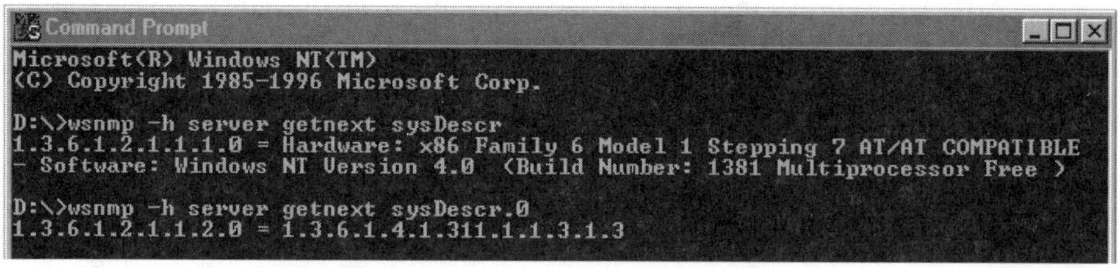

Figure 6.9 Using GetNextRequest to Access Server sysDescr

value returned tells us the IAB authoritative value of the network management subsystem for the IBM IntelliStation Server.

The discussion above highlights one of the problems with the GetRequest command in contrast to the GetNextRequest command: With the GetRequest command, if there is no value for the object requested, "null" and an error indication is returned. So if we wanted to access a number of values using the GetRequest command and there was no value for any one of the objects requested, then no values would be returned. The GetNextRequest command provides a way to circumvent this problem as shown in what follows using the System group in **Figure 6.10**.

Consider the command:

GetNextRequest (sysDescr, sysObjectID, sysUpTime)

The GetResponse to this command should be:

GetResponse ((sysDescr.0 = value), (sysObjectID.0 = value), (sysUpTime.0 = value)).

Now suppose the sysDescr object requested by this device was wrong or was "not accessible" to the requesting Management Station and the same command were given:

GetNextRequest (sysDescr, sysObjectID, sysUpTime).

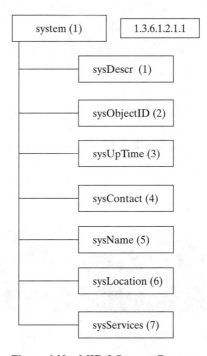

Figure 6.10   MIB-2 System Group

The GetResponse from the Agent would be:

> GetResponse ((sysObjectID.0 = value), (sysObjectID.0 = value), (sysUpTime = value)).

The first (sysObjectID.0 = value) in the GetResponse is returned because it is the next object with a value after the invalid sysDescr object, according to the following lexicographical order beginning at the top.

sysDescr	[1.3.6.1.2.1.1.1]
sysDescr.0	[1.3.6.1.2.1.1.1.0]
sysObjectID	[1.3.6.1.2.1.1.2]
sysObjectID.0	[1.3.6.1.2.1.1.2.0]

Let's see what we actually get using the command:

> wsnmp −h server getnext sysDescr.1 sysObjectID sysUpTime.

The command and the result are shown in **Figure 6.11**. Since sysDescr.1 is not a valid instance identifier, the getnext command retrieved the value of the next object in lexicographical order instead which is sysObjectID.0. The other two objects requested are correct so the values retrieved were as expected.

The example we have just seen implies a powerful feature of the GetNextRequest command: It can be used to obtain all values in a MIB in lexicographical order, starting from any point. Using ipRouteTable in **Table 6.1** again as an example, the command:

> GetNextRequest (ipRouteTable).

will result in:

> GetResponse (ipRouteDestination.10.3.4.3 = 10.3.4.3).

In other words, since SNMP cannot return all values in a table or all values in any row, it will return the instance of the next available object in lexicographical order. This is the instance in the first row and first column of the table. Now using GetNextRequest repeatedly, all values in the table can be accessed.

Figure 6.11 Using GetNextRequest to Access Three Server Objects

As another example of this concept, using the following GetNextRequest command:

GetNextRequest (ipRouteDestination.10.3.4.5),

the GetResponse will be:

GetResponse (ipRouteifIndex.10.3.4.3 = 1),

since this is the next instance in lexicographical order.

6.5.1 Set Command

The Set command is used to write the value of an object. For example, if you wanted to change sysContact for a device you would use the command:

SetRequest (sysContact = name).

The response to this command would be:

GetResponse (sysContact = name).

Thus the VarBindList pair for these two commands would both be sysContact|name.

It is also possible to use the SetRequest command in SNMP to add or delete a row from a table. However, the result is Management Agent implementation dependent **[Ref 12].** This topic is discussed in **Chapter 12** where we examine and demonstrate SNMPv2 and SNMPv3.

6.6 SECURITY

> **Note**
>
> When reading the following section, review the configuration of SNMP on SERVER in Chapter 4

As we saw in **Figure 6.2**, the SNMP message contains a Community Name field. This field is one of the security measures provided by SNMP. The first two columns of **Table 6.2** show all the SNMP security measures.

Authentication provides the first line of security protection in SNMP. The Community Name authenticates messages between Management Stations and Agents. The receiver must have the Community Name used by the sender in its database or the message will be discarded. The Community Name defines an

Table 6.2 SNMP Security Parameters

Authentication	Authorization (Rights)	MIB Access
• Community Name	• SNMP Access Mode ❑ Read-Only ❑ Read-Write	• read-only • read-write • write-only • not-accessible
	• MIB View ❑ Object ❑ Object 2 • • ❑ Object N	

SNMP Community Profile = MIB View + SNMP Access Mode
SNMP Access Policy = SNMP Community + SNMP Community Profile

SNMP Community which is a relationship between a Management Agent and a set of Management Stations. Thus more than one Management Station may have access to information on the Management Agent. Likewise, more than one Management Station may receive trap messages from a Management Agent.

Authorization provides the second line of security protection. The second column in **Table 6.2** lists the authorization measures. Authorization determines the rights that a Management Station has relative to MIB objects. **SNMP Access Mode** determines one set of rights **[Ref 6-7].** The Management Agent can choose to assign either Read-Only or Read-Write access modes to MIB objects. The other set of rights is determined by the **MIB View** assignment. A MIB View is a set of MIB objects. The MIB view may limit the objects that the Management Station can access using an SNMP Access Mode.

An **SNMP Community Profile** is defined to be a combination of SNMP Access Mode and MIB View. Finally, an **SNMP Access Policy** is defined to be a combination of SNMP Community and SNMP Community Profile.

The Management Agent must maintain a table of SNMP Access Policies. This table is a mapping of Community Names to SNMP Access Policy. Thus when the Management Agent receives a message, it looks in the table for the community name in the message and, if found, the Management Station's access to MIB objects is limited by the corresponding Access Policy.

The third column in **Table 6.2** is **MIB Access**. As you can see, MIB Access is not the same as SNMP Access Mode. RFC 1155, "Structure and Identification of Management Information for TCP/IP-Based Internets," defines the structure of MIB objects. The access clause in this document defines the MIB Access choices listed under MIB Access in **Table 6.2**. RFC 1157, "A Simple Network Management Protocol (SNMP)" **[Ref 6]** resolves these differences according to **Table 6.3**.

Therefore, what this table is saying is that SNMP Access Modes Read-Only or Read-Write provided by an agent to a manager may be influenced by how the Access Clause of the object macro has been written.

Table 6.3 Resolution of SNMP Access Mode and MIB Access

SNMP Access Mode	MIB Access	Resolution
Read-Only	Read-Only	Object available for Get and Trap operations
	Read-Write	Object available for Get and Trap operations
	Write-Only	Object available for Get and Trap operations but the value is implementation-dependent
	Not-accessible	Object is unavailable
Read-Write	Read-Only	Object available for Get and Trap operations
	Read-Write	Object available for Get, Set and Trap operations
	Write-Only	Object available for Get, Set and Trap operations but the value is implementation-dependent for Get and Trap operations
	Not-accessible	Object is unavailable

Management Agents can serve as Proxies for other devices on the network. A **Proxy** collects object values from devices that do not support SNMP management when a request for those values is made by a Management Station. For example, devices may use proprietary Agents or may wish access to be controlled by the proxy so that the performance of the device will not be reduced by management overhead. The proxy maintains SNMP Access Policies for the proxied devices.

6.7 SNMP NMS APPLICATIONS

Now that we have explored the use of an SNMP command line interface, we will appreciate how helpful NMS applications can be. Most NMSs, such as the one used in this book, include a MIB browser application. That application provides graphical views of MIBs from which an object value for retrieval can simply be highlighted. **Figure 6.12** shows an example of such a screen for SERVER that has the IP address 192.192.192.242.

At the top of the screen, you see the IP address 192.192.192.242 of SERVER. That choice was made on another Meterware screen that you will see later. The left panel of the screen shows a partial listing of the MIB tree that begins at iso as we saw in **Figure 6.6**. The system group is expanded and the object sysName is highlighted. Highlighting this object generates the data for it in the right panel. This data is included in the SMI definition of an object as you will see in the next chapter. For example, as you saw in **Figure 6.10**, the OID is 1.3.6.1.2.1.1.5 and as you saw in **Table 6.2**, the SNMP Access Mode for this object is Read-Write.

After highlighting an object, clicking the Get button (green button in upper right) will create a GetRequest or GetNextRequest command that is sent to SNMP. SNMP creates the appropriate PDU and delivers it to the Agent on the highlighted device. There is also a Set button (blue/red button in upper right) to change the value of a MIB object that is highlighted. Results are returned in the bottom panel of the screen. Note that button colors are visable when the Meterware CD is used.

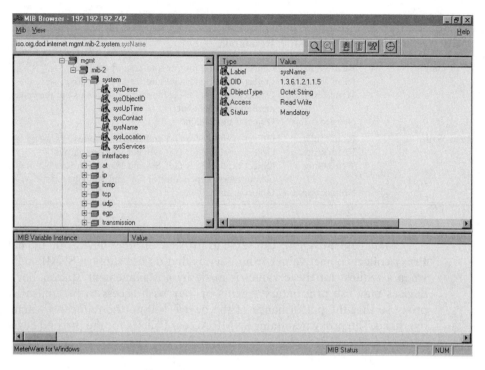

Figure 6.12 Meterware MIB Browser Screen

6.8 SNMP MESSAGE CAPTURE

It will be helpful to see how the SNMP message format shown in **Figures 6.2** and **6.3** compares with some actual messages. We have constructed **Tables 6.4** and **6.5** to help with this comparison. For the demonstration, we will "Get" the value of **sysName** of SERVER from a Management Station. We want to capture the GetRequest or Get-NextRequest message sent when the Get button is clicked and the GetResponse message is returned by the Management Agent on SERVER. To do this, we started Fastmeter capturing frames just before the Get button in **Figure 6.12** was clicked.

At the top of the screen in **Figure 6.13** is the IP address of Fastmeter. This is because Fastmeter is the device that has been selected to do the capturing. The top panel shows the frames that were captured. You see only communications between WS2-3 and SERVER because we created a filter to capture only these frames. The "3" in WS2-3 refers to the Ethernet interface of WS2. We will discuss the details of capturing and filtering in Chapter 8: RMON. Frames #1 and #2 contain the information we are looking for. Frame #1 was sent to SERVER when the MIB variable sys-Name was highlighted and the Get button clicked.

The middle panel in **Figure 6.13** provides the Meterware decodes of the packets in the frame sent from WS2-3 to SERVER. There are three packet types: IP, UDP and SNMP. UDP, rather than TCP, is the Transport layer protocol used by

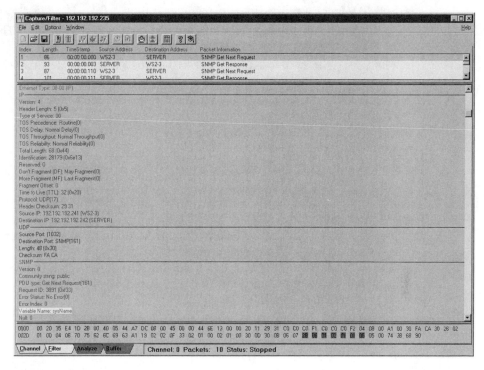

Figure 6.13 Meterware Decode of GetNextRequest Message from WS2-3 to Server

SNMP to minimize the overhead of management frames. You will notice at the bottom of the IP packet decode that the IP address of the Source computer is that of WS2-3, namely 192.192.192.241 and that the IP address of the destination computer is that of SERVER, namely 192.192.192.242.

   Table 6.4 provides a comparison of the GetNextRequest message decode, shown in the SNMP section of **Figure 6.13**, with the fields shown in **Figures 6.2 and 6.3**.

Table 6.4 Comparison of Figures 6.2 and 6.3 with the SNMP Message decode in Figure 6.13

Figures 6.2 and 6.3	Figure 6.13 GetNextRequest Message Decode
SNMP Version	0
Community String	public
PDU Tag*	GetNextRequest (161)
Request ID	3891
Error Status	No Error (0)
Error Index	0
VarBindList	sysName/Null 0

* Labeled PDU Type in Figure 6.13

- SNMP Version—represented by the integer 0
- Community String—the community "public" to which WS2 belongs. This must be the same as Server Read-Only community string.
- PDU Tag—the GetNextRequest PDU has the tag 161 in decimal. (Tags are discussed in **Appendix D**)
- Request ID—a number assigned to the GetNextRequest message in order to correlate it with the correct GetResponse message
- Error Status—has the value 0 in a request frame
- Error Index—has the value 0 in a request frame
- VarBindList—the pair sysName and Null, represented by 0. Null is used for the Variable value in a request packet

The bottom panel in **Figure 6.13** is the BER encoding of the frame in hexadecimal notation. You will notice that sysName is highlighted in the SNMP packet decode section. This causes its hexadecimal representation to be highlighted also.

The top panel in **Figure 6.14** shows the GetResponse packet from SERVER to WS2-3 highlighted. It was the next frame captured. The middle panel is the Meterware protocol analysis of this frame.

The IP packet decode shows, in this case, that the Source IP address is 192. 192.192.242, that of SERVER and that the Destination IP address is 192.192.192.241,

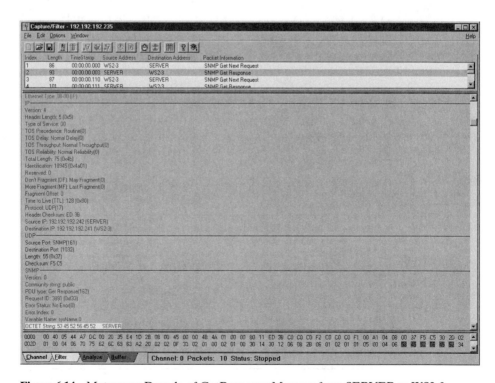

Figure 6.14   Meterware Decode of GetResponse Message from SERVER to WS2-3

Table 6.5 Comparison of Figures 6.2 and 6.3 with the SNMP Message Decode in Figure 6.14

Figures 6.2 and 6.3	Figure 6.14 GetNextRequest Message Decode
SNMP Version	0
Community String	public
PDU Tag*	Get-Response(162)
Request ID	3891
Error Status	No Error (0)
Error Index	0
VarBindList	sysName.0/SERVER

* Labeled PDU Type in Figure 6.14

that of WS2-3 as expected. **Table 6.5** provides a comparison of the Get-Response SNMP message decode in **Figure 6.14**, with the fields shown in **Figures 6.2 and 6.3**.

- SNMP—is represented by the integer 0
- Community String—the community to which SERVER belongs. Thus SERVER and WS2-3 belong to the same community. Otherwise the request from WS2-3 would have been discarded by SERVER
- PDU Tag—the GetResponse PDU Tag has the decimal value 162
- Request ID—The same ID as in the request packet to show that they are pairs
- Error Status—has the value 0 to indicate that there were no errors in the request frame
- Error Index—is 0 because Error Status is 0
- VarBindList—sysName.0 is the reference to the instance of sysName. SERVER is the value of sysName.0.

The bottom panel in **Figure 6.14** is the BER encoding of the frame in hexadecimal notation. You will notice that SERVER is highlighted in the SNMP protocol decode. This causes its hexadecimal representation to be highlighted also.

The reader should be aware that protocol analyzers in general and Meterware, in particular, only decode the hexadecimal code of object values. For a discussion of the complete hexadecimal decode, see **Appendix D** where the Basic Encoding Rules (BER) are explained.

In this chapter, MIB-2 was introduced. In the next chapter we will examine the structure of MIBs in detail.

CHAPTER SUMMARY

The basic components of the network management environment were reviewed. The format of SNMP messages used for communication between a Management Station and a Management Agent were examined. We saw that a Management

Station must belong to a community that is recognized by a Management Agent in order to access MIB values. We also saw that not all communities are equal. A community name has rights associated with it that determine the type of access a Management Station is allowed. For example, the values of some variables can only be read by a Management Station while others may be changed. We also saw that SNMP can be configured to limit access to certain IP addresses. These constraints provide another level of security for the Management Agent. However the security is minimal. As can be seen in Chapter 12, SNMPv3 provides a rigorous security measure. However, SNMPv3 is not widely implemented yet. Most of the network community uses SNMPv1 because of its long-standing use and ease of use. The SNMP commands used by a Management Station were explained and demonstrated. The structure of MIB-2 and the format of MIB object identifiers were discussed. The format of SNMP commands and arguments and how they are used was reviewed. The use of Meterware and Fastmeter were introduced so that we could capture and examine SNMP messages sent between the Management Agent and the Management Station.

REVIEW QUESTIONS

1. Which layer of the OSI Reference Model contains management applications?
2. Which layer of the OSI Reference Model contains SNMP?
3. How is the Agent process distinguished from SNMP?
4. What is the function of the MIB on the Management Agent?
5. What is the function of the MIB on the Management Station?
6. What fields does the VarBindList in the SNMP PDU contain and what is the content of those fields?
7. How many commands does SNMPv1 provide?
8. What is the purpose of the Trap command?
9. Why is there a need for proprietary MIBs?
10. How many objects does MIB-2 contain?
11. What significant capability is provided by the GetNextRequest command?
12. What field in the SNMPv1 packet authenticates the Management Station to the Management Agent?
13. What authorization options are available to the Management Agent?
14. Relative to Table 6.3 and Section 6.5, what is an example of an unavailable object?

EXERCISES

1. Using a table of ASCII code, convince yourself that the hexadecimal code for SERVER, in the last line of the SNMP Section of Figure 6.14, is actually SERVER. Then locate that code in the total decode of the captured frame.

2. Although there is a snmp group in MIB-2, there are no objects in the group that correspond to READ or WRITE Community Names. Check the community name on your PC by:
- Double-clicking the Network icon in Control Panel
- Highlighting the SNMP Service
- Clicking Properties to see the SNMP configuration
- Document the SNMP configuration that you find

3. As explained in Chapter 5, connect the serial port on your PC to another device using a crossover cable as necessary. Alternatively, use a Telnet client to connect to a Telnet Server on the device.
- Determine the SNMP Community Name(s) with which the device has been configured.
- If the device has not been configured and if you have permission do so, configure it.
- Document your configuration.

4. Start Meterware/Analyzer, open Summary View from the View Menu and double-click the device configured in Exercise #3. An Information screen for the device opens. Click Resolve. This will poll (send GetRequest packets to) the device for information on the Information Screen. One of the packets returned by the device will be the Read and Write Community Names. See that they are the ones you configured on the device.

> **Note**
>
> The flexibility to configure the SNMP agent on a device depends on the device and the SNMP agent version.

5. In the SNMP decoded section of Figure 6.14, you see that the name of the system, sysName, was requested in the GetNextRequest command.
- Open the Meterware MIB Browser from the Summary View Tools Menu
- Highlight sysName in the mib-2 system group for one of your devices
- Click the Get button and see that what is returned is the name of your system

6. In Meterware Summary View:
- Click MIB Browser on the Tools menu.
- Under mib-2, select ip.
- Under ip, select ipAddrTable.
- Select ipAddrEntry.
- Select ipAdEntAddr.
- Click the Get button
- See that what is displayed in the bottom panel are the IP addresses of the interfaces on the device you queried.

REFERENCES

1. ISO/IEC 7498-1 "Open Systems Interconnection-Basic Reference Model."

2. ISO/IEC 7498-4 "Management Framework."

3. "SNMP, SNMPv2 and CMIP: The Practical Guide to Network Management Standards," William Stallings, Addison Wesley, 1993.

4. ISO/IEC 8825-1 "Information Technology-ASN.1 Encoding Rules: Specification of Basic Encoding Rules (BER), Canonical Encoding Rules (CER) and Distinguished Encoding Rules (BER).

5. "The Simple Book: An Introduction to Network Management," Second Edition, Marshall T. Rose, Prentice Hall, 1994, pp. 295–313.

6. RFC 1157, "A Simple Network Management Protocol"

7. Op. cit. [3], p. 143.

8. RFC 1215 "A Convention for Defining Traps for use with the SNMP."

9. RFC 1155, "The Structure of Management Information."

10. ISO/IEC 8824-1 "Information Technology-Abstract Syntax Notation One (ASN.1): Specification of basic notation."

11. "Total SNMP," by Sean Harnedy, CBM Books, 1994.

12. Op. cit. [3], p. 153.

CHAPTER 7

MANAGEMENT INFORMATION BASE (MIB)

This chapter includes:

- Structure of Management Information (SMI)
- Formal Definition of MIB Objects
- Expanded Use of the MIB Browser
- MIB II objects
- Enterprise objects
- MIB Compiler
- MIB Editor

In Chapter 6, we examined some of the structure of the SMIv1 tree (Figure 6.6) and, in particular, some nodes in the mib-2 branch that are of interest for this book. The purpose of this chapter is to learn how MIB objects are created, how to use this knowledge to monitor and change MIB objects, how to add new MIBs to a Network Management System (NMS) and expanded use of the MIB Browser.

Because of the almost unlimited number of device parameters that network managers might want to monitor, the number of objects in the mib-2 branch could become very large. Aside from data structure organizational issues, there is significant additional memory and processor load incurred if there is a large number of managed objects and the size of those objects is also large, which is the case for tables. Device vendors would not want device performance to suffer in order to monitor device objects. Thus to have a practical network management system, it was realized that the number of mib-2 managed objects had to be limited and that a consensus on which objects to include was necessary.

7.1 STRUCTURE OF MANAGEMENT INFORMATION

Figure 6.6 of Chapter 6 has been reproduced here, with a small amount of additional detail, as **Figure 7.1**. The three nodes below the root node are labeled: **ccitt (0)**, **iso (1)** and **joint-iso-ccitt (2)**. Both ccitt and iso had been developing the

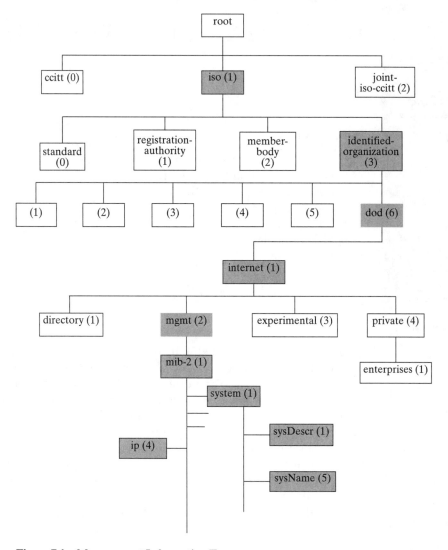

Figure 7.1 Management Information Tree

ISO/IEC OSI standards for the management of information before SNMP evolved in the United States. Thus ccitt and iso had produced network management documents that included definitions of MIB object data structures. Also, as previously discussed, there was a working model of an Application layer network management protocol (CMIP) for the OSI Reference Model. Given the work by the ISO/IEC, the Internet Activities Board (IAB) in the United States decided to base the Internet Structure of Management Information (SMI) on the work by the ISO. For purposes of this book, we are only interested in nodes under the iso node. However, the nodes under joint-iso-ccitt are important for the OSI management structure.

As was mentioned in Chapter 6, the National Institute of Standards and Technology (NIST) and the Department of Defense (DoD) were the agencies first identified under the **identified-organizations** node. Because of the original packet switching work by DoD, supported by ARPA, the Internet node came under DoD purview and DoD was assigned the management of that node. The Internet node is now the responsibility of the Internet Activities Board (IAB). The mgmt node and mib-2 were thus assigned to the Internet node. Therefore the prefix to all mib-2 objects is: **iso.org.dod.internet.mgmt.mib-2.**

Under iso (1),

- **standard (0)** has a subordinate node assigned to each International Standard
- **registration-authority (1)** is reserved for OSI registration authorities as they are created
- **member-body (2)** has a subordinate node assigned to each member body of the ISO/IEC. These nodes represent countries
- **identified-organization** has a subordinate node for any organization that can justify it. Currently there are only two identified-organizations, the National Institute of Standards and Technology (NIST) and the U.S. Department of Defense (DoD)

Under dod (6), there is one subordinate node.

- **internet (1)** is managed by the IAB.

Under internet (1),

- **directory (1)** is reserved for DoD directory services.
- **management (2)** contains nodes defined in IAB documents such as RFCs. The Internet Assigned Numbers Authority (IANA) is the administrator for this branch.
- **experimental (3)** contains nodes that are objects in the testing or research phase. They are registered by the IANA.
- **private (4)** contains nodes identified with enterprises that are using proprietary MIBs on their devices. These enterprises are labeled **enterprises (1).**

Under management (2), there is currently,

- **mib-2 (1)** which contains the Internet standard MIB objects which are the principal subject of this chapter. mib-2 includes the objects in mib-1, its predecessor.

Although the Structure of Management Information (SMI) was introduced in the previous chapter, we need to look more closely at this subject in this section. In particular, we need to learn how an information object is defined in general. Information objects are not limited to mib-2 objects. For example, an information object can be a document such as an RFC as mentioned above in this chapter.

The most comprehensive approach to defining data types and values for an information object is provided by the ISO/IEC standard 8824, parts 1-4. **[Ref 1]** This standard describes Abstract Syntax Notation 1 (ASN.1). **Appendix B** gives the reader some appreciation of the ASN.1 terminology and the references listed there will provide as much depth on the subject as desired.

SMI uses a subset of ASN.1 to define mib-2 information objects. This subset is chosen to provide the minimum number of objects and constructs that are needed for a practical and simple approach to network management. Such an approach is consistent with the philosophy of the developers of SNMP.

Figure 7.2 is a copy of the OBJECT-TYPE MACRO used by SMI. It is shown and explained in **Appendix B.** (For a more in-depth treatment of this subject, see **[Ref 2].**) Each line in the figure is called a clause.

The abstract syntax notation in **Figure 7.2** certainly does not make easy reading. That might be another reason for calling it abstract. However, if you are going to do network management, you ought to know something about how the objects you will be using are defined. Each object that is managed has to be constructed using the notation in **Figure 7.2**. The MIB on the Management Station contains instances of the object MACRO that define specific objects. Object values are stored on the Management Agent.

All objects in mib-2 are constructed using the clauses in **Figure 7.2** except the clauses ReferPart and DefValPart. ReferPart is a reference to another MIB module definition and DefValPart is a default value that is assigned if no value has been given to an object. These objects may be used in later MIB versions. The DescrPart is optional but it is typically used to give a semantic description of the object in readable text. The IndexPart is used only when the object is constructed, e.g., a table in which one or more column objects must be used as indices to make it possible to uniquely identify a row in the table. The use of lower case and caps is defined in ASN.1.

> **Note**
>
> A good way to think about the OBJECT-TYPE MACRO is as a template. You pick the clauses in the template you need to create a macro instance, i.e., an object.

```
OBJECT-TYPE  MACRO :: =
BEGIN
TYPE NOTATION :: = "SYNTAX"  type ( TYPE ObjectSyntax )
                   "ACCESS"    Access
                   "STATUS"    Status
                   DescrPart
                   ReferPart
                   IndexPart
                   DefValPart
                   DisplayString


VALUE NOTATION :: = value  (VALUE  ObjectName )
Access  :: =  "read-only"
              | "read-write"
              | "write-only"
              | "not-accessible
Status  :: =  "mandatory"
              | "optional"
              | "obsolete"

DescrPart :: = "DESCRIPTION"  value (description DisplayString | empty )

ReferPart :: = "REFERENCE"  value ( reference DisplayString | empty )

IndexPart :: = "INDEX"  "{" IndexTypes "}"

IndexTypes :: = IndexType | IndexTypes "," IndexType

IndexType :: = value ( indexobject ObjectName ) | type ( IndexType )

DefValPart :: = "DEFVAL"  "{" value (defvalue ObjectSyntax ) "}" | empty

DisplayString :: =  OCTET STRING  SIZE  (0..255)
END
```

Figure 7.2 Object-Type MACRO

7.2 OBJECT EXAMPLES

We will now use the OBJECT-TYPE MACRO as a template for developing some example mib-2 object definitions. In addition to providing some object practice, we will get an appreciation for the information that is stored in an object. We will learn how to construct a new object definition and how to compile object source code so that a new object can be added to an NMS.

Let's start with a simple object, the sysDescr object which is one of the nodes shown in **Figure 7.1**. In the examples that follow, the (—) indicates a comment which a MIB compiler will ignore. Using **Figure 7.2**, the **sysDescr** object is written as shown in **Figure 7.3.**

So we have now taken the MACRO Definition and created a specific object named sysDescr which has the value {system 1} or {1.3.6.1.2.1.1.1}.

sysDescr OBJECT-TYPE	—the object has the ObjectName sysDescr and is of type —OBJECT-TYPE, i.e., its type is defined by the OBJECT- —TYPE MACRO. All mib-2 objects are of —OBJECT-TYPE. As opposed to the C language, the type —of objects is put after the object name.
SYNTAX DisplayString (SIZE (0..255)	—the MACRO says that this type is ObjectSyntax. —ObjectSyntax type is defined in RFC 1155 as a CHOICE —between a number of types. One of these types is —DisplayString (see **Appendix B**)
ACCESS read-only	—read-only is one of the options provided by the Access —production. Productions are supporting assignments —which complete ("resolve" is the formal word) type and —value definitions in the assignment list by using more —detailed assignments.
STATUS mandatory	—this is one of the options provided by the Status —production
DESCRIPTION	"A textural description of the entity. This value should include the full name and version identification of the system's hardware type, software operating system and networking software. Description should only contain printable ASCII characters."
value {system 1}	—the MACRO definition says that VALUE is ObjectName —type. ObjectName is defined in RFC 1155 to be OBJECT —IDENTIFIER type which has the value {system 1}for —this object as seen in **Figure 7.1**

Figure 7.3 sysDescr object formal definition

> **Note**
>
> This is a good place to point out that ASN.1 use of words can be confusing no matter how many times one reads their definitions. The words: variables, names, values and instances are among these. We hope the explanations that follow are useful.
>
> - Instances—an object is an instance of a MACRO. In general, an instance is the representation of object.
> - Names—the name of an object. It is of type Object Identifier, a string of numbers separated by dots (.)
> - Values—an instance of a MACRO has a value. For example, sysDescr has the value {system.1} or (1.3.6.1.2.1.1).
> - Variable—an Object Identifier. The value of the variable is stored on the Management Agent.

Let's create another object in the system group, namely **sysName (5)** as shown in Figure 7.4. This is the object that was requested by Meterware from SERVER using the GetRequest command and captured by the Fastmeter probe in **Chapter 6**: SNMP.

sysName OBJECT-TYPE	— the object has the name sysName and is of type — OBJECT-TYPE, i.e., the MACRO name.
SYNTAX DisplayString (SIZE (0..255)	—the MACRO says that this type is ObjectSyntax. This —ObjectSyntax type is defined in RFC 1155 as a CHOICE —between a number of types. One of these is DisplayString. —see **Appendix B.**
ACCESS read-write	— this is one of the options provided by the Access — production.
STATUS mandatory	— this is one of the options provided by the Status — production.
DESCRIPTION	"An administratively assigned name for this managed node. By convention, this is the node's fully qualified domain name."
value {system 5}	— the MACRO says that value is ObjectName type —ObjectName is defined in RFC 1155 to be OBJECT —IDENTIFIER which is {system 5} for this object as seen — in **Figure 7.1**

Figure 7.4 sysName object

Now let's create a more complex object, a table object. A good example for this is the **ipAddrTable** that is in the ip Group Conceptionally, this table looks like **Table 7.1.**

The numbers in braces { } in the column headings are the column OBJECT IDENTIFIERS. In the information management tree in **Figure 7.1**, the Object Identifier of the ipAddrTable is {mib-2.4.20}. Each entry (row) in the table has the Object Identifier ipAddrEntry (1) so each row has the Object Identifier {mib-2.4.20.1}. The Object Identifier of an object in, say, the column ipAdEntNetMask, would have the Object Identifier {mib-2.4.20.1.3}.

As was discussed in **Chapter 6** for the ipRouteTable, the value of at least one column object is used as an Index object that will identify the row to associate with the column object whose instance we want to access. The Index object specified by RFC1213 (see **Appendix C**) for ipAddrTable is ipAdEntIndex. The values in this column are of type INTEGER and numbered from 1 to N beginning with 1 in the first row of the table. Thus, if the Management Station wanted to access a value of ipAdEntNetMask for example for the Interface 3, the Object Identifier placed in the SNMP GetRequest packet would be **mib-2.4.20.1.3.3.** (See **Chapter 6** for a discussion of the format of the GetRequest command)

Now let's look at how the ipAddrTable object is created by using **Figure 7.2** as a template (see **Figures 7.5** and **7.6**).

MIB-II objects are defined in RFC 1213 "Management Information Base for Network Management of TCP/IP-based internets: MIB-II" **[Ref 3].** These definitions begin on page 12 of that document. It is well written, comprehensive and instructive for those using MIBs for the first time. The complete version of RFC1213 is given in **Appendix C**. Let's look at the beginning of RFC1213.

> **Note**
>
> Compiled versions of MIB-II objects are usually built into a network management system. In case they are not, you can go to this RFC, save all of the object definitions as text files to a floppy, and compile them using the network management system compiler. We will do compiling later in this chapter.

Table 7.1   ipAddrTable {mib-2.4.20}

ipAdEntAddr {mib-2.4.20.1.1}	ipAdEntIndex {mib-2.4.20.1.2}	ipAdEntNetMask {mib-2.4.20.1.3}	IpAdEntBcastAddr {mib-2.4.20.1.4}	ipAdEntReasm MaxSize {mib-2.4.20.1.5}
	1			
	2			
	3			
	4			

ipAddrTable OBJECT-TYPE	
SYNTAX SEQUENCE OF ipAddrEntry	—a SEQUENCE OF is a constructed ASN.1 —type which is a list of objects of the same —type. In the case of a table, it means a list —of the rows in the table. ipAddrEntry is —another object defined in **Figure 7.6.**
ACCESS not-accessible	—rows are not accessible. Only objects in a —row are accessible
STATUS mandatory	—must be included in the object
DESCRIPTION	"The table of addressing information relevant to this entry's IP addresses"
value {ip 20}	— ip is the object under mib-2 that contains —the object ipAddrTable which has the —OBJECT IDENTIFIER {ip 20}

Figure 7.5   ipAddrTable Object

The beginning of RFC 1213 is shown in **Figure 7.7**. RFC1213 is a good example of an ASN.1 MIB module. The clauses in **Figure 7.7** are explained in **Table 7.2**. The remainder of RFC 1213 is a listing of othe other MIB-II object definitions given in **Appendix C. Table 7.2** describes the clauses in **Figure 7.7.**

You have now seen how a MIB module is constructed and that this particular module, RFC 1213, lists the definitions of all MIB-II objects. Thus if a Management System does not provide MIB-II objects, you can copy the module from the standard, load it into the Management System as is, and then compile it.

Let's now look at the iso branch of the SMI MIB tree as displayed by the network management application Meterware/Analyzer.

7.3   NMS PRESENTATION OF THE SMI

The view of the iso branch provided by Meterware is shown in **Figure 7.8**. We see this view expanded in the diagram of **Figure 7.1** also.

The panel on the left can display the tree branches in any detail desired. When a node is checked, as is mib-2 in the figure, the children of the node are shown in the right panel. In this case the children of mib-2 are its groups. One can see the children of any node by clicking the (+) sign in the left panel next to the node. Only the value of a terminal (leaf) node can be accessed by SNMP. To get a

ipAddrEntry OBJECT-TYPE	—this MACRO defines the object —ipAddrEntry. It is the name of any —row in the table
SYNTAX ipAddrEntry	—ipAddrEntry is of type SEQUENCE as —defined below in the next panel
ACCESS not accessible	— previously defined
STATUS mandatory	— previously defined
DESCRIPTION	"Information relative to one of the IP Addresses in the table. This information includes the IP Address itself."
INDEX {ipAdEntAddr}	—referring to the template in **Figure 7.2**, —IndexTypes resolves to ipAdEntAddr. In other —words, there is only one index type in this case. —As we see in the next panel, this Index Type is of —type ipaddress which is defined elsewhere to be —OCTET STRING of SIZE 4. Here we see an —example of nesting type-definitions which occur —frequently in MIB object definitions. Thus in this —case, only ipAdEntAddr is used to determine the —desired row.
value {ipAddrTable 1}	—ipAddrTable 1 is the Object Identifier of all rows —in the table
ipAddrEntry : : = SEQUENCE {	—a SEQUENCE is a list of objects that may be of —different types In this example, the SEQUENCE —corresponds to the following objects in one row —of the table
ipAdEntAddr ipAddress ipAdEntIfIndex INTEGER ipAdEntNetMask ipAddress ipAdEntBcastAddr INTEGER ipAdEntReasmMaxSize INTEGER (0 .. 65535)	—ObjectName and type —ObjectName and type —ObjectName and type —ObjectName and type —ObjectName and type

Figure 7.6 ipAddrEntry Object

```
      RFC1213-MIB DEFINITIONS ::= BEGIN
      IMPORTS
            mgmt, NetworkAddress, IpAddress, Counter, Gauge,
            TimeTicks
            FROM RFC1155-SMI

            OBJECT-TYPE
            FROM RFC-1212;
```

— This MIB module uses the extended OBJECT-TYPE
  macro as defined in [14]; (**Author's Note:** [14] is a
  reference at the end of this RFC. See **Appendix C** for the
  complete RFC.)

— MIB-II (same prefix as MIB-I)

mib-2 OBJECT IDENTIFIER ::= { mgmt 1 }

— textual conventions

DisplayString ::= OCTET STRING
—This data type is used to model textual information
—taken from the NVT ASCII character set. By
—convention, objects with this syntax are declared as —
having SIZE (0..255)

```
SNMP Working Group                                    [Page12]
RFC 1213                    MIB-II              March 1991
```

PhysAddress ::= OCTET STRING
—This data type is used to model media addresses.
—For many types of media, this will be in a binary
—representation. For example, an ethernet address
—would be represented as a string of 6 octets.

— groups in MIB-II

system   OBJECT IDENTIFIER ::= { mib-2 1 }

interfaces   OBJECT IDENTIFIER ::= { mib-2 2 }

at   OBJECT IDENTIFIER ::= { mib-2 3 }

ip   OBJECT IDENTIFIER ::= { mib-2 4 }

icmp   OBJECT IDENTIFIER ::= { mib-2 5 }

tcp   OBJECT IDENTIFIER ::= { mib-2 6 }

udp   OBJECT IDENTIFIER ::= { mib-2 7 }

egp   OBJECT IDENTIFIER ::= { mib-2 8 }

— historical (some say hysterical)

(continued)

Figure 7.7   Beginning of RFC 1213: MIB-II Module

```
— cmot        OBJECT IDENTIFIER ::= { mib-2 9 }

transmission OBJECT IDENTIFIER ::= { mib-2 10 }

snmp         OBJECT IDENTIFIER ::= { mib-2 11 }

— the System group

—Implementation of the System group is mandatory for
—all systems. If an agent is not configured to have a
—value for any of these variables, a string of length
—0 is returned.

sysDescr OBJECT-TYPE
        SYNTAX  DisplayString (SIZE (0..255))
        ACCESS  read-only
        STATUS  mandatory

DESCRIPTION
        "A textual description of the entity.
        This value should include the full name
        and version identification of the system's
        hardware type, software operating-system,
        and networking software.  It is mandatory
        that this only contain printable ASCII
        characters."
::= { system 1 }
```

Figure 7.7 *Continued*

Table 7.2 Description of Clauses in RFC1213

Clause	Description
IMPORTS mgmt, NetworkAddress, IpAddress, Counter, Gauge, TimeTicks **FROM** RFC1155-SMI	• mgmt is the **ObjectName** of the mgmt node under Internet in the MIB tree • NetworkAddress, IpAddress, Counter, Gauge and TimeTicks are **ObjectTypes** • The definitions of these items are obtained (imported) from RFC1155-SMI.
IMPORTS OBJECT-TYPE **FROM** RFC-1212	• OBJECT-TYPE is the name of the MACRO that defines the abstract data structure of MIB objects
— This MIB module.....	• Refers to the OBJECT-TYPE format shown in **Figure 7.2**
— MIB-II.....	• MIB-II is a superset of MIB-I
DisplayString ::= OCTET STRING	• This definition is provided to make it clear that the OCTET STRING, defined in RFC1155, means that only printable characters shall be used.
PhysAddress ::= OCTET STRING	• As explained in RFC 1213
— groups in MIB-II	• This list gives ObjectNames (e.g. system) to the OBJECT IDENTIFIERs of the MIB-II groups
sysDescr OBJECT-TYPE	• Gives the ObjectName sysDescr to the OBJECT IDENTIFIER • Uses the name OBJECT-TYPE to define the abstract data structure that is being used to specify sysDescr • Defines the object sysDescr

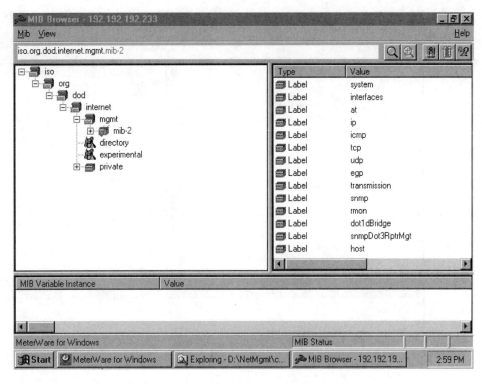

Figure 7.8 Meterware Presentation of the iso branch of the SMI tree

value of a terminal (leaf) node, the device must first be selected on another screen. For example the IP address can be used to select the device. We will see that screen later in this chapter.

The top of the screen in **Figure 7.8** shows that the selected device has the IP address 192.192.192.233 (WS1). To get the value of an object on this device, the ObjectName in the left panel is highlighted and the GetRequest command is executed automatically by clicking the button with the green cross (+) in the top right tool bar.

Clicking the (+) sign next to mib-2 expands it into its groups as shown in **Figure 7.9**. mib-2 originally contained 10 groups, from system down to snmp. Thirteen extension groups have been added. Three of these are: dot1dbridge, snmpDot3Rptr-Mgmt and host. dot1dbridge is the managed bridge objects group. The dot1 terminology refers to the IEEE 802.1 draft standard for managing bridges connecting LAN segments. snmpDot3RptrMgmt is the group of objects for managing hubs (repeaters). The notation Dot 3 comes from the related standard IEEE 802.3. The host group refers to the Host Resources MIB. We will see this group in Chapter 10 when we discuss the desktop management protocol. An excellent reference to all mib-2 groups and its extensions is given in **[Ref 4].**

Now let's use the NMS Meterware to get information about some objects in mib-2. We will focus on the ip group and in particular the ipAddrTable so that we

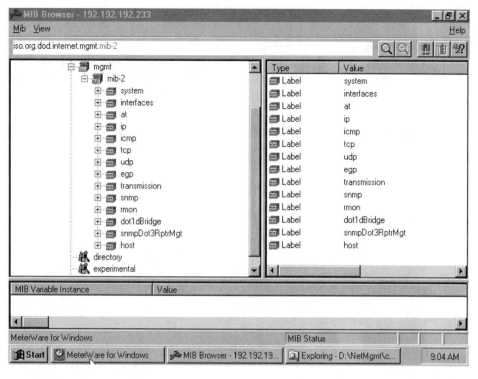

Figure 7.9 mib-2 groups

can make use of what we learned earlier when discussing that table (**Table 7.1.**) We expand the ip group in **Figure 7.9** until we get the ipAddrEntry objects shown in **Figure 7.10**.

A convenient feature of this NMS is the listing of the key components of the object definition that appears in the right panel when the object is highlighted. The object **IpAddrEntry** contains **column** objects. Column objects label columns in the table. For every interface on a device there will be a row identified by one or more instances of column objects in that row appended to the column Object Identifier. Such column objects are called Index objects as we saw in Chapter 6. You see what they are for the ipAddrTable in **Figure 7.11**. We now use Meterware to fill in **Table 7.1** for WS1.

Let's start by getting the instances in the ipAdEntNetMask column. To do that we highlight **ipAdEntNetMask** in **Figure 7.10** and click the GetRequest button (green +). The result is shown in **Figure 7.11**. Note that colors are shown when the Meterware CD is used.

The Get Response from WS1 contains the results shown in the bottom panel. The instance identifiers (variables) on the left are associated with the instances (values) on the right. A MIB Variable Instance Identifier identifies a specific instance associated with a MIB column object. MIB Variable Instance Identifiers are what the NMS passes to the SNMP Agent. A GetResponse returns the instance (value). As we saw in **Chapter 6**, a MIB Variable Instance Identifier is a concatena-

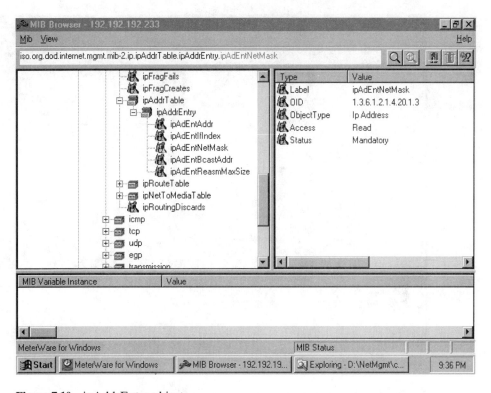

Figure 7.10   ipAddrEntry objects

tion of the Object Identifier of a column object (e.g., ipAdEntNetMask) with an index object (ipAdEntAddr) instance (value) to identify the desired instance in the table. From the identifiers on the left of the bottom panel in **Figure 7.11**, we see that this table has one Index object, the IP address object ipAdEntAddr.

Table 7.3 shows the completed ipAddrTable for WS1. The elements in the table are explained as follows:

ipAdEntAddr

- 127.0.0.1 is the IP loopback address for WS1 internal communications
- 192.192.192.233 is the IP address of the Ethernet NIC

ipAdEntIfIndex

- 1 is the integer that identifies the interface 127.0.0.1 in the ifTable
- 2 is the integer that identifies the interface 192.192.192.233 in the ifTable

ipAdEntNetMask

- 255.0.0.0 is the net mask for the interface 1. It says that the address 127.0.0.1 is a Class A IP address in which the first byte refers to networks and the last three bytes refer to devices on one of the networks.

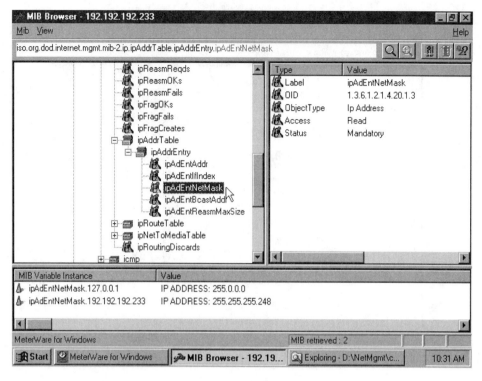

Figure 7.11 ipAdEntNetMask instances for WS1

- 255.255.255.248 is the netmask for the demonstration network used in the book. It is a Class C network, see Appendix A for a discussion.

ipAdEntBcastAddr

- In both rows, 1 means that the IP broadcast address is all ones.

ipAdEntReasmMax Size

- In both rows, 65535 is the maximum number of bytes that can be reassembled into a complete datagram from partial datagrams.

Table 7.3 WS1 ipAddrTable {1.3.6.1.2.1.4.20}

ipAdEntAddr {1.3.6.1.2.1.4.20.1.1}	ipAdEntIfIndex {1.3.6.1.2.1.4.20.1.2}	ipAdEntNetMask {1.3.6.1.2.1.4.20.1.3}	ipAdEntBcastAddr {1.3.6.1.2.1.4.20.1.4}	ipAdEntReasmMax Size {1.3.6.1.2.1.4.20.1.5}
127.0.0.1	1	255.0.0.0	1	65535
192.192.192.233	2	255.255.255.248	1	65535

Note: Each row in the table has the OBJECT IDENTIFIER {1.3.6.1.2.1.4.20.1} for ipAddrEntry

A good question at this point is "How does the NMS know the Index object instance to append to the column Object Identifier to construct the Object Instance Identifier?" It may be able to access it from the device database. If not, as we saw in **Chapter 6**, it will use the GetNextRequest command:

GetNextRequest (ipAdEntNetMask)

to get the first instance, ipAdEntNetMask.1, in the ipAdEntNetMask column and then use:

GetNextRequest (ipAdEntNetMask.1)

to get the second instance, ipAdEntNetMask.2. The rest of **Table 7.3** can be obtained in similar manner.

7.4 NMS METERWARE NETWORK VIEW

Up to this point, we have only made use of the MIB Browser application of our NMS. It is now time to examine its features in general because we are ready to make use of them.

Figure 7.12 shows the main Meterware screen, the Summary View that is the portal to all of its network management tools. All of the devices on the demonstration network and what the NMS knows about them are shown on this screen. Devices that host RMOM MIB objects were discovered automatically when Meterware starts and broadcasts GetRequest packets. These devices automatically appear on the Summary View screen and their data is stored in the Meterware database. Other devices are added by the user with the New Device command on the Edit Menu. The New Device command launches the New Device Information Screen shown in **Figure 7.13**.

The screen as depicted has some default values filled in. The user enters a Device Name and IP address, clicks the Resolve button and Meterware sends SNMP packets to the device. The GetResponse packets contain the remaining information that is available. If information is missing, the user fills it in and clicks Resolve again to see that there are no conflicts with what was configured on the device in Chapters 4 or 5. Apply is then clicked to store the correct information in the device database. It is important to be sure that Read and Write community names returned by the GetResponse packets are identical to those you configured for the device in either Chapter 4 or Chapter 5. The device will not respond to GetRequest messages otherwise. We will use this screen often in this and the following chapters. Its other features will be explained as we demonstrate them.

When you want to Get or Set object values for a device, the device is identified in **Figure 7.12** by highlighting it. Then, for example, the MIB Browser for the device is opened by selecting it from the Tools Menu. The screen that opens, in this case for Switch 2 (192.192.192.244), is shown in **Figure 7.14**.

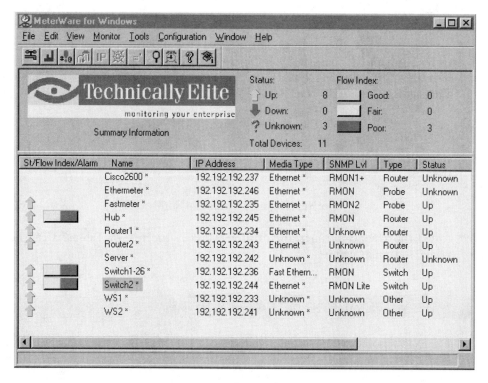

Figure 7.12 Meterware Summary View Screen

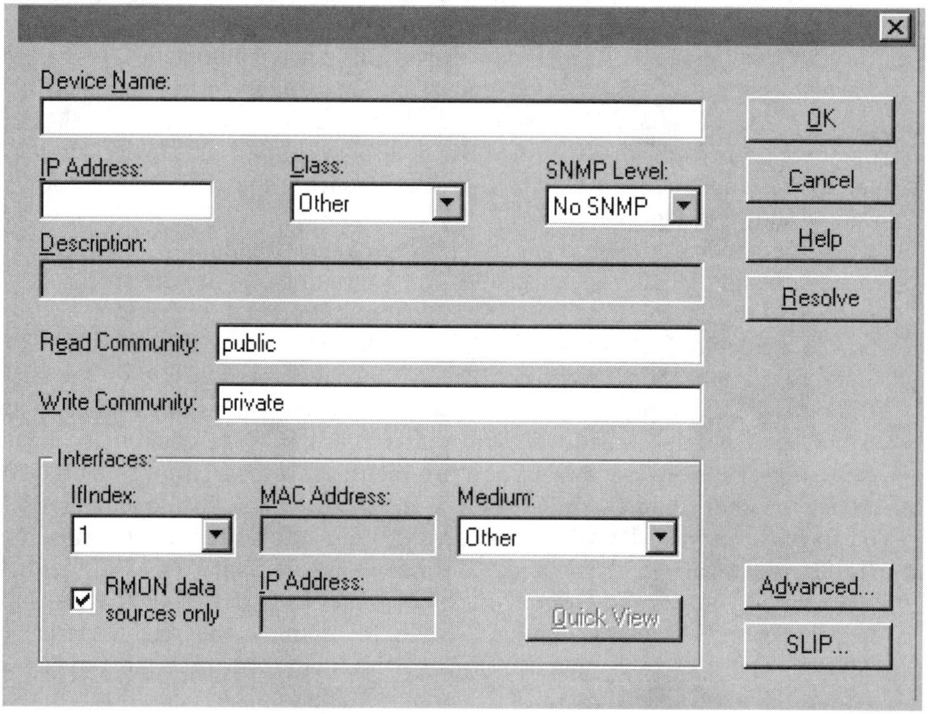

Figure 7.13 New Device Information Screen

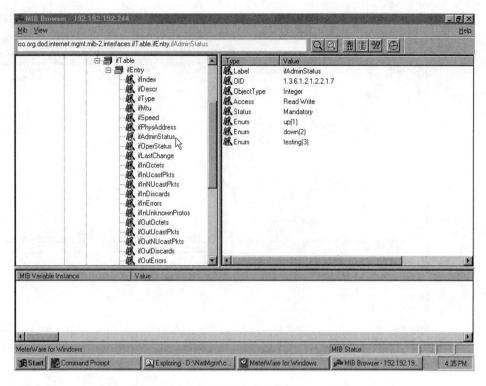

Figure 7.14   MIB Browser for Switch 2 (192.192.192.244)

7.5 SET COMMAND

We will use **Figure 7.14** and the object ifAdminStatus to explore the Set command.

In the left panel, ifAdminStatus (interface Administrative Status) is highlighted. Notice in the right panel that the Definition of this object provides three enumerations for its possible values: up(1), down (2) and testing (3). The object is Read Write. ifAdminStatus is a useful object because it provides a mechanism for the network manager to shut down a port if it is not performing properly or if unauthorized frames are being received on that port. First let's "Get" ifAdminStatus of Switch 2 by clicking the Get button. The result is shown in **Figure 7.15**.

ifAdminStatus for the 27 ports of Switch2 is shown in the bottom panel. If we were to scroll down we would see that all instances are of type INTEGER and all instances are 1. Thus all ports are "administratively up." This does not mean that all are connected to devices. For this network, only ports 3 and 25 are connected. Port 3 is connected to SERVER and port 25 (AUI) is connected to the 10BASE2 cable.

To check the status of port 3 another way, lets use the PING.EXE command that was referred to earlier. Executing PING.EXE with the argument 192.192.192.242 from WS1 will cause ICMP messages to be sent to SERVER. ICMP is the Internet Control Message Protocol which is one of the protocols in the IP layer of the TCP/IP protocol stack. ICMP sends a series (four in this configuration)

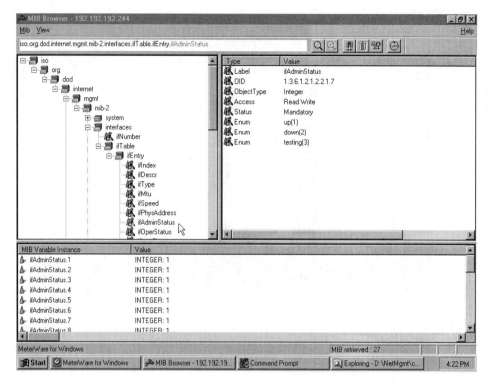

Figure 7.15   ifAdminStatus Values for the ports of Switch 2

of text messages to the IP address identified in the argument of the Ping command and waits for four identical replies to be returned. **Figure 7.16** shows the MSDOS Command Line screen, the PING command and the results.

As we see, SERVER received the messages and replied successfully to WS1. Now let's suppose that we Set port 3 on Switch 2 to administratively down. We return to **Figure 7.15**, highlight ifAdminStatus.3 and click the Set button on the top right of the screen. The Set-Value Input dialog box opens as shown in **Figure 7.17**. There we enter the type of the object, INTEGER, type in the instance 2 which will down the interface and click the Send button.

Immediately after clicking Send, **Figure 7.17** changes to **Figure 7.18**. You see that the instance of ifAdminStatus for Port 3 is now 2 which is equivalent to down. If you could now see the LED over Port 3 you would see that it is amber showing that it is down. (See **Chapter 5**.)

Let's use PING.EXE again to send an ICMP messages to SERVER from WS1. The results are shown following **Figure 7.19**. As can be seen, SERVER did not receive the ICMP messages from WS1 because port 3, the connection to Server, is down and thus there were no return messages to WS1.

As we have said, most, if not all NMSs come with MIB-II objects installed. This is not true of enterprise objects. Enterprise objects are those that have been

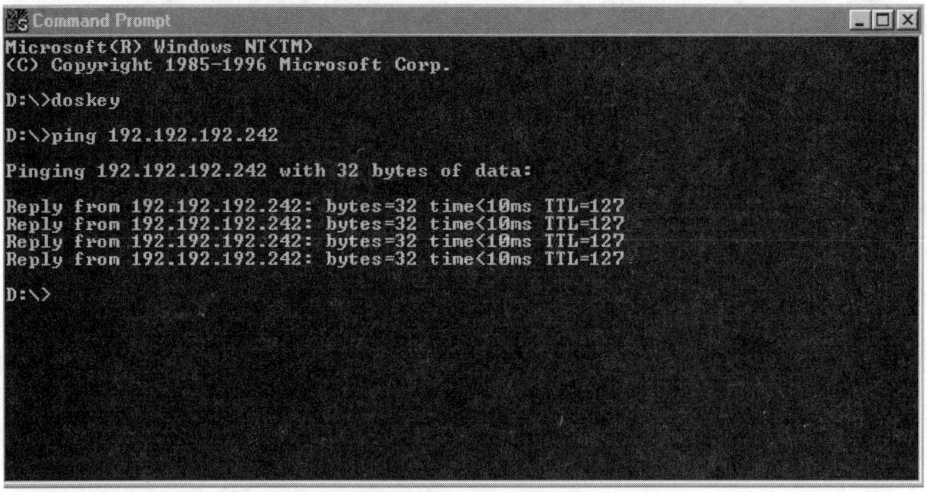

Figure 7.16 ICMP Messages Returned to WS1 by Server

created by vendors specifically for their products. These objects will provide network managers with additional information about device status and performance. The definitions of these objects will usually follow the format used in RFC 1213 and are usually available from the vendor.

In the next section we examine the CISCO mib for the Catalyst Switches on our network. This mib and others for CISCO products can be accessed and downloaded from the CISCO Website. **[Ref 5].** The mib that follows is called ESSWITCH-MIB.MY by CISCO.

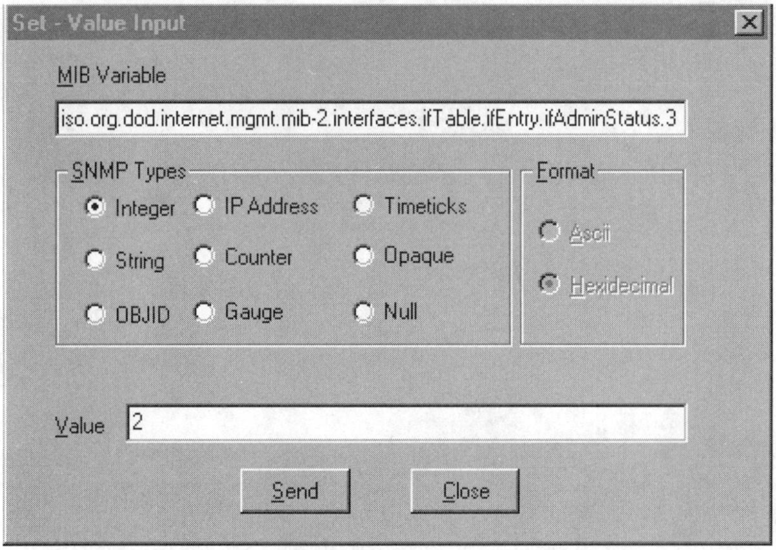

Figure 7.17 Set Dialog Screen

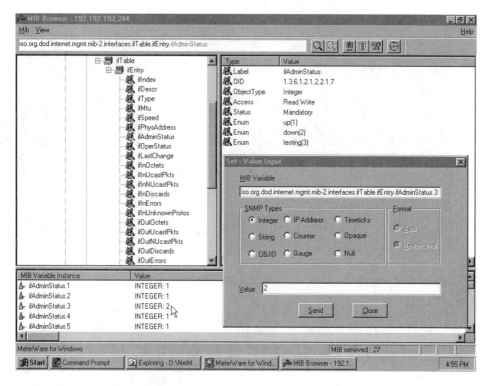

Figure 7.18 Port 3 Set to Down (2)

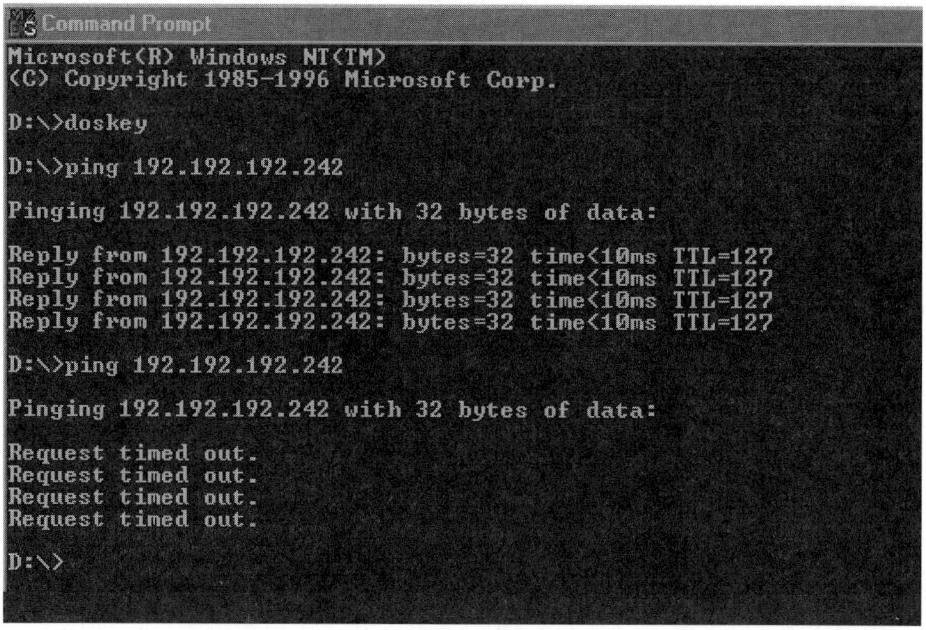

Figure 7.19 ICMP Messages from Server to WS1

7.6 ENTERPRISE MIBS

What follows in Fiure 7.20 is the first part of the CISCO Catalyst Switch mib. The total CISCO mib is 146KB in size. Explanations of the clauses in the first part of the Catalyst mib are provided in Table 7.4.

If we expand the private branch of the mib-2 branch in **Figure 7.8** and then expand its enterprises branch, we get the screen shown in **Figure 7.21**. The nodes nat, natTm, tecElite and sync are nodes specific to the enterprise Apptitude (previously Technically Elite) The node hp is specific to Hewlett Packard products. As you see there is no Cisco enterprise node. We will now compile the Cisco Catalyst switch mib ESSWITCH-MIB.MY that was downloaded from the WebPage given in **[Ref 6]** and add it to the enterprises branch. The screen that allows us to do MIB compiling is shown in **Figure 7.22**. It is obtained by clicking **MIB Compiler** on the Tools Menu on the **Summary View** screen.

You see in the left panel that there are already files that have been compiled and loaded into the SMI tree. The first of these, MAIN.MB, provides the mib-2 objects. The others are the Apptitude enterprise MIBs just discussed.

Table 7.4 Description of Clauses in Cisco Catalyst Switch mib module

Clause	Description
IMPORTS enterprises, Counter, Gauge, IpAddress, TimeTicks **FROM** RFC1155-SMI	• enterprises is a node under private under Internet where all MIBs specific to vendor products are listed • The object types Counter, Gauge, IpAddress and TimeTicks were also imported by RFC 1213 From RFC 1155 as we saw in **Table 7.1**
IMPORTS TRAP-TYPE **FROM** RFC-1215	• RFC-1215, "A Convention for Defining Traps for use with the SNMP," defines a MACRO with the name TRAP-TYPE. Objects that use this MACRO are listed near the end of the Catalyst Switch mib module
IMPORTS OBJECT-TYPE **FROM** RFC-1212	• RFC-1212 has the title "Concise MIB Definitions." This is where the MACRO with the name OBJECT-TYPE was first defined
IMPORTS Timeout **FROM** BRIDGE-MIB	• BRIDGE-MIB is a mib extracted from RFC1493 by Cisco
IMPORTS sysName, ifIndex, DisplayString **FROM** RFC1213-MIB	• sysName is the fully qualified domain name of the system • ifIndex is a column object in the ifTable. It provides an integer that identifies each device interface represented by the table • DisplayString was discussed previously
grandjunction	• The ObjectName of the Cisco enterprise object
products	• The ObjectName of the Cisco products object
fastLink	• The ObjectName of a set of Cisco products
seriesG2xx	• The ObjectName of a set of fastLink products
Series2000	• The ObjectName of a second set of fastLink products. This set contains the Catalyst switches
sysInfo, sysConfig, port, netMgmt, upgrade, vlan, bandwidthUsage, bridgeGroup	• The ObjectNames of the series2000 groups

```
—STAND-ALONE-ETHERNET-SWITCH-MIB
        —REVISION 1.00

DEFINITIONS ::= BEGIN

IMPORTS
        enterprises, Counter, Gauge, IpAddress, TimeTicks
                FROM RFC1155-SMI
        TRAP-TYPE
                FROM RFC-1215
        OBJECT-TYPE
                FROM RFC-1212
        Timeout
                FROM BRIDGE-MIB
        sysName, ifIndex, DisplayString
                FROM RFC1213-MIB;

grandjunction   OBJECT IDENTIFIER ::= { enterprises 437 }

—categories

products        OBJECT IDENTIFIER ::= { grandjunction 1 }

        —product family

        fastLink        OBJECT IDENTIFIER ::= { products 1 }

        —groups

        seriesG2xx      OBJECT IDENTIFIER ::= { fastLink 2 }
        series2000      OBJECT IDENTIFIER ::= { fastLink 3 }

        — LAST-UPDATED       "9708040000Z"
        — ORGANIZATION       "Cisco Systems, Inc."
        — CONTACT-INFO
        —          "      Cisco Systems
                          Customer Service
        —
                   Postal: 170 W Tasman Drive
        —                  San Jose, CA  95134
        —                  USA
        —
                   Tel: +1 800 553-NETS
        —
                   E-mail: cs-snmp@cisco.com"
—          DESCRIPTION
—              "MIB for the Catalyst 1900 and 2820,
—               Catalyst 2100 and 2800,
—               EtherSwitch 12XX and 14XX"
sysInfo         OBJECT IDENTIFIER ::= { series2000 1 }
sysConfig       OBJECT IDENTIFIER ::= { series2000 2 }
port            OBJECT IDENTIFIER ::= { series2000 3 }
netMgmt         OBJECT IDENTIFIER ::= { series2000 4 }
upgrade         OBJECT IDENTIFIER ::= { series2000 5 }
```

Figure 7.20   First Part of Cisco Catalyst mib

```
vlan             OBJECT IDENTIFIER ::= { series2000 6 }
bandwidthUsage   OBJECT IDENTIFIER ::= { series2000 7 }
bridgeGroup      OBJECT IDENTIFIER ::= { series2000 8 }

— the following group manages G2xx modules
esModuleBasic    OBJECT IDENTIFIER ::= { seriesG2xx 1 }

—+++++++++++++++++++++++++++++++++++++++++++++++++++++++++++

—                General System Information

—+++++++++++++++++++++++++++++++++++++++++++++++++++++++++++

sysInfoFwdEngineRevision OBJECT-TYPE
        SYNTAX   INTEGER
        ACCESS   read-only
        STATUS   mandatory
        DESCRIPTION
                "Returns the revision number of the forwarding
                engine ASIC."

        ::= { sysInfo 1 }

sysInfoBoardRevision OBJECT-TYPE
        SYNTAX   INTEGER
        ACCESS   read-only
        STATUS   mandatory
        DESCRIPTION
                "Returns the revision number of the switch main
                board on which the system firmware resides."

        ::= { sysInfo 2 }

sysInfoTotalNumberOfPorts OBJECT-TYPE
        SYNTAX   INTEGER
        ACCESS   read-only
        STATUS   mandatory
        DESCRIPTION
                "The total number of physical network ports.
                fixed configuration    - 27, 15 or 14 ports,
                modular configuration  - 25 - 41 ports
                This object does NOT represent the upper bound
                of indices into port tables. See
                sysInfoNumberOfSwitchPorts and
                sysInfoNumberOfSharedPorts for that purpose."

        ::= { sysInfo 3 }
```

Figure 7.20 *Continued*

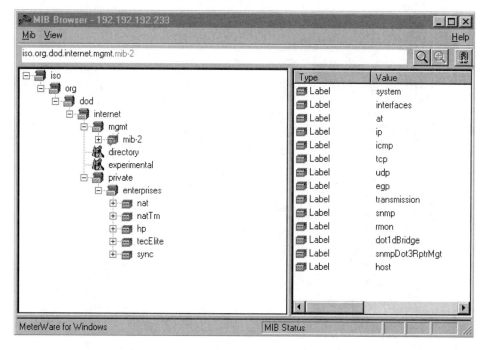

Figure 7.21 Enterprises Branch

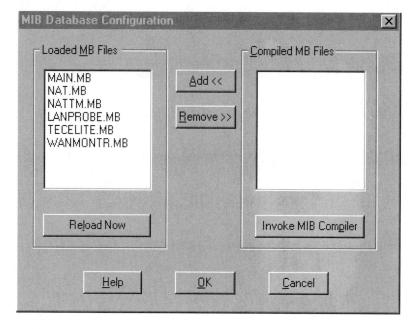

Figure 7.22 MIB Database Configuration

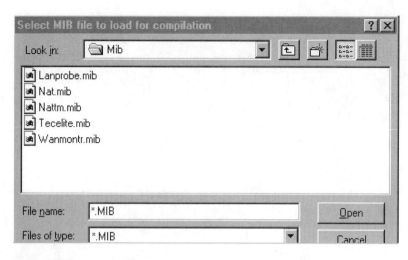

Figure 7.23   MIB Directory

To compile the ESSWITCH-MIB.MY mib, click on the "Invoke MIB Compiler" in **Figure 7.22**. This provides the current MIB directory shown in **Figure 7.23,** that is in <Install Directory\Program Files\Mware\,

In our case, the file to be compiled is on the floppy in A: drive so we tell the compiler to look there by typing the A:\filename in the "Look in Box" The file name is ESSWITCH-MIB-MY2.txt. To compile this text file, click Open. The screen in **Figure 7.24** shows the result if there are no syntax errors in the text file. If there are, error messages and explanations are provided that can be read by clicking the Help button.

Figure 7.24 tells us that a tree, rooted at enterprises, was saved to D:\Progam Files\Mware\mib\ESSWITCH-MIB-MY2.MB. and that the tree has 246 nodes. The

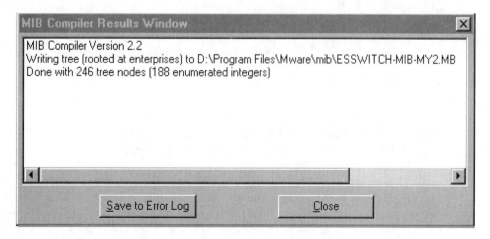

Figure 7.24   Results of compiling ESSWITCH-MIB-MY2.txt

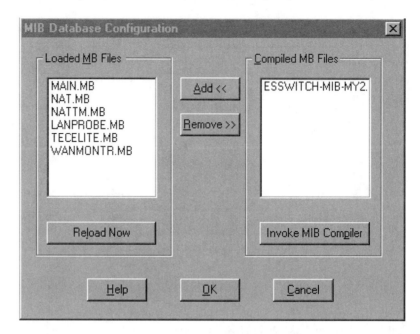

Figure 7.25   After Compiling ESSWITCH-MIB-MY2.txt

extension .MB tells us that this is the compiled binary version of the .txt file. We now
have to go back to **Figure 7.22**, which now looks like the screen shown in **Figure 7.25**.

In the Compiled MIB Files on the right we see that the file has been compiled. We now need to load it into the MIB database by clicking Add. After doing
that we see the screen in **Figure 7.26** showing that ESSWITCH-MIB-MY.MB has
been included in the MIB Database.

Opening the MIB Browser again from Summary View, we see what is shown
in **Figure 7.27**. The new node added to enterprises is **grandjunction**. If you look
back at the first panel of **Figure 7.20**, you see that grandjunction is the ObjectName
of object {enterprise.437} where 437 is the enterprise number assigned to CISCO.
Expanding the grandjunction node we get the result shown in **Figure 7.28**.

The Catalyst switch1900 objects are included in the series 2000 node. The children of this node are shown in **Figure 7.29**. These children are object groups, in addition to those contained in mib-2, that CISCO has decided it needs to monitor the
series 2000 products. Let's expand the **sysInfo** group to get its children, some of
which are shown in **Figure 7.30** for Switch2 that has IP Address 192.192.192.244.

Now let's highlight sysInfoNumberOfSwitchPorts and click the Get button.
The result is shown in the bottom panel of the screen in **Figure 7.31**.

The result is 27. This result is a trivial example since we can count the number
of switch ports by examining the switch if it is local. However, what if the switch
were on a remote network? Then this would be a very convenient way for a network manager to get this information. We will be using other CISCO enterprise
mib objects and mib-2 groups to examine instances of our switch objects in later
chapters.

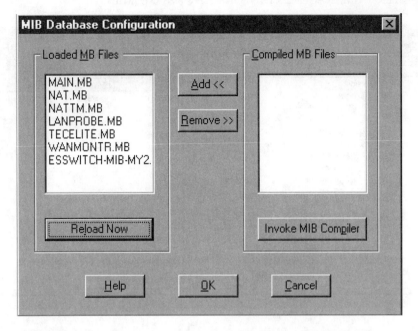

Figure 7.26   MIB Database Configuration After Loading ESSWITCH-MIB-MY2.MB

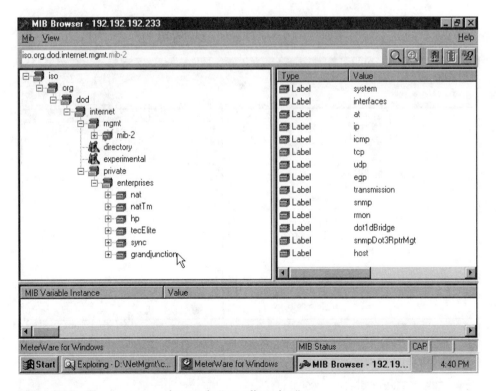

Figure 7.27   The new enterprises node "grandjunction"

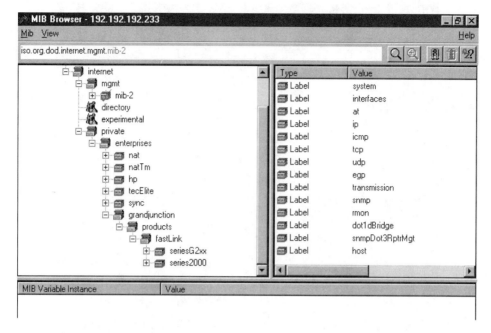

Figure 7.28 grandjunction children

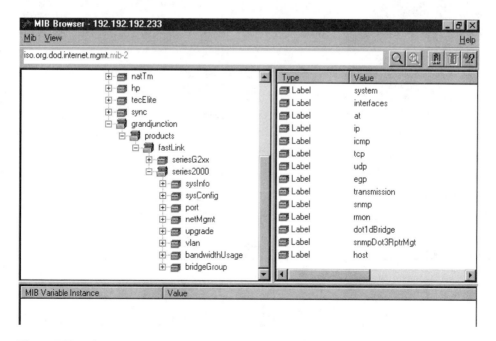

Figure 7.29 Children of series 2000 node

Figure 7.30   Left panel: Children of sysInfo node

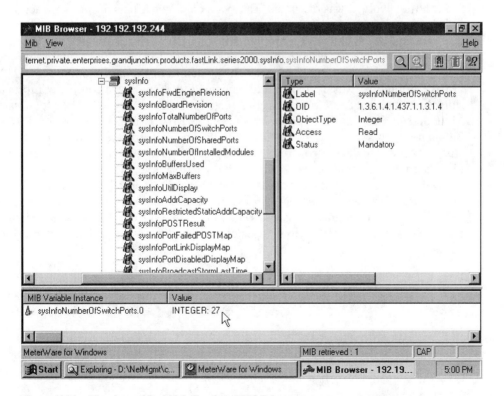

Figure 7.31   Number of Switch2 Catalyst 1900 Ports

7.7 MIB EDITOR

You have seen how the ASN.1 language is used to construct syntactically correct MIB objects in text format. Thus, one can always create and edit MIB objects this way. Like the tools that exist to make it easier to create and edit the source code for a computer language, MIB editors exist that provide a user-friendly interface and automatically create syntactically correct object source code. Such MIB editors may be stand-alone or an integral part of Network Management Systems. An example of a stand-alone MIB editor, made by MG-Soft Corporation, can be found at **[Ref 7]**. See **Table 3.9** in **Chapter 3** for a list of other possible vendors of editor software as well as **[Ref 8]**.

CHAPTER SUMMARY

A primary goal of this chapter was to explain an important but complex subject, the formal definition of a MIB object, so that the student can make informed use of any Network Management System or a command line interface to an SNMP program. The rationale for how the Structure of Management Information (SMI) for the Internet evolved was discussed. The syntax and constructs of the Abstract Syntax Notation.1 (ASN.1) language, necessary to create SMI objects, were explained. The principal ASN.1 ideas of a module and a macro were introduced. The use of a macro to create objects was analyzed and then used to create the actual syntax of simple and constructed mib-2 objects. The structure of the mib module RFC1213: "MIB Definitions" was examined and explained to show how a complete information object, not just a mib object, is constructed using ASN.1 syntax. The Meterware Main Screen, Summary View, was introduced. A MIB Browser was accessed from Summary View and used to retrieve simple and constructed mib-2 objects instances. An example of a constructed mib-2 object is a table. In addition to mib-2 objects, enterprise objects were examined. As an example, the CISCO mib module for switches was downloaded from the CISCO Website, compiled and added to the Meterware MIB Database. The clauses in this module were explained. We then used the objects contained to access switch information from the Catalyst switches on our network. Finally the advantages of a MIB editor were explained and references given.

REVIEW QUESTIONS

1. Why is the iso node the parent of the SMI nodes discussed in this chapter?
2. An SMI object has a value and an instance. What is the difference?
3. What is an Index object and how is it used?
4. What is the value of the sysName object in the mib-2 system group?

5. How many types can the type SEQUENCE OF contain?
6. How many types can the type SEQUENCE contain?
7. Why is it not possible to use SNMPv1 to access an entire table at one time?
8. Is it possible to access a row of a table at one time using SNMPv1?
9. Is the definition of RFC 1213 in Figure 7.7 a MACRO or a Module definition?
10. What is the meaning of the ASN.1 symbol **::=**?
11. What information must be contained in the argument of a GetRequest for an instance of a table column object?
12. How does a GetNextRequest differ from a GetRequest?

EXERCISES

1. Construct the numerical dotted-decimal Object Identifier for the column object **ipRouteDest** in the ip group.
2. Construct the numerical dotted-decimal Object Identifier for the column object **snmp-InBadCommunityNames** in the snmp group.
3. Construct the numerical dotted-decimal Object Identifier for the MIB node **enterprises**.
4. Determine the Ethernet Address of a device:
   • Use a MIB Browser to access the mib-2 **ifTable** on a network device. Use the PC hosting Meterware if you like.
   • Determine the physical (Ethernet) address that corresponds to the IP address of the device.
5. Working with your instructor:
   • Identify a MIB object that has MIB Access: READ-WRITE.
   • Use the Set command to change the current value of that object.
   • Use the Get command to see if you get the new object value that you set.
6. Use the MACRO Object Type to write a definition for a fictitious new object.

REFERENCES

1. ISO/IEC 8824 "Information Technology-Abstract Syntax Notation One (ASN.1), Parts 1-4, http://www.ansi.org.
2. "Understanding SNMP MIBs," David Perkins and Evan McGinnis, Prentice Hall PTR, 1997.
3. RFC 1213 "Management Information Base for Network Management of TCP/IP-based internets: MIB-II," http://www.csl.sony.co.jp/cgi-bin/hyperrfc?rfc-index.txt
4. "Total SNMP," by Sean Harnedy, CBM Books, 1994.
5. http://www.cisco.com
6. http://www.cisco.com/public/sw-center/netmgmt/cmtk/mibs.shtml.
7. "MG-Soft Corporation home page," http://www.mg-soft.com/
8. "mibCentral: A Free SNMP Search Engine," http://www.mibcentral.com/index.shtml

CHAPTER 8

REMOTE MONITORING (RMON1)

This chapter includes the following topics:

- Limitations of the original SNMP MIB
- Capabilities provided by RMON1 MIB Groups
- Examination of the following RMON1 Groups and demonstration of their use
  - ❑ Statistics Group
  - ❑ History Group
  - ❑ Host Group
  - ❑ Matrix Group
  - ❑ Capture Group
  - ❑ Filter Group
  - ❑ Alarm Group
  - ❑ Event Group
  - ❑ HostTopN Group

In Chapter 6: SNMP and Chapter 7: Management Information Base (MIB), we learned to use the objects in mib-2. These objects allowed the Management Station to collect statistical information about devices on which agents were installed. However, these statistics told us little about the sources of received packets, the application protocols that initiated them or the content of the packets. They also told us nothing about the traffic on the network between the source and destination devices. The RMON1 and RMON2 MIBs provide these significant enhancements to mib-2. (RMON stands for Remote Monitor). RMON1 objects provide new information at the MAC layer. RMON2 objects provide new information at the network layer and all layers above. In this chapter, we discuss at length the RMON1 objects and demonstrate their use. In Chapter 9, we do the same for RMON2 objects. Although we refer to the first RMON MIB as RMON1, RMON1 is usually called RMON.

RMON devices are devices attached to a subnet whose only function is to promiscuously read frames on that subnet and store values of objects defined by RMON1 or RMON2 MIBs. These values are then accessed from Management Stations. Probe 1 and Probe 2 on the demonstration network are RMON devices. Probe 1 hosts both RMON1 and RMON 2 MIBs. Probe 2 hosts only the RMON 1 MIB. There are multifunctional devices, such as PCs, hubs, switches and routers, having agents that typically collect a subset of RMON1 or RMON2 object values. We will examine both types of devices. The RMON1 MIB contains ten groups **[Ref 1]**. This book does not address group 10, Token Ring. The RMON2 MIB, **[Ref 2]**, makes a major addition to RMON1 by providing analysis up to the OSI Application layer and adding nine groups of objects to those defined in the RMON1 standard.

8.1 RMON GROUPS

Figure 8.1 is an enhanced diagram of the demonstration network that you have seen in previous chapters. Because we will be referring to details of this diagram in this chapter and the next, we have added that detail to the figure. For example, the last three decimal digits of the IP address have been added to each device label. The WAN part of the diagram has been removed.

The RMON probes are highlighted. You see that Probe 2 (Ethermeter) is attached to Subnet 2 through the Hub and Probe 1 (Fastmeter) is attached to Subnet 1 through Switch 1. Probe 1 is actually two probes in one. It has two monitor ports that can independently collect frames from two subnets. In **Figure 8.1**, Probe 1 can be used to collect frames captured from the mirror ports of Switch 1 and Switch 2 (See Chapter 5 for a discussion of the configuration of mirror ports on these switches.) However, as you will see, we have used Probe 2 in most of this chapter because it is a dedicated RMON1 probe.

To begin our discussion, let's use **Figure 8.2** to put the RMON1 and RMON2 MIBs in perspective relative to original mib-2 groups. The figure shows that the complete object identifier of the mib-2 object is **1.3.6.1.2.1.** The object identifiers of the other groups in mib-2 are written as mib-2.x where x represents the additional integer that identifies the specific group object. Thus, for example, the object identifier of the system group is 1.3.6.1.2.1.1 or mib-2.1.

The groups shown on the left of **Figure 8.2** are the original mib-2 groups, Those shown on the right are extensions that have been added over time. The extension groups shown are those you first saw in **Figure 7.9** and that are included in the version of Meterware we are using. As of this writing, there are 93 mib-2 groups. The rmon group includes RMON1 and RMON2 objects. See **[Ref 3]** for a complete listing of all mib objects assigned by the Internet Assigned Numbers Authority **(IANA)**

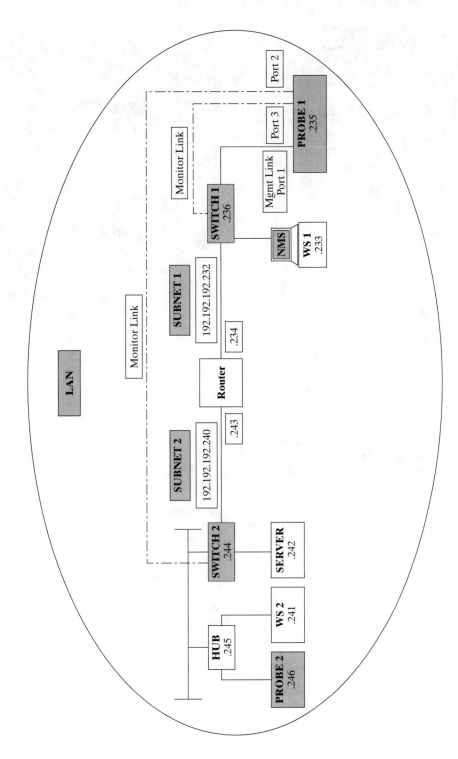

Figure 8.1 The LAN Used in this Book

209

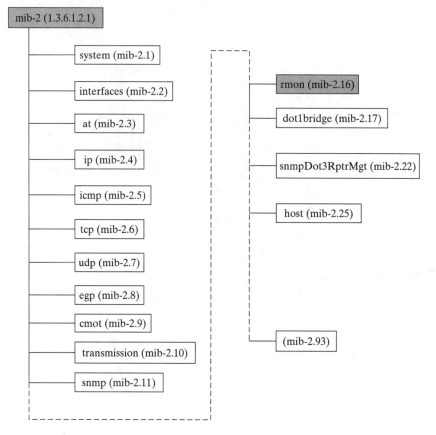

Figure 8.2 Current mib-2 Groups

The RMON1 group gives the network manager a tremendous range of management capability. However, trying to make use of this range effectively can be confusing. There are many tables and many objects in each table. In addition, a new table type, the control table, is introduced. Thus, getting some perspective on the subject takes time. The principal purpose of **Table 8.1** is to give the reader an overview of the groups before jumping into the details. We have put this information in tabular form in order to make it easier for the reader to quickly refer back to the key features of each group. We will see each of the groups in detail later in the chapter. Other comprehensive information about these groups can be obtained from **[Refs 4-5].**

[Ref 1] is the RFC that defines the RMON1 standard and lists all of its groups and objects. We will examine and demonstrate the use of the Ethernet RMON1 objects throughout this chapter. The first column in **Table 8.1** lists the Ethernet RMON1 groups, the second column describes the principal features of the objects in the group and the third column states, in a nutshell, the function of the group.

Table 8.1 RMON1 MIB Group (The Object Identifier of mib-2 is 1.3.6.1.2.1)

Group	Description	Function
Statistics group (mib-2.16.1)	• Consists of the **etherStatsTable**. • There is one table entry (row) for each Ethernet subnetwork to which the RMON1 device is connected. • Each row consists of values of column objects for a subnetwork. • The column objects are counter objects. An example column object is the counter **etherStatsPkts**, which is the number of ethernet packets received since the RMON1 device was first started. • There are 21 column objects in the table.	Counts packets with characteristics defined by objects in the etherStatsTable. The packet count is for all frames read regardless of source.
History group (mib-2.16.2)	• Consists of two tables: the **historyControlTable** and the **etherHistoryTable.** • The management application uses the historyControlTable to specify for example the subnetwork interface that will be monitored, the sampling interval and how many sampling intervals. • The etherHistoryTable has 15 column objects. Each of these objects is sampled in the sampling interval. • A row in the etherHistoryTable consists of the values of the column objects for one sampling interval. Thus, for each interface, there are as many rows in the etherHistoryTable as sampling intervals.	Develops a history of each etherHistoryTable object. Does this by counting packets for each object over a number of defined sampling intervals
Alarm group (mib-2.16.3)	• Consists of the **alarmTable.** • The management application creates a row in the table by defining the object to be monitored, the sampling interval and the alarm thresholds. • Other column objects define how the threshold and object values during a sampling interval are to be compared. • Alarms can be generated and actions taken, depending on the result of the comparison, by referencing rows in the **eventTable.**	Identifies selected object values that become greater or less than thresholds during the sampling interval.
Host group (mib-2.16.4)	• This group gathers statistics specific to hosts on the LAN that is being monitored. • It consists of three tables: **hostControlTable, hostTable** and **hostTimeTable.** • The remote monitor learns about hosts from reading MAC addresses in packets it receives. • The host Table has one row for each host discovered. • The values of column objects in a hostTable row are statistics for a specific host. An example would be the number of packets received, **hostInPkts.** • The hostTimeTable contains the same information as the hostTable. However, the rows are ordered by the time the host was detected.	Records MAC Address and statistics for packets received or transmitted for each host detected on the subnet.
HostTopN group (mib-2.16.5)	• This group consists of two tables: **hostTopNControlTable** and **hostTopNTable.** • The statistics that are compiled make use of the values of objects in the host group. • The management station uses the hostTopNControlTable to specify the maximum number of hosts, N, to monitor, the sampling interval, a variable from the hostTable to monitor and the change of that variable during the sampling interval. • The hostTopNTable ranks the results for the topN hosts relative to a selected variable such as hostInPkts.	Determines the most active N hosts during every sampling interval for a specified variable such as "in-packets."

(*continued*)

Table 8.1 *Continued*

Group	Description	Function
Matrix group (mib-2.16.6)	• This group contains three tables: **matrixControlTable, matrixSDTable** and **matrixDSTable.** (SD = source>destination and DS = destination>source). • The matrixControlTable functions like control tables described for other groups. • The matrixSDTable and matrixDSTable present a logical matrix of source and destination addresses to the management application. • The matrixSDTable and matrixDSTable contain the same information. • The matrixSDTable and the matrixDSTable are indexed differently so that the management application can quickly access the desired data for a particular communication. • Included among the column objects are the MAC source and destination addresses of the hosts involved in communication. There is one row for each communication in the matrixSDTable and matrixDSTable.	Records host MAC Addresses and statistics, such as "in-packets," for conversations between hosts.
Filter group (mib-2.16.7)	• Consists of two control tables: **filterTable** and **channelTable.** • Objects in the filterTable allow the management application to define what packets will be processed by the monitor based on the content of the fields in the packets. • Two types of content filters are applied to define a channel: the **data** filter and the **status** filter. There can be multiple filters applied by creating multiple data and status filters. • Data filters filter on bit patterns in the packet. • Status filters filter on errors such as CRC errors. • Packets that pass a data/status filter combination constitute a **channel.** • Each channel has a capture buffer for its packets. • Packets in a channel can be retrieved from the capture buffer by the NMS using capture group objects. • Packets that match filters can produce events defined in the event group.	Defines the characteristics of read packets that should be processed by the probe. Such characteristics determine a channel.
Capture group (mib-2.16.8)	• This group has two tables: **bufferControlTable** and **captureBufferTable.** • Each row of the bufferControlTable defines the capture characteristics of one buffer. For example, one object defines how much of a packet will be captured and another object how much of that will be returned to the management application in a SNMP GetResponse message. • Each buffer has a captureBufferTable. Each row in this table is assigned to a packet in that buffer. One object, for example, defines the length of the packet.	Defines how much of a channel packet is captured and how much is transmitted to the Management Station.
Event group (mib-2.16.9)	• This group contains the **eventTable** and the **logTable.** • A row in the eventTable defines the parameters of an event. • A row in the logTable defines the event type and the specific event of that type and stores data about the event. • Trap messages generated by an event can be used to control objects in other groups.	Defines and logs events that are generated by objects in other groups and initiates actions.

We now begin a detailed examination of the Ethernet RMON1 group objects and demonstrate their use. We start with the statistics group.

8.1.1 Statistics Group

The statistics group is probably the simplest of the RMON1 groups. Its objects are mostly counters that store numbers of packets, octets, errors, etc., detected in frames on the subnet. These numbers do not differentiate between hosts and are totals for all hosts. The **etherStatsTable** shows the categories for which the numbers are totaled. A review of these categories by the network manager provides a quick and broad view of how well the network is performing. To show the etherStatsTable for Ethermeter, we open the Meterware Summary View, highlight Ethermeter, click on the Tools menu and then click MIB Browser to get the screen shown in **Figure 8.3**.

A probe characterizes packets according to these object names, counts them and puts them into the appropriate "bin." There are 21 etherStatsTable objects. For example, a large number of etherStatsCollisions would immediately tell the network manager that the subnet is overloaded. The last item in the left panel is etherStats2Table. etherStats2Table is a small table that has been added to the RMON1 Statistics group by RMON2. We will discuss the objects in that table when we discuss RMON2.

As mentioned in the introduction to this chapter, control objects and control tables are major features of both RMON1 and RMON2. They determine how data is to be collected by the probe and who is responsible for defining the choices. They are also an important feature because they determine how well the data collection will satisfy the needs of the network manager. **Table 8.2** lists the control objects in

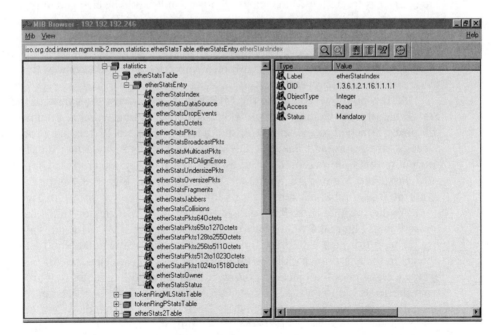

Figure 8.3   etherStatsTable Column Objects

Table 8.2 etherStatsTable Control Objects

Object	Description
etherStatsDataSource	• An integer that formally identifies the device interface from which the data is to be processed. • Has the same value as ifIndex in the ifTable in mib-2 for this device.
etherStatsOwner	• A string that identifies the creator of the table row that is associated with etherStats-DataSource. • Is either the agent with the name monitor or a Management Station name and IP address.
etherStatsStatus	• An integer that specifies the status of the row. Its values can be either valid (1), createRequest (2) underCreation (3) or invalid (4). • The row creator uses a SetRequest to set the value of this object to createRequest (2). • The agent then sets the value to underCreation(3) until the creator is finished. • The creator must then set the value to valid(1) for the row objects to begin to collect data.

Figure 8.3. In the case of the etherStatsTable, the control objects are included in the table. Other groups have separate control tables.

In general, if a Management Station wants data to be collected from a specific subnetwork, it should first examine the values of the group's current control table objects to see if the current values are satisfactory. This can avoid creating a new row and using up precious probe storage. Monitor created rows are expected to have a longer life than rows created by Management Stations and should be changed only with care.

If we were using a command line version of SNMP, as we did in Chapter 6, and wanted to create new etherStatsTable control objects (a new row), the Set-Request command would be applied to each control object. Since we are using a management application with a graphical interface, we will see how this is done using a control table screen later.

At this point, we could use the MIB Browser to access the values of the ether-StatsTable objects. Counts of these objects are continuously being accumulated by the probe attached to the subnet. Instead, let's examine a Meterware program that accesses, integrates, and analyzes the values of objects in the etherStatsTable. The procedure that follows is used for access to all RMON1 group graphical applications.

First, the Meterware Summary View shown in **Figure 8.4** is opened. Then Ethermeter is double-clicked to get its Information screen as shown in **Figure 8.5**.

At the top of **Figure 8.5**, you see the tab RMON. Clicking that takes you to the screen in **Figure 8.6** where buttons for selecting the RMON1 groups are shown.

The buttons activate programs that will automatically poll default Ethermeter objects in these groups with SNMP GetRequests when we click one of them. However, we could choose objects to poll by editing MIB Polling tables that are accessed from the Tools Menu on the Summary View screen. We will see these tables later.

To start Meterware using SNMP GetRequest commands to get etherStats-Table object values, we click the Statistics button. Meterware then constructs the graphs shown in **Figure 8.7**. Utilization of the subnet to which Ethermeter is at-

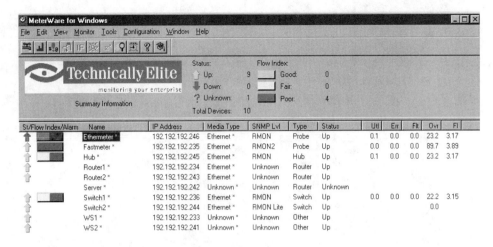

Figure 8.4 Meterware Summary View

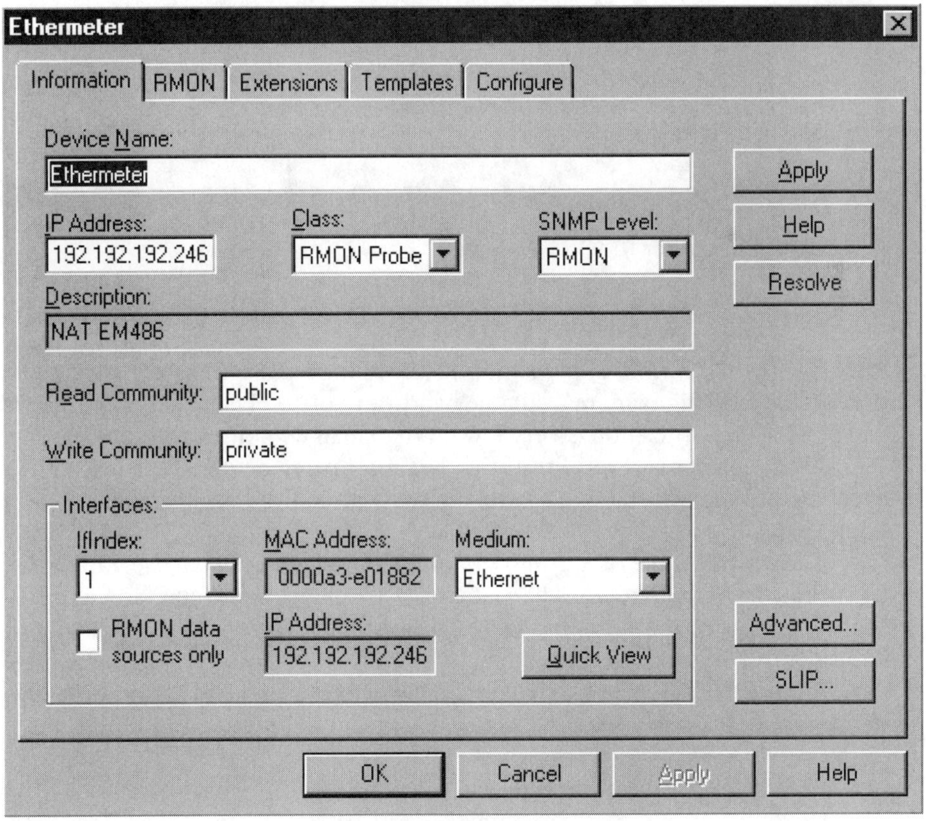

Figure 8.5 Ethermeter Information Screen

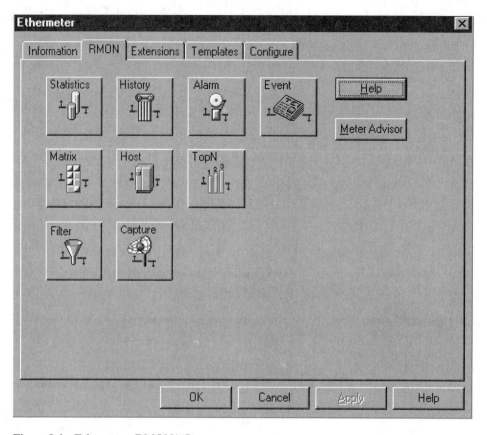

Figure 8.6   Ethermeter RMON1 Groups

tached, 192.192.192.240, is presented in the top graph. Utilization represents the percentage of the maximum available bandwidth of 10mb/sec that is being used. As can be seen, the utilization is very low on this small demonstration subnet. The bottom graph represents several statistics. The most prominent is the Packet Rate that averages between 2 and 3 packets/sec. We will analyze such graphs later in the book.

The control table of a group can always be accessed from the Table Menu or by clicking the icon that looks like a table on the menu bar of the screen that is presented after the group's icon in **Figure 8.6** is clicked. **Figure 8.8** shows the etherStatsTable control objects and values.

Since Ethermeter has only one interface to the subnet, there is only one row in the control table. We see that:

etherStatsOwner = **monitor**
etherStatsStatus = **valid**
etherStatsDataSource = **ifIndex.1**
etherStatsIndex = **1**

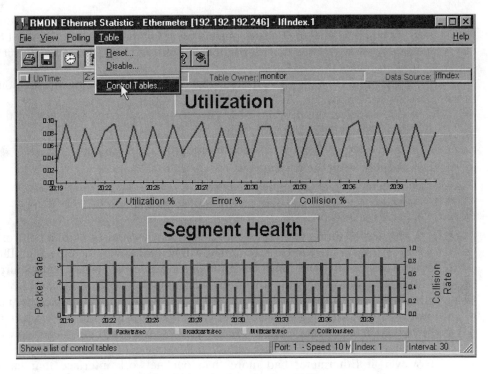

Figure 8.7 Analysis of Object Values in the etherStatsTable.

We know from the fact that the value of etherStatsOwner is "monitor," that the agent on Ethermeter has automatically created and taken ownership of this row of the control table. It has set etherStatsDataSource equal to ifIndex.1, the instance identifier in the mib-2 ifTable for the Ethermeter interface to subnetwork 192.192.192.240. The Index object etherStatsIndex = 1 because this row is the first row in the table. etherStatsStatus is set to "valid" so that Ethermeter will store data

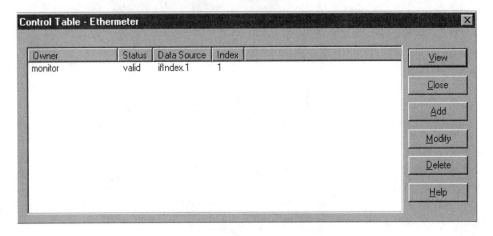

Figure 8.8 Control Objects and Values in the Ethermeter etherStatsTable

in the in the etherStatsTable objects. If you were to read all of the instance identifiers for the Ethermeter Statistics objects using **Figure 8.3** and GetRequest SNMP messages, you would see that all of them are indexed by 1, the Index object in the etherStatsTable.

The buttons on the right of **Figure 8.8** provide the following information:

- **View**—select the row and click View to start collecting Statistics for the control objects defined for that row
- **Add**—open a window in which another row can be added
- **Modify**—edit the current row
- **Delete**—delete the highlighted row
- **Help**—get help on how to use the above buttons

Figure 8.9 shows the more general case for the Statistics group control table. For every row in the control table, there will be one row in the etherStatsTable. In other words, for every distinct set of the object values of Owner, Data Source and Index, there will be another row in the control table and an associated row in the etherStatsTable. If the network manager decides that he is going to create another owner for the same values of the other control objects, that will cause a new row to be created in the control table and the etherStatsTable. The data in each row would, of course, be the same and that would be a poor use of probe memory resources. However, if Ethermeter had more than one network interface that had Data Source ifIndex.2, that interface would provide new data and it would therefore make sense to have another control table row with an associated etherStatsTable row for the new data.

Recognize that the etherStatsTable Control Table is a virtual table because there is no distinct control table. The rows in this virtual table correspond to dis-

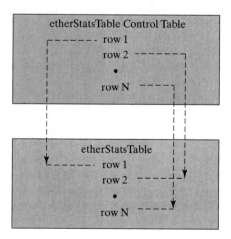

Figure 8.9 Relationship Between etherStatsTable Control Table Rows and etherStatsTable Rows

tinct sets of the objects {Owner, Data Source and Index}. There is only one row in the case of Ethermeter. The values shown in the Control Table for Ethermeter were created automatically. If they had not been set by the monitor's agent, the Management Station would have had to create a row.

The format of the material presented above for the Statistics group is typical of what will be presented for the other RMON1 groups. Now let's examine the History Group.

8.1.2 History Group

As its name implies, the History Group enables the network manager to build a record of what is happening on the network over time. It does this by building a history of each etherHistoryTable object. Packets are counted for each object over a number of defined sampling intervals thus, its objects are very useful for monitoring the time dependence of network performance and determining if additional resources are needed. Some of the etherHistoryTable objects are the same as those in the etherStatsTable. The big difference is that the time dependence of etherHistoryTable object values can be tracked.

The MIB Browser shows the highest level objects in the History group in **Figure 8.10**. Five tables are listed. For Ethernet RMON1 purposes, we are only interested in the **historyControlTable** and the **etherHistoryTable.** The History group has a separate control table. You also see that there is a historyControl2Table that has been added to RMON1 by RMON2 and will be discussed in Chapter 9.

- **historyControlTable**

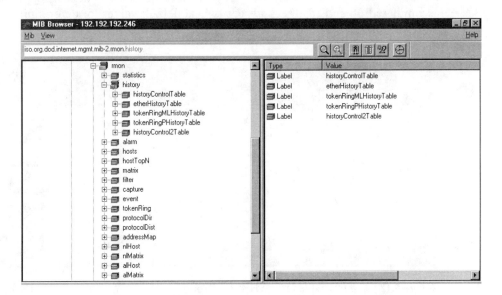

Figure 8.10   MIB Browser View of History Group

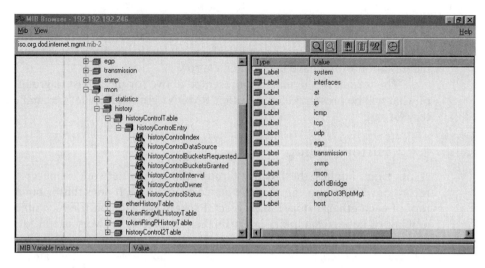

Figure 8.11   historyControlTable Column Objects

Figure 8.11 shows the column objects in the historyControlTable. We access the History control table just as we did for the Statistics control table from the screen in **Figure 8.6**. This time we click the History button and select Control Table from the Table Menu on the screen provided. The result is **Figure 8.12**.

Table 8.3 describes these objects. There is one row in the historyControlTable for each distinct set of control object values. Thus, there are two rows in **Figure 8.12**, one for each historyControlInterval of 30 and 1800 seconds. historyControlInterval is the time during which counts for the column objects in the etherHistoryTable are accumulated. 30 and 1800 seconds are typical default values for determining short-

Owner	Status	Interval	Granted	Request	Data Source	Index	
monitor	valid	30	120	120	ifIndex.1	1	View
monitor	valid	1800	120	120	ifIndex.1	2	Close
							Add
							Modify
							Delete
							Help

Figure 8.12   Control Table for the History Group

Table 8.3 historyControlTable Objects

Object	Row 1	Row 2	Description
historyControlIndex	1	2	• Index object for the rows
historyControlDataSource	ifIndex.1	ifIndex.1	• Interface to subnet 192.192.192.240 • Has the value of ifIndex. in the mib-2 ifTable
historyControlInterval	30 sec	1800 sec	• There are two Sampling interval lengths. One for short-term history and one for long-term history
historyControlBuckets Requested	120	120	• Number of sampling intervals requested
historyControlBuckets Granted	120	120	• Number of sampling intervals granted. Determines how long the sampling will be done and thus how much probe memory is granted. Granted buckets can be less than requested buckets
historyControlStatus	valid(1)	valid(1)	• An integer that specifies the status of the row • Its values can be either valid (1), createRequest (2) underCreation (3) or invalid (4). • The row creator uses a SetRequest to set the value of this object to createRequest (2) • The agent then sets the value to underCreation(3) until the creator is finished • The creator then sets the value to valid(1).

term and long-term histories. **Figure 8.13** shows the relationship between historyControlTable, etherHistoryTable and the number of granted buckets in the historyControlTable for the data in **Figure 8.12**.

The first row in the control table shows that 120 buckets (intervals of 30 seconds) have been granted to the historyControlTable row with the historyControlIndex having the value 1. The second row says that 120 buckets (intervals of 1800 seconds) have been granted to the historyControlTable row with the historyControlIndex having the value 2. Thus, the etherHistoryTable will have 240 rows. **Figure 8.14** shows the etherHistoryTable objects.

Table 8.4 relates some of these etherHistoryTable objects to those in the historyControlTable. Both etherHistoryIndex and etherHistorySampleIndex are index objects whose values are concatenated to all column object instance identifiers in the etherHistoryTable. For example, you see in the bottom panel of **Figure 8.14**, an instance of the etherHistoryPkts identified as etherHistoryPkts.1.262 with the value of 161. (.1) refers to the value of etherHistoryIndex and (.262) refers to the value of etherHistorySampleIndex sample number 262. (Sample numbers do not necessarily correspond to the number of rows because in this example there are 240 rows. However, each sample number is unique.)

Figure 8.15 shows the result of clicking the History button in **Figure 8.6** to produce a history report by polling Ethermeter for the data it has collected from ifIndex.1 for 30-second-sample historyControlIntervals. The report is constructed from the default MIB Polling Tables mentioned above. There are no collisions or

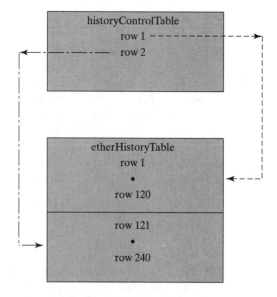

Figure 8.13 Relationship Between Rows in historyControlTable and etherHistoryTable for historyControlTable in Figure 8.12.

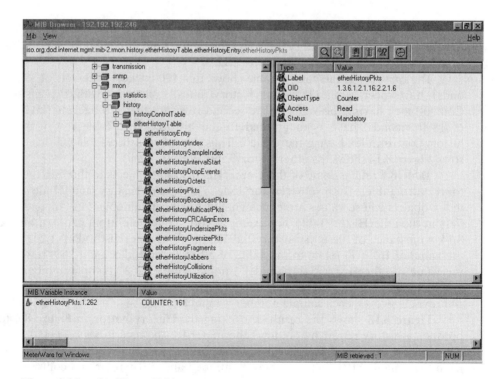

Figure 8.14 etherHistoryTable

Table 8.4 Connection between etherHistoryTable and historyControlTable Objects

Object	Description
etherHistoryIndex	• Identifies etherHistoryTable rows with a row in the historyControlTable. • etherHistoryIndex = historyControlIndex • It is an Index object for the etherHistoryTable
etherHistorySampleIndex	• etherHistoryIndex and etherHistorySampleIndex taken together identify the buckets to associate with a row in the historyControlTable • It is an Index object for the etherHistoryTable
etherHistoryIntervalStart	• The value of sysUpTime object in the Systems group at the start of the sample interval
etherHistoryDropEvents	• The number of times it was detected that the monitor dropped a packet due to lack of resources.

errors to report. The network manager can use such reports to correlate high traffic with time of day. For example, although the packet rate at 19:14 is only about 11 packets/sec, it is more than twice as high as the average packet rate. One might want to investigate the reason for this.

Let's do a little calculation relative to the peak utilization of 0.3 % that we see in the upper graph.

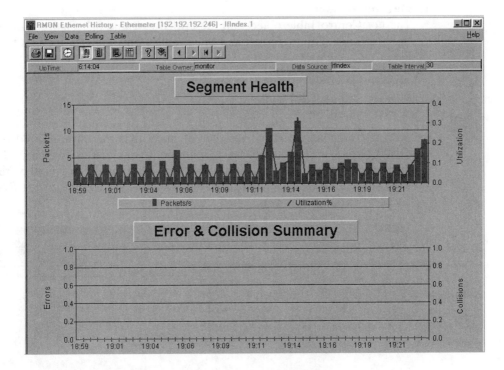

Figure 8.15 Ethermeter 30-second-sample History Report

1. The typical packet captured during the sampling intervals was about 300 octets.
2. The peak number of packets/sec is about 12 packets/sec.
3. At 8 bits/octet, the number of bits/sec = $300 \times 8 \times 12 = 28{,}800$ bits/sec.
4. Utilization = bits per sec./link speed = 28,800bits per sec/10MBps = 0.0029 or 0.29%, which is what the graph shows.

Thus, the peak traffic is only about what a 28.8Kb/s modem supports.

Now let's continue our investigation of the RMON1 groups with the Host Group.

8.1.3 Host Group

The Host group objects identify traffic statistics with the host that is detected on the subnet. This is the first group we have discussed to make the connection between traffic and host. Having this data, one can now ask questions like "Why is host X transmitting so many packets compared to other hosts on the subnet?" **Figure 8.16** shows the objects in the Host Group. There are four tables in this group: the hostControlTable, the hostTable, the hostTimeTable and the hostControl2Table. The last table was added by RMON2 and will be discussed in Chapter 9. We look at the hostControlTable first in **Figure 8.17**

a. hostControlTable

The hostControlTable objects are described in **Table 8.5**. **Figure 8.18** shows the hostControlTable objects and their values. This table introduces the objects:

$$\textbf{hostControlTableSize} = 11$$
$$\textbf{hostControlLastDeleteTime} = 0$$

hostControlTableSize is the number of hosts that have transmitted or received frames on the subnet since Ethermeter was first "powered up." This number is determined by counting distinct MAC addresses in the frames read. hostControlLastDeleteTime is the value of sysUpTime in the System

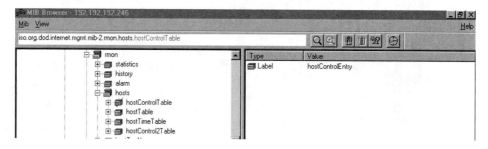

Figure 8.16   Host Group objects

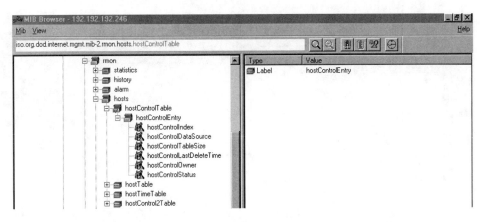

Figure 8.17   hostControlTable objects

group of mib-2 at which a row in the hostTable was deleted. There have been no deletions so this value is 0. The value of the object hostControlIndex on the far right cannot be seen without scrolling. Its value is 1. **Figure 8.19** shows the **hostTable** objects.

b. hostTable

Three objects in the hostTable needing definition are shown in **Table 8.6**. The rest of the object values in hostTable are the statistics collected for each host. By highlighting hostAddress in the MIB Browser and clicking the GetRequest button at the top right of the screen, we get the listing, shown in the bottom panel of **Figure 8.19**. The values on the right are detected host MAC addresses in hexadecimal notation. This is a complicated but useful listing because it enables us to examine SNMP object instance identification. Let's look at the second item in the list as an example.

Table 8.5   hostControlTable Objects

Object	Description
hostControlIndex	• An integer that identifies a row in hostControlTable and the probe interface to the subnet
hostControlDataSource	• An integer that identifies the probe interface to the subnet. It is equal to the value of ifIndex in the ifTable in mib-2
hostControlTableSize	• The number of rows (hosts) in the hostTable detected on hostControlDataSource
hostControlLastDeleteTime	• The value of sysUpTime at which an entry in the hostTable was deleted • Agent does deletion if monitor resources become scarce • Information is needed by hostTimeTable
hostControlOwner	• The creator of the hostControlTable row
hostControlStatus	• As we have seen in other control tables, the status must be set to valid(1) in order for the probe to collect data for the hostTable.

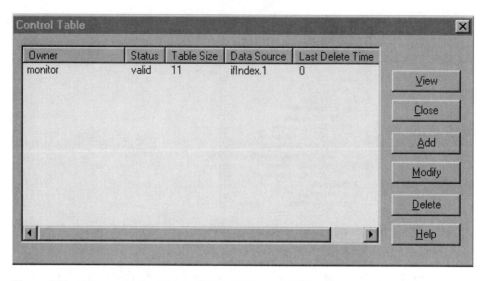

Figure 8.18   Ethermeter hostControlTable Objects and Values

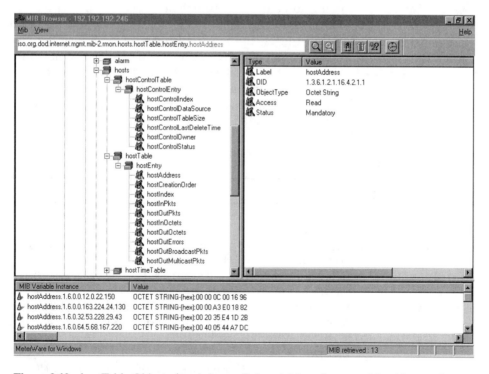

Figure 8.19   hostTable Objects (top left panel); hostAddress Instance Identifiers and Values (bottom panel)

Table 8.6 hostTable Object Descriptions

Object	Description
host Address	• The MAC address of the host
hostCreationOrder	• An integer between 1 and hostControlTableSize specifying the order in time in which the host was detected on the interface. The smaller the integer, the earlier the host was detected
hostIndex	• All hosts detected on the same interface have the same integer value, i.e., hostIndex = hostControlIndex

MIB Variable Instance	Value
hostAddress.1.6.0.0.163.224.24.130	Octet String (hex) 00 00 A3 E0 18 82

The value on the right is the MAC hostAddress expressed in hex as usual. hostAddress is an Index object used in object instance identifiers of hostTable values The other Index object is hostIndex. This is 1 for the Ethermeter interface. The other two things we need to know are: 1) a MAC address Index object expressed in decimal notation, and 2) the prefix to this decimal notation. The prefix is the number of octets in the MAC address. In the case of Ethernet addresses, the prefix is 6. Thus, we can breakdown the MIB Variable Instance Identifier shown above in **Table 8.7**.

The object identifier for hostAddress is 1.3.6.1.2.1.16.4.2.1.1. Thus, the complete instance identifier for the hostAddress in the first row of the hostTable is:

1.3.6.1.2.1.16.4.2.1.1.1.6.0.0.163.224.24.130.

It is certainly nice to have an NMS graphical interface, such as Meterware's MIB Browser, so that we are not required to type such detailed arguments into SNMP GetRequest commands. **Figure 8.20** shows the other table in the Host Group, the **hostTimeTable**.

c. hostTimeTable

The hostTimeTable contains the same objects as the hostTable. The reason for its existence is to make use of a different Index object, **the hostTime-CreationOrder,** rather than hostAddress. This enables the appearance of new hosts on the subnetwork to be easily recognized by the Management Station. **Table 8.8** describes some hostTimeTable objects.

The Index Objects for the hostTimeTable are hostTimeCreationOrder and hostTimeIndex. Highlighting hostTimeAddress and then clicking the GetRequest

Table 8.7 Instance Identifier for the hostTable MIB Variable "hostAddress"

Column Object Name	hostIndex	hostAddress (decimal)
hostAddress	1	6.0.0.163.224.24.130

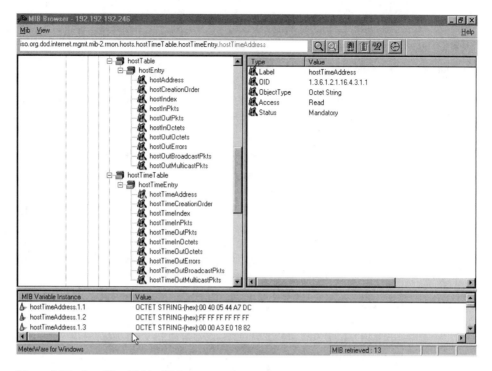

Figure 8.20 hostTimeTable Objects

button on the top right of the screen, the MIB Variable Instance Identifiers and their values are displayed in the bottom panel of **Figure 8.20**. Notice that the second index in the MIB Variable Instance identifier is now an integer, the hostTime-CreationOrder, rather than hostAddress as in the hostTable.

If there are so many hosts on the subnet that probe memory resources are being depleted, the probe will use hostTimeCreationOrder to drop hosts from the list of hosts it maintains. The host dropped first will be that least recently used. This will cause the value of the Index object hostTimeCreationOrder for other hosts to decrease. Thus, the Management Station could use the wrong instance identifier for

Table 8.8 hostTimeTable Objects

Object	Description
hostTimeAddress	• The MAC address of the host
hostTimeCreationOrder	• An integer between 1 and hostControlTableSize specifying the order in time in which the host was identified on the interface. The smaller the integer, the earlier the host was detected • Index object for the hostTimeTable
hostTimeIndex	• All hosts detected on the same interface have the same value. • Index object for the hostTimeTable • hostTimeIndex = hostIndex = hostControlIndex

the value it wanted. To protect against this, it monitors the hostControlLastDelete-Time object value in the hostTable. If it has not downloaded a complete hostTable since that time, it must do so in order to keep the hostTable in sync.

Now let's look at how Meterware displays the hostTable. Returning to **Figure 8.6** and clicking the Host icon, produces the screen shown in **Figure 8.21**. This screen provides a convenient display of all host activity on subnet 192.192.192.240. For each host it displays: Status (St), MAC address, number of transmitted packets, number of transmitted bytes, number of received packets, number of received bytes, number of packet errors, number of packets broadcast and number of packets multicast since the time the host was first detected. The list is sorted according to which host has the largest statistics indicated by the down-arrow. The list can be sorted for other columns also. This listing provides a quick look at who is putting how much traffic on the network. The Address column is the name of the device if that has been resolved, an IP address or the MAC address. If MAC address, sometimes the "vendor" part of the address, the first six hexadecimal digits, will be displayed.

If the display has a blue ellipse in the status (St) column, it means not enough information about the device has been collected yet by polling it. If the status is green, the device is answering most polls for statistical data. If the status is red, the device is not responding. If the status is yellow, the device has not recently sent or received packets.

RMON Host - Ethermeter [192.192.192.246] - IfIndex: 1

File View Polling Table   Help

UpTime: 3:26:31   Table Owner: monitor   Data Source: ifIndex

St	Address	MAC Address	Out Packets↓	Out Bytes	In Packets	In Bytes	Errors	Broadcast	Multicast
○	Router1-3	00000c-001696	12698	4080308	10602	4176439	0	439	1238
○	Switch2-25	005050-e0f559	6374	417161	0	0	0	0	6374
○	192.192.192.244	005050-e0f540	5279	2522357	5267	2302103	0	3	0
○	Ethermeter	0000a3-e01882	2795	640039	2788	586311	0	2	0
○	Server-2	002035-e41d2b	1733	413029	1637	371353	0	140	108
○	WS2-3	004005-44a7dc	1014	247757	909	311539	0	375	0
○	Hub	08004e-07b7e6	936	409959	931	364410	0	16	0
○	0180c2-00004f	0180c2-000000	0	0	6169	394816	0	0	0
○	01000c-cccccc	01000c-cccccc	0	0	205	22345	0	0	0
◉	030000-000001	030000-000001	0	0	101	13759	0	0	0
○	DODINET.000118	01005e-000118	0	0	7	453	0	0	0
○	DODINET.000005	01005e-000005	0	0	1238	101516	0	0	0
○	broadcast	ffffff-ffffff	0	0	975	85545	0	0	0

*** Waiting to Poll ***   Total: 13

MeterWare for Windows   Port: 1 · Speed: 10 M Index: 1   Interval: 30

Figure 8.21 Hosts Detected by Ethermeter on Subnet 192.192.192.240

You see a host with the name WS2-3. The 3 means that this host has three ports and the information presented is for port 3 or ifIndex.3. This is the Ethernet interface for WS2. Likewise, the switches on the demonstration network have 27 ports and you see a host with the name Switch2-25 referring to port 25 or ifIndex.25. Not all of our network devices show in this figure because some have not been turned on. Some hosts shown in this figure are not directly related to devices on our demonstration network. For example, the Address 030000-000001 is the address of Master Browser on this network. The Addresses starting with DODINET refer to hardware addresses on root Domain Name Service (DNS) servers of the Internet. These appear here because SERVER, the DNS server on this network has not been able to resolve a DNS request for an IP address. It has tried to contact a root server to do so by sending a DNS packet to Router2, the default router. Broadcast is the sum of all broadcast packets received by a device. You can combine the information in this view with frames captured using the capture and filter groups discussed below to do a superb job of monitoring and troubleshooting your network.

8.1.4 HostTopN Group

This group makes it possible to calculate the rate at which host traffic for one of the variables listed in the hostTable is increasing or decreasing. The data is presented for a specific sampling interval of the Host Group and changes with each sampling interval. As you will see, Meterware provides a convenient table and pie chart from which the network manager can quickly ascertain this information. For each row in the hostTopNControlTable there are N rows in the hostTopNTable, one for each host included in the calculation. N is a configurable number. **Figure 8.22** shows the HostTopN tables. **Table 8.9** describes the hostTopNControlTable objects. **Figure 8.23** shows the Meterware view of the hostTopNControlTable.

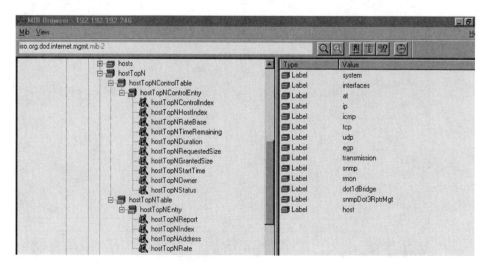

Figure 8.22   HostTopN Tables

Table 8.9 Description of hostTopNControlTable Objects

Object	Description
hostTopNControlIndex	• An integer that identifies a row in the hostTopNControlTable • Each row in that table defines the data that will be reported for N-hosts on one interface
hostTopNHostIndex	• An integer that refers to the interface on which the N-hosts are observed. It is the same for each of the N-hosts • hostTopNHostIndex = hostControlIndex
hostTopNRateBase	• An integer that specifies one of the seven variables in the hostTable to count in the sampling interval to determine the hostTopNRateBase (packets/second in the hostTopNTable) • Choices are: ❑ hostTopNInPkts (1) ❑ hostTopNOutPkts(2) ❑ hostTopNInOctets (3) ❑ hostTopNOutOctets (4) ❑ hostTopNOutErrors (5) ❑ hostTopNOutBroadcastPkts (6) ❑ hostTopNOutMulticastPkts (7)
hostTopNTimeRemaining	• Number of seconds remaining in the sampling interval
hostTopNDuration	• The sampling interval in seconds
hostTopNRequestedSize	• The number of hosts, N, requested to include in the report
hostTopNGrantedSize	• The number of hosts granted
hostTopNStartTime	• sysUpTime when this report sampling was started.
hostTopNOwner	• Monitor or Management Station that creates the row in the hostTopN-ControlTable
hostTopNStatus	• An integer that specifies the status of the control table row • Its values can be either valid (1), createRequest (2) underCreation (3) or invalid (4) • The row creator uses a SetRequest to set the value of this object to createRequest (2) • The agent then sets the value to underCreation(3) until the creator is finished • The creator then sets the value to valid(1)

Note

Because views of hostTopN objects are time-dependent, views may not correspond to one another in time.

We see in **Figure 8.23** that:

topNBaseRate = "In Packets"
Host (hostTopNHostIndex) = 1 and
Index (hostTopNControlIndex) = 175

Index is a number generated by the Ethermeter agent. It identifies a row in the hostTopNControlTable and will not necessarily be a small number. On this screen, the number is large enough that all of it is not shown. It is a unique number. It is the

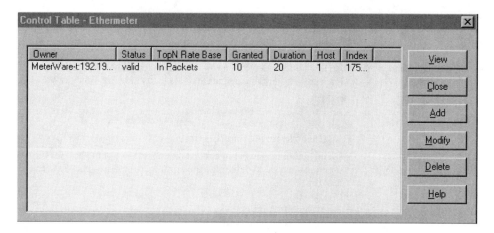

Figure 8.23   Meterware View of hostTopNControlTable Objects and Values

number called index at the bottom right of the Distribution of Top N Object Values that will be shown below. Every time you create a Distribution of Top N Object Values, the agent will generate a new hostTopNControlIndex that is not necessarily ordered sequentially.

Table 8.10 describes the objects in the hostTopNTable. **Figure 8.24** is the Meterware pie chart showing the distribution of the top five hosts based on the "in-packets" rate-base. The pieces of the pie show the "in-packets/sec" during the sampling interval for each of the hosts. Thus the largest was 1 unit/sec for WS2-3, which corresponds to about 20 "in-packets" during the sampling interval of 20 seconds. The traffic for WS2-3, was 38.4% of the total traffic. You can click on the other pieces of the pie to see their traffic percentage. You can click the Modify button on the Control Table screen to change what data are collected or the Add button to create additional pie charts using other hostTopNRateBase choices, for example hostTopNOutErrors (5). A pie chart like this is obviously much more useful on a network with more traffic or for longer sampling intervals.

The Index = 1724 at the bottom is the hostTopNControlIndex. Interval = 20 is the length of the sampling interval in seconds.

To see how the Index objects for the hostTopNTable are used, let's look at a MIB Browser view in **Figure 8.25**.

Table 8.10   Description of hostTopNTable Objects

Object	Description
hostTopNReport	• An integer that identifies the report
	• hostTopNReport = hostTopNControlIndex
hostTopNIndex	• An integer that identifies the data from one host included in the hostTopNReport
hostTopNAddress	• The MAC address associated with the host identified by hostTopNIndex
hostTopNRate	• The amount of change in the hostTopNRateBase in packets/second during the sampling interval.

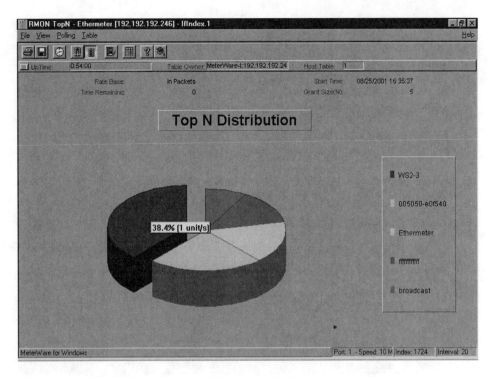

Figure 8.24   Distribution of hostTopN In-Packet Traffic for N=5

The address values listed on the right of the bottom panel are the hosts with the greatest number of "in-packets." MIB Variable Instance Identifiers for those hosts are listed on the left. The Index objects are hostTopNReport and hostTop-NIndex in that order. Therefore, the breakdown of MIB Variable Instance Identifiers as shown in **Table 8.11** where hostTopNReport = hostTopNControlIndex. In other words, the report is for one interface that is identified by 1915 and for the hosts detected on that interface identified by the hostTopNIndex of 1. In this case, there are six hosts being reported. There were probably 10 hosts granted but only six had any traffic.

The Host group and the hostTopNTable objects provided us with information about traffic transmitted and received by individual hosts. Now let's look at the Matrix Group whose objects provide us with information that identifies the specific hosts that are communicating with one another.

8.1.5 Matrix Group

The capability to determine the source and destination of a communication is accomplished by three tables in the Matrix Group. They are shown in **Figure 8.26**.

This group adds another dimension to network management because we will now know which conversations are causing the most traffic, not just which hosts. It is often the case that who is talking to whom is the most important information.

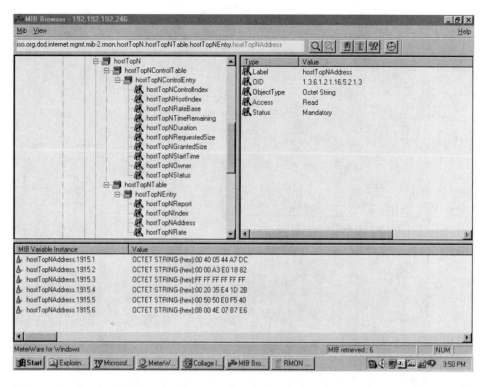

Figure 8.25   hostTopNTable (top left panel) and hostTopNAddress values (bottom panel)

The objects in the **matrixControlTable** are identical to those in the hostControlTable and used for the same purposes. The information in the **matrixSDTable** is identical to that in the **matrixDSTable.** The Index objects for the two tables are also the same. The distinction between these tables is in the order of appending Index objects to the column object name.

In Tables 8.12 and 8.13 we give an example of the logical view of how these tables are used to store probe data for four hosts. The numbers in parentheses in the column headings indicate the order in which the Index objects are appended to the column object name. The letters A,B,C,D represent hosts. In the matrixSDTable, the MAC source address in the detected frame is stored in the first column. The MAC destination address in the frame is stored in the second column. For the same interface, the matrixSDIndex is the same for all rows. Packets, octets and errors for any frame sent from A→B for example, are added to those already in the remaining three columns: matrixSDPkts, matrixSDOctets, and matrixSDErrors.

In the matrixDSTable, the direction of the communication in each row is reversed relative to that in the corresponding row in the matrixSDTable. Thus, columns 1

Table 8.11   Composition of hostTopNAddress MIB Variable Instance Identifiers

hostTopNAddress	hostTopNReport	hostTopNIndex	Value
1.3.6.1.2.1.16.5.2.1.3	1915	1	00 40 05 44 A7 DC

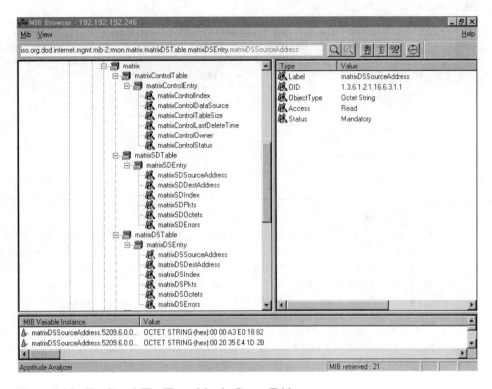

Figure 8.26 Top Panel: The Three Matrix Group Tables

and 2 are interchanged and the source in the matrixSD table becomes the destination in the matrixDSTable. This arrangement makes it easy for the management station to access the reversed direction information. For example if the management station wants conversations from B→A instead of from A→B, it chooses the column object matrixDSDestAddress and reverses the order of matrixSDSourceAddress and matrixDSDestAddress Index objects in the instance identifier field of the GetRequest.

Recognize that **Tables 8.12 and 8.13** provide a logical view of the storage, the probe may actually store all this information in one table and in another order. The only important thing is that the data can be accessed logically and quickly.

Figure 8.27 shows the result of a GetRequest for the matrixSDDestAddress. Meterware uses the GetNextRequest repeatedly to get all instances of this object in lexicographical order. For this example, we are using the Fastmeter interface #3 to the Switch2 monitor port to collect frames on subnet 192.192.192.240.

The results in **Figure 8.27** are a snapshot of all MAC addresses in the destination field of frames detected on Fastmeter interface # 3 connected to the mirror port of Switch2. As **Table 8.12** indicates, the Index object values in the MIB Variable Instance identifier that is highlighted are:

3 = matrixSDIndex
6.0.32.53.228.29.43 = matrixSDSourceAddress
6.0.64.5.68.167.220 = matrixSDDestAddress

Table 8.12 matrixSDTable

matrixSD Source Address (2)	matrixSD DestAddress (3)	matrixSD Index (1)	matrixSD Pkts	matrixSD Octets	matrixSD Errors
A	B				
A	C				
A	D				
B	C				
B	D				
C	D				

This entry in the matrixSDTable was generated by pinging WS2 from SERVER. Clicking the Matrix button on the RMON screen in **Figure 8.20** opens the Management Station application that constructs the view shown in **Figure 8.28** from data in the matrixSDTable and matrixDSTable.

The highlighted conversation is the ping message sent from SERVER to WS2. The conversation just below it contains the response from WS2 to Server.

Sometimes, we need to know more details about frames than what is provided by the RMON Host and Matrix tables. MAC addresses may not be enough to track down a problem. For these more detailed looks into the traffic, we use the Filter and Capture Groups.

8.1.6 Filter and Capture Groups

We talk about these groups together because they are usually used together. The **Capture** Group objects define how a probe captures frames and downloads them from buffers on the probe to buffers on the Management Station for examination. The **Filter** Group enables the user to select what types of frames should be captured. When there is high traffic, this selective approach makes finding frames of interest easier and reserves buffer space for those frames. We will spend a considerable

Table 8.13 matrixDSTable

matrixDS Source Address (3)	matrixDS DestAddress (2)	matrixDS Index (1)	matrixDS Pkts	matrixDS Octets	matrixDS Errors
B	A				
C	A				
D	A				
C	B				
D	B				
D	C				

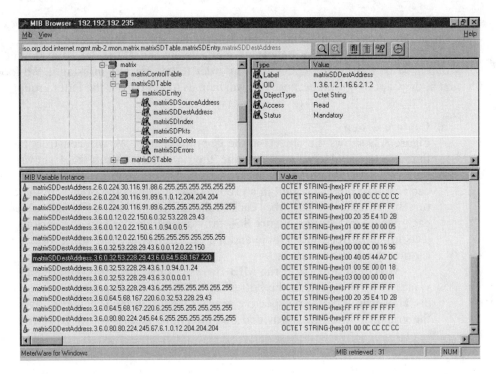

Figure 8.27 matrixSDDestAddress Instance Identifiers and Values

St	Source	SRC MAC	Destination	DST MAC	Pkts↓	Octets	Errors
○	WS2-3	004005-44a7dc	broadcast	ffffff-ffffff	401	31955	0
○	Router2-3	00000c-001696	DODINET.000005	01005e-000005	388	31885	1
○	Server-2	002035-e41d2b	WS2-3	004005-44a7dc	387	158521	0
○	WS2-3	004005-44a7dc	Server-2	002035-e41d2b	383	145136	1
○	Router2-3	00000c-001696	broadcast	ffffff-ffffff	154	10756	0
○	Server-2	002035-e41d2b	broadcast	ffffff-ffffff	129	19464	0
○	Server-2	002035-e41d2b	030000-000001	030000-000001	106	12489	0
○	Switch2-3	005050-e0f543	01000c-cccccc	01000c-cccccc	65	7020	0
●	Server-2	002035-e41d2b	Router2-3	00000c-001696	46	3484	0
●	Router2-3	00000c-001696	Server-2	002035-e41d2b	19	1406	0
●	XYZ.e0f540	005050-e0f540	broadcast	ffffff-ffffff	4	256	0
●	Server-2	002035-e41d2b	dodinet	01005e-000118	4	258	0

*** Waiting to Poll ***   Total: 12

Figure 8.28 Pairwise Traffic between Hosts Observed on Fastmeter Interface #3 Connected to Switch2 Mirror Port

amount of time on these groups for two reasons: 1) the capture of packets provides a tremendous amount of information that is not obtainable in any other way. Thus, it is worth knowing the details of how to do it effectively and 2) the details of the filter group must be thoroughly understood in order to be effective in using it. We look first at the Capture group because this will help us to appreciate the Filter group.

a. Capture Group

Figure 8.29 shows the objects in the Capture Group. We will construct tables that list these objects and describe their purposes. **Table 8.14** shows the bufferControlTable for the Capture Group. There is one row in this table for each capture buffer created in a probe. **Table 8.15** lists the objects in the captureBufferTable and describes each of them. There is one row in this table for each packet in a buffer. **Figure 8.30** provides an idea of how the various objects in the bufferControlTable and the captureBufferTable work together to capture the desired packets.

We could now go to the MIB Browser views shown in **Figure 8.29**, set values of MIB objects in the bufferControlTable, and begin to capture packets. However, a better perspective of what we are doing is achieved by using the graphical interfaces provided by Meterware. Access to the RMON Cap-

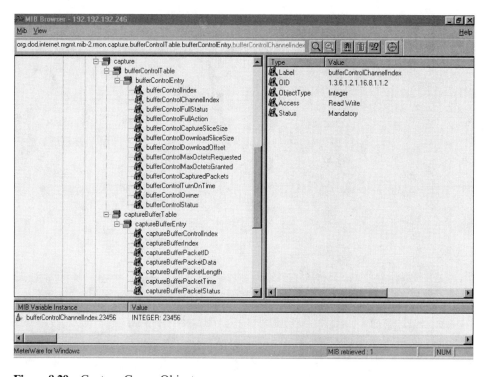

Figure 8.29 Capture Group Objects

Table 8.14   bufferControlTable

Object	Description
bufferControlIndex	• The integer that identifies a row in the bufferControlTable • There is one buffer for each defined channel • A channel is defined by the filter(s) that are applied to determine which packets are captured in the buffer
bufferControlChannelIndex	• An integer that identifies the channel that is supplying the buffer with packets
bufferControlFullStatus	• A Status value of (1) means space is available in the buffer • If the value is (2), the buffer is full
bufferControlFullAction	• A value of (1) means the buffer is locked when full and will accept no further packets • A value of (2) means the buffer will wrap and discard old packets to make room for new
bufferControlCaptureSliceSize	• Maximum number of octets in each packet that will be captured in the buffer
bufferControlDownloadSliceSize	• Maximum number of octets in the buffer that will be downloaded to the management station in a single SNMP GetResponse
bufferControlDownloadOffset	• The offset, in octets, of the first octet that will be retrieved in a single SNMP GetResponse
bufferControlMaxOctetsRequested	• The size of buffers, in octets, requested by the management station
bufferControlMaxOctetsGranted	• Number of buffer octets granted by the probe agent
bufferControlCapturedPackets	• Number of packets currently in the buffer
bufferControlTurnOnTime	• The value of sysUpTime (System Group object) when this buffer was first turned on
bufferControlOwner	• The creator of the buffer (see Control Table)
bufferControlStatus	• An integer that specifies the status of the row • Its values can be either valid (1), createRequest (2) underCreation (3) or invalid (4). • The row creator uses a SetRequest to set the value of this object to createRequest (2) • The agent then sets the value to underCreation(3) until the creator is finished • The creator then sets the value to valid(1).

ture Group interface is obtained from **Figure 8.20**, the RMON tab. Click the Capture button to get the screen shown in **Figure 8.31**. The center panel shows that we can create up to 10 channels. We create a channel by highlighting it and clicking the Edit button to get the screen shown in **Figure 8.32**.

The name of Channel 0 at the top of the figure is the IP address of the Management Station, WS2 in this case. If you compare the choices on this screen with the bufferControlTable objects in **Table 8.14**, you will see that **Figure 8.32** provides a convenient way to set values of those objects. Usually the default values are satisfactory. The Filter Criteria provides an option to Accept or Reject a packet that satisfies the Filter. We will discuss this later.

Table 8.15 captureBufferTable

Object	Description
captureBufferControlIndex	An integer that identifies the buffer that holds this packet. It has the same value as the bufferControlIndex that identifies the buffer
captureBufferIndex	The integer that uniquely identifies this packet
captureBufferPacketID	The integer that identifies the order in which packets were received on the interface regardless of the buffer in which stored.
captureBufferPacketData	The actual packet data
captureBufferPacketLength	The actual length of the packet in octets
captureBufferPacketTime	The number of milliseconds from the time the buffer was turned on until this packet was captured
captureBufferPacketStatus	A number that represents the number of errors detected in the packet. See RFC 1271 for details about how this number is calculated.

The Event button provides a screen that allows configuration of an event to take place if this channel receives a certain packet. We will discuss this during examination of the Event group.

To create a channel with the default values shown, click the Create button that produces the screen shown in **Figure 8.33**. Here you see: 1) the Status of channel 0 is "Stopped," meaning that no packets are being captured by this channel; 2) the buffer size of 16,896 octets requested in **Figure 8.32** has been granted; and 3) the whole buffer is currently available.

Notice that the Create button has changed to an Attach button. This allows you to attach a filter to the channel that was created before. Clicking the Free button will free up the memory resources reserved by the agent for the channel. Clicking the Run button will start the capture process. Clicking the tabs at the bottom of **Figure 8.33** does the following:

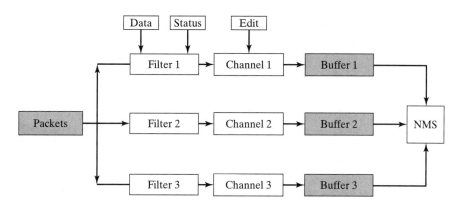

Figure 8.30 Capturing the Desired Packets on the Subnet

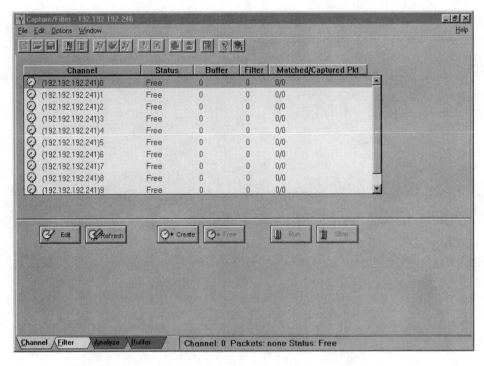

Figure 8.31   Capture/Filter Channels for Ethermeter

Figure 8.32   Channel Edit Screen

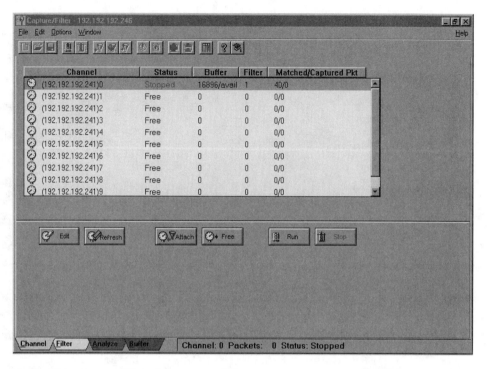

Figure 8.33 Capture/Filter Channels for Ethermeter (192.192.192.246) after editing the channel

- **Filter Tab**—opens the screen where filters for a channel can be constructed.
- **Buffer Tab**—opens the screen where the packets that are captured and the protocols they contain are shown. We have seen some of these in Chapters 6 and 7.
- **Analyze Tab**—opens a screen where captured packets can be more precisely filtered for specific analyses.

The way channel 0 is configured at this moment, if capturing were started by clicking the Run button, all packets seen by Ethermeter on interface ifIndex.1 would be captured until the requested buffer was full. This is a perfectly acceptable approach because the captured packets can be scanned by the user and the ones of interest examined. This is what we did in previous chapters. However, packets of interest may be missed if this method is used if the buffer becomes full. That leads us to the subject of filtering. We will come back to the Channel, Buffer and Analyze tabs later.

b. Filter Group

As we have done in previous sections, a good way to start the discussion of the Filter Group is to look at its objects. This group contains two tables: the **filterTable** and the **channelTable**. The MIB Browser shows the objects in these tables in **Figure 8.34**. **Table 8.16** is a listing of the filterTable objects and their description.

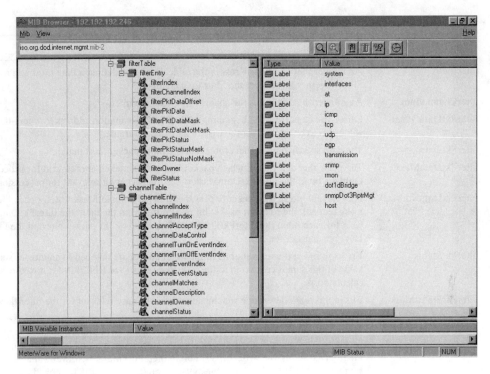

Figure 8.34 Filter Group Objects

We now construct a similar table for the channelTable objects. Each row in the channelTable, **Table 8.17**, defines one channel.

captureBufferPacketData Object

Tables 8.14 through **8.17** describe the objects we need to know about to capture packets effectively. However, these tables provide so much information that it may be helpful to put their objects in a logical order, which might actually be used in practice. Whether you use them in the MIB Browser or you use the graphical filter and channel interfaces, you still have to have a procedure for using them effectively. We provide such a procedure, with example, in **Table 8.18**. The on-line User Guide that comes with Meterware is also very helpful here.

A principal goal of **Table 8.18** is to show how the user's actions when using Meterware's graphical interfaces relate to the capture/filter objects. The steps in the procedure seem rather laborious in the beginning but they become second nature and are quickly implemented after you have used the graphical interfaces and the MIB Browser for a little while. Figures 8.35 through 8.38 are referenced there.

A number of interesting things can be learned from examining the buffer screen created by clicking the Buffer tab. This screen is shown in **Figure 8.39**. First, from the top panel, it looks like the filters have worked correctly, capturing only packets to and from WS2-3 and Ethermeter. To see how many packets were captured, we can expand the top panel summary as shown in **Figure 8.40**.

Table 8.16   filterTable Objects

Object	Description
filterIndex	An integer that identifies a row in the table. Each row defines a data filter and a status filter. Together these form the filter for a channel.
filterChannelIndex	An integer that identifies the channel that uses the filter.
filterPktDataOffset	Offset, in octets, from the beginning of the MAC destination address to where the filter will begin to be applied for the case of an Ethernet frame.
filterPktData	The data specified in the data filter that the input packet must match.
filterPktDataMask	The mask that determines which packet bits to be matched are relevant for processing. Only if a bit in the filterPktDataMask is 1 is the packet bit relevant for processing.
filterPktDataNotMask	For relevant bits in the packet to pass the filterPktDataNotMask test, for each bit in this mask that is 1, the relevant packet bit must differ from the bit in the filterPktData. Likewise, for each bit in the filterPktDataNotMask that is 0, the packet bits and the filterPktData bits must differ.
filterPktStatus	Errors found in the relevant bits of the input packet are mapped to an integer sum. The value of this sum is compared to the filterPktStatus. (See RFC2819 for how the sum is calculated.)
filterPktStatusMask	Bits in this mask determine which packet input bits are relevant for the filterPktStatus test.
filterPktStatusNotMask	For the relevant bits in the input packet to pass the filterPktStatusNotMask test, for each bit in this mask that is 1, the bits in the integer sum must all differ from the bits in the filterPktStatus. Likewise, for each bit in the filterPktStatusNotMask that is 0, the sum bits and the filterPktStatus bits must differ. (See RFC 2819 for how the sum is calculated.)
filterOwner	The entity that configured this table. It could be the probe agent or the Management Station.
filterStatus	• An integer that specifies the status of the row. • Its values can be either valid (1), createRequest (2) underCreation (3) or invalid (4) • The row creator uses a SetRequest to set the value of this object to createRequest (2) • The agent then sets the value to underCreation(3) until the creator is finished • The creator then sets the value to valid(1).

There are 28 packets and indeed, they all satisfy the filters we built. All packets from WS2-3 to Ethermeter, except the last, are SNMP GetRequest packets that are polling Ethermeter for values of various objects. All packets from Ethermeter to WS2-3 are GetResponse SNMP packets returning the current values of the requested objects.

Figure 8.41 shows much of the content of the SNMP PDU in frame #2. The first item of interest is that the community string used by WS2 is public. Public is the correct READ community string for Ethermeter. WS2 obtained this information from the device database that was built for each device shown in Summary View. What are shown are requests for values of channelTable objects.

Figure 8.42 shows the content of the SNMP PDU in frame #3, a GetResponse to WS2 from Ethermeter. We see that the community string used in this PDU is public which is the READ community string configured for WS2. Values of the channelTable objects are returned to the NMS on WS2.

Table 8.17   channelTable Objects

Object	Description
channelIndex	An integer that identifies one row in the table. A row corresponds to a channel.
channelIfindex	An integer that identifies the interface through which the monitor is receiving packets. The value of channelIfindex is the same as the value of ifIndex for this interface in the mib-2 ifTable.
channelAcceptType	The value of this object determines how the filters for the channel are to function. There are two possible integer values: **acceptMatched (1)** and **acceptFailed (2)**. If the value is set to 1, the packet must pass both the data and status filters associated with the channel to be accepted by the channel, If the value is set to (2), the packet will be accepted by the channel only if it fails either the data or status filter associated with the channel.
channelDataControl	There are two possible integer values: **on (1)** and **off (2)**. The channel must be "on" for data, status and events to "flow through" the channel.
channelTurnOnEventIndex	An integer that identifies the event in the Event group that will turn the channelDataControl from **off to on** when the event occurs. **channelTurnOnEventIndex** has the same value as the **eventIndex** object in the Event Group (to be discussed) that identifies the same event. In other words, if the event associated with eventIndex occurs, channelDataControl is turned on and the channel **passes** filtered packets.
channelTurnOffEventIndex	An integer that identifies the event in the Event group that will turn the channelDataControl from **on to off** when the event occurs. **channelTurnOffEventIndex** has the same value as the **eventIndex** object in the Event Group that identifies the same event. In other words, if the event associated with eventIndex occurs, channelDataControl is turned off and the channel passes no further packets.
channelEventIndex	An integer that identifies the event that is generated when the channelDataControl is on and the packet is matched. **channelEventIndex** has the same value as **eventIndex** in the Event Group.
channelEventStatus	There are three possible integer values for this object: **eventReady (1); eventFired (2); and eventAlwaysReady (3)**. If the value is 1, a single event may be generated and then the probe will set the value to 2. No further events may be generated until this object is reset to 1. If the value of the object is 3, events may continue to be generated.
channelMatches	The number of times a packet matches this channel. The number of matches continues to be updated even if channelDataControl is set to off.
channelDescription	Comments about the channel.
channelOwner	The entity that configured the channel such as a Management Station.
channelStatus	• An integer that specifies the status of the row. • Its values can be either valid (1); createRequest (2); underCreation (3); or invalid (4). • The row creator uses a SetRequest to set the value of this object to createRequest (2). • The agent then sets the value to underCreation (3) until the creator is finished. • The creator then sets the value to valid(1).

Table 8.18 Procedure for Use of Filter and Capture Group Objects

Step	Action	Result
1	Double-click device in Summary or Map View	Produces the device information screen
2	Click the RMON button	Provides the graphical interfaces to RMON Groups
3	Click either the Filter or Capture button	Provides the Capture/Filter Channel screen. Here a channel is selected for edit and we begin to set MIB variables.
4	Click the Edit button	The channel Edit screen shown in **Figure 8.32** opens. There we see the first of the objects that can be set. They are: • **Filter Criteria**—channelTable/channelAcceptType • **Action on Full Buffer**—bufferControlTable/bufferControlFullStatus • **Capture Slice Size**—bufferControlTable/bufferControlCaptureSliceSize • **Download Slice Size**—bufferControlTable/bufferControlDownloadSliceSize • **Request Buffer Size**—bufferControlTable/bufferControlMaxOctetsRequested • **Buffer Size Granted**—bufferControlTable/bufferControlMaxOctetsGranted • **Buffer Status**—bufferControlTable/bufferControlStatus The default values are usually acceptable. You can check that these values have been set according to your choices by examining the object values in the MIB Browser.
5	Click the Create button	You are returned to the Capture/Filter Channel screen, Figure 8.33. There you see: • The channel has been given the name 192.192.192.241(0). This is the IP address of the owner of the channel, the Management Station that created it. • The requested buffer size of 16, 896 octets has been granted and it is currently all available. • One filter has been set. This is the default filter: Ethernet-type packets with any framing. • The count of packets that match the filter and the number of these packets that have been captured. No packets have been captured because we have not clicked the Run button. In other words, the channel is not turned on.
6	On Capture/Filter Channel screen, select RMON Tables from Windows menu	Provides a screen showing the RMON Control Table in **Figure 8.35**
7	Highlight Owner and click "View Details" button in **Figure 8.35**	Provides screen shown in **Figure 8.36** containing additional Capture and Filter objects that should be set. These are: • **Owner**—channelTable/channelOwner • **Interface Index**—channelTable/channelIfIndex • **Channel Index**—channelTable/channelIndex • **Status**—channelTable/channelStatus. Valid(1) means the channel has been created. • **Packet Matches**—channelTable/channelMatches • **Accept Type**—channelTable/channelAcceptType • **Data Flow Control**—channelTable/channelDataControl. The channel is "off(2)" which means the Run button on the Capture/Filter has not been clicked. No packets are being captured. • **Turn On Event Index**—channelTable/channelTurnOnEventIndex. There is no event selected to turn channelDataControl from "off(2)" to "on(1)" when the appropriate packet is matched. • **Turn Off Event Index**—channelTable/channelTurnOffEventIndex. There is no event selected to turn channelDataControl from "on(1)" to "off(2)."

Step	Action	Result
		• **Generated Event Index**—channelTable/channelEventIndex. There has been no event configured in the Event Group to be generated by a matched packet. • **Generated Event Status**—channelTable/channelEventStatus. Options are eventReady(1), eventFired(2) or eventAlwaysReady(3).
8	From the Capture/Filter Channel screen, click the Filter Tab	This is our first look at the screen that allows us to set up filters for a channel. Rather than look at all packets, we create a filter that selects packets. The first example is packets from Ethermeter to WS2 and from WS2 to Ethermeter. To build the **first** filter, we select the following choices from the pull down menus in **Figure 8.37**: • **Link Layer**—ifTable/ifType = ethernet-csma (6) • **Protocol**—filterTable/filterPktData = IP = 08 00 h • **Sub-protocol**—filterTable/filterPktData = UDP = 11 h • **Source address**—filterTable/filterPktData = Ethermeter ❑ (MAC) 00 00 a3 e0 18 82 hex ❑ (IP) 192.192.192.246 decimal ❑ (IP) C0 C0 C0 F6 hex • **Destination Address**—filterTable filterPktData = WS2-3 ❑ (MAC) 00 40 05 44 a7 dc hex ❑ (IP) 192.192.192.241 decimal ❑ (IP) C0 C0 C0 F1 hex filterPktData is the data part of the filter that is to be matched to the incoming packet. The above selections built this object as the text boxes were completed from the pull down menus and the adjacent (✓) was clicked. This process also enters the data in the middle panel and locates it where it is in the Ethernet II frame. • **Allow Packets**—filterTable/filterPktStatus = Any Packets = 0 To build the **second** filter, the data in **Figure 8.37** is modified to what is shown in **Figure 8.38** and then the "Modify" button is clicked to set the new values. Now any packets that satisfy data and status sub-filters of either filter built in these two figures will be captured.
9	Click the Run button on the Capture/Filter Channel Screen	• **Run**—channelTable/channelDataControl = on(1)
10	Click the Stop Button on the Capture/Filter screen	• **Stop**—channelTable/channelDataControl = off(2)
11	Select the Buffer tab	• Review the content of captured packets.

Figure 8.43 shows the content of the SNMP PDU in frame #28, the last frame captured. This PDU is a SetRequest from WS2 to Ethermeter. The first thing to notice is that the community string is private. This is the Ethermeter WRITE community string that is required in a Set Request. The other point is that the value of channelDataControl is 2. Thus when the Stop button on the Capture/Filter screen was clicked, a SetRequest containing the Variable Binding pair, channelDataControl.232|off(2) was sent to Ethermeter. 232 is the value of the channelIndex Index object for the channelTable.

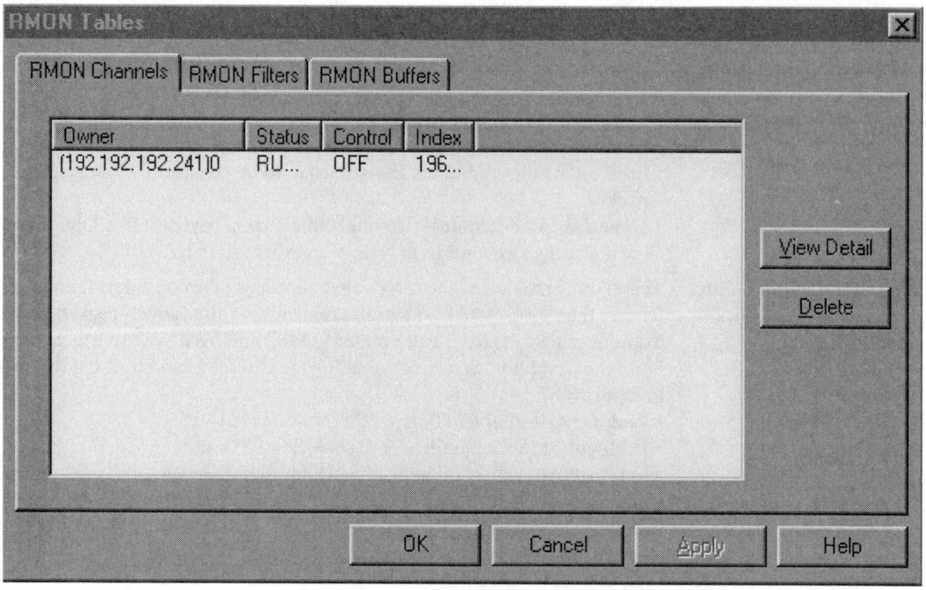

Figure 8.35 RMON Channels

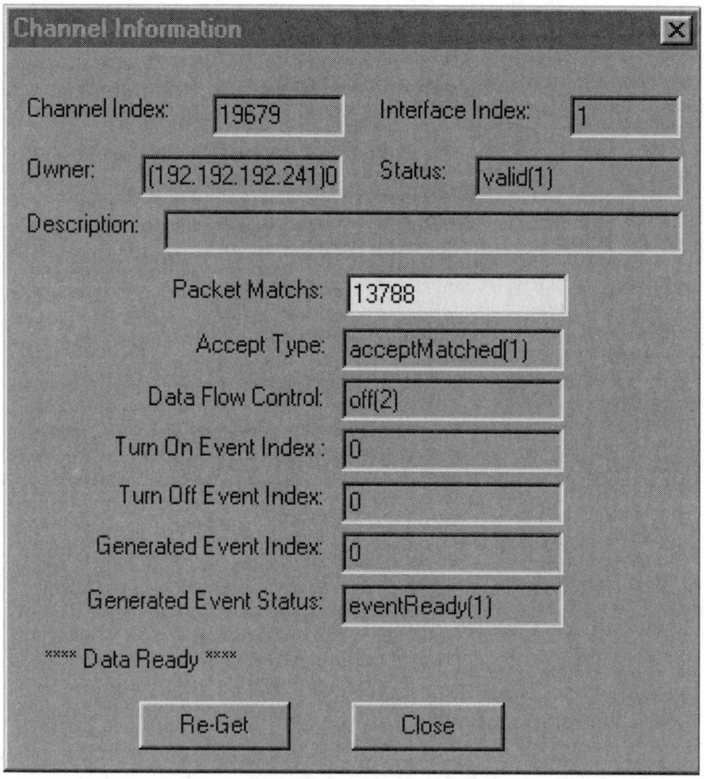

Figure 8.36 Channel Information

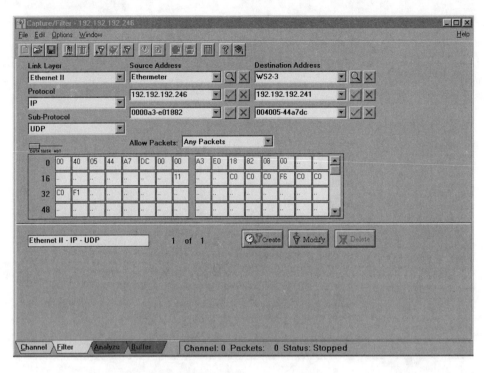

Figure 8.37   Capture/Filter-Filter Screen: Filter #1

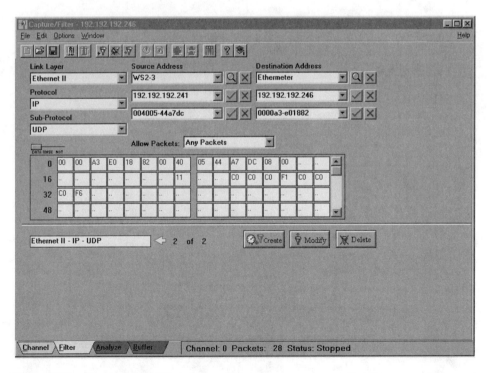

Figure 8.38   Capture/Filter-Filter Screen: Filter #2

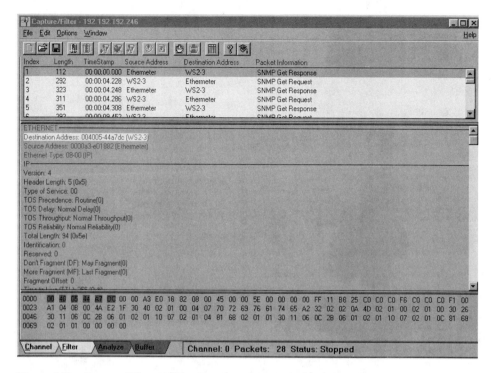

Figure 8.39   Capture/Filter: Buffer Screen - WS2-3/Ethermeter Traffic

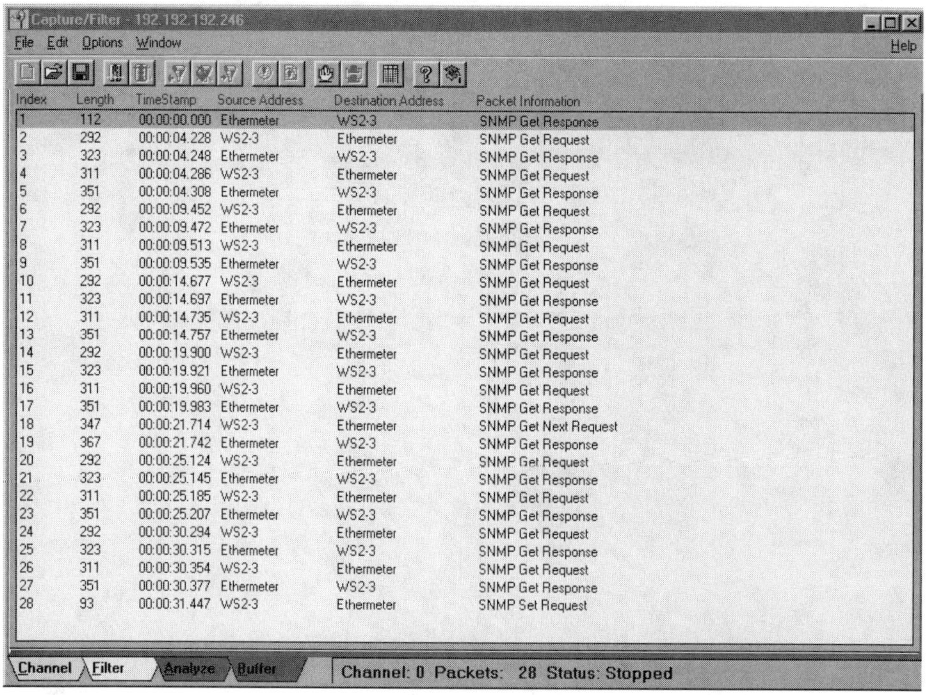

Figure 8.40   All WS2-3/Ethermeter Frames Captured

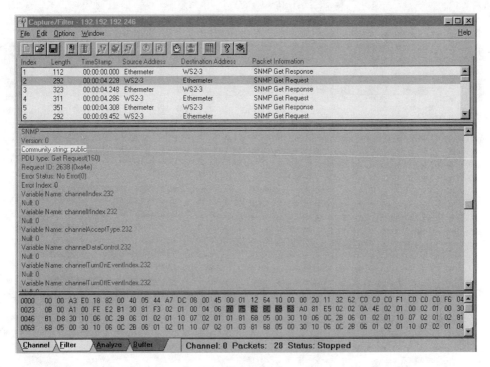

Figure 8.41 Content of SNMP PDU in Frame #2

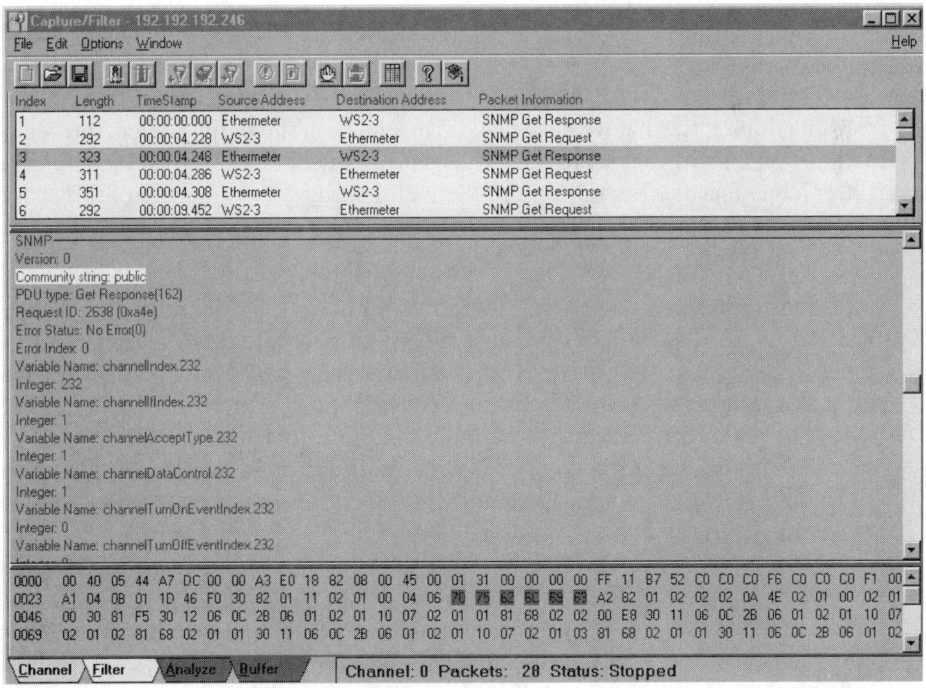

Figure 8.42 Content of SNMP PDU in Frame #3

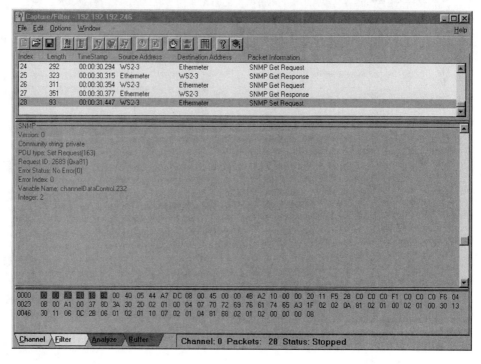

Figure 8.43 Content of SNMP PDU in Frame #28

In addition to what we have just discussed about the buffer screen, further examination would show that it provides values for many bufferControlTable and captureBufferTable objects. You will explore them in the exercises at the end of this chapter.

8.1.7 Analysis of Captured Frames

Captured frames can be further filtered using the screen obtained by clicking the Analyze tab. In **Figure 8.44**, we have shown an example. The lower right window displays the frame (#10 out of 28) that has been selected from the captured frames summary shown on the buffer screen. The top right text boxes allow the user to build a protocol for further filtering. We continue to select the Ethernet II frame and the IP and UDP protocols so there is no other protocol filtering. Clicking the (√) adjacent to the top text box, adds the selection to the expression window on the top left of the screen.

Now suppose we want to filter UDP packets that have a two-octet **length** field with the value **00 fe** h. The simplest way to do that is to find a frame on the buffer screen that has that UDP PDU length, highlight it so that it appears in the lower right window of the Analyze screen, click on the length and it appears in the Data Build text box in the upper left. Next click the adjacent (√) which adds the length to the expression window.

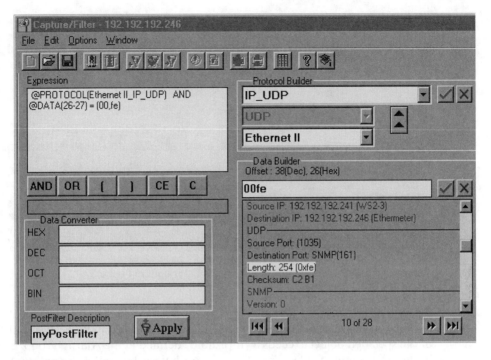

Figure 8.44 Analyze Screen

We must also insert an AND logic operator in between the first and second expressions so that only packets that meet both criteria are selected. We do that by clicking the AND button. Then click the Apply button, button left, and the frames that meet both criteria appear in the top panel on the buffer screen. As you see, there are only six frames in **Figure 8.45** that match the new filter built in **Figure 8.44**.

You can now see that using the capture and filter groups, combined with the analyze screen allows one, with patience, to focus down on frames with some very specific characteristics.

There are two other RMON groups that we must discuss because of their value to network troubleshooting. These are the Alarm Group and the Event Group. The Alarm and Event groups can be considered action groups that produce responses to values of objects that occur in other RMON groups. Configuring Alarms and associated Events that result in trap messages being sent to the network manager is the principal mechanism of Fault Management. We will start our discussion with the Alarm Group.

8.1.8 Alarm Group

Figure 8.46 shows the objects in the Alarm Group. This group consists of one table, the alarmTable. Generally speaking, the values of objects in the Alarm table having

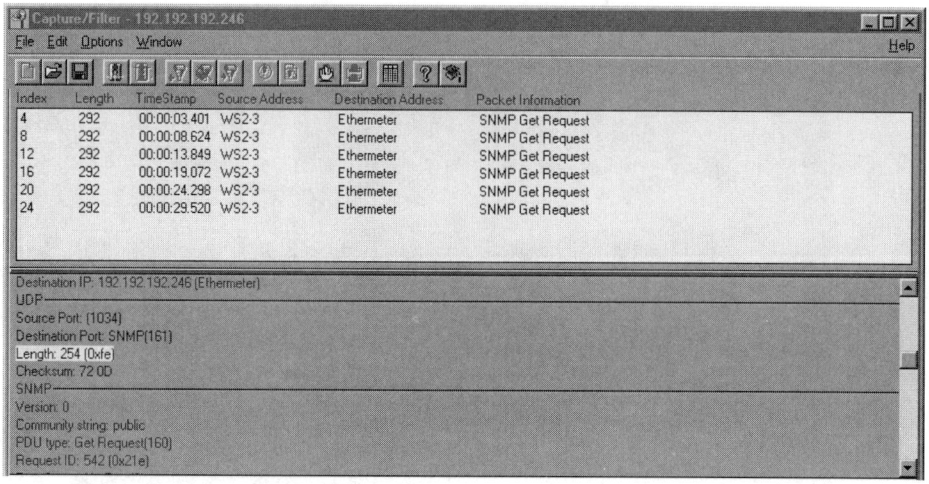

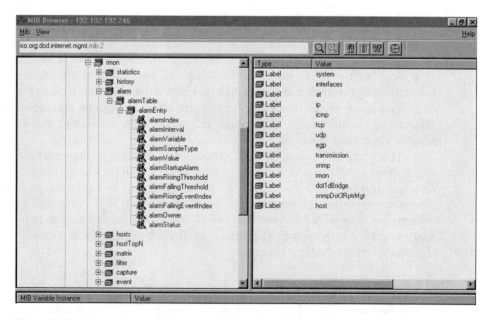

Figure 8.45 Captured Frames Matching the Filter built in Figure 8.44

"threshold" in their names are compared by the RMON agent to values of objects in other groups and an alarm packet is sent to the Management Station if the value of the specified object exceeds a "threshold" defined in the Alarm Group. Each row in the Alarm table is identified 1) by a threshold value and 2) by an object that is sampled for a specified interval. **Table 8.19** describes the objects in the Alarm table.

Now let's relate the Alarm Group objects to the Event Group Objects.

Figure 8.46 Alarm Group Objects

Table 8.19 Alarm Table Objects

Object	Description
alarmIndex	An integer that identifies a row in the table
alarmInterval	The time interval over which the variable is sampled
alarmVariable	The object identifier of the variable to be sampled
alarmSampleType	There are two types: • absoluteValue (1)—value of object is compared directly with the threshold. • deltaValue (2)—difference between values of object after current sample and last sample is compared to the threshold.
alarmValue	• The value of the object sampled at the end of the last sampling period
alarmStartupAlarm	There are three types: • risingAlarm(1)—is generated if the first sample after the row becomes "valid" equals or exceeds the alarmRisingThreshold. • fallingAlarm(2)—is generated if the first sample after the row becomes "valid" is less than or equal to the alarmFallingThreshold • risingOrFallingAlarm(3)—is generated if either of the thresholds are violated
alarmRisingThreshold	• The rising threshold is exceeded by the variable
alarmFallingThreshold	• The falling threshold is greater than the variable
alarmRisingEventIndex	• The value of this object is employed when the alarmRisingThreshold is crossed • This value is the same as an eventIndex object in the eventTable. Thus, the alarmRisingEventIndex will trigger an event in the eventTable
alarmFallingEventIndex	• The value of this object is employed when the alarmFallingThreshold is crossed • This value is the same as an eventIndex object in the eventTable. Thus the alarmFallingEventIndex will trigger an event in the eventTable
alarmOwner	• Monitor or Management Station that created a row in the alarmTable
alarmStatus	• An integer that specifies the status of the row. • Its values can be either valid (1), createRequest (2) underCreation (3) or invalid (4) • The row creator uses a SetRequest to set the value of this object to createRequest (2) • The agent then sets the value to underCreation(3) until the creator is finished • The creator then sets the value to valid(1)

8.1.9 Event Group

Figure 8.47 shows the objects in the Event group. The Event group consists of two tables: the **eventTable** and the **logTable**. This group is used to define events that can be triggered by objects in the Alarm group. Events can also trigger actions defined elsewhere.

Table 8.20 lists and describes the objects in the eventTable and the logTable. The principal mechanism for an event in the eventTable to cause an action is the trap message. The trap message must be configured to do this. A good example is the channelTurnOffEventIndex in **Table 8.17**. The value of this index can be set equal to that of an eventIndex in the eventTable with an eventType of trap(3). Then, when a packet matches a channel, a trap will be sent to the Management Station. The Management Station can be configured to send an SNMP SetRequest

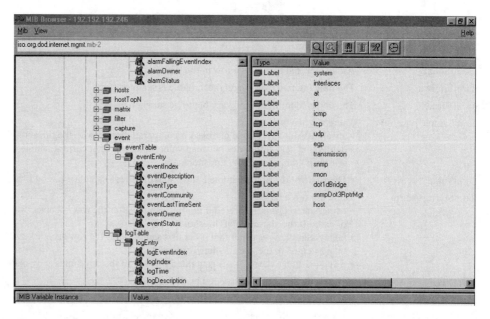

Figure 8.47 Event Group Objects

Table 8.20 eventTable and logTable Objects

Object	Description
eventIndex	• An integer that identifies a row in the eventTable
eventDescription	• Text description of the event defined by this row
eventType	There are 4 types: • none (1)—no event has been defined • log (2)—an entry is made in the corresponding row of the logTable • snmp-trap (3)—a trap is sent to one or more management stations • log-and-trap (4)—entry is made and trap is sent
eventCommunity	• the community string that is to be entered in the trap message. Must be the same as what is configured for the trap recipient
eventLastTimeSent	• the value of the sysUpTime object in the mib-2 system group when the event defined by eventIndex was last triggered.
eventOwner	• Monitor or Management Station that created this row in the eventTable
eventStatus	• Must be "valid (1)" for event to be triggerable
logEventIndex	• Has same value as eventIndex for the event that triggered the log entry
logIndex	• An integer that identifies this entry among other entries of the same eventType, i.e., none, log, trap or log-and-trap
logTime	• The value of sysUpTime in the mib-2 system group when this entry was generated
logDescription	• A description of the event that caused this entry in the logTable.

causing the channelDataControl object value to be changed from on (1) to off (2). No further packets for this channel will be processed.

We have not configured events up to this time. You will do that in Exercise # 10 at the end of this chapter.

This completes our examination of the RMON1 groups. In the next chapter, we examine and demonstrate the use of the RMON2 groups. These groups provide significant additions to our monitoring and troubleshooting tools and address state-of-the-art networking management needs.

CHAPTER SUMMARY

This chapter discussed all of the Ethernet RMON1 groups and demonstrated the use of their objects to examine network traffic. The objects in each group were displayed using the Meterware MIB Browser. Then, a table format was constructed so that the purpose of each object could be described. A major component of this chapter was a demonstration of the relationship between RMON group objects and the functions and displays implemented by using Meterware's graphical interfaces or the graphical interfaces of any NMS. In particular, a table was constructed that showed a procedure for coordinating the use of the filter and capture group objects with the filter and capture graphical interfaces. Exercise #7 was designed to demonstrate the coordinated use of the Alarm and Event groups to create an alarm threshold and generate a trap message event when the threshold was exceeded.

REVIEW QUESTIONS

1. Why is a probe called a remote monitor?
2. Are probes the only devices that collect network segment traffic information?
3. What object values are available from the agent on a PC or server?
4. What was the principal benefit of adding RMON1 groups to mib-2?
5. Give an example of what can be done because of RMON1 objects in mib-2
6. What is the complete numerical object identifier of the rmon group in mib-2?
7. How many groups are there now in mib-2 if you include RMON1
8. We have emphasized that configuration of Control Tables is a critical aspect of using RMON1 objects. What are the functions of objects in Control Tables?
9. How many rows are there in the etherHistoryTable for each row in the historyControlTable?
10. What does the hostTopNRateBase in the hostTopNControlTable define?
11. What does the hostTopNRate in the hostTopNTable define?
12. What is the rule of thumb about utilization on an Ethernet network? In other words, when is the utilization too high for acceptable throughput?
13. What is the difference between the matrixSDTable and the matrixDSTable?

14. The word index is often used in the names of objects in the RMON1 groups. What is your view of how this word is used?

15. What is an Index object? How is it used?

16. How are buffers used by a probe?

17. How are buffers used by a management application?

18. What defines a channel?

19. A channel filter contains two kinds of sub-filters. How are the sub-filters used?

20. How is the object filterPktData used?

21. When the Run button on the Meterware Capture/Filter Channel screen is clicked, what object in the channelTable is changed and how is it changed?

22. How is an event, triggered by a channel, made known to the Management Station?

EXERCISES

1. Using the Control Table of the History Group in Meterware, your NMS or the historyControlTable in a MIB Browser directly:
  a. "Add" another row in the historyControlTable with the instances:
   ❑ "Status" = createRequest (2)
   ❑ "Owner" = Management Station IP Address
   ❑ Sampling "interval" = 60 seconds
   ❑ Bucket "request" = 50.
  b. Set "Status" to "valid(1)."
  c. Highlight the row you created.
  d. "View" the development of the history chart by clicking the "View" button or return to the Meterware Information Screen for your RMON 1 device and click the RMON button.

2. Using your MIB Browser, determine the hostTimeCreationOrder for the host that was first observed by the probe on your network. What is the MAC address of that host?

3. Using the Host group and either the MIB Browser or the graphical display of the hostTable, determine the host on your network that has received the most in-packets.

4. Convince yourself that the decimal form of the destination MAC address in the highlighted entry in Figure 8.27 is correct by translating it to the hexadecimal MAC address value.

5. If you look at the Capture/Filter buffer screen after capturing some packets, you will see under the Index heading that the packets are numbered in order. This index is the captureBufferIndex object in the captureBufferTable. It identifies a packet. This index does not necessarily reflect the order in which packets that were captured were detected. Use the MIB Browser to examine the captureBufferPacketIDs and determine the order in which the captured packets were captured relative to packets that were only observed.

6. Use the Capture/Filter Filter screen to create a filter with the following parameters for your RMON I agent:
  a. Ethernet II frame
  b. IP Network Layer
  c. UDP Transport Layer
  d. Source and Destination addresses specified
  e. Status sub-filter = Any Packets

7. Examine the Data Sub-filter field that was configured in Exercise 6 to see if your configuration of the filter is correctly represented.

8. Click "Mask"(next to "Data") in the screen created in Exercise 6 to get the values of the corresponding filterPktDataMask object in the Mask fields. Compare the mask fields to the Data fields in Figure Chp8Ex6. Is the mask correct?

9. Return to the Capture/Filter Channel screen and click Run. Capture some packets and then click Stop. Click the Buffer tab to examine the packets that have been captured. Are the captured packets consistent with the filter you set?

10. In this exercise, you will configure an alarm table and an event table for a device that will cause a trap to be logged and trigger a trap message to your management station if the device has been configured to send traps.

   a. Double-click your hub, switch, router or probe in Summary View. Select the RMON tab and then click the Alarm icon shown in Figure 8.6.

   b. In the Alarm/Event Control table that appears, click the Add button.

   c. On the Add Alarm/Event screen that appears, you must select a variable to monitor. Click the MIB Browser button on the right of the screen to get to the object etherStatsPkts in the RMON Statistics group and highlight it. Then click the Get Mib button to put "etherStatsPkts" in the Variable Text Box.

   d. Return to the Add Alarm/Event screen to see that the etherStatsPkts.1 identifier has been inserted in the Variable Text Box. **Why is the dot 1 (.1) there?**

   e. Select a Rising Threshold to which to compare etherStatsPkts.1. The Rising Threshold is a number in units per second where units are what you set in Variable Text Box and Interval is the sampling time. It is the product (units) of these two that you want to be notified about if it exceeds a value that you choose. *For the exercise to work, the product must be exceeded so that a trap will be logged.*

   f. For sampling, select "absolute" where absolute means the number of units in a given sampling will be compared to the threshold.

   g. For Alarm type select Rising or Falling.

   h. Under Rising Event Rules, type in the "community string" that you have set for trap messages to be received by your management station.

   i. Select Log and Trap.

   j. Select OK to complete the configuration.

   k. Use the Channel, Edit and Filter screens to create your desired filter, if any.

   l. Run the channel until the number of captured packets exceeds the "threshold" you set.

   m. In the Event Table of the Alarm/Event Control Table screen, highlight the rising etherStatsPkts event and click the View Log button.

   n. There you should see the object identifier for etherStatsPkts associated with rising alarm, the time the event occurred relative the device up time and the index of the event.

   o. In addition, if you have configured your device to send trap messages to your NMS Management Station, bringing up Meterware Summary View should show a clock icon next to your device indicating that it sent a trap to the management station.

REFERENCES

1. Request for Comments: *1757,* "Remote Network Monitoring Management Information Base," February 1995, Category: Standards Track. Obsoletes RFC *1271*

2. Request for Comments: 2021, "Remote Network Monitoring Management Information Base Version 2 using SMIv2."

3. "Network Management Parameters," http://www.iana.org/assignments/smi-numbers

4. "SNMP, SNMPv2 and CMIP: The Practical Guide to Network Management Standards," Chp 7, William Stallings, Addison Wesley, 1993.

5. "SNMP, SNMPv2 and RMON," second edition, William Stallings, Addison Wesley, 1996.

CHAPTER 9

RMON2

This chapter discusses and demonstrates the RMON2 Groups:

- protocolDir
- protocolDist
- addressMap
- nlHost
- nlMatrix
- alHost
- alMatrix
- usrHistory
- probeConfig

RMON1 group objects give us the capability to examine the MAC layer properties of network traffic. The focus of RMON2 objects is examination of traffic at the network and higher layers of the OSI Reference Model. To make the most effective use of bandwidth, it is becoming important to know which applications are using the most bandwidth, what services are being requested by those applications, and whether or not the services guaranteed by Service Level Agreements are being provided. It is also important to have a handle on traffic at each OSI layer so that levels of service can be requested, granted and managed. You will see that the RMON2 capabilities provided by Apptitude's Fastmeter are matched to the needs of state-based traffic analysis being required by today's networks.

9.1 RMON2 IMPLEMENTATION

Figure 9.1 shows a MIB Browser view of all rmon groups. RMON2 adds nine groups to RMON1. These include **protocolDir** through **probeConfig.** As we did for RMON1, we first examine RMON2 groups using the MIB Browser to learn how to relate RMON 2 objects to NMS graphical applications. We begin our exploration with the Meterware Summary View shown in **Figure 9.2**.

We use the probe Fastmeter to explore RMON2 objects. Notice in the second line of Figure 9.2 that the Meterware device discovery process has detected that Fastmeter is an RMON2-type device. The clocks next to some of the device Names indicate they have sent traps to Meterware. In this case, the traps indicate the device is "Up." Double-clicking Fastmeter provides the screen shown in **Figure 9.3**.

At the top of this screen, you see both RMON1 and RMON2 tabs because Fastmeter can decode both types of MIB objects. Notice the Read and Write community strings that were configured for Fastmeter from its console port in Chapter 5. These strings are configured to enable the network administrator to define the MIB View that is presented to the user. This is the only device on our network that allows SNMPv1 view configuration. rmon_admin security level allows all objects on the probe to be read including captured frames. tei_admin provides a total view as well as set (write) privileges. Views with more constraints can be configured. For ex-

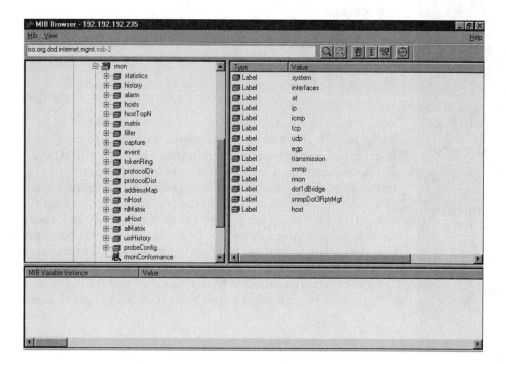

Figure 9.1   MIB Browser view of all rmon Groups

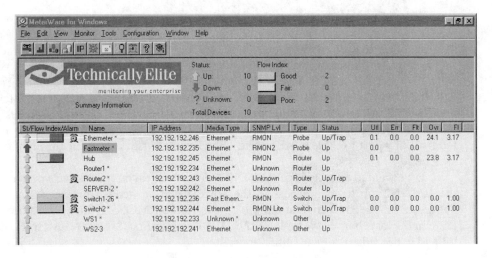

Figure 9.2 Meterware Summary View of Devices on Network 192.192.192.0

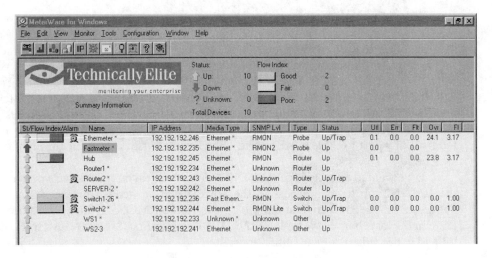

Figure 9.3 Fastmeter Information Screen

ample, you can configure a view that allows all objects except capture buffers to be read.

Another feature of Fastmeter is its two Fast Internet (100Mb/sec) interfaces that are used as monitor ports for other devices. Under ifIndex in **Figure 9.3**, if you were to select either port 2 or port 3, you would see that Medium becomes Fast Ethernet. On our network, these ports are connected to mirror ports on Switch1 and Switch2. As you may remember from the configuration of these switches in Chapter 5, the switches are configured to copy all frames received on or transmitted from any port to these mirror ports. Thus, Fastmeter sees all traffic through both switches.

If we wanted to access the RMON2 group graphical interfaces, we would click the RMON2 tab to gain access to the RMON2 group icon. However, as stated above, we first need to understand the objects in the RMON2 groups. Therefore, as done in the last chapter, we will use the MIB Browser first. So, lets return to **Figure 9.1** and expand the Protocol Directory group.

9.2 PROTOCOLDIR GROUP

9.2.1 Protocol Directory Group

We start with this group because its objects, and especially the graphical interface used later, provide an excellent overview of RMON2 protocols and capabilities. The objects in the Protocol Directory group are listed in **Figure 9.4**.

A good discussion of this and other RMON2 groups is given in **[Ref 1]**. **[Ref 2]** is the RMON2 RFC that should be consulted as the authoritative source. The reference for our examination of the protocolDir group is **[Ref 3]**, RFC 2895 "Remote Network Monitoring MIB Protocol Identifier Reference." A good description of this RFC and its purpose is given in the abstract:

"This memo defines a notation describing protocol layers in a protocol encapsulation, specifically for use in encoding INDEX values for the protocolDirTable, found in the RMON-2 MIB (Remote Network Monitoring Management Information Base) [RFC2021]. The definitions for the standard protocol directory base layer identifiers are also included. This document is intended to identify the encoding rules for the OCTET STRING objects protocolDirID and protocolDirParameters."

As the reader will see, the protocolDirID Index objects define a hierarchical tree of all OSI layer protocols that the probe can decode. Since there are so many of these protocols, an organizational methodology is essential. This hierarchy is not only useful for the mechanics of defining an Index object of the protocolDirTable but more generally for the management of the protocols listed in this table.

Table 9.1 describes the protocolDir group objects.

Table 9.1 protocolDir group objects

Object	Description
protocolDirLastChange	The **sysUpTime** at which the last change was made in the directory listing of protocols. Protocols can be inserted or deleted from the directory.
protocolDirTable	Protocol Table Entries.
protocolDirEntry	There is an entry in protocolDirTable for every protocol that the probe supports.
protocolDirID	**Octet string in dotted-decimal notation** that is similar to mib Object Identifiers. The protocols have a hierarchical relationship to one another that is expressed by the ID. protocolDirID is an **Index object** for the protocolDirTable.
protocolDirParameters	**Octet string in dotted-decimal notation**. This is the second **Index object** of protocolDirTable. protocolDirID and protocolDirParameters are concatenated to form the instance identifier for each object in the protocolDirTable.
protocolDirLocalIndex	This is a unique integer, defined locally by the probe, that identifies the protocol.
protocolDirDescr	Textual description of the protocol.
protocolDirType	protocolDirType is defined by two bits that can be **set** as follows: • If High Order Bit 0 = 1, children of this protocol can be defined in the protocolDirTable (by either the agent or the manager). • If Low Order Bit 1 = 1, the protocol is addressRecognitionCapable (indicates that this protocol can be used to generate network addresses for use by host and matrix table entries)
protocolDirAddressMap Config	• If the protocol is a network layer protocol, the value of this object is an integer that determines if the probe supports decoding of network addresses and, if so, is the support turned on or off. The values for the object are as follows: ❑ notSupported (1) ❑ supportedOff (2) ❑ supportedOn (3)
protocolDirHostConfig	The value of this object is an integer used as follows: • notSupported (1) • supportedOff (2) • supportedOn (3) • notSupported (1) means that the probe will not provide network addresses for use by the network layer and application layer Host Tables
protocolDirMatrixConfig	The value of this object is an integer used as follows: • notSupported (1) • supportedOff (2) • supportedOn (3) • notSupported (1) means that the probe will not provide network addresses for use by the network layer and application layer Matrix Tables
protocolDirOwner	The entity that created this row in the table
protocolDirStatus	The status of the protocol entry. It must be "active(1)" for statistics to be collected and for all other objects that depend on the status to exist.

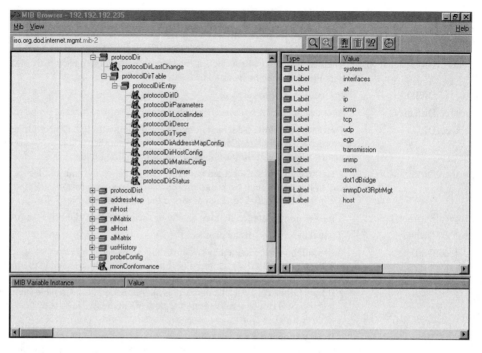

Figure 9.4   protocolDir group

> **Note**
>
> In the descriptions of protocolDirAddressMapConfig, protocolDirHost-
> Config and protocolDirMatrixConfig, supportedOff (2) is the default
> setting because this frees up considerable memory resources for the
> probe and increases its processing speed. We see later how to toggle be-
> tween supportedOff (2) and supportedOn (3)

Let's look at the protocolDirTable objects in turn.

a. protocolDirID

As mentioned above, each protocol is part of a hierarchical protocol tree. A
protocolDirID is a concatenation of the following in the order shown.

1. An octet that is the count of octets in the protocolDirID
2. Four octets in dotted-decimal notation that identify the base layer protocol (e.g., Ethernet)
3. Four octets that identify the network layer protocol (e.g., IP)
4. Four octets for every other protocol layer except the highest
5. Four octets identifying the port number of the highest layer protocol.

All protocol numbers and port numbers can be found in **[Ref 4]** by clicking
on the alphabet letter **P** on that Website home page.

Table 9.2   protocolDirID for snmp

Octet Count	ether2	ip	udp	snmp port
16	0.0.0.1	0.0.8.0	0.0.0.17	0.0.0.161

The following is an example of a **protocolDirID** for the protocol **snmp** encapsulated in an Ethernet II frame, encapsulated in the IP network layer protocol header, encapsulated in the UDP transport layer protocol:

protocolDirID = **16.0.0.0.1.0.0.8.0.0.0.0.17.0.0.0.161**

Table 9.2 dissects this ID. There are 16 octets in protocolDirID. The Data Link protocol, in this case ether2 (Ethernet II), is called the base layer protocol. The format for this protocol and its description, taken from **[Ref 3]**, is shown in **Figure 9.5**.

"The first octet ('f') is the special function code described below. The next two octets ('op1' and 'op2') are operands for the function. If not used, an operand must be set to zero. The last octet ('m') is the enumerated value for a particular base layer encapsulation. All four octets are encoded in network-byte-order."

There are two possible values for 'f' at this time: Zero means that there is no function applied to the protocol identifier in the last octet. A non-zero value of 'f' means a function, with the operands indicated, is applied. There is currently only one value of 'f'' = 1, which corresponds to a "wildcard" base layer. When used, it means that counts of any base layer identifier used with the same network layer identifier will be aggregated. **Figure 9.6** lists the currently possible values for ('m') in the base identifier. The second part of instance identifiers is the Index object **protocolDir Parameters** that we now discuss.

b. **protocolDirParameters**

As stated in **Table 9.1**, the encoding of protocolDirParameters is combined with the encoding of protocolDirID to produce the instance identifier for each object instance (row) in the protocolDirTable. Let's see how protocolDirParameters is encoded. protocolDirParameters contains one octet for each protocol layer included in the protocolDirID. Each bit in an octet can be used to identify some capability of the protocol layer with which it is associated. The octet bit is **set** to indicate the capability is provided. Let's assume

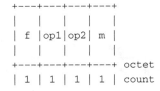

Figure 9.5   base-layer protocol format

```
Name            ID
------------------------
ether2          1
llc             2
snap            3
vsnap           4
ianaAssigned    5
```

Figure 9.6 Base Layer Encoding Values for ('m')

the protocolDirID shown in **Table 9.2**. The protocolDirParameters object would then have the following value:

protocolDirParameters = **4.0.1.0.0**

according to **Table 9.3**. The fields in **Table 9.3** are explained as follows:

❑ **Octet Count = 4** because there are four octets, one for each of the four protocol layers
❑ **ether2 octet = 0** because ether2 has no parameters
❑ **ip octet = 1** because there is one bit in the ip octet that can be set. The value one means "ip countsFragments." This means that even if a message is fragmented, it is guaranteed that the probe will count the number of packets containing higher layer protocols correctly.
❑ **udp octet = 0** means udp has no parameters
❑ **snmp octet = 0** means snmp has no parameters

Coding of protocolDirParameters is described in **[Ref 3]**. See this reference for other possible values of the protocolDirParameters octets. The Fastmeter probe uses all the information in these two Index objects to identify and count protocolDirIDs when a frame is detected on the subnet. To get a better feel for the protocol hierarchy, let's draw part of the protocol tree as shown in **Figure 9.7**. Each shaded group of numbers is the protocolDirID for the protocol encapsulations in the column. For example in the far left column, the encapsulation is ether2.ip.udp.snmp. Concatenating the codes for each protocol, we get 1.0.0.1.0.0.8.0.0.0.0.17.0.0.0.161. Notice that this is a wildcard encoding of ether2 so those snmp packets encapsulated in any Ethernet base protocol will be aggregated. This is not the case for the ether2 encapsulation with the code 0.0.0.1 shown in the third column from the left. The other base identifier protocols are llc for Logical Link Control; snap for Subnetwork Address Pro-

Table 9.3 protocolDirParameters for protocolDirID in Table 9.2

Octet Count	ether2 octet	ip octet	udp octet	snmp octet
4	0	1	0	0

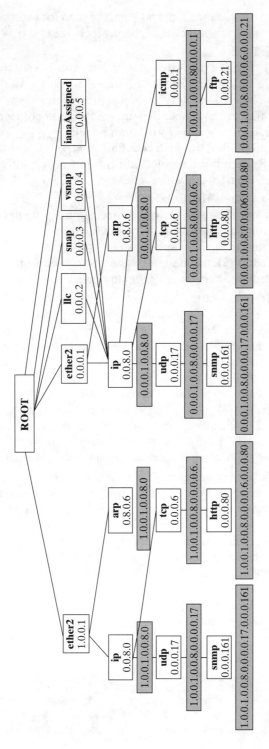

Figure 9.7 Part of the protocolDirID Tree

269

tocol; vsnap for vendor snap; and ianaAssigned for protocols that do not fit in the other base-layer branches of the protocol tree.

c. **protocolDirType**

This object specifies the Attributes of a protocol. See **[Ref 3]** for a listing of the possible Attributes. The Attributes are also conveniently shown in the RMON 2 Protocol Directory graphical presentation as we will see below. The Attributes that are available depend on the protocol layer. For example, for the **ip** layer, there are two bits that can be set:

❑ **hasChildren (0):** if this high order bit is set, ip encapsulates other protocols

❑ **addressRecognitionCapable(1):** if this low order bit is set, ip is capable of decoding the network address field

d. **protocolDirAddressMapConfig**

This object specifies whether the device can map the network address to the MAC address. The following are the possibilities:

❑ **notSupported(1):** the mapping is not supported

❑ **supportedOff(2):** the mapping is supported but is off

❑ **supportedOn(3):** the mapping is supported and is on

e. **protocolDirHostConfig**

This object specifies whether the device will provide network addresses for the network layer host table and the application layer host table instance identifiers. The following are the possibilities with respect to the network layer and application layer host tables:

❑ **notSupported(1):** network layer addresses are not supplied for the network layer or application layer host tables

❑ **supportedOff(2):** network layer addresses are supplied for the network layer and application layer host tables but the support is off

❑ **supportedOn(3):** network layer addresses are supplied for the network layer and application layer host tables and the support is on

f. **protocolDirMatrixConfig**

This object specifies whether the network layer and application layer matrix tables are supported by network addressing. The following are the possibilities:

❑ **notSupported(1):** network addresses will not be available to network layer and application layer matrix instance identifiers

❑ **supportedOff(2):** network addresses are available but the support is turned off

❑ **supportedOn(3):** network addresses are available and the support is turned on

> **Note**
>
> When network addresses are supplied to network and application layer host tables and matrix tables, it is typical that the addresses are only available in Index objects and are not part of the tables.

In order to get an appreciation for how the protocolDir objects are used, we need to employ the MIB Browser. So let's return to **Figure 9.4**. From the point of view of our lengthy discussion of protocolDirID and protocolDir-Parameters, it is important to take note of the object **protocolDirLocalIndex**. As mentioned in **Table 9.1**, this integer is a locally defined index to proto-colDirID.[*] In **Figure 9.4**, we highlight protocolDirLocalIndex and click the GetRequest button to get the objects displayed in the bottom panel of **Figure 9.8**.

g. protocolDirLocalIndex

The bottom panel in **Figure 9.8** shows some of the instance identifiers for pro-tocolDirLocalIndex and its values. protocolDirLocalIndex is a useful object in RMON2 because it is a convenient shorthand for the lengthy instance iden-tifiers. Also it is an Index object for many tables. Notice at the bottom right of the screen that the probe Fastmeter lists 1151 unique values of protocolDir-LocalIndex. The first object instance identifier in **Figure 9.8** is

protocolDirLocalIndex.4.0.0.0.1.1.0

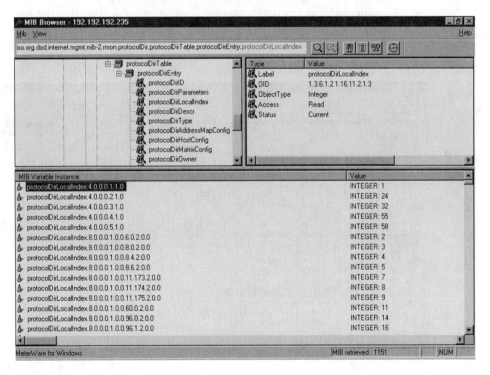

Figure 9.8 protocolDirLocalIndex Instance Identifiers and Values

---

[*] Our appreciation to Andy Bierman for clarifying the important distinction between protocolDirID and protocolDirLocalIndex.

Its **value** is one, the number that identifies the protocol ether2. Referring to **Tables 9.2** and **9.3** as guides, the interpretation of the numerical string is:

❏ The number of octets in protocolDirID is 4
❏ protocolDirID = 0.0.0.1, where 0.0.0.1 is the ether2 (Ethernet II) base identifier protocol
❏ The number of octets in protocolDirParameters is 1
❏ protocolDirParameters = 0, where 0 is the value of the octet because ether2 has no parameters.

In **Figure 9.9**, we have used GetRequest to obtain other values of protocolDirLocalIndex. They are shown in the bottom panel. The highlighted instance identifier is described below. Its protocolDirLocal Index is 749.

1. protocolDirID octets =   16
2. protocolDirID =   **1.0.0.1**.0.0.8.0.0.0.0.17.0.0.0.161
3. protocolDirParameters octets =   4
4. protocolDirParameters =   0.1.0.0

The protocolDirID is almost the same as that shown in **Table 9.2**. What is new is the octet string **1.0.0.1** that identifies the link layer protocol. **[Ref 3]** defines a "wildcard" link layer identifier indicated by a value = 1 for the first octet. A wildcard identifier results in a count of protocol traffic at the next higher

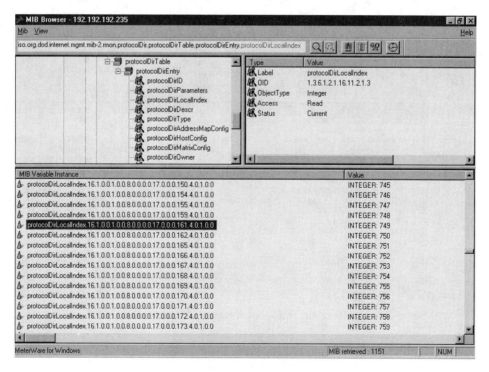

Figure 9.9   More protocolDirLocalIndex instance identifiers and their Values

layer being aggregated for any encapsulating link layer. According to the RMON2 specifications, the fourth octet in the link layer identifier should be the lowest link layer number that is expected on the subnetwork to which the device is attached. The fourth octet has a value = 1 which represents the ether2 link layer.

Now let's look at how Meterware displays the information we have been discussing in its Protocol Directory Administration graphical interface.

h. Protocol Directory Administration

To access this application, we go to the screen shown in **Figure 9.3**, click the RMON2 tab and then click the protocolDir button. This generates the screen shown in **Figure 9.10**. The top left pane shows a small number of the protocols in the hierarchical list that the probe Fastmeter is capable of processing. These are network layer protocols encapsulated in ether2. You can click on any of the protocols in these folders or in the bottom left screen to get the related protocolDirTable object values in the top right pane. This is a lot easier than having to collect them with the MIB Browser.

The bottom left pane lists the protocols that have been seen by the probe on either port 2 or port 3 during previous sampling intervals. Here, E = Ether2, and A = any base encoding of Ethernet. We have highlighted the application layer protocol **A-SNMP-u,** where A = "SNMP over any Ethernet

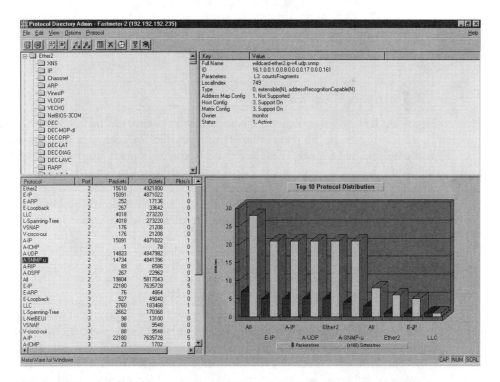

Figure 9.10   Protocol Directory Administration Graphical Interface

base encoding" and u = "SNMP over UDP." When A-SNMP-u is double-clicked, the protocolDirTable object values appear in the top right panel. Notice the values of Address Map Config, Host Config and Matrix Config objects that are Not Supported, Support On and Support On, respectively. You can toggle the last two values by clicking the buttons over the top left panel in **Figure 9.10**. Notice also the value of Parameters: L3 countsFragments. This means that the network layer (L3) guarantees that higher layer PDUs will be counted correctly even if fragmented. What octet in protocolDirParameters shows this?

The lower right panel shows a histogram of packets/sec and octets/sec for the top10 protocols that generated the most traffic during the last sampling interval. The sampling interval can be set on the Options menu at the top of the screen. At the time that this screen was captured, it was 30sec. The top10 Protocol histogram appears to show duplicates of some protocols. This is because protocol traffic for both Fastmeter port 2 connected to Switch1 and Fastmeter port 3 connected to Switch 2, are being shown. As can be seen, the traffic on our small demonstration network is small as expected. Starting from the left in the histogram, the equality of #2 packets/sec or #2 octets/sec through #6 packets/sec or #6 octets/sec, shows that almost all the traffic on port 2 is from **ether2.ip.udp.snmp** packets. The Protocol Directory Administration Screen has integrated a lot of information that would have taken a long time to collect with the MIB Browser alone.

The TopN packet histogram is calculated from values collected in the lower left pane and these values are derived from the objects in the protocolDist Group. So let's look at this group.

9.2.2 protocolDist Group

Figure 9.11 shows the protocolDistControlTable and the protocolDistStatsTable. There is one row in the protocolDistControlTable for each interface on which the probe is detecting frames. There are two interfaces or ports from which Fastmeter is collecting data. These are ports 2 and 3 indicated in the lower left pane of **Figure 9.10**. The number of packets or octets seen by either port for each protocol is the total number seen by that port since the probe was turned on. The number of packets comes from the values of the Counter objects listed in the bottom panel of **Figure 9.11**.

For example, lets look at the second MIB Variable Instance **protocolDistStatsPkts.2.3** and break it down according to **Table 9.4**. This table also helps us to see how the terminology is used.

protocolDistStatsPkts is the column object whose instances are being counted. protocolDistControlIndex = 2 identifies row 2 in the protocolDistControlTable. protocolDir Local Index = 3 tells us that protocolDirID is ether2.ip. In summary, **Figure 9.11** tells us that 11571 packets included ip encapsulated in ether2.

The Protocol Directory Administration screen provides an impressive and useful array of information. One could argue that this information is all that a network

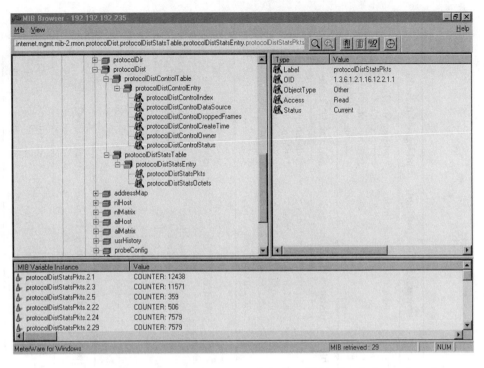

Figure 9.11 protocolDistControlTable, protocolDistStatsTable (top left panel) and Instances of protocolDistStatsPkts (bottom panel)

manager needs to know about protocols on the network. In some cases it is. In other cases, for example a production network that has a lot of traffic and more potential problems, a deeper understanding of protocol traffic is required. For example, one may need to know which hosts are making use of which protocols and to what extent. In addition, one may want to know which applications are causing the most traffic between which hosts. We will now explore the RMON2 objects and applications that enable the network manager to examine these questions. We will start the examination with the nlHost group objects. First, however, we make a brief digression into the subject of Index objects. We have created **Table 9.5** to help with this.

Table 9.4 protocolDistStatsPkts

Column Object	Index Objects	Index Object Values	Port	protocol DirID	Instance Value
protocolDistStatsPkts	protocolDist Control Index	2	2		
	protocolDirLocal Index	3		ether2.ip	11571

Table 9.5 Summary of RMON2 Index Objects

protocolDirTable	protocolDistControlTable	protocolDistStatsTable	addressMapControlTable	addressMapTable
1. protocolDirID 2. protocolDirParameters	1. protocolDistControlIndex	1. protocolDistControl Index 2. protocolDirLocalIndex	1. addressMapControlIndex	1. addressMapTimeMark 2. protocolDirLocalIndex 3. addressMapNetworkAddress 4. addressMapSource

nlHostControlTable	nlHostTable	nlMatrixControlTable	nlMatrixSDTable	nlMatrixDSTable
1. nlHostControlIndex	1. nlHostControlIndex 2. nlHostTimeMark 3. protocolDirLocalIndex 4. nlHostAddress	1. nlMatrixControlIndex	1. nlMatrixControlIndex 2. nlMatrixSDTimeMark 3. protocolDirLocalIndex 4. nlMatrixSDSourceAddress 5. nlMatrixSDDestAddress	1. nlMatrixControlIndex 2. nlMatrixSDTimeMark 3. protocolDirLocalIndex 4. nlMatrixSDDestAddress 5. nlMatrixSDSourceAddress

nlMatrixTopNControl Table	nlMatrixTopNTable	alHostTable	alMatrixSDTable	alMatrixDSTable
1. nlMatrixTopNControl Index	2. nlMatrixTopNControl Index 3. nlMatrixTopNIndex	1. nlHostControlIndex 2. alHostTimeMark 3. protocolDirLocalIndex (nl) 4. nlHostAddress 5. protocolDirLocalIndex (al)	1. nlMatrixControlIndex 2. alMatrixSDTimeMark 3. protocolDirLocalIndex (nl) 4. nlMatrixSDSourceAddress 5. nlMatrixSDDestAddress 6. protocolDirLocalIndex (al)	1. nlMatrixControlIndex 2. alMatrixSDTimeMark 3. protocolDirLocalIndex (nl) 4. nlMatrixSDDestAddress 5. nlMatrixSDSourceAddress 6. protocolDirLocalIndex (al)

alMatrixTopNControl Table	alMatrixTopNTable	usrHistoryControlTable	usrHistoryObjectTable	usrHistoryTable
1. alMatrixTopNControl Index	1. alMatrixTopNIndex	1. usrHistoryControlIndex	1. usrHistoryControlIndex 2. usrHistoryObjectIndex	1. usrHistoryControlIndex 2. usrHistorySampleIndex 3. usrHistoryObjectIndex

9.2.3 Index Objects

As we have seen, Index objects play an important role in accessing instances of mib objects in general and RMON2 objects in particular. The use of Index objects can be confusing, especially when there are many of them for a given table. Therefore, **Table 9.5** was constructed to provide an overview of them and how they relate. The objects are numbered in the order in which they appear when concatenated with a column object to provide an instance identifier for that column object.

The following are main points about Index Objects:

1. The number of Index objects for a given table is the minimum necessary to identify an object instance in all situations. Even so, some tables have six of them.

2. The Index objects for each table are ordered lexicographically. This order is used when concatenating them with the name of an object to form the instance identifier.

3. An Index Object in RMON2 is not necessarily an object in the table for which it is being used. It may be an object in another table. A good example of this is the Index Object **protocolDirLocalIndex**. It is an object in many other tables.

4. Tables contain objects whose ACCESS is "not accessible," but these objects may be Index objects. An example of this situation is the **nlHostAddress** object in the nlHostTable. Its ACCESS is "not accessible," but it is an Index object of the nlHostTable so its values will appear in all instances of objects in that table and can therefore be accessed that way.

5. Take note that some tables have two protocolDirLocalIndex objects. One is part of the instance identifier for a network layer (nl) protocol and the other is part of the instance identifier for an application layer(al) protocol.

6. Be aware that in the nlMatrixSDTable and the alMatrixSDTable, the nlMatrixSDSourceAddress Index Object and the alMatrixSDSourceAddress Index Object, respectively, come before the nlMatrixSDDestAddress and the alMatrixSDDestAddress Index Objects. The opposite is true for the nlMatrixDSTable and the alMatrixDSTable.

Now let's proceed with discussion of the nlHost Group.

9.2.4 nlHost Group

The nlHost objects become important when it is desirable to know the source of a packet that is not on the local network, i.e., the source is on the other side of a router attached to the local network. When network addresses are decoded (e.g., IP addresses), the location of the source anywhere in the world will be known. This knowledge provides the network manager with a more critical look at subnet traffic with which to question the presence of traffic from other networks. The objects in the nlHostControlTable and the nlHostTable are shown in **Figure 9.12**.

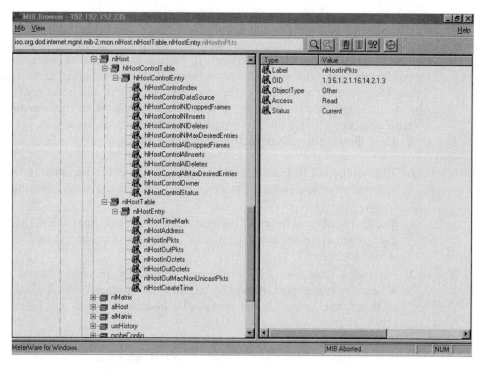

Figure 9.12 nlHostControlTable and nlHostTable objects (left panel)

As we have come to expect by now, there is a control table, the **nlHostControlTable**, and data table, the **nlHostTable**. There is, as usual, one row in the nlHost-ControlTable for each interface of the probe to the network. There is one row in the nlHostTable for each distinct set of its four Index objects listed in **Table 9.5**.

In the next screen, we have the results of sending a GetRequest to Fastmeter for values of nlHostInPkts. **Table 9.6** gives the breakdown of the highlighted MIB Variable Instance in the bottom panel of **Figure 9.13**. The Index objects in **Table 9.6** are in order from left to right, the order in which they are concatenated to the Object Identifier.

- nlHostControlIndex = 2 means that this data came from port 2 on Fastmeter
- nlHostTimeMark = 31 means that this data is current as of relative time 31 since the probe was started. The higher the value of nlHostTimeMark the later the host was detected on the network.

Table 9.6 nlHostInPackets.2.31.3.4.192.192.192.241 Instance Identifier and Value

nlHostControl Index	nlHostTime Mark	protocolDir LocalIndex	nlHost Address	nlHostIn Packets
2	31	3	4.192.192.192.241	29717

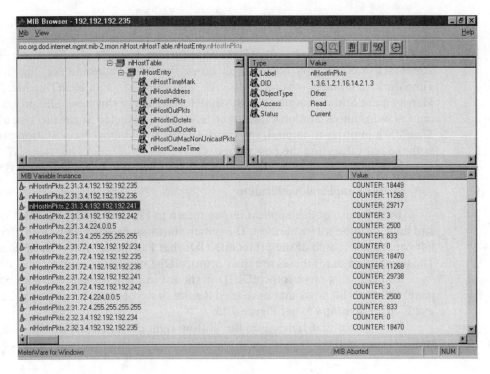

Figure 9.13 nlHostTable objects (top left panel) and Instances of nlHostInPkts (bottom panel)

- protocolDirLocalIndex = 3 is the index to protocolDirID ether2.ip
- nlHostAddress = 4.192.192.192.241 specifies that the network address has 4 octets and that the IP address 192.192.192.241.
- nlHostInPackets = 29717 is the count of packets encapsulated in ether2.ip4 seen on port 2

You can determine the network address of the host that received 29717 **nlHostInPackets** from the instance identifier in **Figure 9.13** as we have just done. You cannot determine the protocolDirID directly from the instance identifier. You determine it indirectly from the value of protocolDirLocalIndex, which is 3 in this example. To identify the protocol from the integer value, you return to the screen shown in **Figure 9.8** or **Figure 9.9** and scroll until you find the Value = 3.

Thus, it is possible to do what we have just done to determine a network address and protocol-identifier associated with a nlHostInPackets value. Doing so for one address and protocol is all right, but doing it for many would take far too much time when you are trying to solve a problem. As you will see in the next section, Meterware and other network management systems (NMS) provide applications that make the job much simpler.

Before leaving this section, there are a couple of interesting points that the instances of the MIB Variable nlHostInPkts present. One is that the octets in the

Index objects are in lexicographical order. The other relates to values of the Index object nlHostTimeMark, the second Index object. For the highlighted instance and others, nlHostTimeMark = 31. Notice that further down in the list starts nlHost-TimeMark = 32. If you could scroll down the list you would see that nlHost-TimeMark continues to increase. At the end of a nlHostTimeMark, the Management Station requests a list of nlHostInPkts in this case. The probe sends only new instances and/or values that have been detected since the last nlHost-TimeMark in order to minimize network traffic. The Management Station presents both the old values and the new values.

Now let's look at an application that saves us a lot of work:

nlHost Graphical Application

To make use of this application, we return to **Figure 9.3**, click the RMON2 tab and then click the nlHost button. The screen shown in **Figure 9.14** is presented. The left panel shows some of the protocolDirIDs that Fastmeter is capable of decoding. The numbers in parentheses are their protocolDirLocalIndex values.

You can click any protocolDirID in the list in the left panel and the top right panel will show all hosts that have used it since the probe was powered up. Let's select **E-ip = ether2/ip4** to get **Figure 9.15**.

First, notice that **Index 2** on the bottom right of the screen indicates that the traffic shown in the top right pane was detected by Fastmeter port 2 connected to

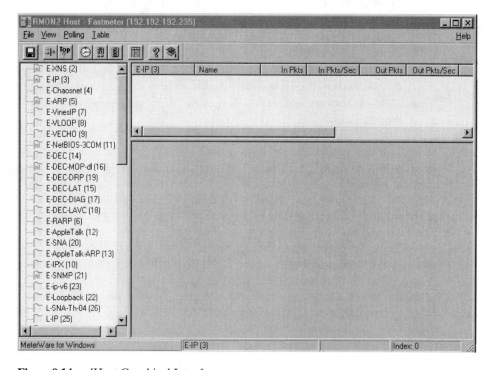

Figure 9.14   nlHost Graphical Interface

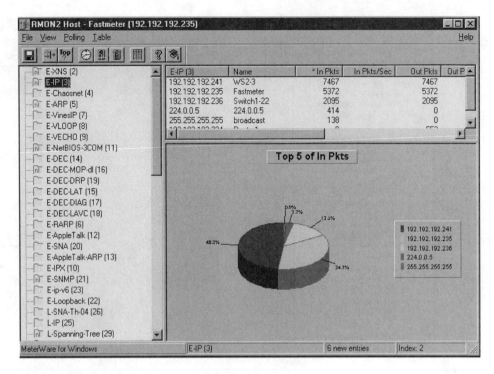

Figure 9.15 Host Traffic for protocolDirID ether2.ip

the Fast Ethernet port on Switch2. This traffic includes any packet whose proto-colDirID included ether2.ip. The pie diagram shows the percentage of In-Pkts using ether2.ip for each of the top 5 hosts. You could change this diagram to represent the percentage of Out-Pkts, for example, by clicking on Out-Pkts in the heading of the top panel. You can immediately see that most of the ether2.ip traffic is to hosts 192.192.192.241 and 192.192.192.235. Why do you think that is?

To take the next step and see how much of this traffic is due to packets using the protocolDirID **ether2.ip.udp,** you would simply go down the list in the left panel until you find this combination and double-click it. Instead of demonstrating this, let's demonstrate what we see by going one step further and asking for hosts using **ether2.ip.udp.snmp.** Scroll down the list in the left panel and select **A-SNMP-u** and double-click it to get **Figure 9.16**. The top panel in **Figure 9.16** shows the network addresses of all hosts that have either sourced or received the protocol **ether2.ip4.up.snmp**.

The list of hosts in the top panel is now much shorter. The pie diagram shows the percentages of In-Packets associated with the top four hosts. Notice that proto-colDirLocalIndex (al) associated with this protocol is 749. The (al) indicates that the probe is decoding the application layer protocol SNMP. You can select which statistics you want to graph by clicking on a column heading. In-Packets is selected in this case as indicated by the (*).

Now, let's send a message using another protocol and see what is detected by Fastmeter. We will create and send Internet Control Message Protocol (ICMP)

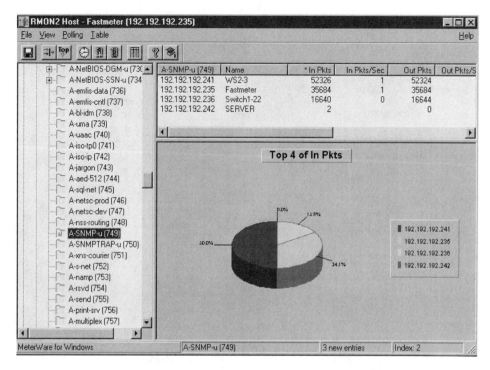

Figure 9.16   Top 4 Hosts Sending or Receiving ether2.ip.udp.snmp packets

frames. To do this, we open the MSDOS window from the Programs Menu in Windows. At the DOS prompt, we type **ping 192.192.192.235** and then Enter to run the ping application. This will send four ICMP messages to Fastmeter from which four response messages will be returned. You will see the responses on your MSDOS screen. The result in nlHost is shown in **Figure 9.17**.

The top panel shows that WS2-3 sent four packets and received four packets. Similarly, Fastmeter received the four packets from WS2-3 and returned four packets. The pie diagram shows that each device sent an equal number of packets, which is correct.

9.2.5 alHost Group

This group is very similar to the nlHost Group except that the focus is on application traffic rather than network traffic. **Figure 9.18** shows the objects in the alHost Group.

It consists of just one table, the **alHostTable**. The nlHostControlTable is the control table for the alHostTable. The alHostTable does not include objects analogous to nlHostAddress or nlHostOutMacNonUnicastPkts objects. There will be one entry in the alHostTable for each application-level protocol transmitted or received by each known network address. Thus, an application-level protocol can be traced to the host that transmitted or received it.

As you see in **Table 9.5**, there are five Index objects for this table: nlHostControlIndex, alHostTimeMark, protocolDirLocalIndex (nl), nlHostAddress and pro-

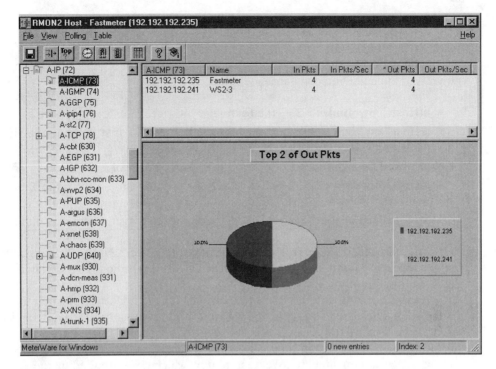

Figure 9.17　ICMP Messages Between 192.192.192.241(WS2-3) and 192.192.192.235 (Fastmeter)

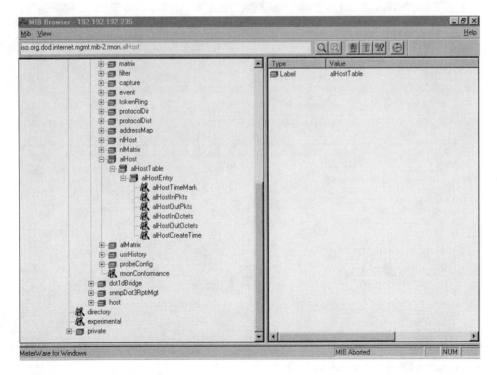

Figure 9.18　alHost Group Objects

tocolDirLocalIndex (al) in that order. Let's use the MIB Browser to get some values of alHostInPkts. The result is shown in **Figure 9.19**. **Table 9.7** describes the components of the highlighted instance identifier.

- **nlHostControlIndex = 2** ⇒ the Fastmeter interface monitoring is port 2
- **alHostTimeMark = 0** ⇒ host was detected during the first time interval after Fastmeter was powered up
- **protocolDirLocalIndex(nl) = 72** ⇒ the network protocol is IP
- **nlHostAddress = 192.192.19.235** ⇒ address of Host that received the application-layer protocol
- **protocolDirLocalIndex(al) = 749** ⇒ the application layer protocol is snmp

You can check the correspondence between protocolDirLocalIndex values and protocols in **Figure 9.10**, Protocol Directory Administration. This is your main database for all protocol information.

As was the case with the RMON1 Host Group, the nlHost Group and the alHost Group objects tell us only about network or application traffic to or from isolated hosts. The nlHost Group objects identify the hosts using network layer protocols. The alHost Group objects identify the hosts using higher layer protocols such as udp, tcp, snmp and http. We do not know which hosts are sending these pro-

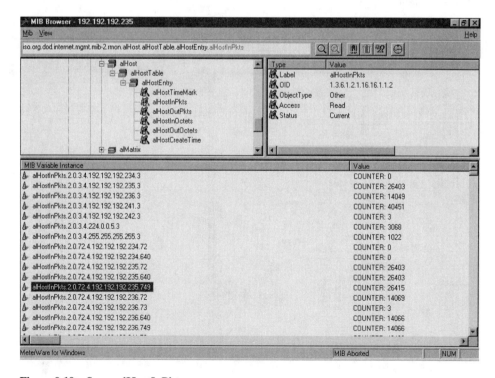

Figure 9.19 Some alHostInPkts

Table 9.7   Components of Highlighted alHostPkts Instance Identifier in Figure 9.19

nlHostControl Index	alHostTime Mark	(nl)protocolDir Local Index	nlHostAddress	(al)protocolDir Local Index
2	0	72	192.192.192.235	749

tocols to communicate. To know that we need to look at the nlMatrix Group and the alMatrix Group.

The nlMatrix and alMatrix groups are very similar and both contain TopN tables that sort and prioritize conversations between pairs of hosts according to packets sent by the source. A few objects in these two groups are not the same as can be seen by comparing the two groups in their respective MIB Browser views. There is no difference in the Meterware nlMatrix and alMatrix graphical interfaces. We will examine the more comprehensive alMatrix group in MIB view and graphical view as this will be sufficient to also see how to use the nlMatrix Group objects.

9.2.6 alMatrix Group

The alMatrix Group objects allow the user to document pairwise conversations between applications. The tables in this group are shown in **Figure 9.20**. The first two tables shown in **Figure 9.20**, the alMatrixSDTable and the alMatrixDSTable are controlled by values of objects in the **nlMatrixControlTable**. The alMatrixTopNTable is controlled by the alMatrixTopNControlTable. This control table has not been expanded in **Figure 9.20**.

As we did for alHostInPkts, let's get some values of alMatrixSDPkts. These are shown in **Figure 9.21**. These instance identifiers identify conversations using one application protocol and one network protocol between identified hosts during a specific time interval. We have highlighted one of these conversations in **Figure 9.21** and have described the components of the instance identifier in **Table 9.8**. The value of the Counter object for this instance shows that there were 174 such conversations during alMatrixSDTimeMark = 2. This is an example of an instance identifier that contains two protocolDirLocalIndex values.

- **nlMatrixControlIndex** = 2 identifies Port 2 of Fastmeter as the port where the conversation was detected
- **alMatrixSDTimeMark** = 2 identifies the time interval during which the conversation took place
- **protocolDirLocalIndex (nl)** = 72 identifies A-ip as the network protocol. A-ip means IP encapsulated in all base-layer protocols.
- **nlMatrixSDSourceAddress** = 4.192.192.192.235 identifies Fastmeter as the source of the conversation
- **nlMatrixSDDestAddress** = 4.192.192.192.241 identifies WS2-3 as the destination of the conversation.

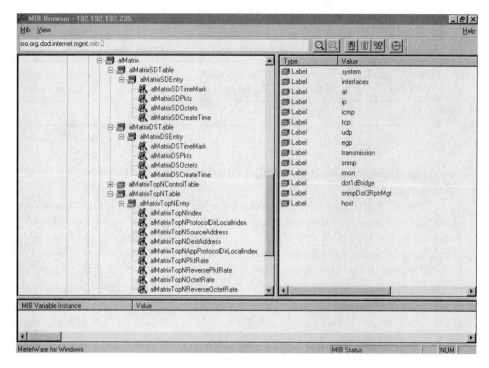

Figure 9.20 alMatrix tables

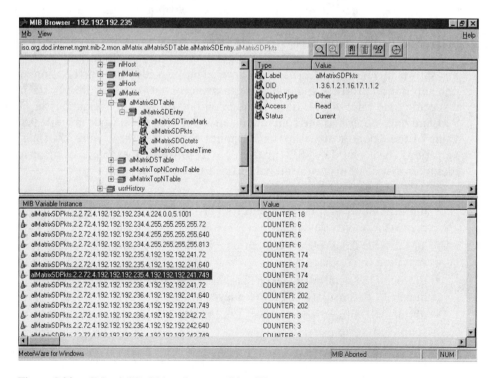

Figure 9.21 alMatrixSD Object Instance Identifiers

Table 9.8   Instance Identifiers for alMatrixSDPkts

nlMatrixControl Index	alMatrixSD TimeMark	protocolDir LocalIndex (nl)	nlMatrixSD SourceAddress	nlMatrixSDDest Address	protocolDir LocalIndex (al)
2	2	72	4.192.192.192.235	4.192.192.192.241	749

- **ProtocolDirLocalIndex (al)** = 749 identifies A-SNMP-u as the application layer protocol used.

Now that you see how the alMatrix group works, let's make use of one of the original application layer protocols in the TCP/IP protocol stack, FTP, and detect it using the alMatrix group. We will send an FTP message from WS2-3 to SERVER that is hosting Microsoft IIS with FTP and WWW sites. **Figure 9.22** shows the message dialog using an FTP command line client that is provided by Microsoft Windows.

You could also produce the same results automatically by opening ftp://192.192.192.242/ in Internet Explorer or Netscape.

The file, **Fig 8.19**.tif, had been placed in the FTP home directory on Server so that it could be accessed. Now we return to **Figure 9.3**, the Fastmeter Information screen, click the RMON2 tab and click alMatrix to get the screen shown in **Figure 9.23**.

In the left panel, under A-TCP, A-FTP is highlighted. We are therefore asking to see all packets detected on Fastmeter port 3 using FTP, encapsulated in TCP, encapsulated in IP, encapsulated in any base layer protocol. The top panel shows the

Figure 9.22   FTP Client Dialog

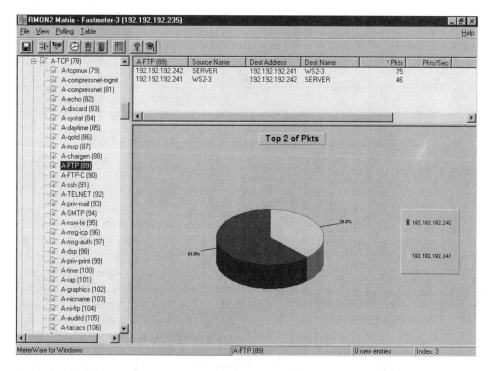

Figure 9.23 FTP Conversation between WS2-3 and Server

request from WS2-3, the response from SERVER and the number of packets sent in each case. Notice in the left panel that the protocolDirLocalIndex for TCP and FTP are 78 and 89, respectively. These are two of the six Index object values used in al-MatrixSDTable instance identifiers. If we were to access the MIB Browser view of a GetRequest or any alMatrixSDTable or alMatrixDSTable object, we would find these TCP and FTP protocolDirLocalIndex values in the instance identifier of this conversation.

Let's make use of the alMatrix group again. This time we will use it to document a conversation between a Web Client and a Web Server. For the Web Client we will use Internet Explorer and the Web Server will be Microsoft IIS. In Internet Explorer, we open http://192.192.192.242. IIS returns the default.htm file in the WWW home directory wwwroot. From the alMatrix tables, Meterware collects the information shown in **Figure 9.24**.

Notice that client 192.192.192.241 sent more packets than server 192.192.192.242 although server was returning the requested default.htm file. This is typical of a TCP session that often requires extra packets to ensure the reliability of the session. The pie chart shows that most of the volume of traffic came from server.

There are other graphical interfaces provided by Meterware that we should examine. **Figure 9.25** shows the TopN communication pairs for the protocol ether2/IP/UDP/SNMP observed on Fastmeter port 3.

The top panel of **Figure 9.25** shows all conversations for the protocolDirectoryID any Ethernet/IP/UDP/SNMP. The bottom panel displays how the conversa-

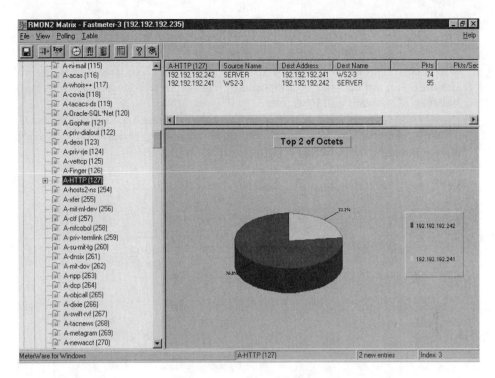

Figure 9.24   HTTP Communication between IE Web Client and IIS Web Server

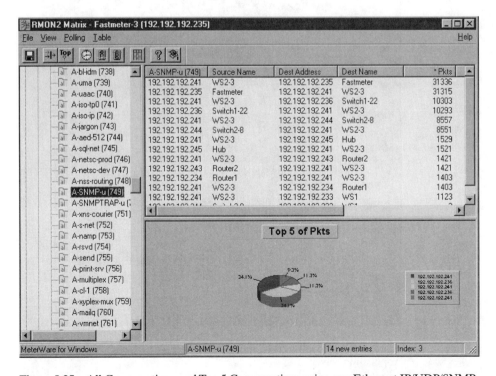

Figure 9.25   All Conversations and Top 5 Conversations using any Ethernet IP/UDP/SNMP

tions are distributed by host. You can immediately see that most of the conversation is between hosts 192.192.192.241 and 192.192.192.235. This is because most of the traffic on the network is composed of pairs of GetRequests and GetResponses between Meterware and Fastmeter.

When there is a lot of traffic on the network, another useful diagram is that shown in **Figure 9.26**. You can access this screen from the Meterware Summary View. On the Monitor Menu, click Top Applications.

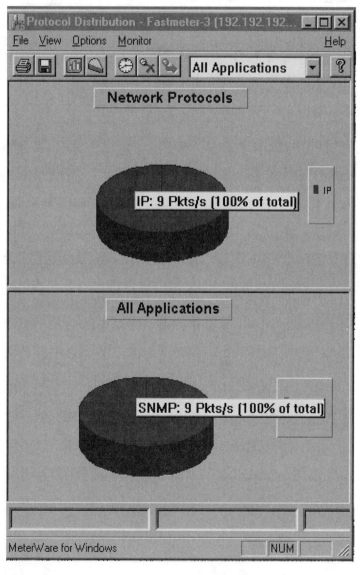

Figure 9.26 Protocol Distribution by Network Layer and Application Layer

The pie diagram in the top panel shows the network protocols in use. You can click on a slice of the pie to see the traffic for a particular network protocol. You can also break that protocol down into the higher level protocols it is supporting. The pie in the bottom panel will show the application protocols in use and their traffic.

Clicking the histogram icon at the top of **Figure 9.26** shows the trend in network and application protocol usage in **Figure 9.27**.

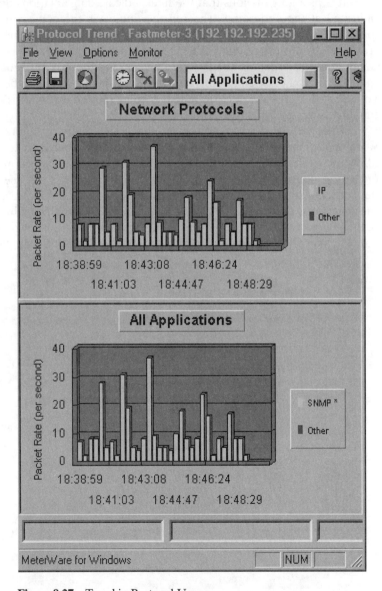

Figure 9.27   Trend in Protocol Usage

Again, we need more traffic to make this diagram interesting. Clicking the pie-shaped icon at the top of **Figure 9.27** creates **Figure 9.28**, the breakdown of application protocols. Finally, a nice graphical interface that supports the alMatrix group is obtained from the Meterware Summary View. On the Monitor menu, click Top Users Matrix to get the screen shown in **Figure 9.29**.

This graphic does not take much time to configure and is extremely useful on a large network. To see how to configure it, go to Table of Contents of the on-line Users Manual and look for the reference to **Top Users Matrix.**

It is probably obvious that the lines indicate conversations between the hosts indicated at the end-points. The red line indicates the conversation that has the most traffic (colors shown on Meterware Analyzer CD). The other colors indicate traffic relative to the red line. Blue is next in traffic followed by yellow. If you click on an end-point such as 192.192.192.241, you get the box showing specifics about that host. If you click on a line, you get the traffic in pkts/sec in both directions. As you see in the left pane, the traffic that is being plotted is for All-IP, i.e., any packets that are using any link layer protocol and the IP network layer protocol.

What we like most about this graphic is the ability to separate traffic by network environment. The top four buttons on the tool bar next to the printer icon allow the traffic to be separated into no filtering (far left), local network filtering, enterprise filtering and Internet filtering. Local filtering is not used since the local network, the subnet on which the probe resides (192.192.192.232), is made part of the enterprise network, 192.192.192.0. **Figure 9.29** is for "no filtering," as can be seen in the status bar at the bottom of the figure. In the pull-down menu on the tool bar, you may also select groups of protocols rather than just a single protocol as has

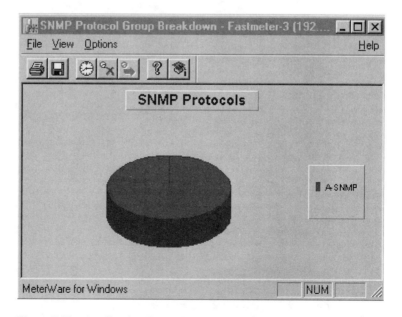

Figure 9.28   Application-Layer Protocols in Use

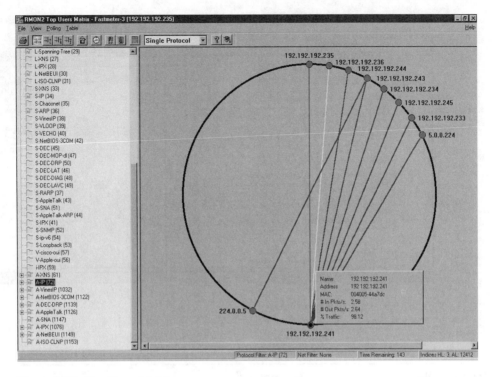

Figure 9.29 Top Users Matrix

been done in the figure. 150 rows of the alMatrixSDTable are included in each sample shown for the sampling interval.

Now let's look at what the **usrHistory group** can do for us.

9.2.7 usrHistory Group

This group was included in the RMON2 specification to enable network managers to collect a history on the activity of any network object that can be counted. The **usrHistoryControlTable** is very similar to the historyControlTable in RMON1 except that it includes the object usrHistoryControlObjects that has integer values to specify how many MIB Variable Instance identifiers will be tracked. The **usrHistoryObjectTable** has one row for each MIB Variable Instance identifier. The **usrHistoryTable** has "usrHistoryControlBucketsGranted" rows for each object in the usrHistoryObjectTable.

   Figure 9.30 shows the MIB Browser view of the usrHistory group. This group will test our understanding of using the MIB Browser because there is no Meterware graphical interface to help us. Also, the RMON2 standard in **[Ref 2]** is not very clear on the use of usrHistory objects. Therefore, we will work our way through it one step at a time. It turns out that there is an order to setting object values in these tables that is important. We will use one table to establish the order and describe the objects and another table to give an example of the process. We will start with the usrHistoryControlTable. usrHistory objects are described in **Tables 9.9, 9.10, and 9.11.**

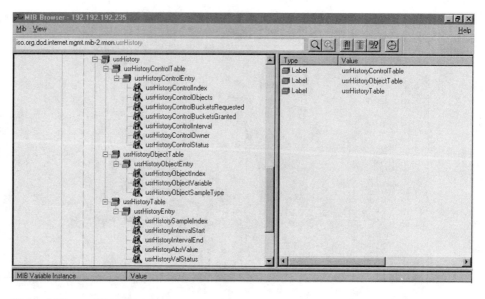

Figure 9.30 usrHistory group

Table 9.9 usrHistoryControlTable Objects (Index Object is usrHistoryControlIndex)

Order	Object	Description
1	usrHistoryControlStatus	This is the first object in the usrHistory Group, which must be set before any others can be configured. Highlight the object and click the SetRequest button at the top right of the MIB Browser screen in **Figure 9.30**. The following are possible object values: • active (1)—objects can be retrieved • notInService(2)—the row is not usable • notReady(3)—setting values of objects is not complete • createAndGo(4)—after values are set, row is made immediately active • createAndWait(5)—after values are set, status must be set to active(1) • destroy(6)—deletes all object values in row.
2	usrHistoryControlOwner	• The string that defines who created the usrHistoryControlTable. A typical value is "monitor."
3	usrHistoryControlObjects	• The integer that specifies the number of objects to be included in the usrHistoryObjectTable. These are the objects whose history will be documented.
4	usrHistoryControlInterval	• The sampling interval, in seconds, during which the objects specified in usrHistoryObjectTable will be counted
5	usrHistoryControlBuckets Requested	• An integer that specifies the number of sampling intervals requested for the objects specified in the usrHistoryObjectTable
N/A	usrHistoryControlBuckets Granted	• This value is set by the probe based on available resources.
N/A	usrHistoryControlIndex	• An integer that specifies a row in the usrHistoryControlTable. • This object is not accessible. It is set by the probe and has values starting from 0.

Table 9.10   usrHistoryObjectTable (Index Objects are: usrHistoryControlIndex and usrHistoryObjectIndex)

Order	Object	Description
6	usrHistoryObjectVariable	• The MIB Variable Instance of the object to be sampled
7	usrHistoryObjectSampleType	There are two possible values: • absoluteValue(1)—value of the variable at the end of the sampling interval • deltaValue(2)—the difference between the variable value at the end of the current interval and the previous interval, i.e., the change in the value.
N/A	usrHistoryObjectIndex	• An integer that uniquely identifies a row in this table • There is no access to this object

The usrHistoryObjectTable has a row for each distinct set of {usrHistoryControlIndex, usrHistoryControlObjects, usrHistoryControlBucketsRequested and usrHistoryControlInterval} created.

We now show how to configure the usrHistory Group to collect a history. We start with the MIB Browser view of the usrHistory Group in **Figure 9.30**. To configure the necessary objects we are going to use the values shown in **Table 9.12** in the order in which they are shown.

Table 9.11   usrHistoryTable (Index Objects are: usrHistoryControlIndex, usrHistorySampleIndex and usrHistoryObjectIndex)

Order	Object	Description
N/A	usrHistorySampleIndex	• An integer that identifies the row of the object in the usrHistoryObjectTable that is being sampled • This index increases by one for each sample taken.
N/A	usrHistoryIntervalStart	• The value of sysUpTime (mib-2 System Group) at the start of the sampling interval
N/A	usrHistoryIntervalEnd	• The value of sysUpTime at the end of the sampling interval
N/A	usrHistoryAbsValue	• The object that stores the samples of usrHistoryObjectVariable • The samples can be either positive or negative • If usrHistoryObjectSampleType is set to absoluteValue(1), the sample is the number of packets of usrHistoryObjectVariable seen during the sampling interval • If usrHistoryObjectSampleType is set to deltaValue(2), the sample is the difference between the number of packets seen during the current sampling interval and the number seen during the previous sampling interval. This difference can be positive or negative • The sign of the difference is the value of usrHistoryValStatus
N/A	usrHistoryValStatus	This object has the possible values: • valueNotAvailable(1) - value has not been determined • valuePositive(2) - value of usrHistoryAbsValue is positive • valueNegative(3) - value of usrHistoryAbsValue is negative

Table 9.12 Configuring the usrHistory Group

Order	Object	Description	Value
1	usrHistoryControlStatus	createAndWait	5
2	usrHistoryControlOwner	monitor	monitor
3	usrHistoryControlObjects	Number of objects	1
4	usrHistoryControlInterval	Seconds	60
5	usrHistoryControlBuckets Requested	Number of Sampling Intervals	50
6	usrHistoryObjectVariable	protocolDistStats Pkts.2.3	1.3.6.1.2.1.16.12.2.1.1.2.3
7	usrHistoryObjectSampleType	absoluteValue	1

What data will we collect by these settings for the usrHistoryControlTable objects? First, we are only collecting data on one object, protocolDistStatsPkts.2.3. This is the number of packets detected on Fastmeter port 2 using the IP network protocol over any Ethernet base layer (3). A sample will be taken for 60 seconds and there will be 50 samples. At the end of a sampling interval, the number of packets counted will be added to the number at the end of the previous sampling interval.

Figure 9.31 shows the procedure for setting usrHistoryControlStatus to createAndWait(5) by highlighting this object and then clicking the SetRequest button to get the screen shown in the lower right foreground.

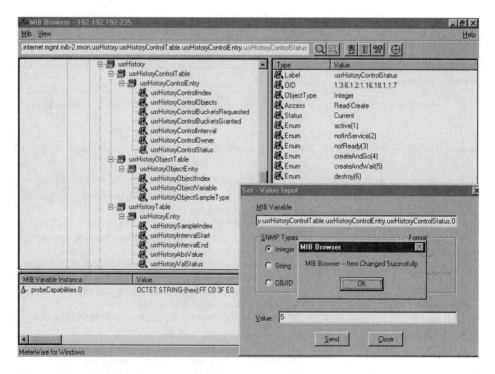

Figure 9.31 Procedure for Setting usrHistory group objects

You see that we have set the value to 5 which is "createAndWait" so that when all control objects are set we must then make the control table entry "valid." You also see that after you "send" this value, there is a response indicating the "set" was a success.

Continuing in the order shown in **Table 9.12**, we use the same procedure to set objects usrHistoryControlOwner through usrHistoryControlBucketsRequested. For reasons that are not clear, to set the next two objects, usrHistoryObjectVariable and usrHistoryObjectSampleType, you must first do a GetRequest to obtain the current values of these objects and then double-click the MIB Variable Instance to get the Set screen.

usrHistory Group is now configured to track the history of protocolDistStats-Pkts.2.3. Let's look at what is collected in **Figure 9.32**, based on two different usrHistoryTable configurations.

usrHistoryAbsValue is an object in the usrHistoryTable. The Index objects for this table are usrHistoryControlIndex, usrHistorySampleIndex and usrHistoryObjectIndex in the order concatenated to the Object Identifier.

The first six MIB Variable Instance values in the bottom panel are for the setting of usrHistoryObjectSampleType equal to absoluteValue(1). As you can see from the time dependence of the COUNTER value, the count of protocolDistStatsPkts.2.3 is always increasing. Although the RMON2 standard does not seem to

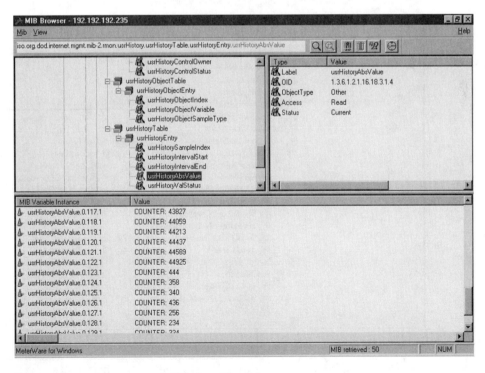

Figure 9.32   Values of protocolDistStatsPkts.2.3

specify this, the count must be the total count of all packets observed since the probe was turned on.

The last seven MIB Variable Instance values are for the setting of usrHistory-ObjectSampleType equal to deltaValue(2). In this case, the count is the difference between the total count at the end of the current interval and the count at the end of the previous interval. You see that these counts are much smaller. Checking the object usrHistoryValStatus shows that all counts are positive.

The usrHistory Group can be used to create a history of any mib-2 object that can be resolved to an Integer32, Counter, Gauge or TimeTicks type and is therefore a very powerful tool.

Now lets examine the last of the RMON2 Groups.

9.2.8 probeConfig Group

Figure 9.33 shows the MIB Browser view of the probeConfig group. The purpose of including this group in the RMON2 specification was to provide standardized objects whose values would make it easier for network managers to coordinate capabilities of NMSs from one vendor with probes from other vendors. Since these

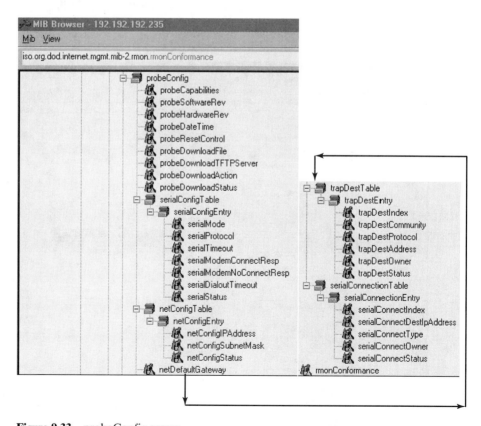

Figure 9.33 probeConfig group

Table 9.13 probeConfig Group object description

Object	Description
probeCapabilities	The right panel in **Figure 9.34** lists Fastmeter RMON1 and RMON2 probeCapabilities. The hex value FF C0 3F E0 of the probeCapabilities MIB Variable Instance in the bottom panel identifies the capabilities if it is converted to binary. Starting with bit 0 on the left, each bit that is 1 indicates support for that capability. For example, if the alarm group is supported, bit 3 would be 1.
probeResetControl	Has the following values: • (1) probe is running • (2) do a warm boot remotely • (3) do a cold boot remotely. Cold booting restores default configuration values in nonvolatile memory
probeDownloadFile	• Name of a the file that will update the probe boot image in flash memory
probeDownloadTFTPServer	• IP address of the TFTP server that will download the updated boot image • Meterware contains a TFTP server • The download can be initiated from either the probe console or from Meterware in the case of Fastmeter
probeDownloadAction	Has the following values: • (1) notDownloading • (2) discontinue normal operation, download the new boot image to PROM, and do a warm boot to restart the new boot image • (3) discontinue normal operation, download the new boot image to RAM but retain the old boot image in PROM
serialConfigTable	• There is one row in the table for each serial interface on the probe • Each row contains objects whose values are set to configure a modem communication link for the probe. This configuration can also be done through the probe console port using a PC in terminal mode such as Windows Hyperterminal
netConfigTable	• There is one row for each network interface on the probe • Objects are used to configure probe network address, subnet mask and default gateway
serialConnectionTable	• Stores the parameters required to initiate a SLIP connection to the management station. An example is: serialConnectionIPAddress—the IP address of the station on the other end of the SLIP connection
trapDestTable	Traps are used by the probe to notify the management station of an event that has been configured in the eventTable. The trapDestTable contains the following objects: • trapDestIndex—a unique integer that identifies a row in the table • trapDestCommunity: a. the community string that is associated with destination IP addresses to which the trap will be sent b. the trap is sent as a result of an event if eventCommunity =trapDestCommunity • trapDestProtocol—choices are: a. ip(1) b. ipx(2) • trapDestAddress—the IP or IPX address to which the trap will be sent.

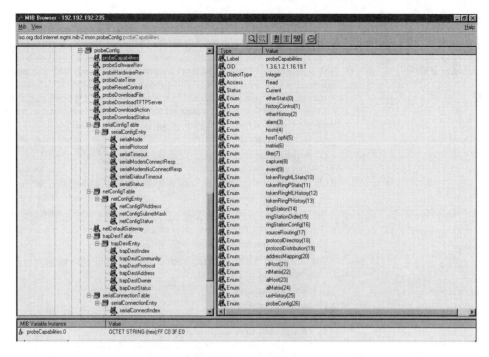

Figure 9.34 Fastmeter RMON and RMON2 Capabilities

objects are helpful for implementation, Table 9.13 is provided to clarify the uses of those that are not obvious. See **[Ref 2]** for more details on probeConfig objects and their use.

probeCapabilities is a very useful object. It identifies all rmon (RMON1 and RMON2) groups that the probe supports. Those for Fastmeter are shown in **Figure 9.34**. As explained in Table 9.13, the MIB Variable Instance probeCapabilites.0 value of FF C0 3F E0 hex identifies all the probe capabilities that are shown in the right panel of the figure. We have explored all of these in this and the preceding chapter.

9.2.9 Other rmon Devices

Probes are dedicated rmon devices. However, there are other devices, such as switches and hubs, which host rmon objects. As time goes on, we can expect to see more devices doing this. However, there is the constraint that serving SNMP polls takes processing time that is critical on switches and routers.

Our demonstration network has three devices that host rmon objects other than the probes: the 2 CISCO Catalyst 1900 switches and the 3COM hub. These devices host only RMON1 groups and only some of groups in the case of the switches. Sometimes, the latter devices are called RMON Lite or mini-RMON.

9.2.10 RMON2 Groups Not Discussed

There are two RMON2 groups that were not discussed in detail: addressMap group and alHost group. We felt that the use of these groups would be clear from others we have discussed. We will summarize their characteristics here.

- ❏ **addressMap group**

  The objects are shown in the addressMap MIB Browser view. The graphical interface to this group is identical to that of many others, for example nlHost. The display of hosts is determined by protocol selection. For every host that has used that protocol, the host IP address and name is listed. For each IP address listing, the hardware address and the Data Source ifIndex object is given.

- ❏ **alHost group**

  The objects are shown in the alHost MIB Browser view. The graphical interface to this group is also identical to that of nlHost group for example. The display of hosts is determined by protocol selection. For every host that has used the protocol, the host IP address, its name, the number of inPkts and outPkts and the number of inOctets and outOctets are listed.

  [Refs 1-2] should be consulted for any details on these groups that are not clear from their MIB Browser view or from what has been said about other groups.

CHAPTER SUMMARY

RMON2 objects enable analysis of traffic at the network and higher layer protocols. There is a large array of RMON2 tables and each contains many objects. Thus, this chapter created tables to organize, coordinate and explain them. The MIB Browser, Meterware and the Fastmeter probe were used to demonstrate how to access network traffic parameters. As in the previous chapter on RMON1, we continued to make use of the MIB Browser to demonstrate fundamental concepts and to relate those demonstrations to how Meterware GUI applications work. The power of those applications is especially clear in this chapter.

The RMON2 protocolDir group serves as entrée into the other groups. Its object values influence the functionality of the rest of the groups. The key objects, protocolDirID and protocolDirParameters, were discussed at length. protocolDirID is a hierarchical system of protocol identifiers that is used in Index Objects to identify the protocol. protocolDirParameters provides an octet of bits for every protocol in a packet. These bits identify capabilities of the protocol such as the ability to process network addresses. The Meterware companion graphical interface to the protocolDir group is called Protocol Directory Administration. This screen shows all protocols that the probe supports, current protocol traffic, all protocolDir object values and a histogram of traffic distributed among the most active protocols. The last encompasses the protocolDist group objects.

RMON2 made use of the SMIv2 **[Ref 5]** to include Index Objects not in the groups whose objects they index. This feature provides added value without adding column objects. Indexing is more complex in RMON2. Because of that, we provided a table that summarizes Index Objects so that they could be compared and referenced as needed.

Key features of RMON2 are the two groups, nlMatrix and alMatrix, which enable host conversations to be detected and analyzed. Conversations were segregated by network layer and higher layer protocols and displayed using graphical interfaces. In addition, trend analyses showed the time-dependence of the distribution of traffic among protocols. These tools were used to analyze traffic that was created by sending ICMP (ping) messages as well as FTP and HTTP messages to the NT4.0 Server IIS.

The usrHistory group is similar to the history group in RMON but allows the user a choice of objects to be sampled over time. Meterware does not provide a graphical interface for the usrHistory group.

Finally, the probeConfig group was examined. This group enables coordination between diverse management applications and probes. A primary object in this group is the probeCapabilities object whose value identifies all the RMON2 groups that a probe supports. It also has objects that specify how the probe is to communicate remotely with a management station using a SLIP interface and a modem

REVIEW QUESTIONS

1. What is the principal functionality added by RMON2 objects relative to that provided by RMON1 objects?
2. How do the Ethermeter and Fastmeter probes differ in their capabilities?
3. What does it mean for a protocol to be extensible?
4. What is the result of setting the object protocolDirAddressMapConfig to supportedOff (2)?
5. What is the Object Identifier for the object protocolDirLocalIndex?
6. True or False? When a column object is also an Index Object, its value is not included in instances of column object.
7. Where can you find all the protocols supported by a probe in the Meterware NMS?
8. Why do some MIB Variable Instance Identifiers have more than one value of the Index Object protocolDirLocalIndex?
9. How does the nlHost group in RMON2 differ from the Host group in RMON1?
10. What reference do you use to find all protocol numbers?
11. What capability does the usrHistory group provide that the history group in RMON does not?
12. What do the Index object values in protocolDistStatsPkts.2.3 in **Figure 9.11** represent?

1. Create the protocolDirID for the protocol ether2/ip4/tcp/icmp.
2. Create the MIB Variable Instance for protocolDistStatsPkts for the UDP protocol and port 3 of Fastmeter.
3. Use **[Ref 3]** to create the protocolDirParameters for the ether2/ip/tcp/HTTP protocol.
4. Use the MIB Browser to access the protocolDirTable. Use the GetRequest message to get the values of protocolDirLocalIndex. Identify an instance of the protocol ether2/ip.
5. Use Meterware alMatrix to view traffic on your network. Select the application A-SNMP-U to filter the traffic. Use the protocolDirLocalIndex to identify the MIB Variable Instance for alMatrixSDPkts in the MIB Browser. Use the instance to create a table like that shown in **Table 9.8**.
6. For each device on your network that you think may have rmon capabilities, see if they support the probeConfig group. If so, use the probeCapabilities object in the group to list the capabilities. Make a table of them for each device. Then access the netConfigTable to determine the IP or IPX addresses of the serial interface. Include that in your table.
7. If the probeConfig group is supported on a probe that you have on your network, identify the IP addresses of the trap destinations from the trapDestTable.
8. Use the usrHistory tables to create the values necessary to track nlHostInPackets for a host of your choice for 15 minutes. Set the sampling interval to 60secs. Set the usrHistoryObjectSampleType to deltaValue. Plot the values of usrHistoryAbsValue as a function of time for 15 minutes.
9. According to the RMON2 specification, protocolDirID has Max-access = not accessible. Thus, it is not directly available to the MIB Browser. However, since it is an Index object, it is indirectly available in every object instance identifier in the protocolDirTable. What is the protocolDirID for ether2.ip.tcp.http?

REFERENCES

1. "SNMP, SNMPv2 and RMON," second edition, William Stallings, Addison Wesley, 1996.
2. "Remote Network Monitoring Management Information Base Version 2 using SMIv2, S. Waldbusser, Request for Comments 2021, January 1997, http://www.cis.ohio-state.edu/cgi-bin/rfc/rfc2021.html
3. "Remote Network Monitoring MIB Protocol Identifier Reference." Request for Comments: 2895, A. Bierman and C. Bucci Cisco Systems, Inc. and R. Iddon, 3COM, Inc., August 2000, http://www.csl.sony.co.ip/rfc/cache/rfc2895.txt.html
4. Internet Assigned Numbers Authority, "Protocol Numbers and Assignment Services," http://www.iana.org/numbers.htm
5. "Structure of Management Information for version 2 of the Simple Network Management Protocol (SNMPv2)." Request for Comments: *1442*, J. Case, SNMP Research, Inc. K. McCloghrie Hughes LAN Systems M. Rose Dover Beach Consulting, Inc. S. Waldbusser Carnegie Mellon University, April 1993.

CHAPTER 10

DESKTOP MANAGEMENT

- Desktop Management Interface (DMI)
- Management Information Files (MIFs)
- DMI Attributes
- DMI Elements
- SNMP Subagents
- Demonstrate MIF to MIB Mapping
- Demonstrate Use of SNMP Extension Agents
- Host MIB
- Demonstrate SNMP Access to DMI Agents

One of the more recently developed network management protocols is called the Desktop Management Interface (DMI). The DMI is a standard developed by a consortium of companies needing access to more information about the desktop system than is provided by mib-2 objects. This consortium is called the Desktop Management Taskforce (DMTF). Their model for DMI management is similar to that of SNMP management. However, they are not identical and are implemented differently. In this chapter we will discuss the DMI model and demonstrate its use.

10.1 THE DESKTOP MANAGEMENT INTERFACE (DMI)

10.1.1 DMI Architecture

The DMI standard is a 254-page document. We could spend as much time discussing and implementing its concepts as we spent on Chapters 6 and 7. We will limit our discussion to the main concepts presented in the standard and then use an IBM implementation of the DMI for demonstration.

The DMI models a system composed of hardware, software and firmware components. A **component** is specified by a Management Information File **(MIF)** that defines the component's **attributes**. A MIF is similar to an SNMP MIB and an attribute is similar to an SNMP object, as we will see in more detail below. A management application such as a browser needs to access component MIF files to determine attribute values. When doing so directly, a browser, for example, sends a Remote Procedure Call (RPC) to the DMI agent. A RPC is a protocol in the TCP/IP Application layer and the DMI agent consists of software components that reside on the desktop being queried. **Figure 10.1** shows the DMI architecture. This figure is modified for our purposes from that accessed from **[Ref 1]** where you can open or download the DMI 2.0s Specification. The figure is on page 11 of that specification. **[Ref 2]** is another useful reference to DMTF documents.

Figure 10.1 suggests that the DMI implementation is composed of three major parts: management (e.g., browser), DMI Service Provider and components. The **DMI Service Provider** controls the communication between management and components.

When the browser is the DMI application on the local desktop, as it is in Figure 10.1, it creates a Remote Procedure Call and RPC Support translates the call for the **Management Interface Server**. This server is a **Management API** that is the primary interface between management software and the DMI Service Provider. The DMI Service Provider passes the request to the **Procedural Component Interface**, a **Component API** that also acts as a switchboard to **Procedural Component Instrumentation (CI).** CIs are code written by vendors to define access

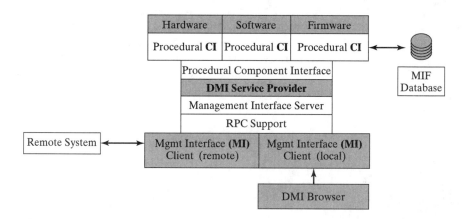

Figure 10.1 DMI Architecture

to manageable aspects of the component (e.g., network card, processor, modem, BIOS) so that MIF files can be written for them.

Figure 10.1 also indicates that a component's MIF can be accessed from a remote system. This can be a DMI browser using a RPC or a management application using SNMP as we will see below

Table 10.1 summarizes the DMI terms and interfaces we have just discussed. The order in the table is from top to bottom in **Figure 10.1**.

As the reader can see from the table, when we breakdown the DMI implementation into its elements, there are many software modules. Of course, this is no different from what is required to implement any complex interface.

10.1.2 The DMI Browser

To gain a better understanding of desktop information that can be accessed using the DMI, we examine what is provided by the DMI browser and the DMI agent on the IntelliStation ZPRO Server on our demonstration network. The browser and the agent were shipped with the ZPRO Server and we installed them. **Figure 10.2** shows the browser opened.

The white labels were inserted by the author. As you can see, icons enable the user to install and uninstall desktop components to be managed. The description of the icon appears when the mouse pointer overlays its button. Newly installed com-

Table 10.1 DMI Architecture Element Description

Elements	Description
Components	• Hardware, software or firmware that make up the computer system • The manageable characteristics of a component are described by a Management Information Format **(MIF)** file • The MIF file is similar to the MIB in SNMP
Procedural Component Instrumentation (CI)	• Created by component vendor to describe access to manageable aspects of the component • Implements component management
Procedural Component Interface	• An API that enables communication between the DMI Service Provider and the Procedural CIs
DMI Service Provider	• Provides the primary software interface between management applications and components • Acts as a layer of abstraction between these two worlds that minimizes the detail necessary to implement DMI management
Management Interface Server	• An API that enables communication between a management application and the DMI Service Provider
RPC Support	• Provides translation between the Management Interface(MI) client that issues the RPC and the Management Interface Server
Management Interface (MI) Client (local or remote)	• Used by management applications that wish to manage a component • Software that supports the RPC request at the local or remote computer
Management Interface (MI) Client (local or remote)	• Used by management applications that wish to manage a component • Software that supports the RPC request at the local or remote computer
DMI Browser	• Application that accesses the attributes of a component.

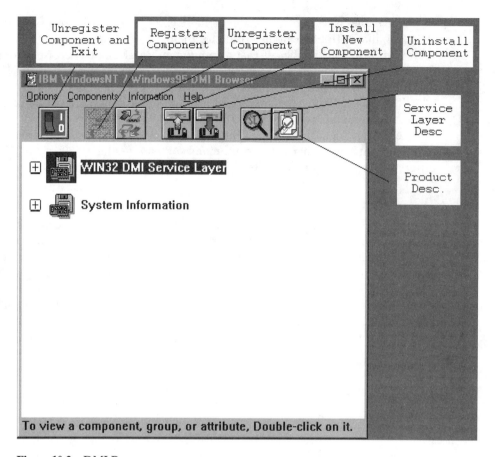

Figure 10.2 DMI Browser screen

ponents must be registered with the DMI Service Provider, using the Register Component icon, for communication between them to take place.

The two items listed on the screen are the DMI Components: WIN32 DMI Service Layer and System Information. (The WIN32 DMI Service Layer is now called the WIN32 Service Provider.) These two components provide all the information currently made available about the IBM IntelliStation ZPRO desktop computer. Let's first discuss the Service Layer component.

10.2 INTELLISTATION ZPRO COMPONENTS

10.2.1 WIN32 DMI Service Layer Component

This component is required to be present in every DMI implementation. Clicking the (+) sign provides a list of the groups in this component, as shown in **Figure 10.3**. DMI groups are similar to SMI groups

For this version of the WIN32 Service Layer there is only one group, ComponentID. Each group contains attributes. Attributes are similar to SMI objects. To get

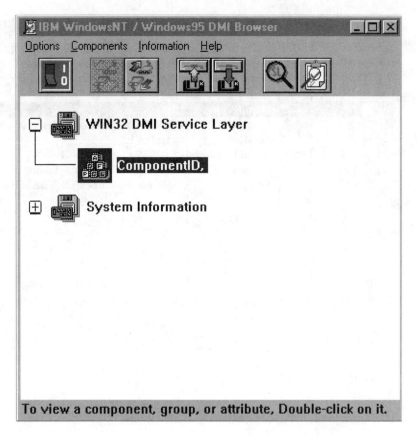

Figure 10.3 ComponentID Group of the WIN32 DMI Service Layer
Component

a list of the attributes of ComponentID, you double-click it. The result is shown in
Figure 10.4.

At the top of **Figure 10.4** is the definition **ID: 0001 - Class: DMTF | Compo-
nentID | 1.0**. This definition specifies that the group has the ID 0001, the group
defining body is the DMTF, the group has the name ComponentID and the version
of the Product is 1.0. Each row in the figure represents an attribute. The elements of
the attributes are listed across the top. Remember that attributes are like SNMP
objects. **Attribute Elements** are like SNMP clauses that define objects. Since not all
elements of the attributes can be seen at the screen resolution used for **Figure 10.4**
and to explain the attributes better, **Table 10.2** was constructed. The orientation of
this table is more familiar because we present the attributes like SMI object definition clauses are presented.

For example, the value for attribute with ID = "5" is the date and time on
which the latest installation of the IBM DMI Browser occurred on the IBM IntelliStation ZPRO computer. The date is 09-23-2001 and the time is 15:06:13 in hours,
minutes and seconds. The numbers 004060 represent time in microseconds. −300
means 300 minutes (5 hours) west of UTC (Greenwich time).

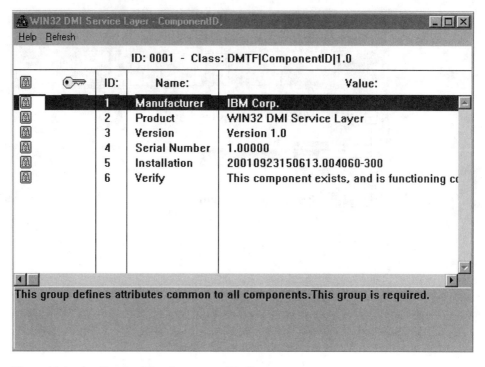

Figure 10.4 Attributes of the ComponentID Group

10.2.2 System Information Component

This component has many groups as suggested by **Figure 10.5,** where only some of them are shown. Scrolling this list shows many other groups. These include memory modules, expansion slots, motherboard and language groups. Slot information is an

Table 10.2 Attributes of the Component ID Group

Attribute Elements	Attributes					
ID	1	2	3	4	5	6
Name	Manufacturer	Product	Version	Serial #	Installation	Verify
Desc.	Product Producer	Name of Component	Component Version	Serial # for this version	Time/Date of last installation	Level of verification
Access	Read-Only	Read-Only	Read-Only	Read-Only	Read-Only	Read-Only
Storage	Common	Common	Common	Specific	Specific	Specific
Type	*String(64)*	*String(64)*	*String(64)*	*String(64)*	Date	Verify Type
Value	IBM Corp.	WIN32 Service Layer	"Version 1.0"	"1.00000"	200109231 50613.0040 60-300	7 (Working)

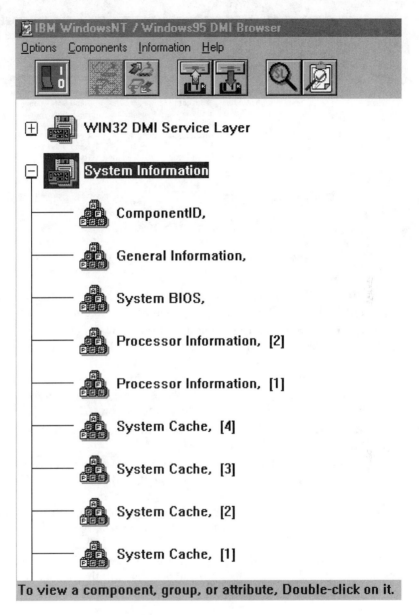

Figure 10.5   Some Groups of the System Information Component

example of something always useful to know without having to open the box even if you can do it locally. **Figure 10.6** shows the attributes of Slot Group [1].

Each row in this figure represents an attribute. Attribute elements are shown across the top of the table starting on the left with ID. The information in this figure is described as follows:

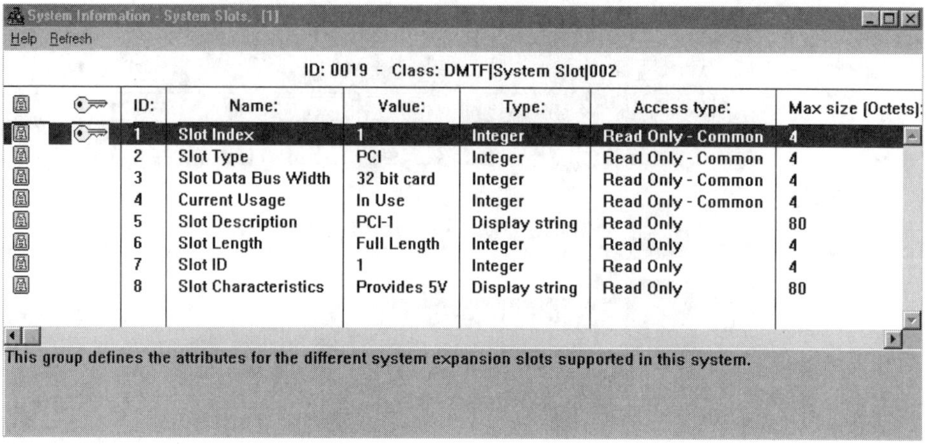
System Information - System Slots, [1]

Help Refresh

ID: 0019 - Class: DMTF|System Slot|002

ID:	Name:	Value:	Type:	Access type:	Max size (Octets):
1	Slot Index	1	Integer	Read Only - Common	4
2	Slot Type	PCI	Integer	Read Only - Common	4
3	Slot Data Bus Width	32 bit card	Integer	Read Only - Common	4
4	Current Usage	In Use	Integer	Read Only - Common	4
5	Slot Description	PCI-1	Display string	Read Only	80
6	Slot Length	Full Length	Integer	Read Only	4
7	Slot ID	1	Integer	Read Only	4
8	Slot Characteristics	Provides 5V	Display string	Read Only	80

This group defines the attributes for the different system expansion slots supported in this system.

Figure 10.6 Attributes of the System Slot Group 1

- **System Information—System Slots, [1]**—specifies that the table describes the attributes in the System Slot #1 group of the System Information component
- **ID: 0019—Class: DMTF | System Slot | 002**—specifies that the ID of this group is 0019, and that its class definition is DMTF|System Slot | 002. DMTF is the organization that created the group, System Slot is the name of the group and 002 is the version of the software that implements access to the group attributes. As the DMI model in **Figure 10.1** shows, this software is called Procedural Component Instrumentation **(CI)**.
- **ID, Name, Value, Type, Access type and Max size (Octets)**—the attribute elements
- **Key**—indicates that the value of Slot Index (1 in this case) is to be used to identify this System Slot group among the others that may exist.

The vendors that make up the DMTF realized that to make the DMI standard viable, access would need to be convenient to large numbers of users. To this end, the DMTF designed software that would enable translation between the SNMP MIB format and the DMTF MIF format so that a management application using SNMP could access DMI attributes transparently. This mapping implementation is discussed in the next section.

10.3 DMI/SNMP MAPPING

The best description of the interoperability required of DMI and SNMP is provided by the following that is quoted from **[Ref 1]**.

"The Desktop Management Framework and the Internet-standard Network Management Framework, commonly known as the "SNMP Management Framework," are standard management frameworks widely deployed to manage computer systems and network devices, respectively. The two frameworks are similar in concept and function. However, while the two frameworks may co-exist on the same system, the two are not inherently interoperable. Despite this, applications that span the heterogeneous nature of system and network management must access management information using both frameworks. Therefore, the objective of this mapping standard is to bridge the interoperability gap between SNMP and DMI-based solutions. For example, by providing the mapping specified in this document, existing SNMP-based applications and/or toolkits can be leveraged to manage DMI-based systems as well as SNMP devices." DMI to SNMP mapping is discussed in **[Ref 3].**

A diagram of DMI to SNMP mapping is provided by **Figure 10.7**. The IBM System View product has used this architecture to implement DMI and the mapping from DMI to SNMP.

The difference between **Figure 10.7** and **Figure 10.1** is indicated by the shaded modules at the bottom of the diagram. The IBM System View implementation provides an SNMP agent, a DMI subagent and a Distributed Protocol Interface (DPI). These modules are typical of the functionality necessary to provide the mapping. Through the DPI, the DMI subagent registers components with the SNMP agent. When the SNMP agent receives a SNMP packet requesting the value of a DMI attribute, the SNMP agent recognizes the component whose attribute is being requested. The SNMP agent then passes the request to the DMI subagent, which in turn maps the request into DMI MIF terminology. The reverse mapping is done when the DMI Service Layer passes the MIF reply to the DMI subagent.

For all this to happen, there must be a translation between MIB Object Identifier (OID) format and MIF attribute format. This is done by creating two mapping files. One is called a DMISA.MAP file by IBM where DMISA stands for DMI Subagent. An example of such a file is shown in **Figure 10.8**.

The top line labels the individual parts of an entry. The second line is an example entry. The third line is an actual entry and the fourth line is the entry we are

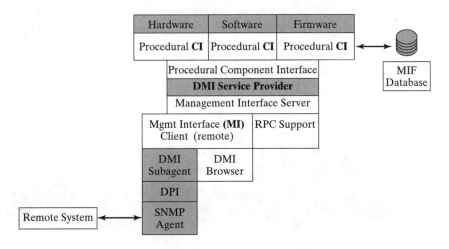

Figure 10.7 DMI Architecture with SNMP Agent and DMI Subagent

```
/* "oid" 1 group-id 1 attribute-id "component-name" key-count keys */
/* "1.3.6.1.4.1.2.5.11.1.5"  1 1 1 1  "PC Systems MIF" 0 0 */

"1.3.6.1.4.1.2.5.11.6"  1 1 1 1  "DMTF Developers - Direct
Interface Version" 0 0

"1.3.6.1.4.1.2.5.11.1.99"  1 1 1 1  "WIN32 DMI Service Layer" 0 0
```

Figure 10.8   IBM DMISA.MAP file

using for our example. The first part of an entry is the OID of the object in the management application MIB. We will see this OID in the Meterware MIB below. The rest of the entry relates the OID to the MIF structure. The most important part is, for our example, the MIF Name "WIN32 DMI Service Layer." If this mapping entry is correct, the SNMP agent will know to pass the SNMP packet it receives to the DMI subagent.

The other requirement is a utility that converts a MIF file into a MIB file that can be used by a MIB Browser. The MIB file is compiled as we did in Chapter 7 and added to the MIB Browser on the management station. First, let's look at the command that produces the MIF-to-MIB translation and then at the corresponding MIF and MIB files for the WIN32 DMI Service Layer component on the ZPRO. **Figure 10.9** shows the screen capture of the translation command.

The MIB hierarchy for the IBM ZPRO SNMP agent requires that new objects become a subtree under **ibmDmiMib.** We have chosen to call the root of the subtree **mydmtfGroups** and to give it the OID 1.3.6.1.4.1.2.5.11.1.99 as shown in the DMISA.MAP file in **Figure 10.8**. The file **win32sl.mif** is the MIF file that will be translated into a MIB file and automatically saved with the name **win32sl.mib.**

Now let's look at the content of these two files so that we can compare MIF format to MIB format and see how they differ. This comparison is important in order to get a better understanding of the DMI operation. **Figure 10.10** shows the win32sl.mif file.

The DMI browser reads a MIF file and presents a screen like that shown in **Figure 10.2**. Text that is bolded in **Figure 10.10** was done by the author to further clarify the start and stop of component, group and attributes sections.

```
Command Prompt                                                        _ □ X
Microsoft(R) Windows NT(TM)
(C) Copyright 1985-1996 Microsoft Corp.

D:\>miftomib "mydmtfGroups = {enterprises ibm(2) ibmArchitecture(5) ibmDmi(11)
ibmDmiMib(1) 99 }" D:\sva\dmi\bin\backup\win32sl.mif
```

Figure 10.9   miftomib command and its parameters

```
start component
    name        = "WIN32 DMI Service Layer"
    description = "This is information about the service layer itself."
///////////////////////////////////////////////
//
//
//              component id group                 //
//
//
///////////////////////////////////////////////
// Component ID Group
// Enumerations for this group
//

  Start Enum
    Name = "Verify_Type"
    Type = Integer
    0x00 = "An error occurred; check status code"
    0x01 = "This component does not exist"
    0x02 = "The verify is not supported"
    0x03 = "Reserved"
    0x04 = "This component exists, but the functionality is untested"
    0x05 = "This component exists, but the functionality is unknown"
    0x06 = "This component exists, and is not functioning correctly"
    0x07 = "This component exists, and is functioning correctly"
  End Enum

  start group
    name    = "ComponentID"
    id      = 1
    class   = "DMTF | ComponentID |1.0"
    description = "This group defines attributes common to all components."
                  "This group is required."

    start attribute
      name    = "Manufacturer"
      id      = 1
      description = "The name of the manufacturer that produces this
                    component."
      access  = READ-ONLY
      storage = COMMON
      type    = STRING(64)
      value   = "IBM Corp."
    end attribute
```

(continued)

Figure 10.10   win32sl.mif file

```
start attribute
  name    = "Product"
  id      = 2
  description = "The name of the component."
  access  = READ-ONLY
  storage = COMMON
  type    = STRING(64)
  value   = "WIN32 DMI Service Layer"
end attribute

start attribute
  name    = "Version"
  id      = 3
  description = "The version for the component."
  access  = READ-ONLY
  storage = COMMON
  type    = STRING(64)
  value   = "Version 1.0"
end attribute

start attribute
  name    = "Serial Number"
  id      = 4
  description = "The serial number for this instance of this
                component."
  access  = READ-ONLY
  storage = SPECIFIC
  type    = STRING(64)
  value   = "1.0000
end attribute

start attribute
  name    = "Installation"
  id      = 5
  description = "The time and date of the last install of this
                component."
  access  = READ-ONLY
  storage = SPECIFIC
  type    = DATE
  value   = ""
end attribute
```

Figure 10.10   *Continued*

```
    start Attribute
      Name = "Verify"
      Id = 6
      Access = Read-Only
      Storage = Specific
      Type = "Verify_Type"
      Description = "A code that provides a level of verification
                    that the component is still installed and working."
      Value = 0x07
    end Attribute

  end group

end component
```

Figure 10.10 *Continued*

Figure 10.11 shows the MIB produced by applying the utility **miftomib** to the MIF described above. The reader can immediately see similarities in MIF and MIB formats. The MIB format is the same as we saw in Chapter 7. At least one of the MIF designers pointed out in a DMTF document that the MIB format would probably have been used by the DTMF if the agreement on attributes could have been resolved.

Once the win32sl.mib file is compiled and added to the Meterware MIB Browser, the MIB Browser display is that shown in **Figure 10.12**. dmtfGroups is an object inserted by the IBM System View Agent MIF to MIB conversion software. "t" **in tComponent** stands for table, which is actually a "Sequence of" in MIB language. The six DMI attributes of the Component ID group are shown as leaves under ecomponentid, where the "e" in **eComponentid** stands for entry.

By clicking the attribute **a1Manufacturer,** we are presented with its OID in the top right panel. "a1" in a1Manufacturer stands for "attribute in the first group of the of WIN Service Layer Component." Notice that its value is that which we placed in the DMISA.MAP file plus four ones. The first "one" means all attributes are in Key order, the second "one" is not defined, the third "one" means this attribute is in group 1 and the fourth "one" is the ID of the attribute. This ID will change when different attributes are selected.

The data in the bottom panel is the result of doing an SNMP GetRequest with a1Manufacturer selected. Thus, the DMI subagent is doing the translation job correctly because it returned the correct value of a1Manufacturer, namely IBM Corp.

In the section just concluded, we have investigated the software designed by IBM to implement the DMI specification and to translate MIF files to MIB files. The reader should explore software other vendors provide to implement the DMI specification for desktop information and to provide access to SNMP management stations. (See **Table 3.9**.)

```
WIN32DMISERVICELAYER-MIB DEFINITIONS ::= BEGIN
— This is information about the service layer itself.
IMPORTS
    OBJECT-TYPE
    FROM RFC-1212
    enterprises
    FROM RFC1155-SMI
    DisplayString
    FROM RFC1213-MIB;
DmiInteger                  ::= INTEGER
DmiDisplaystring       ::= DISPLAYSTRING
DmiDate                            ::= OCTET STRING (SIZE (28))
DmiComponentIndex      ::= INTEGER

mydmtfGroups         OBJECT IDENTIFIER ::=  { enterprises
ibm(2)ibmArchitecture(5) ibmDmi(11) ibmDmiMib(1) 99 }
dmtfGroups           OBJECT IDENTIFIER ::= {mydmtfGroups  1}

SComponentid ::= SEQUENCE {
    a1Manufacturer                          DmiDisplaystring,
    a1Product                               DmiDisplaystring,
    a1Version                               DmiDisplaystring,
    a1SerialNumber                          DmiDisplaystring,
    a1Installation                          DmiDate,
    a1Verify                                DmiInteger
}

tComponentid OBJECT-TYPE
    SYNTAX        SEQUENCE OF SComponentid
    ACCESS        not-accessible
    STATUS        mandatory
    DESCRIPTION   "This group defines attributes common to all components.
                  This group is required."
    ::= {dmtfGroups 1}

eComponentid OBJECT-TYPE
    SYNTAX        SComponentid
    ACCESS        not-accessible
    STATUS        mandatory
    DESCRIPTION   ""
    INDEX         {DmiComponentIndex}
    ::= {tComponentid 1}

a1Manufacturer OBJECT-TYPE
    SYNTAX        DmiDisplaystring
    ACCESS        read-only
    STATUS        mandatory
    DESCRIPTION   "The name of the manufacturer that produces this
                  component."
    ::= {eComponentid 1}
```

Figure 10.11   win32sl.mib file

```
a1Product OBJECT-TYPE
     SYNTAX          DmiDisplaystring
     ACCESS          read-only
     STATUS          mandatory
     DESCRIPTION     "The name of the component."
     ::= {eComponentid 2}

a1Version OBJECT-TYPE
     SYNTAX          DmiDisplaystring
     ACCESS          read-only
     STATUS          mandatory
     DESCRIPTION     "The version for the component."
     ::= {eComponentid 3}

a1SerialNumber OBJECT-TYPE
     SYNTAX          DmiDisplaystring
     ACCESS          read-only
     STATUS          mandatory
     DESCRIPTION     "The serial number for this instance of this component."
     ::= {eComponentid 4}

a1Installation OBJECT-TYPE
     SYNTAX          DmiDate
     ACCESS          read-only
     STATUS          mandatory
     DESCRIPTION     "The time and date of the last install of this
                     component."
     ::= {eComponentid 5}

a1Verify OBJECT-TYPE
     SYNTAX          INTEGER {
          vAnErrorOccurredCheckStatusCode           (0),
          vThisComponentDoesNotExist                (1),
          vTheVerifyIsNotSupported                  (2),
          vReserved                                 (3),
          vThisComponentExistsButTheFunctionalityI  (4),
          vThisComponentExistsButTheFunctionality1  (5),
          vThisComponentExistsAndIsNotFunctioningC  (6),
          vThisComponentExistsAndIsFunctioningCorr  (7)
     }
     ACCESS          read-only
     STATUS          mandatory
     DESCRIPTION     "A code that provides a level of verification that the
                     componentis still installed and working."
     ::= {eComponentid 6}

END
```

Figure 10.11 *Continued*

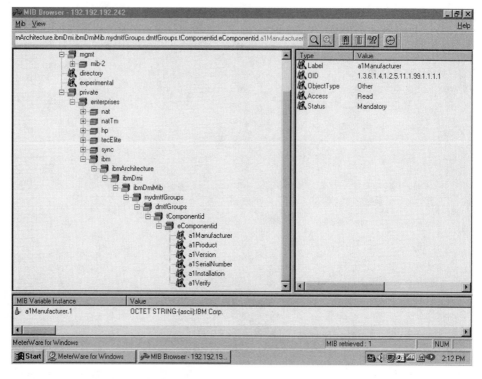

Figure 10.12 Meterware MIB Browser on WS2 showing the ibm(2) tree added to the enterprise group.

IBM no longer supports System View Agent because it has chosen to concentrate most of its network management development efforts on its high-end Tivoli Network Management System. Nevertheless, the concepts we have described for System View Agent apply to DMI implementations by other vendors. An on-line reference to Tivoli can be found in **Table 3.9**.

It is also possible for a vendor to extend an SNMP agent on a desktop that normally accesses only mib-2 standard objects to access objects of vendor interest. We look at such an extension in the next section.

10.4 DESKTOP SNMP EXTENSION AGENTS

Windows NT 4.0 Server (or the separate CD-ROM Server Resource Kit that was employed here) provides three enterprise SNMPv1 extension agents: one for the Windows Name Service (WINS), one for the Dynamic Host Configuration Protocol (DHCP) and one for the Internet Information Server (IIS). We compiled the associated MIBs using Meterware's compiler (see Chapter 7 for the discussion of how to do this) and added them to the Meterware MIB Browser under the microsoft/software subtree as shown in **Figure 10.13**.

The node labeled "grandjunction" in **Figure 10.13** is the Cisco enterprise node that we explored in Chapter 7. Each of the Microsoft nodes dhcp, intenetServer and wins contain many objects that can be used to examine Server activities. As an example, let's expand the **wins** node and its **par**(ameter) subnode in **Figure 10.14**. We have highlighted leaf node **parWinsTotalNoOfReq,** which has the OID of 1.3.6.1.4.1.311.1.2.1.12 and executed a GetRequest from SERVER. parWinsTotal-NoOfReq stands for the "total number of requests to WINS for NetBIOS name to IP address." Counter has the value 5 indicating there have been five requests of WINS for IP addresses associated with device NetBIOS names. The node 1.3.6.1.4.1.311 is the OID assigned to Microsoft by the IETF.

As you can see, there are many objects whose values describe the WINS application. These values are not available from Windows NT 4.0. It should also be clear that there is no end to the number of desktop components and their attributes that could be added to the DMI environment. **[Ref 4]** provides some recently developed desktop software products.

In addition to SNMP extension agents and the DMI 2.0 Specification, the Host MIB provides objects whose values characterize a desktop system. Let's take a brief look at this MIB.

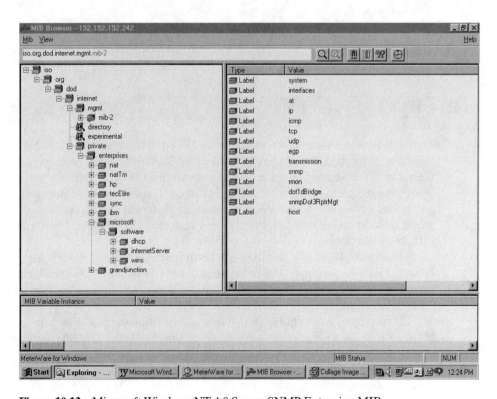

Figure 10.13 Microsoft Windows NT 4.0 Server SNMP Extension MIBs

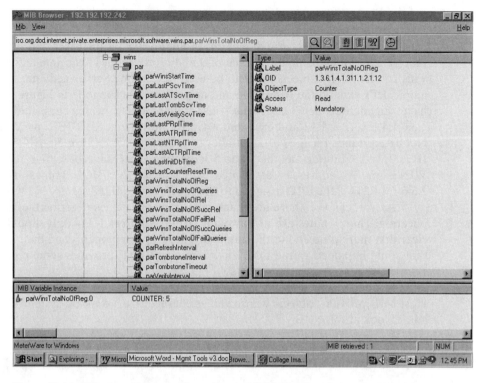

Figure 10.14 Windows Internet Name Service (WINS) "par" Subnode Objects

10.5 HOST MIB

The MIB Browser view shown in **Figure 10.15** shows objects in the Host MIB **[Ref 5]**. We have expanded hrStorageTypes and hostStorageTable to give you a feel for their objects. hrStorageTypes certainly provide useful information about the types of storage media that the desktop has installed. The entries in hrStorageTable contain column objects whose values characterize different storage allocations. Entries might include disk partitions, file systems, ram and virtual store for paging. Again, valuable information.

Figure 10.16 shows another interesting set of objects under the hrDevice branch. Here, for example, the hrPartitionTable tell us partition sizes and the associated file system. hrFSTypes lists all known file systems such as the File Allocation Table (FAT) system.

Unfortunately, vendors have infrequently implemented this mib-2 standard MIB. In fact, in spite of the availability of this MIB, the DMI Specification and SNMP extension agents, this desktop information is not uniformly available.

In the next chapter, we look at another recent addition to the set of network management tools. This addition is entitled Web-based Management because it can be implemented using HTTP from any computer with a web browser.

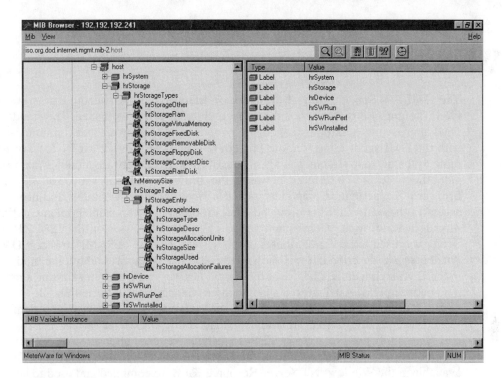

Figure 10.15 Host MIB

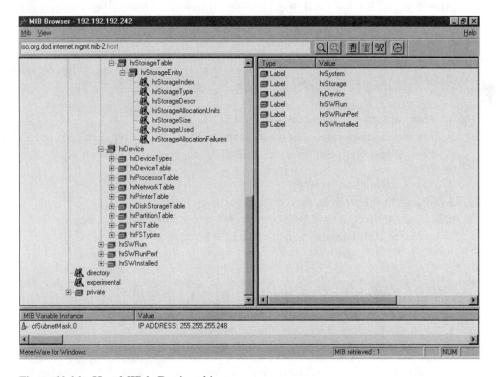

Figure 10.16 Host MIB hrDevice objects

CHAPTER SUMMARY

The DMI 2.0s Specification of the Desktop Management Architecture was examined. The purpose of each module in the architecture was explained. The standard DMI approach to desktop management involves a DMI Browser that communicates with the DMI agent using Remote Procedure Calls. The browser can be local or remote to the desktop system. The agent consists of a set of software modules that provide the necessary interfaces between the browser and hardware, software or firmware Components. Components are described by their Attributes and browser access to these attributes is provided by a Procedural Component Implementation module written by the Component vendor. The DMI Browser on the IBM ZPRO Server was used to access Attributes of this system. The use of SNMP to access DMI Attributes was described. It was shown that such access requires additional modules in the DMI architecture. The use of these modules was explained. In addition, a mapping between DMI Attributes in a Component Management Information File (MIF) and a MIB is required. The creation of this mapping was explained and demonstrated. The resulting MIB was compiled, loaded into the Meterware MIB Browser and successfully used to access a ZPRO attribute. Vendors often provide SNMP extension agents containing additional management objects for their products. Those available in the Windows NT Server Resource Kit were compiled and used to access some additional object values of the WINS Server. Finally, we examined mib-2 Host MIB objects. Like the DMI Specification attributes and SNMP extension agent objects, the values of these objects characterize desktop features.

REVIEW QUESTIONS

1. What was the purpose of establishing the DMTF?
2. How would you describe the primary functionality difference between DMI and SNMP?
3. What Application layer protocol is used to communicate between DMI client and server?
4. What is a DMI "component"?
5. What is the function of a Procedural Component Interface?
6. Describe the hierarchy of DMI components, groups, attributes and elements.
7. Relate the DMI hierarchy to that of the MIB hierarchy.

EXERCISES

1. Windows operating systems provide an SNMP agent.
   a. See if your computer came with a DMI utility.
   b. If you have a DMI utility, find out if it provides the capability to map a MIF file to MIB format. If so, do the mapping and document it. Use the DMI Help file to guide you in this mapping.

   c. Compile the MIB and add it to the Meterware/Analyzer MIB Browser as was done in Chapter 7 for the Cisco Enterprise MIB.
   d. Try to access a system attribute as we did in this chapter.
   e. If none of this is available to you, proceed to Exercise # 2.

2. Table 3.9 in Chapter 3 provides many vendors of network management software.
   a. Examine the table to find a potential vendor of DMI software.
   b. Use the provided URL to check on availability.
   c. See if a demonstration copy is available.
   d. If so, load the demonstration copy and see if its capabilities will enable you to do Exercise 1.

3. See if your Windows operating system provides any SNMP extension agents. If so:
   a. Compile one of its MIBs.
   b. Add it to the Meterware/Analyzer MIB Browser.
   c. Access one of the extension agent objects.

REFERENCES

1. DMI 2.0s Specification, http://www.dmtf.org/standards/spec.php
2. Desktop Management Interface (DMI) Standards, http://www.dmtf.org/standards/standard_dmi.php
3. DMI-to-SNMP Mapping Specification, http://www.dmtf.org/standards/snmp.php
4. Network World Fusion; Desktop management updates, Part 2, http://www.nwfusion.com/newsletters/nsm/2001/01156794.html
5. Host Resources MIB, Request for Comments: 1514, P. Grillo, Network Innovations Intel Corporation and S. Waldbusser, Carnegie Mellon University, September 1993, http:// www.cis.ohio-state.edu/cgi-bin/rfc/rfc1514.html

CHAPTER 11

WEB-BASED MANAGEMENT

- Web Server Access on a LAN
- Web Server Management Modules
- SNMP Configuration
- Monitor Port Configuration
- Web Browser/Web Server Communication

The advantage to Web-based Management is that no special management or agent software is required. The management client is a Web browser and the agent is a Web server stored in flash memory on the device. Thus if a vendor normally has a flash memory module installed because that is the only non-volatile memory on the device, it is convenient to include a Web server. This is normally the case for routers, switches and high-end servers. Having a Web server, a device can be managed from any computer on the network. We will examine Web-based management of a Cisco Catalyst 1900 switch on our network.

11.1 SETTING-UP LAN ACCESS

If you have a direct connection to the Internet and are using Internet Explorer for example, just type in the domain name or IP address of the device in the Address box and click "Go." The web server will respond with its home page. If Internet Explorer has been configured for dial-up networking and you want to access a Web server on your LAN, a couple of configuration changes are necessary as shown in the next section.

First open Internet Explorer to get the Dial-up Connection screen that is shown in **Figure 11.1**. Click the Settings button and select the "General" tab to get **Figure 11.2**. Change the home page address to the IP address of the device whose embedded Web server you want to access. In the case of this example, it is 192.192.192.244, the IP address of Switch 2. Then click the "Connections" tab to get **Figure 11.3**.

On the Connections tab, change from "Always dial my default connection" to "Never dial a connection" to avoid an attempt by Dial-up connection to dial your IPS. Now exit Internet Explorer and open it again. You should get the screen that will enable you to make a LAN connection to the Web server of the selected device. That screen is shown in **Figure 11.4**. From this time on, whenever you open Internet Explorer, that screen will appear. To get back to your normal dial-up connection, just change the two configuration corrections you made back to what they were.

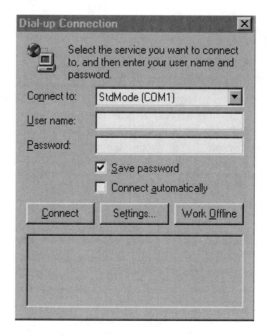

Figure 11.1   Dial-up Connection Screen

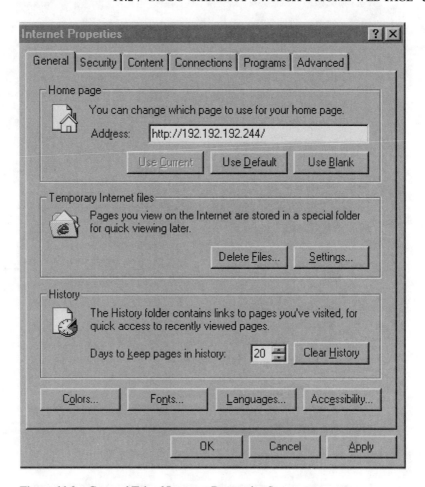

Figure 11.2   General Tab of Internet Properties Screen

On **Figure 11.4**, enter the ID and Password configured on the device and click "OK." The HTTP connection to the selected IP address is made. **Figure 11.5** shows the result for this example, the web page of Cisco Catalyst Switch 2.

11.2 CISCO CATALYST SWITCH 2 HOME WEB PAGE

Starting with this screen, you can configure the switch remotely as we did directly from its Console port in Chapter 5. At the bottom of **Figure 11.5**, you see an image of Switch 2. It is an active image when accessed from your web browser, on which you can access ports, by clicking them. On this switch ports that are connected to the network are colored green. Ethernet port 3, third from the left, is connected to SERVER. The FastEthernet port, port 27 on the far right, is connected to a

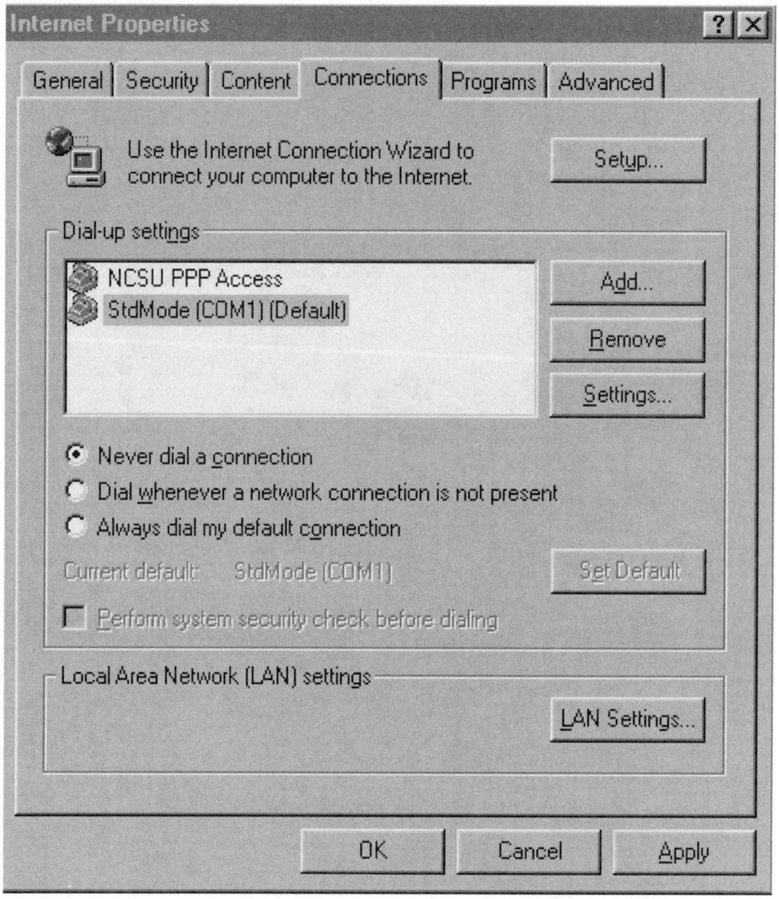

Figure 11.3 Connections Tab of Internet Properties Screen

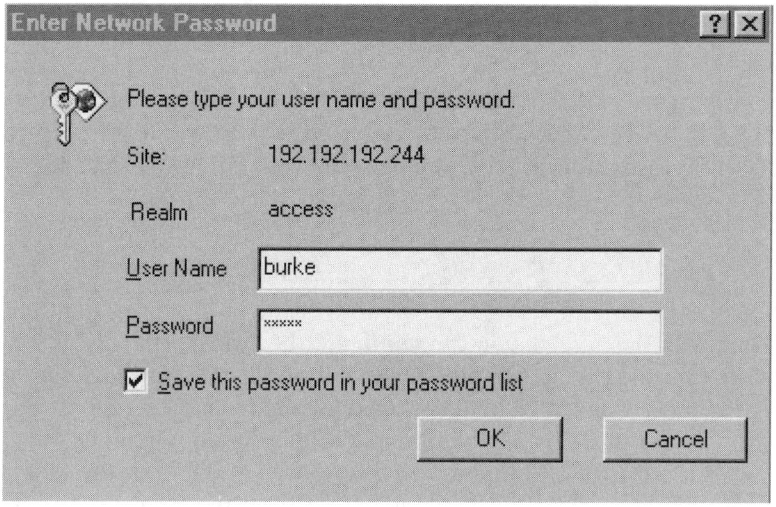

Figure 11.4 Access Screen for IP Address 192.192.192.244

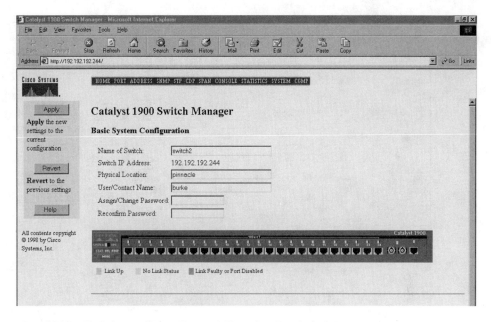

Figure 11.5   Web Server Home Page of Cisco Catalyst Switch 2

monitoring port of the probe Fastmeter that we used extensively in Chapters 8 and 9 to monitor switch traffic. The menu bar at the top of the screen shows the various items that you can access for detailed configuration of the switch.

Let's first click port 3 to see what information that provides. **Figure 11.6** shows the result. As we see from this figure, clicking one port provides management access for all ports. The top table shows data for the two FastEthernet ports, 26 and 27. Notice that port 26 has its linkbeat disabled because it is not connected to any device. This port is an optical fiber port. Auto-negotiate is configured for port 27 and full duplex is assigned. Auto-negotiate means that the switch will negotiate with devices attached to that port for the fastest link that will work. As we have mentioned, ports 26 and 27 are 100 Mb/s capable and so are Fastmeter ports 2 and 3. Thus, this speed has been established for the link between Switch 2, port 27 and Fastmeter, port 3.

The column labeled "Flood Unknown MACs," enables ports to be configured to: 1) reject a frame received with a MAC address not in its database of devices that can be reached through the port, or 2) transmit all received unicast or multicast frames with unknown MAC addresses. Port 27 is configured to flood only unicast packets. Notice in the column labeled "Port Name/Description," that port 27 has the name Fastmeter.

Enhanced Congestion Control is disabled for both ports. If it were enabled, the switch would send packets to the attached device to reduce packet rate if the switch started dropping packets due to the rate being too high.

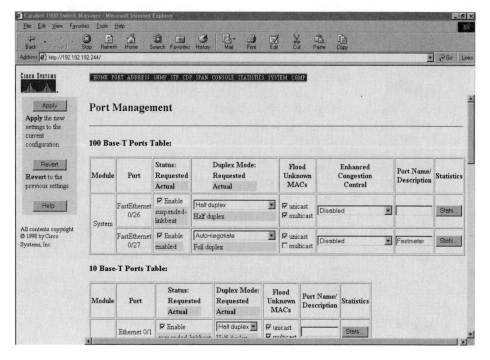

Figure 11.6 Port Management Tables showing the 100BASET and some 10BASET Ports

On the left of the figure, are the buttons Apply, Revert and Help and their explanations. By clicking a Statistics button on the far right, we get the statistics about the chosen port as discussed in the next section.

- Port Statistics

The result of clicking the Statistics button for port 27 is shown in **Figure 11.7**.

First, notice that there are no "Receive Statistics" for this port. This is because, if you remember from Chapter 5, this port was configured to be a mirror port. As such, it only transmits copies of frames received by other ports to Fastmeter, port 3. There are no framing, address or collision errors.

Now let's scroll down to the Ethernet ports table shown previously in **Figure 11.6**. **Figure 11.8** shows as much of that table as we can get on the screen. Here we see that the only Ethernet port enabled is port 3. Of course, port 27 is also enabled. Port 3 is connected to the server ZPRO and it is a half-duplex connection as required for 10BASET ports. (See Chapter 1.) Let's look at the statistics for this port by clicking the Stats button. The statistics are shown in **Figure 11.9**.

As expected for this port, we see both Receive and Transmit statistics. Notice that "Total good frames" is the same as "Good frames forwarded." If that were not the case, the network manager might be concerned that frames were being dropped

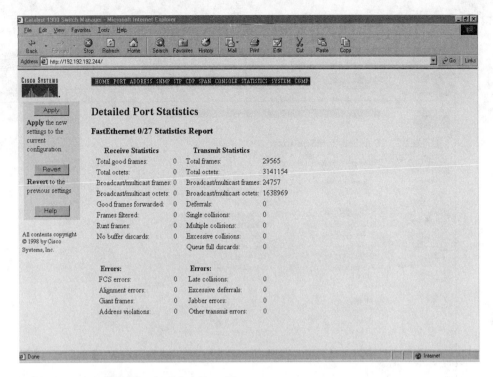

Figure 11.7 Statistics for Switch 2, Port 27

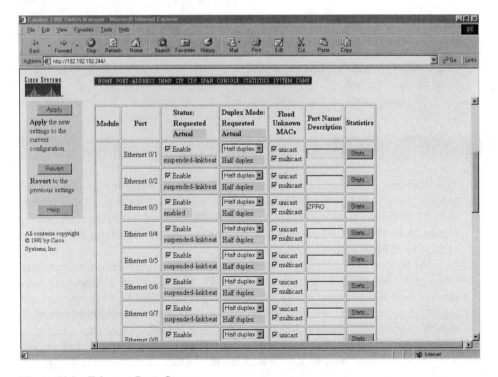

Figure 11.8 Ethernet Ports Summary

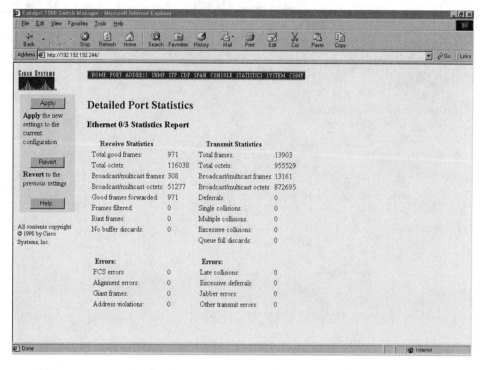

Figure 11.9 Statistics for Ethernet Port 3 Connected to server ZPRO

due to heavy traffic or frames containing MAC addresses unknown to the switch were being received.

Next, let's look at the important task of configuring SNMP using this tool.

11.3 SNMP CONFIGURATION

The Web-based management interface offers a very convenient way to check or modify the SNMP configuration of a device. One often forgets what configuration was set originally and is surprised when the SNMP agent refuses a GetRequest. **Figure 11.10** shows the data provided by clicking the SNMP menu on the menu bar at the top of **Figure 11.9**.

At the top of the Figure 11.10, you see the community strings we configured in Chapter 5 that must by used by any SNMP Management Station that wants to READ or WRITE object values on the switch. In the middle of the screen, you see the IP addresses of stations that will be sent trap messages and the community strings that the switch will use in the trap message. Just below, you see the selected occurrences for which a trap message will be sent. These occurrences do not include the RMON alarms that may be configured for the switch as discussed in Chapter 8 and

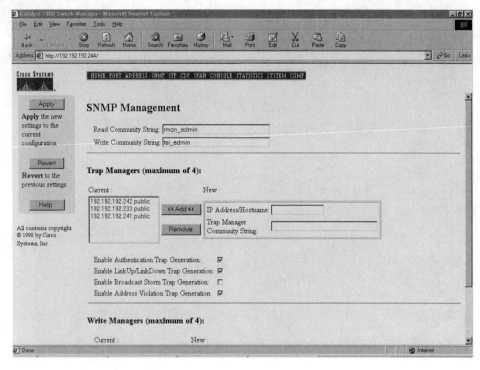

Figure 11.10   SNMP Configuration of Switch 2

that may also cause a trap to be sent. On the right of the "Current" Management Stations, are "New" windows where you can "Add" or "Remove" Management Stations.

The Management Stations that have privileges to write (set) values on the switch are shown at the bottom of **Figure 11.11**. As a final Web-based Management example, click SPAN on the menu bar at the top of **Figure 11.11** to get the web page shown in **Figure 11.12**.

11.4 SWITCHED PORT ANALYZER (SPAN)

As the reader can see, this is a more convenient format for configuring SPAN than what was available directly from the switch console connection (see Chapter 5). It shows, as expected, that the 100BASET port 27 on Switch 2, is the monitor port selected for the "Select Monitoring Port" window.

In the "Ports Monitored" window, you add the ports that you want to be monitored. These ports send a copy of received or transmitted frames to port 27. Care must be taken on a production network with the number of ports that are monitored. Too many can cause collisions in the switch and dropped frames. In general, ports should only be monitored for diagnostic purposes.

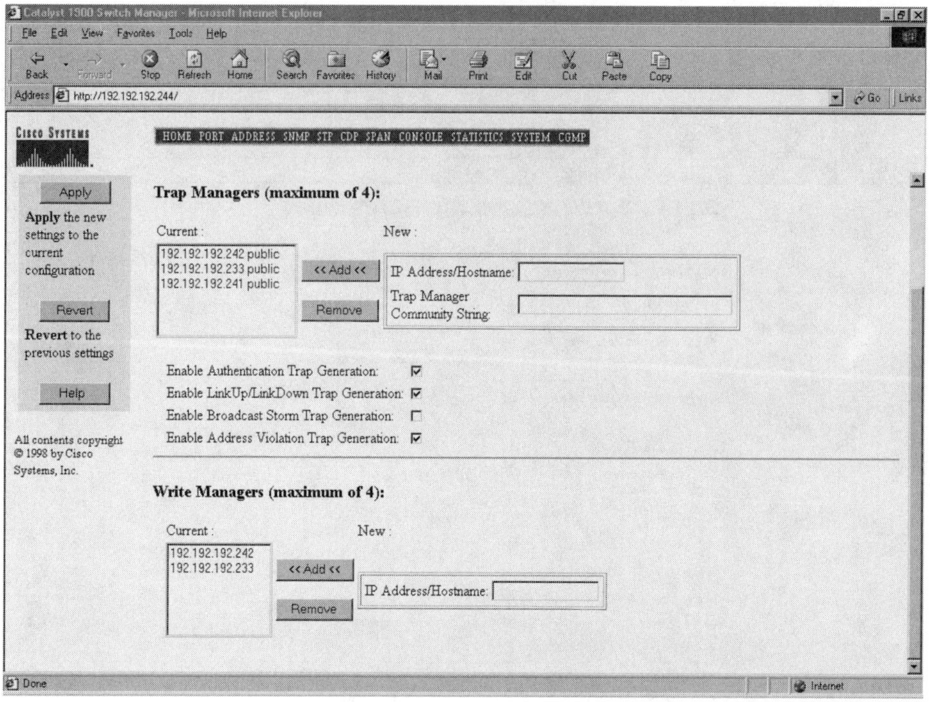

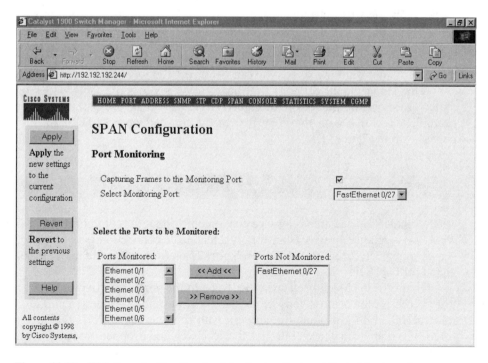

Figure 11.11 Managers Allowed to Write (Set) SNMP Object Values on Switch 2

Figure 11.12 Web Page for Configuring Monitoring Port and Ports Monitored

It is interesting to use the RMON tools we studied in Chapters 8 and 9 to see what actually happens when a Web browser application and HTTP are used to access the embedded Web server of a device. What happens is exactly what happens when we use a Web browser to access the web page of a device on the Internet.

11.5 WEB BROWSER/WEB SERVER COMMUNICATION

When you access a web page, it is surprising how many packets must be transferred to completely display even a typical page. Let's examine this for the HTTP request made of Switch 2 at 192.192.192.244. **Figure 11.13** shows captures of packets sent from WS2 to Switch 2.

The top panel shows only a few of the packets sent from WS2 to Switch 2. Packet 75 is displayed in more detail. As we have seen in previous chapters, a complete display of a frame captured by Fastmeter shows Ethernet and IP sections above the UDP or TCP section. In the second line of the TCP section, you see that the target port is the "well-known port" HTTP(80). In the HTTP section, you see that packet # 75 is requesting the graphic **bar.htm.** This is presumably the menu bar image in figures such as Figure 11.12. We can see the HTTP packet decode because Fastmeter supports RMON 2 and thus decodes "Application Layer" protocols.

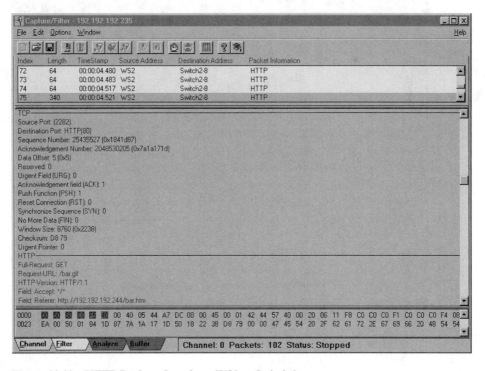

Figure 11.13   HTTP Packets Sent from WS2 to Switch 2

To see how many packets are exchanged when Internet Explorer on WS2 requests the Switch 2 Home Page, we will make use of the RMON2 utiliy alMatrix. In the hierarchy of protocols in the left panel of **Figure 11.14,** we have selected the filter A-HTTP (127) that references the protocol node **ethernet-wildcard/ip/tcp/http** (see Chapter 9). The top right panel shows the number of packets captured that make up the matrix of conversations satisfying this filter.

Figures 11.13 and 11.14 indicate the capabilities of two powerful troubleshooting utilities. The RMON2 alMatrix utility allows us to capture all conversations between all devices that are communicating with protocols of interest. Then we can ask, should these devices be communicating using these protocols? If not, what information is being transmitted? The RMON1 Capture/Filter utlility allows us to decode the conversations between specific hosts to examine this information. Using these utilities together provides an example of achieving effective and precise Security Management on the network.

In today's networking environment, there is concern, for example, about which applications on which devices are using what bandwidth and are communication policies actually being implemented. The utilities just discussed can be used to address such concerns.

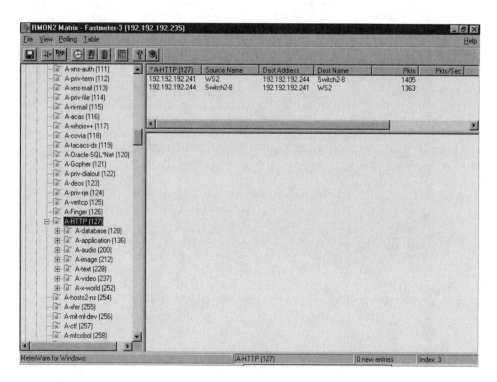

Figure 11.14 Using the RMON 2 alMatrix Utility to Display HTTP Packets between WS2 and Switch 2

CHAPTER SUMMARY

Web-based Management was explored using the Web Server on Cisco Catalyst 1900 Switch 2 on the demonstration network and the Internet Explorer web browser on WS2. The Netscape browser could have been used also. Web-base management requires that the device to be managed has a Web server installed. This installation is convenient for routers, switches and servers that have a flash memory module. For access to the Web Server on a device on the same LAN, the setup procedure was shown. Following this, the Home Page of Switch 2 was accessed. The Home Page provides an image of the switch ports that can be accessed by clicking them. This produces a page that is an entrée' to management of all switch ports. One aspect of this management view shows which ports are enabled. Another aspect provides management of SNMP configuration of community strings and trap managers. The capability to select the monitor port and the ports to be monitored was examined. The RMON1 Capture/Filter utility was used to capture HTTP packets between the web browser and the switch web server using Fastmeter. The RMON2 alMatrix utility was used to count packets that satisfied the filter ethernet-wildcard/ip/tcp/http.

REVIEW QUESTIONS

1. What is the primary advantage to web-based management?
2. What does a device require in order to be managed this way?
3. When you access a web server on any device using its IP address, why do you receive its web page?
4. When you do not receive a web page when you access the device's web page, what is a possible reason?
5. Why is web-based management convenient?
6. If web-based management is not available, what approach other than SNMP might you take?
7. Why might you want to have the managed device reject the unknown IP address of a client?
8. What is the meaning of RequestURL/bar.gif in Figure 11.13?

EXERCISES

1. Configure a web browser to access an embedded web server on your network as we did in this chapter.

2. If you do not know which devices on your network have an embedded web server, try to access some with the web server you just configured. Try routers, switches, and hubs as likely candidates.

3. Document the SNMP configuration of a device. For example, what is the community string required to change(set) the configuration?

CHAPTER **12**

SNMPv3

with David Spakes of SNMP Research

In this chapter we will:

- Review the standardization process for Internet protocols
- Review the history of SNMPv2 and SNMPv3 development
- Describe SNMPv2 operational enhancements to SNMPv1
- Review SMIv2
- Discuss Security Threats and Authentication and Privacy Protocols
- Explore the future beyond SNMPv3
- Describe SNMPv3 Terminology
- Describe the SNMPv3 User-based Security Model
- Explain the SNMP Framework Architecture
- Explain the SNMPv3 message format
- Describe MIBs that support SNMPv3
- Explain and demonstrate the authentication of users and encryption of messages
- Configure Users for an SNMPv3 agent on a Cisco Router
- Demonstrate the use of an SNMPv3 Configuration Wizard
- Demonstrate SNMPv3 Management Using the SNMP Research EnterPol NMS
- Demonstrate automated Enterprise Configuration using an EnterPol application

12.1 TRANSITION FROM PREVIOUS CHAPTERS

In previous chapters, we focused on the use of SNMPv1 to demonstrate and analyze network management implementation. This chapter deals with newer versions of SNMP that were the result of years of effort to improve the management protocol. Many good ideas were tried in SNMPv2, but ultimately it was SNMPv3 that brought a new standard for management with industrial-strength security and administration features. In addition to RFCs and textbooks referenced throughout, see the textbooks listed at the end for good discussions of some of the topics we cover.

We are now in a period of transition during which SNMPv1 will continue to be a pervasive network management protocol. This transition will last for several years, but SNMPv3 is expected to replace SNMPv1 and all other previous versions of the protocol because of the ever-increasing concern for the security of network communications.

12.2 SNMPv2, SNMPv3, AND BEYOND

In the late 1980s, as we saw in Chapter 2, SNMP was the protocol whose time had come. It was a common, unifying solution that filled an enormously important need in the networking industry. Through SNMP, it became possible for the first time for a Network Operator to diagnose and correct problems in physically distant machines of any general type. As an open Internet Standard, any original equipment manufacturer (OEM) could include SNMP support in their device, and any software vendor could produce management applications to control that device. The need for a common management protocol was so great, SNMP became the most rapidly standardized of all Internet protocols.

Within weeks after SNMP had been declared a fully Standard Internet protocol, the SNMP authors were hard at work again. Users of this new technology began to identify operational limitations. In addition, the original SNMP included no real security mechanisms, which would be essential to ensure that the protocol would be adopted for use in government agencies and some large enterprises.

By April 1993, a specification for SNMP Version 2 (SNMPv2) was published as a Proposed Standard. This specification included a variety of new features to address the operational limitations of the original SNMP (henceforth called SNMPv1). SNMPv2 introduced security mechanisms including strong authentication and message encryption. The vision of the SNMP authors was that SNMPv2 would coexist with SNMPv1 for a time, but eventually would replace SNMPv1 completely.

If events in the mid-1990s had transpired in a slightly different way, the history of SNMP would end with SNMPv2. However, as we will see later in this chapter, disagreement over some of the details of SNMPv2 security forced the authors of SNMPv2 to put their vision on hold. It would take a few more years and the birth of SNMPv3 to bring this management protocol to its intended and current state of functionality.

12.2.1 Standardization Process Overview

A review of the standardization process is important in order to understand the relationship of SNMPv2 and SNMPv3. SNMPv3 has now become an Internet Standard. This results in previous versions of SNMP being given the official status of "Historic." These standards are set by an organization called the Internet Engineering Steering Group (IESG). For a protocol to become an Internet Standard, it normally must endure a long process of implementation experience and scrutiny lasting a few years. The purpose of this process is to ensure that an Internet Standard (which may simply be referred to as a Standard) is characterized by a high degree of technical maturity and by a generally held belief that the specified protocol or service provides significant benefit to the Internet community.

A specification for a protocol that is intended to become a Standard follows an obstacle course called the "standards track." There are four hurdles. First, a Working Group must be formed by the Internet Engineering Task Force (IETF) to develop the specification in an open forum. The IETF assigns a chairperson to oversee the development process. When the specification is initially completed and approved by the IETF, the next step is for the specification to be published as a Proposed Standard in a numbered document called a Request for Comments (RFC). When significant portions of the protocol have been implemented and some positive experience gained, the specification can be published again (in another RFC) as a Draft Standard. At this stage, all portions of the specification must be implemented, and it must be demonstrated to the IETF that multiple independent implementations exist that can interoperate successfully. When this has been achieved, after a minimum waiting period, and after a "last call" in which objections are heard and discussed, the IETF can recommend to the IESG that the protocol advance to a Standard state. On approval of the IESG, the specification is published again (in another RFC) and the protocol becomes Standard.

A protocol that is on the standards track may not always advance forward. At each stage, the IETF may determine that the specification requires additional work, keeping it at its present level of maturity or possibly reducing it to a level of lesser maturity. The IETF can also move the specification off the standards track completely, to a state of Informational or Experimental. In this case, if the work is continued, the protocol would have to re-enter the standards track at the beginning. Even a protocol that is Standard may eventually be retired and moved off the standards track to the Historic state.

Familiar protocols such as FTP and Telnet became Standards through the process just described. Other protocols such as HTTP and POP3 are on the standards track.

12.2.2 SNMPv2: A Brief History

If you were to speak with a typical software developer today who is tasked with implementing SNMP in a piece of equipment under development, and if you were to ask him or her to comment about the latest developments in SNMP technology, there is a high degree of probability that the response would be erroneous. Many developers today are completely unaware that there exists any version of SNMP beyond SNMPv1. Some developers know that a secure version of SNMP exists, but almost all will tell you that it is called SNMPv2, and they will refer you to an RFC that is Historic.

In truth, SNMPv2 did introduce security, as well as a number of other improvements to both the protocol and to the Structure of Management Information (SMI): (the grammar for writing MIB documents). The original SNMPv2 was published as a Proposed Standard **[Ref 1-11].** A number of books describing SNMPv2 were also published.* When the time came to consider advancing SNMPv2 to a Draft Standard state, however, there was significant disagreement on security issues. The Working Group fell into chaos, and the work surrounding SNMPv2 began to crumble. Consequently, **the protocol of SNMPv2 never became a Standard.**†

While no one in the SNMPv2 Working Group could agree on the security issues, everyone agreed that the other parts of SNMPv2 were both mature and vitally important to meet the immediate needs of the Network Management community. The IETF decided to allow parts of SNMPv2 to advance forward on the standards track, but the other parts would be held back to receive additional work. The Structure of Management Information Version 2 (SMIv2) defined for SNMPv2 did eventually become an Internet Standard **[Ref 12-14].** In addition, most of the other features of SNMPv2 were incorporated into SNMPv3. The topic of SNMPv2 is still very relevant, so we will explore it further.

SNMPv2 Goals

The Proposed Standard SNMPv2 published in 1993 provided three basic types of improvements over SNMPv1. First, there were new and improved **protocol operations**. Second, there was an **expanded grammar** for writing MIB documents defined by a second version of the Structure of Management Information, **SMIv2**. Third, SNMPv2 introduced **strong security**.

Improved Protocol Operations. The protocol operations of the original SNMPv2 exist today in SNMPv3. They are:

1. A GetBulk operator for large data retrieval
2. A 64-bit data type
3. Acknowledged trap messages, called Informs
4. Improved error handling
5. Contexts
6. A new kind of SNMP Proxy

GetBulk PDU The purpose of the GetBulk operator is to perform "bulk data retrieval." With GetBulk, the Management Station can safely retrieve large amounts of SNMP data using minimal network traversion and protocol overhead.

---

*Books published about the original SNMPv2 are still in circulation today and almost certainly contribute to the confusion of many software developers.

†Today, we refer to this version of SNMPv2 as *Party-based SNMPv2*, or SNMPv2p.

For each GetBulk request it receives, the SNMP agent packs the Response with as many encoded variable bindings as it can fit in the message, up to the number requested. The number of variable binding pairs that can be returned in a single response message depends on the following factors:

1. The upper limit on the size of an SNMP message exchanged between a particular agent and manager, called the maximum message size. The limit is determined by the programming of the SNMP agent and manager. It is also determined by the network configuration.
2. The lengths of the object identifiers involved influences the number of variable bindings that can be returned. The longer the OIDs, the fewer that can be encoded within the maximum message size.
3. The types and values of the MIB objects being returned. For example, if the SNMP agent were packing the Response PDU with octet strings of length 100, fewer variable bindings would fit into the message than if the agent were packing the Response PDU with integer objects.

It is typical for an SNMP manager to request more data from the agent than will fit into a single Response message. The power of GetBulk is that the SNMP manager will receive a Response containing the most data that it can safely receive in a single message.

The format of the GetBulkRequest message is shown in **Figure 12.1** The response message has the same format as used in SNMPv1 that we saw in Chapter 6.

The highlighted fields are new in this SNMPv2 PDU. They determine how the message is to be processed. The GetBulkRequest PDU accesses object values in a manner similar to the GetNextRequest PDU. That is, the object value that is returned is the one in next lexicographical order to the Object Identifier specified in the variable binding.

Object values can be retrieved in two ways. One way is to retrieve only **one** value of an object instance, that of the object instance in next lexicographical order to that specified in the variable binding. The number of such values to be retrieved in this way is determined by the integer in the **non-repeaters** field. So for example, if you specify "3" for this integer, you will receive a value for one object in next lexicographical order for each of the first three variable-bindings in the PDU ("non-repeaters"). The second way to retrieve values makes use of **max-repetitions.** This integer specifies the **number** of values of object instances to be accessed in next lexicographical order for each of the remaining variable-binding pairs in the PDU.

version (1)	community	request-id	PDU Type	non-repeaters	max-repetitions	variable-bindings

Figure 12.1   GetBulkRequest Message Format (shown here for SNMPv2c).

Therefore, in a simple scenario, the number of values you expect to be returned is:

$$N + (R * M),$$

where N = non-repeaters, R = number of bindings in the PDU in excess of non-repeaters, and M = max repetitions. More specifically, M is the number of instances of each of the R column objects requested. When the amount of data requested is greater than what will fit into a single Response message, the number of values returned is governed by the following principle:

$$E + H \leq \min(MMS_N, \min(MMS_A, MMS_M)),$$

where E = the length of the encoded Response PDU, H = the size of the SNMP message header, MMS_A = maximum message size supported by the SNMP Agent, MMS_M = maximum message size supported by the SNMP Manager, and MMS_N = maximum message size of the network above which IP fragmentation occurs.

Many readers at this point are likely to question the necessity of maximum message size and the use of phrases like "safely receive." Why not simply program the agent and manager to handle SNMP messages of an arbitrary size? The reason is rather simple, if not intuitive. The time when network management is most needed is when the network is not functioning properly. In a network where there is a high degree of packet loss, SNMP is far more likely to function properly if the packets exchanged between manager and agent are smaller than the threshold of IP fragmentation.

A packet traversing the network is fragmented, or split up, when it is too large to be processed as a whole by the network equipment; e.g., when the packet is larger than an Ethernet frame, or when the packet exceeds the size of a network stack buffer in a router. On the receiving side of a network transmission, a fragmented packet must be reassembled from its fragments. If there is packet loss, the probability that all of the fragments will reach a destination and be reassembled successfully is less than the probability that a single, smaller message that isn't fragmented will reach its destination.

Jeffrey Case, one of the authors of SNMP and SNMPv2, likes to describe the GetNextRequest PDU as the "the powerful GetNext operator" and the GetBulkRequest PDU as "the awesome GetBulk operator." Both operators can discover objects and instances in the SNMP agent. GetBulk makes it possible to safely retrieve large amounts of data with the minimum network traversion and protocol overhead. **[Ref 15]** provides further discussion of the GetBulk operator. An example of the use of this operator can be found on pages 366–370 of this reference.

Counter64 The technology of computer hardware is constantly improving, and with it, the speed of networks continues to grow. It is little wonder that as SNMPv2 was being designed, the authors of the protocol were asked to add a 64-bit data type. Consider a MIB object such as ifOutOctets, which is a count of the number of bytes of data that has been transmitted through a network interface. On a network where 10 megabit per second throughput is possible, a count of bytes could reach the maximum value represented by 32 bits in under an hour. Now consider that 100 megabit Ethernet is commonplace, and gigabit Ethernet is available. Thus, the Counter64 type was incorporated into the SNMPv2 specification and exists today as part of SNMPv3. When designing a MIB, the rule of thumb is that if your Counter32 would wrap in under a few minutes, use a Counter64 instead.

Inform Requests Notifications in SNMPv2 and SNMPv3 are either Traps or **Informs**. An "Inform Request" is essentially an acknowledged trap. The Inform request was an idea that originated in the IETF Working Group for Distributed Management (DISMAN). **Manager-to-manager communication** is a fundamental requirement to implement distributed management, and the Inform message was intended to be the way for one SNMP manager to send information to another SNMP manager.

As it turned out, most people were far more concerned that their Traps would be lost in the network by the "unreliable" UDP transport than they were about getting their SNMP managers talking to one another. Therefore, the use of the Inform was adapted over time to meet this perceived need. Today, both agents and manager can send and receive Inform messages.

An Inform request works very much like a Trap. Both types of messages can be used to send unsolicited notifications about alarms and other events. Both types of messages use the SNMPv2-Trap PDU. The difference is that when an SNMP entity sends an Inform request, it expects to receive a Response PDU in reply. If it does not receive the Response PDU within a certain time, it will retransmit the Inform request, and this cycle continues until the reply message is received or until a specified retry count is exceeded.

Improved Error Handling SNMPv2 improved the way that SNMP agents respond to Get and Set requests. The agent has a richer set of values it can insert into the error status field of a Response message. In addition, the variable bindings in a Response message can contain **exceptions** in addition to object identifiers and values.

ERROR STATUS/ERROR INDEX In SNMPv1, there are only a few values that can be assigned to the error status of a Response message. In many situations, the only error message that was appropriate to return was the "generic error."

In the original SNMPv2, and today in SNMPv3, there are a larger number of values for error status that provide meaningful information in the case of failure. As an example, consider the situation in which a Set request, containing two or more variable bindings, encounters an error as it is being processed by the SNMP agent. In SNMPv1, the response would be "generic error," which is meaningless since it communicates no information about the current state of the device. In SNMPv2 and SNMPv3, there are two appropriate responses for this situation. If the agent is able to "clean up" the resulting mess and return the device to its original state before the Set request began to be processed, then the agent returns an error status value of "commit failed." If the agent is not able to roll back to the previous state, then the agent returns an error status value of "undo failed." By examining the value of error status, the SNMP manager can decide if any corrective action is necessary. Receiving a "commit failed" is better than receiving an "undo failed," because the former means that the device's state has not been changed. On receiving an "undo failed" message, the SNMP manager must refresh its notion of the state of the device by sending GetRequests to assess the current values of the MIB objects.

EXCEPTIONS   As was discussed in Chapter 6 of this book, if multiple object values are requested in a SNMPv1 GetRequest message and one of the values is not available, an error is returned, but the Response PDU contains no values for any of the objects in the GetRequest. As we saw, the GetNextRequest message was the way to avoid this problem.

SNMPv2 mostly corrected this GetRequest problem. If there is a problem with any variable binding pair, SNMPv2 and SNMPv3 return the values of the other objects requested, and insert an OID value of noSuchObject, noSuchInstance or endOfMibView in the value field(s) of the problem variable binding(s). As with SNMPv1, the error-index field indicates the first variable binding at which the first error occurred. However, there are other SNMPv2 PDU errors that still cause no values to be returned. See page 362 in **[Ref 15]** for a discussion of these.

Contexts   In human conversation, it is natural to respond to the same question in different ways, depending on the context of the question. For example, if your boss asks you what you accomplished today, the context is "information related to your employment," and you would likely talk about particular work-related goals that you met, such as implementing a feature in a program. When you arrive home from work and your spouse asks you the same question, "What did you accomplish today?" the context is likely to be different. For example, the context of the question may be "the errand you were supposed to run over your lunch break."

The concept of context also exists in SNMP. For example, you may want to know how many network interfaces are installed in a piece of network equipment. To form the proper "question," you would send an SNMP Get request for ifNumber.0 to the device; the answer may be "5." But perhaps you would like to know how many of those interfaces are Ethernet interfaces. A brute force way to obtain this information would be to Get-Next through all of the instances of the object ifType and count each response in which the type of the interface was Ethernet.

Another way to obtain this information might be to send an SNMP Get request for ifNumber.0 in the Ethernet context. For this to work, however, the SNMP agent would have to have special programming to modify its answer based on the context of the question.

SNMP agent developers who needed this type of functionality in their SNMPv1 agents would commonly program the agent to modify its response based on the community string found in the request message. This was an unintended overloading of the community string, which was designed to be used for authentication purposes. So, the authors of SNMPv2 decided to add a field to the SNMP message header to carry the context information for each request.

Formally defined, an SNMP **context** is a collection of management information (objects) accessible by an SNMP entity. An item of management information may exist in more than one context. To access objects in different contexts, the SNMP request is qualified by some type of context parameter. In the original SNMPv2 protocol message, there were two context parameters called contextLocalEntity and contextLocalTime.* In SNMPv3, the context parameter is called contextName.

A New Kind of SNMP Proxy   Traditionally, an "SNMP Proxy" is an SNMP agent that exposes the data in some software application as MIB objects. But this term is very loosely applied to several different kinds of fronting relationships involving SNMP, and a general discussion about proxy is beyond the scope of this chapter. However, we will briefly mention a new type of SNMP Proxy that was introduced by SNMPv2.

PACKET FORWARDING   SNMP agent developers would sometimes modify their SNMPv1 agents to overload the community string in yet another way. For some SNMP agents, a particular community string meant "go ask another SNMP agent for its information." One purpose of this type of proxy was to perform local caching of MIB object values found in remote SNMP agents. Another purpose of this type of proxy was to obtain management information from SNMP agents in a different type of network. For example, if a Management Station attached to a TCP/IP network needed to ascertain the health of a device contained in an IPX network, the SNMP manager would send its SNMP messages to an SNMP Proxy with a special community string that would cause the proxy to retransmit the SNMP message onto the IPX network.

Again, the authors of SNMPv2 decided to add a field to the SNMP message header to carry this type of context information for each request. In SNMPv2, the context parameter was an object identifier. In SNMPv3, the context parameter is an **Octet String** called contextSnmpEngineID.

PROTOCOL TRANSLATION: SNMPv2->SNMPv1   The SNMPv2 authors had an additional purpose in mind for this new type of proxy. It was expected that at some point, SNMPv1 would disappear, and everyone would use SNMPv2. However, they recognized that migrating from SNMPv1 to SNMPv2 usage would not occur immediately but that it would be a gradual process occurring over time. SNMPv2 is incompatible with SNMPv1. However, it was believed that there would be situations in which a Management Station would want to use SNMPv2 to access data found in an SNMPv1 agent. To this end, it was specified that an SNMP Proxy forwarding messages between managers and agents would be capable of performing the necessary protocol translation; e.g., converting SNMPv2 request messages into SNMPv1, and converting SNMPv1 response messages into SNMPv2 response messages. This type of protocol translation is also defined for SNMPv3, and the function performed by this type of SNMP Proxy is called proxy forwarding.

SMIv2.   The Structure of Management Information Version 2 (SMIv2) defined for SNMPv2 applies today to SNMPv3. The primary differences between the original Concise MIB definitions **[Ref 16-18]** and SMIv2 are summarized here:

---

*The contextLocalTime parameter was ill defined, but the intention was to allow an agent response to vary based on the time. For example, a Set request could cause the device to change state now or on the next reboot.

1. SMIv2 has an enhanced OBJECT-TYPE macro.

2. SMIv2 incorporates several new macros from ASN.1, including MODULE-COMPLIANCE and AGENT-CAPABILITIES to define more precisely what is expected of an SNMP agent that supports SNMPv2 or SNMPv3.

3. Using SMIv2, one can refine the definitions of SNMP data types using a formal TEXTUAL-CONVENTION macro.

More From ASN.1   The conformance statement document for SNMPv2, **[Ref 14]**, defines four new macros: the **NOTIFICATION-GROUP, OBJECT-GROUP, MODULE-COMPLIANCE** and **AGENT-CAPABILITIES** macros. Up to this point in the book, we have only been concerned with the OBJECT-TYPE macro. The following definitions briefly explain the functionality of these new macros:

- *NOTIFICATION-GROUP macro:* Specifies a collection of notifications, each of which is defined by another macro, the **NOTIFICATION-TYPE** macro. The NOTIFICATION-TYPE macro, defined below, replaces the TRAP-TYPE macro described in the Informational RFC 1215. This macro is used to assign an object identifier to an exceptional condition and hang it in the MIB tree.

- *NOTIFICATION-TYPE macro:* SNMPv2 introduced two new types of PDUs. The SNMPv2-TRAP PDU was created so that traps were more like other SNMP messages, having generic OIDs instead of special-purpose fields like Generic Trap, Specific Trap, and Enterprise. As mentioned above, the Inform Request PDU was originally created for manager-to-manager communication, but its use changed to become a more general "acknowledged trap." A corresponding change to the MIB grammar was needed to support these new PDU types. The change was the addition of the NOTIFICATION-TYPE macro.

- *OBJECT-TYPE macro:* SMIv2 has enhanced this macro relative to SMI as follows:
  - ❏ A MAX-ACCESS clause is used instead of an ACCESS clause to provide these choices: "not-accessible" | "accessible-for-notify" | "read-only" | "read-write" | "read-create."
    - ⇒ "not-accessible" means that there is no access to an object of this type. It is the type used for table index objects where the value can be derived from the instance identifier. Its purpose is to eliminate the "Grant's Tomb" effect and optimize SNMP data retrieval. (The Grant's Tomb effect means getting redundant information when you walk a table defined by an SMIv1 MIB. The value of an Index object will be specifically returned in addition to it being available in the instance identifier.)
    - ⇒ "accessible-for-notify" means that there is no direct access to an object of this type, but an instance of the object can be delivered to another SNMP entity in the payload of a Trap or Inform message. The delivery of object data in a notification can be constrained by MIB views in the security service layer.
    - ⇒ "read-write" implies read access and write access, but the level of access can be constrained by MIB views in the security service layer.

⇒ "read-create" implies read access, write access, and create access, but the level of access can be constrained by MIB views in the security service layer. The "read-create" mode enables the manager to create rows in a table and set values for the row column objects. We saw examples of a create capability provided by the RMON specifications in Chapters 8 and 9. This new feature in SMIv2 is based on the RMON create mode. Not all SNMPv2 implementations enable the "read-create" access mode for managers. Some limit this mode to agent internal processing only.

❑ An AUGMENTS clause is added to the OBJECT-TYPE MACRO that can be substituted for the INDEX clause. The AUGMENTS clause allows the MIB designer to add column objects to an existing table. This is a valuable feature because, for example, it would allow vendors to add objects of particular interest to them to a standard table and thus reduce the number of enterprise table objects.

- *OBJECT-GROUP macro:* defines related MIB objects that are supported by the agent.
- *NOTIFICATION GROUP macro:* defines related notifications that are supported by the agent.
- *MODULE-COMPLIANCE macro:* defines agent compliance with respect to the objects in the OBJECT-GROUP. An agent that complies with a MODULE-COMPLIANCE macro instance must support all objects defined in the OBJECT-GROUP macro.
- *AGENT-CAPABILITIES macro:* defines the agent's actual capabilities in support of objects in an OBJECT-GROUP.

Row Status and other Textual Conventions   SMIv2 also introduces a new macro called **TEXTUAL-CONVENTION [Ref 12-13]**, or "TC" for short. The macro format is designed to allow more extensive and precise information to be given about an object. For example, there is a TC called DisplayString, which is an Octet String of any length from zero to 255 that can only contain textual information taken from the NVT ASCII character set as defined in RFC 854 on pages 4 and 10–11.

Two Textual Conventions are defined to support the "read-create" value of the MAX-ACCESS clause of an OBJECT-TYPE MACRO. One is called **StorageType**, an enumerated integer that can be set to any of the following values:

- **volatile**(2), which stores a newly created row in RAM where data is lost upon reboot.
- **non-volatile**(3), which stores a newly created row in a type of storage (e.g., in NVRAM or a disk file) where the data is persistent across reboots.
- **permanent**(4), which means that the row can not be deleted, but it can be modified.
- **readOnly**(5), which means that the row is completely in ROM and cannot be deleted or modified.

The other TC defined specifically for "read-create" is **RowStatus**. The Row-Status is an enumerated integer that not only reports on the current status of a row, but influences the row creation process and also provides the means whereby a table row can be deleted.

When rows are configured by a management station with Set requests, the object of type RowStatus—typically the last column object in the table—must be set first to either **createAndWait**(5) or **createAndGo**(4) while other objects in the row are set. The Row Status object is set to **active**(1) to enable access to its objects if RowStatus was **createAndWait**(5). If all of the object values required to enable a row have not been set, the status is **notReady**(3), and the row can not be made active. Any time after the row has been made active, it can be explicitly de-activated by setting the value of the RowStatus object to **notInService**(2). At any time, the row can be deleted entirely by setting the value of the RowStatus object to **destroy**(6). The TC text describes a finite state machine that governs the behavior of objects of type RowStatus.

Security.　Networks can be a target for unlawful activity by disgruntled employees, electronic thieves, hackers, or even terrorists. SNMP Set requests are a potential means whereby these kinds of individuals can carry out malicious acts. SNMPv1 provided no real security mechanisms, so many SNMP agents created in the past were programmed to simply not accept Set requests, reducing SNMP to a monitoring protocol.

SNMPv2 introduced security mechanisms designed to protect against a variety of threats. The threats identified by SNMPv2 and the security mechanisms used in SNMPv2 apply to SNMPv3 today.

Network Management Threats　There are four potential threats related to network management:

- **Masquerade**: A malicious person pretends to be an authorized user when performing network management operations.
- **Message payload modification**: A malicious person modifies the contents of an SNMP request that is "in flight."
- **Message stream modification**: A malicious person changes the intended delivery sequence of SNMP requests. For example, a replay attack is the resending of a valid SNMP request at a later time to elicit an identical response (e.g., a reboot).
- **Disclosure**: A malicious person views sensitive information carried in an SNMP request, response, or notification.

Strong Authentication (MD5)　The defense against the first three of the four threats is **strong authentication**. An SNMP message is considered authentic if the following are true:

- The receiver of the message knows with a high degree of certainty the sender of the message is who he or she claims to be.
- The receiver of the message knows with a high degree of certainty that the message has not been modified.

- The receiver of the message knows with a high degree of certainty that the message has been received in a timely manner.

In the SNMP message header, there are two fields containing information that allows the receiver to verify that the message is authentic. The first field is a time stamp indicating when the message was sent. The second field is a message digest, which is a hash value computed using the bytes of the message, the time stamp, and a private key known only to the sender and to the authorized receiver of the message.

The hash is computed using a one-way algorithm so the original operands can not be derived from the resulting value. The algorithm used for SNMPv2 is called Message Digest Algorithm 5 (MD5). There are currently two algorithms that are standard for SNMPv3. One is MD5. The other is the Secure Hash Algorithm (SHA-1).

Before the sender transmits the message, the hash computation is performed, and the digest is inserted into the message. Upon receiving the message, the receiver performs the same hash computation and compares the resulting digest to the one that it finds in the message. If the digest values are the same, the receiver treats the message as authentic. If the digest values are not the same, the message is discarded.* This process will be described in more detail when SNMPv3 is discussed.

Note that for this security mechanism to provide a realistic defense against the threats, there are a few assumptions that must be true. First, the sender and the receiver (i.e., the SNMP agent and the SNMP manager) must have the same notion of the current time. Second, the private key must be genuinely private. If key values are chosen that are easy to guess, or if they are written down on sticky notes and stuck to the monitor of the network management console, the security is easily compromised.

Encryption (DES)   The defense against the last of the four threats, disclosure, is **encryption**. The contents of an encrypted SNMP message (captured by a malicious person) can not be viewed. The payload is "scrambled" in such a way that the information is meaningless until the message is returned to its original form, i.e., decrypted.

Encryption is performed using a reversible algorithm called Data Encryption Standard (DES). Specifically, SNMP security uses DES in 56-bit Cypher-Block Chaining (CBC) mode. The algorithm requires another private key known only to the sender and to the authorized receiver of the message. The same key is used to both encrypt and decrypt the message.

Before the sender transmits the message, encryption is performed on the payload using the private key. Upon receiving the message, the receiver decrypts the payload using the same private key. If the resulting message is unscrambled properly and therefore understandable, then it is processed. If a key used to decrypt the

---

*In SNMPv3, the receiver responds with a Report PDU to indicate to the sender of the original message that the message was discarded and why.

message is not the same as the key used to encrypt the message, the resulting message will again be an array of meaningless bytes, and the message is discarded.*

Note that for this security mechanism to provide a realistic defense against disclosure, the private key must again be genuinely private. Also, note that it is senseless to allow encryption in absence of authentication. If you can unscramble an encrypted message but cannot verify that the message is authentic, what have you accomplished? For this reason, SNMPv2 defined only the following three modes of security (still true for SNMPv3):

- no authentication, "noAuthNoPriv"
- authentication with no privacy, "authNoPriv"
- authentication with privacy, "authPriv"

The original SNMPv2: SNMP Parties are No Fun Earlier in this chapter, we touched on the fact that a disagreement on security issues prevented SNMPv2 from advancing to the Draft Standard state, so the protocol never became a standard. Everyone agreed that the underlying security mechanisms—the MD5 and DES algorithms and their application—were technologically sound. What people did not agree on, however, was the encapsulation of the technology.

In the original SNMPv2, the security principal was the **party**. The idea for parties was derived from early 20th century telephone jargon, in which a *party* was a circuit that serviced one or more homes, and when one wanted to place a call, it was proper to say that one "party" would ask the operator to connect them to another "party." Unlike the username-password model, the party model was a unfamiliar concept that contributed to general confusion and misunderstanding of SNMPv2 security.

The implementation details of SNMP parties also did not appeal to members of the SNMPv2 Working Group. The identification of a party was an object identifier (OID). Also, the authentication keys and encryption keys were represented only as a string of sixteen binary numbers each. Therefore, to begin to establish communication between an SNMP manager and an SNMP agent, one was required to configure three OIDs (two parties and a context) and two binary keys in two configuration datastores—one for the manager and one for the agent. These two configurations were identical, except that the order of the party OIDs had to be reversed in one of the configurations. In addition, the agent had to be configured with MIB view and access control parameters. All of these details were overwhelming, even to technically oriented members of the Working Group. As a result, someone coined the phrase that "SNMP parties are no fun," expressing a sentiment that eventually led to the decision not to advance SNMPv2 as a whole on the standards track.

In the years that followed there were many proposed replacements for SNMPv2 Security. Some examples are SNMPv2c, SNMPv2u and SNMPv2*, none of which included parties. A brief history of these versions can be found in

---

*Again in SNMPv3, the receiver responds with a Report PDU.

[Ref 27]. Of these, only SNMPv2c survives (where "c" stands for community). This version uses the community string for security implementation just as SNMPv1 does.

The User-based Security Model. The user-based security model (USM) introduced by SNMPv2u and SNMPv2* exists today in SNMPv3. This encapsulation employs the **user** as a security principal.

For noAuthNoPriv messages, the user has no passphrase. This mode of operation is intended for accessing public information from an SNMP agent, such as the device name or type. For authNoPriv messages, the user has one passphrase,* which is the **authentication passphrase**. This passphrase is transformed into the binary authentication key that is needed for the MD5 or SHA-1 algorithm, but an operator rarely needs to deal with this secret key in its binary form. For authPriv messages, the user has two passphrases: an authentication passphrase and a **privacy passphrase**. The privacy passphrase is transformed into the binary encryption key that is needed for the DES algorithm. Again, the operator rarely needs to deal with this secret key in its binary form.

SNMPv3

SNMPv3 was published in January 1998 in RFC 2261-2265 as a Proposed Standard. It was immediately published again in RFC 2271-2275 to correct some editorial errors, but again as a Proposed Standard. Code writers followed suit by releasing their implementations over the next couple of months. SNMP Research had been a constant participant in the SNMPv3 design effort,† so it was possible to deliver source code to anxious customers the same week that the RFCs were published.

In April 1999, SNMPv3 advanced on the standards track when it was published as a Draft Standard in RFC 2571-2575. Two other RFCs were also published. RFC 2570 is an Informational introduction to SNMPv3 that provides some of the same historical background that we have discussed so far through this chapter. RFC 2576 **[Ref 28]** added a Proposed Standard specification for the coexistence of SNMPv3 with SNMPv1 and SNMPv2c, where SNMPv3 included a MIB for configuring community strings for SNMPv1 and SNMPv2c agents. At about the same time that SNMPv3 was being published as a Draft Standard, a few public domain implementations were released from various university development projects, including the University of California, Davis (which later became the basis for Net-SNMP) and the University of Quebec, Montreal.

Finally, in December 2002, SNMPv3 became a full Internet Standard. With the approval of the IESG having been announced eight months earlier, the documents went through their final round of edits and were published one last time as RFC 3410-3418 **[Ref 22-27, 30-32].**

---

*We normally think of a user as having a password, but in SNMPv3, the secret string can contain embedded spaces, so "**passphrase**" is a more accurate descriptor.
†It has been noted frequently that SNMP Research's source code is based on the standards, but often the standards are based on SNMP Research's source code.

Full Standard Status

As an Internet Standard protocol, SNMPv3 will enjoy the same high level of acceptance as did its predecessor, SNMPv1. Already, other specifications such as the DOCSIS standard for cable modem equipment requires the support of SNMPv3 with DES encryption. Many products being produced to connect to computer networks will support SNMPv3 for secure monitoring and remote control.

Deployment: the Old Chicken-and-Egg Problem

New devices being created today will first be installed in networks where there is a large presence of devices that support SNMPv1 and SNMPv2c, but no SNMPv3. Software on the Network Management platform controlling these networks is unlikely to take advantage of the features of an SNMPv3 agent. So there will be a period of time in which equipment manufacturers will be inclined to postpone the implementation of SNMPv3 in their devices to minimize short-term production costs.

Vendors of software for Network Management platforms are faced with a similar scenario. Most networks that their software would monitor and control are saturated by devices that support SNMPv1 and SNMPv2c, but few if any devices in the network support SNMPv3. Anticipating low demand for SNMPv3 support in the short term, these vendors are also inclined to postpone the implementation of SNMPv3 in their software to minimize production costs.

This situation in which vendors are waiting on one another to be the first to release SNMPv3 is a classic example of the "chicken-and-egg problem." In absence of strong demand by network managers, these vendors will tend to put off the development of SNMPv3 indefinitely. It is expected, however, that the advancement of SNMPv3 with security to full Standard coincidentally at a time of increased awareness of worldwide terrorism will prompt consumers of the technology to apply considerable pressure to the vendors to turn the specifications and existing implementations into product features.

12.2.3 What to Expect in the Future

This section provides a quick glimpse at other trends and developments that are anticipated for the near future.

SNMPv1 and SNMPv2 via Proxies

SNMPv1 and SNMPv2c provide no security in their operation and should be replaced. The IETF sent this message to the Internet community by moving the original SNMP Standard to the Historic state. The official recommendation by the people who make standards is to no longer use the community-based SNMP protocols, but instead to use SNMPv3.

Yet, as mentioned above, implementations of SNMPv1 and SNMPv2c are embedded in a large number of existing networkable devices, and they will continue to exist and be in use until all of that equipment is replaced. So how can networks be made secure today? Many companies disallow all SNMP traffic through their firewalls. This is extremely limiting and often undesirable. SNMPv3 and the packet-forwarding SNMP Proxy concept provide the mechanism for a safe and easy migration.

A device containing an SNMPv1 agent can be placed behind a firewall so that no malicious person can attack the system from the outside. At the firewall, the SNMP Proxy is configured to translate inbound SNMPv3 Get and Set requests received from the public network to SNMPv1 and to forward them to the SNMPv1 agent. Responses transmitted by the SNMPv1 agent are converted back to SNMPv3 before they are relayed back into the public network. Also, trap messages transmitted by the SNMPv1 agent are converted to SNMPv3 before they are forwarded to SNMP managers in the public network. Through this technique, access to existing SNMPv1 agents can be made secure for as long as the existing device provides useful service to its owner.

Even Better Security for SNMPv3

Another trend we are likely to witness in the near future is the development of stronger security algorithms for SNMPv3. A decade ago, it was computationally infeasible for a malicious person to crack the encryption of the 56-bit DES algorithm, but 10 years later, DES is considered by some to provide security that is barely adequate. A stronger version of DES called 3-DES is one candidate for addition to the Standard. Fortunately, SNMPv3 was designed to allow extensions of its security subsystem so this would be possible.

While security becomes stronger, it is desirable for the configuration and administration of security to become easier as well. Diffie-Helman is an extension of the User-based Security Model (USM) that allows the initial set of passphrases for a user to be distributed to remote SNMP entities securely. Adoption of extensions such as Diffie-Helman will make SNMPv3 easier to deploy and use in the real world.

Experiments Will Continue

Experiments in SNMP will continue for years to come. An effort called "Evolution of SNMP (EOS)" is now attempting to define the next-generation features that should be added to SNMPv3, including a Structure of Management Information Version 3 (SMIv3). Another group of people is attempting to define a standard for exchanging SNMP information through the connection-oriented TCP protocol instead of using the connectionless UDP protocol. Experiments such as these will shape the thoughts of implementers and will help define SNMP in the future.

12.3 SNMPv3

12.3.1 New Terminology

We first explore some other SNMPv2 innovations in order to appreciate the use of SNMPv3. We start with the SNMP Framework Architecture shown in **Figure 12.2**. This figure is taken from RFC 3411 "An Architecture for Describing SNMP Frameworks" **[Ref 22].**

The SNMP Framework Architecture, whose concepts have evolved over the development of the different versions, embodies the intended modularization of past, present, and future versions. Two principal concepts of this architecture are that it will support any version of SNMP and that other Security Subsystems and Access Control Subsystems can be substituted for those currently in use. This concept is also true for the Applications. The Message Processing Subsystem currently handles SNMP versions 1, 2 and 3 messages. The Security Subsystem currently uses the User-based Security Model (USM) to provide authentication and encryption of messages for the Message Processing Subsystem. The Access Control Subsystem is currently the View-based Access Control System and supports the Message Processing Subsystem. The Dispatcher sends messages to the network, receives messages from the network and hands them off to the Message Processing Subsystem. This architecture supports community-string-based security and user-based security.

Managers and Agents are called SNMP entities in SNMPv3 terminology. An entity is made up of two parts: 1) an SNMP Engine and 2) Applications that provide the required functionality of the engine. An SNMP Engine consists of a **Dispatcher, Message Processing Subsystem, Security Subsystem** and **Access Control Subsystem.** The Applications consist of **commands** that generate Requests, Notifications and Informs and that receive responses. **[Refs 24-26]** and **[Ref 29]** provide the details of these subsystems. The snmpEngine node in the snmpv2 subtree shown in **Figure 12.3,** contains many objects because of the need to define values for the many system engine components and its applications. One particularly important object is snmpEngineID.

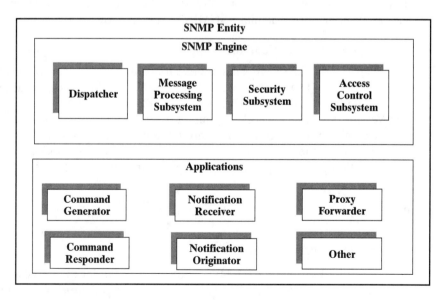

Figure 12.2 Components of the SNMP Framework Architecture

SNMP Engine

The Message Processing and Dispatcher (MPD) in the snmpEngine sends and receives SNMP messages. It also dispatches SNMP PDUs to SNMP applications in the same entity for processing. When an outgoing SNMP message needs to be constructed or when data needs to be extracted from an SNMP message, the Dispatcher delegates these tasks to a **version-specific** Message Processing Module within the Message Processing Subsystem. Versions can be SNMPv1, SNMPv2c or SNMPv3 as we will see in our demonstrations. Coordination with the Security Subsystem is also part of message processing.

Every SNMP entity has a unique identifier called an snmpEngineID. If an entity supports SNMPv3, then its identifier is exposed as a scalar MIB object called **snmpEngineID.0** that is important for the configuration of authentication and encryption in the User-based Security Model (as we shall see). Even if an SNMP entity does not support SNMPv3, its SNMP Engine ID is important for other purposes. For example, an SNMP manager can use SNMP Engine IDs to correlate events reported through Trap and Inform messages. In addition, for an entity to be accessible through a proxy forwarder, the entity's SNMP Engine ID must be configured in the proxy's configuration.

Figure 12.3 shows the snmpEngineID object in relation to other internet subtrees of a modern SNMP entity.

SNMP Applications

An SNMP Application is the embodiment of functionalities that are common in SNMP entities. The following are the types of SNMP Applications:

1. A **command generator** sends SNMP Get, GetNext, GetBulk, and Set requests.
2. A **command responder** receives and processes SNMP Get, GetNext, GetBulk, and Set requests. Upon successful completion of the command, the command responder sends a Response message.
3. A **notification originator** sends SNMP Trap and Inform messages.
4. A **notification receiver** receives SNMP Trap and Inform messages. On receipt of an Inform message, a notification receiver sends a Response message.
5. A **proxy forwarder** receives SNMP Get, GetNext, GetBulk, and Set request messages and Response messages and forwards them to exactly one other destination. A proxy forwarder also receives Trap and Inform messages and forwards them to one or more destinations.

A traditional SNMP Manager is an SNMP entity that contains a command generator application and a notification receiver application. A traditional SNMP Agent is an SNMP entity that contains a command responder application and a notification originator application. Hybrid applications are also possible. For example, a **Mid-Level Manager** is a special-purpose SNMP entity for hierarchical management organizations, a concept promoted since the early 1990s by

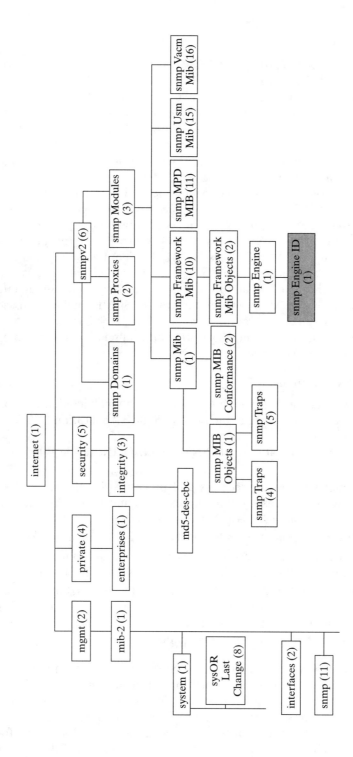

Figure 12.3 Objects in the Internet Subtree Relevant to this Chapter

the DIStributed MANagement (DISMAN) Working Group. Most of the time, a mid-level manager acts in the manager role, so it contains a command generator application and notification receiver application that allows it to monitor and control lower-order SNMP agents (e.g., in a LAN). A mid-level manager sometimes needs to be monitored and controlled by a higher-order manager (e.g., from across a WAN), so the mid-level manager also contains a command responder application and a notification originator application so it can act in an agent role.

12.3.2 SNMPv3 Messages

SNMPv3 messages communicate more information between SNMP entities than did SNMPv1 or SNMPv2 messages. For example, the SNMPv3 message header contains the snmpEngineID of the entity that is the intended final recipient of the message (contextEngineID) as well as the snmpEngineID of the "next hop"—if the message is to be delivered via one or more proxy forwarders—which is used for security purposes. It is labeled msgAuthoritativeEngineID, which is commonly shortened to "authEngineID". There is also a new PDU type for SNMPv3 messages called a Report. In this section we will briefly examine the features of SNMPv3 messages.

SNMPv3 Message Format

Figure 12.4 shows the format of the SNMPv3 message. The following is a description of each of the fields in the SNMPv3 header.

- **msgVersion** specifies the version of SNMP used to create the message. The receiving entity then knows which Message Processing Module to call, SNMPv1="0," SNMPv2c="1," SNMPv2u/SNMPv2*="2," SNMPv3="3."
- **msgID** provides the mechanism to coordinate replies with requests. It also offers some protection against a message being captured and replayed.
- **msgMaxSize** specifies the largest message size that can be sent or replied to by the sender. This was discussed earlier when the GetBulk PDU was described.

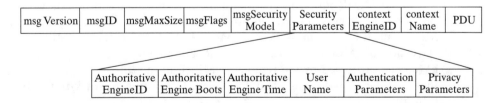

Figure 12.4 SNMPv3 Message Format

- **msgFlags** is a one-byte field. Three of these bits are currently used to set reportableFlag, authFlag, and privFlag. If reportableFlag is set, a receiver must transmit a Report back to the sender in the event of an error; for example, it is used to report that a scoped PDU cannot be decrypted (more about this later). If authFlag is set, the message is sent with authentication. If privFlag is set, the message is sent with authentication and privacy. The last two flags alert the receiver to apply the same security level when the contents are processed or when replying.

- **msgSecurityModel** is an integer that identifies the security model that the sender is using to generate the message. The options are SNMPv1/SNMPv2c="1," SNMPv2u/SNMPv2*="2," and SNMPv3="3."

- **Security Parameters**
  - ❏ **msgAuthoritativeEngineID** is the snmpEngineID of the authoritative entity. The authoritative entity is the agent for Get, GetNext, Set, GetBulk and Trap messages. The manager is the authoritative entity for Inform messages.
  - ❏ **msgAuthoritativeEngineBoots** is the number of times an snmp engine has been reinitialized since snmpEngineID was last configured
  - ❏ **msgAuthoritativeEngineTime** is the number of seconds since the value of snmpEngineBoots last changed.
  - ❏ **msgUserName** is the user on whose behalf the message is being sent
  - ❏ **msgAuthenticationParameters** contains the Message Access Code created by the applying the authentication protocol and the secret key
  - ❏ **msgPrivacyParameters** contains the "salt." **[Ref 27]** See discussions below for how the salt is created by applying a privacy protocol and a secret key.

- **contextEngineID** specifies the snmpEngineID of the entity that has management access to a specified context of objects. The contextEngineID and the snmpEngineID may not be the same if the agent is managing objects on another device such as when it acts as a proxy.

- **contextName** specifies the name of the accessible context of managed objects.

- **PDU** is the message content.

- **scopedPDU** includes the PDU, contextName and contextEngineID. It is the scopedPDU that is encrypted when confidentiality is required.

If an SNMPv1 or SNMPv2c entity receives no reply when it sends a message to another SNMP entity, the reason for the lack of response is not known. The message may have been lost during network transit before it reached the remote SNMP entity. Or, the message may have reached the remote SNMP entity, which chose not to respond (because of authentication failure, etc.). Or, the message may have been processed by the remote SNMP entity, a reply message may have been sent, and the reply message may have been lost during network transit on the return trip.

If the response to a Get message is not received, the command generator may simply retry the original request. Even after multiple retries, however, it is impossible to diagnose the problem with certainty.* If the response to a Set message is not received, the command generator has the added uncertainty of not knowing if a change of state occurred in the remote SNMP entity.

The Report PDU was added to the SNMP protocol to correct this flaw. When a command responder receives a Get or Set request message and determines that it will not send a Response message, it responds to the command generator with a Report message instead of "silently dropping" the original message. Likewise, when a notification receiver receives an Inform message and determines that it will not send a Response message, it responds to the notification originator with a Report message instead of "silently dropping" the Inform.

The VarBind list of the Report PDU contains a counter MIB object that indicates which type of error occurred:

"snmpUnavailableContexts" means that the message could not be processed, because the contextName specified in the SNMPv3 message, while known to the SNMP entity, was unavailable when the message was received; e.g., a Subagent was not running.

"snmpUnknownContexts" means that the message could not be processed, because the SNMP entity does not support the contextName specified in the SNMPv3 message.

"usmStatsUnsupportedSecLevels" means that the message could not be processed because the Security Subsystem of the receiving SNMP entity does not support the security level requested by the sending SNMP entity.

"usmStatsNotInTimeWindows" means that the message could not be processed because it was not received in a timely manner and the receiving SNMP entity is defending itself against a potential replay attack. The sender of the original message should update its notion of the receiver's current time and retransmit the message.

"usmStatsUnknownUserNames" means that the message could not be processed because the user name specified in the SNMPv3 message is not configured or not active in the receiver's usmUserTable.

"usmStatsUnknownEngineIDs" means that the message could not be processed because the receiver did not recognize one of the SNMP Engine ID values specified in the SNMPv3 message. If the contextEngineID is different from the authEngineID, this indicates that the SNMP entity does not contain a proxy forwarder application.

"usmStatsWrongDigests" means that the message could not be processed because a failure occurred in the authentication layer of the Security Subsystem. The authentication key found in the SNMPv3 message is not the user's correct key as configured in the recipient's usmUserTable.

---

*An SNMP entity that listens for ICMP messages could determine that the host or network is down if it receives a "destination unreachable" message, or it could determine that an SNMP agent isn't running on the host if it receives a "port unreachable" message, but if no ICMP message is received, the cause remains unknown.

"usmStatsDecryptionErrors" means that the message could not be processed because the encrypted portion of the message could not be decrypted. The privacy key found in the SNMPv3 message is not the user's correct key as configured in the recipient's usmUserTable.

12.3.3 VACM and USM

The User-based Security Model and the View-based Access Control Model together define how secure access to managed object values is to be provided. Implementation of this security is obtained by configuring five tables:

- vacmContextTable
- vacmSecurityToGroupTable
- vacmAccessTable
- vacmViewTreeFamilyTable
- usmUserTable

Context was introduced previously. We now discuss it in more detail along with the related concept of a MIB view.

- A **context** is a collection of management objects. An agent may have access to more than one context. For example, it may have one context that provides access to all objects on the device that hosts it as well as another context that includes objects on another device through a proxy mechanism. An agent's vacmContextTable can be configured with vacmContextName(s) that reference these specific sets of objects. In an SNMP agent that implements the Master Agent/Subagent paradigm, vacmContextName rows can be added automatically as each new Subagent is loaded or connects to the Master Agent. The Subagent's MIB objects may extend the default context or may exist in a different context.

    If an SNMPv3 scoped PDU contains a contextName and if the agent supports user-configured contexts, that name must be in the agent's vacmContextTable or no access to any objects will be allowed. If a contextName is not specified in a PDU or the agent does not support user specification of it, then user-specified context does not limit access to managed objects. The default contextName is the empty string " ".
- A **MIB view** is a set of managed objects (and optionally, the specific instances of objects) **within a context** that determine objects accessible by the user. MIB views are named in the vacmAccessTable and are specified, in terms of the MIB subtrees they contain, in the vacmViewTreeFamilyTable. The MIB view limits the access of a user defined in the vacmSecurityToGroupTable to the objects specified in the view.
- A **View Subtree** is part of a view and is the set of all MIB object instances that have a common OBJECT IDENTIFIER prefix to their names. "A view subtree is identified by the OBJECT IDENTIFIER which has the longest

OBJECT IDENTIFIER prefix that is common to all (potential) MIB object instances in that subtree."

- A **ViewTreeFamily** is a set of view subtrees defined by the pairing of an OBJECT IDENTIFIER value (called the vacmViewTreeFamilyViewName) with a bit string value (called the vacmViewTreeFamilyMask.) The mask defines which sub-identifiers of the vacmViewTreeFamilyViewName are significant to the family's definition.

  For each possible managed object instance, that instance belongs to a particular ViewTreeFamily if both of the following conditions are true:
  - ❑ the OBJECT IDENTIFIER name of the managed object instance contains at least as many sub-identifiers as does the family name, and
  - ❑ each sub-identifier in the OBJECT IDENTIFIER name of the managed object instance matches the corresponding sub-identifier of the family name whenever the corresponding bit of the associated family mask is non-zero. When the configured value of the family mask is all ones, the view subtree family is identical to the single view subtree identified by the family name.

It will be helpful (if not essential) at this point to provide a simple example of how these definitions are used. We use **Figure 12.5** to do that.

1. Let **X** represent the root OBJECT IDENTIFIER of a context defined on an SNMP agent.

2. Assume we want to limit the access of users to some of the objects in the context

3. Let one user have the view defined by the subtree identified by OBJECT IDENTIFIER **X.1**. Let the other user have the view defined by the subtree identified by OBJECT IDENTIFIER **X.2**.

4. A family of subtrees to which a user may have access is defined by a combination of the object vacmViewTreeFamilyViewName and vacmViewTreeFamilyMask.

5. For a subtree to be in the family, the OBJECT IDENTIFIER that goes with the vacmViewTreeFamilyViewName defined in the vacmAccessTable must be the prefix common to every OBJECT IDENTIFIER in the subtree.

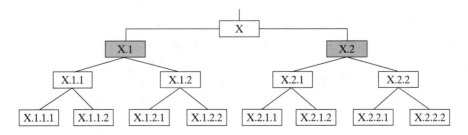

Figure 12.5   A vacmContext and MIB Subtrees

Thus, in **Figure 12.5**, if **X.1** is the OBJECT IDENTIFIER that goes with the vacmViewTreeFamilyViewName, **X.1.1** and **X.1.2** are subtrees of the family with the OBJECT IDENTIFIER X.1.

The vacmViewTreeFamilyMask would be (1100) where the "1" bits specify the sub-identifiers for each object that must be the same as the family OBJECT IDENTIFIER. Bits that are "0" are wildcards.

Figure 12.6 shows the VACM tables discussed above and their location in snmpVacmMIB (16). **Figure 12.7** shows the objects in the snmpUsmMIB (15) sub-tree. The following describe the content and functionality of the objects shown in **Figure 12.7:**

- **snmpAuthProtocols(3)** includes objects that specify the current protocol choices for authenticating users. These protocol choices and their OIDs are:
  ❑ usmNoAuthProtocol {1.3.6.1.6.3.10.1.1.1}
  ❑ usmHMACMD5Auth Protocol {1.3.6.1.6.3.10.1.1.2}
  ❑ usmHMACSHAAuth Protocol {1.3.6.1.6.3.10.1.1.3}
- **snmpPrivProtocols(4)** include the objects that specify the protocols that en-crypt message PDUs to keep their contents confidential. The current protocol choices and their OIDs are:
  ❑ usmNoPrivProtocol {1.3.6.1.6.3.10.1.2.1}
  ❑ usmDESPrivProtocol {1.3.6.1.6.3.10.1.2.2}
  [**Ref 25**] should be consulted for the details of how these protocols work. Good discussions of these topics at the fundamental level are included in

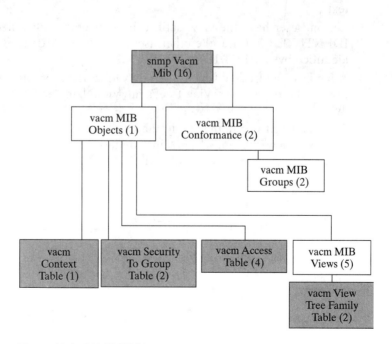

Figure 12.6   VACM Tables

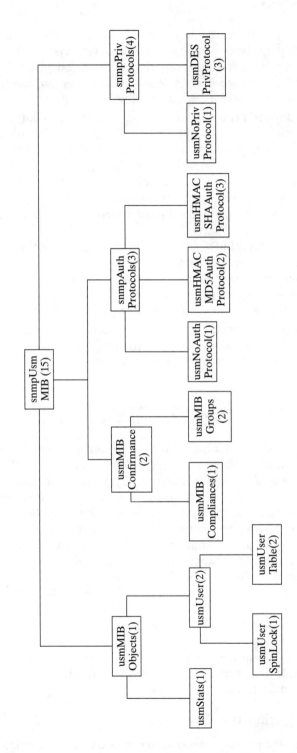

Figure 12.7 snmpUsmMIB Subtree

[Refs 19-20] As discussed earlier in this chapter, both the authentication protocols and the privacy protocols involve secret keys held by the user and the agent. When authentication is used, these keys establish that the user is who he claims to be. When privacy (confidentiality) is also used, the PDU is encrypted and decrypted using a secret key.

- **usmMIBObjects(1)** As the name suggests, this node contains the objects defined in the OBJECT-TYPE macro for the snmpUsmMIB module (see Chapter 7 and Appendix B for macro and module definitions). These objects are of particular importance to security imlementation as we will show.
  - ❏ **usmStats** objects accumulate statistics about messages that have not met various security requirements configured on the agent. Such statistics are potentially important indicators of misuse of network management.
  - ❏ **usmUser** contains two nodes:
    - ⇒ **usmUserSpinLock** values enable managers to avoid conflict when writing to the usmUserTable.
    - ⇒ **usmUserTable** This is one of the critical configuration tables mentioned above that will be discussed below in detail. A useful discussion can also be found in **[Ref 20]** on pages 161–182.
- **usmMIBConformance(2)** includes the objects that specify how agents are to comply with the standards and the groups (usmMIBGroups) of objects that must be supported as part of this compliance.

12.4 CONFIGURING SNMPv3 SECURITY

This section shows the reader how to use the concepts discussed above to configure user access to managed objects on an SNMPv3 agent. The SNMPv3 agent is installed on the Cisco 2611 router shown in **Figure 12.8.** We will configure the five VACM and USM tables listed in the previous section to achieve this.

The first user of a device agent must be configured on the agent using an 'out-of-band' or 'non-SNMP' mechanism. For example, the user could be configured manually in the agent's local configuration datastore (LCD), perhaps using a text editor to modify a flat ASCII text file. This is what is done on the Cisco router configured in this chapter. In an embedded system, the first user is likely to be configurable from the device console using a menu. The latest Data Over Cable Service Interface Specification (DOCSIS) for Cable Modems and other cable equipment requires the use of the Diffie-Helman mechanism to enable secure installation of the first user across the network.

After the first user has been configured, other users can then be configured remotely using SNMP set commands or an NMS. We will see command-line configuration in the demonstrations that follow.

12.4.1 Configuring the First User

As mentioned in the above paragraph, routers are typically configured through the console-based command line interface. To configure the router, it is necessary to have a password to access its configuration mode. In the text that follows, router

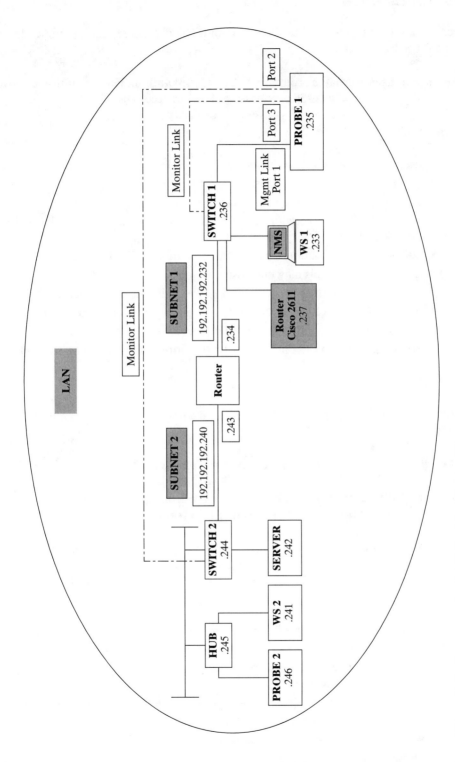

Figure 12.8 Demonstration LAN Used for Chapter 12

command reserved words are shown in bold. The first router command needed has the format:

snmp-server user username groupname {v1 | v2 | v3} **auth {md5 | sha}** auth-password **priv des56** priv-password **access** access-list,

where :

- username is vacmSecurityName as specified in Table 12.2
- groupname is vacmGroupName as specified in Table 12.2
- **snmp-server** refers to the router agent
- v1, v2 and v3 are choices for the SNMP version to be used (SNMPv1, SNMPv2c, or SNMPv3)
- **auth** specifies that authentication will be used (for SNMPv3 only)
- **md5** or **sha** protocols may be chosen for auth
- auth-password is the password used in the authentication process
- **priv des56** specifies the DES 56 bit encryption protocol will be used
- priv-password is the password used in the encryption process
- **access** specifies that an access-list of IP addresses will be used (for SNMPv3 only)
- access-list is the list of IP addresses

Only some of the parameters available in the command were used. Thus, the actual command was:

snmp-server user burke pinnacle v3

since no authorization, privacy or access-list was configured for user "burke."
The second router command used has the format:

snmp-server group [groupname {**v1 | v2 | v3 [auth | noauth | priv]**}] [**read** readview] [**write** writeview] [**notify** notifyview] [**access** access-list],

where:

- **group** specifies a group will be configured
- groupname is the name of the group
- {**v1|v2|v3 [auth|noauth|priv]**} requires selection of SNMP version to be used and auth, noauth, or priv if v3.
- **read** specifies a read-MIB view will be configured
- readview is the name of the MIB view
- **write** specifies a write-MIB view will be configured
- writeview is the name of the MIB view

- **notify** specifies a notify-MIB view will be configured
- notifyview is the name of the MIB view

The actual command used was:

snmp-server group pinnacle v3 noauth **read** internetR **write** internetW **notify** notify.

This command defines the group "pinnacle." When users in the group "pinnacle" access the device using SNMP version "v3" and using a security level of NoAuthentication ("noauth"), those users will receive access to MIB views as follows: readview "internetR," write-view "internetW" and notify-view "notify."

The next command specifies the objects included in or excluded from named MIB views.

snmp-server view view-name oid-tree {**included | excluded**}

where:

- view-name is a named MIB view as specified in the previous command (e.g., "internetR")
- oid-tree is the OBJECT IDENTIFIER of the subtree that will be included in or excluded from view-name

The command used for each view-name was:

snmp-server view view-name 1.3.6.1 included,

Thus, each of the three views is of the internet {1.3.6.1} subtree.

With these router commands, the user "burke" has configured the VACM vacmSecurityToGroupTable, vacmAccessTable and vacmViewTreeFamilyTable for the group "pinnacle." Notice that a vacmContextName was not configured because this router does not support a user-configured vacmContextTable. However, we will describe this table.

There are many other router configuration commands, for example, for Traps and Informs. Thus all router configuration can be done locally on the router or using Telnet remotely with the appropriate password. However, for the configuration demonstrations that follow, we will use command line utilities to demonstrate the details of configuration, and then a network management system. The first rows of the VACM table configurations shown below, include the instances configured locally with the router commands for the first user. The next section describes configuration of other users remotely.

12.4.2 Configuration of Other Users

vacmContextTable

In most cases, the vacmContextTable (Table 12.1) is not to be configured by the user but by the agent. Its primary purpose is to show what contexts are available.

Table 12.1   vacmContextTable {1.3.6.1.6.3.16.1.1}

vacmContextName(1)
" "
"mgr"

It is useful to access it via Get PDUs to obtain values of vacmContextName(s) that can be used to guide selection of vacmAccessContextPrefix values in the vacmAccessTable.

The Index Object for the table is:

1. vacmContextName (1)

vacmContextName can be any alphanumeric string up to 32 bytes. Zero or more vacmContextName instances may be added to the table. We have configured the empty string, " ", for the vacmContextName in all the tables we are configuring.

vacmSecurityToGroupTable

After configuration of this table is complete, the vacmSecurityToGroupTable will look like that shown as Table 12.2 below.

The Index objects for this table are:

1. vacmSecurityModel
2. vacmSecurityName

The following paragraphs describe the column objects:

vacmSecurityModel (1) is specified by one of four integers: 0, 1, 2, or 3. The User-based Security Model is indicated by the integer "3." It is used in SNMPv3 to provide user authentication and PDU privacy. SNMPv1 and SNMPv2 use integers "1" and "2," respectively and "any security model" is "0." The value "0" is a special case and not arbitrarily usable.

vacmSecurityName (2) identifies a user in group vacmGroupName.

vacmGroupName (3) specifies the group of which vacmSecurityName is a user.

Table 12.2   vacmSecurityToGroupTable {1.3.6.1.6.3.16.1.2}

vacmSecurity Model (1)	vacmSecurity Name (2)	vacmGroup Name (3)	vacmSecurityTo GroupStorageType (4)	vacmSecurityTo GroupStatus (5)
3	burke	pinnacle	non-volatile	active
3	abc	def	non-volatile	active
3	molly	safe	non-volatile	active
3	anni	safe	non-volatile	active

vacmSecurityToGroupStorageType (4) is one of the five types described below.

vacmSecurityToGroupStatus (5) is of Type RowStatus. It and other Textual Conventions **[Ref 13]** are described in Section 12.2.2.1.2.2. When this column object is set to "active," all instances of column objects in the row are valid for defining the security-to-group relationship.

- vacmSecurityToGroupTable—First Row

  The first row in **Table 12.2** reflects the configuration produced by the router commands described earlier. The router SNMPv3 agent automatically configures the **non-volatile** default instance of vacmSecurityToGroupStorageType if no other choice is made and sets vacmSecurityToGroupStatus to **active** to make the row valid or enabled.

  We saw in Section 12.2.2 that four types of vacmSecurityToGroupStorageType can be chosen:

  ❑ volatile(2)
  ❑ non-volatile(3)
  ❑ permanent(4)
  ❑ readOnly(5).

  The last three are backed up by permanent storage. A row that is "permanent" can be changed but not deleted, and a row that is "readOnly" cannot be changed or deleted.

- vacmSecurityToGroupTable—Second Row—creating a new user

  The second row of **Table 12.2** will be configured remotely by the user "burke" that was configured in row 1. We will use command line interface utilities to do this configuration in order to demonstrate the details of the process. The steps used to create this row demonstrate most of the principles of creating a row in any table. The steps are shown in **Figure 12.9**.

  The usage line at the top of the figure shows the format of the SNMP utility **setany*** that allows any number of objects in the table to be set in one command if desired. The use of the parameters available is as follows:

  ❑ [-v1], [-v2] and [-v3] provide selection of SNMPv1, SNMPv2c or SNMPv3 messages to be sent between the management station and the agent. An SNMPv3 agent will be often be multilingual so that it can process any of the three protocols.
  ❑ Parameters on the next line provide the option to include contextEngineID and contextName values.
  ❑ Parameters on the third line provide options to specify a timeout for a set response and a number of tries of the **setany** command.
  ❑ Parameter [-pkt_size number] specifies the maximum PDU in bytes that is to be used in a single set message
  ❑ agent_addr and community/UserName must specify the IP address of the agent and either the community name for SNMPv1 and SNMPv2 or the user name for SNMPv3.

---

*SNMP Research utility

```
D:\>setany
usage:  setany [-v1] [-v2c] [-v3] \
        [-ctxid contextID] [-ctx contextName] \
        [-d] [-timeout seconds] [-retries number] \
        [-pkt_size number] \
        agent_addr community/userName \
        variable_name type value [variable_name type value . . .]
                where type is:
                    -b - bit string
                    -i - integer
                    -o - octet string
                    -d - object identifier
                    -a - ip_addr
                    -c - counter
                    -g - gauge
                    -t - time_ticks
                    -D - Display String
                    -N - NULL

D:\>setany -v3 192.192.192.237 burke vacmSecurityToGroupStatus.3.3.97.98.99 -i 5
Enter Authentication password :
vacmSecurityToGroupStatus.3.3.97.98.99 = createAndWait(5)

D:\>setany -v3 192.192.192.237 burke vacmGroupName.3.3.97.98.99 -D def
Enter Authentication password :
vacmGroupName.3.3.97.98.99 = def

D:\>setany -v3 192.192.192.237 burke vacmSecurityToGroupStorageType.3.3.97.98.99 -i 3
Enter Authentication password :
vacmSecurityToGroupStorageType.3.3.97.98.99 = nonVolatile(3)

D:\>setany -v3 192.192.192.237 burke vacmSecurityToGroupStatus.3.3.97.98.99 -i 1
Enter Authentication password :
vacmSecurityToGroupStatus.3.3.97.98.99 = active(1)
```

Figure 12.9 Configuration of the second row in Table 12.2.

❑ variable_name is the name of each object (concatenated with Index object values) that is to be set.
❑ type is that of the object being set
❑ value is that assigned to the object

Following the usage format in Figure 12.9, there are four setany commands. As mentioned above, we could have combined all of these commands into one.

Table 12.3 shows the values of the parameters used in the first setany command. When rows are configured remotely by SNMP commands, the object of type RowStatus, the last column object in the table, must be set first to either **create and wait (5)** or **create and go (4)** while other objects in the row are set **[Ref 13]**. The response to the command, create and wait (5) is shown on the third line of the first setany command indicating that the create-and-wait status was set.

Table 12.3 setany SNMPv3 command parameters

SNMP Version	agent addr	user Name	variable name	vacmSecurity Model (Index Object)	vacmSecurity Name (Index Object)	type	value
v3	192.192.192.237	burke	vacmSecurity ToGroupStatus	3	3.97.98.99	integer	5

In order to set the value of vacmSecurityToGroupStatus to create and wait (5), it was necessary to identify the row using values of the two Index objects vacmSecurityModel and vacmSecurityName. This was done by concatenating the Index object values to the variable name vacmSecurityToGroupStatus. The value of "3" for vacmSecurityModel indicates that the User-based Security Model **[Ref 25]** is being used for authentication and privacy of messages, when applied. The value of vacmSecurityName indicates the format to be used for setting octet string values. Its first sub identifier, "3," specifies the number of sub identifiers to follow. Each of those following sub identifiers is an ASCII representation of a letter. Thus, 97.98.99 represents the vacmSecurityName "abc."

In summary, the four setany commands in **Figure 12.9** were used to configure a new user and group in row 2 of **Table 12.2** as follows:

1. The first setany command:
   - Set vacmSecurityToGroupStatus to the integer(i) value "createAndWait(5)"
   - Used the Index object vacmSecurityModel to specify the User-based Security Model (3)
   - Used the Index object vacmSecurityName to specify the user "abc.".
2. The second setany command created the literal (D) value vacmGroupName "def" for user "abc."
3. The third setany command configured the integer (i) "nonvolatile(3)" for vacmSecurityToGroupStorageType.
4. The fourth setany command configured the integer (i) "active (1)" for vacmSecurityToGroupStatus, enabling the row for the Access Control Subsystem of the router's SNMPv3 agent.

Therefore, four setany commands configured a second user in a second group in the vacmSecurityToGroupTable. This second user is not yet recognized by the agent because more user configuration, described below, is necessary.

In the next section we examine the vacmAccessTable and demonstrate its configuration.

vacmAccessTable

After configuration, the vacmAccessTable will appear as shown in **Table 12.4.** The Index objects for this table are:

- vacmGroupName
- vacmAccessContexPrefix
- vacmAccessSecurityModel
- vacmAccessSecurityLevel

The column objects vacmAccessContextPrefix and vacmAccessContextMatch are used as follows:

- vacmAccessContextPrefix is an octet string. It can be part or all of any contextName defined on the agent
- vacmAccessContextMatch defines the use of vacmAccessContextPrefix. The value "exact(1)" means the value of vacmAccessContextPrefix must exactly match the contextName in the scoped PDU of the message received. The value "prefix(2)" means the octets in vacmAccessContextPrefix need only match the contextName octets specified in vacmAccessContextPrefix.

Thus, for example, if contextName in the received SNMPv3 request message is "internet," then any row of the vacmAccessTable in which vacmAccessContextMatch is "prefix" and "vacmAccessContextPrefix" is "int," meets the criteria for the contextName in the message.

The columns of the vacmAccessTable called vacmAccessReadViewName, vacmAccessWriteViewName and vacmAccessNotifyViewName identify specific views in the vacmViewTreeFamilyTable discussed later. These names are arbitrary, but in Table 12.4 we have tried to make them mnemonic. For example, the choice of value internetR for vacmAccessReadViewName for read access to the "internet" (1.3.6.1) subtree.

Let's look at user "burke" setting instances in the second row of **Table 12.4**. The following SNMP command sets the second row into create-and-wait (5) status.

setany -v3 192.192.192.237 burke vacmAccessStatus.3.100.101.102.0.3.1 -i 5
This command is not shown in **Figure 12.10**.

Notice first that we are using the recognized user "burke" to do the configuration. Notice the values of the Index objects used in the first setany command. The first Index object is vacmGroupName. Its value, 3.100.101.102, indicates that vacmGroupName is coded as three values in dotted-decimal notation. In ASCII, 100.101.102 = **def**, the vacmGroupName we chose for the second row in **Table 12.2**. The values vacmAccessContextPrefix = " " (zero is the length of the empty string), vacmAccessSecurityModel = 3 and vacmAccessSecurityLevel = 1 were configured by the agent using the Index object values provided in the "create and wait (5)" command shown just above.

The first three setany commands in **Figure 12.10** configure the view names "internet," "restricted" and "notify."

Table 12.4 vacmAccessTable {1.3.6.1.6.3.16.1.4}. (the prefix of each ObjectName is vacmAccess)

Context Prefix (1)	Security Model (2)	Security Level (3)	Context Match (4)	ReadView Name (5)	WriteView Name (6)	NotifyView Name (7)	Storage Type (8)	Status (9)
" "	3	1[a]	exact(1)	internetR	internetW	notify	non-volatile	active
" "	3	1	exact(1)	internet	restricted	notify	non-volatile	active
" "	3	2[b]	exact(1)	internet	restrictedA	notify	non-volatile	active

(a) = noAuthNoPriv, (b) = authNoPriv

```
D:\>setany -v3 192.192.192.237 burke vacmAccessReadViewName.3.100.101.102.0.3.1 -D internet
Enter Authentication password :
vacmAccessReadViewName.3.100.101.102.0.3.1 = internet

D:\>setany -v3 192.192.192.237 burke vacmAccessWriteViewName.3.100.101.102.0.3.1 -D restricted
Enter Authentication password :
vacmAccessWriteViewName.3.100.101.102.0.3.1 = restricted

D:\>setany -v3 192.192.192.237 burke vacmAccessNotifyViewName.3.100.101.102.0.3.1 -D notify
Enter Authentication password :
vacmAccessNotifyViewName.3.100.101.102.0.3.1 = notify

D:\>setany -v3 192.192.192.237 burke vacmAccessStatus.3.100.101.102.0.3.1 -i 1
Enter Authentication password :
vacmAccessStatus.3.100.101.102.0.3.1 = active(1)
```

Figure 12.10   Setting object values for the second row of vacmAccessTable (Table 12.4)

The last setany command in **Figure 12.10** changes vacmAccessStatus from "create-and-wait (5) status to "active" status.

The user, **abc**, a member of a group **def**, is now configured with Read, Write and Notify View names, that employ the Security Model "User-based Security Model" with a Security Level of **noAuth(1)**. Now we need to map view subtrees to these view names. The following section describes the vacmViewTreeFamilyTable that will be configured to accomplish this mapping.

vacmViewTreeFamilyTable

This table is used to map which subtrees are to be included in or excluded from the vacmViewTreeFamilyViewName listed in the first column of **Table 12.5**.

The Index objects for this table are:

- vacmViewTreeFamilyViewName
- vacmViewTreeFamilySubtree.

Instances of vacmViewTreeFamilyViewName, that were configured in **Table 12.4**, are shown in the first column of **Table 12.5**. The second column lists the subtrees

Table 12.5   vacmViewTreeFamilyTable: {1.3.6.1.6.3.16.1.5.2} (the prefix of each object name is vacmViewTree)

FamilyView Name(1)	FamilySubtree (2)	FamilyMask (3)	FamilyType (4)	FamilyStorage Type(5)	FamilyStatus (6)
internetR	1.3.6.1	" "	1[a]	non-volatile	active
internetW	1.3.6.1	" "	1	non-volatile	active
notify	1.3.6.1	" "	1	non-volatile	active
internet	1.3.6.1	" "	1	non volatile	active
restricted	vacmSecurityTo GroupTable {1.3.6.1.6..3.16.1.2}	" "	1	non-volatile	active
restrictedA	snmpModules {1.3.6.1.6.3}	" "	1	non-volatile	active

(a) "1" = included

that are mapped to the names in the first column. The other column objects were discussed earlier in the chapter.

Notice how the FamilySubtree(2) instances in the second column have been used. The first four vacmViewTreeFamilyViewNames have read, write, notify and read access respectively to the internet subtree {1.3.6.1}. The vacmViewTreeFamily-ViewName "restricted" has write access to the objects in the vacmSecurity-ToGroupTable in the SNMPv2 MIB tree. The vacmViewTreeFamilyViewName "restrictedA" has write access to the snmpModules subtree in the SNMPv2 MIB tree. Looking back at **Table 12.4** the reader can see some logic behind the mapping choices. For example, since the view-name "restrictedA" requires authentication (vacmAccessSecurityLevel =2), it has been given a larger write view than the view-name "restricted" which has no authentication (vacmAccessSecurityLevel =1). Al-though convenient for the configuration purposes of this chapter, it is not a good idea to give read and write access to the same subtree as was done for the first two vacmViewTreeFamilyViewNames in column 1.

As **Table 12.5** shows, the vacmViewTreeFamilyViewName "notify" is a vac-mAccessNotifyViewName. Objects in the subtree {1.3.6.1} can therefore be in-cluded in Notification PDUs sent by the router agent.

We have now completed the discussion of the vacmMIBObjects(1) tables. It will be useful at this point to review the process of creating the VACM Tables be-cause the number of steps and tables that had to be completed made the process complicated.

Figure 12.11 diagrams the steps and the tables used.

1. From Table 12.2, the user to clone, "abc," is selected.
2. Table 12.6 associates noAuthNoPriv with user "abc."
3. Table 12.4 defines the names of Read, Write, and Notify views and associates a security level with each. The views shown are accessible by security level noAuthNoPriv and therefore by user "abc."
4. Table 12.5 associates the noAuthNoPriv views with the subtrees shown.
5. User "abc" can therefore access objects in these subtrees of the router MIB.

To complete the configuration of a new user we must configure the **usm-UserTable**. The content of this table will be discussed in the next section and its configuration will follow.

usmUserTable

Table 12.6 shows the usmUserTable and some instances of the column objects. We discuss these instances later in the chapter. First, we examine the meaning of the column objects.

The Index objects for this table are:

- usmUserEngineID
- usmUserName.

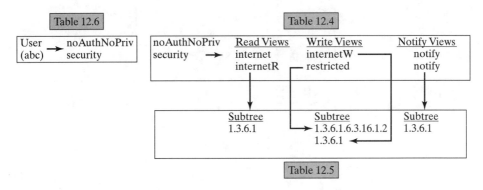

Figure 12.11 Configuration of View-based Access Control for User "abc"

There are 13 objects in the usmUserTable. A complete description of these objects is provided in **[Ref 29]**. We provide brief summaries of them below.

- **usmUserEngineID** is the snmpEngineID shown in the snmp Modules subtree of **Figure 12.3**. It is the ID of the **authoritative** SNMP entity. The authoritative SNMP entity monitors the **integrity** of SNMPv3 messages. A non-authoritative engine can determine the ID of the authoritative entity by sending a message to the authoritative entity that includes the following fields and values:

$$securityLevel = noAuthNoPriv$$
$$msgUserName = `` ''$$
$$msgAuthoritativeEngineID = `` ''$$

  The authoritative engine returns a message with the value fields completed.
- **usmUserName** is the name of a user on the management station. It is a alphanumeric text string of 1 to 32 bytes.
- **usmUserSecurityName** is normally the same as usmUserName. If not, it can be mapped to usmUserName.
- **usmUserCloneFrom** is the object that enables a new user to be created from a recognized user. Its value is a pointer to the clone-from row. A new user in the usmUserTable must be created (cloned-from) a user that already is recognized by the agent. After the new user row is initially cloned, the values of its instances will be the same as those of the row cloned-from.

  Authentication and/or privacy keys of the clone-from user must be changed. This is the purpose of the Key Change objects in the table.

  An instance of usmUserCloneFrom is the instance of usmUserEngineID including instances of Index objects usmUserEngineID and usmUserName for an existing row **[Ref 25]**.

  The security level of the usmUserSecurityName in the clone-from row must be equal to or greater than the security level in the new user row. Also

Table 12.6 usmUserTable { 1.3.6.1.6.3.15.1.2.2} (Each column object name has the prefix **usmUser**)

EngineID (1)	Name (2)	Security Name (3)	Clone From (4)	Auth Protocol (5)	AuthKey Change (6)	OwnAuth Key Change (7)	Priv Protocol (8)	PrivKey Change (9)	OwnPriv Key Change (10)	Public (11)	Storage Type (12)	Status (13)
80000009 03000050 0f0b6960	burke	burke	0.0	usmNoAuth Protocol	" "	" "	usmNoPriv Protocol	" "	" "	" "	non-volatile	active
80000009 03000050 0f0b6960	abc	abc	1.3.6.1.6.3. 15.1.2.2.1.1. usmUser EngineID. usmUser Name	usmNoAuth Protocol	" "	" "	usmNoPriv Protocol	" "	" "	" "	non-volatile	active

Index Objects
- usmUserEngineID
- usmUserName

the usmUserAuthProtocol and usmUserPrivProtocol must be the same in both the clone-from row and the new row (unless the authentication protocol is "noauth" or the privacy protocol is "nopriv" in the new row).

- **usmUserAuthProtocol** specifies the authentication protocol to be used. As we have seen in **Figure 12.7**, the choices are currently:

usmNoAuthProtocol,
usmHMACMD5AuthProtocol, or
usmHMACSHAAuthProtocol.

In HMACMD5-96, H stands for the hashing function used to generate the Message Access Code (MAC) using MD5, the Message Digest algorithm, version 5. In HMACSHA, the NIST Secure Hash Algorithm (SHA) is used. For details on these algorithms in particular and network security in general, see **[Refs 19-20]**.

- **usmUserAuthKeyChange**. The authentication key in the new row is initially the same as that in the cloned row. Thus it must be changed and that is the purpose of this object. The basis for authentication in SNMPv3 is the **password** (passphrase) created by the user. If the clone-from user has a password, this password will be digitally repeated and the result hashed by the chosen hashing algorithm e.g. HMACMD5, to produce a **secret key** for the new user.

The secret key is prepended and appended to the snmpEngineID value of the agent entity and, for example, HMACMD5 applied to obtain another key, the **authKey**. This key is unique to the agent. This process is described in RFC 3414 **[Ref 25]**.* Further hashing on derivatives of authKey and the whole message to be sent produces a 12-octet **message access code (MAC)**. The MAC is sent with the message in the **msgAuthenticationParameters** field (see Figure 12.4). The diagram in **Figure 12.12** shows the steps in the process just described.

When the agent receives the message it repeats the steps shown in **Figure 12.12**. If the same MAC is generated, the message is authenticated as being what was originally sent.

There is no mechanism to provide a new authKey for the cloned row directly. It is done indirectly with the aid of the usmUserAuthKeyChange object. In the case of the first user "burke" in **Table 12.6**, if it had not been configured with router commands, a template row should have been provided by the device vendor from which to clone a row for user "burke." This template row should contain values similar to the following:

❑ usmUserEngineID = the snmpEngineID value for the agent entity
❑ usmUserName = "template"

---

*SNMP Research has a utility that performs these functions.

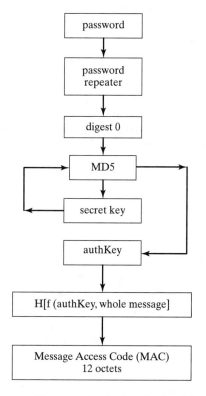

Figure 12.12 Steps to Generate the Authentication Message Access Code (MAC)

❏ usmUserSecurityName = "template"
❏ usmUserCloneFrom = "0.0"
❏ usmUserAuthProtocol = " "
❏ usmUserAuthKeyChange = " "
❏ usmUserOwnAuthKeyChange = " "
❏ usmUserPrivProtocol = " "
❏ usmUserPrivKeyChange = " "
❏ usmUserOwnPrivKeyChange = " "
❏ usmUserPublic = "OCTET STRING"
❏ usmUserStorageType = "permanent"
❏ usmUserStatus = "active"

In the case of user "burke," the empty string values for:

❏ usmUserAuthProtocol
❏ usmUserAuthKeyChange

❑ usmUserOwnAuthKeyChange

❑ usmUserPrivProtocol

❑ usmUserPrivKeyChange

❑ usmUserOwnPrivKeyChange

indicate that there was no authentication or privacy configured for user "burke."

- **usmUserOwnAuthKeyChange** differs from usmUserAuthKeyChange only in that the Index object for the row, usmUserName, must match the value of usmUserName for the row. This is the object value that is changed if the user doing the configuration is the user in the clone-from row.
- **usmUserPrivProtocol** specifies the privacy protocol to use for encrypting the PDU in the message. As shown in **Figure 12.7**, the choices for the values of this object are currently:

usmNoPrivProtocol, or

usmDESPrivProtocol

where DES stands for the NIST Data Encryption Standard.

- **usmUserPrivKeyChange**
  The approach shown in **Figure 12.12** is also used to generate a **privKey**. The first 8-octets of the privKey are used as the DES key.
  A 16-bit Initialization Vector (**IV**) is then created. It is comprised of the last 8-octets of the privKey and a **"salt."** The salt is added to the "recipe" to ensure that the IV is unique to the message (see **Ref 31**).
  The salt is generated by concatenating the first 4-octets in the snmp-EngineBoots object value with the first 4-octets of a locally generated integer. The salt constitutes the **msgPrivacyParameters** field of the message
  The scopedPDU part of the message is to be encrypted according to the specification. To encrypt the scopedPDU, the IV is XOR-ed with the first 64-bit block of the plain text, scopedPDU. This cyphertext block is then XOR-ed with the next 64-bit block of plain text to produce the next cyphertext block etc until the entire scopedPDU is encrypted.
  To change the privKey of a user, the procedure described above for the usmUserAuthKeyChange is followed.
- **usmOwnPrivKeyChange** is implemented as described for usmUserOwnAuthKeyChange
- **usmUserPublic** is used to check that a change to authKey or privKey has actually taken place. If usmUserPublic is included in a set message and its value changes to the set value, then the variable authKey or privKey has changed since all or no variables will change.
- **usmUserStorageType** has the same storage types that we have discussed for previous tables
- **usmUserStatus** is of RowStatus type and its possible values are the same as those discussed for previous tables.

Configuration Implementation: No Authentication and No Privacy The usm-UserTable maps a user and an agent's snmpEngineID to the authentication and privacy protocols and their keys, if any, that will be employed by messages sent between user and agent. This mapping is the last step in the process of making a user recognizable by the agent. As described above, a new user row must be cloned from a current user row.

In this section, we will clone a new user from a row that does not use authentication or privacy. The clone-from user name is "burke" and the new user name is "abc." **Figure 12.13** shows the use of a SNMP Research utility **"getmany"**** that accesses all values of all objects in a table. The first line in Figure 12.13 shows the get-many command usage. -v3 specifies that SNMPv3 is to be used, 192.192.192.237 is the IP address of the Cisco 2611 router, burke is the userName, and usmUserTable is the object to be accessed. getmany uses the GetNextRequest PDU repeatedly. The results obtained are the usmUserTable column object values for the row with user "burke." The values for user "burke" were configured earlier in the chapter using Cisco router commands.

Notice the line of **Figure 12.13** beginning with usmUserSecurityName. The coding of the Index objects usmUserEngineID and usmUserName are:

$$\text{usmUserEngineID} = 12.128.0.0.9.3.0.0.80.15.11.105.96$$
$$\text{usmUserName} = 5.98.117.114.107.101$$

The usmUserEngineID is the decimal encoding of the Cisco router agent Engine ID. Its hexadecimal value is 80000009030000500fob6960.

Since this row has usmUserAuthProtocol set to usmNoAuthProtocol and usmUserPrivProtocol set to usmNoPrivProtocol, all key-type objects have the value " ". The value of non-volatile for usmUserStorageType was configured by the agent automatically. According to Ref [25] for the clone-from row, usmUserClone-From is set to 0.0. The value " " has been set for usmUserPublic. usmUserStatus has been set to "active." to enable access to the object values by the management station.

To clone a new user "abc" from the clone-from row, the **setany** commands in **Figure 12.14** are used. The first **setany** command sets usmUserStatus to createAnd-Wait(5) status. The second **setany** command shows how the usmUserAuthProtcol object is set by providing its OBJECT IDENTIFIER from Figure 12.7. The third setany command shows how to set the usmUserCloneFrom column object value. [**Ref 13**] says that the value of the usmUserCloneFrom column object in the new row should be the instance identifier of the object in the first column of the row being cloned-from. This instance identifier is:

$$\text{usmUserEngineID.12.128.0.0.9.3.0.0.80.15.11.105.96.5.98.117.114.107.101}$$

where decimal notation is used to express the snmpEngineID as before.

---

*SNMP Research utility.

```
D:\>getmany -v3 192.192.192.237 burke usmUserTable
Enter Authentication password :
usmUserSecurityName.12.128.0.0.9.3.0.0.80.15.11.105.96.5.98.117.114.107.101 = burke
usmUserCloneFrom.12.128.0.0.9.3.0.0.80.15.11.105.96.5.98.117.114.107.101 = 0.0
usmUserAuthProtocol.12.128.0.0.9.3.0.0.80.15.11.105.96.5.98.117.114.107.101 = usmNoAuthProtocol
usmUserAuthKeyChange.12.128.0.0.9.3.0.0.80.15.11.105.96.5.98.117.114.107.101 =
usmUserOwnAuthKeyChange.12.128.0.0.9.3.0.0.80.15.11.105.96.5.98.117.114.107.101 =
usmUserPrivProtocol.12.128.0.0.9.3.0.0.80.15.11.105.96.5.98.117.114.107.101 = usmNoPrivProtocol
usmUserPrivKeyChange.12.128.0.0.9.3.0.0.80.15.11.105.96.5.98.117.114.107.101 =
usmUserOwnPrivKeyChange.12.128.0.0.9.3.0.0.80.15.11.105.96.5.98.117.114.107.101 =
usmUserPublic.12.128.0.0.9.3.0.0.80.15.11.105.96.5.98.117.114.107.101 =
usmUserStorageType.12.128.0.0.9.3.0.0.80.15.11.105.96.5.98.117.114.107.101 = nonVolatile(3)
usmUserStatus.12.128.0.0.9.3.0.0.80.15.11.105.96.5.98.117.114.107.101 = active(1)
```

Figure 12.13   Column object values in the clone-from row of the usmUserTable

The fourth setany command puts the new row into the active(1) state. Now let's check that the new user, "abc" is recognized by the router. We do that with the getone command in **Figure 12.15.**

This command requests the value of vacmGroupName.3.3.97.98.99 for the new row with the usmUserName "abc." The return of the correct value "def" shows that the new user "abc" is recognized by the router (see Table 12.2).

Configuration: Authentication and No Privacy   In this section, we want to configure a row in the usmUserTable for a user with security level authNoPriv. We cannot do this by cloning from a current row in the table because all users have a lower security level. Thus we must create such a user from scratch. We will do this by using the router's SNMP configuration commands. However, it could be done by creating a template row first. We start with **Table 12.2** that is repeated at the top of the next page.

The Index objects for this table are:

```
  Command Prompt
Microsoft(R) Windows NT(TM)
(C) Copyright 1985-1996 Microsoft Corp.

D:\>setany
usage:   setany [-v1] [-v2c] [-v3] \
         [-ctxid contextID] [-ctx_contextName] \
         [-d] [-timeout seconds] [-retries number] \
         [-pkt_size number] \
         agent_addr community/userName \
         variable_name type value [variable_name type value . . .]
                  where type is:
                          -b - bit string
                          -i - integer
                          -o - octet string
                          -d - object identifier
                          -a - ip_addr
                          -c - counter
                          -g - gauge
                          -t - time_ticks
                          -D - Display String
                          -N - NULL

D:\>setany -v3 192.192.192.237 burke usmUserStatus.12.128.0.0.9.3.0.0.80.15.11.105.96.3.97.98.99 -i 5
Enter Authentication password :
usmUserStatus.12.128.0.0.9.3.0.0.80.15.11.105.96.3.97.98.99 = createAndWait(5)

D:\>setany -v3 192.192.192.237 burke usmUserAuthProtocol.12.128.0.0.9.3.0.0.80.15.11.105.96.3.97.98.99 -d 1.3.6.1.
6.3.10.1.1.1
Enter Authentication password :
usmUserAuthProtocol.12.128.0.0.9.3.0.0.80.15.11.105.96.3.97.98.99 = usmNoAuthProtocol

D:\>setany -v3 192.192.192.237 burke usmUserCloneFrom.12.128.0.0.9.3.0.0.80.15.11.105.96.3.97.98.99 -d usmUserEngi
neID.12.128.0.0.9.3.0.0.80.15.11.105.96.5.98.117.114.107.101
Enter Authentication password :
usmUserCloneFrom.12.128.0.0.9.3.0.0.80.15.11.105.96.3.97.98.99 = usmUserEngineID.12.128.0.0.9.3.0.0.80.15.11.105.9
6.5.98.117.114.107.101

D:\>setany -v3 192.192.192.237 burke usmUserStatus.12.128.0.0.9.3.0.0.80.15.11.105.96.3.97.98.99 -i 1
Enter Authentication password :
usmUserStatus.12.128.0.0.9.3.0.0.80.15.11.105.96.3.97.98.99 = active(1)
```

Figure 12.14   Cloning user "abc" from the user "burke"

Table 12.2 vacmSecurityToGroupTable {1.3.6.1.6.3.16.1.2}

vacmSecurity Model (1)	vacmSecurity Name (2)	vacmGroup Name (3)	vacmSecurityTo GroupStorageType (4)	vacmSecurityTo GroupStatus (5)
3	burke	pinnacle	non-volatile	active
3	abc	def	non-volatile	active
3	molly	safe	non-volatile	active
3	anni	safe	non-volatile	active

1. vacmSecurityModel
2. vacmSecurityName

Table 12.2, row three, is configured using the router commands as follows:

snmp-server group safe **v3** auth **read** internet **write** restrictedA **notify** notify
snmp-server user molly safe **v3 auth md5** gonzaga

Table 12.7 is **Table 12.6** with a new row added for user "molly" that was configured with these router commands.

To see if the row for groupname "safe" has been accepted by the agent, we execute the getone command with username "molly" shown in **Figure 12.16**.

In the first command, no password was entered at the line "Enter Authentication password." and an "AUTHORIZATION_ERROR: 1 was the response. In the second command, the authentication password "gonzaga" was entered and the correct vacmGroupName.3.5.109.111.108.108.121 = "safe" is returned. Therefore, "molly" is a completely configured router agent SNMP user. Other users with security level "authNoPriv" could now be cloned from this user "molly" row in the usmUserTable.

To be able to clone users with security level "authPriv," a user with "authPriv" security level could be created on the router with router commands to produce the clone-from row. Instead, we will demonstrate a Wizard in development at SNMP Research that simplifies the process.

```
D:\>getone
usage:   getone [-v1] [-v2c] [-v3] \
         [-ctxid contextID] [-ctx contextName] \
         [-d] [-timeout seconds] [-retries number] \
         [-pkt_size number] \
         agent_addr community/userName \
         variable_name [variable_name . . .]

D:\>getone -v3 192.192.192.237 abc vacmGroupName.3.3.97.98.99
Enter Authentication password :
vacmGroupName.3.3.97.98.99 = def
```

Figure 12.15   getone command with usmUserName "abc"

Table 12.7 usmUserTable {1.3.6.1.6.3.15.1.2.2} (Each column object name has the prefix **usmUser**) This is Table 12.6 with the row for user "molly" added.

EngineID (1)	Name (2)	Security Name (3)	Clone From (4)	Auth Protocol (5)	AuthKey Change (6)	OwnAuth Key Change (7)	Priv Protocol (8)	PrivKey Change (9)	OwnPriv Key Change (10)	Public (11)	Storage Type (12)	Status (13)
80000009 03000050 0f0b6960	burke	burke	0.0	usmNoAuth Protocol	" "	" "	usmNoPriv Protocol	" "	" "	" "	non-volatile	active
80000009 03000050 0f0b6960	abc	abc	1.3.6.1.6.3. 15.1.2.2.1.1. usmUser EngineID. usmUser Name	usmNoAuth Protocol	" "	" "	usmNoPriv Protocol	" "	" "	" "	non-volatile	active
80000009 03000050 0f0b6960	molly	molly	0.0	HMACMD5 Auth Protocol	" "	" "	usmNoPriv Protocol	" "	" "	" "	non-volatile	active

Index Objects
- usmUser EngineID
- usmUser Name

```
D:\>getone -v3 192.192.192.237 molly vacmGroupName.3.5.109.111.108.108.121
Enter Authentication password :
Error code set in packet - AUTHORIZATION_ERROR: 1.

D:\>getone -v3 192.192.192.237 molly vacmGroupName.3.5.109.111.108.108.121
Enter Authentication password : gonzaga
Enter Privacy password       :
vacmGroupName.3.5.109.111.108.108.121 = safe
```

Figure 12.16 Requesting vacmGroupName.3.5.109.111.108.108.121

12.5 A WIZARD FOR CONFIGURING SNMPv3 SECURITY

In this section, we demonstrate an SNMPv3 Configuration Wizard.* It will be used to clone an authenticated user "anni" from the authenticated user "molly." The reader will see how easy this makes the process relative to using command line utilities. This wizard can be used to configure a user with "noAuthNoPriv," "authNoPriv" or "authPriv" security level. We will use it to configure user "anni" with authNoPriv from user "molly" with authNoPriv. Self-explanatory instructions are provided on the screens. **Figure 12.17** is the first of the configuration screens.

After entering the device host name or IP address, the "Next" button will be highlighted. Click "Next." On the screen shown in **Figure 12.18,** we enter the username that we configured with router commands as the username for the SNMPv3 Configuration Wizard to use to send SNMP set commands to the SNMPv3 agent.

The screen shown in **Figure 12.19** asks for the security level that the SNMPv3 Configuration Wizard should use to send SNMP set commands to the router agent. Since molly was configured with only an authentication password and not a privacy password, the first choice is the only choice that will work (authNoPriv).

On the screen shown in **Figure 12.20,** we enter molly's password so the SNMPv3 Configuration Wizard can successfully send SNMP set commands in molly's name. The password (passphrase) is automatically converted to a secret key using the HMACMD5 algorithm as discussed earlier.

The screen shown in **Figure 12.21** sets up GET/SET and/or TRAP/INFORM packets for use by user "anni." of the type we have constructed in previous command-line get and set commands.

The screen in **Figure 12.22** shows the current recognized users and their security levels. To create user "anni," the Create New" button is clicked. The next two screens generated by the wizard (not shown) request:

1. the name of the new user ("anni"), and
2. the security level that should be configured (authNoPriv). The screen after that (not shown) requests the name of the user to clone from. In our case, that is "molly." The following screen is:

On the next two screens (shown in **Figure 12.23** and **Figure 12.24**), we enter molly's authentication password again (this time for the purpose of generating a

---

*A product of SNMP Research International.

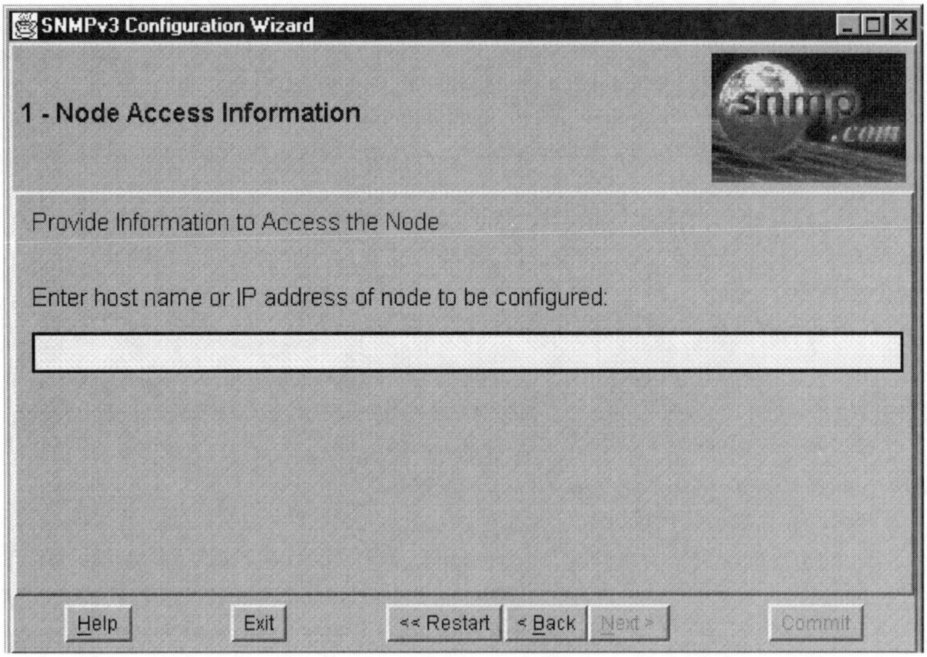

Figure 12.17   Host Name or IP address of device (192.192.192.237 in our case)

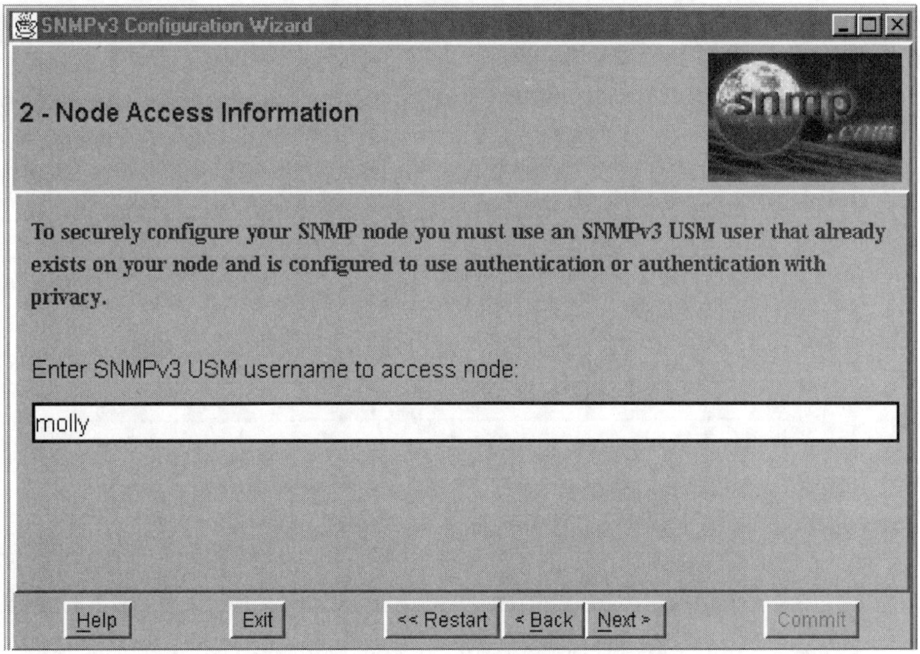

Figure 12.18   Entering authenticated user "molly" to enable access to the router

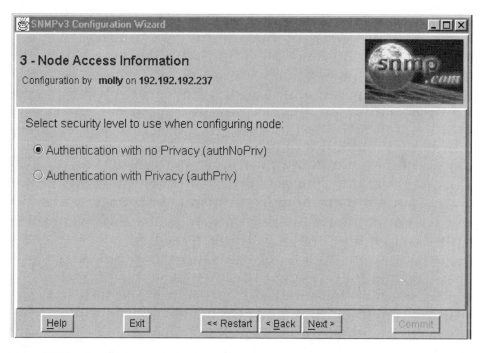

Figure 12.19   Configuring authNoPriv security level for user "anni"

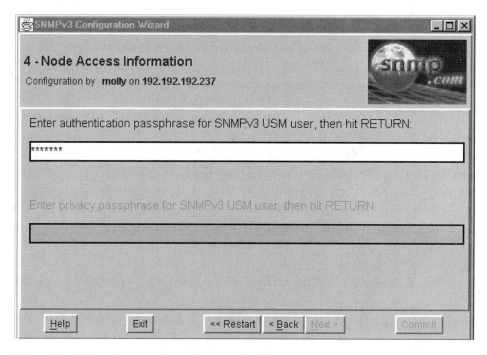

Figure 12.20   Entering passphrase for recognized user "molly"

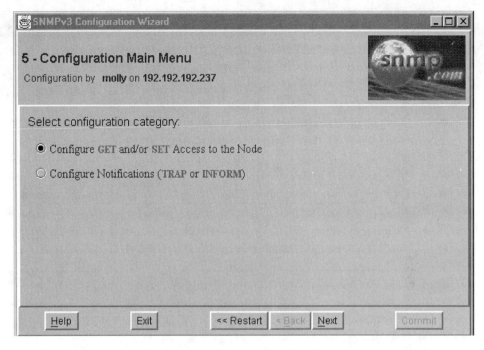

Figure 12.21 Request for configuration of Get/Set and/or Trap/Inform commands

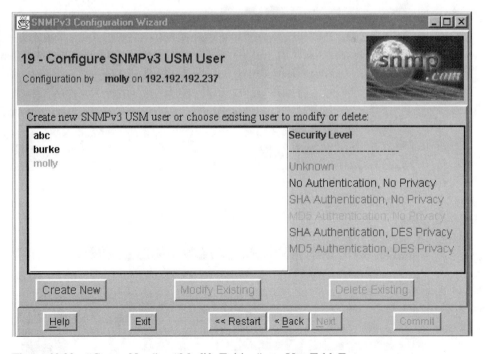

Figure 12.22 "Create New" or "Modify Exiting" usmUserTableEntry

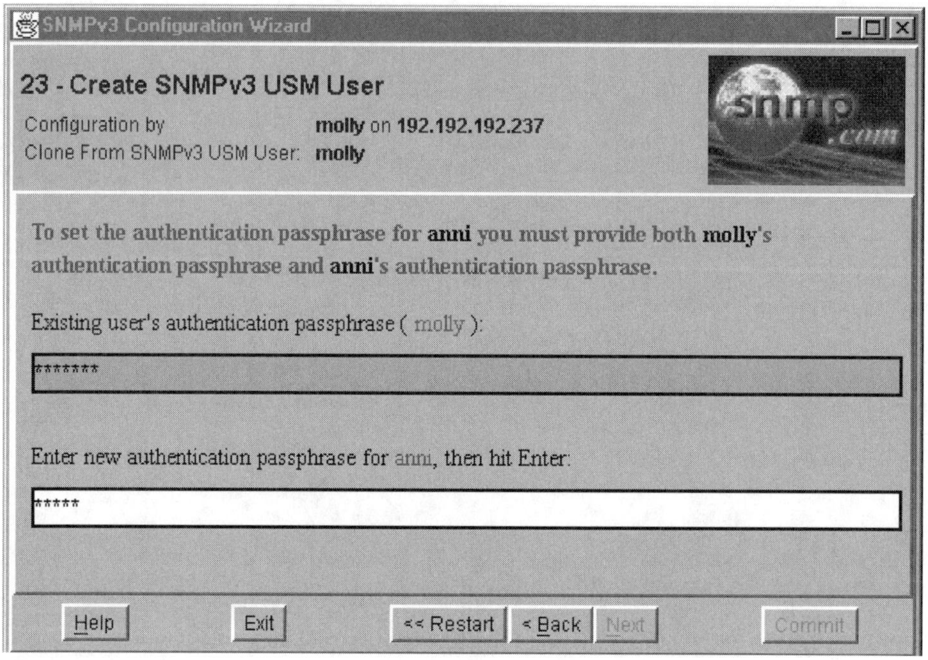

Figure 12.23 Passwords to be used in creating usmUserAuthKeyChange

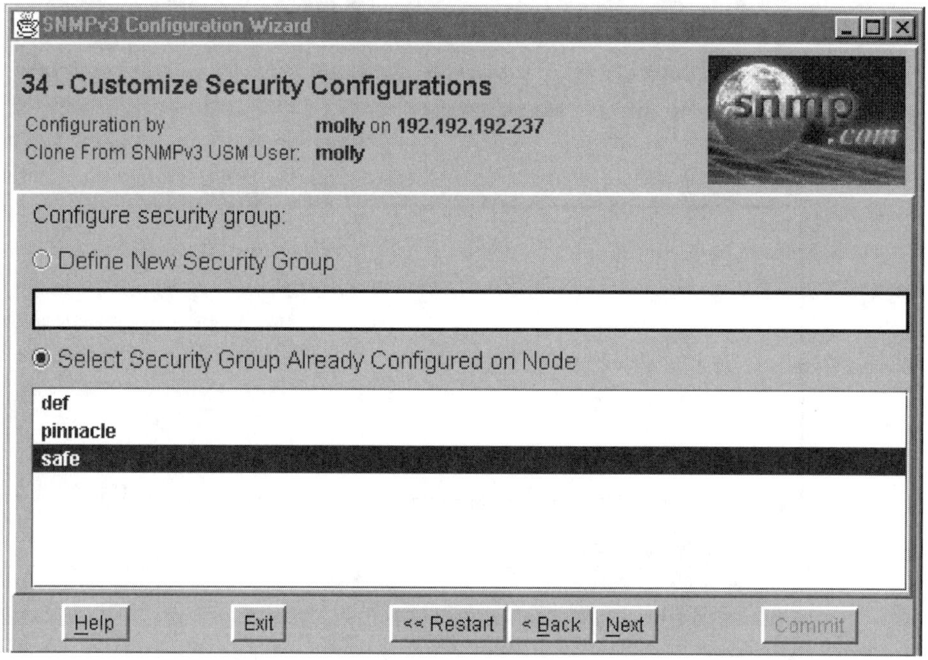

Figure 12.24 Selection of the vacmGroupName "safe" for new user "anni"

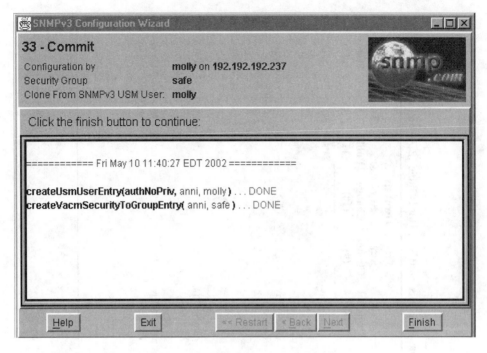

Figure 12.25 View of configurations that were completed

KeyChange value for anni), and we select an existing security group in which to assign the new user anni. Finally, on the screen shown in **Figure 12.25,** we see that the SNMPv3 Configuration Wizard has finished creating the user anni.

Cloning a new user for the usmUserTable from the command line is probably the most difficult SNMPv3 configuration task. The SNMPv3 Wizard makes it easy.

Let's check that the cloning took place. To do that, we return to the command line interface and use the "getone" command shown in **Figure 12.26**.

As you see in the first command, if a password is not used, there is an AUTHORIZATION_ERROR. In the second command, the configured passphrase "dijon" for user "anni" is entered and the correct vacmGroupName "safe" is returned.

The usmUserTable should now have the configuration shown in **Table 12.8** which shows the user "anni," cloned from user "molly," added to the table. In this case, the SNMPv3 Configuration Wizard created a usmUserAuthKeyChange for user "anni" from molly's and anni's password. The usmUserAuthKeyChange is not

```
D:\>getone -v3 192.192.192.237 anni vacmGroupName.3.4.97.110.110.105
Enter Authentication password :
Error code set in packet - AUTHORIZATION_ERROR: 1.

D:\>getone -v3 192.192.192.237 anni vacmGroupName.3.4.97.110.110.105
Enter Authentication password : dijon
Enter Privacy password        :
vacmGroupName.3.4.97.110.110.105 = safe
```

Figure 12.26 User "anni" accessing vacmGroupName .3.4.97.110.110.105

Table 12.8 usmUserTable {1.3.6.1.6.3.15.1.2.2} (Each column object name has the prefix **usmUser**) This is Table 12.7 with user "anni" added.

EngineID (1)	Name (2)	Security Name (3)	Clone From (4)	Auth Protocol (5)	AuthKey Change (6)	OwnAuth Key Change (7)	Priv Protocol (8)	Priv Key Change (9)	OwnPriv Key Change (10)	Public (11)	Storage Type (12)	Status (13)
80000009 03000050 0f0b6960	burke	burke	0.0	usmNoAuth Protocol	" "	" "	usmNoPriv Protocol	" "	" "	" "	non-volatile	active
80000009 03000050 0f0b6960	abc	abc	1.3.6.1.6.3. 15.1.2.2.1.1. usmUser EngineID. usmUser Name	usmNoAuth Protocol	" "	" "	usmNoPriv Protocol	" "	" "	" "	non-volatile	active
80000009 03000050 0f0b6960	molly	molly	0.0	HMACMD5 Auth Protocol	" "	" "	usmNoPriv Protocol	" "	" "	" "	non-volatile	active
80000009 03000050 0f0b6960	anni	anni	1.3.6.1.6.3. 15.1.2.2.1.1. usmUser EngineID. usmUser Name	HMACMD5 Auth Protocol	" "		usmNoPriv Protocol	" "	" "	" "	non-volatile	active

Index Objects
- usmUser EngineID
- usmUser Name

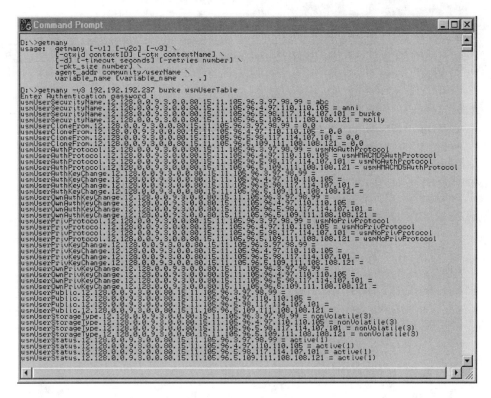

Figure 12.27 **Getmany** utility showing final configuration of usmUserTable on Cisco 2611 router

shown in the table. The final state of the usmUserTable is determined by using the getmany command to access the table. The result is shown in **Figure 12.27**.

You see, at the top of the returned data, the four users that were configured on the SNMPv3 Cisco 2611 router: "abc," "anni," "burke" and "molly." You also see a few lines down that users "anni" and "molly" are configured with the usm-HMACMD5AuthProtocol.

In the next section, we look at the Enterpol NMS that provides a GUI for SNMPv3 management.

12.6 ENTERPRISE-WIDE SNMPv3 SECURITY CONFIGURATION

In this section we describe and demonstrate another product available from SNMP Research: Enterpol* for Windows NT 4.0. Enterpol is an NMS that supports all SNMP versions and that includes a number of comprehensive applications. It

---

*The screens shown in the rest of this chapter are taken from Enterpol version 1.0, a product currently available from SNMP Research. Enterpol version 2.0 is under development. It is expected that the screens for the Simple PolicyPro application will change slightly in the next version of Enterpol.

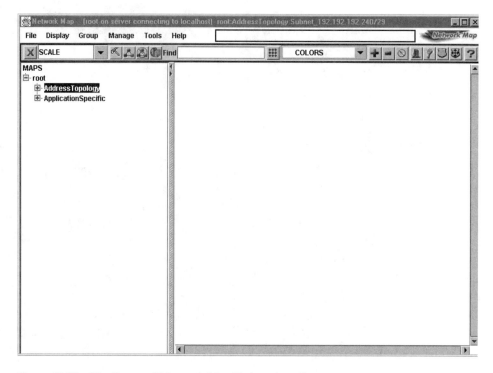

Figure 12.28 The Enterpol Network Map Before Autodiscovery

was provided for our evaluation of its SNMPv3 capabilities by using it with this chapter.

Figure 12.28 shows the Enterpol Network Map. This is a network map of the type we described for Meterware/Analyzer in Appendix F. It is blank because Enterpol has just started. Its autodiscover utility sends ICMP and SNMP messages to all active devices on the network to determine their SNMP capabilities such as version, community string, username as well as IP address and subnet mask.

The left panel of this figure will show the hierarchy of subnets on the network. The right panel will show icons for devices on those subnets. At the top of screen, in the middle of the menu bar, is a set of the icons. The icon on the far right of this set provides a "Parent Map." This map is a connected diagram of icons representing subnets and routers. You can click any subnet to see its devices.

The set of icons on the far right of the menu bar represents choices of Enterpol NMS applications. One application, to be discussed below, is "Simple Policy Pro." It is an application that allows user configuration and policy to be configured uniformly across the enterprise.

Enterpol includes a user configurable autodiscover executable. The autodiscover.cnf file allows the user to customize details of the autodiscover process. For example, it allows the user to control the geographical extent of autodiscover. One feature that the author found helpful is the ability to display real-time queries for device SNMP configuration data to see if the results are consistent with what was actually configured.

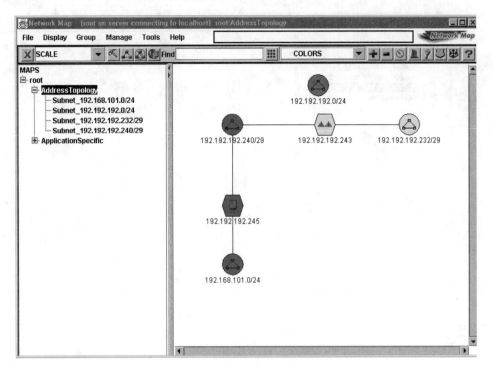

Figure 12.29   Network Map after Autodiscovery

Figure 12.29 shows the Network Map after autodiscover has detected all devices on our demonstration network. At the top of the right panel, you see the network IP address 192.192.192.0/24 where "24" is the number of network mask bits. Just below the network IP address, you see the two subnets on the demonstration network, 192.192.192.240/29 and 192.192.192.232/29 connected by the router. "29" is the number of bits in the subnet mask. The device with the IP address 192.192.192.245 is the hub. It appears here because it is the gateway to a network with the IP address 192.168.101.0/24. This is the network connected to the SLIP connection on the hub.

If you double click the icon labeled 192.192.192.240/29, the devices on that subnet are displayed in **Figure 12.30**.

Similarly, if you double click the icon labeled 192.192.192.232/29 or the corresponding subnet under Address Topology in the left panel, the devices on that subnet are displayed as shown in **Figure 12.31**.

Not all of the devices on this subnet were active at this time. The device with the address 192.192.192.237 is the Cisco 2611 router configured with the SNMPv3 agent. To determine what the autodiscover process learned about this device, double click on the icon to get the menu shown in **Figure 12.32**.

One can **ping** the node to check connectivity, run **trace** to determine the number of router hops between the management station and the node, check to see the number of **events** that the node has logged, examine the **properties** of the node determined by autodiscover and open a **mib browser** to access values of the node's MIB objects.

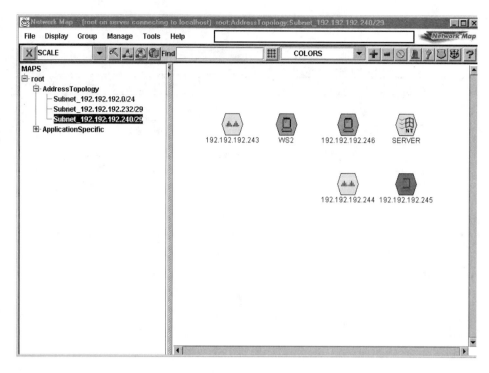

Figure 12.30   Devices on Subnet 192.192.192.240/29

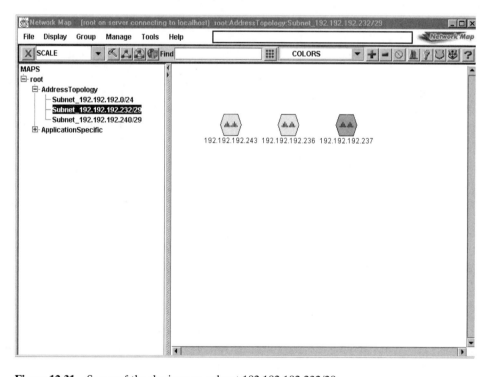

Figure 12.31   Some of the devices on subnet 192.192.192.232/29

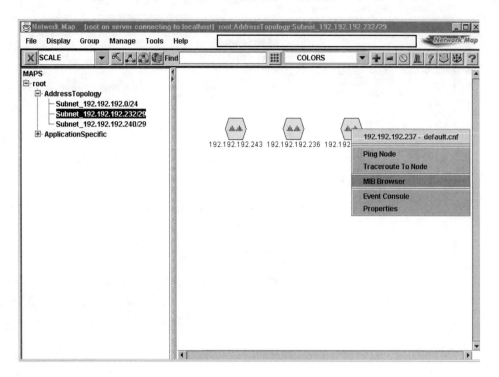

Figure 12.32 Management options for device 192.192.192.237 (Cisco 2611 router)

Clicking Properties displays the screen in **Figure 12.33**. This is the typical set of information that is provided. The first two items in the list are the DNS Name and the IP address of the node. The next five items are mib-2 system group object values. The next line says that autodiscover has detected an SNMP agent on the device. This is followed by lines that describe configurations of all SNMP versions found. There would also be lines for the users "molly" and "anni" if we had configured the "autodiscover.cnf" file with information about users with security level higher than noAuthNoPriv, the security level of user "burke." The next line may show MIBs supported by the device. Finally, other capabilities and characteristics of the device may be shown. This is quite a comprehensive list and one that enables the manager to quickly assess the networking capabilities of the device.

Finally, we access MIB objects on the device by selecting the MIB Browser menu item. This launches the web browser as shown in **Figure 12.34**. This screen shows the MIB-II and SNMPv3 MIBs that can be accessed currently. Scrolling shows access to other SNMP information. Clicking "User-based Security Model MIB" sends SNMPv3 messages that collect object values beginning at this level of the MIB. **Figure 12.35** shows the results for the usmUserTable we configured. Clicking a folder on the far left generates a list of all instance values for that row.

The next section describes one of Enterpol's applications, Simple Policy Pro, that should make a significant contribution to secure network management in the enterprise.

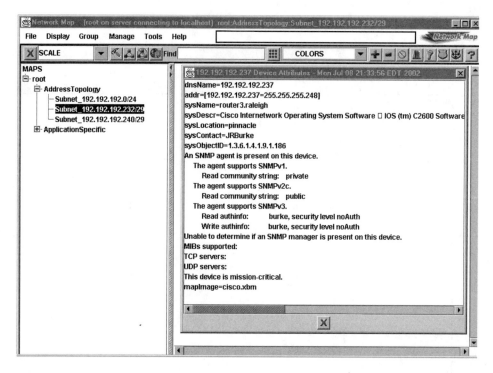

Figure 12.33   Properties of device 192.192.192.237

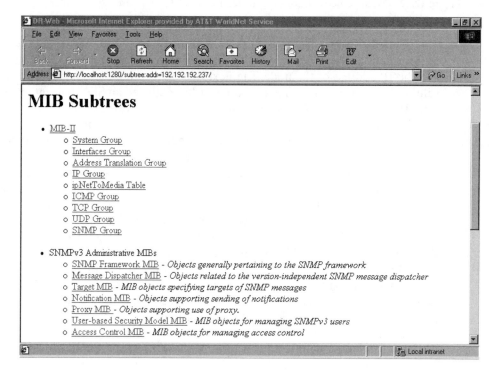

Figure 12.34   MIBs currently accessible from the Enterpol MIB Browser

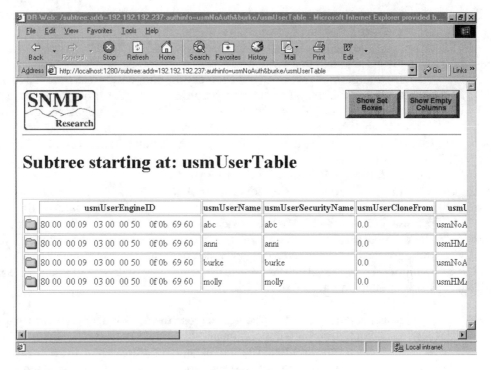

Figure 12.35   usmUserTable configured for device 192.192.192.237

12.7 SIMPLE POLICYPRO

Earlier in this chapter, we saw how the SNMPv3 Configuration Wizard could be used to configure an SNMPv3 user on a single device with an access control profile that allowed the user to perform basic SNMP Get and Set requests. Simple PolicyPro is an EnterPol application that performs the same configuration but on a much larger scale.

Imagine for a moment that you are the network administrator for a large company, or enterprise, which has hundreds, thousands, or perhaps tens of thousands of hosts connected to the network. In such an environment, you are probably not working alone. Under your supervision are several network operators and field technicians, each of whom needs various levels of SNMP access to each host. There are also numerous software tools that use SNMP to automatically monitor different aspects of network health, and each of these needs their own level of access to each host. Finally, some small office groups within the company may insist on having autonomy to check problems with their own printers, etc., that could require minimal SNMP access.

In a large enterprise, security is almost certainly a vital concern. There are the obvious threats that come from outside the company—corporate spies and hackers—but increasingly there is a danger from within the company by disgruntled employees and white-collar criminals. To be truly secure means that you don't stop with the initial SNMPv3 configuration, but periodically you change the management passwords installed on each host within the network. In addition, as employees come and go, you must be prepared to add and delete user configuration instantly at the touch of a button.

If configuring network management in the enterprise-wide environment seems like a monumental task, that's because it is. Forget trying to use command-line manager utilities like **setany**. Some brazen individuals might think about using a tool like the SNMPv3 Configuration Wizard to tackle this job, but it would be like trying to chop down a giant sequoia tree with a small hatchet. The best choice is an application that is designed from the ground up to meet the demands of this important and difficult job. Simple PolicyPro is such a tool.

In the current version of Enterpol, the graphical interface for Simple PolicyPro presents a stack of tabbed panes that guide the operator through the process of deploying SNMP security configuration information throughout the network. The discussion of these panes provided below will give the reader a feel for this application. As expected, however, it is necessary to go through one's own configuration to see exactly how to use the panes. An overview of each pane is provided in the paragraphs that follow.

Select Agents. The first step is to choose the SNMP agents for which security configuration will be managed by Simple PolicyPro. A list of all known hosts is presented. The names and IP addresses of these hosts are discovered by Enterpol's autodiscovery engine or are extracted from the database of a complimentary Network Management System, such as HP/OpenView. The properties of a host—does it support SNMPv1, SNMPv2c, or SNMPv3, and is the agent configurable—are discovered by Enterpol's autodiscovery engine. **Figure 12.36** shows the "Select Agents" pane for our demonstration network. The Cisco 2611 router with IP Address 192.192.192.237 is the "Agent Chosen for Management" by highlighting it and clicking the button with two arrows pointing right.

Select Managers. The second step is to choose the SNMP managers. Simple PolicyPro can configure into any SNMPv3 agent the IP address of any specified SNMP manager as a target for certain notifications.* Simple PolicyPro can also configure into *configurable managers* the authentication and privacy passwords necessary to receive all other types of notifications and to send commands without prompting the user of that system for his or her passwords.

Configurable managers are SNMPv3 manager entities that can receive new configuration information through SNMP Set requests. Configurable managers have an embedded command responder application, or they have access to a separate process that provides command responder services. An example of this is SNMP Research's BRASS prod-

---

*Non-configurable managers can receive SNMPv1 Traps, SNMPv2c Traps, SNMPv2c Informs, and SNMPv3 Informs with No authentication and No privacy. If a manager is configurable, it can receive SNMPv3 Traps and Informs with authentication and privacy enabled.

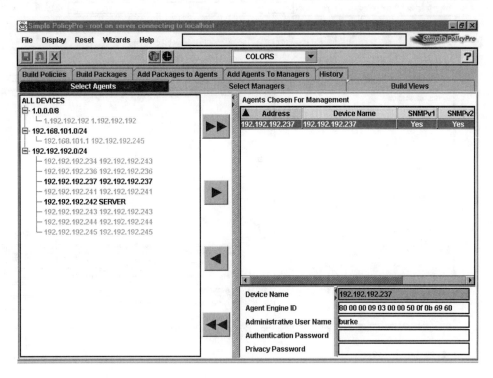

Figure 12.36 Select Agents for Management

uct. The BRASS Server is the SNMP engine for all of SNMP Research's Network Management Systems—including Enterpol—and it is also a Subagent in order for it to be a configurable manager.

Figure 12.37 shows the "Select Managers" pane where SERVER is the "Manager Chosen for Management." You see in the bottom right pane that there is a user, "CharlieDChief," configured with two passwords for the "authPriv" security level. This configuration was done in the autodiscover.cnf file for SERVER and the user automatically became a recognized user. This is not currently the case for agents configured in autodiscover.cnf for security levels higher than noAuthNoPriv as mentioned above.

Build Views. The third step is to define MIB views. A MIB **view** is a collection of MIB *subtrees* that will be "visible" to users accessing the SNMP agent with Get or Set commands. **Figure 12.38** shows the "Build Views" screen for our configuration of the VACM and USM tables.

Build Policies. The fourth step is to define policies. A **policy** is a collection of MIB *views* and the **users** who have identical privileges to perform management operations within those views. For example, one could create a "Helpdesk" policy for all company employees who work at the help desk. All such employees would have only a low to medium security clearance, so they may have a modest MIB view for SNMP Get operations and a tiny MIB view for performing only essential Set operations.

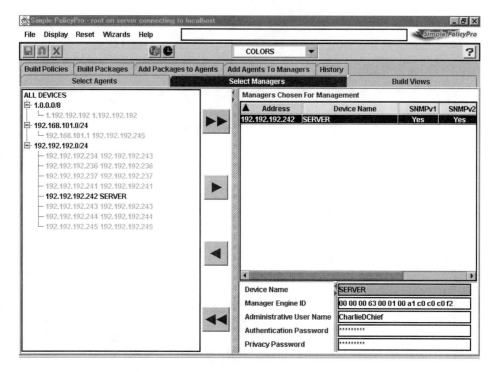

Figure 12.37   Select Manager

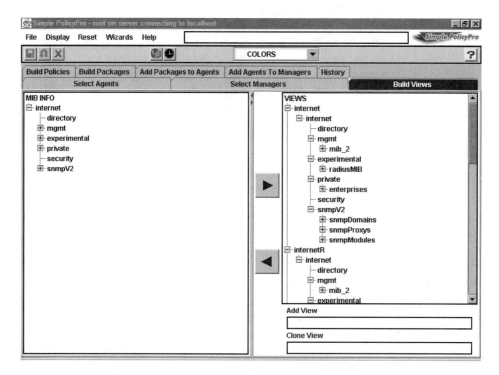

Figure 12.38   Build Views for Users

These users may have an all-inclusive MIB view for receiving notifications, however. All of these users and their MIB views would be contained together in the policy. Users may exist in only one policy. MIB views can be used in many policies and many times in each policy to establish degrees of access in different security levels. **Figure 12.39** shows the "Build Policies" screen for the demonstration network. The Policies shown in the pane on the far right are constructed from combinations of Groups, Views and Users chosen from other panes and screens as described in this paragraph.

Build Packages. The fifth step is to define policy packages. A policy package is a collection of policies that are deployed together. For example, one could create a "DayShift" package containing "Helpdesk" users, "SysAdmin" users, and so on. **Figure 12.40** shows the "Build Packages" pane for Cisco router with SNMPv3 agent. The Policies defined in the left pane have been combined into one Policy Package for the router.

Add Packages to Agents. The sixth step is to deploy policy packages to configurable SNMPv3 agents. Assigning a package to an agent causes Simple PolicyPro to send all of the necessary SNMP Set requests to the agent (potentially hundreds for each policy) to configure the USM and VACM MIBs for the command responder application. If any of the policies include a MIB view for SNMPv1 or SNMPv2c access to a multilingual device, Simple PolicyPro will also send SNMP Set requests to the agent to

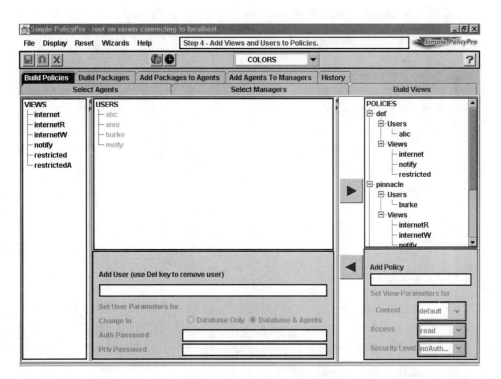

Figure 12.39   Build Policies for Users

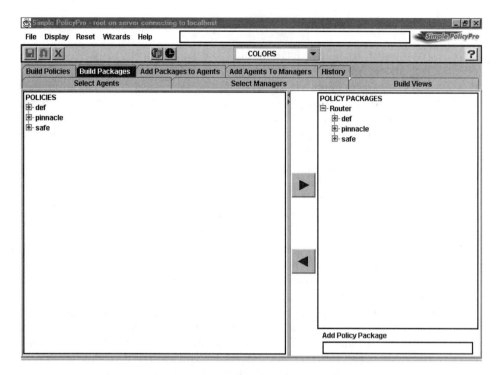

Figure 12.40 Build Packages for Agents

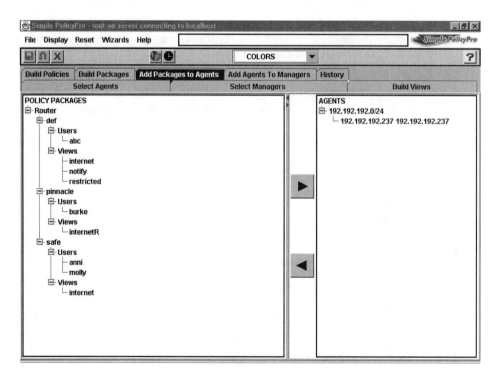

Figure 12.41 Deploy Packages to Agents

configure the COMMUNITY MIB [Ref 28]. **Figure 12.41** shows the "Add Packages to Agents" pane in which Policy Packages on the left can be selected for addition to the Cisco router.

Add Agents to Managers. The seventh and last step is to assign SNMP agents to SNMP managers. This causes Simple PolicyPro to configure the notification originator application for an agent's USM, VACM, NOTIFY, and TARGET MIBs and each manager's IP and SNMP Engine ID. If any of the SNMP managers are configurable managers, then Simple PolicyPro also sends the necessary SNMP Set requests to the manager to configure each user's authentication and privacy keys and each agent's SNMP Engine ID. **Figure 12.42** shows the "Add Agents to Managers" pane in which the Cisco router SNMPv3 agent has been added to the Manager "SERVER."

Once a configuration has been deployed, any changes to existing and deployed views, users, policies, or packages are updated as quickly as possible in the SNMP agents and managers. So, if a user forgets his or her pass phrase, it can be updated almost immediately in every configured host simply by going to the "Build Policies" pane and entering a new pass phrase for the user. Just as easily, a user can be deleted from all hosts if necessary. Through the interface, periodic changes of security information can be performed with relative ease.

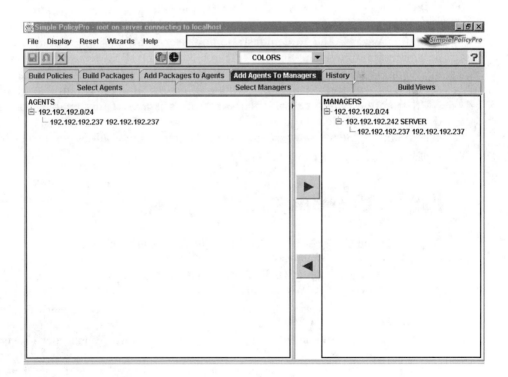

Figure 12.42   Add Agents to Managers

In conclusion, Simple PolicyPro enables the network administrator to manage security keys and access control policies for a very large number of hosts in an enterprise-wide configuration. Simple PolicyPro automates to the level of point-and-click the process of configuring SNMPv3 entities that we have presented in detail in this chapter.

CHAPTER SUMMARY

The focus of this chapter was the introduction of the reader to the new SNMPv3 Internet Standard and to demonstrate its use. To do that, it was also necessary to review the capabilities provided by SNMPv2 that are implemented by SNMPv3. Various versions of SNMPv2 were developed during its evolution and some of the history of that evolution was described because it served as the foundation for SNMPv3. The architecture of SNMPv3 was described and it was emphasized that its modular design enables easy implementation of SNMP versions 1, 2, and 3 as well as future innovations in security approaches. The SNMPv2 MIB subtree of the internet MIB was described because the values assigned to its objects are important to the configuration of the SNMPv3 agent database. There are five tables in the SNMPv2 MIB that were configured to demonstrate how a NMS user obtains access to objects on a SNMPv3 configured device. Command-line utilities, available from SNMP Research were used to demonstrate the details of the configuration process. These demonstrations were followed by using the SNMP Research SNMPv3 Configuration Wizard GUI to demonstrate how user usmUserTable configuration can be greatly simplified. The SNMP Research NMS EnterPol was used to show automatic configuration of a network map for the demonstration network and access to SNMP device characteristics and configurations. Another important feature of this NMS, from the point of view of large networks, is a GUI that enables configurations to be distributed throughout the enterprise. Configuration of this application, called Simple PolicyPro, was demonstrated using configurations set earlier in the chapter.

REVIEW QUESTIONS

1. SNMPv1 and SNMPv2c use community strings for security in their PDUs. What are the significant security advantages provided by SNMPv3?
2. What delayed the approval of SNMPv2 as an Internet Standard?
3. What is the principal difference between SNMPv2 capability and SNMPv3 capability?
4. Do you think that the use of SNMPv3 will increase the use of network management over the Internet? If so, why?
5. Of the network intrusion techniques addressed by SNMPv3, do you think one is most important and if so why?
6. Of the network intrusion techniques addressed by SNMPv3, which do you think have been adequately addressed by SNMPv3—any, all, none?

7. Explain how intrusion has been addressed by SNMPv3 procedures.

8. We have said that five tables are required to configure users of a SNMPv3 agent. Is the use of these tables clear, or would you recommend another approach? If the use of these tables is not clear, identify what is confusing.

9. We have said that EnterPol provides a utility that enables policy-based management across the network. What is policy-based management?

10. How does authentication differ from encryption and which do you think is most important?

11. Why is it necessary to initially configure an SNMPv3 agent directly rather than remotely using SNMPv3?

12. What is the value of configuring views for users?

13. Name some of the values of having an snmpEngineID.

14. How does a contextEngineID differ from an authEngineID?

15. What is the advantage of a proxy forwarder in the case of SNMPv3?

EXERCISES

1. If you have a device with an agent that supports SNMPv3, configure the agent locally for one user using commands provided by the device for the security level authNoPriv.

2. If you have SNMPv3 utilities, attempt to access the value of an object with this user.

3. When successful with exercise 2, create a new user remotely with authNoPriv security level.

4. Attempt to access the value of an object with the new user and a command line utility.

5. If you have access to an NMS that supports SNMPv3, access the same object value with the NMS and compare the experience with exercise 4.

6. You see from these suggested exercises what software/hardware is needed to implement SNMPv3 device management. Discuss these requirements with your instructor if you are in a classroom or with your supervisor if you are part of the IT organization in your corporation and obtain the necessary software, if possible.

7. Make a list of observations from your experiences with the above exercises when you have the necessary software.

REFERENCES

1. "Introduction to version 2 of the Internet-standard Network Management Framework Network," Request for Comments: *1441* (HISTORIC), J. Case, SNMP Research, Inc., K. McCloghrie, Hughes LAN Systems, M. Rose, Dover Beach Consulting, Inc., S. Waldbusser, Carnegie Mellon University, April 1993.

2. "Structure of Management Information for version 2 of the Simple Network Management Protocol (SNMPv2)." Request for Comments: *1442* (PROPOSED STANDARD), J. Case, SNMP Research, Inc., K. McCloghrie, Hughes LAN Systems, M. Rose, Dover Beach Consulting, Inc., S. Waldbusser, Carnegie Mellon University, April 1993. Obsoleted by RFC 1902, RFC 2578 [REF 12].

3. "Textual Conventions for version 2 of the Simple Network Management Protocol (SNMPv2)," Request for Comments: *1443* (PROPOSED STANDARD), April 1993,

J. Case, SNMP Research, Inc., K. McCloghrie, Hughes LAN Systems, M. Rose, Dover Beach Consulting, Inc., S. Waldbusser, Carnegie Mellon University. Obsoleted by RFC 1903, RFC 2579 [REF 13].

4. "Administrative Model for version 2 of the Simple Network Management Protocol (SNMPv2)" Request for Comments: *1445* (HISTORIC), J. Galvin, Trusted Information Systems, K. McCloghrie, Hughes LAN Systems, April 1993.

5. "Security Protocols for version 2 of the Simple Network Management Protocol (SNMPv2)." Request for Comments: *1446* (HISTORIC), J. Galvin, Trusted Information Systems, K. McCloghrie, Hughes LAN Systems, April 1993.

6. "Party MIB for version 2 of the Simple Network Management Protocol (SNMPv2)," Request for Comments: *1447* (HISTORIC), K. McCloghrie, Hughes LAN Systems, J. Galvin, Trusted Information Systems, April 1993.

7. "Protocol Operations for version 2 of the Simple Network Management Protocol (SNMPv2)," Request for Comments: *1448* (PROPOSED STANDARD), J. Case, SNMP Research, Inc., K. McCloghrie, Hughes LAN Systems, M. Rose, Dover Beach Consulting, Inc., S. Waldbusser, Carnegie Mellon University, April 1993. Obsoleted by RFC 1905, RFC 3416 [REF 30].

8. "Transport Mappings for version 2 of the Simple Network Management Protocol (SNMPv2)," Request for Comments: *1449* (PROPOSED STANDARD), J. Case, SNMP Research, Inc., K. McCloghrie, Hughes LAN Systems, M. Rose, Dover Beach Consulting, Inc., S. Waldbusser, Carnegie Mellon University, April 1993. Obsoleted by RFC 1906, RFC 3417 [REF 31].

9. "Management Information Base for version 2 of the Simple Network Management Protocol (SNMPv2)," Request for Comments: *1450* (PROPOSED STANDARD), J. Case, SNMP Research, Inc., K. McCloghrie, Hughes LAN Systems, M. Rose, Dover Beach Consulting, Inc., S. Waldbusser, Carnegie Mellon University, April 1993. Obsoleted by RFC 1907, RFC 3418 [REF 32].

10. "Manager-to-Manager Management Information Base," Request for Comments: *1451* (HISTORIC), J. Case, SNMP Research, Inc., K. McCloghrie, Hughes LAN Systems, M. Rose, Dover Beach Consulting, Inc., S. Waldbusser, Carnegie Mellon University, April 1993.

11. "Coexistence between version 1 and version 2 of the Internet-standard Network Management Framework," Request for Comments: *1452* (PROPOSED STANDARD), J. Case, SNMP Research, Inc., K. McCloghrie, Hughes LAN Systems, M. Rose, Dover Beach Consulting, Inc., S. Waldbusser, Carnegie Mellon University, April 1993. Obsoleted by RFC 1908, RFC 2576 [REF 28].

12. "Structure of Management Information Version 2 (SMIv2)." Request for Comments: *2578*, STD: 58, April 1999. K. McCloghrie, Cisco Systems, D. Perkins, SNMP info, and J. Schoenwaelder, TU Braunschweig. Authors of previous version: J. Case, SNMP Research, Inc., K. McCloghrie, Cisco Systems, M. Rose, First Virtual Holdings, and S. Waldbusser, International Network Services. Obsoletes: RFC 1902, RFC 1442 [REF 2].

13. "Textual Conventions for SMIv2," Request for Comments: *2579*, April 1999, K. McCloghrie, Cisco Systems, D. Perkins, SNMPinfo, J. Schoenwaelder, TU Braunschweig, STD: 58, Obsoletes: RFC 1903, RFC 1443 [REF 3].

14. "Conformance Statements for SMIv2," Request for Comments: *2580*, Editors of this version: STD: 58, Obsoletes: *1904*, K. McCloghrie, Cisco Systems, D. Perkins, Category: Standards Track SNMPinfo, J. Schoenwaelder, TU Braunschweig. Authors of previous version: J. Case, SNMP Research, Inc., K. McCloghrie, Cisco Systems, M. Rose, First Virtual Holdings, S. Waldbusser, International Network Services, April 1999.

15. "SNMP, SNMPv2 and RMON," William Stallings, Addison Wesley, 1996.

16. "Structure and Identification of Management Information for TCP/IP-based Internets, Network, Request for Comments: *1155*, Obsoletes: RFC 1065, M. Rose, Performance Systems International, K. McCloghrie, Hughes LAN Systems, May 1990.

17. "Concise MIB Definitions," Request for Comments: *1212*, M. Rose, Performance Systems International, K. McCloghrie, Hughes LAN Systems, Editors, March 1991.

18. "A Convention for Defining Traps for use with the SNMP," Request for Comments: *1215* M. Rose, Editor, Performance Systems International, March 1991.

19. "Network Security: Provate Communication in a Public World," C. Kaufman, R. Perlman and M. Speciner, Prentice Hall, 1995.

20. "Network and Internetwork Security: Principles and Practice," William Stallings, Prentice Hall, 1995.

21. "Introduction to Community-based SNMPv2," Request for Comments: *1901*, Category: (HISTORIC), J. Case, SNMP Research, Inc., K. McCloghrie, Cisco Systems, Inc., M. Rose, Dover Beach Consulting, Inc., S. Waldbusser, International Network Services, January 1996.

22. "An Architecture for Describing SNMP Management Frameworks" Request for Comments: *3411*, STD0062, December 2002 (STANDARD). D. Harrington, Enterasys Networks, R. Presuhn, BMC Software, Inc., B. Wijnen, Lucent Technologies. ftp://ftp.isi.edu/in-notes/rfc3411.txt. Obsoletes: RFC 2571, RFC 2271, RFC 2261.

23. "Message Processing and Dispatching for the Simple Network Management Protocol (SNMP)," Request for Comments: *3412*, STD0062, December 2002 (STANDARD). J. Case, SNMP Research Inc., D. Harrington, Enterasys Networks, R. Presuhn, BMC Software, Inc., and B. Wijnen, Lucent Technologies. ftp://ftp.isi.edu/in-notes/rfc3412.txt. Obsoletes: RFC 2572, RFC 2272, RFC 2262.

24. "SNMP Applications," Request for Comments: *3413*, STD0062, December 2002 (STANDARD), D. Levi, Nortel Networks, P. Meyer, Secure Computing Corporation, and B. Stewart, Retired. ftp://ftp.isi.edu/in-notes/rfc3413.txt. Obsoletes: RFC 2573, RFC 2273, RFC 2263.

25. "The User-Based Security Model for Version 3 of the Simple Network Management Protocol (SNMPv3)," RFC *3414*, STD0062, December 2002 (STANDARD). U. Blumenthal, and B. Wijnen, Lucent Technologies, ftp://ftp.isi.edu/in-notes/rfc3414.txt. Obsoletes: RFC 2574, RFC 2274, RFC 2264.

26. "View-based Access Control Model for the Simple Network Management Protocol (SNMP)," RFC *3415*, STD0062, December 2002 (STANDARD). B.Wijnen, Lucent Technologies, R. Presuhn, BMC Software, Inc., and K. McCloghrie, Cisco Systems, Inc. ftp://ftp.isi.edu/in-notes/ rfc3415.txt. Obsoletes: RFC 2575, RFC 2275, RFC 2265.

27. "Introduction and Applicability Statements for Internet Standard Network Management Framework." Request for Comments: *3410*, December 2002 (INFORMATIONAL), J. Case, SNMP Research, Inc., R. Mundy, Network Associates Laboratories, D. Partain, Ericsson, and B. Stewart, Retired.

28. "Coexistence between Version 1, Version 2, and Version 3 of the Internet-standard Network Management Framework," Request for Comments: *2576*, Category: Standards Track, R. Frye, CoSine Communications, D. Levi, Nortel Networks, S. Routhier, Integrated Systems Inc., Wijnen, Lucent Technologies, March 2000. Obsoletes: RFC 2089, RFC 1908, RFC 1452 [REF 11].

29. "A Practical Guide to SNMPv3 and Network Management," David Zeltserman, Prentice Hall, 1999.

30. "Version 2 of the Protocol Operations for the Simple Network Management Protocol (SNMP)," RFC *3416*, STD0062, December 2002 (STANDARD). J. Case, SNMP Research, Inc., K. McCloghrie, Cisco Systems, Inc., M. Rose, Dover Beach Consulting, Inc., S. Waldbusser, International Network Services, and R. Presuhn, BMC Software, Inc.

(Editor of this version). ftp://ftp.isi-edu/in-notes/rfc3416.txt. Obsoletes: RFC 1905, RFC 1448 [REF 7].

31. "Transport Mappings for the Simple Network Management Protocol (SNMP)," RFC *3417*, STD0062, December 2002 (STANDARD). J. Case, SNMP Research, Inc., K. Mc-Cloghrie, Cisco Systems, Inc., M. Rose, Dover Beach Consulting, Inc., S. Waldbusser, International Network Services, and R. Presuhn, BMC Software, Inc. (Editor of this version). ftp://ftp.isi-edu/in-notes/rfc3417.txt. Obsoletes: RFC 1906, RFC 1449 [REF 8].

32. "Management Information Base (MIB) for the Simple Network Management Protocol (SNMP)," RFC *3418*, STD0062, December 2002 (STANDARD). J. Case, SNMP Research, Inc., K. McCloghrie, Cisco Systems, Inc., M. Rose, Dover Beach Consulting, Inc., S. Waldbusser, International Network Services, and R. Presuhn, BMC Software, Inc. (Editor of this version). ftp://ftp.isi-edu/in-notes/rfc3418.txt. Obsoletes: RFC 1907, RFC 1450 [REF 9].

RECOMMENDED TEXTBOOKS

1. "Network Management," Mani Subramanian, Addison Wesley, 2000.

2. "A Practical Guide to SNMPv3 and Network Management," David Zeltserman, Prentice Hall, 1999.

3. "SNMP, SNMPv2, SNMPv3, and RMON 1 and 2," William Stallings, 3rd ed. Addison-Wesley, 1999. ISBN 0-201-48534-6.

4. "SNMP, SNMPv2 and CMIP," William Stallings, Addison Wesley, 1993.

APPENDIX A

IP ADDRESSING, ARP, AND RARP

A.1 IP ADDRESSING

An IP address is 32 bits (four bytes) long and belongs to one of three classes. The 32 bits are divided into four fields of eight bits each as indicated in **Figure A.1.** Thus, in principle, an IP address has 256 choices for the decimal values of each field. By convention, fields are separated by dots (.) from other fields. For example, an IP address might be:

192.192.192.186

The format of the IP address was defined so that it would unambiguously specify both the address of the network and the address of a device attached to that network.

Class A means that the first eight bits of the address determine the network address and the other twenty-four bits determine the address of a device on that network. Thus a Class-A address will have the largest number of devices. A **Class-B** address uses the first 16 bits to determine the network address and the remaining 16 bits to determine the address of a device on that network. A **Class-C** address uses the first 24 bits to determine the network address and the remaining 8 bits to determine the address of a device on the network. Thus a network with a Class-C address has the smallest number of devices available.

The vertical lines in the first field of each class represent the bits that identify the class. For a Class-A address, the first bit is 0. For a Class-B address the first two bits are 1 and 0. For a Class-C address, the first three bits are 1,1 and 0. Thus when a router reads these bits, it immediately knows the class of the IP address. Once it knows the class, it knows how many bits in the address represent the network address.

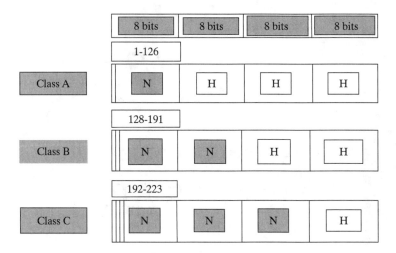

Figure A.1 IP Address Classes

Use of the first bits in the IP address for class identification of course reduces the number of possible network addresses for each class. The numbers above the first field in each class in **Figure A.1** give the possible values for that field. To further describe IP addressing, consider **Figure A.2.**

There are three networks in **Figure A.2.** Network 192.192.192.0 has two subnets that are discussed in more detail below. The router is connected to a point-to-point network that connects it to the router on the network labeled Internet. The network labeled Internet is intended to represent any other network on the Internet. Network 192.192.192.0 is a Class-C network, the point-to-point network is a Class-B network and the network labeled Internet is a Class-A network.

Let's say a router on the network labeled Internet receives a packet. It looks in its routing table and determines that the packet is destined for a network with

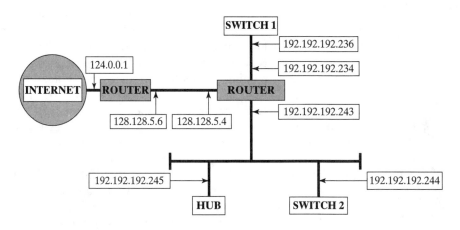

Figure A.2 IP Addressing

address 192.192.192.0. and that the shortest path to that network is through the router with the network address 124.0.0.1. Therefore the packet is sent to that router. This router looks in its routing table and finds that the shortest path to network 192.192.192.0 is out the port with the network address 128.128.5.6. Once the packet is received at port 128.128.5.4, it must have some way of knowing which subnet is to receive the packet. Thus the router must have a way of distinguishing subnets based on the IP address of the packet. This brings us to the topic of subnet addressing.

A.2 SUBNET ADDRESSING

There is an oversight administration responsible for assigning Internet addresses or for delegating that responsibility to other certified organizations to do so. Once a network administrator is assigned such a network address, he or she can divide it into subnets if so desired. To do this the administrator "steals" some of the device part of the IP address to create subnet addresses. This extends the network address space by using some of the bits at the front of the device part of the IP address.

The router learns what subnet should receive a packet by using what is called a **subnet mask** that is stored on the router in its **routing table.** You will see how the router uses the subnet mask as we discuss the content of **Table A.1.**

Suppose the IP address in the packet received by the router on our network is 192.192.192.245 as shown in the table. The binary address corresponding to this decimal address is shown in the last four columns of the table.

The subnet mask in decimal format is given in columns 2 through 5 and in binary format in the last four columns. When the router is configured, the subnet mask value is assigned by the network administrator. It is the binary value of the subnet mask that is of most interest. Any digit that is a one in the subnet mask means that that digit in the IP address is part of the network address in the received packet. Notice first that the first three binary fields in the subnet mask are all ones. This should of course be the case because we know that the first three fields of a Class-C address define the network part of an IP address if there are no subnets.

The last field in the subnet mask has ones in the first five places. This tells us that the network administrator has created subnets by using five of the eight bits in the device part of the Class C address. How many subnets have been created by using these five bits? Using five bits would normally provide 2^5 or 32 subnets. However, the rules are that no network address, subnet address or device address can

Table A.1 Determination of Subnet Addresses

	Decimal Format				Binary Format			
IP Address	192	192	192	245	11000000	11000000	11000000	11110101
Subnet Mask	255	255	255	248	11111111	11111111	11111111	11111000
Logical AND	192	192	192	240	11000000	11000000	11000000	11110000

have all ones or all zeros because these addresses are for special purposes. We don't need to discuss that subject here. So actually there are only 30 possible subnets. There are three bits left to identify devices on each of the 30 subnets. However, since a device address cannot have all ones or all zeroes, there can be only six, not eight, devices on each of the subnets.

Out of the possible 30 subnets, we have arbitrarily chosen the following subnet addresses 192.192.192.240 and 192.192.192.232 for the network used in this book. When the router on the network 192.192.192.0 receives a packet, it performs a logical **AND** operation on the binary format of the IP address in the packet and the subnet mask. A logical AND operation compares the same two bits of the IP address and the subnet mask. If the two bits are both ones the result is a 1. If either bit is not a one the result is 0. The result of this AND operation is shown in the last row of Table A.1. In this case, the packet would be routed correctly to the subnet 192.192.192.240 and then to the device with the IP address 192.192.192.245.

There are probably five main points to be remembered about the above discussion of IP addressing.

1. An IP address consists of a network part and a device part.
2. The IP address consists four fields with each field potentially having a decimal value ranging from 0 to 255.
3. The first few bits in the first field of an IP address determine which fields of the address identify the network part of the address. The rest of the bits identify the device part.
4. A network administrator may use some of the bits of the device part to create subnets.
5. If there are subnets on a network, the network administrator must create a subnet mask that the router uses to direct a packet to the right subnet.

To proceed in our discussion, let's look in more detail at the TCP/IP protocol stack as shown in **Figure A.3.** As can be seen, we have identified some of the protocols in each layer.

A.3 ARP

The Network Interface layer includes the Address Resolution Protocol **(ARP).** This is the protocol that establishes the mapping between an IP address and a hardware address. Let's use the router in our network as an example of how this works. When the Internet layer on the router receives a packet from another network, it knows only the IP address of the destination device. We have seen above how the router determines the subnet to which the device is attached. However, the MAC layer on the router port attached to that subnet needs the MAC address of the destination device to insert it in IEEE 802.3 frame MAC header. To obtain this hardware address, the IP process makes a call to the ARP process in the Network

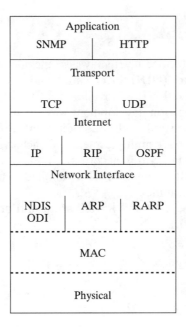

Figure A.3 TCP/IP Protocol Stack and the Ethernet MAC and Physical Layers

Interface layer. The ARP process creates a packet that includes the device IP address and passes it to the MAC layer, where it is encapsulated in the MAC frame and broadcast to all devices on the subnet. The hardware broadcast destination address is all ones. All devices read the ARP message. The device that has the IP address in the message inserts its hardware address in the received message and returns it to the router. The router then sends the packet, along with the received hardware address, to the MAC layer. The MAC layer creates a new frame and uses the received hardware address as the MAC destination address and the hardware address of the router as the MAC source address.

The router stores the new hardware address in its ARP cache. Thus if it receives another packet for the same destination device, it will find the hardware address in the ARP cache and will not have to use ARP. However, addresses cached in an ARP table are only kept for a finite time.

A.4 RARP

Another Network Interface layer protocol is the Reverse Address Resolution Protocol **(RARP).** RARP is implemented when the hardware address of the destination device is known but the IP address is not. The message is sent to a RARP server on the network that maintains IP address/Hardware address pairs.

A.5 ODI AND NDIS

The Network Interface layer may also include the implementations of the Open Data-link Interface **(ODI)** Specification and the Network Device Interface Specification **(NDIS).** ODI was a Novell and 3 COM-led specification development and the NDIS specification development was inspired by Microsoft. The intent of both specifications was similar, although different. Both allow multiple protocol stacks to communicate over multiple media. To achieve this, the protocol stack and the NIC driver must be written according to one of these specifications. These specifications reduced the number of NICs that had to be produced and greatly increased network interoperability.

ODI, NDIS, ARP and RARP are useful not only to routers but also to any host on the network.

APPENDIX **B**

ABSTRACT SYNTAX NOTATION 1 (ASN.1)

In this Appendix, the basic concepts of the ASN.1 language will be discussed. The purpose of this language is to provide a structure for information that is independent of any encoding technique used to represent the data. Thus ASN.1 can be used for many purposes.

Specifications for ASN.1 are described in ISO/IEC 8824, part 1-4. **[Ref 1-2]** The Introduction to that standard states: "This Recommendation|International Standard presents a standard notation for the definition of data types and values." This notation is used by the Structure of Management Information (SMI), described in RFC 1155, to define MIB objects **(see Appendix C).** It is also used to specify management information documents such as RFCs and the OSI Application layer Protocol Data Units (PDUs) that are passed from the Application layer to the Presentation layer.

ASN.1 is a comprehensive and complex language. Thus we could not do it justice in a short appendix. What we can do, however, is describe the ASN.1 concepts that are used by RFC 1155 to define objects that make up a MIB. SMI is a subset of ASN.1 Several references to ASN.1 will be given at the end of this Appendix.

ASN.1 is used to define data structures. Some of these structures are of a form familiar from other languages such as C and C++. An example is the "structure" type in the C language. An ASN.1 module is used to create an information object. Objects in MIB-II are examples of information objects.

B.1 ASN.1 MODULES

The module has the form:

```
<modulereference> DEFINITIONS ::=
     BEGIN
          EXPORTS
          IMPORTS
          Assignment List
     END
```

modulereference is the name of the module that allows the complete module to be referenced and used by another module in a library.

DEFINITIONS, BEGIN and **END** are ASN.1 keywords used as shown in the above module template.

EXPORTS is a keyword that introduces a list of names of type and value definitions in the module that can be exported and used by other modules in a module library.

IMPORTS is a keyword that introduces a list of names of type and value definitions that are imported from other modules in the library.

Assignment List is a list of assignments of names to type and value definitions. Included in the list are other supporting assignments (productions) which complete ("resolve" is the formal word) type and value definitions in the assignment list by using more detailed assignments.

One of the assignments in the Assignment List may be a MACRO. MACROs define other abstract data types in terms of basic ASN.1 types. The MACRO construct is used to define the data structure of new MIB information objects. Thus, as mentioned above, the MACRO is analogous to the structure type in the C language. All objects in MIB-II are defined using the OBJECT-TYPE MACRO defined below. The ASN.1 requirement for the use of lower and upper case letters is indicated in these examples. When something is enclosed in quotes it means that it should appear as written in the resulting MIB-II object text.

B.2 MACRO

The MACRO construct has the form:

```
OBJECT-TYPE  MACRO :: =
BEGIN
    TYPE NOTATION :: = "SYNTAX"    type ( TYPE ObjectSyntax )
                       "ACCESS"    Access
                       "STATUS"    Status
                       "DescrPart"
                       "ReferPart"
                       "IndexPart"
                       "DefValPart"
                       "DisplayString"

    VALUE NOTATION :: = value  (VALUE  ObjectName )

    Access   :: =  "read-only"
                |  "read-write"
                |  "write-only"
                |  "not-accessible"

    Status   :: =   "mandatory"
                |  "optional"
                |  "obsolete"
```

```
DescrPart ::= "DESCRIPTION"  value (description DisplayString | empty )

ReferPart ::= "REFERENCE"  value ( reference DisplayString | empty )

IndexPart ::= "INDEX"   "{" IndexTypes "}"

IndexTypes ::= IndexType | IndexTypes  ","  IndexType

IndexType ::= value (indexobject ObjectName ) | type (IndexType)

DefValPart ::= "DEFVAL"  "{"  value ( defvalue ObjectSyntax )  "}"
                 |  empty

DisplayString ::= OCTET STRING SIZE ( 0..255 )
END
```

The first letter in the name of a type is capitalized. If the type name is a compound name, the first letter in each part of the name is capitalized, e.g. **NameOfType, DisplayString etc.**

The first letter in the name of a value is lower case. If the value name is a compound name, subsequent first letters are capitalized, e.g. **nameOfValue.**

::= is the assignment operator, analogous to the equals sign (=) in typical computer languages

OBJECT-TYPE is the actual name of the MACRO. This name should be in caps.
MACRO indicates that what follows is the MACRO. MACRO should be in caps.
BEGIN and **END** are keywords that enclose the body of the MACRO. Keywords are always in caps.
TYPE NOTATION, followed by the assignment operator **(:: =),** is the clause that defines the object type as follows:

"SYNTAX" specifies the MIB object type. Notice that "SYNTAX" is in quotes and thus will appear in the actual MIB object.

(TYPE ObjectSyntax) states that the object type is to be one of the types defined by ObjectSyntax).

ObjectSyntax is the name assigned to the CHOICE production which is defined as:

CHOICE {
nameOfObject1 ObjectType1
nameOfObject2 ObjectType2
•
•
nameOfObjectN ObjectTypeN
}
For example, nameOfObject1 could be "number" and ObjectType1 could be "INTEGER."

ACCESS is the name given to the production defined by Access as shown above.
STATUS is the name given to the production defined by Status as shown above.
DescrPart is defined to be "DESCRIPTION" which has a value that is of type DisplayString or is empty (i.e., no description is given). A "DESCRIPTION" is optional.

ReferPart is defined to be "REFERENCE" which has a value of type DisplayString or is empty. ReferPart provides a reference to another document for example. This is not used by MIB-II.

IndexPart is defined to be "INDEX" {IndexTypes}
    IndexTypes ::= IndexType | IndexTypes , IndexType
      IndexType ::= value (indexObject ObjectName}
        ObjectName ::= OBJECT IDENTIFIER

If you carefully write down this nesting of type definitions, you will see that it resolves to IndexPart meaning "INDEX" followed by a list of table column object types enclosed in { }. These column objects are those that are used to determine which row in a table is to be selected to determine the instance of a column object.

    DefValPart is defined to be "DEFVAL" followed by value where value is another CHOICE production. Since MIB-II does not use DefValPart, this CHOICE production is not shown here.

VALUE NOTATION, followed by the assignment operator (::=), specifies the value of the object.

    value is of type specified by ObjectName
      ObjectName ::= OBJECT IDENTIFIER , the location of the object in the **iso** information tree.

So, for example, if the name of the MIB object is **sysDescr** it is of type **OBJECT IDENTIFIER** and has the value {**system 1**}.

REFERENCES

1. ISO/IEC 8824 "Information Technology-Abstract Syntax Notation One (ASN.1), Parts 1-4, http://www.ansi.org.
2. "SNMP, SNMPv2 and CMIP: The Practical Guide to Network Management Standards," William Stallings, Addison Wesley, 1993, p. 568.

APPENDIX C

RFC 1213

Network Working Group   K. McCloghrie
Request for Comments: 1213   Hughes LAN Systems, Inc.
Obsoletes: RFC 1158   M. Rose
                                        Performance Systems International
                                                                  Editors
                                                               March 1991

              Management Information Base for Network Management
                        of TCP/IP-based internets:
                                  MIB-II

Status of this Memo

This memo defines the second version of the Management Information
Base (MIB-II) for use with network management protocols in TCP/IP-
based internets. This RFC specifies an IAB standards track protocol
for the Internet community, and requests discussion and suggestions
for improvements. Please refer to the current edition of the "IAB
Official Protocol Standards" for the standardization state and status
of this protocol. Distribution of this memo is unlimited.

Table of Contents

1. Abstract

This memo defines the second version of the Management Information
Base (MIB-II) for use with network management protocols in TCP/IP-
based internets. In particular, together with its companion memos
which describe the structure of management information (RFC 1155)
along with the network management protocol (RFC 1157) for TCP/IP-
based internets, these documents provide a simple, workable
architecture and system for managing TCP/IP-based internets and in
particular the Internet community.

2. Introduction

As reported in RFC 1052, IAB Recommendations for the Development of
Internet Network Management Standards [1], a two-prong strategy for
network management of TCP/IP-based internets was undertaken. In the
short-term, the Simple Network Management Protocol (SNMP) was to be
used to manage nodes in the Internet community. In the long-term,
the use of the OSI network management framework was to be examined.
Two documents were produced to define the management information: RFC
1065, which defined the Structure of Management Information (SMI)
[2], and RFC 1066, which defined the Management Information Base
(MIB) [3]. Both of these documents were designed so as to be
compatible with both the SNMP and the OSI network management
framework.

This strategy was quite successful in the short-term: Internet-based
network management technology was fielded, by both the research and
commercial communities, within a few months. As a result of this,
portions of the Internet community became network manageable in a
timely fashion.

As reported in RFC 1109, Report of the Second Ad Hoc Network
Management Review Group [4], the requirements of the SNMP and the OSI
network management frameworks were more different than anticipated.
As such, the requirement for compatibility between the SMI/MIB and
both frameworks was suspended. This action permitted the operational
network management framework, the SNMP, to respond to new operational
needs in the Internet community by producing this document.

As such, the current network management framework for TCP/IP-based
internets consists of: Structure and Identification of Management
Information for TCP/IP-based internets, RFC 1155 [12], which
describes how managed objects contained in the MIB are defined;
Management Information Base for Network Management of TCP/IP-based
internets: MIB-II, this memo, which describes the managed objects
contained in the MIB (and supercedes RFC 1156 [13]); and, the Simple
Network Management Protocol, RFC 1098 [5], which defines the protocol
used to manage these objects.

3.   Changes from RFC 1156

Features of this MIB include:

(1)   incremental additions to reflect new operational
      requirements;

(2)   upwards compatibility with the SMI/MIB and the SNMP;

(3)   improved support for multi-protocol entities; and,

(4)   textual clean-up of the MIB to improve clarity and
      readability.

The objects defined in MIB-II have the OBJECT IDENTIFIER prefix:

    mib-2   OBJECT IDENTIFIER ::= { mgmt 1 }

which is identical to the prefix used in MIB-I.

3.1.   Deprecated Objects

In order to better prepare implementors for future changes in the
MIB, a new term "deprecated" may be used when describing an object.
A deprecated object in the MIB is one which must be supported, but
one which will most likely be removed from the next version of the
MIB (e.g., MIB-III).

MIB-II marks one object as being deprecated:

    atTable

As a result of deprecating the atTable object, the entire Address
Translation group is deprecated.

Note that no functionality is lost with the deprecation of these
objects: new objects providing equivalent or superior functionality
are defined in MIB-II.

3.2. Display Strings

In the past, there have been misinterpretations of the MIB as to when
a string of octets should contain printable characters, meant to be
displayed to a human. As a textual convention in the MIB, the
datatype

    DisplayString ::=
        OCTET STRING

is introduced. A DisplayString is restricted to the NVT ASCII
character set, as defined in pages 10-11 of [6].

The following objects are now defined in terms of DisplayString:

    sysDescr
    ifDescr

It should be noted that this change has no effect on either the
syntax nor semantics of these objects. The use of the DisplayString
notation is merely an artifact of the explanatory method used in
MIB-II and future MIBs.

Further it should be noted that any object defined in terms of OCTET
STRING may contain arbitrary binary data, in which each octet may
take any value from 0 to 255 (decimal).

3.3 Physical Addresses

As a further, textual convention in the MIB, the datatype

    PhysAddress ::=
        OCTET STRING

is introduced to represent media- or physical-level addresses.

The following objects are now defined in terms of PhysAddress:

    ifPhysAddress
    atPhysAddress
    ipNetToMediaPhysAddress

It should be noted that this change has no effect on either the
syntax nor semantics of these objects. The use of the PhysAddress
notation is merely an artifact of the explanatory method used in
MIB-II and future MIBs.

3.4. The System Group

Four new objects are added to this group:

    sysContact
    sysName
    sysLocation
    sysServices

These provide contact, administrative, location, and service
information regarding the managed node.

3.5. The Interfaces Group

The definition of the ifNumber object was incorrect, as it required
all interfaces to support IP. (For example, devices without IP, such
as MAC-layer bridges, could not be managed if this definition was
strictly followed.) The description of the ifNumber object is
changed accordingly.

The ifTable object was mistaken marked as read-write, it has been
(correctly) re-designated as not-accessible. In addition, several
new values have been added to the ifType column in the ifTable
object:

> ppp(23)
> softwareLoopback(24)
> eon(25)
> ethernet-3Mbit(26)
> nsip(27)
> slip(28)
> ultra(29)
> ds3(30)
> sip(31)
> frame-relay(32)

Finally, a new column has been added to the ifTable object:

> ifSpecific

which provides information about information specific to the media
being used to realize the interface.

3.6. The Address Translation Group

In MIB-I this group contained a table which permitted mappings from
network addresses (e.g., IP addresses) to physical addresses (e.g.,
MAC addresses). Experience has shown that efficient implementations
of this table make two assumptions: a single network protocol
environment, and mappings occur only from network address to physical
address.

The need to support multi-protocol nodes (e.g., those with both the
IP and CLNP active), and the need to support the inverse mapping
(e.g., for ES-IS), have invalidated both of these assumptions. As
such, the atTable object is declared deprecated.

In order to meet both the multi-protocol and inverse mapping
requirements, MIB-II and its successors will allocate up to two
address translation tables inside each network protocol group. That
is, the IP group will contain one address translation table, for
going from IP addresses to physical addresses. Similarly, when a
document defining MIB objects for the CLNP is produced (e.g., [7]),
it will contain two tables, for mappings in both directions, as this
is required for full functionality.

It should be noted that the choice of two tables (one for each
direction of mapping) provides for ease of implementation in many

cases, and does not introduce undue burden on implementations which realize the address translation abstraction through a single internal table.

3.7. The IP Group

The access attribute of the variable ipForwarding has been changed from read-only to read-write.

In addition, there is a new column to the ipAddrTable object,

    ipAdEntReasmMaxSize

which keeps track of the largest IP datagram that can be re-assembled on a particular interface.

The descriptor of the ipRoutingTable object has been changed to ipRouteTable for consistency with the other IP routing objects. There are also three new columns in the ipRouteTable object,

    ipRouteMask
    ipRouteMetric5
    ipRouteInfo

the first is used for IP routing subsystems that support arbitrary subnet masks, and the latter two are IP routing protocol-specific.

Two new objects are added to the IP group:

    ipNetToMediaTable
    ipRoutingDiscards

the first is the address translation table for the IP group (providing identical functionality to the now deprecated atTable in the address translation group), and the latter provides information when routes are lost due to a lack of buffer space.

3.8. The ICMP Group

There are no changes to this group.

3.9. The TCP Group

Two new variables are added:

    tcpInErrs
    tcpOutRsts

which keep track of the number of incoming TCP segments in error and the number of resets generated by a TCP.

3.10. The UDP Group

A new table:

    udpTable

is added.

3.11. The EGP Group

Experience has indicated a need for additional objects that are
useful in EGP monitoring. In addition to making several additions to
the egpNeighborTable object, i.e.,

    egpNeighAs
    egpNeighInMsgs
    egpNeighInErrs
    egpNeighOutMsgs
    egpNeighOutErrs
    egpNeighInErrMsgs
    egpNeighOutErrMsgs
    egpNeighStateUps
    egpNeighStateDowns
    egpNeighIntervalHello
    egpNeighIntervalPoll
    egpNeighMode
    egpNeighEventTrigger

a new variable is added:

    egpAs

which gives the autonomous system associated with this EGP entity.

3.12. The Transmission Group

MIB-I was lacking in that it did not distinguish between different
types of transmission media. A new group, the Transmission group, is
allocated for this purpose:

    transmission OBJECT IDENTIFIER ::= { mib-2 10 }

When Internet-standard definitions for managing transmission media
are defined, the transmission group is used to provide a prefix for
the names of those objects.

Typically, such definitions reside in the experimental portion of the
MIB until they are "proven," then as a part of the Internet
standardization process, the definitions are accordingly elevated and
a new object identifier, under the transmission group is defined. By
convention, the name assigned is:

    type OBJECT IDENTIFIER ::= { transmission number }

where "type" is the symbolic value used for the media in the ifType
column of the ifTable object, and "number" is the actual integer
value corresponding to the symbol.

3.13. The SNMP Group

The application-oriented working groups of the IETF have been tasked
to be receptive towards defining MIB variables specific to their
respective applications.

For the SNMP, it is useful to have statistical information. A new group, the SNMP group, is allocated for this purpose:

```
snmp   OBJECT IDENTIFIER ::= { mib-2 11 }
```

3.14. Changes from RFC 1158

Features of this MIB include:

(1) The managed objects in this document have been defined using the conventions defined in the Internet-standard SMI, as amended by the extensions specified in [14]. It must be emphasized that definitions made using these extensions are semantically identically to those in RFC 1158.

(2) The PhysAddress textual convention has been introduced to represent media addresses.

(3) The ACCESS clause of sysLocation is now read-write.

(4) The definition of sysServices has been clarified.

(5) New ifType values (29-32) have been defined. In addition, the textual-descriptor for the DS1 and E1 interface types has been corrected.

(6) The definition of ipForwarding has been clarified.

(7) The definition of ipRouteType has been clarified.

(8) The ipRouteMetric5 and ipRouteInfo objects have been defined.

(9) The ACCESS clause of tcpConnState is now read-write, to support deletion of the TCB associated with a TCP connection. The definition of this object has been clarified to explain this usage.

(10) The definition of egpNeighEventTrigger has been clarified.

(11) The definition of several of the variables in the new snmp group have been clarified. In addition, the snmpInBadTypes and snmpOutReadOnlys objects are no longer present. (However, the object identifiers associated with those objects are reserved to prevent future use.)

(12) The definition of snmpInReadOnlys has been clarified.

(13) The textual descriptor of the snmpEnableAuthTraps has been changed to snmpEnableAuthenTraps, and the definition has been clarified.

(14) The ipRoutingDiscards object was added.

(15) The optional use of an implementation-dependent, small positive integer was disallowed when identifying instances of the IP address and routing tables.

4. Objects

Managed objects are accessed via a virtual information store, termed
the Management Information Base or MIB. Objects in the MIB are
defined using the subset of Abstract Syntax Notation One (ASN.1) [8]
defined in the SMI. In particular, each object has a name, a syntax,
and an encoding. The name is an object identifier, an
administratively assigned name, which specifies an object type. The
object type together with an object instance serves to uniquely
identify a specific instantiation of the object. For human
convenience, we often use a textual string, termed the OBJECT
DESCRIPTOR, to also refer to the object type.

The syntax of an object type defines the abstract data structure
corresponding to that object type. The ASN.1 language is used for
this purpose. However, the SMI [12] purposely restricts the ASN.1
constructs which may be used. These restrictions are explicitly made
for simplicity.

The encoding of an object type is simply how that object type is
represented using the object type's syntax. Implicitly tied to the
notion of an object type's syntax and encoding is how the object type
is represented when being transmitted on the network.

The SMI specifies the use of the basic encoding rules of ASN.1 [9],
subject to the additional requirements imposed by the SNMP.

4.1. Format of Definitions

Section 6 contains contains the specification of all object types
contained in this MIB module. The object types are defined using the
conventions defined in the SMI, as amended by the extensions
specified in [14].

5. Overview

Consistent with the IAB directive to produce simple, workable systems
in the short-term, the list of managed objects defined here, has been
derived by taking only those elements which are considered essential.

This approach of taking only the essential objects is NOT
restrictive, since the SMI defined in the companion memo provides
three extensibility mechanisms: one, the addition of new standard
objects through the definitions of new versions of the MIB; two, the
addition of widely-available but non-standard objects through the
experimental subtree; and three, the addition of private objects
through the enterprises subtree. Such additional objects can not
only be used for vendor-specific elements, but also for
experimentation as required to further the knowledge of which other
objects are essential.

The design of MIB-II is heavily influenced by the first extensibility
mechanism. Several new variables have been added based on
operational experience and need. Based on this, the criteria for

including an object in MIB-II are remarkably similar to the MIB-I criteria:

(1)   An object needed to be essential for either fault or configuration management.

(2)   Only weak control objects were permitted (by weak, it is meant that tampering with them can do only limited damage). This criterion reflects the fact that the current management protocols are not sufficiently secure to do more powerful control operations.

(3)   Evidence of current use and utility was required.

(4)   In MIB-I, an attempt was made to limit the number of objects to about 100 to make it easier for vendors to fully instrument their software. In MIB-II, this limit was raised given the wide technological base now implementing MIB-I.

(5)   To avoid redundant variables, it was required that no object be included that can be derived from others in the MIB.

(6)   Implementation specific objects (e.g., for BSD UNIX) were excluded.

(7)   It was agreed to avoid heavily instrumenting critical sections of code. The general guideline was one counter per critical section per layer.

MIB-II, like its predecessor, the Internet-standard MIB, contains only essential elements. There is no need to allow individual objects to be optional. Rather, the objects are arranged into the following groups:

      - System
      - Interfaces
      - Address Translation (deprecated)
      - IP
      - ICMP
      - TCP
      - UDP
      - EGP
      - Transmission
      - SNMP

These groups are the basic unit of conformance: This method is as follows: if the semantics of a group is applicable to an implementation, then it must implement all objects in that group. For example, an implementation must implement the EGP group if and only if it implements the EGP.

There are two reasons for defining these groups: to provide a means of assigning object identifiers; and, to provide a method for

implementations of managed agents to know which objects they must
implement.

6. Definitions

```
        RFC1213-MIB DEFINITIONS ::= BEGIN
        IMPORTS
                mgmt, NetworkAddress, IpAddress, Counter, Gauge,
                        TimeTicks
                    FROM RFC1155-SMI
                OBJECT-TYPE
                        FROM RFC-1212;

        --   This MIB module uses the extended OBJECT-TYPE macro as
        --   defined in [14];

        --   MIB-II (same prefix as MIB-I)

        mib-2       OBJECT IDENTIFIER ::= { mgmt 1 }

        -- textual conventions

        DisplayString ::=
            OCTET STRING
        -- This data type is used to model textual information taken
        -- from the NVT ASCII character set.  By convention, objects
        -- with this syntax are declared as having
        --
        --      SIZE (0..255)

        PhysAddress ::=
            OCTET STRING
        -- This data type is used to model media addresses.  For many
        -- types of media, this will be in a binary representation.
        -- For example, an ethernet address would be represented as
        -- a string of six octets.

        -- groups in MIB-II

        system      OBJECT IDENTIFIER ::= { mib-2 1 }

        interfaces  OBJECT IDENTIFIER ::= { mib-2 2 }

        at          OBJECT IDENTIFIER ::= { mib-2 3 }

        ip          OBJECT IDENTIFIER ::= { mib-2 4 }

        icmp        OBJECT IDENTIFIER ::= { mib-2 5 }

        tcp         OBJECT IDENTIFIER ::= { mib-2 6 }

        udp         OBJECT IDENTIFIER ::= { mib-2 7 }

        egp         OBJECT IDENTIFIER ::= { mib-2 8 }

        -- historical (some say hysterical)
        -- cmot      OBJECT IDENTIFIER ::= { mib-2 9 }

        transmission OBJECT IDENTIFIER ::= { mib-2 10 }
```

```
snmp          OBJECT IDENTIFIER ::= { mib-2 11 }

-- the System group

-- Implementation of the System group is mandatory for all
-- systems.  If an agent is not configured to have a value
-- for any of these variables, a string of length 0 is
-- returned.

sysDescr OBJECT-TYPE
    SYNTAX  DisplayString (SIZE (0..255))
    ACCESS  read-only
    STATUS  mandatory
    DESCRIPTION
            "A textual description of the entity.  This value
            should include the full name and version
            identification of the system's hardware type,
            software operating-system, and networking
            software.  It is mandatory that this only contain
            printable ASCII characters."
    ::= { system 1 }

sysObjectID OBJECT-TYPE
    SYNTAX  OBJECT IDENTIFIER
    ACCESS  read-only
    STATUS  mandatory
    DESCRIPTION
            "The vendor's authoritative identification of the
            network management subsystem contained in the
            entity.  This value is allocated within the SMI
            enterprises subtree (1.3.6.1.4.1) and provides an
            easy and unambiguous means for determining 'what
            kind of box' is being managed.  For example, if
            vendor 'Flintstones, Inc.' was assigned the
            subtree 1.3.6.1.4.1.4242, it could assign the
            identifier 1.3.6.1.4.1.4242.1.1 to its 'Fred
            Router.'"
    ::= { system 2 }

sysUpTime OBJECT-TYPE
    SYNTAX  TimeTicks
    ACCESS  read-only
    STATUS  mandatory
    DESCRIPTION
            "The time (in hundredths of a second) since the
            network management portion of the system was last
            re-initialized."
    ::= { system 3 }

sysContact OBJECT-TYPE
    SYNTAX  DisplayString (SIZE (0..255))
    ACCESS  read-write
    STATUS  mandatory
```

```
    DESCRIPTION
            "The textual identification of the contact person
            for this managed node, together with information
            on how to contact this person."
    ::= { system 4 }


sysName OBJECT-TYPE
    SYNTAX  DisplayString (SIZE (0..255))
    ACCESS  read-write
    STATUS  mandatory
    DESCRIPTION
            "An administratively-assigned name for this
            managed node.  By convention, this is the node's
            fully-qualified domain name."
    ::= { system 5 }


sysLocation OBJECT-TYPE
    SYNTAX  DisplayString (SIZE (0..255))
    ACCESS  read-write
    STATUS  mandatory
    DESCRIPTION
            "The physical location of this node (e.g.,
            'telephone closet, 3rd floor')."
    ::= { system 6 }


sysServices OBJECT-TYPE
    SYNTAX  INTEGER (0..127)
    ACCESS  read-only
    STATUS  mandatory
    DESCRIPTION
            "A value which indicates the set of services that
            this entity primarily offers.

            The value is a sum.  This sum initially takes the
            value zero, Then, for each layer, L, in the range
            1 through 7, that this node performs transactions
            for, 2 raised to (L - 1) is added to the sum.  For
            example, a node which performs primarily routing
            functions would have a value of 4 (2^(3-1)).  In
            contrast, a node which is a host offering
            application services would have a value of 72
            (2^(4-1) + 2^(7-1)).  Note that in the context of
            the Internet suite of protocols, values should be
            calculated accordingly:

                layer  functionality
                  1    physical (e.g., repeaters)
                  2    datalink/subnetwork (e.g., bridges)
                  3    internet (e.g., IP gateways)
                  4    end-to-end  (e.g., IP hosts)
                  7    applications (e.g., mail relays)
```

```
                        For systems including OSI protocols, layers 5 and
                        6 may also be counted."
            ::= { system 7 }

    -- the Interfaces group

    -- Implementation of the Interfaces group is mandatory for
    -- all systems.

    ifNumber OBJECT-TYPE
        SYNTAX   INTEGER
        ACCESS   read-only
        STATUS   mandatory
        DESCRIPTION
                "The number of network interfaces (regardless of
                their current state) present on this system."
        ::= { interfaces 1 }

    -- the Interfaces table

    -- The Interfaces table contains information on the entity's
    -- interfaces.  Each interface is thought of as being
    -- attached to a 'subnetwork.'  Note that this term should
    -- not be confused with 'subnet' which refers to an
    -- addressing partitioning scheme used in the Internet suite
    -- of protocols.

    ifTable OBJECT-TYPE
        SYNTAX   SEQUENCE OF IfEntry
        ACCESS   not-accessible
        STATUS   mandatory
        DESCRIPTION
                "A list of interface entries.  The number of
                entries is given by the value of ifNumber."
        ::= { interfaces 2 }

    ifEntry OBJECT-TYPE
        SYNTAX   IfEntry
        ACCESS   not-accessible
        STATUS   mandatory
        DESCRIPTION
                "An interface entry containing objects at the
                subnetwork layer and below for a particular
                interface."
        INDEX   { ifIndex }
        ::= { ifTable 1 }

    IfEntry ::=
        SEQUENCE {
            ifIndex
                INTEGER,
            ifDescr
                DisplayString,
```

```
            ifType
                INTEGER,
            ifMtu
                INTEGER,
            ifSpeed
                Gauge,
            ifPhysAddress
                PhysAddress,
            ifAdminStatus
                INTEGER,
            ifOperStatus
                INTEGER,
            ifLastChange
                TimeTicks,
            ifInOctets
                Counter,
            ifInUcastPkts
                Counter,
            ifInNUcastPkts
                Counter,
            ifInDiscards
                Counter,
            ifInErrors
                Counter,
            ifInUnknownProtos
                Counter,
            ifOutOctets
                Counter,
            ifOutUcastPkts
                Counter,
            ifOutNUcastPkts
                Counter,
            ifOutDiscards
                Counter,
            ifOutErrors
                Counter,
            ifOutQLen
                Gauge,
            ifSpecific
                OBJECT IDENTIFIER
        }


    ifIndex OBJECT-TYPE
        SYNTAX  INTEGER
        ACCESS  read-only
        STATUS  mandatory
        DESCRIPTION
                "A unique value for each interface.  Its value
                ranges between 1 and the value of ifNumber.  The
                value for each interface must remain constant at
```

```
                    least from one re-initialization of the entity's
                    network management system to the next re-
                    initialization."
          ::= { ifEntry 1 }

    ifDescr OBJECT-TYPE
        SYNTAX  DisplayString (SIZE (0..255))
        ACCESS  read-only
        STATUS  mandatory
        DESCRIPTION
                    "A textual string containing information about the
                    interface.  This string should include the name of
                    the manufacturer, the product name and the version
                    of the hardware interface."
          ::= { ifEntry 2 }

    ifType OBJECT-TYPE
        SYNTAX  INTEGER {
                    other(1),            -- none of the following
                    regular1822(2),
                    hdh1822(3),
                    ddn-x25(4),
                    rfc877-x25(5),
                    ethernet-csmacd(6),
                    iso88023-csmacd(7),
                    iso88024-tokenBus(8),
                    iso88025-tokenRing(9),
                    iso88026-man(10),
                    starLan(11),
                    proteon-10Mbit(12),
                    proteon-80Mbit(13),
                    hyperchannel(14),
                    fddi(15),
                    lapb(16),
                    sdlc(17),
                    ds1(18),             -- T-1
                    e1(19),              -- european equiv. of T-1
                    basicISDN(20),
                    primaryISDN(21),    -- proprietary serial
                    propPointToPointSerial(22),
                    ppp(23),
                    softwareLoopback(24),
                    eon(25),             -- CLNP over IP [11]
                    ethernet-3Mbit(26),
                    nsip(27),            -- XNS over IP
                    slip(28),            -- generic SLIP
                    ultra(29),           -- ULTRA technologies
                    ds3(30),             -- T-3
                    sip(31),             -- SMDS
                    frame-relay(32)
                }
```

```
    ACCESS  read-only
    STATUS  mandatory
    DESCRIPTION
            "The type of interface, distinguished according to
            the physical/link protocol(s) immediately 'below'
            the network layer in the protocol stack."
    ::= { ifEntry 3 }

ifMtu OBJECT-TYPE
    SYNTAX  INTEGER
    ACCESS  read-only
    STATUS  mandatory
    DESCRIPTION
            "The size of the largest datagram which can be
            sent/received on the interface, specified in
            octets.  For interfaces that are used for
            transmitting network datagrams, this is the size
            of the largest network datagram that can be sent
            on the interface."
    ::= { ifEntry 4 }

ifSpeed OBJECT-TYPE
    SYNTAX  Gauge
    ACCESS  read-only
    STATUS  mandatory
    DESCRIPTION
            "An estimate of the interface's current bandwidth
            in bits per second.  For interfaces which do not
            vary in bandwidth or for those where no accurate
            estimation can be made, this object should contain
            the nominal bandwidth."
    ::= { ifEntry 5 }

ifPhysAddress OBJECT-TYPE
    SYNTAX  PhysAddress
    ACCESS  read-only
    STATUS  mandatory
    DESCRIPTION
            "The interface's address at the protocol layer
            immediately 'below' the network layer in the
            protocol stack.  For interfaces which do not have
            such an address (e.g., a serial line), this object
            should contain an octet string of zero length."
    ::= { ifEntry 6 }

ifAdminStatus OBJECT-TYPE
    SYNTAX  INTEGER {
                up(1),        -- ready to pass packets
                down(2),
                testing(3)    -- in some test mode
            }
    ACCESS  read-write
```

```
     STATUS  mandatory
     DESCRIPTION
            "The desired state of the interface.  The
            testing(3) state indicates that no operational
            packets can be passed."
     ::= { ifEntry 7 }

ifOperStatus OBJECT-TYPE
     SYNTAX  INTEGER {
                 up(1),        — ready to pass packets
                 down(2),
                 testing(3)    — in some test mode
             }
     ACCESS  read-only
     STATUS  mandatory
     DESCRIPTION
            "The current operational state of the interface.
            The testing(3) state indicates that no operational
            packets can be passed."
     ::= { ifEntry 8 }

ifLastChange OBJECT-TYPE
     SYNTAX  TimeTicks
     ACCESS  read-only
     STATUS  mandatory
     DESCRIPTION
            "The value of sysUpTime at the time the interface
            entered its current operational state.  If the
            current state was entered prior to the last re-
            initialization of the local network management
            subsystem, then this object contains a zero
            value."
     ::= { ifEntry 9 }

ifInOctets OBJECT-TYPE
     SYNTAX  Counter
     ACCESS  read-only
     STATUS  mandatory
     DESCRIPTION
            "The total number of octets received on the
            interface, including framing characters."
     ::= { ifEntry 10 }

ifInUcastPkts OBJECT-TYPE
     SYNTAX  Counter
     ACCESS  read-only
     STATUS  mandatory
     DESCRIPTION
            "The number of subnetwork-unicast packets
            delivered to a higher-layer protocol."
     ::= { ifEntry 11 }
```

```
ifInNUcastPkts OBJECT-TYPE
    SYNTAX   Counter
    ACCESS   read-only
    STATUS   mandatory
    DESCRIPTION
            "The number of non-unicast (i.e., subnetwork-
            broadcast or subnetwork-multicast) packets
            delivered to a higher-layer protocol."
    ::= { ifEntry 12 }

ifInDiscards OBJECT-TYPE
    SYNTAX   Counter
    ACCESS   read-only
    STATUS   mandatory
    DESCRIPTION
            "The number of inbound packets which were chosen
            to be discarded even though no errors had been
            detected to prevent their being deliverable to a
            higher-layer protocol.  One possible reason for
            discarding such a packet could be to free up
            buffer space."
    ::= { ifEntry 13 }

ifInErrors OBJECT-TYPE
    SYNTAX   Counter
    ACCESS   read-only
    STATUS   mandatory
    DESCRIPTION
            "The number of inbound packets that contained
            errors preventing them from being deliverable to a
            higher-layer protocol."
    ::= { ifEntry 14 }

ifInUnknownProtos OBJECT-TYPE
    SYNTAX   Counter
    ACCESS   read-only
    STATUS   mandatory
    DESCRIPTION
            "The number of packets received via the interface
            which were discarded because of an unknown or
            unsupported protocol."
    ::= { ifEntry 15 }

ifOutOctets OBJECT-TYPE
    SYNTAX   Counter
    ACCESS   read-only
    STATUS   mandatory
    DESCRIPTION
            "The total number of octets transmitted out of the
            interface, including framing characters."
    ::= { ifEntry 16 }
```

```
ifOutUcastPkts OBJECT-TYPE
    SYNTAX   Counter
    ACCESS   read-only
    STATUS   mandatory
    DESCRIPTION
            "The total number of packets that higher-level
            protocols requested be transmitted to a
            subnetwork-unicast address, including those that
            were discarded or not sent."
    ::= { ifEntry 17 }

ifOutNUcastPkts OBJECT-TYPE
    SYNTAX   Counter
    ACCESS   read-only
    STATUS   mandatory
    DESCRIPTION
            "The total number of packets that higher-level
            protocols requested be transmitted to a non-
            unicast (i.e., a subnetwork-broadcast or
            subnetwork-multicast) address, including those
            that were discarded or not sent."
    ::= { ifEntry 18 }

ifOutDiscards OBJECT-TYPE
    SYNTAX   Counter
    ACCESS   read-only
    STATUS   mandatory
    DESCRIPTION
            "The number of outbound packets which were chosen
            to be discarded even though no errors had been
            detected to prevent their being transmitted.  One
            possible reason for discarding such a packet could
            be to free up buffer space."
    ::= { ifEntry 19 }

ifOutErrors OBJECT-TYPE
    SYNTAX   Counter
    ACCESS   read-only
    STATUS   mandatory
    DESCRIPTION
            "The number of outbound packets that could not be
            transmitted because of errors."
    ::= { ifEntry 20 }

ifOutQLen OBJECT-TYPE
    SYNTAX   Gauge
    ACCESS   read-only
    STATUS   mandatory
    DESCRIPTION
            "The length of the output packet queue (in
            packets)."
    ::= { ifEntry 21 }
```

```
ifSpecific OBJECT-TYPE
     SYNTAX   OBJECT IDENTIFIER
     ACCESS   read-only
     STATUS   mandatory
     DESCRIPTION
             "A reference to MIB definitions specific to the
             particular media being used to realize the
             interface.  For example, if the interface is
             realized by an ethernet, then the value of this
             object refers to a document defining objects
             specific to ethernet.  If this information is not
             present, its value should be set to the OBJECT
             IDENTIFIER { 0 0 }, which is a syntatically valid
             object identifier, and any conformant
             implementation of ASN.1 and BER must be able to
             generate and recognize this value."
     ::= { ifEntry 22 }

-- the Address Translation group

-- Implementation of the Address Translation group is
-- mandatory for all systems.  Note however that this group
-- is deprecated by MIB-II. That is, it is being included
-- solely for compatibility with MIB-I nodes, and will most
-- likely be excluded from MIB-III nodes.  From MIB-II and
-- onwards, each network protocol group contains its own
-- address translation tables.

-- The Address Translation group contains one table which is
-- the union across all interfaces of the translation tables
-- for converting a NetworkAddress (e.g., an IP address) into
-- a subnetwork-specific address.  For lack of a better term,
-- this document refers to such a subnetwork-specific address
-- as a 'physical' address.

-- Examples of such translation tables are: for broadcast
-- media where ARP is in use, the translation table is
-- equivalent to the ARP cache; or, on an X.25 network where
-- non-algorithmic translation to X.121 addresses is
-- required, the translation table contains the
-- NetworkAddress to X.121 address equivalences.

atTable OBJECT-TYPE
     SYNTAX   SEQUENCE OF AtEntry
     ACCESS   not-accessible
     STATUS   deprecated
     DESCRIPTION
             "The Address Translation tables contain the
             NetworkAddress to 'physical' address equivalences.
             Some interfaces do not use translation tables for
             determining address equivalences (e.g., DDN-X.25
             has an algorithmic method); if all interfaces are
```

```
                    of this type, then the Address Translation table
                    is empty, i.e., has zero entries."
         ::= { at 1 }

   atEntry OBJECT-TYPE
         SYNTAX  AtEntry
         ACCESS  not-accessible
         STATUS  deprecated
         DESCRIPTION
                    "Each entry contains one NetworkAddress to
                    'physical' address equivalence."
         INDEX   { atIfIndex,
                     atNetAddress }
         ::= { atTable 1 }

   AtEntry ::=
         SEQUENCE {
             atIfIndex

                 INTEGER,
             atPhysAddress
                 PhysAddress,
             atNetAddress
                 NetworkAddress
         }

   atIfIndex OBJECT-TYPE
         SYNTAX  INTEGER
         ACCESS  read-write
         STATUS  deprecated
         DESCRIPTION
                    "The interface on which this entry's equivalence
                    is effective.  The interface identified by a
                    particular value of this index is the same
                    interface as identified by the same value of
                    ifIndex."
         ::= { atEntry 1 }

   atPhysAddress OBJECT-TYPE
         SYNTAX  PhysAddress
         ACCESS  read-write
         STATUS  deprecated
         DESCRIPTION
                    "The media-dependent 'physical' address.

                    Setting this object to a null string (one of zero
                    length) has the effect of invaliding the
                    corresponding entry in the atTable object.  That
                    is, it effectively dissasociates the interface
                    identified with said entry from the mapping
                    identified with said entry.  It is an
                    implementation-specific matter as to whether the
                    agent removes an invalidated entry from the table.
```

Accordingly, management stations must be prepared
to receive tabular information from agents that
corresponds to entries not currently in use.
Proper interpretation of such entries requires
examination of the relevant atPhysAddress object."
    ::= { atEntry 2 }

atNetAddress OBJECT-TYPE
    SYNTAX NetworkAddress
    ACCESS read-write
    STATUS deprecated
    DESCRIPTION
            "The NetworkAddress (e.g., the IP address)
            corresponding to the media-dependent 'physical'
            address."
    ::= { atEntry 3 }

-- the IP group

-- Implementation of the IP group is mandatory for all
-- systems.

ipForwarding OBJECT-TYPE
    SYNTAX INTEGER {
                forwarding(1),   -- acting as a gateway
                not-forwarding(2) -- NOT acting as a gateway
            }
    ACCESS read-write
    STATUS mandatory
    DESCRIPTION
            "The indication of whether this entity is acting
            as an IP gateway in respect to the forwarding of
            datagrams received by, but not addressed to, this
            entity. IP gateways forward datagrams. IP hosts
            do not (except those source-routed via the host).

            Note that for some managed nodes, this object may
            take on only a subset of the values possible.
            Accordingly, it is appropriate for an agent to
            return a 'badValue' response if a management
            station attempts to change this object to an
            inappropriate value."
    ::= { ip 1 }

ipDefaultTTL OBJECT-TYPE
    SYNTAX INTEGER
    ACCESS read-write
    STATUS mandatory
    DESCRIPTION
            "The default value inserted into the Time-To-Live
            field of the IP header of datagrams originated at
            this entity, whenever a TTL value is not supplied
            by the transport layer protocol."
    ::= { ip 2 }

```
ipInReceives OBJECT-TYPE
    SYNTAX  Counter
    ACCESS  read-only
    STATUS  mandatory
    DESCRIPTION
            "The total number of input datagrams received from
            interfaces, including those received in error."
    ::= { ip 3 }

ipInHdrErrors OBJECT-TYPE
    SYNTAX  Counter
    ACCESS  read-only
    STATUS  mandatory
    DESCRIPTION
            "The number of input datagrams discarded due to
            errors in their IP headers, including bad
            checksums, version number mismatch, other format
            errors, time-to-live exceeded, errors discovered
            in processing their IP options, etc."
    ::= { ip 4 }

ipInAddrErrors OBJECT-TYPE
    SYNTAX  Counter
    ACCESS  read-only
    STATUS  mandatory
    DESCRIPTION
            "The number of input datagrams discarded because
            the IP address in their IP header's destination
            field was not a valid address to be received at
            this entity.  This count includes invalid
            addresses (e.g., 0.0.0.0) and addresses of
            unsupported Classes (e.g., Class E).  For entities
            which are not IP Gateways and therefore do not
            forward datagrams, this counter includes datagrams
            discarded because the destination address was not
            a local address."
    ::= { ip 5 }

ipForwDatagrams OBJECT-TYPE
    SYNTAX  Counter
    ACCESS  read-only
    STATUS  mandatory
    DESCRIPTION
            "The number of input datagrams for which this
            entity was not their final IP destination, as a
            result of which an attempt was made to find a
            route to forward them to that final destination.
            In entities which do not act as IP Gateways, this
            counter will include only those packets which were
            Source-Routed via this entity, and the Source-
            Route option processing was successful."
    ::= { ip 6 }
```

```
ipInUnknownProtos OBJECT-TYPE
    SYNTAX  Counter
    ACCESS  read-only
    STATUS  mandatory
    DESCRIPTION
            "The number of locally-addressed datagrams
            received successfully but discarded because of an
            unknown or unsupported protocol."
    ::= { ip 7 }

ipInDiscards OBJECT-TYPE
    SYNTAX  Counter
    ACCESS  read-only
    STATUS  mandatory
    DESCRIPTION
            "The number of input IP datagrams for which no
            problems were encountered to prevent their
            continued processing, but which were discarded
            (e.g., for lack of buffer space).  Note that this
            counter does not include any datagrams discarded
            while awaiting re-assembly."
    ::= { ip 8 }

ipInDelivers OBJECT-TYPE
    SYNTAX  Counter
    ACCESS  read-only
    STATUS  mandatory
    DESCRIPTION
            "The total number of input datagrams successfully
            delivered to IP user-protocols (including ICMP)."
    ::= { ip 9 }

ipOutRequests OBJECT-TYPE
    SYNTAX  Counter
    ACCESS  read-only
    STATUS  mandatory
    DESCRIPTION
            "The total number of IP datagrams which local IP
            user-protocols (including ICMP) supplied to IP in
            requests for transmission.  Note that this counter
            does not include any datagrams counted in
            ipForwDatagrams."
    ::= { ip 10 }

ipOutDiscards OBJECT-TYPE
    SYNTAX  Counter
    ACCESS  read-only
    STATUS  mandatory
    DESCRIPTION
            "The number of output IP datagrams for which no
            problem was encountered to prevent their
            transmission to their destination, but which were
```

```
             discarded (e.g., for lack of buffer space).  Note
             that this counter would include datagrams counted
             in ipForwDatagrams if any such packets met this
             (discretionary) discard criterion."
     ::= { ip 11 }

ipOutNoRoutes OBJECT-TYPE
     SYNTAX   Counter
     ACCESS   read-only
     STATUS   mandatory
     DESCRIPTION
             "The number of IP datagrams discarded because no
             route could be found to transmit them to their
             destination.  Note that this counter includes any
             packets counted in ipForwDatagrams which meet this
             'no-route' criterion.  Note that this includes any
             datagarms which a host cannot route because all of
             its default gateways are down."
     ::= { ip 12 }

ipReasmTimeout OBJECT-TYPE
     SYNTAX   INTEGER
     ACCESS   read-only
     STATUS   mandatory
     DESCRIPTION
             "The maximum number of seconds which received
             fragments are held while they are awaiting
             reassembly at this entity."
     ::= { ip 13 }

ipReasmReqds OBJECT-TYPE
     SYNTAX   Counter
     ACCESS   read-only
     STATUS   mandatory
     DESCRIPTION
             "The number of IP fragments received which needed
             to be reassembled at this entity."
     ::= { ip 14 }

ipReasmOKs OBJECT-TYPE
     SYNTAX   Counter
     ACCESS   read-only
     STATUS   mandatory
     DESCRIPTION
             "The number of IP datagrams successfully re-
             assembled."
     ::= { ip 15 }

ipReasmFails OBJECT-TYPE
     SYNTAX   Counter
     ACCESS   read-only
     STATUS   mandatory
```

```
     DESCRIPTION
             "The number of failures detected by the IP re-
             assembly algorithm (for whatever reason: timed
             out, errors, etc).  Note that this is not
             necessarily a count of discarded IP fragments
             since some algorithms (notably the algorithm in
             RFC 815) can lose track of the number of fragments
             by combining them as they are received."
     ::= { ip 16 }

ipFragOKs OBJECT-TYPE
     SYNTAX  Counter
     ACCESS  read-only
     STATUS  mandatory
     DESCRIPTION
             "The number of IP datagrams that have been
             successfully fragmented at this entity."
     ::= { ip 17 }

ipFragFails OBJECT-TYPE
     SYNTAX  Counter
     ACCESS  read-only
     STATUS  mandatory
     DESCRIPTION
             "The number of IP datagrams that have been
             discarded because they needed to be fragmented at
             this entity but could not be, e.g., because their
             Don't Fragment flag was set."
     ::= { ip 18 }

ipFragCreates OBJECT-TYPE
     SYNTAX  Counter
     ACCESS  read-only
     STATUS  mandatory
     DESCRIPTION
             "The number of IP datagram fragments that have
             been generated as a result of fragmentation at
             this entity."
     ::= { ip 19 }

-- the IP address table

-- The IP address table contains this entity's IP addressing
-- information.

ipAddrTable OBJECT-TYPE
     SYNTAX  SEQUENCE OF IpAddrEntry
     ACCESS  not-accessible
     STATUS  mandatory
     DESCRIPTION
             "The table of addressing information relevant to
             this entity's IP addresses."
     ::= { ip 20 }
```

```
ipAddrEntry OBJECT-TYPE
    SYNTAX   IpAddrEntry
    ACCESS   not-accessible
    STATUS   mandatory
    DESCRIPTION
            "The addressing information for one of this
            entity's IP addresses."
    INDEX    { ipAdEntAddr }
    ::= { ipAddrTable 1 }

IpAddrEntry ::=
    SEQUENCE {
        ipAdEntAddr
            IpAddress,
        ipAdEntIfIndex
            INTEGER,
        ipAdEntNetMask
            IpAddress,
        ipAdEntBcastAddr
            INTEGER,
        ipAdEntReasmMaxSize
            INTEGER (0..65535)
    }

ipAdEntAddr OBJECT-TYPE
    SYNTAX   IpAddress
    ACCESS   read-only
    STATUS   mandatory
    DESCRIPTION
            "The IP address to which this entry's addressing
            information pertains."
    ::= { ipAddrEntry 1 }

ipAdEntIfIndex OBJECT-TYPE
    SYNTAX   INTEGER
    ACCESS   read-only
    STATUS   mandatory
    DESCRIPTION
            "The index value which uniquely identifies the
            interface to which this entry is applicable.  The
            interface identified by a particular value of this
            index is the same interface as identified by the
            same value of ifIndex."
    ::= { ipAddrEntry 2 }

ipAdEntNetMask OBJECT-TYPE
    SYNTAX   IpAddress
    ACCESS   read-only
    STATUS   mandatory
    DESCRIPTION
            "The subnet mask associated with the IP address of
            this entry.  The value of the mask is an IP
```

```
                address with all the network bits set to 1 and all
                the hosts bits set to 0."
        ::= { ipAddrEntry 3 }


ipAdEntBcastAddr OBJECT-TYPE
        SYNTAX  INTEGER
        ACCESS  read-only
        STATUS  mandatory
        DESCRIPTION
                "The value of the least-significant bit in the IP
                broadcast address used for sending datagrams on
                the (logical) interface associated with the IP
                address of this entry.  For example, when the
                Internet standard all-ones broadcast address is
                used, the value will be 1.  This value applies to
                both the subnet and network broadcasts addresses
                used by the entity on this (logical) interface."
        ::= { ipAddrEntry 4 }


ipAdEntReasmMaxSize OBJECT-TYPE
        SYNTAX  INTEGER (0..65535)
        ACCESS  read-only
        STATUS  mandatory
        DESCRIPTION
                "The size of the largest IP datagram which this
                entity can re-assemble from incoming IP fragmented
                datagrams received on this interface."
        ::= { ipAddrEntry 5 }

-- the IP routing table

-- The IP routing table contains an entry for each route
-- presently known to this entity.


ipRouteTable OBJECT-TYPE
        SYNTAX  SEQUENCE OF IpRouteEntry
        ACCESS  not-accessible
        STATUS  mandatory
        DESCRIPTION
                "This entity's IP Routing table."
        ::= { ip 21 }


ipRouteEntry OBJECT-TYPE
        SYNTAX  IpRouteEntry
        ACCESS  not-accessible
        STATUS  mandatory
        DESCRIPTION
                "A route to a particular destination."
        INDEX   { ipRouteDest }
        ::= { ipRouteTable 1 }
```

```
IpRouteEntry ::=
    SEQUENCE {
        ipRouteDest
            IpAddress,
        ipRouteIfIndex
            INTEGER,
        ipRouteMetric1
            INTEGER,
        ipRouteMetric2
            INTEGER,
        ipRouteMetric3
            INTEGER,
        ipRouteMetric4
            INTEGER,
        ipRouteNextHop
            IpAddress,
        ipRouteType
            INTEGER,
        ipRouteProto
            INTEGER,
        ipRouteAge
            INTEGER,
        ipRouteMask
            IpAddress,
        ipRouteMetric5
            INTEGER,
        ipRouteInfo
            OBJECT IDENTIFIER
    }

ipRouteDest OBJECT-TYPE
    SYNTAX  IpAddress
    ACCESS  read-write
    STATUS  mandatory
    DESCRIPTION
            "The destination IP address of this route.  An
            entry with a value of 0.0.0.0 is considered a
            default route.  Multiple routes to a single
            destination can appear in the table, but access to
            such multiple entries is dependent on the table-
            access mechanisms defined by the network
            management protocol in use."
    ::= { ipRouteEntry 1 }

ipRouteIfIndex OBJECT-TYPE
    SYNTAX  INTEGER
    ACCESS  read-write
    STATUS  mandatory
    DESCRIPTION
            "The index value which uniquely identifies the
            local interface through which the next hop of this
            route should be reached.  The interface identified
```

```
                  by a particular value of this index is the same
                  interface as identified by the same value of
                  ifIndex."
        ::= { ipRouteEntry 2 }

ipRouteMetric1 OBJECT-TYPE
     SYNTAX   INTEGER
     ACCESS   read-write
     STATUS   mandatory
     DESCRIPTION
                  "The primary routing metric for this route.  The
                  semantics of this metric are determined by the
                  routing-protocol specified in the route's
                  ipRouteProto value.  If this metric is not used,
                  its value should be set to -1."
        ::= { ipRouteEntry 3 }

ipRouteMetric2 OBJECT-TYPE
     SYNTAX   INTEGER
     ACCESS   read-write
     STATUS   mandatory
     DESCRIPTION
                  "An alternate routing metric for this route.  The
                  semantics of this metric are determined by the
                  routing-protocol specified in the route's
                  ipRouteProto value.  If this metric is not used,
                  its value should be set to -1."
        ::= { ipRouteEntry 4 }

ipRouteMetric3 OBJECT-TYPE
     SYNTAX   INTEGER
     ACCESS   read-write
     STATUS   mandatory
     DESCRIPTION
                  "An alternate routing metric for this route.  The
                  semantics of this metric are determined by the
                  routing-protocol specified in the route's
                  ipRouteProto value.  If this metric is not used,
                  its value should be set to -1."
        ::= { ipRouteEntry 5 }

ipRouteMetric4 OBJECT-TYPE
     SYNTAX   INTEGER
     ACCESS   read-write
     STATUS   mandatory
     DESCRIPTION
                  "An alternate routing metric for this route.  The
                  semantics of this metric are determined by the
                  routing-protocol specified in the route's
                  ipRouteProto value.  If this metric is not used,
                  its value should be set to -1."
        ::= { ipRouteEntry 6 }
```

```
ipRouteNextHop OBJECT-TYPE
    SYNTAX   IpAddress
    ACCESS   read-write
    STATUS   mandatory
    DESCRIPTION
            "The IP address of the next hop of this route.
            (In the case of a route bound to an interface
            which is realized via a broadcast media, the value
            of this field is the agent's IP address on that
            interface.)"
    ::= { ipRouteEntry 7 }

ipRouteType OBJECT-TYPE
    SYNTAX   INTEGER {
                other(1),      -- none of the following

                invalid(2),    -- an invalidated route

                               -- route to directly
                direct(3),     -- connected (sub-)network

                               -- route to a non-local
                indirect(4)    -- host/network/sub-network
            }
    ACCESS   read-write
    STATUS   mandatory
    DESCRIPTION
            "The type of route.  Note that the values
            direct(3) and indirect(4) refer to the notion of
            direct and indirect routing in the IP
            architecture.

            Setting this object to the value invalid(2) has
            the effect of invalidating the corresponding entry
            in the ipRouteTable object.  That is, it
            effectively dissasociates the destination
            identified with said entry from the route
            identified with said entry.  It is an
            implementation-specific matter as to whether the
            agent removes an invalidated entry from the table.
            Accordingly, management stations must be prepared
            to receive tabular information from agents that
            corresponds to entries not currently in use.
            Proper interpretation of such entries requires
            examination of the relevant ipRouteType object."
    ::= { ipRouteEntry 8 }

ipRouteProto OBJECT-TYPE
    SYNTAX   INTEGER {
                other(1),      -- none of the following

                               -- non-protocol information,
                               -- e.g., manually configured
```

```
            local(2),        -- entries

                             -- set via a network
            netmgmt(3),      -- management protocol

                             -- obtained via ICMP,
            icmp(4),         -- e.g., Redirect

                             -- the remaining values are
                             -- all gateway routing
                             -- protocols
            egp(5),
            ggp(6),

            hello(7),
            rip(8),
            is-is(9),
            es-is(10),
            ciscoIgrp(11),
            bbnSpfIgp(12),
            ospf(13),
            bgp(14)
        }
    ACCESS   read-only
    STATUS   mandatory
    DESCRIPTION
            "The routing mechanism via which this route was
            learned.  Inclusion of values for gateway routing
            protocols is not intended to imply that hosts
            should support those protocols."
    ::= { ipRouteEntry 9 }


ipRouteAge OBJECT-TYPE
    SYNTAX   INTEGER
    ACCESS   read-write
    STATUS   mandatory
    DESCRIPTION
            "The number of seconds since this route was last
            updated or otherwise determined to be correct.
            Note that no semantics of 'too old' can be implied
            except through knowledge of the routing protocol
            by which the route was learned."
    ::= { ipRouteEntry 10 }


ipRouteMask OBJECT-TYPE
    SYNTAX   IpAddress
    ACCESS   read-write
    STATUS   mandatory
    DESCRIPTION
            "Indicate the mask to be logical-ANDed with the
            destination address before being compared to the
            value in the ipRouteDest field.  For those systems
```

that do not support arbitrary subnet masks, an
agent constructs the value of the ipRouteMask by
determining whether the value of the correspondent
ipRouteDest field belong to a class-A, B, or C
network, and then using one of:

```
mask             network
255.0.0.0        class-A
255.255.0.0      class-B
255.255.255.0    class-C
```

If the value of the ipRouteDest is 0.0.0.0 (a
default route), then the mask value is also
0.0.0.0. It should be noted that all IP routing
subsystems implicitly use this mechanism."
::= { ipRouteEntry 11 }

ipRouteMetric5 OBJECT-TYPE
    SYNTAX   INTEGER
    ACCESS   read-write
    STATUS   mandatory
    DESCRIPTION
            "An alternate routing metric for this route. The
            semantics of this metric are determined by the
            routing-protocol specified in the route's
            ipRouteProto value. If this metric is not used,
            its value should be set to -1."
    ::= { ipRouteEntry 12 }

ipRouteInfo OBJECT-TYPE
    SYNTAX   OBJECT IDENTIFIER
    ACCESS   read-only
    STATUS   mandatory
    DESCRIPTION
            "A reference to MIB definitions specific to the
            particular routing protocol which is responsible
            for this route, as determined by the value
            specified in the route's ipRouteProto value. If
            this information is not present, its value should
            be set to the OBJECT IDENTIFIER { 0 0 }, which is
            a syntatically valid object identifier, and any
            conformant implementation of ASN.1 and BER must be
            able to generate and recognize this value."
    ::= { ipRouteEntry 13 }

-- the IP Address Translation table

-- The IP address translation table contain the IpAddress to
-- 'physical' address equivalences. Some interfaces do not
-- use translation tables for determining address
-- equivalences (e.g., DDN-X.25 has an algorithmic method);
-- if all interfaces are of this type, then the Address
-- Translation table is empty, i.e., has zero entries.

```
ipNetToMediaTable OBJECT-TYPE
    SYNTAX   SEQUENCE OF IpNetToMediaEntry
    ACCESS   not-accessible
    STATUS   mandatory

    DESCRIPTION
            "The IP Address Translation table used for mapping
            from IP addresses to physical addresses."
    ::= { ip 22 }

ipNetToMediaEntry OBJECT-TYPE
    SYNTAX   IpNetToMediaEntry
    ACCESS   not-accessible
    STATUS   mandatory
    DESCRIPTION
            "Each entry contains one IpAddress to 'physical'
            address equivalence."
    INDEX    { ipNetToMediaIfIndex,
                 ipNetToMediaNetAddress }
    ::= { ipNetToMediaTable 1 }

IpNetToMediaEntry ::=
    SEQUENCE {
        ipNetToMediaIfIndex
            INTEGER,
        ipNetToMediaPhysAddress
            PhysAddress,
        ipNetToMediaNetAddress
            IpAddress,
        ipNetToMediaType
            INTEGER
    }

ipNetToMediaIfIndex OBJECT-TYPE
    SYNTAX   INTEGER
    ACCESS   read-write
    STATUS   mandatory
    DESCRIPTION
            "The interface on which this entry's equivalence
            is effective.  The interface identified by a
            particular value of this index is the same
            interface as identified by the same value of
            ifIndex."
    ::= { ipNetToMediaEntry 1 }

ipNetToMediaPhysAddress OBJECT-TYPE
    SYNTAX   PhysAddress
    ACCESS   read-write
    STATUS   mandatory
    DESCRIPTION
            "The media-dependent 'physical' address."
    ::= { ipNetToMediaEntry 2 }
```

```
ipNetToMediaNetAddress OBJECT-TYPE
    SYNTAX   IpAddress
    ACCESS   read-write
    STATUS   mandatory
    DESCRIPTION
            "The IpAddress corresponding to the media-
            dependent 'physical' address."
    ::= { ipNetToMediaEntry 3 }


ipNetToMediaType OBJECT-TYPE
    SYNTAX   INTEGER {
                other(1),        -- none of the following
                invalid(2),      -- an invalidated mapping
                dynamic(3),
                static(4)
            }
    ACCESS   read-write
    STATUS   mandatory
    DESCRIPTION
            "The type of mapping.

            Setting this object to the value invalid(2) has
            the effect of invalidating the corresponding entry
            in the ipNetToMediaTable.  That is, it effectively
            dissasociates the interface identified with said
            entry from the mapping identified with said entry.
            It is an implementation-specific matter as to
            whether the agent removes an invalidated entry
            from the table.  Accordingly, management stations
            must be prepared to receive tabular information
            from agents that corresponds to entries not
            currently in use.  Proper interpretation of such
            entries requires examination of the relevant
            ipNetToMediaType object."
    ::= { ipNetToMediaEntry 4 }

-- additional IP objects


ipRoutingDiscards OBJECT-TYPE
    SYNTAX   Counter
    ACCESS   read-only
    STATUS   mandatory
    DESCRIPTION
            "The number of routing entries which were chosen
            to be discarded even though they are valid.  One
            possible reason for discarding such an entry could
            be to free-up buffer space for other routing

            entries."
    ::= { ip 23 }
```

```
-- the ICMP group

-- Implementation of the ICMP group is mandatory for all
-- systems.

icmpInMsgs OBJECT-TYPE
    SYNTAX   Counter
    ACCESS   read-only
    STATUS   mandatory
    DESCRIPTION
            "The total number of ICMP messages which the
            entity received.  Note that this counter includes
            all those counted by icmpInErrors."
    ::= { icmp 1 }

icmpInErrors OBJECT-TYPE
    SYNTAX   Counter
    ACCESS   read-only
    STATUS   mandatory
    DESCRIPTION
            "The number of ICMP messages which the entity
            received but determined as having ICMP-specific
            errors (bad ICMP checksums, bad length, etc.)."
    ::= { icmp 2 }

icmpInDestUnreachs OBJECT-TYPE
    SYNTAX   Counter
    ACCESS   read-only
    STATUS   mandatory
    DESCRIPTION
            "The number of ICMP Destination Unreachable
            messages received."
    ::= { icmp 3 }

icmpInTimeExcds OBJECT-TYPE
    SYNTAX   Counter
    ACCESS   read-only
    STATUS   mandatory
    DESCRIPTION
            "The number of ICMP Time Exceeded messages
            received."
    ::= { icmp 4 }

icmpInParmProbs OBJECT-TYPE
    SYNTAX   Counter
    ACCESS   read-only
    STATUS   mandatory
    DESCRIPTION
            "The number of ICMP Parameter Problem messages
            received."
    ::= { icmp 5 }
```

```
icmpInSrcQuenchs OBJECT-TYPE
    SYNTAX  Counter
    ACCESS  read-only
    STATUS  mandatory
    DESCRIPTION
            "The number of ICMP Source Quench messages
            received."
    ::= { icmp 6 }

icmpInRedirects OBJECT-TYPE
    SYNTAX  Counter
    ACCESS  read-only
    STATUS  mandatory
    DESCRIPTION
            "The number of ICMP Redirect messages received."
    ::= { icmp 7 }

icmpInEchos OBJECT-TYPE
    SYNTAX  Counter
    ACCESS  read-only
    STATUS  mandatory
    DESCRIPTION
            "The number of ICMP Echo (request) messages
            received."
    ::= { icmp 8 }

icmpInEchoReps OBJECT-TYPE
    SYNTAX  Counter
    ACCESS  read-only
    STATUS  mandatory
    DESCRIPTION
            "The number of ICMP Echo Reply messages received."
    ::= { icmp 9 }

icmpInTimestamps OBJECT-TYPE
    SYNTAX  Counter
    ACCESS  read-only
    STATUS  mandatory
    DESCRIPTION
            "The number of ICMP Timestamp (request) messages
            received."
    ::= { icmp 10 }

icmpInTimestampReps OBJECT-TYPE
    SYNTAX  Counter
    ACCESS  read-only
    STATUS  mandatory
    DESCRIPTION
            "The number of ICMP Timestamp Reply messages
            received."
    ::= { icmp 11 }

icmpInAddrMasks OBJECT-TYPE
    SYNTAX  Counter
```

```
    ACCESS   read-only
    STATUS   mandatory
    DESCRIPTION
            "The number of ICMP Address Mask Request messages
            received."
    ::= { icmp 12 }

icmpInAddrMaskReps OBJECT-TYPE
    SYNTAX   Counter
    ACCESS   read-only
    STATUS   mandatory
    DESCRIPTION
            "The number of ICMP Address Mask Reply messages
            received."
    ::= { icmp 13 }

icmpOutMsgs OBJECT-TYPE
    SYNTAX   Counter
    ACCESS   read-only
    STATUS   mandatory
    DESCRIPTION
            "The total number of ICMP messages which this
            entity attempted to send.  Note that this counter
            includes all those counted by icmpOutErrors."
    ::= { icmp 14 }

icmpOutErrors OBJECT-TYPE
    SYNTAX   Counter
    ACCESS   read-only
    STATUS   mandatory
    DESCRIPTION
            "The number of ICMP messages which this entity did
            not send due to problems discovered within ICMP
            such as a lack of buffers.  This value should not
            include errors discovered outside the ICMP layer
            such as the inability of IP to route the resultant
            datagram.  In some implementations there may be no
            types of error which contribute to this counter's
            value."
    ::= { icmp 15 }

icmpOutDestUnreachs OBJECT-TYPE
    SYNTAX   Counter
    ACCESS   read-only
    STATUS   mandatory
    DESCRIPTION
            "The number of ICMP Destination Unreachable
            messages sent."
    ::= { icmp 16 }

icmpOutTimeExcds OBJECT-TYPE
    SYNTAX   Counter
    ACCESS   read-only
```

```
        STATUS  mandatory
        DESCRIPTION
                "The number of ICMP Time Exceeded messages sent."
        ::= { icmp 17 }


icmpOutParmProbs OBJECT-TYPE
        SYNTAX  Counter
        ACCESS  read-only
        STATUS  mandatory
        DESCRIPTION
                "The number of ICMP Parameter Problem messages
                sent."
        ::= { icmp 18 }


icmpOutSrcQuenchs OBJECT-TYPE
        SYNTAX  Counter
        ACCESS  read-only
        STATUS  mandatory
        DESCRIPTION
                "The number of ICMP Source Quench messages sent."
        ::= { icmp 19 }


icmpOutRedirects OBJECT-TYPE
        SYNTAX  Counter
        ACCESS  read-only
        STATUS  mandatory
        DESCRIPTION
                "The number of ICMP Redirect messages sent.  For a
                host, this object will always be zero, since hosts
                do not send redirects."
        ::= { icmp 20 }


icmpOutEchos OBJECT-TYPE
        SYNTAX  Counter
        ACCESS  read-only
        STATUS  mandatory
        DESCRIPTION
                "The number of ICMP Echo (request) messages sent."
        ::= { icmp 21 }


icmpOutEchoReps OBJECT-TYPE
        SYNTAX  Counter
        ACCESS  read-only
        STATUS  mandatory
        DESCRIPTION
                "The number of ICMP Echo Reply messages sent."
        ::= { icmp 22 }


icmpOutTimestamps OBJECT-TYPE
        SYNTAX  Counter
        ACCESS  read-only
```

```
        STATUS  mandatory
        DESCRIPTION
                "The number of ICMP Timestamp (request) messages
                sent."
        ::= { icmp 23 }

icmpOutTimestampReps OBJECT-TYPE
        SYNTAX  Counter
        ACCESS  read-only
        STATUS  mandatory
        DESCRIPTION
                "The number of ICMP Timestamp Reply messages
                sent."
        ::= { icmp 24 }

icmpOutAddrMasks OBJECT-TYPE
        SYNTAX  Counter
        ACCESS  read-only
        STATUS  mandatory
        DESCRIPTION
                "The number of ICMP Address Mask Request messages
                sent."
        ::= { icmp 25 }

icmpOutAddrMaskReps OBJECT-TYPE
        SYNTAX  Counter
        ACCESS  read-only
        STATUS  mandatory
        DESCRIPTION
                "The number of ICMP Address Mask Reply messages
                sent."
        ::= { icmp 26 }

-- the TCP group

-- Implementation of the TCP group is mandatory for all
-- systems that implement the TCP.

-- Note that instances of object types that represent
-- information about a particular TCP connection are
-- transient; they persist only as long as the connection
-- in question.

tcpRtoAlgorithm OBJECT-TYPE
        SYNTAX  INTEGER {
                    other(1),     -- none of the following

                    constant(2),  -- a constant rto
                    rsre(3),      -- MIL-STD-1778, Appendix B
                    vanj(4)       -- Van Jacobson's algorithm [10]
                }
        ACCESS  read-only
        STATUS  mandatory
```

```
        DESCRIPTION
                "The algorithm used to determine the timeout value
                used for retransmitting unacknowledged octets."
        ::= { tcp 1 }

    tcpRtoMin OBJECT-TYPE
        SYNTAX  INTEGER
        ACCESS  read-only
        STATUS  mandatory
        DESCRIPTION
                "The minimum value permitted by a TCP
                implementation for the retransmission timeout,
                measured in milliseconds.  More refined semantics
                for objects of this type depend upon the algorithm
                used to determine the retransmission timeout.  In
                particular, when the timeout algorithm is rsre(3),
                an object of this type has the semantics of the
                LBOUND quantity described in RFC 793."
        ::= { tcp 2 }

    tcpRtoMax OBJECT-TYPE
        SYNTAX  INTEGER
        ACCESS  read-only
        STATUS  mandatory
        DESCRIPTION
                "The maximum value permitted by a TCP
                implementation for the retransmission timeout,
                measured in milliseconds.  More refined semantics
                for objects of this type depend upon the algorithm
                used to determine the retransmission timeout.  In
                particular, when the timeout algorithm is rsre(3),
                an object of this type has the semantics of the
                UBOUND quantity described in RFC 793."
        ::= { tcp 3 }

    tcpMaxConn OBJECT-TYPE
        SYNTAX  INTEGER
        ACCESS  read-only
        STATUS  mandatory
        DESCRIPTION
                "The limit on the total number of TCP connections
                the entity can support.  In entities where the
                maximum number of connections is dynamic, this
                object should contain the value -1."
        ::= { tcp 4 }

    tcpActiveOpens OBJECT-TYPE
        SYNTAX  Counter
        ACCESS  read-only
        STATUS  mandatory
```

```
         DESCRIPTION
                 "The number of times TCP connections have made a
                 direct transition to the SYN-SENT state from the
                 CLOSED state."
         ::= { tcp 5 }

tcpPassiveOpens OBJECT-TYPE
         SYNTAX  Counter
         ACCESS  read-only
         STATUS  mandatory
         DESCRIPTION
                 "The number of times TCP connections have made a
                 direct transition to the SYN-RCVD state from the
                 LISTEN state."
         ::= { tcp 6 }

tcpAttemptFails OBJECT-TYPE
         SYNTAX  Counter
         ACCESS  read-only
         STATUS  mandatory
         DESCRIPTION
                 "The number of times TCP connections have made a
                 direct transition to the CLOSED state from either
                 the SYN-SENT state or the SYN-RCVD state, plus the
                 number of times TCP connections have made a direct
                 transition to the LISTEN state from the SYN-RCVD
                 state."
         ::= { tcp 7 }

tcpEstabResets OBJECT-TYPE
         SYNTAX  Counter
         ACCESS  read-only
         STATUS  mandatory
         DESCRIPTION
                 "The number of times TCP connections have made a
                 direct transition to the CLOSED state from either
                 the ESTABLISHED state or the CLOSE-WAIT state."
         ::= { tcp 8 }

tcpCurrEstab OBJECT-TYPE
         SYNTAX  Gauge
         ACCESS  read-only
         STATUS  mandatory
         DESCRIPTION
                 "The number of TCP connections for which the
                 current state is either ESTABLISHED or CLOSE-
                 WAIT."
         ::= { tcp 9 }

tcpInSegs OBJECT-TYPE
         SYNTAX  Counter
         ACCESS  read-only
```

```
        STATUS   mandatory
        DESCRIPTION
                "The total number of segments received, including
                those received in error.  This count includes
                segments received on currently established
                connections."
        ::= { tcp 10 }

tcpOutSegs OBJECT-TYPE
        SYNTAX   Counter
        ACCESS   read-only
        STATUS   mandatory
        DESCRIPTION
                "The total number of segments sent, including
                those on current connections but excluding those
                containing only retransmitted octets."
        ::= { tcp 11 }

tcpRetransSegs OBJECT-TYPE
        SYNTAX   Counter
        ACCESS   read-only
        STATUS   mandatory
        DESCRIPTION
                "The total number of segments retransmitted - that
                is, the number of TCP segments transmitted
                containing one or more previously transmitted
                octets."
        ::= { tcp 12 }

-- the TCP Connection table

-- The TCP connection table contains information about this
-- entity's existing TCP connections.

tcpConnTable OBJECT-TYPE
        SYNTAX   SEQUENCE OF TcpConnEntry
        ACCESS   not-accessible
        STATUS   mandatory
        DESCRIPTION
                "A table containing TCP connection-specific
                information."
        ::= { tcp 13 }

tcpConnEntry OBJECT-TYPE
        SYNTAX   TcpConnEntry
        ACCESS   not-accessible
        STATUS   mandatory
        DESCRIPTION
                "Information about a particular current TCP
                connection.  An object of this type is transient,
                in that it ceases to exist when (or soon after)
                the connection makes the transition to the CLOSED
                state."
```

```
        INDEX   { tcpConnLocalAddress,
                  tcpConnLocalPort,
                  tcpConnRemAddress,
                  tcpConnRemPort }
        ::= { tcpConnTable 1 }


TcpConnEntry ::=
    SEQUENCE {
        tcpConnState
            INTEGER,
        tcpConnLocalAddress
            IpAddress,
        tcpConnLocalPort
            INTEGER (0..65535),
        tcpConnRemAddress
            IpAddress,
        tcpConnRemPort
            INTEGER (0..65535)
    }


tcpConnState OBJECT-TYPE
    SYNTAX  INTEGER {
                closed(1),
                listen(2),
                synSent(3),
                synReceived(4),
                established(5),
                finWait1(6),
                finWait2(7),
                closeWait(8),
                lastAck(9),
                closing(10),
                timeWait(11),
                deleteTCB(12)
            }
    ACCESS  read-write
    STATUS  mandatory
    DESCRIPTION
            "The state of this TCP connection.

            The only value which may be set by a management
            station is deleteTCB(12).  Accordingly, it is
            appropriate for an agent to return a 'badValue'
            response if a management station attempts to set
            this object to any other value.

            If a management station sets this object to the
            value deleteTCB(12), then this has the effect of
            deleting the TCB (as defined in RFC 793) of the
            corresponding connection on the managed node,
```

resulting in immediate termination of the
connection.

As an implementation-specific option, a RST
segment may be sent from the managed node to the
other TCP endpoint (note however that RST segments
are not sent reliably)."
::= { tcpConnEntry 1 }

tcpConnLocalAddress OBJECT-TYPE
    SYNTAX   IpAddress
    ACCESS   read-only
    STATUS   mandatory
    DESCRIPTION
            "The local IP address for this TCP connection. In
            the case of a connection in the listen state which
            is willing to accept connections for any IP
            interface associated with the node, the value
            0.0.0.0 is used."
    ::= { tcpConnEntry 2 }

tcpConnLocalPort OBJECT-TYPE
    SYNTAX   INTEGER (0..65535)
    ACCESS   read-only
    STATUS   mandatory
    DESCRIPTION
            "The local port number for this TCP connection."
    ::= { tcpConnEntry 3 }

tcpConnRemAddress OBJECT-TYPE
    SYNTAX   IpAddress
    ACCESS   read-only
    STATUS   mandatory
    DESCRIPTION
            "The remote IP address for this TCP connection."
    ::= { tcpConnEntry 4 }

tcpConnRemPort OBJECT-TYPE
    SYNTAX   INTEGER (0..65535)
    ACCESS   read-only
    STATUS   mandatory
    DESCRIPTION
            "The remote port number for this TCP connection."
    ::= { tcpConnEntry 5 }

-- additional TCP objects

tcpInErrs OBJECT-TYPE
    SYNTAX   Counter
    ACCESS   read-only

```
       STATUS   mandatory
       DESCRIPTION
               "The total number of segments received in error
               (e.g., bad TCP checksums)."
       ::= { tcp 14 }

tcpOutRsts OBJECT-TYPE
       SYNTAX   Counter
       ACCESS   read-only
       STATUS   mandatory
       DESCRIPTION
               "The number of TCP segments sent containing the
               RST flag."
       ::= { tcp 15 }

-- the UDP group

-- Implementation of the UDP group is mandatory for all
-- systems which implement the UDP.

udpInDatagrams OBJECT-TYPE
       SYNTAX   Counter
       ACCESS   read-only
       STATUS   mandatory
       DESCRIPTION
               "The total number of UDP datagrams delivered to
               UDP users."
       ::= { udp 1 }

udpNoPorts OBJECT-TYPE
       SYNTAX   Counter
       ACCESS   read-only
       STATUS   mandatory
       DESCRIPTION
               "The total number of received UDP datagrams for
               which there was no application at the destination
               port."
       ::= { udp 2 }

udpInErrors OBJECT-TYPE
       SYNTAX   Counter
       ACCESS   read-only
       STATUS   mandatory
       DESCRIPTION
               "The number of received UDP datagrams that could
               not be delivered for reasons other than the lack
               of an application at the destination port."
       ::= { udp 3 }

udpOutDatagrams OBJECT-TYPE
       SYNTAX   Counter
       ACCESS   read-only
```

```
        STATUS  mandatory
        DESCRIPTION
                "The total number of UDP datagrams sent from this
                entity."
        ::= { udp 4 }

    -- the UDP Listener table

    -- The UDP listener table contains information about this
    -- entity's UDP end-points on which a local application is
    -- currently accepting datagrams.

    udpTable OBJECT-TYPE
        SYNTAX  SEQUENCE OF UdpEntry
        ACCESS  not-accessible
        STATUS  mandatory
        DESCRIPTION
                "A table containing UDP listener information."
        ::= { udp 5 }

    udpEntry OBJECT-TYPE
        SYNTAX  UdpEntry
        ACCESS  not-accessible
        STATUS  mandatory
        DESCRIPTION
                "Information about a particular current UDP
                listener."
        INDEX   { udpLocalAddress, udpLocalPort }
        ::= { udpTable 1 }

    UdpEntry ::=
        SEQUENCE {
            udpLocalAddress
                IpAddress,
            udpLocalPort
                INTEGER (0..65535)
        }

    udpLocalAddress OBJECT-TYPE
        SYNTAX  IpAddress
        ACCESS  read-only
        STATUS  mandatory
        DESCRIPTION
                "The local IP address for this UDP listener.  In
                the case of a UDP listener which is willing to
                accept datagrams for any IP interface associated
                with the node, the value 0.0.0.0 is used."
        ::= { udpEntry 1 }

    udpLocalPort OBJECT-TYPE
        SYNTAX  INTEGER (0..65535)
        ACCESS  read-only
        STATUS  mandatory
```

```
        DESCRIPTION
                "The local port number for this UDP listener."
        ::= { udpEntry 2 }

-- the EGP group

-- Implementation of the EGP group is mandatory for all
-- systems which implement the EGP.

egpInMsgs OBJECT-TYPE
    SYNTAX   Counter
    ACCESS   read-only
    STATUS   mandatory
    DESCRIPTION
            "The number of EGP messages received without
            error."
    ::= { egp 1 }

egpInErrors OBJECT-TYPE
    SYNTAX   Counter
    ACCESS   read-only
    STATUS   mandatory
    DESCRIPTION
            "The number of EGP messages received that proved
            to be in error."
    ::= { egp 2 }

egpOutMsgs OBJECT-TYPE
    SYNTAX   Counter
    ACCESS   read-only
    STATUS   mandatory
    DESCRIPTION
            "The total number of locally generated EGP
            messages."
    ::= { egp 3 }

egpOutErrors OBJECT-TYPE
    SYNTAX   Counter
    ACCESS   read-only
    STATUS   mandatory
    DESCRIPTION
            "The number of locally generated EGP messages not
            sent due to resource limitations within an EGP
            entity."
    ::= { egp 4 }

-- the EGP Neighbor table

-- The EGP neighbor table contains information about this
-- entity's EGP neighbors.

egpNeighTable OBJECT-TYPE
    SYNTAX   SEQUENCE OF EgpNeighEntry
    ACCESS   not-accessible
```

```
           STATUS   mandatory
           DESCRIPTION
                   "The EGP neighbor table."
           ::= { egp 5 }

       egpNeighEntry OBJECT-TYPE
           SYNTAX   EgpNeighEntry
           ACCESS   not-accessible
           STATUS   mandatory
           DESCRIPTION
                   "Information about this entity's relationship with
                   a particular EGP neighbor."
           INDEX    { egpNeighAddr }
           ::= { egpNeighTable 1 }

       EgpNeighEntry ::=
           SEQUENCE {
               egpNeighState
                   INTEGER,
               egpNeighAddr
                   IpAddress,
               egpNeighAs
                   INTEGER,
               egpNeighInMsgs
                   Counter,
               egpNeighInErrs
                   Counter,
               egpNeighOutMsgs
                   Counter,
               egpNeighOutErrs
                   Counter,
               egpNeighInErrMsgs
                   Counter,
               egpNeighOutErrMsgs
                   Counter,
               egpNeighStateUps
                   Counter,
               egpNeighStateDowns
                   Counter,
               egpNeighIntervalHello
                   INTEGER,
               egpNeighIntervalPoll
                   INTEGER,
               egpNeighMode
                   INTEGER,
               egpNeighEventTrigger
                   INTEGER
           }

       egpNeighState OBJECT-TYPE
           SYNTAX   INTEGER {
                       idle(1),
                       acquisition(2),
```

```
                    down(3),
                    up(4),
                    cease(5)
                }
    ACCESS   read-only
    STATUS   mandatory
    DESCRIPTION
            "The EGP state of the local system with respect to
            this entry's EGP neighbor.  Each EGP state is
            represented by a value that is one greater than
            the numerical value associated with said state in
            RFC 904."
    ::= { egpNeighEntry 1 }

egpNeighAddr OBJECT-TYPE
    SYNTAX   IpAddress
    ACCESS   read-only
    STATUS   mandatory
    DESCRIPTION
            "The IP address of this entry's EGP neighbor."
    ::= { egpNeighEntry 2 }

egpNeighAs OBJECT-TYPE
    SYNTAX   INTEGER
    ACCESS   read-only
    STATUS   mandatory
    DESCRIPTION
            "The autonomous system of this EGP peer.  Zero
            should be specified if the autonomous system
            number of the neighbor is not yet known."
    ::= { egpNeighEntry 3 }

egpNeighInMsgs OBJECT-TYPE
    SYNTAX   Counter
    ACCESS   read-only
    STATUS   mandatory
    DESCRIPTION
            "The number of EGP messages received without error
            from this EGP peer."
    ::= { egpNeighEntry 4 }

egpNeighInErrs OBJECT-TYPE
    SYNTAX   Counter
    ACCESS   read-only
    STATUS   mandatory
    DESCRIPTION
            "The number of EGP messages received from this EGP
            peer that proved to be in error (e.g., bad EGP
            checksum)."
    ::= { egpNeighEntry 5 }

egpNeighOutMsgs OBJECT-TYPE
    SYNTAX   Counter
    ACCESS   read-only
```

```
        STATUS   mandatory
        DESCRIPTION
                "The number of locally generated EGP messages to
                this EGP peer."
        ::= { egpNeighEntry 6 }


    egpNeighOutErrs OBJECT-TYPE
        SYNTAX   Counter
        ACCESS   read-only
        STATUS   mandatory
        DESCRIPTION
                "The number of locally generated EGP messages not
                sent to this EGP peer due to resource limitations
                within an EGP entity."
        ::= { egpNeighEntry 7 }


    egpNeighInErrMsgs OBJECT-TYPE
        SYNTAX   Counter
        ACCESS   read-only
        STATUS   mandatory
        DESCRIPTION
                "The number of EGP-defined error messages received
                from this EGP peer."
        ::= { egpNeighEntry 8 }


    egpNeighOutErrMsgs OBJECT-TYPE
        SYNTAX   Counter
        ACCESS   read-only
        STATUS   mandatory
        DESCRIPTION
                "The number of EGP-defined error messages sent to
                this EGP peer."
        ::= { egpNeighEntry 9 }


    egpNeighStateUps OBJECT-TYPE
        SYNTAX   Counter
        ACCESS   read-only
        STATUS   mandatory
        DESCRIPTION
                "The number of EGP state transitions to the UP
                state with this EGP peer."
        ::= { egpNeighEntry 10 }


    egpNeighStateDowns OBJECT-TYPE
        SYNTAX   Counter
        ACCESS   read-only
        STATUS   mandatory
        DESCRIPTION
                "The number of EGP state transitions from the UP
                state to any other state with this EGP peer."
        ::= { egpNeighEntry 11 }
```

```
egpNeighIntervalHello OBJECT-TYPE
    SYNTAX   INTEGER
    ACCESS   read-only
    STATUS   mandatory
    DESCRIPTION
            "The interval between EGP Hello command
            retransmissions (in hundredths of a second).  This
            represents the t1 timer as defined in RFC 904."
    ::= { egpNeighEntry 12 }

egpNeighIntervalPoll OBJECT-TYPE
    SYNTAX   INTEGER
    ACCESS   read-only
    STATUS   mandatory
    DESCRIPTION
            "The interval between EGP poll command
            retransmissions (in hundredths of a second).  This
            represents the t3 timer as defined in RFC 904."
    ::= { egpNeighEntry 13 }

egpNeighMode OBJECT-TYPE
    SYNTAX   INTEGER { active(1), passive(2) }
    ACCESS   read-only
    STATUS   mandatory
    DESCRIPTION
            "The polling mode of this EGP entity, either
            passive or active."
    ::= { egpNeighEntry 14 }

egpNeighEventTrigger OBJECT-TYPE
    SYNTAX   INTEGER { start(1), stop(2) }
    ACCESS   read-write
    STATUS   mandatory
    DESCRIPTION
            "A control variable used to trigger operator-
            initiated Start and Stop events.  When read, this
            variable always returns the most recent value that
            egpNeighEventTrigger was set to.  If it has not
            been set since the last initialization of the
            network management subsystem on the node, it
            returns a value of 'stop'.

            When set, this variable causes a Start or Stop
            event on the specified neighbor, as specified on
            pages 8-10 of RFC 904.  Briefly, a Start event
            causes an Idle peer to begin neighbor acquisition
            and a non-Idle peer to reinitiate neighbor
            acquisition.  A stop event causes a non-Idle peer
            to return to the Idle state until a Start event
            occurs, either via egpNeighEventTrigger or
            otherwise."
    ::= { egpNeighEntry 15 }

-- additional EGP objects
```

```
egpAs OBJECT-TYPE
    SYNTAX  INTEGER
    ACCESS  read-only
    STATUS  mandatory
    DESCRIPTION
            "The autonomous system number of this EGP entity."
    ::= { egp 6 }

-- the Transmission group

-- Based on the transmission media underlying each interface
-- on a system, the corresponding portion of the Transmission
-- group is mandatory for that system.

-- When Internet-standard definitions for managing
-- transmission media are defined, the transmission group is
-- used to provide a prefix for the names of those objects.
-- Typically, such definitions reside in the experimental
-- portion of the MIB until they are "proven", then as a
-- part of the Internet standardization process, the
-- definitions are accordingly elevated and a new object
-- identifier, under the transmission group is defined. By
-- convention, the name assigned is:
--
--     type OBJECT IDENTIFIER    ::= { transmission number }
--
-- where "type" is the symbolic value used for the media in
-- the ifType column of the ifTable object, and "number" is
-- the actual integer value corresponding to the symbol.

-- the SNMP group

-- Implementation of the SNMP group is mandatory for all
-- systems which support an SNMP protocol entity.  Some of
-- the objects defined below will be zero-valued in those
-- SNMP implementations that are optimized to support only
-- those functions specific to either a management agent or
-- a management station.  In particular, it should be
-- observed that the objects below refer to an SNMP entity,
-- and there may be several SNMP entities residing on a
-- managed node (e.g., if the node is hosting acting as
-- a management station).

snmpInPkts OBJECT-TYPE
    SYNTAX  Counter
    ACCESS  read-only
    STATUS  mandatory
    DESCRIPTION
            "The total number of Messages delivered to the
             SNMP entity from the transport service."
    ::= { snmp 1 }

snmpOutPkts OBJECT-TYPE
    SYNTAX  Counter
    ACCESS  read-only
```

```
      STATUS   mandatory
      DESCRIPTION
              "The total number of SNMP Messages which were
              passed from the SNMP protocol entity to the
              transport service."
      ::= { snmp 2 }

snmpInBadVersions OBJECT-TYPE
      SYNTAX   Counter
      ACCESS   read-only
      STATUS   mandatory
      DESCRIPTION
              "The total number of SNMP Messages which were
              delivered to the SNMP protocol entity and were for
              an unsupported SNMP version."
      ::= { snmp 3 }

snmpInBadCommunityNames OBJECT-TYPE
      SYNTAX   Counter
      ACCESS   read-only
      STATUS   mandatory
      DESCRIPTION
              "The total number of SNMP Messages delivered to
              the SNMP protocol entity which used a SNMP
              community name not known to said entity."
      ::= { snmp 4 }

snmpInBadCommunityUses OBJECT-TYPE
      SYNTAX   Counter
      ACCESS   read-only
      STATUS   mandatory
      DESCRIPTION
              "The total number of SNMP Messages delivered to
              the SNMP protocol entity which represented an SNMP
              operation which was not allowed by the SNMP
              community named in the Message."
      ::= { snmp 5 }

snmpInASNParseErrs OBJECT-TYPE
      SYNTAX   Counter
      ACCESS   read-only
      STATUS   mandatory
      DESCRIPTION
              "The total number of ASN.1 or BER errors
              encountered by the SNMP protocol entity when
              decoding received SNMP Messages."
      ::= { snmp 6 }

-- { snmp 7 } is not used

snmpInTooBigs OBJECT-TYPE
      SYNTAX   Counter
      ACCESS   read-only
      STATUS   mandatory
```

```
    DESCRIPTION
            "The total number of SNMP PDUs which were
            delivered to the SNMP protocol entity and for
            which the value of the error-status field is
            'tooBig'."
    ::= { snmp 8 }

snmpInNoSuchNames OBJECT-TYPE
    SYNTAX  Counter
    ACCESS  read-only
    STATUS  mandatory
    DESCRIPTION
            "The total number of SNMP PDUs which were
            delivered to the SNMP protocol entity and for
            which the value of the error-status field is
            'noSuchName'."
    ::= { snmp 9 }

snmpInBadValues OBJECT-TYPE
    SYNTAX  Counter
    ACCESS  read-only
    STATUS  mandatory
    DESCRIPTION
            "The total number of SNMP PDUs which were
            delivered to the SNMP protocol entity and for
            which the value of the error-status field is
            'badValue'."
    ::= { snmp 10 }

snmpInReadOnlys OBJECT-TYPE
    SYNTAX  Counter
    ACCESS  read-only
    STATUS  mandatory
    DESCRIPTION
            "The total number valid SNMP PDUs which were
            delivered to the SNMP protocol entity and for
            which the value of the error-status field is
            'readOnly'.  It should be noted that it is a
            protocol error to generate an SNMP PDU which
            contains the value 'readOnly' in the error-status
            field, as such this object is provided as a means
            of detecting incorrect implementations of the
            SNMP."
    ::= { snmp 11 }

snmpInGenErrs OBJECT-TYPE
    SYNTAX  Counter
    ACCESS  read-only
    STATUS  mandatory
    DESCRIPTION
            "The total number of SNMP PDUs which were
            delivered to the SNMP protocol entity and for
```

```
               which the value of the error-status field is
               'genErr'."
     ::= { snmp 12 }


snmpInTotalReqVars OBJECT-TYPE
     SYNTAX   Counter
     ACCESS   read-only
     STATUS   mandatory
     DESCRIPTION
               "The total number of MIB objects which have been
               retrieved successfully by the SNMP protocol entity
               as the result of receiving valid SNMP Get-Request
               and Get-Next PDUs."
     ::= { snmp 13 }


snmpInTotalSetVars OBJECT-TYPE
     SYNTAX   Counter
     ACCESS   read-only
     STATUS   mandatory
     DESCRIPTION
               "The total number of MIB objects which have been
               altered successfully by the SNMP protocol entity
               as the result of receiving valid SNMP Set-Request
               PDUs."
     ::= { snmp 14 }


snmpInGetRequests OBJECT-TYPE
     SYNTAX   Counter
     ACCESS   read-only
     STATUS   mandatory
     DESCRIPTION
               "The total number of SNMP Get-Request PDUs which
               have been accepted and processed by the SNMP
               protocol entity."
     ::= { snmp 15 }


snmpInGetNexts OBJECT-TYPE
     SYNTAX   Counter
     ACCESS   read-only
     STATUS   mandatory
     DESCRIPTION
               "The total number of SNMP Get-Next PDUs which have
               been accepted and processed by the SNMP protocol
               entity."
     ::= { snmp 16 }


snmpInSetRequests OBJECT-TYPE
     SYNTAX   Counter
     ACCESS   read-only
     STATUS   mandatory
```

```
        DESCRIPTION
                "The total number of SNMP Set-Request PDUs which
                have been accepted and processed by the SNMP
                protocol entity."
        ::= { snmp 17 }

snmpInGetResponses OBJECT-TYPE
        SYNTAX  Counter
        ACCESS  read-only
        STATUS  mandatory
        DESCRIPTION
                "The total number of SNMP Get-Response PDUs which
                have been accepted and processed by the SNMP
                protocol entity."
        ::= { snmp 18 }

snmpInTraps OBJECT-TYPE
        SYNTAX  Counter
        ACCESS  read-only
        STATUS  mandatory
        DESCRIPTION
                "The total number of SNMP Trap PDUs which have
                been accepted and processed by the SNMP protocol
                entity."
        ::= { snmp 19 }

snmpOutTooBigs OBJECT-TYPE
        SYNTAX  Counter
        ACCESS  read-only
        STATUS  mandatory
        DESCRIPTION
                "The total number of SNMP PDUs which were
                generated by the SNMP protocol entity and for
                which the value of the error-status field is
                'tooBig.'"
        ::= { snmp 20 }

snmpOutNoSuchNames OBJECT-TYPE
        SYNTAX  Counter
        ACCESS  read-only
        STATUS  mandatory
        DESCRIPTION
                "The total number of SNMP PDUs which were
                generated by the SNMP protocol entity and for
                which the value of the error-status is
                'noSuchName'."
        ::= { snmp 21 }

snmpOutBadValues OBJECT-TYPE
        SYNTAX  Counter
        ACCESS  read-only
        STATUS  mandatory
```

```
    DESCRIPTION
            "The total number of SNMP PDUs which were
            generated by the SNMP protocol entity and for
            which the value of the error-status field is
            'badValue'."
    ::= { snmp 22 }

-- { snmp 23 } is not used

snmpOutGenErrs OBJECT-TYPE
    SYNTAX  Counter
    ACCESS  read-only
    STATUS  mandatory
    DESCRIPTION
            "The total number of SNMP PDUs which were
            generated by the SNMP protocol entity and for
            which the value of the error-status field is
            'genErr'."
    ::= { snmp 24 }

snmpOutGetRequests OBJECT-TYPE
    SYNTAX  Counter
    ACCESS  read-only
    STATUS  mandatory
    DESCRIPTION
            "The total number of SNMP Get-Request PDUs which
            have been generated by the SNMP protocol entity."
    ::= { snmp 25 }

snmpOutGetNexts OBJECT-TYPE
    SYNTAX  Counter
    ACCESS  read-only
    STATUS  mandatory
    DESCRIPTION
            "The total number of SNMP Get-Next PDUs which have
            been generated by the SNMP protocol entity."
    ::= { snmp 26 }

snmpOutSetRequests OBJECT-TYPE
    SYNTAX  Counter
    ACCESS  read-only
    STATUS  mandatory
    DESCRIPTION
            "The total number of SNMP Set-Request PDUs which
            have been generated by the SNMP protocol entity."
    ::= { snmp 27 }

snmpOutGetResponses OBJECT-TYPE
    SYNTAX  Counter
    ACCESS  read-only
    STATUS  mandatory
```

```
        DESCRIPTION
                "The total number of SNMP Get-Response PDUs which
                have been generated by the SNMP protocol entity."
        ::= { snmp 28 }

snmpOutTraps OBJECT-TYPE
        SYNTAX  Counter
        ACCESS  read-only
        STATUS  mandatory
        DESCRIPTION
                "The total number of SNMP Trap PDUs which have
                been generated by the SNMP protocol entity."
        ::= { snmp 29 }

snmpEnableAuthenTraps OBJECT-TYPE
        SYNTAX  INTEGER { enabled(1), disabled(2) }
        ACCESS  read-write
        STATUS  mandatory
        DESCRIPTION
                "Indicates whether the SNMP agent process is
                permitted to generate authentication-failure
                traps.  The value of this object overrides any
                configuration information; as such, it provides a
                means whereby all authentication-failure traps may
                be disabled.

                Note that it is strongly recommended that this
                object be stored in non-volatile memory so that it
                remains constant between re-initializations of the
                network management system.""
        ::= { snmp 30 }
END
```

APPENDIX D

BASIC ENCODING RULES (BER)

The Application layer is unique in that its data is described with Abstract Syntax Notation (ASN.1). **[Ref 1]**. ASN.1 is said to be abstract because its syntax is independent of programming languages and computer architectures. This approach allows all applications on all computers that make use of this standard to communicate. We have seen in **Appendix B** how ASN.1 is used to define the structure of MIB objects that are used by SNMP.

Abstract Syntax Notation must be encoded in binary format for use by the transport components of the protocol stacks on the communicating computers. This binary format is called the **Transfer Syntax** and the rules for encoding are called the Basic Encoding Rules **(BERs) [Ref 2].** We are now going to apply these Basic Encoding Rules to SNMP messages. One can ask why it is necessary to do this if the protocol analyzer translates between the binary format, created by applying the BER, and readable text. The answer is that you may want to be able to interpret all of the binary format which is presented in hexadecimal format. Protocol analyzers, like Meterware, typically translate only the data essential to the user. Application layers need more information to be able to communicate.

All ASN.1 data items are encoded using the following format: (see Figure D.1)

- The **TAG** field includes the ASN.1 data type, the class to which that data type belongs and a bit which specifies if the data type is simple or constructed. **[Ref 3]** A simple data type is, for example, a scalar like Integer. A constructed data type would, for example, be a list of simple data types.

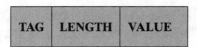

Figure D.1   BER Encoding Format for ASN.1 Data Items

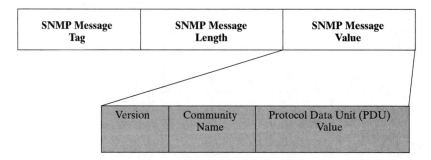

Figure D.2   The BER Encoding of the SNMP Message

- The **LENGTH** field is the number of octets (bytes) in the VALUE field
- The **VALUE** field may be structured. Thus the word "VALUE" is used in a very general way. The structure of this field depends on the ASN.1 data type as we will see.

Let's apply this discussion to the SNMP message in **Figure D.2 (Figure 6.2)**

The entire SNMP message is an ASN.1 data item that has a Tag and a Length and a Value, where Length is the length, in octets, of the Value field. This diagram provides a good picture of what is meant by a structured "Value" where there is more than one component to the "Value." The BERs actually call this a constructed value. Each component of the SNMP Message Value has a Tag, Length and Value. Thus the procedure we are following is recursive in which we keep expanding Value fields into Tag. Length and Value fields until we get to the actual data values. This process is called the BER Tag, Length, Value (TLV) encoding approach.

Continuing this process, **Figure D.3** shows the TLV encoding of the SNMP Message Value field.

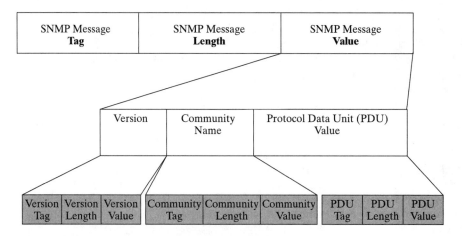

Figure D.3   TLV Encoding of the SNMP Message Value Field

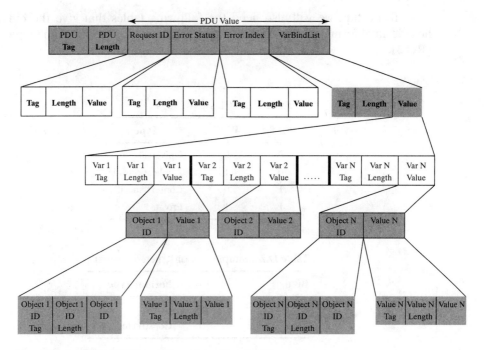

Figure D.4 BER TLV Encoding of the VarBindList

We have now completed the BER encoding of the Version and Community Name fields because their value fields, as we will see below, have only one component. However the PDU Value field has four components so we expand it into its TLV components in **Figure D.4.**

Figure D.4 shows the four fields of the PDU Value, Request ID, Error Status, Error Index and VarBindList. There is no need to expand the Value fields of Request ID, Error Status and Error Index because they are integers with one value. However, the VarBindList has a number of pairs of values, the number depending on the number of values requested by a Management Station or being returned by the Management Agent in response to such a request. As shown, each variable in the list has a TLV encoding. The value field of each variable contains two components, the Object ID and the Value of the Object. Each of these has a TLV encoding. The value field in the Object ID TLV encoding contains the SMI location of the object in the MIB tree. The value field in the Value TLV encoding contains the actual value of the object.

Protocol Analyzers decode the atomic or leaf TLV encodings. For the VarBindList component of the PDU "Value" in **Figure D.4,** only the value of the Object ID and the value of the object are decoded. Thus, there are a lot of hexadecimal characters in the SNMP packet and other Application layer packets that are not examined by the protocol analyzer. These are the Tag and Length characters in the TLV format. We will use the hexadecimal code in the Get-Response frame from SERVER to WS2-3 shown in **Figure 6.14** to examine these characters in the light of the discussion above.

To do this, we will also need the following tables that give the binary and hexadecimal formats for some ASN tags which are associated with the types shown **[Ref 3].**

Table D.1 Classes of Tags

Bit 8	Bit 7	Type
0	0	Universal
0	1	Applicationwide
1	0	Context-specific
1	1	Private

Table D.2 Simple or Constructed Format

Bit 6	Format Type
0	Simple
1	Constructed

Table D.3 Universal Class Tag Numbers

Type	Bit 5	Bit 4	Bit 3	Bit 2	Bit 1	Decimal	Format
Integer	0	0	0	1	0	2	simple
Octet String	0	0	1	0	0	4	simple
Null	0	0	1	0	1	5	simple
Object Identifier	0	0	1	1	0	6	simple
Sequence, Sequence of	1	0	0	0	0	16	constructed

Table D.4 Context-Specific Class Tag Numbers

Type	Bit 5	Bit 4	Bit 3	Bit 2	Bit 1	Decimal	Format
Get-Request PDU	0	0	0	0	0	0	constructed
Get-Next-Request PDU	0	0	0	0	0	1	constructed
Get-Response PDU	0	0	0	1	0	2	constructed
Set-Request PDU	0	0	0	1	1	3	constructed
Trap PDU	0	0	1	0	0	4	constructed

Now lets combine these tables into one that will help us to interpret the hexadecimal code more easily.

Table D.5 Binary, Hexadecimal and Decimal Formats for Some BER Tags

Tag Type	Bit 8	Bit 7	Bit 6	Bit 5	Bit 4	Bit 3	Bit 2	Bit 1	hex	decimal
Integer	0	0	0	0	0	0	1	0	**02**	2
Octet String	0	0	0	0	0	1	0	0	**04**	4
Null	0	0	0	0	0	1	0	1	**05**	5
Object Identifier	0	0	0	0	0	1	1	0	**06**	6
Sequence Sequence of	0	0	1	1	0	0	0	0	**30**	48
Get-Request	1	0	1	0	0	0	0	0	**A0**	160
Get-Next-Request	1	0	1	0	0	0	0	1	**A1**	161
Get-Response	1	0	1	0	0	0	1	0	**A2**	162
Set-Request	1	0	1	0	0	0	1	1	**A3**	163
Trap	1	0	1	0	0	1	0	0	**A4**	164

We now use **Table D.5** and **Figure 6.14,** included again here as Figure D.5, to interpret the hexadecimal code shown in that figure. The result is shown in **Table D.6**. All the hex values shown are also shown in Figure D.5.

There are 47 octets in the SNMP Message part of the hexadecimal data in the bottom panel of Figure 6.14. It begins with h30 on the far right of the first line and ends with h52 on the far right of the second line. Of the 47 octets, 26 octets are decoded by the Meterware application in the SNMP section of Figure D.5. Thus 21 octets represent Tag and Length values.

Table D.6 Explanation of SNMP Message in Figure 6.14 Bottom Panel

Field	SNMP Message Decode					
	TAG (binary)			TAG (hex)	Length (hex) # of Value bytes	Value (hex)
	Class	Format	Type			
Message	00	1	10000	30	2D	Constructed
Version	00	0	00010	02	01	00
Community Name	00	0	00100	04	06	70 75 62 6C 69 63 (public)
PDU	10	1	00010	A2	20	Constructed
Request ID	00	0	00010	02	02	of 33
Error Status	00	0	00010	02	01	00
Error Index	00	0	00010	02	01	00
VarBind List	00	1	10000	30	14	Constructed
Variable 1	00	1	10000	30	12	Constructed
Object 1 ID	00	0	00110	06	08	2B 06 01 02 01 01 05 00 (sysName.0)
Value 1	00	0	00100	04	06	53 45 52 56 45 52 (SERVER)

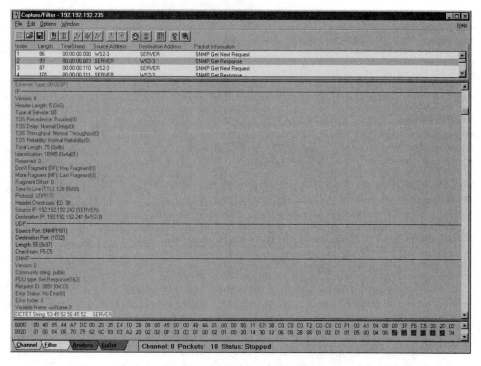

Figure D.5 Meterware Decode of GetResponse Message from Server to WS2-3

The Tag and Length values enable the Management Station to provide a consistent storage data structure for access by management applications.

REFERENCES

1. ISO/IEC 8824-1:1998, "Information technology—Abstract Syntax Notation One (ASN.1): Specification of basic notation," p. vii.

2. ISO/IEC 8825-1:1998, "Information Technology—ASN.1 encoding Rules: Specification of Basic Encoding Rules (BER), Canonical Encoding Rules (CER) and Distinguished Encoding Rules (DER)."

3. "Total SNMP," Sean Harnedy, CBM Books, 1994, pp. 48–50.

APPENDIX E

INFORMATION MANAGEMENT INITIATIVES

There are other important network management initiatives of which the reader should be aware. Their subject matter is not directly relevant to the purpose of this book; therefore, they were not included in the chapters. In addition, we could not have done justice to them in any reasonable number of pages. Because of their importance, however, this appendix provides a brief introduction to their capabilities.

E.1 TELECOMMUNICATIONS MANAGEMENT NETWORK (TMN)

The Telecommunications Management Network (TMN) concept was proposed to the International Telecommunications Union (ITU-T) in 1986 [Ref 1]. At that time, the ITU-T was called the CCITT. ITU-T Recommendation M.3010 "Principles for TMN" was published in 1992. M.3010 23/4 "Principles for a Telecommunications Management Network," that contained general principles for planning, operating and maintaining a TMN, was published somewhat later. Thus, the beginnings of this management activity in the ITU overlapped the beginnings of proposed network management activities in the United States. (See Chapter 2 for a review of U.S. activities.)

As telephony and data communications began to merge, the TMN Study Group activities began to include more effort in data communication management. Thus the TMN and the Internet Activities Board (IAB) in the United States continue to perform parallel but synergistic activities. This synergism can only increase as computer-based telephony continues to grow. In contrast to the focus of this book on LAN network management, the focus of TMN is naturally on WAN network management. A book on WAN network management, of the type we have written here, would certainly be of benefit to many readers.

In this book, we have discussed the Structure of Management Information (SMI) and the ASN.1 language used to construct SMI objects. However, because of the complexity of enterprise network management, over the past decade there have been industry-based initiatives to define comprehensive object-oriented architectures that would intrinsically incorporate the distributed and heterogeneous nature of the problem. We discuss some of these initiatives below.

E.2 WEB-BASED ENTERPRISE MANAGEMENT INITIATIVE (WBEM)

[Ref 2] introduces the Web-Based Enterprise Management Initiative **(WBEM)** and provides detailed references for it. The following statements from this reference effectively summarize the intent of the initiative.

"WBEM is a set of management and internet standard technologies developed to unify the management of enterprise computing environments. WBEM provides the ability for the industry to deliver a well-integrated set of standard management tools leveraging the emerging web technologies. The DMTF (Desktop Management Task Force) has developed a core set of standards that make up WBEM. These include a data model, the Common Information Model **(CIM)** standard; xmlCIM Encoding Specification; and a transport mechanism called **CIM operations over HTTP.**"

"CIM is a data model, a conceptual view of the managed environment, that attempts to unify and extend the existing instrumentation and management standards (SNMP, DMI. CMIP etc.) using object-oriented constructs and design."

"The value of CIM stems from its object orientation....Relationships between objects are extremely powerful concepts. Before CIM, management standards captured relationships in multi-dimensional arrays or cross-referenced data tables. The object paradigm offers a more elegant approach in that relationships and associations are directly modeled."

The Common Information Model **(CIM)** is described in **[Ref 3].** This reference provides tutorials on several levels depending on the interests of the reader. The CIM is divided into a **Core Model** and a **Common Model.** The Core Model captures notions that are applicable to all domains of management. The Common Model captures notions that are applicable to particular management domains that are independent of technology or implementation. The Common Models include Systems, Applications, Devices, Users and Networks There are also **Extension Models** that are technology and/or implementation specific.

The xmlCIM encoding specifications define XML Elements that can be used to represent CIM classes and instances. The CIM operations over HTTP define a mapping of CIM operations onto HTTP that allow these operations to interoperate in an open environment.

In Chapter 10, we examined the Desktop Management Interface (DMI). This interface is based on CIM, as you will see from **[Ref 3].** This reference comments on the classes Component ID and System Information that we saw when we used the DMI MIB Browser hosted by SERVER on our network.

In addition, when demonstrating Web-based management in Chapter 11, we implemented one of the WBEM concepts, CIM operations over HTTP, to manage the Cisco Catalyst 1900 switch (Switch 2) on our network.

E.3 COMMON OBJECT RESOURCE BROKER ARCHITECTURE (CORBA)

Some of the early work that led to CORBA was provided by Microsoft's Common Object Model (COM) and Distributed COM. COM and DCOM underlie Object Linking and Embedding (OLE), ActiveX and DirectX. **[Ref 4]** is an excellent introduction to the relationship between COM, DCOM and CORBA and to distinctions between COM and CORBA.

CORBA was designed by the Object Management Group (**OMG**)**[Ref 5]**. Like the DMTF, the OMG is a non-profit organization whose members are organizations that have an interest in establishing open standard models for computer communication networks that are based on the use of objects. The approach is not identical to that of the DMTF, but the founding principal is the same: developing a high-level model that can be used to guide the development of open and interoperable implementations in enterprise network management. A good introduction to the components of CORBA is provided by **[Ref 6]**. **[Ref 5]** provides access to statements by a large number of companies, by industry sector, which have made use of the CORBA approach.

E.4 INTEGRATION OF MANAGEMENT INFORMATION

The number of enterprise ISPs and telephony networks in today's IT environment is certainly large. Commensurate with this number, is the need to manage an even larger number of devices and software applications on these networks and evaluate their performance and availability to the user. Such management is usually done on a network by network basis using tools, such as SNMP, that have been discussed in this book. The problem with the network-by-network approach to management is not the technology or a lack of data-gathering tools, but the lack of a comprehensive and intelligent data management plan. To put it another way, as is typical of our society, there is too much data and not enough knowledge.

Tools such as IBM's "Tivoli Manager for Network Hardware" **[Ref 7]** address part of this problem. It provides the capability to store enterprise-wide inventory data in a central location. Information is available through a common user interface that makes use of the Desktop Management Taskforce (DMTF) Common Information Model (CIM) discussed above. It also couples Network Management Applications (NMAs) that provide a common data format and open interfaces with the centralized repository that holds data from all NMAs.

Tools by Micromuse, under the name Netcool, **[Ref 8],** address the problem by creating a dynamic repository of trap messages from trap agents throughout the enterprise and analyzing the traps to determine the critical faults from various enterprise perspectives. **Figure E.1,** copied with permission from a Netcool/OMNIbus™ Users Manual, provides an overview of the Netcool/OMNIbus Integrated Architecture.

In the middle-left of the figure is the Netcool **Object Server™.** It is the core of the system where all trap events are stored and managed. A Netcool **Probe™** is software resident on servers that collect trap messages from network Management Stations and forward them to the Netcool Object Server for analysis. Netcool **Monitors™** are server resident applications that act as users of services to test their availability. Netcool **Gateways™** are server-resident software that provide transparent connectivity with other Netcool Object Servers, complimentary applications, Relational Database Management Systems, help desk systems and other management systems using, for example, SNMP or CMIS. A suite of applications can be used on UNIX, Java or NT 4.0 operating systems platforms. These applications interact with Object Servers to provide the user with graphical views of network events and analyses of these events.

In summary, the purpose of Netcool/OMNIbus and other Netcool tools is to provide integration of fault management events in service provider and enterprise networks that can be analyzed and addressed before they cause a failure in service. The solution comprises a combination of tools and Netcool Object Server to enable

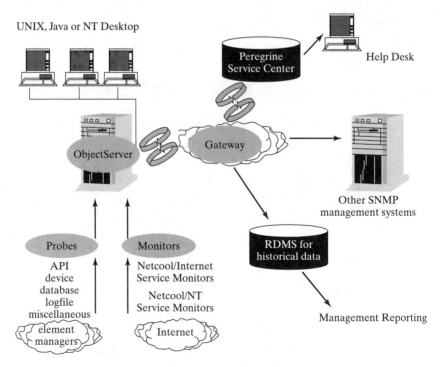

Figure E.1 The Micromuse Netcool/OMNIbus™ Architecture. (Reprinted with permission from Micromuse Inc. 2002 Copyright Micromuse Inc. All rights reserved.)

rapid analysis of a large number of events quickly to determine those that are critical to the business model of the operation being monitored. The traps that are analyzed are generated by RMON1 Alarm and Event group objects that we studied.

REFERENCES

1. "ITU TMN Roadmap," http://www.itu.int/TMN/.
2. "Web-Based Enterprise Management (WBEM) Initiative," http://www.dmtf.org/standards/standard_wbem.php.
3. "Education: CIM Tutorial," http://www.dmtf.org/education/cimtutorial/using/conc.php# Object-OrientedModeling.
4. "COM vs. CORBA : A Decision Framework," http://www.quoininc.com/company/articles/COM_CORBA.pdf.
5. "Object Management Group," http://www.corba.org./.
6. "CORBA : Getting Started," http://www.omg.org/gettingstarted/corbafaq.htm.
7. "Tivoli Manager for Network Hardware," http://www-4.ibm.com/software/sysmgmt/products/mgr_netinventory.html.
8. "Micromuse: Netcool Solutions," http://www.micromuse.com/.

APPENDIX F

ADDITIONAL METERWARE TOOLS

When Meterware was used in the chapters of this book, we focused on the tools that were most instructive for those chapters. In this Appendix, we examine other useful features in more detail

F.1 DEVICE DISCOVERY

You have seen from the Meterware Summary View (e.g., Figure 7.12 in Chapter 7), that when Meterware first opens, it gradually displays which devices are "up," the names of the devices, their IP addresses, the type of media to which the device is connected, the SNMP capability of the device, etc. This and other information, such as the number of device interfaces, the physical address of the interfaces and the SNMP Read and Write community names of the devices are displayed on the device Information screen (e.g., Figure 7.13 in Chapter 7) that can be accessed by double-clicking the device in Summary View.

The data for these initial displays are obtained from SNMP Get-Request messages that Meterware sends to each of its "seed" addresses. This Discovery process is only possible if at least one seed IP address is provided as requested by Meterware during the start-up process. The seed address must be that of a device that supports the RMON1 standard and at a minimum collects data for and supports the RMON1 statistics group. Such devices include the Cisco switches and routers, 3Com Hub and the Technically Elite probes 1 and 2 on the demonstration network.

The SNMP packets sent to one or more seeds collect information about other RMON devices about which the seeds know. Eventually, all RMON devices on the network are known and the Port Summary View for discovered RMON devices is complete. Recognize that this process can be extremely bandwidth demanding for a large network and may not be always be a practical solution.

Even when this approach is practical, it is still necessary to identify devices that do not support the RMON standard. Identification of such devices is a manual process that is accomplished using the Edit menu of Meterware and selecting New Device. Using the palette of new devices provided on the right side of the New Device screen, devices such as PCs and Workstations can be added to the Summary View. All that is necessary is to complete the Infromation screen for the device. Although manually intensive, this is a reliable approach to device identification.

Throughout this book, we have used the Meterware Summary screen. Meterware also provides another screen called MAP View. This view is a graphical representation of Summary View. For our network, MAP View is as shown in **Figure F.1** except for Chapter 12 where another Cisco router is added.

The devices that support the RMON1 standard are automatically placed in this view during startup of Meterware. Such devices, in the case of our network, are Ethermeter, Fastmeter, Switch 2, Switch 1 and the Router interfaces (Router1 and Router2). Other devices must be manually added by using the Edit menu and selecting New Device as stated above.

The palette on the right allows you to select the icon you want for a device if you so desire. Otherwise, the Information window will provide the icon. The connections between devices must also be done manually. Click the Help menu and select Help on this Screen to see how to make connections. The drawing palette on the left allows you to add text as was done here to identify the subnets. Select the

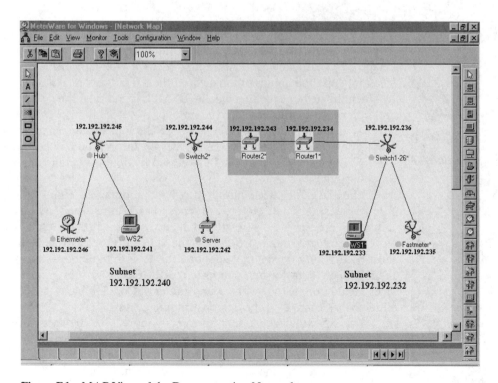

Figure F.1 MAP View of the Demonstration Network

"A" icon to do that. The router is shown as two routers. This is a characteristic of Meterware that requires an icon for each interface. The colored dots next to each device indicate its status. A green dot indicates the device is up. A red dot indicates it is down. A blue dot indicates the status is unknown. A yellow dot indicates the device sent a trap to management stations. You can clear the yellow dots by right-clicking the device and then clicking "Clear Alarms." The result will be a colored dot that indicates device staus. All dots are green in this map so all devices are "up." (Because color is not used in this text, you will not be able to see the colors in MAP View but you will be able to do so when using the NMS software provided.)

The MAP View is typical of a screen that is used to monitor the status of devices on large networks. By the color of the dot in this case or of the icon in other management applications, it is immediately obvious which devices need attention. Problems with such devices can be often be corrected remotely.

There are many other features of the Meterware MAP View that can be explored with the Users Guide on the CD-ROM. For example, for large production networks with may subnets, you can make a multilevel network diagram in which each level is represented in the main diagram by the appropriate icon from the palette on the right of **Figure F.1.**

F.2 TEMPLATES

We have used the MIB Browser to get values of selected MIB variables for a device. The use of templates is a convenient way to access the values of a set of MIB objects of regular interest, automatically. There are pre-defined standard and device-dependent templates provided by Meterware. It is also possible to create custom templates. We look first at a pre-defined standard template.

Starting with the Summary View screen of Meterware, from the Tools menu, select Template Editor to get the screen shown in **Figure F.2.**

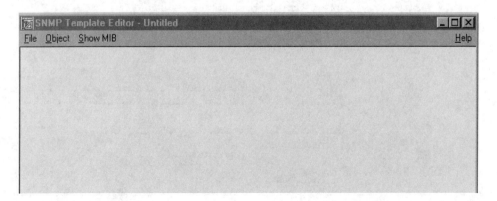

Figure F.2 Template Editor Screen

We will add MIB objects to this screen. From the File menu, select open to see some of the list of pre-defined templates as shown in **Figure F.3.** All the template files have the extension .tpl and are stored in the Mware.tpl directory.

We have selected one of the simplest templates, udp.tpl, so that we can use it to access MIB information from any device. We will use WS2 as the example device. Clicking the Open button in **Figure F.3** generates the screen in the background of **Figure F.4.**

The background screen shows the four SNMP udp scalar MIB object labels and the udp table object label. GET in the center column indicates objects that are scalar objects, i.e., only one answer is returned whereas TABLE indicates that many values may be contained in this object. The right column contains the OIDs for the objects. No OID is shown for the table object. The foreground screen shows the two column objects in the udp table, their OID and the number of rows allotted to each.

To collect values of these MIB objects from WS2, we go to the Meterware Summary View screen and double click WS2 to get its Information screen and then click the Templates to get **Figure F.5.** In this figure, the template udp.tpl is selected. Click View to get **Figure F.6.**

In the boxes in the upper part of the figure, you see the values of the four scalar objects that were requested from the agent on WS2. These are a snapshot of the totals at the time this screen was captured. Two important things to notice are that the number of errors detected (udpNoErrors) is zero and that udpNoPorts is 303. udpNoPorts represents the number of datagrams that were received for which there was no application listening at the port where they were received. There

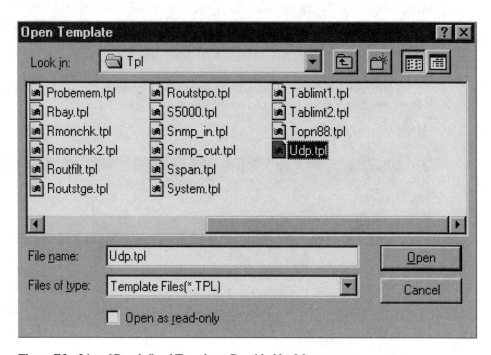

Figure F.3 List of Pre-defined Templates Provided by Meterware

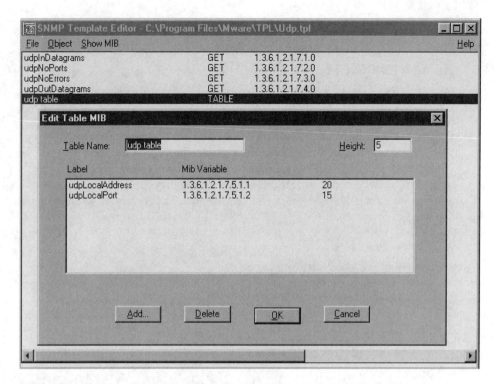

Figure F.4 "Background Screen": Listing of Available MIB Objects. "Foreground Screen": Listing of MIB Objects in the udp table.

could be good or bad reasons for there being so many udpNoPorts. A network manager might want to know which is true.

The udpLocalPort 1032 in the udptable is a **"Registered port,"** i.e., a port registered by the **Internet Assigned Numbers Authority [Ref 1]** to another organization. Port 69 is the **"Well Known"** port "Bootstrap Protocol Client" If WS2 were a computer without permanent storage media, port 69 would be used by the associated Bootstrap server to download an operating system that would boot WS2. Ports 161 and 162 are SNMP and Trap "Well Known Ports," respectively. The SNMP agent listens on these ports. Ports 137 and 138 are the "Well Known" NetBIOS Name Service and NetBIOS Datagram Service ports, respectively. The IP address 192.192.192.241 is the IP address of WS2 on network 192.192.192.0.

Things get a little more interesting if we use Dial-up to create a network between WS2 and an ISP using Internet Explorer. The results are shown in **Figure F.7.**

Here we see that WS2 has udpLocalAddress 12.93.73.244 and udpLocalAddress 192.192.192.241. Thus, WS2 is connected to our demonstration network and to a network between WS2 and an ISP, i.e., it is multihomed. Both networks are communicating with the NetBIOS Name Service port 137 to relate the name and IP address of WS2 and with NetBIOS Datagram Service port 138 to send and or receive messages using the udp transport protocol.

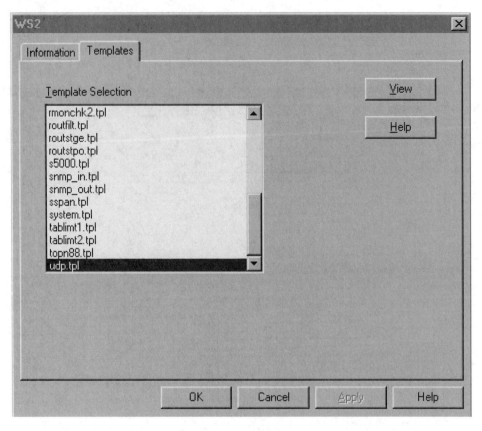

Figure F.5 Pre-defined Template Selection for WS2

Figure F.6 udp Template View for WS2

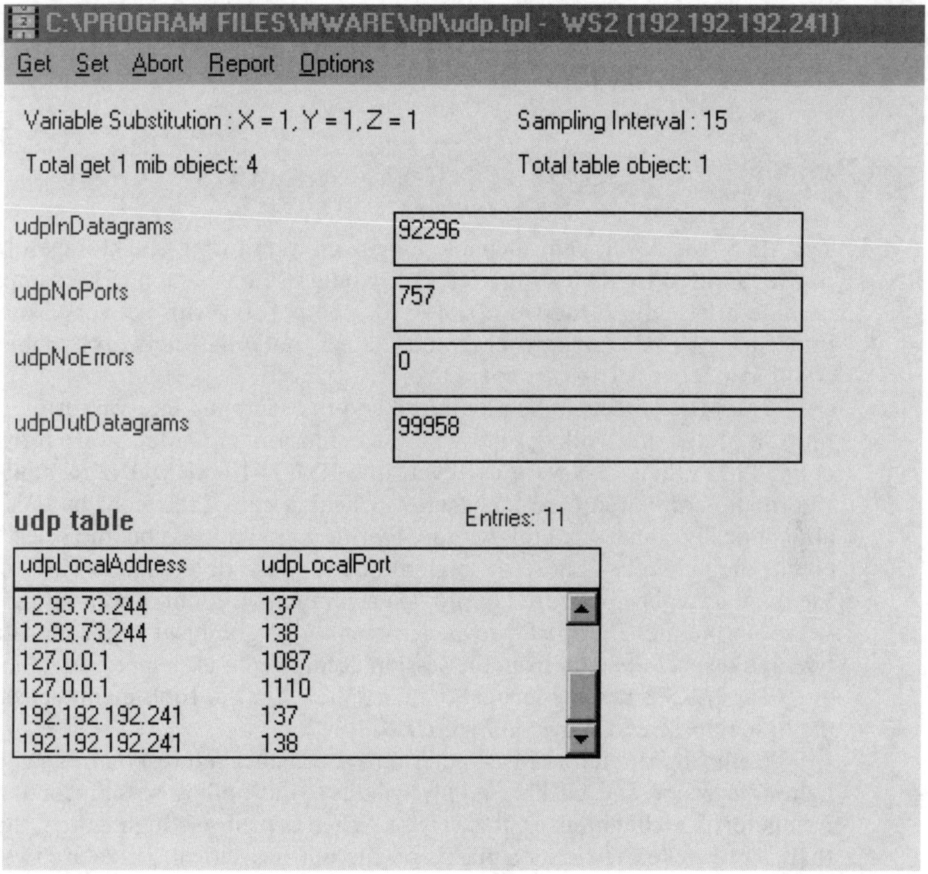

Figure F.7   Another udp Template View for WS2

IP address 127.0.0.1 is the "Loopback Address" that is used by processes internal to WS2 to communicate. In this example, port 1087 is being used for communication by the "CPL Scrambler." Presumably, this application provides encryption/decryption of messages between the ISP site and WS2. The "Loopback Address" is also being used to "keep alive" communications between the ISP and WS2. The purpose of this simple example is for the reader to see that a simple template, such as udp.tpl, can provide a check on both LAN and WAN communications.

The principal advantage of using a template is to group together MIB objects whose values are important and that you want to access readily. Therefore, you may want to create custom templates for some devices that include only objects important to you. Now that you have seen what a pre-defined template can do for you, you can create your own templates, **See pages 278–286 of the on-line Users Manual** on the Meterware/Analyzer CD for instructions on how to do that.

In the next section, we examine the Meterware Reporting System **(MRS).** MRS will enable you to create documentation based on the results of polling MIB objects on devices of particular interest.

F.3 METERWARE REPORTING SYSTEM (MRS)

The **MRS** was developed to enable long-term monitoring and storage of network traffic captured by RMON probes. One would use this system, for example, to determine a baseline of network traffic for comparison with network samples captured later. This comparison could detect potential network problems that additional network capacity could avoid.

The MIB objects to be monitored and the sampling interval for them are defined in **Meterware Polling Files** with the extension .mpf. Meterware provides predefined **MPF** files that were used with the RMON1 or RMON2 tabs on a device Information screen in Chapters 8 and 9. Clicking one of the icons on those screens automatically starts a polling session. During a polling session, the selected probe counts the number of packets received for each MIB object in the MPF file. Either the session can be configured to provide a cumulative count or a count for an interval set in the file. The MRS provides a number of graphical applications that analyze and display the data from the session according to user specified criteria.

The MRS is accessed from Summary View. On the Tools menu, select Reporting to see the screen shown in **Figure F.8.**

Both Ethermeter and Fastmeter have been checked (✓) on this screen. Highlighting a probe and clicking Apply will start the polling session for that probe. Fastmeter is highlighted on this screen. When a probe is highlighted, the reports that can be generated are highlights on the buttons shown. There are two types of reports; Trends and Station. Station reports focus on individual devices. The availability of the reports depends on the amount of time that has been configured for data to be captured by the MIB Poller. Clicking on the View Sessions shows the MIB Poller screen in **Figure F.9** when Ethermeter is highlighted.

The top panel shows the MPF file named ERMON1.MPF. It contains the three tables shown in the bottom panel. The configuration of the RmonHost table, for example, is shown in **Figure F.10.**

Interval = 600 sec means the MIB Poller application will poll the SNMP agent on Ethermeter every 600 sec (10 minutes) for values of the MIB Names shown in **Figure F.10.** Type = Delta means that the difference between the value of the Counter for each MIB object at the start of interval and at the end of the interval will be presented. To see these records, you would double-click RmonHost in **Figure F.10.**

The Reporting System in **Figure F.8** can be used to generate reports about the highlighted subjects, such as Utilization, that are based on the records the MIB Poller collects. The screens provided by the Reporting System can be graphed in a variety of ways that are chosen from its menu bar. As mentioned above, such graphs can be used as archives of network traffic to which future traffic patterns can be compared.

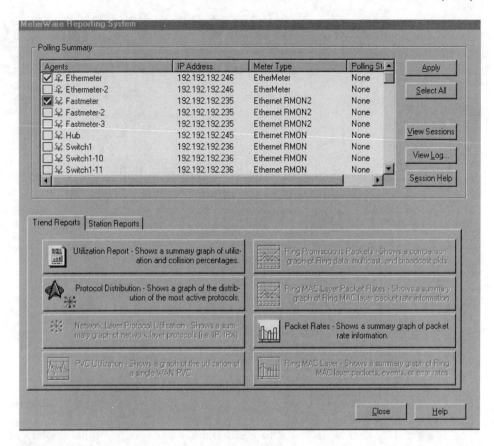

Figure F.8   Meterware's Reporting System Screen

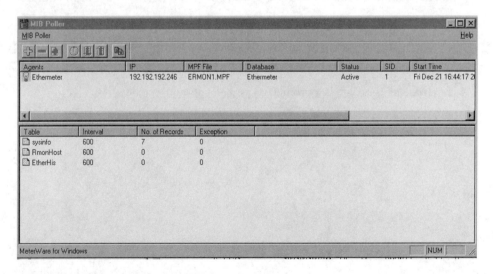

Figure F.9   MIB Poller Screen for Ethermeter

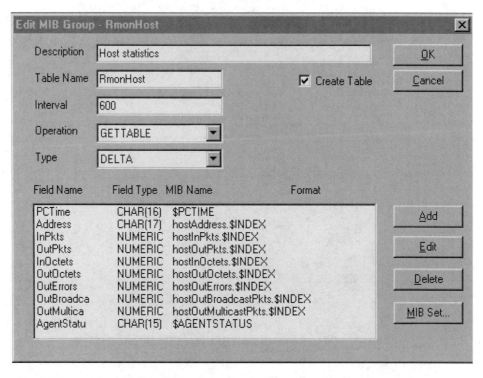

Figure F.10   Ethermeter RmonHost MIB Objects File

With this section, and what has been demonstrated in previous chapters, most of the capabilities of Meterware/Analyzer have been covered. However, there are more capabilities that you can use as you gain experience with your network.

REFERENCE

1. "Port Numbers," http://www.iana.org/assignments/port-numbers.

ACRONYMS

ANSI   American National Standards Institute
API   Application Program Interface
ARP   Address Resolution Protocol
ARPA   Advance Research Projects Agency
AS   Autonomous System
ASCII   American Standard Code for Information Interchange
ASN.1   Abstract Syntax Notation.1
ATM   Asynchronous Transfer Mode
AUI   Attachment Unit Interface
BDC   Backup Domain Controller
BER   Basic Encoding Rules
BGP   Border Gateway Protocol
BIOS   Basic Input/Output System
BNC   Bayonet-Neill-Concelman connector
CBC   Cypher Block Chaining
CCITT   Consultative Committee for Telegraphy and Telephony (now ITU-T)
CI   Component Interface
CIM   Common Interface Model
CMIP   Common Management Information Protocol
CMOT   CMIP over TCP
COM   Microsoft Common Object Model
CORBA   Common Object Resource Broker Architecture
CSMA/CD   Carrier Sense Multiple Access with Collision Detection
DBMS   Database Management System
DCE   Data Circuit Terminating Equipment
DCOM   Microsoft Distributed Common Object Model
DES   Data Encryption Standard

DHCP   Dynamic Host Configuration Protocol
DISMAN   Distributed Management Working Group
DMA   Direct Memory Access
DMI   Desktop Management Initiative
DMISA   Desktop Management Interface Subagent
DMTF   Desktop Management Task Force
DNS   Domain Name Service
DOCSIS   Digital Over Cable System Interface Specification
DPI   Distributed Protocol Interface
DQDB   Dual Queue Dual Bus
DTE   Data Terminal Equipment
EGP   Exterior Gateway Protocol
EIA   Electronics Industries Association
EOS   Evolution of SNMP
FCS   Frame Check Sequence
FDDI   Fiber Distributed Data Interface
FTAM   File Transfer Access Management
FTP   File Transfer Protocol
HMACMD5   Hashing Function that generates the Message Access Code (MAC) using Message Digest Version 5
HMACSHA   Hashing Function that generates the Message Access Code (MAC) using the Secure Hashing Algorithm
HTTP   Hypertext Transfer Protocol
IAB   Internet Activities Board
IANA   Internet Assigned Numbers Authority
ICMP   Internet Control Message Protocol
IEC   International Electrotechnical Commission
IEEE   Institute of Electrical and Electronic Engineers
IESG   Internet Engineering Steering Group
IETF   Internet Engineering Task Force
IGRP   Inteior Gateway Routing Protocol
IIS   Microsoft Internet Information Server
IP   Internet Protocol
IPS   Internet Service Provider
IPX   Internet Packet Exchange
IRP   Interior Routing Protocol
IRQ   Interrupt Request
ISA   Industry Standard Architecture
ISO   International Organization for Standardization
ITU   International Telecommunication Union
LAN   Local Area Network
LCD   Local Configuration Datastore
LLC   Logical Link Control
MAC   Message Access Code
MAC   Medium Access Control
MD   Message Digest

MI   Management Interface
MIB   Management Information Base
MIF   Management Information File
MPD   Message Processing and Dispatcher
MTBF   Mean Time Between Failures
NBT   NetBIOS over TCP/IP
NDIS   Network Device Interface Specification
NIC   Network Interface Card
NID   Network Intrusion Detector
NIST   National Institute of Standards and Technology
NMS   Network Management System
NVT   Network Virtual Terminal
ODI   Open Datalink Interface
OID   Object Identifier
OLE   Object Linking and Embedding
OMG   Object Management Group
OSI   Open System Interconnection protocol
OSPF   Open Shortest Path First routing protocol
PCI   Peripheral Component Interface
PDC   Primary Domain Controller
PDU   Protocol Data Unit
PING   Packet Internet Groper
POP   Post Office Protocol
PPP   Point-to-Point Protocol
PSTN   Public Switched Telephone Network
QoS   Quality of Service
RARP   Reverse Address Resolution Protocol
RFC   Request for Comment
RIP   Routing Information Protocol
RMON   Remote Monitoring
ROSE   Remote Operations Service Element
RPC   Remote Procedure Call
SAME   System Application Management Entity
SGMP   Simple Gateway Management Protocol
SHA   Secure Hash Algorithm
SLA   Service Level Agreement
SLIP   Serial Line Internet Protocol
SMDS   Switched Multi-megabit Data Service
SMI   Structure of Management Information
SMTP   Simple Mail Transport Protocol
SNAP   Subnetwork Address Protocol
SNMP   Simple Network Management Protocol
SONET   Synchronous Optical Network
SPAN   Switched Port Analyzer
SPX   Sequenced Packet Exchange
TC   Textual Convention

TCP   Transmission Control Protocol
TFTP   Trivial File Transfer Protocol
TIA   Telecommunications Industries Association
TLV   Tag, Length, Value coding
TMN   Telecommunications Management Network
TOS   Type of Service
UART   Universal Asynchronous Receiver/Transmitter
UDP   User Datagram Protocol
USM   User-Based Security Model
VACM   View-Based Control Model
VLAN   Virtual Local Area Network
VSNAP   Vendor Subnetwork Address Protocol
WAN   Wide Area Network
WBEM   Web Based Enterprise Management Initiative
WINS   Windows Internet Name Service
XML   Markup Language of Type X

GLOSSARY

Address Resolution Protocol (ARP)   Broadcasts a MAC destination address. Receiver with that address returns its IP address.

alMatrix Group (RMON 2)   Objects that characterize communications between hosts at the Application layer.

Area   Set of devices in an Autonomous System. Areas and Autonomous Systems are used by OSPF to confine routing table traffic.

arpa   Router configuration parameter specifying that the Ethernet II frame is to be used in all communications with this router.

Attribute   In the context of the Desktop Management Interface (DMI), a set of Elements that characterizes a host component, i.e., hardware, software of firmware.

authKey   Key unique to the user and a SNMPv3 agent that is derived from the "clone-from" user authentication password.

Autodiscovery   Network Management System (NMS) process that broadcasts SNMP "Get-Requests" to determine what devices are attached to the network and queries existing SNMP agents for values of MIB objects that determine the SNMP configuration of the agent.

Autonomous System   A set of one or more networks that use the same routing protocol.

Border Gateway Protocol (BGP)   Used by Boundary Routers to communicate between Autonomous Systems.

Border Routers   Link OSPF Areas.

Boundary Router   Connects Autonomous Systems.

Capture Group (RMON 1)   Objects that configures how a probe is to use capture buffers.

Channel   Probe buffer that stores packets characterized by values of objects in the RMON buffer Control Table.

Clause   An ASN.1 construct that is used by a MACRO to specify an object data type and its value.

Column Object   MIB table object name.

Common Object Resource Broker (CORBA)   Architecture designed by the non-profit organization Object Management Group (OMG) to establish open networking standards based on the use of objects.

Community Name   An SNMP password used in SNMPv1 messages to limit access to Management Agents.

Console   Serial port on a device that is used by a host computer to monitor and configure the device.

Context   A collection of MIB objects accessible by a SNMP entity. The SNMPv3 PDU contains a context field that can be completed to limit the number of MIB objects being returned.

Control Table   RMON MIB object whose entries determine what data in related tables is captured by a probe.

Desktop Extension Agent   Vendor-specific software that adds SNMPv1 MIB objects to those supported by the original equipment manufacturer (OEM)

DMI Attribute Elements   Elements define "attributes" in DMI the way "clauses" define objects in a MIB.

DMI Component   Manageable hardware, software or firmware.

DMI Component Instrumentation (CI)   Vendor-specific code that provides access to the manageable aspects of a "component."

Dynamic Address   MAC destination address that will be dropped from an address table in a configured time after storage unless another frame from that source address has been received.

Enterprise   A Management Information Tree object that contains objects defined by private organizations.

Filter   Values of objects in the RMON MIB filter table that filter a Channel buffer to specified packets.

Filter Group (RMON 1)   Object that specify the details of which packets are to be captured and stored in a buffer.

Flooding   Distributing a frame received by a switch out of all ports if the MAC destination address in the frame is not contained in the switch table.

Full-Duplex   Link that supports communications in both directions simultaneously.

getmany   SNMP Research Command-line executable that implements multiple SNMP Get-Next-Request commands for values of all objects in a MIB table for all SNMP versions

getone   SNMP Research Command-line executable that implements the SNMP Get-Request command for all SNMP versions.

Group   Set of related MIB objects.

Half-Duplex   Link that supports communications in both directions but only one direction at a time.

Host MIB   Objects that specify host resources such as device and storage characteristics.

Hub   Device that provides a centralized LAN implementation using an Ethernet configuration.

Index Object   An object whose value is concatenated with a Column Object name and other Index Objects to identify a column object value in a MIB Table.

IP Class Leading bits of the network part IP address used by a router to determine the network class.

IP Subnet Addressing Enables the creation of subnetwork addresses within the host address space.

IP Subnet Mask Thirty-two bit set of "1s" and "0s" used with the IP address to determine the subnetwork address.

Local Area Network (LAN) A geographically small network that provides interconnection of a variety of communicating devices.

MACRO (OBJECT-TYPE) ASN.1 type used to define MIB objects.

Management Agent Software that manages the storage and retrieval of information about the host on which it is installed.

Management Information Base (MIB) Virtual Database of information collected about a device by protocols in the protocol stack on the device.

Management Information File (MIF) Defines the "attributes" of a Desktop Management Interface (DMI) hardware, software or firmware "component."

Matrix Group (RMON 1) Objects that identify and characterize communications at the network level between specific hosts.

MIF Attribute Analogous to a MIB object in DMI.

module An ASN.1 construct that includes Export, Import, and Assignment List clauses. The Export clause specifies definitions that can be used by other modules. The Import clause specifies definitions that can be used with "this" module. The Assignment List assigns names to types and values.

Monitor Port Port on a switch to which copies of traffic received or transmitted by other specified ports are sent for monitoring by a device such as a probe.

Network Management System (NMS) A set of applications residing on a Management Station that configures, accesses, displays and analyzes information on a Management Agent device.

nlHost Group (RMON 2) Objects that characterize communications between hosts at the OSI Network layer.

OBJECT IDENTIFIER Set of integers, separated by dots (.), that describes the location of the object in the Management Information Tree of OBJECT IDENTIFIERS.

Object Instance Identifier The concatenation of a Column Object name with values of Index Objects, separated by dots, that identifies a Column Object value in a MIB Table.

Open Shortest Path First (OSPF) A routing protocol that is more comprehensive than RIP. It differs primarily as follows: 1) Distributes only changes in routing table and 2) computes "path cost" by integrating a number of variables such as number of hops, throughput and link traffic.

Open System Interconnection (OSI) Reference Model Seven-layer stack of protocols specified by the ISO to guide the development of interoperable communication standards.

Package Collection of Policies to be distributed to an SNMP agent for implementation.

Packet (SNMP) Consists of three fields: Protocol Version, Community Name and Protocol Data Unit (PDU).

Path Cost Measure of the bandwidth of a port. Used by the Spanning Tree Protocol to determine which port to disconnect when eliminating a loop in the network. Path Cost = 1000/Port Bandwidth in Mbits/sec.

PDU Type Choice of Get-Request, Get-Response, Get-Next-Request, Set-Request or Trap commands.

Ping Executable that determines communication connectivity between peer IP layers.

Policy Collection of MIB Views and users who have identical privileges to perform management operations within those views.

Primary Domain Controller (PDC) In Windows NT 4.0, a computer that hosts the Server Operating System and controls access to its resources, those of other computers in the domain and those of computers in other domains.

privKey Key unique to the user and a SNMPv3 agent that is derived from the "clone-from" user encryption password.

Probe Device that is configurable by an NMS to capture network traffic statistics specific to an OSI protocol layer.

Protocol Data Unit (SNMPv1) Consists of five fields: PDU Type, Request ID, Error Status, Error Index and VarBindList.

protocolDirGroup (RMON 2) Objects that characterize protocol encapsulations in all layers of the OSI Reference Model.

protocolDirID (RMON 2) Object that defines protocols and their hierarchical order in a frame.

protocolDirParameters (RMON 2) Object that specifies capabilities of a particular protocol in the protocolDirID.

protocolDirType (RMON 2) Object that specifies particular attributes of a protocol relative to others in the protocolDirID.

Proxy For example, 1) a SNMP Agent that supports access to MIB objects on devices that do not implement an Agent or 2) an SNMP Agent that translates between different SNMP versions.

Restricted Address MAC destination address that is associated with a list of ports that may send frames to the restricted address.

RMON1 MIB Contains objects that describe network traffic at the OSI Data Link layer such as MAC Addresses.

RMON2 MIB Contains objects that describe network traffic at all layers of the OSI Reference Model.

Router Device that establishes connections to other routers based on the destination network address.

Routing Information Protocol (RIP) Sends the entire routing table every thirty seconds to routers on adjacent networks. These routers likewise distribute their routing tables. Thus, all routing tables are quickly distributed throughout the network. Routing paths are selected based on "path cost." In RIP, path cost is the number of hops between routers to reach the destination network.

Routing Table Mapping of router ports to destination network addresses.

setany SNMP Research Command-line executable that implements the SNMP Set operation for all SNMP versions.

Simple Network Management Protocol (SNMP)   A protocol of the TCP/IP Application Layer that implements connectionless communication of management information between network devices.

SMIv2   Structure of Management Information for SNMPv2.

SNMP Engine   Consists of the agent processes that handle message control, message processing, security and access.

SNMPv2   Enhanced version of SNMPv1 providing improved protocol operations.

SNMPv3   The latest SNMP standard that provides "industrial strength" security using Strong Authentication and encryption.

Spanning Tree Protocol (STP)   Reconfigures bridge or switch ports as necessary to eliminate network loops.

Static Address   MAC destination address that will remain stored in a switch address table.

Strategy (Implementation)   An evaluation of resources required and technology available to provide a cost-effective management strategy to support the corporate business model.

Strategy (Management)   Evaluation of what management information is necessary in order to maintain performance required to meet the demands of the corporate business model.

Structure of Management Information (SMI)   Specification of how information is to be managed. Information is described by a data structure of objects whose content is formally specified by Abstract Syntax Notation.1.

Subagent   Manages a set of functionally related objects that describe part of all objects managed by an Agent.

Switch   Conventionally, a device that establishes connections between it's ports based on the destination hardware address. Other layers of protocols are used in current switches.

Switched Port Analyzer (SPAN)   Monitor port on a Cisco switch that collects copies of frames received or transmitted by configured ports for analysis by an attached probe.

Telecommunications Management Network (TMN)   General principles for telecommunications network management that originally dealt with telephony management of WAN's when proposed to the CCITT (now ITU-T) in 1986. Data management is now involved also.

TLV   Basic Encoding Rules (BER) schema that prepends Tag and Length fields to the SNMP Value field (the message) to construct the Transfer Syntax that will be sent over the "wire." The hexadecimal code at the bottom of all Analyzer Capture screens is TLV coding.

Transmission Control Protocol (TCP)/Internet Protocol (IP)   A four layer stack of protocols that implements either connection-oriented or connectionless communication between network devices.

Trap   An informative, unsolicited message from a Management Agent to a Management Station.

User Based Security Model (USM)   Employs a passphrase (password) and an SNMP Engine ID to configure authentication and encryption for the user of a device that hosts an SNMPv3 agent.

View   A set of managed objects, within a Context, that specifies the objects accessible to the user and the access rights to those objects.

View-based Access Control Model (VACM)   Implemented by the objects in a (four) table set that includes the vacmContextTable, vacmAccessTable, vacmViewTreeFamilyTable, vacmSecurityToGroupTable to control user access.

VLAN   LANs that can be connected to one another by intra-switch circuits. Each Virtual LAN is isolated as if by a firewall.

Web Based Enterprise Management Initiative (WBEM)   Initiative to deliver a set of well-integrated management and Internet standard technologies leveraging emerging Web technologies.

Wide Area Network (WAN)   A network of unlimited size in which circuit switches and/or packet switches route messages between smaller networks such as LANs.

Windows Internet Name Service (WINS)   Provides a mapping of NetBIOS device names on the local network to IP addresses.

wsnmp   IBN System View Command-line executable that provides SNMPv1 operations.

INDEX

Pearson Prentice Hall License Agreement and Limited Warranty

READ THE FOLLOWING TERMS AND CONDITIONS CAREFULLY BEFORE OPENING THIS SOFTWARE PACKAGE. THIS LEGAL DOCUMENT IS AN AGREEMENT BETWEEN YOU AND PEARSON EDUCATION, INC. (THE "COMPANY"). BY OPENING THIS SEALED SOFTWARE PACKAGE, YOU ARE AGREEING TO BE BOUND BY THESE TERMS AND CONDITIONS. IF YOU DO NOT AGREE WITH THESE TERMS AND CONDITIONS, DO NOT OPEN THE SOFTWARE PACKAGE. PROMPTLY RETURN THE UNOPENED SOFTWARE PACKAGE AND ALL ACCOMPANYING ITEMS TO THE PLACE YOU OBTAINED THEM FOR A FULL REFUND OF ANY SUMS YOU HAVE PAID.

1. GRANT OF LICENSE: In consideration of your purchase of this book, and your agreement to abide by the terms and conditions of this Agreement, the Company grants to you a nonexclusive right to use and display the copy of the enclosed software program (hereinafter the "SOFTWARE") on a single computer (i.e., with a single CPU) at a single location so long as you comply with the terms of this Agreement. The Company reserves all rights not expressly granted to you under this Agreement.

2. OWNERSHIP OF SOFTWARE: You own only the magnetic or physical media (the enclosed media) on which the SOFTWARE is recorded or fixed, but the Company and the software developers retain all the rights, title, and ownership to the SOFTWARE recorded on the original media copy(ies) and all subsequent copies of the SOFTWARE, regardless of the form or media on which the original or other copies may exist. This license is not a sale of the original SOFTWARE or any copy to you.

3. COPY RESTRICTIONS: This SOFTWARE and the accompanying printed materials and user manual (the "Documentation") are the subject of copyright. The individual programs on the media are copyrighted by the authors of each program. Some of the programs on the media include separate licensing agreements. If you intend to use one of these programs, you must read and follow its accompanying license agreement. You may not copy the Documentation or the SOFTWARE, except that you may make a single copy of the SOFTWARE for backup or archival purposes only. You may be held legally responsible for any copying or copyright infringement which is caused or encouraged by your failure to abide by the terms of this restriction.

4. USE RESTRICTIONS: You may not network the SOFTWARE or otherwise use it on more than one computer or computer terminal at the same time. You may physically transfer the SOFTWARE from one computer to another provided that the SOFTWARE is used on only one computer at a time. You may not distribute copies of the SOFTWARE or Documentation to others. You may not reverse engineer, disassemble, decompile, modify, adapt, translate, or create derivative works based on the SOFTWARE or the Documentation without the prior written consent of the Company.

5. TRANSFER RESTRICTIONS: The enclosed SOFTWARE is licensed only to you and may not be transferred to any one else without the prior written consent of the Company. Any unauthorized transfer of the SOFTWARE shall result in the immediate termination of this Agreement.

6. TERMINATION: This license is effective until terminated. This license will terminate automatically without notice from the Company and become null and void if you fail to comply with any provisions or limitations of this license. Upon termination, you shall destroy the Documentation and all copies of the SOFTWARE. All provisions of this Agreement as to warranties, limitation of liability, remedies or damages, and our ownership rights shall survive termination.

7. MISCELLANEOUS: This Agreement shall be construed in accordance with the laws of the United States of America and the State of New York and shall benefit the Company, its affiliates, and assignees.

8. LIMITED WARRANTY AND DISCLAIMER OF WARRANTY: The Company warrants that the SOFTWARE, when properly used in accordance with the Documentation, will operate in substantial conformity with the description of the SOFTWARE set forth in the Documentation. The Company does not warrant that the SOFTWARE will meet your requirements or that the operation of the SOFTWARE will be uninterrupted or error-free. The Company warrants that the media on which the SOFTWARE is delivered shall be free from defects in materials and workmanship under normal use for a period of thirty (30) days from the date of your purchase. Your only remedy and the Company's only obligation under these limited warranties is, at the Company's option, return of the warranted item for a refund of any amounts paid by you or replacement of the item. Any replacement of SOFTWARE or

media under the warranties shall not extend the original warranty period. The limited warranty set forth above shall not apply to any SOFTWARE which the Company determines in good faith has been subject to misuse, neglect, improper installation, repair, alteration, or damage by you. EXCEPT FOR THE EXPRESSED WARRANTIES SET FORTH ABOVE, THE COMPANY DISCLAIMS ALL WARRANTIES, EXPRESS OR IMPLIED, INCLUDING WITHOUT LIMITATION, THE IMPLIED WARRANTIES OF MERCHANTABILITY AND FITNESS FOR A PARTICULAR PURPOSE. EXCEPT FOR THE EXPRESS WARRANTY SET FORTH ABOVE, THE COMPANY DOES NOT WARRANT, GUARANTEE, OR MAKE ANY REPRESENTATION REGARDING THE USE OR THE RESULTS OF THE USE OF THE SOFTWARE IN TERMS OF ITS CORRECTNESS, ACCURACY, RELIABILITY, CURRENTNESS, OR OTHERWISE.

IN NO EVENT, SHALL THE COMPANY OR ITS EMPLOYEES, AGENTS, SUPPLIERS, OR CONTRACTORS BE LIABLE FOR ANY INCIDENTAL, INDIRECT, SPECIAL, OR CONSEQUENTIAL DAMAGES ARISING OUT OF OR IN CONNECTION WITH THE LICENSE GRANTED UNDER THIS AGREEMENT, OR FOR LOSS OF USE, LOSS OF DATA, LOSS OF INCOME OR PROFIT, OR OTHER LOSSES, SUSTAINED AS A RESULT OF INJURY TO ANY PERSON, OR LOSS OF OR DAMAGE TO PROPERTY, OR CLAIMS OF THIRD PARTIES, EVEN IF THE COMPANY OR AN AUTHORIZED REPRESENTATIVE OF THE COMPANY HAS BEEN ADVISED OF THE POSSIBILITY OF SUCH DAMAGES. IN NO EVENT SHALL LIABILITY OF THE COMPANY FOR DAMAGES WITH RESPECT TO THE SOFTWARE EXCEED THE AMOUNTS ACTUALLY PAID BY YOU, IF ANY, FOR THE SOFTWARE.

SOME JURISDICTIONS DO NOT ALLOW THE LIMITATION OF IMPLIED WARRANTIES OR LIABILITY FOR INCIDENTAL, INDIRECT, SPECIAL, OR CONSEQUENTIAL DAMAGES, SO THE ABOVE LIMITATIONS MAY NOT ALWAYS APPLY. THE WARRANTIES IN THIS AGREEMENT GIVE YOU SPECIFIC LEGAL RIGHTS AND YOU MAY ALSO HAVE OTHER RIGHTS WHICH VARY IN ACCORDANCE WITH LOCAL LAW.

ACKNOWLEDGMENT

YOU ACKNOWLEDGE THAT YOU HAVE READ THIS AGREEMENT, UNDERSTAND IT, AND AGREE TO BE BOUND BY ITS TERMS AND CONDITIONS. YOU ALSO AGREE THAT THIS AGREEMENT IS THE COMPLETE AND EXCLUSIVE STATEMENT OF THE AGREEMENT BETWEEN YOU AND THE COMPANY AND SUPERSEDES ALL PROPOSALS OR PRIOR AGREEMENTS, ORAL, OR WRITTEN, AND ANY OTHER COMMUNICATIONS BETWEEN YOU AND THE COMPANY OR ANY REPRESENTATIVE OF THE COMPANY RELATING TO THE SUBJECT MATTER OF THIS AGREEMENT.

Should you have any questions concerning this Agreement or if you wish to contact the Company for any reason, please contact in writing at the address below.

Robin Short
Pearson Prentice Hall
One Lake Street
Upper Saddle River, New Jersey 07458